THE BUDDHIST PUBLICATION SOCIETY

The BPS is an approved charity dedicated to making known the Teaching of the Buddha, which has a vital message for all people.

Founded in 1958, the BPS has published a wide variety of books and booklets covering a great range of topics. Its publications include accurate annotated translations of the Buddha's discourses, standard reference works, as well as original contemporary expositions of Buddhist thought and practice. These works present Buddhism as it truly is—a dynamic force which has influenced receptive minds for the past 2500 years and is still as relevant today as it was when it first arose.

For more information about the BPS and our publications, please visit our website, or write an e-mail or letter to:

The Administrative Secretary
Buddhist Publication Society
P.O. Box 61
54 Sangharaja Mawatha
Kandy • Sri Lanka

E-mail: bps@sltnet.lk
web site: http://www.bps.lk
Tel: 0094 81 223 7283
Fax: 0094 81 222 3679

FACETS OF BUDDHIST THOUGHT

Collected Essays
of
K. N. Jayatilleke

Facets of Buddhist Thought

Collected Essays

of

K. N. Jayatilleke

Buddhist Publication Society
Kandy • Sri Lanka

Buddhist Publication Society
P.O. Box 61
54, Sangharaja Mawatha
Kandy, Sri Lanka

This collection contains all the essays found in *The Message of the Buddha: A posthumous work edited by Ninian Smart* (ISBN 955–24–0204–2), first published in 1975 by George Allen & Unwin Ltd. BPS edition published in 2000 with the permission of the editor, Prof. Ninian Smart, and the author's widow, Mrs. Patricia Jayatilleke. It also contains other essays published earlier by the BPS in the Wheel Publications series as well as the essay "The Principles of International Law in Buddhist Doctrine," included here with the permission of Mrs. Jayatilleke.

National Library of Sri Lanka-Cataloguing in Publication Data

Jayatilleke, K.N.
Facets of Buddhist thought / K.N. Jayatilleke; ed. by Ninian Smart & Bhikkhu Nyanatusita.- Kandy: Buddhist Publication Society Inc., 2009.- 506p; 22cm.

ISBN 978-955-24-0335-4 Price:

i. 181.043 DDC 21 ii. Title
iii. Smart, Ninian - ed. iv. Bhikkhu Nyanatusita-ed
01. Buddhist Philosophy

Printed by
Samayawardana Printers,
Colombo 10.

Contents

Sources

Ch. 1: "Buddhism and the Scientific Revolution" in *Buddhism and Science,* Wheel Publication No. 3, BPS, 1958, 1959, 1967, 1980.

Ch. 2: "The Historical Context of the Rise of Buddhism" in *The Message of the Buddha,* BPS, 2000.

Chs. 3–8: "The Buddhist Conception of Truth," "The Buddhist Attitude to Revelation," "The Buddhist Conception of Matter and the Material World," "The Buddhist Analysis of Mind," "The Buddhist Conception of the Universe," and "The Buddhist Attitude to God" in *Facets of Buddhist Thought,* Wheel Publication No. 162/164, BPS, 1971, 1984.

Ch. 9: "Nibbāna" in *The Message of the Buddha.*

Ch. 10–12: "The Buddhist View of Survival," "The Buddhist Doctrine of Karma," and "The Case for the Buddhist Theory of Karma and Survival" in *Survival and Karma in Buddhist Perspective,* Wheel Publication No. 141/143, BPS, 1969, 1970, 1980.

Ch. 13: "The Conditioned Genesis of the Individual" in *The Message of the Buddha.*

Chs. 14–18: "The Buddhist Ethical Ideal of the Ultimate Good," "The Basis of Buddhist Ethics," "The Buddhist Conception of Evil," "The Criteria of Right and Wrong," and "The Ethical Theory of Buddhism" in *Ethics in Buddhist Perspective,* Wheel Publication No. 175/176, BPS, 1972, 1984.

Ch. 19: "Some Aspects of the *Bhagavad Gīta* and Buddhist Ethics" in *Aspects of Buddhist Social Philosophy*, Wheel Publication 128/129, BPS, 1969, 1984. Reprinted with permission from *University of Ceylon Review*, Vol. XIII, 2/3 (1955).

Ch. 20: "Toynbee's Criticism of Buddhism" originally published as "A Recent Criticism of Buddhism" in *Aspects of Buddhist Social Philosophy*, Wheel Publication 128/129, BPS, 1969, 1984. Reprinted with permission from *University of Ceylon Review*, Vol. XV, 3/4 (1957).

Ch. 21: "The Buddhist Attitude to Other Religions" in *The Buddhist Attitude to Other Religions*, Wheel Publication No. 216, BPS, 1975, 1991.

Ch. 22: "Buddhism and Peace" in *Buddhism and Peace*, Wheel Publication No. 41, BPS, 1962, 1969, 1983.

Ch. 23: "The Significance of Vesākha" originally published as "The Significance of Vesak" in *The Significance of Vesak*, Wheel Publication No. 178, BPS, 1972, 1984.

Ch. 24: "Buddhism and the Race Question" (co-authored with G. P. Malalasekera) in *Buddhism and the Race Question*, Wheel Publication No. 200/201, BPS, 1974. Reprinted with permission from *Buddhism and the Race Question* (UNESCO 1958), pp. 32–73.

Ch. 25: "The Principles of International Law in Buddhist Doctrine" in *Recueil des Cours*, Tome 12, pp. 300–426, p. 356. The Hague Academy of International Law, The Hague, Netherlands, 1967. Privately reprinted as an offprint. Reprinted as *Dhamma, Man and Law*, Singapore, 1988.

Preface

The BPS is pleased to print this collection of Prof. Jayatilleke's essays. Many of these essays were published earlier by the BPS as Wheel Publications, which then were published in 1979 as a volume of bound *Wheel Publications* called *Facets of Buddhist Thought.* In 2000 the BPS republished *The Message of the Buddha*, a collection of essays by Prof. Jayatilleke edited by Ninian Smart, which included many of the essays from the Wheel Publication series and a few essays not published earlier.

The present collection contains all the essays from *The Message of the Buddha* (chapters 2 to 15), some others from the Wheel Publication series which were included in *Facets of Buddhist Thought* (chapters 1 and 16 to 24) as well as a long essay on the principles of international law in Buddhism (chapter 25), which had earlier been published in an academic law journal.

BPS Editor

Foreword

After more than a century of Western academic study of Buddhism representing an attempt to unravel the mysteries surrounding the teachings of Gotama Buddha, Professor K. N. Jayatilleke, with his *Early Buddhist Theory of Knowledge* (1963), opened a new chapter in its interpretation. Until the publication of this epoch-making work, most Western Buddhist scholars, especially those who began with and, in most cases, confined themselves to the Mahāyāna, utilized the concepts available in the idealistic as well as the existentialist traditions of Western Europe in their interpretation of Buddhism. Very few ventured to compare Buddhism with the tenets of the empiricist and positivist traditions, except Prof. T. W. Rhys Davids, who alone, working through the earliest discourses of the Buddha, occasionally observed their similarities. After being trained in the empiricist and analytic schools of philosophy in England, and coming under the direct influence of Ludwig Wittgenstein at Cambridge, Jayatilleke was the first to provide a comprehensive analysis and interpretation of the early Buddhist epistemological speculations, providing a new dimension to the interpretation of early Buddhism and shedding new light upon its contemporary relevance. Jayatilleke's excellent training in Oriental Languages, especially Pali and Sanskrit, and his expertise in the Western philosophical traditions combined to make him unique among Buddhist scholars and enabled him to perceive trends of thought in Buddhism that came to be submerged as a result of centuries of tradition, both Theravādin and Mahāyānist.

The series of articles included in the present volume belongs to the periods prior to as well as posterior to his famous work, *Early Buddhist Theory of Knowledge*. For this reason, the present work should enable the reader to perceive the manner in which his thinking evolved. In the very first paper on "Buddhism and the Scientific Revolution," which also represents his first major publication as a Lecturer in Philosophy at the University of Ceylon, Jayatilleke comes to grips with one of the most important problems he faced, namely the manner in which one could save the teachings of Buddha in the face of the rather devastating scientific revolution that shattered many basic tenets of the Christian religious tradition.

Here Jayatilleke was able to peg himself on to an idea which he developed with great enthusiasm and at length in his later writings. To quote his own words:

> "I say this because I find that early Buddhism emphasizes the importance of the scientific outlook in dealing with the problems of morality and religion. Its specific 'dogmas' are said to be capable of verification. And its general account of the nature of man and the universe is one that accords with the findings of science rather than being at variance with them."

Jayatilleke was convinced that the verificationist method of the positivists was not different from the method by which the Buddha attempted to eliminate perennial metaphysical issues. And he not only compiled the *Early Buddhist Theory of Knowledge*, setting out in detail the method itself, but also compiled a series of articles, published under the title *Facets of Buddhist Thought* (chapters 3–8), all of which were intended to explain the manner in which this method was utilised by the Buddha to explain the nature of the universe, conceptions of matter and mind, etc. He not only perceived the existence of a positivist method in the early discourses of the Buddha, but also attempted to expand that method to include phenomena that the positivists with a bias for physicalism refused to recognise. This, he believed, was the most significant contribution of early Buddhism to Western thought.

One of the major criticisms levelled against the Buddha by modern interpreters of Buddhism is that Buddha "took for granted" the doctrines of karma and rebirth as found in the mainstreams of the Indian religio-philosophical thought. Jayatilleke was a vehement critic of this view and spent years researching into the problems of karma and presented, what he believed to be, a very scientific explanation of these phenomena. The lengthy articles dealing with karma and survival in Buddhist perspective (chapters 10–12) embody this research where he insisted upon distinguishing the Buddha's explanation of such phenomena from the animistic and substantialist presentations found in the earlier Indian traditions.

The recognition of phenomena such as karma and survival enabled Jayatilleke to dismiss the notion of theistic determinism when explaining ethics. But he was faced with the age-old problem of how to reconcile ethical life, which involves a recognition of human free will, with the basic doctrine of natural determinism (*paṭicca-samuppāda*). In his *Early Buddhist Theory of Knowledge*, Jayatilleke, primarily because of his sympathy with the analytical tradition in philosophy where human behaviour is placed outside the sphere of natural determinism, favoured an "action theory" where he tried to explain the existence of free will because of the indeterminism of human behaviour. But in his essay on dependent origination (chapter 13) and the essays on ethics in Buddhist perspective (chapters 14–18), he abandons this view, recognizing causal conditioning (*paṭicca-samuppāda*) in regard to physical as well as psychic phenomena.

In the four essays entitled "Toynbee's Criticism of Buddhism," "Some Aspects of the Bhagavad Gīta and Buddhist Ethics," "Buddhism and the Race Question" (co-authored by G. P. Malalasekera), and "The Principles of International Law in Buddhist Doctrine"—all dealing with the Buddha's social philosophy—Jayatilleke faithfully carries through his positivist approach in dealing with these topics.

"The Buddhist Altitude to Other Religions," "Buddhism and Peace," and "The Significance of Vesākha" may be considered the exultations of a man who is now convinced that the best thing that could have happened to the world is the appearance of Buddhism.

In this volume, though it contains a series of articles written at different times on varied topics, we perceive the origin and evolution of the views of a scholar who is destined to influence future studies of the Buddha's teachings. As a student, colleague and close friend of Jayatilleke, it gives me unbounded pleasure to introduce these essays to the academician as well as to the layman interested in Buddhism. The readers owe a debt of gratitude to Venerable Nyanaponika as well as to Mr. Richard Abeysekera for their perceptivity to the need of putting together these scattered writings of one of the greatest Buddhist scholars of the twentieth century.

David Kalupahana
Professor and Chairman
Dept. of Philosophy
University of Hawaii

I

Buddhism and the Scientific Revolution

It is a historical fact that the scientific revolution which took its rise in the seventeenth century in the West was largely responsible for upsetting the earlier religious conception of the universe. Not only did science controvert the specific dogmas of Western religion, but it seemed to have undermined the foundations as well as the fundamental concepts implicit in the religious outlook on things.

The new cosmology of Copernicus, Galileo and their successors altered the geocentric picture of the universe, although it was pronounced to be "contrary to the Holy Scriptures." The new biology (the theory of evolution) upset the doctrines of the special creation and the fall of man. And the new psychology seemed to show that man's mind like his physical body worked on a pattern of causal law and that however deep one plumbed into its depths there was not discoverable in it an unchanging soul which governed its activities entirely.

But much more serious was the effect of the scientific outlook on the general religious attitude which involved a belief in a personal God, in purpose and in the objectivity of moral values. Science made its discoveries and progressed quite comfortably on the assumption of universal causation without the necessity for teleological explanations or divine intervention. It dealt with an amoral universe indifferent to the aspirations of men. As among men, moral values like economic values were subjective since they were dependent on the needs and desires of men, and an ethical humanism was the best that could be hoped for. Even such an ethics need not be universal, for, as anthropologists discovered, different societies seem to have followed different moral codes which suited them and ethical relativism was the scientific truth about the nature of moral values.

Of course, there are those who still cling to the dogmas in the face of science or believe in them in a non-literal sense. But the position remains very much the same, although people are no longer optimistic (after two world wars and in the throes of a third) about the ability of science to usher in a brave new world of peace and plenty. It has also been granted that mechanistic explanations of the universe need not necessarily rule out teleological ones. Science too has given up the crude materialism of the eighteenth century and scientists no longer attempt to explain the universe on machine models, while some scientists have denied that strict determinism holds in the sphere of the atom. But all this is still a far cry from religion.

What place would Buddhism occupy in such a context? Are its dogmas and attitudes no better or no worse than those of any other religion? Some Western writers on religion seem to have assumed that this was so, but if one reads through the Buddhist texts, one begins to wonder whether the scientific revolution would have at all affected religion adversely if it had taken place in the context of early Buddhism.

I say this because I find that early Buddhism emphasises the importance of the scientific outlook in dealing with the problems of morality and religion. Its specific dogmas are said to be capable of verification. And its general account of the nature of man and the universe is one that accords with the findings of science rather than being at variance with them.

To take this last point first, we find for instance that the early Buddhist conception of the cosmos is in essence similar to the modern conception of the universe. In the Pali texts that have come down to us we are literally told that hundreds and thousands of suns and moons, earths, and higher worlds, constitute the minor world system, that a hundred thousand times this is the middling world system, and a hundred thousand times the middling world system is the major world system. In modern terminology it would seem as if a minor world system (*cūḷanikā-loka-dhātu*) is a galaxy of which we observe about a hundred million through our best telescopes. The Buddhist conception of time is equally immense.

There is, of course, no theory of biological evolution as such mentioned in the Buddhist texts, but man and society as well as worlds are pictured as changing and evolving in accordance with causal laws.

Then in psychology we find early Buddhism regarding man as a psycho-physical unit whose "psyche" is not a changeless soul but a dynamic continuum composed of a conscious mind as well as an unconscious in which is stored the residua of emotionally charged memories going back to childhood as well as into past lives. Such a mind is said to be impelled to act under the influence of three types of desires—the desire for sense-gratification (*kāma-taṇhā*), the desire for self-preservation (*bhava-taṇhā*) and the desire for destruction (*vibhava-taṇhā*). Except for the belief in rebirth, this conception of the mind sounds very modern, and one cannot also fail to observe the parallel between the threefold desire in Buddhism and the Freudian conceptions of the *eros*, *libido*, and *thanatos*.

I have brought out these similarities not with the intention of showing that Buddhism teaches modern science, but that the scientific revolution does not have the same adverse effect on Buddhism as it had on another religious traditions.

Now let us turn to the content of Buddhism as a theory about the nature and destiny of man. First of all it holds that the honest impartial search for truth even in matters moral and religious is no bar to one's spiritual progress. On more than one occasion the Buddha has admonished honest seekers after the truth in the following words: "You have raised a doubt in a situation in which you ought to be uncertain. Do not accept anything because it is rumoured so, because it is the traditional belief, because the majority hold to it, because it is found in the scriptures, because it is the product of metaphysical argument and speculation, or after a superficial investigation of facts, or because it conforms with one's inclinations, because it is authoritative or because of the prestige value of your teacher." Critical investigation and personal verification were to be the guide to true morality and religion. "If anyone were to speak ill of me, my doctrine and my order," says the Buddha, "do not bear any ill-will towards him, be upset or perturbed at heart, for if you were to be so, it will only cause you harm. If on the other hand anyone were to speak well of me, my doctrine and my order, do not be overjoyed, thrilled or elated at heart, for if so it will only be in your way of forming a correct judgement as to whether the qualities praised in us are real and actually found." A scientific outlook was thus considered necessary not only for discovering the truly moral and religious life but even for the continual self-examination which such an outlook demands.

The field of moral and religious phenomena is, again, not a realm of mystery but one in which the law of cause and effect holds. The principle of causal determination, namely that A is the cause of

B if "whenever an event A occurs an event B occurs, and B does not occur unless A has occurred" is laid down by the Buddha in these very terms, and he further states that he "speaks only of causes and of things which arise from causes." Thus all phenomena, including moral and spiritual experience (with the sole exception of Nibbāna, which is not a conditioned phenomenon), are said to be conditioned by causal laws. Such laws are classified according to their sphere of operation as physical laws (*utu-niyāma*), biological laws (*bīja-niyāma*), psychological laws (*citta-niyāma*) and moral and spiritual laws (*dhamma-niyāma*).

Now, there are three laws which are said to govern the life and destiny of the individual. They are the law of continuity which makes for the persistence of individuality (*bhava*), the law of moral retribution (*kamma*), whereby morally good acts tend to result in pleasant consequences for the individual and morally evil acts in unpleasant consequences, and finally, the law of causal genesis (*paṭicca-samuppāda*), which is intended to explain the above two laws.

The law of continuity, popularly known as rebirth, ensures the persistence of the dynamic unconscious of the individual with the death of the physical body. If this unconscious is not attuned to higher worlds by the moral and spiritual development of the individual, it is said generally to persist in the spirit-sphere (*petti-visaya*) as a discarnate spirit, and subsequently gets reborn as a human. Critics of Buddhism often suggest that this theory of rebirth is dogmatically accepted or taken for granted in Buddhism but a careful study of the texts would show that this is not the case.

Buddhism arose at a time when there was intense speculation on the problem of survival. There were also several schools of materialism, all of which denied survival altogether and there were the sceptics who merely doubted the possibility of survival. Even experiments such as the weighing of the body immediately before and after death were performed in order to discover any evidence of survival. One of the materialist theories mentioned and dismissed by the Buddha was that consciousness was a by-product of the material elements being mixed up in certain proportions to form the organic body—in the same way in which the red colour is produced by suitable mixtures of betel, areca-nut and lime (none of which is red). Several such materialistic theories, as well as a number of one-life-after-death-theories, some of which held that the soul was conscious after death, others that it was unconscious (but existing), and yet others that it was super-conscious after death, are examined and disposed of by the Buddha. The theory of rebirth is offered as one capable of being verified by developing the faculty of seeing our former births, a potentiality which is said to be within the reach of all of us.

Rebirth is therefore not a dogma to be accepted on faith but a hypothesis capable of being scientifically verified. The available evidence for rebirth today is roughly of two sorts.

There is the spontaneous evidence of numerous people from both East and West who have claimed to remember their past lives, in some cases of which the memories have been confirmed by further investigation (e.g., the case of Shanti Devi, *Illustrated Weekly of India*, December 15, 1935. The case of Nellie Horster, *Milwaukee Sentinel*, September 25, 1892). There is also the more reliable and more abundant evidence of psychiatrists and psychologists who have discovered that under hypnotic trance the subject's memories can be traced back not only to childhood but to prior earth lives as well, in some cases of which the facts have been verified (e.g., A. de Rochas, *Les Vies Successives*, Paris, 1911; Ralph Shirley, *The Problem of Rebirth*, London, 1936; Theodore Flournoy, *Des Inde a la planete Mars,* Paris, 1900; Charles E. Cory, "A Divided Self," in *Journal of Abnormal Psychology*, Vol. XIV, 1919).

The law of moral retribution or kamma as taught in Buddhism has also been criticised on the grounds that it amounts to fatalism. This again is due to ignorance of the Buddhist teaching. Causation in Buddhism is carefully distinguished by the Buddha on the one hand from strict determinism and on the other from indeterminism. The Buddha argues that, if everything was determined, then there would be no free will and no moral or spiritual life would be possible and we would be slaves of the past; and on the other hand, if everything was undetermined (*adhicca-samuppanna*) or fortuitous, then again the moral and spiritual life would not be possible, for the cultivation of moral and spiritual values would not result in moral and spiritual growth. It is because the world is so constituted that everything is not strictly determined or completely undetermined that the religious life is possible and desirable, according to the Buddha.

In order to explain rebirth and kamma, some of the Upanishadic thinkers who accepted these doctrines had to recourse to the concept of *ātman* or a changeless soul. The individual continued to be the same because he had a permanent soul which was the agent of all the actions of the individual as well as the experiencer of their fruits. The Buddha was quick to see that such metaphysical entities explained nothing and that it was meaningless to assert or deny an unverifiable entity. He therefore rejected the concept of soul while maintaining the doctrine of the observable continuity of the individuality, and explained the above two laws of continuity and moral retribution in terms of all the verifiable phenomenal factors which determine the continued genesis and growth of the individual. This is too elaborate to be set out in detail. In brief, it describes how the individual is conditioned by his psychological past (going back to past lives which set the general tone of his character) and the genetic constitution of his body derived from his parents, and continues to act in and react with his environment accumulating the experiences of this life in his evolving consciousness (*saṃvaṭṭanika-viññāṇa*), which continues after the death of the body if the threefold desires in it be still active.

Personal and direct knowledge of the operation of these three laws constitutes the threefold knowledge (*tisso vijjā*) which the Buddha and his disciples claimed to have. The awareness of the fact that and the way in which one is being conditioned is said to result in one ceasing to be conditioned, a state which corresponds to the attainment of the unconditioned and supreme felicity of Nibbāna. This is salvation in Buddhism, which is literally salvation from the bondage of finite conditioned existence.

Strictly, Nibbāna is said to be beyond description or conception, the reason given being that it is a state so radically different from the type of existent things which we can conceive of that no meaningful description or definition of it can be given in conceptual terms. It is said that to say that one "exists" in Nibbāna is wrong, for existence is a concept that applies to phenomenal things and has reference to space and time, for Nibbāna is "timeless, in that one cannot speak of it as being in the past, present or future," is not located in space and is not causally conditioned unlike all phenomenal things: but it is also said to be equally wrong to say that one "does not exist" in Nibbāna since this implies a state of oblivion and annihilation. Nevertheless both positive as well as negative descriptions are given, though they are not to be taken as exact definitions, as Nibbāna is—beyond the scope of logic.

Negatively, Nibbāna is the absence of all unhappiness, and all phenomenal existence is said to be infected with unhappiness; we are unhappy either because we experience mental or physical pain and have forebodings for the future, or because the pleasant experiences that we have are insecure and never lasting. This is to take a realistic view of life even in the face of the fact that as the Buddha says "human beings enjoy on the whole more pleasant experiences than unpleasant ones," and therefore it would not be correct to call it pessimism since it has nothing to do with wishful thinking. Positively, Nibbāna is described as a state of "supreme felicity" (*paramaṃ sukhaṃ*).

The way of salvation is described as an eightfold path in which the first step is that of right understanding and living in accordance with the true philosophy of life, and as a result having right aspirations, right speech, right actions, right mode of living, and right mindfulness, culminating in the growth of religious joy and the spiritual and intuitive awareness of right meditation or contemplation. The full fruit of right contemplation, however, can be reaped by those giving up the active social life for the contemplative life. This meditative life is characterized by the stages of personal mystical consciousness (*rūpa-jhāna*) and impersonal mystical consciousness (*arūpa-jhāna*) culminating in the attainment of Nibbāna. With the growth of his mind and spirit there are said to emerge certain faculties latent in him, such as telepathy and clairvoyance and the ability to see his past lives. These cognitive faculties, as explained earlier, make it possible for the individual to realise the conditioned state in which he is, and thereby to attain the Unconditioned. Considering the requirements of the path, the Way to Nibbāna is therefore described as the culmination of a person's moral development (*sīla*), intuitional or spiritual development (*samādhi*) as well as his intellectual or cognitive development (*paññā*). The Buddha was once asked "whether he hoped to save one-third of the world, one-half of the world or the whole world by offering this Way of Salvation," to which he replied that he did not claim to save one-third of humanity, but that just as a skilful doorkeeper guarding the only entrance to the palace knows that all those who seek the haven of this palace must enter by this door, even so all those in the past who were saved, who in the present are being saved and who in future will be saved, have entered, are entering and will enter by this door.

Such is the teaching of early Buddhism, which is offered as a self-consistent scientific hypothesis touching the matters of religion and morality which each person can verify for himself. In fact, not being based on revelation, the fact that it has been verified by him and hundreds of his disciples and is capable of being verified by every earnest seeker is put forward as the criterion of its truth by the Buddha. The empirical and pragmatic test of science is, for the Buddha, the test of true religion. The faith that he requires is the trust that is required to put to the test a certain philosophy of life by devoting one's entire being to living it every moment of one's life. And its worth is to be realised by its fruits by each person for himself. Like the scientists working in other fields, the Buddhas or the Perfect Ones have merely discovered these truths, which are there for all time, and have preached them for the good of the world. Each one has to seek and work out his own salvation; no one can save another and the Perfect Ones do merely point the way.

It would be seen that such a religion is in accord with the temper and the findings of science, so that Buddhism is not likely to be at variance with science so long as scientists confine themselves to their methodology and their respective fields without making a dogma of materialism.

As for purpose, the Buddhist view is that the world as such has no purpose to accomplish though individuals in it may choose their own ends and thus make their lives purposeful, the end recommended by Buddhism being Nibbāna. The Buddha would argue that if the world had a purpose to be attained in a final consummation, then either salvation would be assured for all or some would be fore-doomed and damned for eternity; but according to the Buddha there is no necessity or inevitability in progress; no one is destined to attain Nibbāna unless he wishes to. But as for moral values Buddhism upholds their objectivity, for according to the law of kamma, a drunkard, for instance, unless he repents (i.e., changes his ways) tends to be reborn as a moron whatever the opinions or wishes of the drunkard or the members of his society may be.

2

The Historical Context of the Rise of Buddhism

Tradition has it that the Buddha was born in a certain historical context, at a certain time and at a certain place when his doctrine was likely to be most needed, understood and appreciated. It was then that the aspirant to Buddhahood came down from the *Tusita* heaven to be born among men. Whatever the truth of this belief may be, there is no doubt that the appearance of the Buddha was preceded by the presence of a diversity of religious and philosophical beliefs about the nature and destiny of man in the universe. In fact, there is hardly any major religious or philosophical view prevalent today, or which has evolved in the course of human thought in the East or West, that was not represented then by some religious or philosophical teacher who had appeared on the scene.

Theists, Materialists and Agnostics

These major views were in fact held by six outstanding religious or philosophical teachers, who are each said to have had a large following and who were the senior contemporaries of the Buddha. There was Makkhali Gosāla, the theist (*issara-kiriyavādin*), according to whom the world was created by a divine fiat and continues to unfold itself like a ball of thread that unwinds when flung on the ground.

Being under the impact of various evolutionary forces over which they have no control, beings gradually evolve under varying conditions of existence until they eventually attain final salvation. In the other extreme was Ajita-Kesakambalī, the materialist, according to whom fools and the wise alike terminate their existence at death and there was no such thing as a "good life," which religious men talk about.

Opposed to both these views was Sañjaya Bellaṭṭhiputta, the sceptic agnostic or positivist, who held that beliefs about an after-life, moral responsibility and ultimate salvation were beyond verification and that, therefore, one could not with reason hold any firm opinion about them. Many people are even today either materialists, theists or sceptics. Their world-view or *Weltanschauung* is in fact basically not different from that put forward by these three leading philosophers at the time of the Buddha.

There are, however, three other leading thinkers referred to in the early Buddhist texts and they too represent certain types of thought met with (still) today as well as in the history of human speculation. There was Pūraṇa Kassapa, who was a natural determinist, holding that everything was strictly determined by natural forces. As a corollary to his determinism he was, like the scientists who held a deterministic view of nature, an amoralist who believed that there was nothing good or evil as such. Pakudha Kaccāyana, on the other hand, was, like Empedocles or Aristotle, a categorialist, who tried to explain and comprehend man and the universe by classifying reality into discrete categories. Lastly, Nigaṇṭha Nātaputta, the historical founder of Jainism, was a relativist in his theory of knowledge, holding that there was some truth in every point of view, and an eclectic in his metaphysics, which tries to combine the truth of all these different, even contradictory standpoints.

All these teachers, it is said, who represent standard types of belief were held in great esteem and veneration by the people, and the religion and philosophy of Buddhism are distinguished from every one of them. Some of the disciples of the Buddha were in fact drawn from among those who adhered to their doctrines. Sāriputta, for instance, the chief disciple of the Buddha, was originally a follower of Sañjaya, the sceptic.

Very often, however, the Buddha classified the teachers of his time into two categories, the eternalists (*sassata-vāda*), who believed in the existence of an integral soul, which survived the death of the body, and the annihilationists (*uccheda-vāda*), who asserted the total destruction of the human personality with the death and dissolution of the body. Among the eternalists were various types of theists and among the annihilationists were various categories of materialists. The views of these two schools of thought were the predominant views of the time and it is in opposition to both of them that the religion and philosophy of Buddhism is presented.

Vedic Tradition

If we examine the non-Buddhist sources, we find that some of these theories are traceable to the Vedic tradition, while others can be traced to the non-Vedic. But these terms, Vedic and non-Vedic, are to some extent misleading. For it is possible or even probable that many of the views within the Vedic tradition evolved under the impact of the non-Vedic, while some of the non-Vedic teachings, on the other hand, can be shown to have branched off from the Vedic.

In this chapter, which concerns the historical context of the rise of Buddhism, we shall very briefly consider what is meant by the Vedic and the non-Vedic traditions and the general attitude of Buddhism to each of them, without going into details. It is generally agreed among scholars that Buddhism arose in the sixth century BCE, during or somewhat after the period when the Upaniṣadic doctrines were being formulated. The Upaniṣads are considered to form the tail-end of the Vedic tradition and are hence known as the Vedanta or the end of the Vedas. But it is held to be the end of the Vedic tradition, not merely in a chronological sense, but because the Vedanta constituted the essence or consummation of the Vedic tradition. Even in the Buddhist texts we find the phrase, *vedantagū-brahmacariyo*, used to denote a person who has gained the heights of spiritual knowledge and as such has consummated his religious life. In an Upaniṣadic context, the phrase would denote one who has mastered the essence of the latter portion of the Vedic tradition and as such has realised the fruits of the religious life. This shows the close relationship between Upaniṣadic and early Buddhist thought.

The Upaniṣads, however, do not present a single view but a variety of views regarding the nature and destiny of man in the universe, although there is a certain homogeneity in the thought of the middle and later Upaniṣadic thinkers. These thinkers were historically separated and geographically isolated from each other and there is evidence that they built upon earlier theories and criticised each other. They are, however, all deemed to belong to the Vedic tradition by virtue of the fact that they owed a general allegiance to the Vedas. With the majority of the middle and later Upaniṣadic thinkers, this allegiance was a very loose one, since they considered the earlier imaginative and discursive type of knowledge as a form of "lower knowledge" (*apara-vidyā*), while their own knowledge was derived from an expansion of consciousness and extra sensory powers of perception. This was due to the practice of Yoga and the intuitive knowledge thus gained was regarded by them as *para-vidyā* or the ultimate knowledge.

One important difference with Buddhism was the fact that it paid no special allegiance to the Vedas. The Buddha, it is said, studied under Yogic teachers presumably of the Vedic tradition, such as Ālāra Kālāma and Uddaka Rāmaputta, but, although he mastered their teachings, he is said to have gone away dissatisfied with them. However, immediately after his enlightenment, it is significant that he first thinks of preaching to these two teachers since he considered that they were very wise and would have soon profited from the Dhamma.

The recognition of the worth of these Upaniṣadic teachings in the Buddhist texts is embodied in the stanza with which Brahmā, the regent of the cosmos, invites the Buddha to preach the Dhamma to the world, which would otherwise be destroyed without it. It reads as follows: "There arose in the past among the Magadhan peoples a Dhamma, which was not perfect and which was conceived by imperfect seers. Open now the door to immortality so that people may listen to the Dhamma, which has been fully comprehended by a Perfect One."

A further recognition of the value of the intuitive insights of some of the Upaniṣadic seers is contained in the Buddhist concept of the *Pacceka* Buddha, which accepts the fact that one may attain salvation and a high degree of enlightenment by one's own efforts, without necessarily depending on the teaching of the Buddha himself. Even the teaching of the Buddha, it may be noted, is only a guide to understanding, "for one has to put forth effort oneself, for the Transcendent Ones are only guides" (*tumhehi kiccaṃ ātappaṃ akkhātāro Tathāgatā*). In one place in the Suttanipāta, the Buddha recognises the fact that not all the recluses and brahmins are involved in decay and death (*na'haṃ bhikkhave sabbe samaṇabrāhmaṇāse jāti-jarāya nivuttā ti brūmi*).

An Ancient Way

Of similar import is the conception of the Buddha or the Enlightened One as a discoverer of an "ancient way" (*purāṇaṃ añjasaṃ*) already discovered in the past. But it is not clear whether the "past" here referred to is the historical past of the present world-cycle or of a previous world-cycle. Buddhism upholds the cyclical oscillating theory of the universe, which expands and contracts during immense periods of time, called *vivaṭṭa* and *saṃvaṭṭa-kappas*, aeons of the expansion and contraction of the universe. One sutta and a very early one states that the Buddha "was the first in the history of the present world to break through the shell of ignorance and attain illumination. In another sutta, however, which belongs to a later stratum, the historical Buddha is represented as the seventh Buddha of the current epoch, while still later in the tradition he becomes the twenty-fourth. It is possible that these latter views were developed under the impact of the Vedic and Jain traditions respectively. For the Vedas are traditionally revealed by seven seers, the *saptarṣi,* and Nigaṇṭha Nātaputta, the founder of Jainism, is held to be the twenty-fourth saviour or Tīrthaṅkara.

Yet the basic Buddhist concept is an inherently rational and plausible one. The Buddha merely discovers by his unaided efforts the truths about the nature and destiny of man in the universe and reveals them out of compassion for mankind. This has been done by countless Buddhas in the past. For according to the oscillating theory of the universe, the universe has no beginning in time, and the further we go back in time there is the possibility of going back still further, with successive and unending expansions and contractions of the universe. Likewise it is inferred that there would be such Buddhas in the future. As for the present, it is stated in the *Mahāvastu*, a work embodying some of the earliest views of Mahāyāna Buddhism, that there are galactic systems (*loka-dhātu*) in space in which Buddhas are presently preaching the Dhamma. This is not a conception that is wholly alien to the Theravada tradition. For even today Sri Lankan Buddhists recite the stanza, "*ye ca Buddhā atītā ca, ye ca Buddhā anāgatā, paccuppannā ca ye Buddhā, ahaṃ vandāmi sabbadā.*" This means: "I revere at all times the Buddhas in the past, the Buddhas in the future and those in the present." It is not implausible to believe that, just as much as there are scientists on this earth who have discovered by experiment and observation certain laws operative in nature, there could be other similar beings who have similarly discovered these laws in an inhabited planet of our galactic system or in an alien galactic system.

To come back to earth and to history, we find that it was the convergence of the two traditions, the Vedic and the non-Vedic, which blossomed forth in Buddhism. And it is a remarkable fact, as we have observed, that towards the end of the Vedic tradition there emerged sincere seekers after truth and immortality, who devoted their entire lives to this quest, renouncing all else.

This quest begins in the *Āraṇyakas* or the early Upaniṣadic period, prior to about 800 BCE, when we meet with the following prayer recorded in the *Bṛhadāraṇyaka Upaniṣad*:

> *From the unreal, lead me to the real!*
> *From darkness, lead me to light!*
> *From death, lead me to immortality!* (1.3.28)

It is in answer, as it were, to this quest that the Buddha circa 528 BCE announced to the world: "Open for them are doors to immortality" (*apārutā tesaṃ amatassa dvārā*). And during the interval of time from 800 to 528 BCE earnest seekers gave up everything for this quest.

A New Era

It marked a new stage in the development and evolution of the human mind, but mankind has still to learn the lessons from the discoveries made by this awakened human intellect about or somewhat prior to the sixth century BCE. It is also at this time that we discover the world over a new awakening of the human race. In Greece, Pythagoras, perhaps influenced by Eastern thought, conceives of philosophy as a way of life, sets up a brotherhood and teaches the doctrine of rebirth, which later influenced Plato. Platonic ideas eventually had an impact on Plotinus, St Augustine and the modern Western world. In Israel, the prophet Isaiah dreams of a time to come when there shall be human brotherhood and all nations shall live in amity and friendship and wars shall be no more. In Persia, Zoroaster views the world as a battleground in which the forces of good and evil contend and is convinced of the eventual victory of good over evil. In India, as we have already seen, the Upaniṣadic seers achieve a breakthrough in human consciousness and one of them predicts that "truth alone shall conquer and never untruth" (*satyam eva jayate nānṛtam, Muṇḍaka Upaniṣad,* 3.I.6). In China, Confucius ethicises human relationships and Lao-tzu speaks of the need for man to live in harmony with eternal values and principles.

This message of the sixth century BCE, which marks the spiritual awakening of man and the consequent faith in the possibility of harmonious living, may appear to be antiquated to some, but it is likely to prove to be more relevant to the modern world than would seem at first sight. It was during this sixth century BCE that the Buddha was born and spoke after his enlightenment in a modern idiom, which is becoming increasingly intelligible to man in the twentieth century.

Buddhist tradition, again, has it that the world at this time was eagerly awaiting the birth of an Enlightened One. The *Suttanipāta* says that the sage Asita predicted that the Buddha-child "was born for the welfare and happiness of mankind" (*manussa-loke hita-sukhatāya jāto*). Certainly the Vedic tradition looked forward to someone who would lead the people from darkness to light and from death to immortality. As H. G. Wells points out in his *A Short History of the World*, "Gautama Buddha ... taught his disciples at Benares in India about the same time that Isaiah was prophesying among the Jews in Babylon ..." (London, 1946, p. 90). Isaiah says that a people who walked in darkness have seen a great light and speaks of a child to be born at the time and who shall be called Wonderful, Counsellor, the Mighty God, the Everlasting Father and the Prince of Peace. Of the increase of his government and of peace, it is said, there will be no end.

It is a curious coincidence that all these epithets have been claimed by or for the Buddha either during his lifetime or a few centuries after his birth. For the Buddha says that he is the *Acchariya-Puggala* or the Wonderful Person and *Satthā devamanussānaṃ*, the Counsellor of gods and men, while he has been called the God among gods (*Brahmātibrahmā, Devātideva*), the Eternal Father (*Ādipita*) and the *Santi-rāja* or *Santi-nāyaka*, the Prince of Peace. The Buddha himself says in the *Bhayabherava Sutta*: "If anyone says that there is born in this world a perfectly enlightened being for the weal and welfare of mankind out of compassion for the world, for the weal, welfare and happiness of gods and men, he may rightly say this of me." In the *Ariyapariyesana Sutta*, the Buddha speaks of going to Kāsi to set up the Kingdom of Rule of Righteousness (*Dhamma-cakkaṃ pavattetuṃ*), which is elsewhere called *Brahma-cakka* or the Kingdom of God, but since Brahmā here does not have a theistic connotation, it would mean the highest or the most sublime kingdom. And it is said that the gradual advance of this Rule of Righteousness cannot be prevented by any religious teacher, angel, Satan (Māra), God (Brahmā) or anyone in this cosmos. The

Mahāvastu interprets this Rule of Righteousness in a political setting when it says that "The Rule of Power ultimately depends on the Rule of Righteousness" (*Balacakraṃ hi nisrāya Dharmacakram pravartate*).

No one would say that the reference in Isaiah's prophecy is a Buddhist interpolation. But a similar statement attributed to Confucius in one of his classics is considered by scholars to be a Buddhist interpolation in the text, though the evidence is far from conclusive. It is said in the Chinese classical text, *Lieh-tzu*, that when the chief minister of the state of Sung visited Confucius, he asked him the question, "Are you a Sage?" to which Confucius is said to have replied: "How would I presume [to call myself] a Sage? In fact, I am only one who has extensively studied and who has [stored up] much knowledge." The minister then asked Confucius whether various kings and emperors of China were Sages, to which he replied in the negative. Finally in exasperation he asked Confucius, "Who then is a Sage?" It is said that Confucius changed countenance at this question and after a pause answered as follows: "Among the people of the West there is a Sage. He does not speak and is yet spontaneously believed, he does not [consciously] convert people and yet [his doctrine] is spontaneously realised. How vast he is! There is none among the people who can find a name for it!" (See E. Zürcher, *The Buddhist Conquest of China*, Leiden, 1959, p. 274.) Some Chinese scholars have taken this to be a reference to Lao-tzu but the Buddhists of China have seen in it a reference to the Buddha, for the Buddha was known as the Sakya-Muni or "the Silent Sage of the Sakyans." An ancient Chinese Buddhist scholar makes the following comment on this text: "To judge from this [text], Confucius was fully aware of the fact that the Buddha was a great Sage. But at that time no opportunity had as yet arisen [to expound the doctrine], so he knew it but remained silent ..." (ibid.).

War of Ideologies

Whatever the historicity of these texts, even if we judge the Buddha by our worldly standards, there is little doubt that the Buddha was a person with the keenest intellect and the kindest heart. He towers above the enlightened thinkers of his age for, in his Dhamma, we have an ideology which is claimed to put an end to all ideologies and which shall eventually be shown to be true when all other ideologies have in the light of reason and experience been shown to be false. The supreme victory in the battle of ideologies (*anuttaro saṅgāmavijayo*), it is claimed, shall be won by the Dhamma. It is for this reason among others that it has been claimed of the Buddha that he is the Enlightened One par excellence or the *Anuttara Sammāsambuddha.*

The doctrines of Buddhism can be better understood if we can see in them the impact of the different theories and practises enunciated in the Vedic and non-Vedic traditions. One of the basic principles of Buddhism has been that of accepting whatever it thinks is sound, good and true from whatever source it comes, and of rejecting what it believes to be unsound, evil and false. On this principle, we can observe that there are some things which are acceptable to Buddhism in the Vedic tradition and others which are rejected. It is the same with the theories of the materialists, sceptics, Ājīvikas and Jains in the non-Vedic tradition. A careful study of what is derived from each of these traditions as well as what is rejected will help us to comprehend the Dhamma with greater clarity and precision.

Chronology

We have already said that in the opinion of most scholars Buddhism arose during or after the Upaniṣadic period of Vedic thought. But this period stretches from about the eighth to the fourth century BCE and the question as to what point in the chronological scale Buddhism comes into being is an important one.

For the question as to whether certain ideas in the Upaniṣads influenced or were influenced by Buddhism can be determined largely from such a chronological framework. For example, it has been surmised, though in my opinion not correctly, that Buddhism was not aware of the impersonal concept of Brahman as the ultimate reality to be realised by attaining union with it in this life itself. If so, then if Buddhism spoke of the ultimate reality beyond space, time and causation as the state of Nibbāna to be realised here and now, rather than as a Heaven of Brahmā or a *Brahma-loka* to be attained after death, someone may conclude that the conception of Brahman as an impersonal reality to be realised here and now was influenced by Buddhism. Such conclusions, however, should not be arrived at on the basis of our preconceptions, but on objective criteria, which can be accepted on the basis of their inherent plausibility in the light of reason and experience.

Traditionally, there are 108 Upaniṣads but in actual fact the number is about 200. Of these, thirteen principal Upaniṣads were commented on by Śaṅkara and have been classified as early, middle and late. Thus *Chāndogya* is early, *Kaṭha* belongs to the middle period, while *Maitrāyaṇi* is late. Where does Buddhism take its rise? Is it contemporary with the early, middle or late Upaniṣads? Or does it appear long after the thirteen principal ones had come into being? All these views have been held by various scholars. But the theory that is most plausible and is consistent with the facts is the one that holds the rise of Buddhism as somewhat prior to the *Maitrāyaṇi Upaniṣad,* which is a late Upaniṣad. For there seems to be good evidence that this particular Upaniṣad refers to a rising Buddhist movement.

The Upaniṣad mentions a sect wearing a "ruddy robe" (*kaṣāya*), which converts people by recourse to "rational arguments and examples" (*tarka-dṛṣtānta*), denies the doctrine of the soul (*nairātmyavāda*), preaches a Dhamma which is destructive of the Vedas and orthodox scriptures (*vedādiśāstra-hiṃsaka-dharmābhidhyānam* ...) and whose goal is the mere attainment of pleasure (*ratimātram phalamasya*).

It can be shown that all these descriptions could apply only to Buddhism in the historical context, although some of them could have applied to other movements. Thus, the materialists may be said to have resorted to rational arguments and examples and posited the attainment of pleasure as their goal, but they did not teach Dhamma or wear a ruddy robe. The Jains, on the other hand, had a Dhamma but they did not deny the existence of the soul nor because of their ascetic way of life did they pursue pleasure. It was the Buddhists, who at this time were being criticised by other religious sects as being addicted to pleasure. Besides, they wore a ruddy robe, the *kaṣāya-vastra.* They used rational persuasion as the means of winning over others to their point of view. They taught a doctrine that denied the validity of the concepts of soul and substance and preached a Dhamma, which was not based on, and in fact denied, the acceptance of the Vedic revelation.

Besides, the *Maitrāyaṇi Upaniṣad* shows evidence of the influence of Buddhism, although it forbids the brahmins from studying what is not of the Veda. So the rise of Buddhism, it may be presumed, is not far removed in time from the *Maitrāyaṇi Upaniṣad,* although it is somewhat prior to it. We may, therefore, regard the period from the *Ṛgveda* to the *Maitrāyaṇi Upaniṣad* as the Vedic tradition that could have had an impact on the rise of Buddhism.

But the non-Vedic tradition is equally important. The materialists, sceptics, the various speculations about time and change in the doctrines of the Ājīvikas and the eclectic theories of the Jains have left their mark on Buddhism, which extracted what was true and valuable in each of these schools of thought, leaving out the dross.

Predominant among these in the non-Vedic tradition were the materialists. There are seven schools of such materialists referred to in the *Brahmajāla Sutta* and the existence of several of them is independently attested in the non-Buddhist literature. The first maintained that the mind was identical with the living body and that there was no mind apart from the body that was alive. The second held that mind was an emergent by-product of the body, which disintegrated at death. There were also mystic materialists, some of whom believed in the possibility of expansions of consciousness by the use of drugs and this was criticised by the Buddhists as *micchā jhāna*—trances attained by wrong means.

It is against the background largely of these two main schools of thought that Buddhism is presented. Buddhism accepted the fact there was some degree of truth in some of their doctrines but showed that the ultimate truth transcended them both. Referring to the *bhava-diṭṭhi* or "the personal immortality view" and the *vibhava-diṭṭhi* or "the annihilationist view," the Buddha says: "These religious and philosophical teachers who fail to see how these two views arise and cease to be, their good points and their defects and how one transcends them both in accordance with the truth are under the grip of greed, hate and ignorance ... and will not attain final redemption from suffering" (MN 11.6–7/M I 65).

Besides these two main views, however, we must not forget the variety of views about the nature and destiny of man in the universe, prevalent at the time. These have been summarised in the *Brahmajāla Sutta,* which refers to sixty-two views and ways of life.

3

The Buddhist Conception of Truth

One of the five precepts that a Buddhist has to undertake to observe is that of "refraining from saying what is false." Stated in its negative as well as positive form, he has to "refrain from saying what is false, assert what is true (*sacca-vādī*), be devoted to the truth (*sacca-sandha*), be reliable (*theta*), trustworthy (*paccayika*) and not be one who deceives the world" (*avisaṃvādako lokassa*) (AN 4:198/A II 209).

The necessity for speaking the truth is one of the Ten Virtues (*dasa kusala-kamma*) that one has to practise for one's own good as well as for the good of society. For it is held that a just social order requires that, among other things, the people in it be honest and speak the truth. In this context there is a social slant in the description given as to why one should speak the truth: "Herein, a certain layman rejects falsehood and, refraining from saying what is false, asserts the truth whether he be in a formal assembly of people or in a crowd or at home among his relatives or in his office or when he is called to witness in a court of law disclaiming to have known or seen what he did not know or see and claiming to have known or seen what he has known or seen. Thus, neither for his own sake nor for the sake of others, nor again for some material gain would he state a deliberate falsehood" (*Sāleyyaka Sutta,* MN 41.13/M I 288).

Right speech, however, is not limited to the requirement of speaking the truth. It is also necessary that (1) one avoids slander, which causes divisions and dissensions among people and confines oneself to statements which bring about social harmony and understanding; (2) one refrains from harsh or foul language and is civil and courteous in one's speech, saying what is pleasant; and (3) one avoids gossip and vain speech and speaks at the right occasion and in accordance with the law what is profitable, righteous and true.

An exception is sometimes made in the case of (2) where it is held that our statements, even when, true may be either pleasant or unpleasant. It is sometimes necessary to say what is true but unpleasant when it is useful, just as much as it is necessary to put one's finger in the throat of a child even when it causes a little pain in order to pull out something that has got stuck there. Thus in the

Abhayarājakumāra Sutta (MN 58), it is pointed out that statements may be true or false, useful or useless and pleasant or unpleasant. This results in eight possibilities are follows:

1. True useful pleasant
2. True useful unpleasant
3. True useless pleasant
4. True useless unpleasant
5. False useful pleasant
6. False useful unpleasant
7. False useless pleasant
8. False useless unpleasant

Of the eight possibilities, it is said that the Transcendent One (Tathāgata) asserts 1. and 2. at the proper time. The text reads: "He would assert at the proper time a statement which he knows to be true, factual, useful, agreeable and pleasant to others," i.e. (1.) ... "He would assert at the proper time a statement which he knows to be true, factual, useful, disagreeable and unpleasant to others," i.e. (2.) Lying is prohibited and the necessity to seek and speak the truth is emphasised because such action promotes one's personal happiness as well as social progress and harmony. Yet, one incurs moral blame only if there is an intention to deceive and cause disharmony. But negligence is also to be avoided so that a Buddhist must act with a high sense of responsibility with regard to what he says, considering its possible social repercussions.

The Nature of the Truth

The statements of Buddhism or the Dhamma are claimed to be true. The central truths of Buddhism, pertaining to its theory of reality and ethics, are asserted in the form of the Four Noble Truths (*cattari ariya-saccāni*). Nibbāna is claimed to be "the Truth" (*sacca*), being the supreme truth (*parama-sacca*). It is also interesting to note that the two things which are claimed to be "eternal values" (*sanantana dhamma*) are truth and love. With regard to the former, it is stated: "Truth, indeed, is immortal speech—this is an eternal value" (*saccaṃ ve amatā vācā—eso Dhammo sanantano*). There is a tendency today to regard what is old as antiquated. This is a mistaken view, for all that is verified and established as true is forever modern irrespective of the age in which these truths were discovered.

What is the nature of truth? We use the words "true" or "false" normally of statements. We say that the statement, "There is a harbour in Colombo," is true, while the statement, "There is a harbour in Kandy" is false. But we also speak of believing, conceiving of and knowing the truth and as such we have experience of truth. Knowledge of truth or even belief in it helps us to act efficiently in our environment without causing trouble to others. When we know the road to Kandy, it helps us to get there without difficulty and without the necessity for troubling others. Knowledge of causal laws operating in us or in nature helps us to control ourselves or nature for our own good as well as that of others.

When we continue to think of any evil that somebody has done to us, we tend to hate him. But if we continue to think of even some good that he has done to us, our hatred tends to disappear. So by understanding the psychology of mental phenomena, we can gradually get rid of our hatred and, thereby, make ourselves as well as others happy. This is why knowledge of the truth both with regard to ourselves as well as the environment is important, since it helps us to control ourselves as well as the environment for our own good as well as that of others. When we are aware of the truth, we have knowledge (or true beliefs). Knowledge gives us control or power and this can help us develop our personal and social freedom and happiness.

What are the characteristics or criteria of truth? Philosophers have put forward four main theories regarding this. Some hold that truth is what accords or corresponds with fact. This is called the correspondence theory. Others hold that truth is what is consistent. This is called the coherence theory. Yet others hold that what is true is useful and what is useful is true. This is called the pragmatic theory. Others, again, hold that truth is verifiable in the light of experience. This is called the verifiability theory of truth.

Correspondence and Coherence

What is the Buddhist theory? Quite clearly, Buddhism maintains that truth is to be defined in terms of correspondence with fact. A theory or statement is true when it is "in accordance with fact" (*yathābhūtaṃ*). It is the object of knowledge—"one knows what is in accordance with fact" (*yathābhūtaṃ pajānāti,* DN 2.97/D I 84). In contrast, a statement, theory, belief or conception would be false when it does not accord with fact. As the *Apaṇṇaka Sutta* states: "When in fact there is a next world, the belief occurs to me that there is no next world, that would be a false belief. When in fact there is a next world, if one thinks that there is no next world, that would be a false conception. When in fact there is a next world, if one asserts that there is no next world, that would be a false statement..." (MN 60.8/M I 402). On the other hand, true beliefs, conceptions or statements correspond with fact: "When in fact there is a next world, if the belief occurs to me that there is a next world, that would be a true belief" (MN 60.10/M I 403).

Although correspondence with fact is considered to be an essential characteristic of truth, consistency or coherence is also held to be a criterion. In contrast, inconsistency is a criterion of falsehood. In arguing with his opponents, the Buddha often shows that their theories lead to inconsistencies or contradictions, thereby demonstrating that they are false using what is known as the Socratic method. In the debate with Saccaka, the Buddha points out at a certain stage in the discussion that "his latter statement is not compatible with a former statement nor the former with the latter" (MN 35.17/M I 232). Citta, one of the disciples of the Buddha arguing with Nigaṇṭha Nātaputta, the founder of Jainism, says, "If your former statement is true, your latter statement is false and if your latter statement is true, your former statement is false" (SN 41:8/S IV 298).

This means that truth must be consistent. Therefore, when a number of theories with regard to the nature of man and his destiny in the universe contradict each other, they cannot all be true, though they could all be false if none of them corresponds with fact. So at a time when a number of different religious teachers and philosophers put forward a variety of theories about man and the universe, the *Suttanipāta* asks: "Claiming to be experts, why do they put forward diverse theories—are truths many and various?" The answer given is: "Truths, indeed, are not many and various. ... Truth is one without a second" (*ekaṃ hi saccaṃ, na dutiyaṃ atthi* Sn 884). Consistency or the lack of contradiction is, therefore, a criterion of truth. It is evident from this that if we take different theories such as materialism, theism, scepticism, Buddhism, etc., not all can be true, though all may be false.

We must, however, distinguish consistency between divergent theories and consistency within each theory. Two theories may be each internally consistent though mutually contradictory. So consistency is a necessary but not a sufficient criterion of truth. In other words, if a theory is internally inconsistent, it is false, but the fact that it is consistent is not sufficient for us to accept it as true. From the same shreds of evidence, two lawyers may concoct two mutually contradictory theories as to what happened. Each of these may be internally consistent but this alone is no criterion of their truth. This was why the Buddha rejected theories based on mere reasoning as unsatisfactory since the reasoning may be valid or invalid and even if valid (in the sense of being internally consistent), it may or may not correspond with fact (*Sandaka Sutta*, MN 76.23–29/M I 520).

While internal theoretical consistency is a necessary but not a sufficient criterion of truth, Buddhism also holds that, with regard to theories which concern human behaviour, there must also be consistency between theory and practise. The Buddha claimed that "he practised what he preached and preached what he practised" (It 4:13/p. 122). He expected his disciples also to follow his example. If I preach against the evils of taking liquor but take it myself, it may imply that I am not fully convinced of the truth of what I say. So if someone asserts a certain theory and acts as if he believes that at least part of it is false, his practise would be inconsistent with the theory he puts forward.

Pragmatism

What does Buddhism have to say about pragmatism? Does it uphold a pragmatic theory of truth? Evidently, it does not, since it does not maintain that all true statements are useful or that all useful statements are true. As we have seen above, there are useless truths and useful falsehoods, according to Buddhism. The pragmatic theory of truth was put forward to accommodate theistic beliefs, but Buddhism does not hold that a theory is true because people like to believe it and it is, therefore, of some use to them.

At the same time we have to stress the fact that the Buddha confined himself to asserting statements which were true and useful, though pleasant or unpleasant, so that the Dhamma is pragmatic, although it does not subscribe to a pragmatic theory of truth. This fact is well illustrated by two parables, those of the arrow and of the raft. The parable of the arrow states that a man struck with a poisoned arrow must be concerned with removing it and getting well rather than with purely theoretical questions (about the nature of the arrow, who shot it, etc.) which have no practical utility. Certain questions concerning matters beyond empirical verification were not categorically answered by the Buddha because this was "not useful, not related to the fundamentals of religion, not conducive to dispassion, peace, higher knowledge, realisation and Nibbāna" (MN 63.8/M I 431).

Even the true statements in the Dhamma are not to be clung to. They are to be used for understanding the world and overcoming it. One should not identify oneself with it by forming a sentiment of attachment (*upādāna*) towards it and make it a basis for mere disputation. The parable of the raft states that a person intending to cross a river and get to the other bank, where it is safe and secure, makes a raft and with its help safely reaches the other bank. But however useful the raft may have been, he would throw it aside and go his way without carrying it on his shoulder. In the same way it is said "those who realise the Dhamma to be like a raft should be prepared to discard even the Dhamma, not to speak of what is not Dhamma" (MN 22.13–14/M I 135). The value of the Dhamma lies in its utility for gaining salvation. It ceases to have value to each individual, though it does not cease to be true, when one's aims have been realised.

Verifiability

The statements of the Dhamma are meaningful (*sappāṭihāriya*) and are supported by reason and experience (*sanidānaṃ*) and are hence verifiable (*ehipassika*). It is the duty of each Buddhist to try and verify their truth in practise. The Buddhist starts with right beliefs in his *sammādiṭṭhi* endeavour gradually to eliminate greed and hatred and ends his quest for truth with right knowledge (*sammāñāṇa*) and emancipation of mind (*sammāvimutti*). In the process, each person has to verify the truths of Buddhism for himself. Verifiability in the light of reason and experience is thus a characteristic of the truths of Buddhism.

Middle Path

Another characteristic of many of the important truths of Buddhism is that they happen to lie midway between two extreme points of view. Extreme realism, which says that "everything exists" (*sabbaṃ atthi*) because everything comes into existence, is one extreme, while extreme nihilism, which asserts that "nothing exists" (*sabbaṃ natthi*) since everything passes away, is the other extreme—the truth is that everything is becoming. Similarly false extreme theories are the doctrines of the eternity of the soul and of annihilationism, the doctrines of the identity of the body and mind and of the duality of the body and mind; strict determinism (whether theistic or natural) and indeterminism, the doctrine that we are entirely responsible personally for our own unhappiness and the doctrine that we are not at all responsible for our own unhappiness; extreme hedonism (*kāmasukhallikānuyoga*) and extreme asceticism (*attakilamathānuyoga*). In all these instances, it is said that the Buddha without falling into any of these two extremes, preaches the Dhamma in the middle (*majjhena*). The truth lies in the mean between two extreme views. The middle way (*majjhima paṭipadā*) is thus a mean, both in the matter of belief as well as of conduct.

We have shown so far that, in the Buddhist texts, truth is defined as correspondence with fact, consistency is a necessary but not a sufficient criterion of truth, and the truths of Buddhism are pragmatic and verifiable.

Partial Truths

As a result of the correspondence theory, statements which strictly correspond with fact are considered to be true and those which do not are considered to be false. All statements would thus be true or false. Aristotelian logic is based on this assumption alone but modern logicians as well as ancient Indian thinkers have discovered that, without prejudice to our definition of truth, we can adopt other conventions.

We can consider statements which strictly correspond with fact (as those of the Dhamma are claimed to do) as absolutely true, while those which do not all correspond with fact would be absolutely false. In that case, those which correspond to some extent with facts would be partially true (or partially false). According to this convention, all statements will be either true, false or partially true. Modern logicians have shown that a system of logic could be constructed on the basis of this fundamental assumption as well—namely, that every statement is either true, false or partially true.

It is on the basis of this convention that the Buddha characterised certain theories held by individuals, religious teachers and philosophers as being partial truths (*pacceka-sacca*). It is in this connection that we have the parable of the blind men and the elephant (Ud 6.4). The men who are born blind touch various parts of the elephant such as the tusks, ears, forehead, etc., and each reports, mistaking the part for the whole, that the elephant was like that part which was felt by him. In the same way, the various religious and philosophical theories contain aspects of truth and are based on the misdescribed experiences of the individuals who propounded them, while the Buddha was able to understand how these theories arose as well as their limitations, since he had a total vision of reality with an unconditioned mind.

The Catuṣkoṭi

When a statement is characterised as true or false, these characteristics (true, false) are called values in logic. So a system of logic which is based on the fundamental assumption that all statements are either true or false is called a two-valued logic. Such a system may have two logical alternatives. We may illustrate this with an example:

First Alternative	1. This person is happy.
Second Alternative	2. This person is not happy.

We notice that in this two-valued logic of two alternatives, when the first alternative is true, the second has to be counted as necessarily false, while if the second alternative is true, the first would be false. But this system of logic would not do justice to the facts, if the person concerned was partly happy and partly unhappy.

In such a situation we cannot dogmatically assert that the first alternative was true because the person is partly unhappy and therefore not wholly happy. Nor can we say that the second alternative is true because the person is partly happy and therefore not wholly unhappy. But according to the laws of logic applicable within this system—namely, the law of excluded middle—either the first alternative or the second alternative must necessarily be true.

In order to have a better classification of the facts in situations such as this, the Buddhists adopted the logic of four alternatives, known as the *catuṣkoṭi*. This is a two-valued logic of four alternatives. According to it, statements can be made in the form of four logical alternatives of which only one will be necessarily true. Thus, speaking of the happiness or unhappiness of a person, we can say:

First Alternative	1. This person is (wholly) happy.
Second Alternative	2. This person is (wholly) unhappy.
Third Alternative	3. This person is (partly) happy and (partly) unhappy.
Fourth Alternative	4. This person is neither happy nor unhappy (e.g., if he experiences only neutral sensations of hedonic tone).

This is one of the examples given in the texts. If we take another historical example, we may state the following four logically alternative possibilities with regard to the extent of the universe:

1. The universe is finite (in all dimensions).
2. The universe is infinite (in all dimensions).
3. The universe is finite (in some dimensions) and infinite (in other dimensions).
4. The universe is neither finite nor infinite (in any dimension). This last alternative would be the case if space or the universe was unreal. In such an eventuality, the universe cannot properly be described as either finite or infinite.

Now, according to Aristotelian logic or the two-valued logic of two alternatives, the logical alternatives would have to be:

1. The universe is finite.
2. The universe is not finite.

Now if we explain "the universe is finite" as "the universe is finite in all dimensions," then the other alternative, "the universe is not finite" can mean one of three things (as above).

The logical alternatives according to this system of logic, therefore, become vague, ambiguous and not clearly defined and distinguished. The logic of four alternatives, or the *catuṣkoṭi,* is thus employed in the Buddhist texts for purposes of classification or discussion, where the subject matter requires it. Scholars like Poussin, who believed that Aristotelian logic represented the one and only system of logic, failed to understand its significance and thought that the Buddhists or the Indians did not know any logic. But the modern developments in the subject have shown that there could be different complementary systems of logic based on different conventions and that they may be employed according to the needs of the subject matter to be discussed. Thus the early Buddhist conception of logic was far in advance of its time.

Conventional and Absolute Truth

Another distinction that is made in the Buddhist texts is that of absolute (*paramattha*) and conventional (*sammuti*) truth. This is because appearances are sometimes deceptive and reality is different from what appearances seem to suggest. In the everyday world of common sense, we not only observe hard objects like stones and tables, which do not seem to change their form and structure, but also different persons who seem to continue as self-identical entities being reckoned the same persons at different times of their existence. But this appearance, and the reasoning based on it, is deceptive and is due partly to the failure to see reality as it is and partly to the failure to understand the limitations of language, which employs static concepts to describe dynamic processes.

Once we see reality for what it is and the limitations of language, we can still employ the conventional terminology without being misled by the erroneous implications of language and the assumptions we make because of our distorted view of reality. So we realise that from a conventional point of view we may speak of persons, who in reality are dynamic processes which change constantly owing to the impact of the physical, social and ideological environment and the internal changes which take place. But from an absolute point of view, there are no such persons who are self-identical entities or souls which persist without change.

In the same way, modern science finds it necessary to distinguish between the conventional conception of stones and tables as hard, inert objects, which undergo no change, and the scientific conception of them as composed of atoms and molecules, whose inner content consists largely of empty space and whose fundamental elements have such a tenuous existence that they may be regarded as particles in some respects and waves in other respects, if it is possible at all to conceptualise their existence. Still, from a conventional standpoint we need to talk of stones and tables and there is no harm in doing so, provided we are aware of the false assumptions and misleading implications. As the Buddha would say, "They are expressions, turns of speech, designations in common use in the world which the *Tathāgata* (the Transcendent One) makes use of without being led astray by them" (DN 9.53/D I 202).

4

The Buddhist Attitude to Revelation

In the *Saṅgārava Sutta*, the Buddha states that there are three types of religious and philosophical teachers, considering the basis of their knowledge, who prescribe divergent ways of life. Firstly, there are the revelationists (*anussavikā*), who claim final knowledge on the basis of revelation, such as, for instance, the brahmins of the Vedic tradition. Secondly, there are the rational metaphysicians (*takkī vīmaṃsī*), who claim final knowledge on the basis of their faith in reason and speculation. Thirdly, there are those who claim final knowledge of things not found in the traditional revealed scriptures (*ananussutesu dhammesu*), based on a personal understanding derived from their extrasensory powers of perception.

It is significant that the Buddha classifies himself as a member of the third group. Referring to this class of religious and philosophical teachers the Buddha says, "I am one of them" (*tesāhaṃ asmi,* MN 100.8/M II 211). It would surely be of interest to Buddhists to know something about this last class of religious and philosophical teachers with whom the Buddha identifies himself. It would also be important to note the difference between the Buddha and the other members of this class. But in order to do this, it would be necessary on the one hand to identify the Buddha's contemporaries and predecessors, who were presumed to belong to it. On the other hand, it is vital to examine the Buddhist attitude to the other two classes of religious and philosophical thinkers.

This would involve an analysis of the means of knowledge recognised in pre-Buddhist thought. For this purpose it would be necessary to look into both the Vedic and the non-Vedic traditions that preceded Buddhism. The pre-Buddhist Vedic tradition comprises the thinkers who paid some sort of allegiance to the Vedas. From the evidence of the Buddhist scriptures and the Vedic texts, they consisted of the thinkers responsible for the literature from the Ṛgveda downwards up to about the *Maitrāyaṇi Upaniṣad.* The pre-Buddhist non-Vedic tradition would comprise the materialists; the sceptics, who are called *amarāvikkhepikā* (i.e. eel wrigglers) in the Buddhist texts and *ajñānavādins* or agnostics in the

Jain texts; the Ājīvikas, who propounded theories about time and change; and the Jains, who had Nigaṇṭha Nātaputta as their leader.

A careful study of the relevant texts of the Vedic and non-Vedic traditions shows that the thinkers who claimed a final knowledge of things not found in the traditional revealed scriptures, based on a personal understanding derived from their extra sensory powers of perception, are to be found in both the Vedic and the non-Vedic traditions prior to Buddhism. They were none other than those who practised *yoga* and claimed to have acquired certain extra sensory faculties of perception and expansions of consciousness. We shall examine later the respects in which the Buddha may be compared and contrasted with them.

Here it is relevant to examine the claims of the authoritarian thinkers, who regarded the Vedas as revealed scriptures, as well as those of the rationalists, who put forward metaphysical theories about the nature and destiny of man in the universe based on speculative reasoning. It is worth remembering at the same time that the authoritarian thinkers and the rationalists were by no means confined to the Vedic tradition. They are to be found in the pre-Buddhist non-Vedic tradition as well. The *Suttanipāta* refers to "the Vedas of the Samanas or recluses, as well as to the Vedas of the brahmins" (*vedāni viceyya kevalāni samaṇānaṃ yaṃ p'atthi brāhmaṇānaṃ*; Sn 529) and there is evidence to show that some of the Ājīvikas had their own authoritative religious and philosophical texts handed down by tradition. Besides, there were rationalists, perhaps the majority of them, in the non-Vedic tradition. The materialists, sceptics and many of the Ājīvikas were rationalists who based their findings on reasoning. So we find the authoritarian thinkers, the rationalists, as well as the empiricists or experientialists, whose knowledge was derived from experience, represented in both the Vedic and the non-Vedic traditions prior to Buddhism.

We shall here examine the authoritarian thinkers of the Vedic tradition and the Buddhist attitude to them. For this attitude illustrates the Buddhist attitude to revelation. It was the belief of the majority of the thinkers of the Vedic tradition that the whole of it was the word uttered or breathed forth by the Great Being, who is the ground of existence. A passage in the *Bṛhadāraṇyaka Upaniṣad* reads as follows: "It is—as from a fire laid with damp fuel, clouds of smoke separately issue forth, so, too, verily, from this Great Being has been breathed forth that which is Ṛgveda, Yajurveda, Sāmaveda, (Hymns) of the Atharvāns and Angirases, Legend, Ancient Lore, Sciences, Upaniṣads, Stanzas, Sūtras, explanations and commentaries. From it, indeed, are all these breathed forth" (2.4.10). Since this Great Being (*Mahād Bhūtaṃ*) is conceived as the source of all knowledge and power, these scriptures were an infallible divine revelation. In a later passage in the same Upaniṣad, which adds to this list, the entire cosmos is said to be breathed forth by the Great Being. Both passages occur in a context in which the highest reality is said to be non-dual (*advaitaṃ*). This impersonal conception is to be found in other works of this period, where the Vedas are said to be a product of the basic structure of the world (*skambha*), time (*kāla*) or logos (*vāk*).

Very much earlier in the Ṛgveda itself, though in a late hymn (RV 10.90), the origin of the Vedas is traced to the sacrifice of the Cosmic Person (*puruṣa*). This led in the Brāhmaṇas to the theory that the Vedas are due to the creation of Prajāpāti, the Lord of all creatures. This Prajāpāti is often identified in the Brāhmaṇas with Brahmā, who according to the Buddhist texts is considered by the theistic brahmins to be creator of the cosmos. In the Upaniṣads, Prajāpāti or the Lord of creation sometimes continues in his role as the creator of the Vedas (*Chāndogya Up.* 4.17.1–2). But Brahmā often gains prominence as the creator of the Vedas, although they are actually revealed to mankind by Prajāpāti. The *Chāndogya* says: "This did Brahmā tell to Prajāpāti, Prajāpāti to Manu, and Manu to human beings" (8.15). Very much later in the *Muṇḍaka Upaniṣad,* Brahmā is still "the first of the gods and the maker of all," who eventually reveals both the higher and lower forms of Vedic knowledge to mankind.

On the internal evidence of the Vedic tradition itself, we find that the claim was made at a certain stage in its history that the texts of the Vedic tradition were divinely revealed. The later Vedic tradition, therefore, considers the *ṛṣis* who composed the Vedic hymns, as "seers" in the literal sense of the term, who see the Vedas by means of extrasensory perception (*atīndriyārthadraṣṭaraḥ ṛṣayaḥ...*). Radhakrishnan gives expression to this traditional point of view when he says that "the *ṛṣi* of the Vedic hymn calls himself not so much the composer of the hymns as the seer of them," but it is a theory that was put forward as early as the Brāhmaṇas.

It is because the Vedic thinkers believed their texts to have been divinely revealed that they looked down with scorn at the claims of certain religious and philosophical teachers to have personally verified the truths of their doctrines by developing their extrasensory powers of perception. In the *Subha Sutta,* the Buddha criticises some of the ethical recommendations of the Upaniṣads on the ground that neither the brahmins at the time, nor their teachers up to several generations, nor even the original seers claimed to know the consequences of practising the virtues referred to by verifying the fact with their paranormal perception. Subha, the brahmin student, is enraged at this and quotes the views of one of the senior brahmins, who treated such claims to verify these facts in the light of paranormal perception with contempt, considering them ridiculous (*hassakaṃ*), for it is impossible for a mere human being (*manussa-bhūto*) to claim such knowledge. The point here is that Vedic knowledge is divinely revealed in contrast with the knowledge of the Buddha, which was merely human and therefore of lesser worth.

It is the same criticism that is sometimes levelled against Buddhism by some of its theistic critics on the basis of theistic presuppositions. It is said that the knowledge of the Buddha was merely human, whereas the knowledge allegedly contained in their respective theistic traditions is divine, implying thereby that it was more reliable.

We may examine the value of this criticism. But let us first assess the value of the Buddhist criticisms of the Vedic tradition in their historical context. In the above context, the Buddha criticises the acceptance of certain statements merely on the ground that they are contained in an allegedly revealed text without their being verified as true. It may be stated here that verifiability in the light of experience is one of the central characteristics of truth according to Buddhist conceptions.

In the *Sandaka Sutta,* Buddhism is contrasted with four types of false religions, and four types of religions which are unsatisfactory though not necessarily false, by claiming that the statements of Buddhism have been verified by the Buddha and many of his disciples and were, therefore, verifiable in principle by anyone with the requisite competence. A statement can be reliably accepted as true only when it is repeatedly verified and not because it is dogmatically declared to be the truth on the grounds of revelation. In the *Caṅkī Sutta,* the Buddha says: "There are five things which have a twofold result in this life. What five? A belief based on faith (*saddhā*), one's likes (*ruci*), on revelation (*anussava*), superficial reflection (*ākāraparivitakka*), and agreement with one's preconceptions (*diṭṭhinijjhānakkhanti*).... For even what I learn to be the truth on the ground of it being a profound revelation may turn out to be empty, hollow and false, while what I do not hear to be a truth on the ground of it being a profound 'revelation may turn out to be factual, true and sound" (MN 95.14/M II 170–71). The Buddha goes on to say that one safeguards the truth by accepting a statement from revelation as such without dogmatically claiming it to be true, which is unwarranted. This means that it is spurious to claim as knowledge the truth of a statement in a revealed text. It is different with a statement which has been reliably verified in the light of one's personal experience. It is noteworthy that the Buddha says that beliefs held on the grounds of faith, one's likes, revelation, etc., are likely to have a dual result, namely to be verified as either true or false in this life itself.

In the *Sandaka Sutta,* a similar conclusion is drawn. One of the reasons why a religion based on revelation is unconsoling or unsatisfactory (*anassāsika*) is that it may prove to be either true or false and one cannot say what it is for certain. It is said: "Herein a certain religious teacher is a revelationist, who holds to the truth of revelation and preaches a doctrine according to revelation, according to what is traditionally handed down, according to the authority of scripture. Now, a teacher who is a revelationist and holds to the truth of revelation may have well-heard it or ill-heard it and it may be true or false. At this, an intelligent person reflects thus—this venerable teacher is a revelationist, etc.... so seeing that his religion is unsatisfactory he loses interest and leaves it." So even the fact that it has been clearly apprehended as a revelation is no guarantee of its truth, for revelation is no criterion of truth. For the statements of revealed scripture may turn out to be true or false.

This is one of the central criticisms of revealed religion as found in the Buddhist texts, which reappears in the context under discussion in the *Subha Sutta.* The second criticism that is made is that neither the brahmins living at that period, nor their teachers up to several generations, nor even the original seers claimed to know the consequence of practising these virtues after realising the fact with their higher knowledge, although the Buddha himself could do so.

While the Vedic tradition, from the time of the Brāhmaṇas onwards, claimed that the composers of the Vedic hymns were in fact seers who intuited the truths or saw the statements which were revealed to them by their extrasensory perception, the Buddhists not only denied any higher insight on the part of the seers but quite emphatically asserted that the hymns were in fact *composed* by them. The original seers (*pubbakā isayo*) are constantly described as "the makers and the utterers of the hymns" (*mantānaṃ kattāro, mantānaṃ pavattāro;* DN 13.20/D I 242). The internal evidence of the Ṛgvedic texts proves this, for in them the Vedic poets merely claim to make (*kṛ*), compose (*tak*), produce (*jan*) and utter (*avadannrāñi*) the hymns. The Vedic Anukramaṇī merely defines a *ṛṣi* as "*an* author of a hymn" (*yasya vākyaṃ sā ṛṣiḥ*). *So* there is no historical justification for the claim that the original authors of the Ṛgveda had any extrasensory vision. The Buddhist criticisms were, therefore, realistic and made in the light of objective facts as they saw them. What is true of the origins of the Vedic tradition is true of other revelational traditions, when their historical origins are objectively examined.

The idea that the Buddha was a "mere human being" is also mistaken. For when the Buddha was asked whether he was a human being, a Brahmā (God) or Māra (Satan), he denied that he was any of them and claimed that he was Buddha, i.e. an Enlightened Being who had attained the Transcendent. This does not, however, make the Buddha unique for it is a status that any human being can aspire to attain. The significance of this claim is brought out in the *Brahmanimantanika Sutta,* where it is shown that even a Brahmā eventually passes away while the Buddha, being one with the Transcendent Reality beyond space, time and causation, is not subject to such vicissitudes.

At the same time, the Buddhist criticism of revelation does not imply that revelations are impossible. According to the Buddhist conception of things, it is possible for beings more developed than us to exist in the cosmos and communicate their views about the nature and destiny of man in the universe through human beings. All that is said is that the fact that something is deemed to be a revelation is no criterion of its truth, and revelation, therefore, cannot be considered an independent and valid means of knowledge. No book on scientific method today regards it as such and even theologians have begun to doubt the validity of such claims. According to Buddhist conceptions, revelations may come from different grades of higher beings with varying degrees of goodness and intelligence. They cannot all be true. This does not mean that they are all necessarily false. For they may contain aspects of truth although we cannot say what these are by merely giving ear to them. This is why Buddhism classifies religions based on revelation as unsatisfactory though not necessarily false.

It is a notorious fact that different revelational traditions and individual revelations contradict each other. If "truth is one" (*ekaṃ hi saccaṃ*), as Buddhism believes to be the case, they cannot all be true though all may be false. There are diverse views on crucial matters even within the same revelational tradition. The Brāhmaṇas and the Upaniṣads, for instance, contain several creation myths and divergent accounts as to how life came into existence on earth. The ideas they contain differ from those of the Babylonian myths with which the Western world is familiar.

One such creation myth, for instance, states that in the beginning, the world was Soul (Ātman) alone in the form of a Person. Human beings are the offspring of Ātman, who first creates a wife to escape from anxiety and loneliness. Later the wife assumes the forms of various animals, while Ātman assumes their male forms in order to make love to her. It is thus that the various species of animals come into being. This account of creation is in a section of the *Bṛhadāraṇyaka Upaniṣad.* The creation myth in the *Aitareya Upaniṣad* is quite different, although this too starts with the story that in the beginning Soul or Atman alone existed and there was no other thing whatsoever. Atman creates the worlds by an act of will and then thinks of creating people to look after them. Then, it is said that "right from the waters he drew forth and shaped a person" (*Aitareya Up.* I.3). Here man is created not by an act of procreation, not out of clay, but out of the waters. The evolutionary account of the origin of life found in a section of the *Taittirīya Upaniṣad* is still different. It says that from the Atman or the Soul there progressively emerged space, wind, fire, water, earth, plants, food, seed and then man.

If we compare and contrast the materialist criticism of the Vedas with the Buddhist, we see the difference in approach. The materialists condemned outright the whole of the Vedic tradition and saw no good in it at all. According to them, the Vedas were the work of fools and knaves or in their own words, *bhaṇḍa-dhurta-nisācaraḥ,* i.e. buffoons, knaves and demons. On the other hand, the Buddhists, while holding that the original seers who were the authors of the Vedas merely lacked a special insight with which they were later credited, in keeping with historical fact, praised them for their virtue and rectitude. The materialists categorically repudiated the Vedas as false, self-contradictory and repetitive (*anṛtavyaghata-punarukta-doṣa*). The Buddhists, while pointing out the contradictions and falsities and repudiating the claims to revelation, did not consider all the traditional beliefs in the Vedic tradition to be wholly false. Among the false beliefs, the materialists would point to the belief in sacrifices, in a soul, in survival, in moral values and moral retribution. The Buddhists, however, criticised the Vedic conception of the sacrifice and denied the necessity for the concept of a soul, but agreed with the Vedas in asserting survival, moral values and moral recompense and retribution, which are among the beliefs which formed part of the right philosophy of life or *sammā diṭṭhi* in Buddhism.

Even with regard to the sacrifice, the materialists saw nothing but deception and fraud in it. The Buddhists, while condemning sacrifices as involving a waste of resources and the needless destruction of animals, were not averse to the simple sacrificial offerings made in good faith by the earliest brahmins who killed no animals for the occasion. Just as much as some of the Upaniṣads reinterpret sacrifice or *yajña* as the religious life, Buddhism conceives of *yajña* at its best to be the highest religious life as advocated in Buddhism.

The difference between the attitude of the Upaniṣads and Buddhism towards sacrifices, despite the similarities indicated, may be described as follows: the Upaniṣads as the *jñāṇa-marga* or "the way of knowledge" tended to regard the earlier Vedic tradition in the Brāhmaṇas, advocating the *karma-marga* or "the way of ritual" and the associated learning as a lower form of knowledge (*aparāvidyā*), while the thought of the Upaniṣads was a higher form of knowledge (*parāvidyā*). But even as a lower form of knowledge, it was not discarded. For us to do so would be to deny the authority of the injunctive assertions of the Vedas, which advocated sacrifices, and thereby question and undermine the belief in Vedic revelation. So even where the Upaniṣads urge the cultivation of compassion, an exception is made with regard to the sacrifice. Paradoxically, it is said that one should not harm any creatures except at the sacrificial altars (*ahiṃsan sarvabhūtanī anyatra tīrthebyaḥ*; *Chāndogya Up.* 8.15.1). So it was the belief in revelation which is ultimately the basis for the belief in animal sacrifices.

The materialists, likewise, saw no basis for a belief in revelation since they counted as real only the observable material world. Buddhism on the other hand did not question the basis of the belief in revelation except for its denial of a personal creator God. It criticised particular claims to revelation and the attempt to regard revelation as a separate valid means of knowledge. In the *Tevijja Sutta,* the brahmins claim to have a diversity of paths for attaining fellowship with Brahmā or God. The Buddha criticises these claims on the ground that not one of them has "seen Brahmā face to face" (*Brahmā sakkhidiṭṭho*, DN 13.12/D I 238). This was true of the brahmins present at the time right up to the original composers of the Vedas. So the claim to revelation is without basis. Although Brahmā is believed to be the creator of the cosmos, he is none other than a temporary regent of the cosmos, an office to which any being within the cosmos could aspire. The knowledge of the Buddha, who has attained the Transcendent, excels that of Brahmā, who is morally perfect (*asaṅkiliṭṭha-citto*) but is neither omniscient nor omnipotent. The Buddha, who has held this office in the past and has verified in the light of his extrasensory powers of perception the conditions required for attaining fellowship with God or Brahmā, could state that there is no diversity of paths all leading to such a state but the one and only path consisting in acquiring purity of mind, cultivating compassion and being selfless or without possessions. What is verifiably true is more reliable than a blind belief in a claim to revelation.

The Buddhist attitude to any such revelation would be that of accepting what is true, good and sound and rejecting what is false, evil and unsound after a dispassionate analysis of its contents without giving way to prejudice, hatred, fear or ignorance. The Buddhist criticism of religions based on authoritarian claims is not limited to a criticism of a claim to revelation. An analysis of the sermon addressed to the Kālāmas shows that it is only the first of the grounds for an authoritarian claim, although it was undoubtedly the most important and, therefore, the one to be examined and criticised in detail. The different kinds of claims to knowledge based on authority are seen in the classification of such claims in the *Kālāma Sutta*, which mentions besides revelation claims made on the grounds of tradition (*paramparā*), common sense, wide acceptance of hearsay (*itikira*), conformity with scripture (*piṭaka-sampadā*) and on the ground of something being a testimony of an expert (*bhavyarūpatā*) or the view of a revered teacher (*samaṇo me garu*). They could not be deemed to be valid means of knowledge and the requirement of safeguarding the truth (*saccānurakkhanā*) demands that beliefs held on such a basis be admitted as such instead of dogmatically claiming them to be true. Such dogmatism leads to undesirable consequences for oneself and society—to intolerance, conflict and violence—and is a departure from sincerity and truth.

5

The Buddhist Conception of Matter and the Material World

We are all familiar with the visible and tangible world around us, which we call the material world. We contrast it with what is mental and consider it to exist independently of our thoughts. We have learnt much about it from science during the last few decades but hope to learn much more about it in the future. A knowledgeable scientist who sums up the modern conception of matter in the light of recent findings of science says, "Matter is the world around us; it is everything we see and feel and touch. It seems thoroughly familiar—until we read in the following pages what the scientists have discovered about it within the last fifty years, the last twenty, the last two. The diamond, for example, seems on the face of it resplendently substantial. But as we read on, we find that the diamond is a patterned arrangement of atoms which are themselves mainly empty space, with infinitesimal dabs of electrons whirling around infinitesimal dabs of protons and neutrons. All this we now know to be matter, but we are by no means sure the picture is complete. Within the minuscule heart of the atom—the nucleus—have been found no fewer than thirty kinds of elementary particlse, and no one can say what more will emerge under nuclear bombardment. The further scientists analyse, the less obvious the answers become." (See R.H. Lapp, *Matter*, Life Science Library, Chicago, 1963, p. 7.)

Buddhist View

The conception of matter that is generally found in the Buddhist tradition, except in the extreme idealist schools of thought (*vijñāna-vāda*), is essentially the same. The objectivity of the material world is affirmed. It is said that *rūpa* or matter is not mental (*acetasika*) and is independent of thought (*citta-vippayutta*).

Such matter is classified into three categories. Firstly, there is the category of matter or material qualities, which are visible (*sanidassana*) and can be apprehended by the senses (*sappaṭigha*), such as colours and shapes. Secondly, there is matter which is not visible (*anidassana*) but reacts to stimuli, such as the five senses, as well as the objects of sense which can come into contact with the appropriate sense organs (excluding the visual objects which fall into the first category). Thirdly, there is matter which is neither visible to the naked eye nor apprehensible by the senses but whose existence can either be inferred or observed by paranormal vision. Such, for example, are the essences (*ojā*) of edible food (*kabaliṅkārāhāra*), which are absorbed by our bodies and sustain it. Today we call them proteins, carbohydrates, vitamins, etc. but in the *Dhammasaṅgaṇī,* the essences (*ojā*) of edible food are classified as subtle (*sukhuma*) matter, which is not directly observed or apprehended by the sense organs. The subtle matter of "the realm of attenuated matter" (*rūpa-dhātu*) would also fall into this last category.

In this same category one would also have to include the atom (*paramāṇu*), which is said to be so small that it occupies only a minute portion of space (*ākāsa-koṭṭhāsika*), as the Commentary to the *Vibhaṅga* (p. 343) states. The subcommentary to the *Visuddhimagga* observes that the atom "cannot be observed by the naked eye but only comes within the range of clairvoyant vision" (*maṃsacakkhussa āpātham nāgacchati dibba-cakkhuss'eva āgacchati*), (p. 286). If this is so, then the Buddhist and some of the Indian atomic theories are not the product of pure rational speculation (like those of the Greeks) but are partly the result of extrasensory perception as well.

Yet what is remarkable about the Buddhist atomic theories as against the other Indian and Western classical atomic theories is that they were able to conceive of the atom as existing in a dynamic state. As one scholar (Prof. A. L. Basham) puts it, "The atom of Buddhism is not eternal as in the other three systems since Buddhism dogmatically asserts the impermanence of all things" (*History and Doctrines of the Ājīvikas*, London, 1951, p. 267). Another scholar (Sir Arthur Berriedale Keith) brought out the essentially dynamic conception of the Buddhist theory of the atom when he said that the atom is conceived as "flashing into being; its essential feature is action or function and, therefore, it may be compared to a focus of energy" (*Buddhist Philosophy,* Oxford, 1923, p. 161). We may compare with it what a modern physicist says of the atom: "The old view of it as simple discrete particles and precise planetary orbits is gone.. The physicist now prefers to view the atom as a ball of energetic and uncertain fluff' (*Matter,* Life Science Library, Chicago, 1963 p. 158). We may recall that even the early Buddhist texts compared matter to a "lump of foam" (*pheṇapiṇḍa*).

Atomic Theory

The atomic theories developed only in the schools of Buddhism which, apart from the general notions that they shared, did not always agree among themselves about the nature of atoms. For example, one school (*Sautrāntikas*) held that atoms have spatial dimensions (*dig-bhāga-bheda*), while their opponents (*Vaibhāṣikas*) denied this, arguing that the atom has no parts and no extension. This dialectical opposition led to a situation in which the Idealists argued that the conception of the atom leads to contradictions. If the atom has some finite dimension, however small this may be, it is further divisible and therefore it is not an indivisible unit or an atom. On the other hand, if the atom had no spatial dimension at all, it is a non-entity and material objects having a spatial dimension cannot be composed of them. So the Idealists argued that the atom was a self-contradictory concept and as such could not exist. Since atoms did not exist, there was no material world. So they concluded that the material world was an appearance created by our own minds, like some of the objects in the mind of a hypnotised subject.

The mistake that all these schools committed was to try and prove or disprove the existence of atoms by pure reasoning. As the Buddha pointed out in the *Kālāma Sutta,* we cannot discover or discern the nature of things as they are by pure speculative reasoning (*takka*). It is only when reasoning is closely tied up with experience that there is a discovery of facts in the objective world. For this reason we have either to follow the method of experimental science, which is a matter of controlled observation guided by reasoning, or of developing our extrasensory powers of perception by meditation, if we are to understand things as they are.

Judging by results the Theravadins seem to have kept their speculations close to the findings of jhānic or extrasensory observation. The Vaibhāṣikas spoke of the ultimate element of matter as the *dravya-paramāṇu* or the "unitary atom" and contrasted with this the *saṅghāta-paramāṇu* or the aggregate atom, which we today call a molecule. It is significant that the Theravadins conceived of even the atom (*dravya-paramāṇu*) as a complex (*rūpa-kalāpa*) and spoke even of "the constituents of this complex atom" (*kalāpaṅga*), at the same time considering such an atom to be in a dynamic state of continuous flux.

A table given in the Commentary to the *Vibhaṅga* makes it possible to compare the size of an atom as conceived of in medieval Buddhism with modern conceptions. If we follow this table, an average of thirty-six *paramāṇus* equal one *aṇu*, thirty-six *aṇus* equal one *tajjāri* and thirty-six *tajjāris* equal one *ratha-reṇu*. A *ratha-reṇu* is a minute speck of dust which we can barely appreciate with the human eye. According to this calculation, there are 46,656 atoms in such a minute speck of dust. Now modern scientists think that an average of about 100 million atoms placed side by side in a row would amount to about an inch in length. If so, there would be ten million atoms in a tenth of an inch and a two-hundredth portion of this would have fifty thousand atoms. Although the comparison is to some extent arbitrary, the figures given in the *Vibhaṅgaṭṭhakathā* do not appear to be far divorced from reality.

Original Buddhism

At the same time, we must not forget that it was not the intention of the Buddha to give a detailed account of the nature of the physical world. As the Buddha pointed out in the Siṃsapā forest, taking a few leaves into his hand, what he taught amounted to the leaves in his hand while what he knew but did not teach was comparable in extent to the leaves in the forest.

If there are priorities in the accumulation of knowledge, man should first and foremost learn more about his own nature and his destiny in the universe rather than about the nature and origin of the universe.

Nevertheless, a general understanding of the nature of the physical world is also useful in that it helps us in knowing the nature of things as they are.

The Buddha himself did not disclose any details of an atomic theory but there are passages in which he points out unmistakably that the minutest portion of matter in the world is in a state of constant flux. On one occasion, a monk asks the Buddha whether there was any form or kind of matter (*rūpa*) which was eternal, stable, lasting, not subject to constant change and everlasting. The

Buddha replies that there is no such matter. He then takes a grain of sand on to the tip of his nail and says, "Even such a minute bit of matter is not eternal, stable or lasting, it is subject to constant change and is not everlasting."

What we claim to know with regard to the physical world would not amount to knowledge if it does not reflect the state of things as they are. But such knowledge, once acquired, is to be made use of for one's moral and spiritual development. The significance of the above statement is that even existence in a subtle-material world is not everlasting and that we cannot hope to attain final salvation by attachment even to such an ethereal body. So while early Buddhism gives a realistic account of the essential nature of the physical world, this is done mindful of the psychological and ethical impact of these teachings.

Definition

The totality of matter is classified in the Buddhist texts with reference to time as past, present and future; with reference to the individual as internal and external; with reference to the nature of matter as gross and subtle; with reference to the value of matter as base and ethereal and with reference to space as near and distant (MN 109.8/M III 16).

At the same time the matter spoken of is not just dead matter but living matter as well. The concept includes both the organic as well as the inorganic realms of matter. In this respect, we must not forget that, according to Buddhist conceptions, life (*jīvitindriya*) is a by-product of matter (*upādārūpa*).

In the *Abhidhamma,* too, we notice in the *Dhammasaṅgaṇī* that regarding the nature of the totality of matter there are references to the psychological and ethical aspects of its impact. Matter is causally conditioned (*sappaccaya*), impermanent and subject to decay (*aniccaṃ eva jarābhibhūtaṃ*). It is to be found in the gross world of sensuous gratification (*kāmāvacara*) as well as in the subtle-material world (*rūpāvacara*). In itself it is morally neutral, being neither good nor evil (*avyākata*). But it can be cognised by the six kinds of cognition, (i.e. by means of the senses and the understanding) and it is the kind of thing around which sentiments can be formed (*upādāniya*). It is also the kind of thing that can act as a fetter (*saññojanīya*), although the fetter does not lie in matter as such but in the attachment to matter.

In the earliest texts, *rūpa*, in its widest sense of "matter" as including the organic body as well as the external physical world, is defined as "what undergoes change" (*ruppati*) under the impact of temperature such as heat and cold; atmospheric changes such as wind and heat; organic affections such as hunger which is defined as "heat inside the belly" (*udaraggi-santāpa*), as well as thirst and the changes effected by the sting and bite of gnats and snakes, etc. The general definition that is adopted in the commentaries is that matter (*rūpa*) is so called because "it undergoes change, i.e. becomes subject to modifications under the impact of cold and heat, etc." (*ruppatīti sīta-uṇhādīhi vikāraṃ āpajjati*).

Primary Material Forces

If we apply the definition at the level of sense-observation or the empirically observable world, matter is what undergoes change under the impact of temperature, i.e. heat or cold. Since there is no metaphysical substance called "matter" apart from the observable objective states, the primary forms would be the states of matter themselves manifested under the impact of temperature changes.

Water when cooled would eventually become frozen and solid. If the frozen ice is heated, it turns into water and the water, if heated, boils and turns into steam or a gaseous state. All elements or forms of matter subjected to changes of temperature are to be found in the solid, liquid or gaseous states. Until the third decade of the twentieth century, physicists concerned themselves only with these three states of matter. But it was realised that with the further application of heat to matter in the gaseous state a further state of matter can be brought into being. This is today called the plasma state. If very great heat is applied to steam, the movement of the water molecules becomes so violent that they start smashing themselves into electrically charged ions. This ionisation is the passage to the fourth state of matter or plasma described as a "swarming mass of hot, electrically-charged particles." The blazing mass of the sun is considered to be in this plasma state.

The conception of matter as what undergoes changes of state under the impact of temperature is therefore logically and empirically sound. Although there is no mention of the plasma state as such in the Buddhist texts, the primary forms of matter are held to be the solid (*paṭhavī*), the liquid (*āpo*), the gaseous (*vāyo*) and the fiery (*tejo*), such as lightning.

We can make use of these notions to classify the material of the body as well as the external world. There are solid states of matter in our own body such as the teeth, nails, hair, flesh, etc. The blood, sweat, tears, bile, pus, etc., would be in a liquid state. The air we breathe in inhaling and exhaling, the wind in the abdomen, etc., would be in a gaseous state. The heat in the body which transmutes food and drink in digestion comes under the fiery state of matter.

While in a general sense the four states are referred to in the above manner, it was observed that the specific characteristic of each state was to be found in some degree in the other states. Thus the specific characteristic of what is solid is extension. It is solid in the sense that it extends or spreads out (*pattharatīti paṭhavī*). The characteristic of the liquid state is that of cohesiveness (*bandhanatta, saṅgaha*), while that of the gaseous state is vibration or mobility (*samudīraṇa, chambhitatta, thambhitatta*). The fiery state is said to have the characteristic of causing changes of temperature or maturation (*paripācana*).

These characteristics, it is argued, are not exclusive of the different states of matter but are their most prominent characteristics. As general characteristics they are to be found in all the states of matter. What is solid is most obviously extended but liquids, gases and fires do not lack extension, nor occupancy of space. Similarly, the matter of what is solid has a certain degree of cohesiveness. It has also a certain degree of dynamism or mobility and has a certain temperature. Extension, cohesiveness, mobility and temperature are thus held to be inseparable but distinguishable characteristics of all material things right down to atoms. Different kinds of material objects, therefore, all have these several characteristics in varying degrees. When it comes to atomic theory, Buddhism would have to say that atoms differ from each other according to the presence of these characteristics in varying degrees.

Derivatives

The four characteristic qualities of extension, cohesiveness, mobility and temperature, which coexist (*aññamañña-sahajāta*), are the four great material forces or forms of energy. In a gross state, the qualities of extension, mobility and temperature can be directly appreciated by the sense of touch, but cohesiveness has to be inferred. When we put our hand in water, we can apprehend its resistance or extension, its pressure or mobility as well as its temperature, but its characteristic of cohesiveness eludes us, and the most prominent characteristic of water has therefore to be inferred from observation.

All material things, whether organic or inorganic, and certain material concepts like space, are said to be dependent on or derived from these primary material forces. But the senses in which they are derived are different. In the case of space, the derivation is purely logical in the sense that *ākāsa* or vacuous space (not ether) is untouched by the four material forces and is in fact to be apprehended as the place in which they are absent. In the case of *jīvitindriya* or life, however, it is a derivation in the sense of being a by-product of the primary material forces. Other characteristics of matter such as weight, plasticity, wieldiness, growth, continuity, decay and impermanence are also by-products of the primary manifestations of energy.

Realism

The sense organs as well as the objects of sense are also made up of them. The matter forming the sensitive parts of the eye (*pasāda*), which react to stimuli (*sappaṭigha*), is intimately bound up with our entire psycho-physical personality (*attabhāva-pariyāpanna*) and is again a by-product of the primary material forces.

The sense of sight, for example, is defined in various ways: (1) It is itself invisible though reacting to stimuli but it is the means by which what is visible and impinges on the eye has been seen, is being seen, will be seen or would be seen; (2) it is the organ on which visible objects which are capable of stimulating it have impinged, are impinging, will impinge or would impinge; (3) it is the organ which has been focused, is being focused, will be focused or would be focused on visible objects capable of stimulating it; (4) it is the organ on account of which visual impressions as well as ideas, feelings, conative and cognitive activities aroused by these impressions have arisen, are arising, will arise or would arise. The accounts given in some respects foreshadow and in other respects are not in conflict with the modern finding regarding the psychology or physiology of perception.

In some respects one feels that the modern accounts need to be re-examined in the light of observations made in these texts. For example, textbooks in modern psychology tell us that the primary tastes are the sweet, sour, salt and bitter. But the *Dhammasaṅgaṇī* while mentioning the tastes sweet (*sādu*), sour (*ambila*), salt (*lonika*) and bitter (*tittaka*) also refer to other tastes such as the astringent (*kasāva*) and pungent (*kaṭuka*). Although what we identify as tastes is partly due to what we appreciate through the skin senses as well as taste in the interior of the mouth, and also partly to odour, it is a moot point as to whether the astringent taste (*kahaṭa-raha*) is a by-product of these or is a separate taste altogether.

It is quite evident from the descriptions given of the objects of sense as well as the general theory of matter that original Buddhism upheld the reality of the physical world. What we apprehend through the senses by way of colours or shapes, sounds, smells, tastes, etc., are all by-products of the four primary material forces, which exist in the objective physical world independently of our perceiving them.

The physical movements of our bodies (*kāyaviññatti*) and our verbal activity (*vacīviññatti*), which are due to our volitional actions, are also due to the operations of material factors, though they are concurrently occasioned and accompanied (*citta-samuṭṭhāna, citta-sahabhū*) by mental activity. It is also significant that none of the books of the *Abhidhamma Piṭaka* included in the Canon mention the heart as the physical basis of mental activity. The *Paṭṭhāna,* while recounting the role of the organ of vision in generating visual cognition, makes specific mention of "the physical basis of perceptual and conceptual activity" (*yam rūpaṃ nissaya manodhātu ca manoviññāṇadhātu ca vattati*) and ignores the cardiac theory of the seat of mental activity, which was widely prevalent at this time. (See *Compendium of Philosophy,* P.T.S., London, 1963, pp. 277–9.)

Physical and Social Environment

While conscious mental activity has a physical basis, what we call a person's mind is also conditioned by the physical environment, according to Buddhist conceptions. The physical objects of the external world among other factors stimulate the senses, generate mental activity, feed the mind and motivate one's behaviour. The mind continues to be conditioned by these impacts, which form part and parcel of one's accumulated mental experiences.

It is also the teaching of Buddhism that the economic and social environment also conditions our behaviour. In the *Cakkavattisīhanāda Sutta,* it is stated that the maldistribution of goods in society produces poverty. This eventually leads to the growth of crime and loss of faith in moral values, which, along with a sound economic basis, are necessary to sustain a well-ordered society. However, Buddhism does not teach a theory of physical or economic determinism, for, despite the fact that man is conditioned by these factors, they do not totally determine his behaviour. Man has an element of freedom, which when exercised with understanding makes it possible for him to change his own nature as well as his physical, economic and social environment for the good and happiness of himself as well as of society[1].

---

1. One of the best books written about the Buddhist conception of matter is Y. Karunadasa, *Buddhist Analysis of Matter,* Colombo, 1967. I do not, however, agree with some of the conclusions that the author has come to.

6

The Buddhist Analysis of Mind

The present concise account of the Buddhist theory of mind is based on the early Buddhist texts and leaves out for the most part the elaborations to be found in the later books of the Theravada tradition such as the *Abhidhammattha-saṅgaha*. The main reason for doing so is that otherwise there is a danger of losing sight of the wood for the trees.

Another reason for this is that some of the later traditions of Buddhism developed only certain aspects of the original teaching, exaggerating their importance to such an extent as to distort other aspects. Such seems to have been the case with the idealist (*Vijñānavāda*) schools of Buddhism, which spoke of a universal mind as a vast reservoir in which the individuals' minds were waves or ripples. In such a universe both the individual minds of various beings as well as the external material world were illusions created by the mind. The entire universe is a creation of the mind (*sarvaṃ buddhimayaṃ jagat*) and physical objects do not exist outside our perceptions of them. In some of the Mahayana schools of thought this universal mind was conceived as the ultimate reality or the eternal Buddha, though never as a creator God.

Realism

Some Western scholars also tried to give an idealistic interpretation to early Buddhism by translating the first verse of the *Dhammapada* to mean "All things are preceded by mind, governed by mind and are the creations of the mind" (*manopubbaṅgamā dhammā mano-seṭṭhā mano-mayā*). But the correct interpretation of this stanza, which is also supported by the commentary (*Dhammapadaṭṭhakathā*), is "Conscious states of mind are led by will, are governed by will and are the products of will; so if one speaks or acts with an evil will, suffering comes after one like the wheel that follows the beast of burden who draws the cart." Besides, it is clear from the early Buddhist texts that original Buddhism was realistic and held that the world of matter existed independently of our mind (*citta-vippayuttaṃ*) and was not an illusion produced by it. Though our perceptions and our language distorted the nature of reality, this was only to the extent that a dynamic material world in a continual state of flux was perceived as permanent, solid and substantial.

Attitude to Tradition

The Theravada tradition, in my opinion, has on the other hand to some extent ignored the conception of the transcendent mind to be found in the early Buddhist texts. This has led to misconceptions on the part of scholars and, perhaps, some Buddhists that Nibbāna was a state of oblivion or annihilation. It is, I think, important that Buddhists, who have been asked by the Buddha not to accept things merely because they are to be found in tradition (*ma paramparāya*), should be prepared to examine their own traditions.

We must not forget that, even in the time of the Buddha, some concise statements made by him regarding matters of doctrine were elaborated and developed by monks and nuns. The Buddha very often commended these expositions of the Dhamma. On the other hand, there were others who made erroneous expositions and came to false conclusions in interpreting the statements of the Buddha. There was Satī, for instance, who thought that "the consciousness of a person ran along and fared on without change of identity" *viññāṇaṃ ... sandhāvati saṃsarati anaññaṃ*) like a permanent soul, whereas the Buddha points out that consciousness is causally conditioned (*paṭicca-samuppāda*) and changes under the impact of environment, etc.

Then there is the case of the monk who argued that the doctrine of *anattā* (no-soul) implies the denial of personal responsibility. It is said that "a certain monk entertained the thought that since body, feelings, strivings (conative acts) and intellect are without self, what self can deeds not done by a self affect?" (MN 109.14/M III 19): The Buddha thought that this was an unwarranted corollary of his teaching since there was the continuity of the "stream of consciousness" (*viññāṇa-sota*) without identity in rebecoming from existence to existence and this was called "the dynamic or evolving consciousness" (*saṃvaṭṭanika-viññāṇa*). Individuality is continuing though the person is "neither the same (*na ca so*) nor another (*na ca añño*)."

Characteristics

One of the main features of the Buddhist theory of mind is that, barring the mind in the Nibbānic state, all mental phenomena are causally conditioned (*paticca-samuppanna*). According to Buddhist tradition, causal laws operate not only in the physical realm (*utu-niyāma*) or biological realm (*bija-niyāma*), but in the psychological realm (*citta-niyāma*) as well. Likewise, mental events are more fleeting than the material events of the body, although as a stream of events they outlast the body, whereas the body disintegrates at death. Yet while past phenomena continue to influence and condition the ever-changing present, there is no substratum which can be called a permanent soul. Nor does it make sense to say that the phenomena are in any way associated with or related to such a soul.

The present is conditioned not merely by the past but also by the factors of heredity and environment. Also, conscious mental phenomena have a physical basis. The *Patthāna* speaks of "the physical basis of perceptual and conceptual activity." There is mutual interaction between the physical basis and the mental activity. The mental phenomena are not mere accompaniments of neural or brain phenomena. The nature of the causal relations that hold among mental phenomena and their relations to the body, the physical, social and ideological environment are also analysed and the correlations explained in terms of them. In short we have the earliest historical account of a naturalistic view of the mind.

This knowledge with regard to the mind is to be had by observation and introspection. Introspection is considered to be an unreliable instrument for the study of mental phenomena, according to Western psychologists. This is partly because introspection can only tell us about our private mental experiences, and since these cannot be checked by others, they cannot be trusted. The Buddhist theory is that introspection can be refined and developed by the culture of the mind. Besides, such mental development results in the emergence of extrasensory powers of perception such as telepathy, clairvoyance, etc. This development of the mind is said to sharpen our observation and widen its range since with the development of telepathy, direct and indirect, the minds of others become amenable to public observation like physical objects. The elimination of personal bias makes one's observations objective. Jhānic introspection is described as follows: "Just as one person should objectively observe another, a person standing should observe a person seated, or a person seated a person lying down, even so, should one's object of introspection be well-apprehended, well-reflected upon, well-contemplated and well-penetrated with one's knowledge" (AN 5:28/A III 27).

Modern Western Psychology

With regard to one's own person, it is true that with the growth of objectivity one's emotions tend to evaporate under the scrutiny of objective observation. As a modern textbook of psychology says: "If affective states are immediately at hand to be observed, their description and interpretation are not easy to come by, for they prove to be remarkably elusive. Try to observe in yourself the turbulent feelings aroused in anger. Ask yourself, 'What does anger consist of?' If you are able, when angry, to get yourself in the frame of mind to ask this question, you are also in a fair way toward dispelling the anger" (Frank A. Geldarad, *Fundamentals of Psychology,* London, 1963, p. 38). It is true that watchfulness (*sati*) regarding one's own emotions tends to dissipate them but this too is an important psychological fact. It is a fact that can be made use of to make our minds more stable and serene.

Many modern textbooks of psychology with a behavioural bias have not only completely discarded the concept of a soul but regard psychology as "the science of human behaviour." This is because human behaviour can be publicly observed and measured while human experience cannot. This orientation has its uses. We have learnt a lot about the physiological, biochemical and neural basis of what we call psychological behaviour. As a result, we have learnt to some extent to control such behaviour by surgical or biochemical means. But despite these advances in psychology, mental tensions and anxiety have been on the increase in societies in which the tempo and philosophies of life give no room for intelligent self-restraint, relaxation, self-analysis and meditation as a means to achieving a healthier mind.

Buddhist psychology, on the other hand, while giving a comprehensive account of the nature of human experience and behaviour also provides the means by which we can understand, control and develop ourselves by a process of self-analysis and meditation, which changes our nature and makes it possible to live happily ourselves and with others.

Psychophysical Unit

Man, according to Buddhism, is a psychophysical unit (*nāmarūpa*). This is made up of three components—the sperm and the ovum which go to make up the fertilised ovum or zygote along with the impact of the stream of consciousness of a discarnate spirit (*gandhabba*) or what is called the relinking consciousness (*paṭisandhi-viññāṇa*).

The psychic and organic physical components grow and mature in a state of mutual interaction. There is reliable evidence that certain children are born with memories of a previous life, which correspond to those of a real life of a dead person, and that they could not have acquired these memories by any social contact with the dead person's friends or relatives in this life (see Ian Stevenson, *Twenty Cases Suggestive of Reincarnation,* New York, 1966). There is also evidence that hypnotised subjects who regressed to a prenatal period give accounts of prior lives which they claimed to have lived and which have been partly historically verified as factual (see Morey Bernstein, *The Search for Bridey Murphy,* New York, 1965; also Dr Jonathan Rodney, *Explorations of a Hypnotist,* London, 1959). The above theory can also be experimentally verified if identical twins brought up in the same environment show some marked differences of character. All the available evidence cannot be more plausibly accounted for than on the above theory, although it has not as yet merited the attention of psychologists as a whole.

The belief that the Buddhist doctrine of *anattā* implies a denial of any kind of survival after death rests on a misunderstanding of this doctrine. The doctrine denies a permanent entity or soul which runs through different existences without change of identity but does not deny the continuity of an evolving consciousness. Although the emotionally charged experiences are more fleeting than the changes in the body, their memories registered in the unconscious mind outlast the body and determine its state of re-becoming in different forms of cosmic existence. As the *Saṃyutta Nikāya* says in one place: "Though his material body is devoured by crows and other animals, yet his mind (*citta*), if long-practised in faith, virtue, learning and renunciation, moves upward and goes to distinction" (SN 55:21/S V 370).

Mental Factors

The components of the mind are classified into four branches (*khandha*) or groups (*kāya*), namely (1) feeling or hedonic tone (*vedanā*); (2) sense-impressions, images or ideas and concepts (*saññā*); (3) conative activities and their concomitants (*saṅkhārā*); and (4) intellectual activity (*viññāṇa*).

Vedanā is the feeling component, which accompanies our impressions and ideas. They range from the pleasant to the unpleasant through the neutral. Its source may be physical or psychological. When we cut our finger we feel physical pain. When we hear that a close friend or relative has died suddenly the anguish we experience has a psychological origin. These feelings are classified as six, according to how they originate in the five senses or in the mind with an idea or concept. Since these may be pleasant, unpleasant or neutral, there would be eighteen in all. As associated with one's family life or with a life of renunciation, there would be 36 and as past, present or future, 108 in all. Likewise, pleasure may be material (*āmisa*) as being associated with the satisfactions of needs or wants, or spiritual (*nirāmisa*) as being associated with a life of selflessness, compassion and understanding. The pleasures experienced in the mystical states of consciousness, personal or impersonal (i.e. *rūpa* or *arūpa jhānas*), are classified in an ascending scale, each one being "higher and more exquisite" (*uttaritaraṃ paṇītataraṃ*) than the lower. Nibbāna is the "highest happiness" (*paramaṃ sukhaṃ*) but the happiness in it is not conditioned. It is not subject to the presence of any conditioned *vedanā,* although the happiness can be positively experienced (*vimuttisukha-paṭisaṃvedī*).

The experience of conditioned pleasant, unpleasant and neutral hedonic tone is associated with the impressions and ideas we have as a result of sense-contacts or the conceptual activity of the mind in imagining, remembering, reasoning, listening to others, reading books, etc. These impressions, ideas and concepts constitute *saññā.*

The last on the list of mental factors is *viññāṇa*, which covers knowledge and belief. Knowledge of moral and spiritual matters constitutes *paññā.* This involves greater depth of understanding regarding the nature of reality. The difference between *saññā, viññāṇa* and *paññā* is well illustrated in the *Visuddhimagga* by the simile of the coin. When a child sees a coin, it is only the colour and shape that interest him. A peasant knows its value as a means of exchange. A master of the mint knows its exact value and nature since he can distinguish between a counterfeit coin and a genuine one. There is a wider sense in which the word *viññāṇa* is used, but we shall examine that below.

Saṅkhārā

We have left out the word *saṅkhārā*, which in a psychological context is used in three senses. Firstly in the sense of volitions as in the sentence *avijjā-paccayā saṅkhārā*, which means that our volitions are conditioned by our true or false beliefs, which constitute ignorance. We sometimes think rightly and do good or think wrongly and commit evil. We tread in *saṃsāra* like a blind man with a stick who sometimes goes on the right and sometimes on the wrong track in trying to reach his destination.

In the second sense, *saṅkhārā* is used to denote our conative or purposive activities. They may be bodily processes and may include reflex actions such as breathing (*assāsa-passāsa*) as well as conditioned behaviour such as habits. They may be verbal activities involving cogitative and discursive thinking in waking life or even in dreams. Finally, they may be purposive thinking or ideation involving impressions, ideas or concepts associated with feelings. These are called *kāya-saṅkhārā, vacī-saṅkhārā* and *citta-saṅkhārā* respectively.

We may perform these actions or indulge in these activities aware that we are doing so (*sampajāna*) or unaware that we are doing so (*asampajāna*). We can walk, aware or unaware that we are walking. We can talk aware that we are talking or unaware as in sleep. We can think or have trains of thought aware or unaware of what we are doing. The latter would constitute unconscious mental processes.

Likewise, we perform these activities with varying degrees of control. Normally we have no control over our reflexes but it is said that the yogin who has attained the fourth jhāna has them under control. Lastly, these activities may be initiated by an internal stimulus (*sayam-kataṃ*) or an external one (*param-kataṃ*).

The third sense of *saṅkhārā* denotes all those factors which accompany conscious volitional activity. If, for example, we are bent on doing a good deed these may be right beliefs (*sammā-diṭṭhi*), some degree of awareness (*satindriya*), or a quantum of selflessness, etc.

Relations

All these psychological states are causally conditioned. They may be conditioned by contact with one's physical, social or ideological environment, by the physiological state of the body which is itself a product of heredity and by our psychological past consisting of our experiences and upbringing in this life or even by the potentialities of prior lives. At the same time we can decide our goals and ideals and direct our courses of action since, despite the conditioning, we have an element of free will which we can exercise in our decisions and effort.

The various relations holding between different types of psychological and physical states have also been analysed. Thus, as we have already stated, there is mutual interaction (*aññamañña-paccaya*) between body and mind. The relation between an appropriate stimulus and the sense organ it can activate is called the object-condition (*ārammaṇa-paccaya*). A dominant purpose that we intend to achieve governs and controls all the subsidiary activity it involves; so the relation between such a purpose and the activity it governs becomes a dominant condition (*adhipati-paccaya*). A gradual development of awareness (*sati*) about our own activity of body, speech or mind reveals to us these intricate relations.

The Conscious and the Unconscious

While, as we have stated above, *viññāṇa* was used in the sense of intellectual activity in a specific sense, in the general sense it denoted the whole of our mental activity, conscious or unconscious.

We have already come across the concept of unconscious mental processes in speaking of ideational activity (*citta-saṅkhārā*) of which we are not aware. In one place it is said that a yogin by observing directly with his mind how the mental *saṅkhārā,* which are disposed in the mind of a particular individual presumably in his unconscious mind, can predict what he will think at the next moment (AN 3:60/A I 171). It is also said of a living person that part of his "stream of consciousness" (*viññāṇa-sota*) is present in this world (*idhaloke patiṭṭhitaṃ*) and part in the world beyond (*paraloke patiṭṭhitaṃ*) without a sharp division into two parts (*ubhayato abbocchinnaṃ*), (DN 28.7/D III 105). This means that a man's stream of consciousness has a conscious and an unconscious component.

Our conscious mental activity gets into this unconscious and accumulates in it, continuing to influence our conscious behaviour.

In the unconscious are also the latent tendencies of the mind, called the *anusayās*, the desire to satisfy our senses and sex (*kāmarāgānusayā*), our egoistic impulses (*bhavarāgānusayā*), or aggression (*paṭighānusayā*), as well as the belief we cling to in the unconscious mind (*diṭṭhānusayā*), doubt (*vicikicchānusayā*), conceit (*mānanusayā*) and ignorance (*avijjānusayā*) (AN 1: 5/A I 9). The goal of the religious life, it is said, is not attained until they are completely eradicated.

There are also several levels of consciousness and the Nibbānic state is distinguished from all of them. There is the level of normal consciousness (*saññā-saññī*) in the average person. Then, it is possible that one is insane, being either a neurotic (*khitta-citta*) or a psychotic (*ummattaka*) and, if so, one has an abnormal "disjointed consciousness" (*visaññasaññī*). There is also the "developed consciousness" (*vibhūtasaññī*) of a person who has cultivated the personal or impersonal forms of mystical consciousness. The Nibbānic mind is distinguished from all of them as well as from a state of coma or oblivion (*asaññī*). It is attained with the cessation of all conditioned forms of ideation.

Dreams

Dreams occur when the mind is not relatively quiescent in a state of deep sleep nor fully awake. The mind is in a dynamic state and the Buddha compares it to a fire which smokes by night and flares up during the day. According to the *Milindapañhā,* dreams are of four types: (1) those due to physiological disturbances in the body; (2) those due to mental indulgence, i.e., wish-fulfilment (*samudāciṇṇa*); (3) those due to intervention of a discarnate angel's spirit (*devata*); and (4) prophetic dreams.

The Ideal

The Nibbānic state is the ideal to be attained by all, being one of supreme perfection and happiness. Being a state beyond space, time and causation, it cannot be conceptually apprehended, since all our concepts are derived from the framework of the space-time-cause world.

Yet in an analogical sense, it is often described as a state of transcendent consciousness. In one place it is said that the conditioned saṃsāric consciousness ceases to be in a state of "infinite omni-luminous consciousness without distinguishing mark" (*viññāṇaṃ anidassanaṃ anantaṃ sabbato-pabhaṃ,* DN 11.85/D I 223; MN 49.25/M I 329). It is this "luminous mind" which is said to be in the case of each one of us "tainted by adventitious defilements" (*pabhassaraṃ idaṃ cittaṃ tañca āgantukehi upakkilesehi upakkiliṭṭhaṃ),* (AN 1:6.1–2/A I 10).

Man is, therefore, compared to a piece of gold ore and just as, when the defilements of that ore (*upakkilesa*) are got rid of, it shines with its natural lustre, the mind, it is said, becomes resplendent (*pabhassara*) when its defilements are eliminated. In the case of the mind, the primary defilements of the mind which weaken intuitive insight (*cetaso upakkilese paññāya dubbalīkaraṇe*), (MN 27.18/M I 181) are passion and various forms of greed, ill-will, sloth and torpor, excitement, perplexity and doubt. It is when these and other more subtle defilements are got rid of that the mind becomes relatively perfect and pure (*citte parisuddhe pariyodāte*), (DN 2.83/D I 76) and acquires its extrasensory powers of perception and activity. It is the culmination of this process which results in the attainment of Nibbāna, a state "beyond measure" (*atthaṃgatassa na pamāṇaṃ atthi*), (Sn 1076), "deep, immeasurable and unfathomable" (MN 72.20/M I 487). This transcendent mind is not a soul because it is not personal and is not a self-identical entity. Nor is it a Creator God.

Theory of Motivation

The ideal state is one in which "the mind is divested of its strivings and has attained the destruction of all desires" (Dhp 154). It is also a state of perfect mental health. Man suffers from mental disease until he has attained Nibbāna.

The goal of Buddhism is, therefore, therapeutic. We have to start with our present condition in which we are impelled to act out of greed, hatred and ignorance. Greed consists of the desire to gratify our senses and sexual desire (*kāma-taṇhā*) as well as to satisfy our egoistic impulses (*bhava-taṇhā*), such as our desire for possessions, for power, for fame, for personal immortality, etc. Hatred consists of our aggressive tendencies (*vibhava-taṇhā*) or the desire to eliminate and get rid of what we dislike. Both greed and hatred are fed by ignorance (i.e. erroneous beliefs, illusions, rationalisations) and vice versa. Indulgence in these desires gives temporary satisfaction, but there is a law of diminishing returns which operates in our attempt to find satisfaction through gratification. The process eventually makes us slaves of our desires as in the case of alcoholics, misers, sex-addicts, etc.

Our endeavour should be gradually to change the basis of our motivation from greed, hatred and ignorance to selflessness (*cāga, alobha*), compassion (*karuṇā, adosa*) and understanding (*paññā, amoha*).

Psychological Types

To do this effectively, we must know what psychological types we are. The earliest historical classification of individuals into different types is in the book called *Puggalapaññatti* (tr. *Human Types*) of the *Abhidhamma Piṭaka.* In the later tradition classifications were based mainly on the degree to which people possessed the traits of greed, hatred and ignorance as well as their opposites. Different meditation exercises are recommended for them to get rid of the evil traits and develop the good traits they have.

There could, of course, be various sub-types. Some greed-types (*rāga-carita*) may have strong sex desires, others the desire for power, etc. The general formula applicable to all would be to sublimate greed by desiring to develop restraint and selflessness, compassion and understanding, to sublimate hate by endeavouring to remove greed, hatred and ignorance, and to aid this process to adopt right beliefs (*samma-diṭṭhi*) in place of erroneous ones about the nature and destiny of man in the universe.

7

The Buddhist Conception of the Universe

The early Indians and Greeks speculated about the nature, origin and extent of the universe. Anaximander, a Greek thinker of the sixth century BCE, is supposed to have contemplated the possibility of "innumerable worlds" successively coming out of (and passing away) into an indefinite substance. About a century later, the Greek atomists, Leucippus and Democritus, who postulated the existence of innumerable atoms and an infinite void, conceived of worlds coming-to-be and passing away throughout the void. These speculations were the product of imagination and reason and the "worlds" they talked of were mere reproductions of the earth and the heavenly bodies such as the sun, moon and stars.

The contemporary Indian speculations prior to Buddhism were on the same lines, except for the fact that some of them were claimed to be based on extrasensory perception as well. Here there appears to have been even a wider variety of views than to be found among the Greeks.

The early Buddhist texts summarise their views according to the Buddhist logic of four alternatives: With regard to the extent of the universe, the following four types of views were current: (1) those who held that the universe was finite in all dimensions; (2) that the universe was infinite in all dimensions; (3) that the universe was finite in some dimensions and infinite in others; and (4) those who rejected all the above three views and held that the universe was neither finite nor infinite.

This last view was held by thinkers who argued that the universe or space was unreal. If so, spatial epithets like "finite" or "infinite" cannot be applied to it. So the universe is neither finite nor infinite.

Similarly, with regard to the origin of the universe, there were thinkers who put forward all four possible views, viz: (1) some held that the universe had a beginning or origin in time; (2) others that it had no beginning in time; (3) still others that the universe had in one sense a beginning and in another sense no beginning in time. This would be so if the universe had relative origins, its substance being eternal, while it came into being and passed away from time to time;

(4) finally, there were those who put forward the theory that since time was unreal it did not make sense to say that the universe was "neither eternal nor not eternal."

It is with original Buddhism that we get for the first time in the history of thought a conception of the universe which can in any way be meaningfully compared with the modern picture as we know it in contemporary astronomy. This is all the more remarkable when we find no other such conception which foreshadowed or forestalled modern discoveries in ancient or medieval thought of the East or West.

"The Universe"

Before we describe the essential features of the Buddhist account of the universe or cosmos, it is necessary to clarify what today we mean by the term "universe," for it did not mean this at all times.

The conception of the universe in the West until the end of the medieval period was geocentric, an idea that was mainly Aristotelian in origin. The earth was deemed to be the fixed centre of the universe and the moon, the planets, the sun and the stars were believed to move with uniform circular velocity in crystalline spheres around it. The universe was also finite in spatial extent. Apollonius and Ptolemy made some minor adjustments in an attempt to account for some of the movements of the planets but the basic conceptions remained the same.

This finite geocentric universe was later considered to be the orthodox theological view of the cosmos and attempts on the part of thinkers to change it were treated as heresy. A change came with Copernicus, who was led by observational findings by and the suggestions of early Greek thinkers, like the Pythagorean Philolaus and Aristarchus of Samos, to conceive of the sun as the centre of the universe. The universe was now the solar system (i.e. the sun with the planets going round it), encircled by the stars.

With the construction of larger telescopes since the time of Galileo, the next advance was made by John Herschel in the late eighteenth century. His observations convinced him and others that the unit of the universe was not the solar system but the galaxy or galactic system composed of clusters of stars, the blazing sun that we see being only one among such stars. On the basis of his observations of stars and the calculation of their distances, he was the first to make a map of our galactic system or "island universe" (as he called it), known as the Milky Way.

He too placed our sun at the centre of the disc, though today we know that it is about half-way between the centre and the edge of this huge galaxy. Astronomical distances are so large that they are measured not in terms of miles but in light-years. Light travels at the rate of about 186,000 miles per second. It is held that light, travelling at this speed, would take about 100,000 years to travel across the diameter of the Milky Way. In other words, our galactic system has a diameter of 100,000 years.

It was left to modern astronomy with its more powerful telescopes, aided by radio, to delve deeper into space and to make more accurate observations of the relative locations and shapes of these galaxies.

In the light of these findings we know that the ten billion galaxies in space are not found in isolation but in clusters. So when we survey the universe, the units we have to deal with are the galaxies. They are now classified as regular and irregular on the grounds of shape, the regular ones being elliptical, round or spiral. The commonest of all galaxies (i.e. about three quarters of them) are spiral. The majority of them are called "dwarf galaxies" because they contain about a million stars.

The progress of astronomy has thus resulted in a gradual development of the concept of the universe. The earliest conception was the geocentric, the universe being the earth and the celestial bodies around it. Next, the heliocentric conception concentrated on the solar system. The real advance was made in the next stage when the solar system was conceived as one of many such systems in an "island universe" or galaxy. Following this there was the concept of the cluster of galaxies and the present conception of the universe as consisting of a number of such clusters.

Buddhist Conception

In the Buddhist texts, the word used to denote the world, the cosmos or the universe is *loka.* Its uses are as various as the English word "world." It would be tedious to enumerate them here since we are concerned only with the sense in which it is used to denote "the world in space." This is called *okāsa-loka* or the "space-world" (i.e. the world in space) in the Commentaries, which illustrate this by reference to a relevant passage in the *Visuddhimagga* (Vism VII.37, quoting MN 49.9/M I 328): "As far as these suns and moons revolve, shining and shedding their light in space, so far extends the thousand-fold universe" (*sahassadhā-loko*)—here the word "*loka*" is used to denote "the world in space."

In another context of this passage, the universe is described in three tiers or stages. The smallest unit is here called *sahassī cūḷanikā loka-dhātu*, i.e. the "thousand-fold minor world-system." This is defined as follows: "As far as these suns and moons revolve, shining and shedding their light in space, so far extends the thousand-fold universe. In it are thousands of suns, thousands of moons ... thousands of *Jambudīpas*, thousands of *Aparagoyānas*, thousands of *Uttarakurus*, thousands of *Pubbavidehas* ..." (AN 3:80/A I 227; AN 10:29/A V 59). *Jambudīpa, Aparagoyāna, Uttarakuru* and *Pubbavideha* are the four inhabited regions or the continents known to the people of North India at the time. From descriptions given about them, it appears to have been believed that these people had different temperaments and ways of living.

So it is as if one were to say today that there were "thousands of Indias, thousands of Arabias, thousands of Russias and thousands of Chinas." Its significance is that there were thousands of inhabited places or planets since the earth was associated with one sun and one moon.

This *cūḷanikā loka-dhātu* or minor world-system, which is the smallest unit in the universe though it contains thousands of suns, moons and inhabited planets, can only be compared with the modern conception of a galaxy, the majority of which have about a million suns.

Most modern astronomers believe that the chances are that there could be life of the form to be found on earth in planets of other solar systems in this as well as other galaxies. Prof. Harlow Shapley says, after making a most conservative estimate: "We would still have after all that elimination, ten billion planets suitable for organic life something like that on earth" (*The View from a Distant Star*, London, 1963, p. 64). Another well-known astronomer, Dr Ernst J. Opik, states: "Many planets may carry life on their surface. Even if there were only one inhabited system in every million, there would be 10,000 million million abodes of life in the universe. What a variety of forms and conditions this implies!" (*The Oscillating Universe*, New York, 1960, p. 114).

Clusters of Galaxies

The next unit in the universe, according to the early Buddhist texts, is described as consisting of thousands of minor-world-Systems. This is called a "twice-a-thousand middling world-system" (*dvi-sahassī majjhimikā loka-dhātu*). It would correspond to a cluster of galaxies according to modern conceptions.

This notion of a cluster of galaxies is a fairly recent one in modern astronomy. As Prof. A.C.B. Lovell said in his *BBC Reith Lectures* in 1955:

"Some years ago we thought that these galaxies were isolated units in space, but now we believe that the galaxies exist in great groups or clusters. In the same way that the earth and planets are bound to the sun and move as a unit through space, so on an inconceivably vaster scale we think that the galaxies are contained in clusters as connected, physical systems. The local group contains the Milky Way system, the Andromeda Nebula, and perhaps two dozen others. It is not very populated, compared, for example, with the Virgo cluster of galaxies, which contains at least a thousand visible galaxies, although occupying only about twice the space of the local group" (*The Individual and the Universe*, London, 1958, pp. 6–7).

In the opinion of Prof. William Bonnor, "The milky way is one of a small cluster of galaxies called the 'local group', which includes all galaxies within about a million light-years from the Earth, and contains about twenty members. Beyond this distance one would have to travel about ten million light years before coming across another galaxy. Other galaxies, too, show a distinct tendency to cluster. The clusters may be small, like the local group, or may contain several hundreds or even thousands of galaxies" (*The Mystery of the Expanding Universe*, New York, 1964, p. 32).

We find that here "thousands" is practically the upper limit since many of the clusters of galaxies contain fewer. On the other hand, with reference to the thousand-fold minor-world-system, "thousand" appeared to be too little. Since the Dhamma is summed up in stereotyped formulae (which recur in the Pali Canonical texts) for easy memorisation, it is possible that "thousand" was selected as a convenient common number to describe the hierarchy of units. However, elsewhere in the Canon smaller numbers of such thousand-fold minor-world-systems to be found in clusters are referred to.

In the *Saṅkhāruppati Sutta* of the *Majjhima Nikāya,* the basic unit is again the thousand-fold world-system (*sahassī-loka-dhātu*) (MN 120.12–16/M III 101). But there is a reference to two, three, four ... up to a hundred such world-systems grouped together (e.g. *sata-sahassi-loka-dhātu*) (ibid.).

Of frequent occurrence is the *dasa-sahassī-loka-dhātu*, which should be translated as "the ten thousand-fold world systems." It is used with reference to the local group of galaxies, which consists of about twenty in all, of which about ten cluster relatively close together. One text in fact refers to "the ten nearest island universes" (Rudolf Thiel, *And There Was Light,* New York, 1957, p. 355).

Cosmos

While the middling world-systems consisted of a few, up to a hundred or even a thousand galaxies, the next unit is the whole cluster of middling world-systems. For it is said that thousands of middling world-systems (i.e. clusters of galaxies) go to form the vast universe or the major world-system (*mahā-loka-dhātu*), which some texts on astronomy refer to as the metagalaxy.

Although some astronomers wonder whether there is a hierarchy of clusters of galaxies within the universe, the general opinion is against this. As Prof. Bonnor points out, "One may ask whether clusters of galaxies are the last in the hierarchy. As stars aggregate into galaxies, and galaxies into clusters, do clusters aggregate into superclusters, and so on? Although astronomers are not quite unanimous, it seems that the clusters are the largest individual entities, and we should not be justified in speaking of clusters of clusters. Thus we have at last reached the unit of cosmology, the cluster of galaxies. In practise the galaxy is usually taken as the unit because galaxies can be recognised more easily than clusters" (Bonnor, op. cit., p. 32).

The modern astronomical descriptions of the universe as well as those of the early Buddhist texts stop here. The modern accounts stop because there is a limit to observability on the part of the telescopes. If, as is inferred to be the case, the galaxies further and further away are receding at greater and greater speeds from us, then as they approach the speed of light, they would pass beyond the range of theoretical observability. So the theoretically observable universe is also limited and what happens beyond this would have to be pure speculation, even according to science.

The early Buddhist texts, too, do not state that the major world-system is all there is in the universe, for the question as to whether the world is finite or infinite (*ananto*) in extent is left unanswered (*avyākata*).

The later commentarial tradition, however, goes a step further. One of the synonyms for a world-system or *loka-dhātu* is *cakkavāḷa*, a word of uncertain etymology meaning a "wheel," "circle" or "sphere." The *Pali Text Society Dictionary* commenting on *loka-dhātu* (s.v.) says that it means "constituent or unit of the universe, a world, sphere"; and adds that *loka-dhātu* is another name for *cakkavāḷa*.

Calling a galaxy a "sphere" or a "wheel" is certainly appropriate, for as we know from modern astronomy a galaxy is like a huge catherine wheel revolving round a centre or hub. But the commentary states that these galaxies or spheres (*cakkavāḷa*) are infinite in number (*anantāni cakkavāḷāni*) (A-a II 342). This is certainly going beyond the standpoint of the early Buddhist texts, which is uncommitted on the question of the origin or extent of the universe. While the later traditions of the Sarvāstivāda and Theravada suggest that the number of galaxies or world-systems is infinite in extent, the Mahayana texts hold that the universe is infinite in time, stating that "the universe is without beginning or end" (*anavarāgra*).

Here again the standpoint of original Buddhism was merely to state that the universe was "without a knowable beginning" (*anamatagga*). The Buddha, it is said, could see worlds without limit "as far as he liked" (*yāvatā ākaṅkheyya*) (Nidd II 356). He could also probe into the past without limit, for the further back that he looked into the past, there was the possibility of going back still further. But to say that the world or universe is infinite in time and space is to go beyond the stand of early Buddhism and give an answer to an unanswered question (*avyākata*).

While all schools of Buddhism retained the general picture of the universe as given in the early Buddhist texts, their detailed accounts and elaborations are not always to be trusted. The Sarvāstivāda accounts given in the *Abhidharmakoṣa* differ from those of the Theravādins. The reason for this is that the simple but stupendous conceptions of the early Buddhist view of the universe got mixed up with popular mythological geography and cosmology in the commentarial traditions of the schools.

The Mahayana texts, for the most part, retain the early view of the galactic systems spread out through space. We only notice that "thousand" is replaced by "million." The *Vajracchedikā,* for example, refers to the universe as "this sphere of a million millions of world-systems" (XIX, XXIV, XXX).

Myth and Fact

While the early Buddhist texts are, therefore, more reliable, we must not forget that the account given of the extent of the material universe exhausts the early Buddhist conception of the cosmos. The passage quoted above from the *Aṅguttara Nikāya* goes on to speak of the subtle-material worlds (*rūpa-loka*) or the worlds of higher spirits or gods (*deva*) as being associated with the material worlds or galaxies. They cannot, however, be observed by human vision.

Are we going to dismiss this aspect of the universe as belonging to the realm of mythology? Did the Buddha have grounds for belief in the existence of devas or was this only a popular belief at the time, to which he did not subscribe? We can see the real attitude of the Buddha by the answers he gives to the Brahmin youth Saṅgārava, who questions him on this subject:

> Saṅgārava: "Tell me, Gotama, are there gods (*deva*)?"
>
> Buddha: "I know on good grounds (*thānaso*) that there are gods."
>
> Saṅgārava: "Why do you say when asked 'whether there are gods' that you know on good grounds that there are gods. Does this not imply that your statement is utterly false?"
>
> Buddha: "When one is questioned as to whether there are gods, whether one replies that 'there are gods' or that 'one knows on good grounds that there are gods,' then surely the deduction to be made by an intelligent person is indubitable, namely that there are gods."
>
> Saṅgārava: "Then, why did not the venerable Gotama plainly say so from the very start?"
>
> Buddha: "Because it is commonly taken for granted in the world that there are gods."

The significance of this reply is that the Buddha holds that there are devas not because of a popular or traditional belief, which he took for granted, but because he was personally convinced of their existence on good grounds.

On the other hand, the Buddha had to make use of some of the traditional terms and coin others to describe the different types of worlds of these devas. There is other evidence to suggest that the Buddha did not take popular conceptions for granted. In one place he says that ignorant people believe that there is a hell (*pātāla,* also "abyss") but asserts that this belief was false. "Hell" (*pātāla*), the Buddha says, "is a term for painful bodily sensations" (SN 36:4/S IV 206). Heavens are better than human forms of existence, where everything one experiences is pleasant (AN 3:23/A I 122), while hells are subhuman forms of existence where everything one experiences is unpleasant. The Buddha claims to see both these kinds of worlds. The danger of being born in these subhuman states of downfall (*vinipāta*) is that it is difficult to emerge to the human level after that. The reason is given: "Because there prevails no practice of the good life, no righteous living, no doing of good works, but just cannibalism, the stronger preying on weaker creatures" (SN 56:61–131/S V 466–78).

Clairvoyance

It is stated that the Buddha's ability to see these world-systems and the beings in them is due to his clairvoyance. It is said: "The Blessed One with his clairvoyant paranormal vision can see one world-system, two, three ... fifty world-systems—the thousand-fold minor world-system, the twice-a-thousand middling world-system and the thrice-a-thousand major world system. He could see as far out into space as he liked. So clear is the clairvoyant vision of the Blessed One. In this way is the Blessed One with his clairvoyant vision one who has his eyes open" (*vivaṭacakkhu*) (Nidd II 355).

The clairvoyant powers of the disciples both according to the texts and commentaries are not unlimited like those of the Buddha. Anuruddha, who was considered the foremost of those who had attained the faculty of clairvoyant vision, could see only as far as the "thousand-fold world-system": "It is by the fact of cultivating and developing these four arisings of mindfulness that I have acquired the ability to see the thousand-fold world-system" (SN 52:11/S V 303).

Cosmic Phenomena

Some of the casual statements made by the Buddha appear to come from one who has in fact observed aspects of cosmic space. In one place, the Buddha says: "Monks, there is a darkness of intergalactic space [Woodward has 'interstellar space'], an impenetrable gloom, such a murk of darkness as cannot enjoy the splendour of this sun and moon" (SN 56:46/S V 455). Modern astronomy would agree with this verdict. We see so much light because we are fortunate enough to be close to a sun.

The uncertainty of life in some of these worlds is sometimes stressed with graphic descriptions of cosmic phenomena. The Buddha says that there comes a time, after a lapse of hundreds of thousands of years, when it would cease to rain and vegetable and animal life in the planet would be destroyed (AN 10:55/A V 102). He also speaks of times when seven suns would appear and the earth, including the biggest of mountains which appears so stable, would go up in smoke without leaving any ashes at all. He speaks as though he has witnessed some of these phenomena. He says: "Who would think or believe that this earth or Sineru, the highest of mountains, would burn up and be destroyed except on the evidence of sight?" (Ibid.). Today we know that suns or stars could become cosmic hydrogen bombs, flare up and explode, burning up their planets, if any, and even affecting neighbouring solar systems. A student of astronomy commenting on this possibility says: "Humanity would at any rate enjoy a solemn and dramatic doom as the entire planet went up in a puff of smoke" (Rudolf Thiel, op.cit, p. 329). These phenomena are called novae and supernovae, which are observed from time to time in galaxies including our own.

Colliding galaxies, of which there is some evidence, also spell such disasters.

Time and Relativity

The destruction of the worlds, however, which will cause such phenomena to be manifested in all the world-systems, comes only at the end of an epoch or aeon, called a *kappa*. Several similes are given to illustrate what an immensely long period an aeon is. One such passage reads as follows: "Suppose there were a city of iron walls one *yojana* in length, one in width and one high filled up with mustard seed, from which a man were to take out at the end of every hundred years a mustard seed. That pile of mustard seed would in this way be sooner done away with and ended than an aeon, so very long is an aeon. And of aeons thus long more than one has passed, more than a hundred, more than a thousand, more than a hundred thousand" (SN 12:16/S II 182).

The cosmos undergoes two major periods of change in time called the aeons of expansion and contraction. The aeon of expansion is the period in which the universe unfolds itself or opens out (*vivaṭṭa-kappa*). The other is the one in which the universe closes in and is destroyed (*saṃvaṭṭa-kappa*). Elsewhere they are described as the four stages of the universe: (1) the period of expansion; (2) the period in which the universe remains in a state of expansion; (3) the period of contraction; and (4) the period in which the universe stays contracted.

There are several models according to which astronomers try to explain the movement within the universe in time. One of them is the cycloidal oscillating model, according to which the universe expands and contracts until, as Prof. Bonnor says, "the contraction slows down, ceases and changes to expansion again." The theory is currently favoured by many astronomers in the light of recent findings.

There is also a reference to the relativity of time in different parts of the universe. But this is a comparison of time on earth with time in the heavenly worlds. One day in one of these different worlds is equated with 50 years, 100 years, 200 years, 400 years and 1,600 years respectively on earth. Such in brief outline is the early Buddhist conception of the universe.

8

The Buddhist Attitude to God

The word "God" is used in so many different ways and so many different senses that it is not possible to define the Buddhist attitude to God without clarifying the meaning of this term. The *Concise Oxford Dictionary* defines its sense in a theistic context as: "Supreme being, Creator and Ruler of the Universe." A theistic text (*The Book of Common Prayer*) gives the following description: "There is but one living and true God, everlasting, without body, parts or passions; of infinite power, wisdom and goodness, the Maker and Preserver of all things both visible and invisible ...." I have left out the rest of the quotation since it concerns the specific dogmas of this particular school of theism.

In this form it would be a definition of the concept of a personal God, common to monotheistic belief with the proviso that the idea of creation varies according to different traditions. According to one tradition, God's creation consists in fashioning coexistent chaotic matter and making an ordered cosmos out of chaos. According to another tradition, God's matter in creation is an emanation or emission (*sṛṣṭi*) from the being of God, while according to yet another tradition, God creates matter out of nothing (*ex nihilo*).

Using the word in the above sense of a Personal Creator God, who is a Supreme Being possessed of the characteristics of omniscience, omnipotence and infinite goodness, if we ask the question, "Does God exist?" there are four possible answers. They are: (1) those theists who say "yes" and affirm God's existence; (2) those atheists who say "no" and deny God's existence; (3) those sceptics or agnostics who say "we do not know" or "we cannot know"; and (4) those positivists who say that the question is meaningless since the meaning of the term "God" is not clear.

Atheism

What is the Buddhist answer to this question? Was the Buddha a theist, an atheist, an agnostic or a positivist? The answer is fairly clear. Given the above definition of God in its usual interpretation, the Buddha is an atheist and Buddhism in both its Theravada and

Mahayana forms is atheism.

Some Western scholars have tried to make out that Mahayana Buddhism came into being about the beginning of the Christian era and that in it the Buddha is deified. Both these conclusions are false. Mahayana Buddhism came into being with the Mahāsanghika Council, when a group of liberals broke away from the conservative elders or the Theravādins about a hundred years after the death of the Buddha and in none of the Mahayana schools is the Buddha conceived of as a Creator God.

This does not mean that the Buddha was a mere human being in either the Theravada or Mahayana schools of thought. Some local Buddhist scholars following nineteenth-century Western rationalists have said so, but according to the early Buddhist texts, when the Buddha was asked whether he was a human being, his answer was that he was not a human being but a Buddha, although he was a human being who became a Buddha (AN 4:36/A II 37). The Buddha as the Tathāgata or "The Transcendent One" is "deep, immeasurable and unfathomable." His body passes away at death and he becomes invisible to gods and men and it is incorrect to say that he ceases to exist (MN 72/M I 483 ff).

In denying that the universe is a product of a Personal God, who creates it in time and plans a consummation at the end of time, Buddhism is a form of atheism.

Gosāla's Theism

That Buddhism is atheistic is also clear from its denunciation of the religion and philosophy of theism put forward by Makkhali Gosāla, one of the six senior contemporaries of the Buddha. It is a remarkable fact that these six teachers put forward prototypes of religious or philosophical theories, which have become widely prevalent in the world. Makkhali was a theist or an *issara-nimmāna-vādin*, i.e. one who posited the theory that the ultimate cause was God. The others consisted of a materialist, an agnostic, a Categorialist (who explained the universe in terms of discrete categories), a natural determinist and an Eclectic.

According to the Jain *Bhagavati Sūtra* and the Commentary to the *Dīgha Nikāya*, Makkhali is called Gosāla because he was born in a cowshed (*go-sālā*). In his teaching he denied moral causation and urged that human beings become corrupted or doomed or become purified or saved miraculously, presumably by the will or grace of God. Human beings lacked initiative or freedom and their future was entirely planned by the will of the creator. All beings evolved in various states of existence under the impact of destiny, circumstances or nature. Eventually, fools and the wise alike completed their *saṃsāric* evolution and attained salvation, making an end of suffering.

It is called the theory of salvation through *saṃsāric* evolution (*saṃsāra-suddhi*) and in one place in the Buddhist texts it is described as follows: "There is no short-cut to Heaven. Await thy destiny. Whether a man experiences joy or sorrow is due to his destiny. All beings will attain salvation through *saṃsāric* evolution, so do not be eager for that which is to come" (J-a VI 229). The same idea is expressed as follows in a theistic text: "Beings originate in the Unmanifest, they evolve in a manifest condition and eventually come to rest in the Unmanifest. So why worry."

Makkhali explicitly states that "there is no question of a person attaining maturity of character by good deeds, vows, penances or a religious life" (DN 2.20/D I 54). Man is merely a product of the creation and will of God and his future is laid out. As Makkhali says, "Just as much as a ball of thread when flung on the ground unravels itself until it comes to an end, so the wise and the fools alike fare on in *saṃsāra* and eventually attain salvation."

Makkhali's theism has several attractive features. Firstly, it is logically consistent. As philosophers have pointed out, God's omniscience and omnipotence strictly imply a rigid deterministic universe. God being omniscient sees the entire future in all its aspects and details. It is unlike human foreknowledge, which is only probable. So the future of the creature is strictly mapped out and God can see it as in the reel of a film. God being omnipotent is entirely responsible for it as well, so that a belief in free will on the part of his creatures is merely illusory. Secondly, God is impartial in that he treats all beings alike for, as Makkhali says, "there are no high and low" (*natthi ukkaṃsāvakaṃse*), since all go through the same course of evolution in various stages of existence. Thirdly, there are no eternal hells and beings do not have to burn in an everlasting hell-fire, for they all attain salvation. There are three hundred hells (*tiṃse nirayasate*), or rather purgatories, along with seven human worlds (*satta-mānuse*) and several heavens to pass through before attaining eventual release.

His theism relieves human beings of the burdens of responsibility, gives them security, solace and the joys of the heavens (mixed with the sorrows of purgatories), before assuring salvation. In this sense, it may be compared with many modern forms of theism, which try to equalise opportunities for all and are very apologetic about eternal hell-fires.

Puppet Argument

Yet the theism of Makkhali is severely criticized by the Buddha since it gave a false sense of security to the people and encouraged complacency by denying free will and the value of human effort. The Buddha says that he knows of no other person than Makkhali born for the detriment and disadvantage of so many people, and compares him to a fisherman casting his net at the mouth of a river for the destruction of many fish (AN I:18/A I 33). Similarly in the *Sandaka Sutta*, the Buddha (as reported by Ānanda) says that there are four types of religion which are false in this world and four types which are unsatisfactory though not necessarily totally false, distinguishing Buddhism from all eight of them.

Two of the types condemned as false refer to two forms of theism. One is the doctrine that salvation is not due to human effort or the moral causation effected by good or evil deeds, but that people are miraculously saved or doomed presumably because of the grace or will of God. The other is the doctrine of predestination or theistic evolutionism.

It would be interesting to see the reasons given for this stand taken against certain forms of theism. There are two main arguments against theism presented in the early Canonical texts. The first may be called the Puppet Argument and is stated as follows: "If God designs the life of the entire world—the glory and the misery, the good and the evil acts, man is but an instrument of his will (*niddesa-kari*) and God (alone) is responsible" (J-a V 238).

Theists who do not take a predestinarian stand (which is logically consistent) try to evade this conclusion by saying that God has endowed man with free will. But it can be shown that the concept of divine providence is not compatible with a notion of human freedom. To be consistent, one has either to give up the belief in theism or the belief in freedom or confess that this is a mystery that one cannot understand, which is a departure from reason.

Antony Flew, who has made the most recent and most comprehensive analysis of the concept of theism, including the case for and against it, states one of his conclusions with regard to this matter as follows:

"The stock image is that of a Supreme Father showing long-suffering tolerance towards his often rebellious children: he has given us, it is said, our freedom; and we—wretched unworthy creatures that we are—too often take advantage to flout his wishes. If this image fitted, there would be no problem. Obviously, it is possible for children to act against their parents' wishes. It is also possible for parents to grant to their children freedoms, which may be abused, by refusing to exercise powers of control which they do possess. But the case of Creator and creature must be utterly different. Here the appropriate images, in so far as any images could be appropriate, would be that of the Creator, either as the Supreme Puppetmaster with creatures whose every thought and move he arranges; or as the Great Hypnotist with subjects who always act out his irresistible suggestions. What makes the first image entirely inept and the other two much less so is crucially that God is supposed to be, not a manufacturer or a parent who may make or rear his product and then let it be, but the Creator. This precisely means that absolutely nothing happens save by his ultimate undetermined determination and with his consenting ontological support. Everything means everything; and that includes every human thought, every human action, and every human choice. For we too are indisputably parts of the universe, we are among the 'all things both visible and invisible' of which he is supposed to be 'the Maker, and Preserver'" (*God and Philosophy,* London, 1966, p. 44).

His final conclusion is the same as what I mentioned above. In his own words: "For it is, as we have argued already, entirely inconsistent to maintain both that there is a Creator; and that there are other authentically autonomous beings" (ibid., p. 54). A careful study of the theistic texts of any tradition will show that often this is directly admitted in certain contexts, despite the contradictions in other places.

According to the Buddhist theory of çausation, man's actions are not strictly determined. The Buddhist theory steers clear of both natural and theistic determinism on the one hand and total Indeterminism on the other. Man has an element of free will, although his actions are conditioned but not determined by external and internal stimuli. By the exercise of this freedom along the right lines man can change his own condition from one of anxiety, unrest and suffering to one of serenity and happiness. This is effected not by invoking the grace of God but by human effort and the comprehension of human psychology. In the *Devadaha Sutta*, the Buddha uses the arguments of the theists against them, saying that, if theists are suffering psychologically, then according to their own theories it must be because God has withheld his grace from them whereas in his own case (if theism were true), "he must have been created by a good God" (*bhaddakena issarena nimmito*) (MN 101.46/M II 227).

Argument from Evil

The second argument against theism found in the Canonical texts is the argument from evil. It proceeds on the presumption that, if the world is created by God, then certain evils are inexplicable. It has several variants but let us take some of them together: "If God (Brahmā) is Lord of the whole world and creator of the multitude of beings, then (1) why has he ordained misfortune in the world without making the whole world happy, or (2) for what purpose has he made the world full of injustice, deceit, falsehood, and conceit, or (3) the Lord of creation is evil in that he ordained injustice when there could have been justice" (J-a VI 208).

Here again, leading modern philosophers endorse the argument after showing that all the attempts to explain away evil are unsatisfactory. It will not do to say that evil is negative or unreal, for suffering, ignorance, poverty and ugliness are as real as their opposites. It will not do to say that evils (like wilful injury) are necessary for the existence of higher-order goods (like forgiveness), for there are still many evils unaccounted for in this fashion. Nor will it do to say that the evils in the world are due to the grant of free will to human beings (quite apart from the difficulty of reconciling this with divine providence, as indicated above). For as Prof. Flew has shown, "There are many evils which it scarcely seems either are or could be redeemed in this way: animal suffering, for instance, especially that occurring before—or after—the human period" (Flew, op. cit., p. 54).

Here again the inability to give a rational explanation leads the theist to a confession that it is a mystery: "The origin of moral evil lies forever concealed within the mystery of human freedom" (J. R. Hick, *Philosophy of Religion,* New York, 1963, p. 43). So there is the mystery or the incompatibility between divine providence and human freedom as well as the mystery or the contradiction between belief in divine goodness and the existence of certain evils.

The result is that while some of the Upaniṣads hold that "the world is enveloped by God" (*īṣāvasyaṃ idaṃ sarvaṃ*), Buddhism held that "the world was without a refuge and without God" (*attāṇo loko anabhissaro*).

Other Arguments

I have stated only the two main arguments to be found in the Canonical texts, which may be attributed to the Buddha himself. But the later literature both of Theravada and Mahayana provides an abundance of arguments against the concept of a Personal Creator God (Īsvara). While positive arguments are adduced to show the truth of atheism, there are others which show the fallacies of the theistic arguments for the existence of God.

Even when we take the arguments for theism in a modern context we find that the ontological argument was a mere definition, which mistakenly regarded existence as an attribute. The cosmological argument contradicted its own premise by speaking of an uncaused cause or using the word "cause" in a non-significant sense. The argument from Design, which is superficially the most appealing, flounders when we consider the waste and cruelty of evolution, with nature "red in tooth and claw." It is impossible to contemplate that a loving God could have created and watched the spectacle of dinosaurs tearing each other to pieces for millions of years on earth.

Inconceivable or Meaningless?

In order to reconcile divine love with the apparent cruelty of nature, a move is often made by theists to say that God's love is inscrutable or is another mystery. A human parent would do whatever he could to relieve the suffering of his child who is in great pain. Would an omnipotent and omniscient being look on without intervention? To say that such a being exists is to equate his love with callousness or cruelty. In such a situation we would not know what meaning to attach to the concept of "love" considered as an attribute of God. This has led theists to say that God's attributes as well as his nature are inconceivable. The *Bodhicāryāvatāra* makes a reductio ad absurdum of this contention arguing that in such a case the concept of a God or creator is meaningless: "If, as theists say, God is too great for man to be able to comprehend him, then it follows, that his qualities also surpass our range of thought, and that we neither know him nor attribute to him the quality of a creator." It follows that if normal meanings are given to the words, all-knowing, all-powerful and infinitely good (or analogous meanings), the evidence points against God's existence, whereas if this is not done, the concept becomes meaningless.

Fruit Test

Another test that Buddhism applies in gauging the validity of a belief is the "fruit test," or the attempt to see what consequences a belief or set of beliefs, when acted upon, has led to. With regard to theism it may be held that it has given people a sense of security, and inspired them to various kinds of activity. This does not prove that the belief is true but suggests that it may be useful. A realistic survey would show that while beliefs in theism have done some good, they have brought much evil in their train as well.

Wars have been fought between the main warring creeds of theism and also among the sects within each in the name of God. In contrast, we may quote the words of Dr Edward Conze about Buddhism: "All those who dwell in Asia can take pride in a religion which is not only five centuries older than that of the West, but has spread and maintained itself without recourse to violence, and has remained unstained by religious wars and crusades" (*A Short History of Buddhism*, London, 1958, p. 111). In addition, a careful study of the literature of theism will show that there is hardly a crime or vice which has not been committed or recommended in the name of God.

Hitler thought that he was merely carrying out the will of God and that he and his party were the instruments of providence. The references are too many to quote and may be found in his speeches (N. H. Baynes, *The Speeches of Adolf Hitler,* Oxford, 1942, s.v *God* in Index). For example, in 1938 Hitler says: "I believe that it was God's will to send a boy from here into the Reich, to let him grow up, to raise him to be the leader of the nation so as to enable him to lead back his homeland into the Reich. There is a higher ordering and we all are nothing else than its agents" (ibid., p. 1458). In 1939, he says: "The National Socialist Movement has wrought this miracle. If Almighty God granted success to this work, then the Party was His instrument" (ibid., p. 426). In his *Mein Kampf* (*My Struggle*), he says: "Thus did I now believe that I must act in the sense of the Almighty Creator. By defending myself against the Jews, I am doing the Lord's work" (London, 1938, p. 36). These thoughts may have greatly relieved his conscience when he ordered the extermination of six million Jews from the face of the earth. Some have argued that the concept of the fatherhood of God leads to the idea of the brotherhood of man. At the same time, human inequalities have also been sanctioned in God's name. Such are the concepts of chosen castes, chosen races, chosen nations, chosen classes, chosen creeds, a chosen sex or a chosen individual. As the Buddhist texts say, if God created the world, he would be responsible for the crime and suffering no less than the acts of goodness and self-sacrifice.

Buddhist Atheism

While Buddhism is atheistic, we must not forget that Buddhist atheism has at the same time to be distinguished from materialistic atheism. Buddhism asserted the falsity of a materialistic philosophy which denied survival, recompense and responsibility as well as moral and spiritual values and obligations, no less than certain forms of theistic beliefs. In its thoroughly objective search for truth it was prepared to accept what was true and good in "the personal immortality view" (*bhavadiṭṭhi*) of theism as well as "the annihilationist view" (*vibhavadiṭṭhi*) of atheistic materialism. "Those thinkers who do not see how these two views arise and cease to be, their good points as well as their defects and how one transcends them in accordance with the truth are under the grip of greed, hate and ignorance … and will not attain final deliverance" (MN 11.7/M I 65).

The Divine Life

Buddhism recognises all that is true, good and valuable in certain forms of theistic doctrine. Among the four types of religions which were unsatisfactory but not necessarily false were those based on a revelational tradition (*anussava*). A religion which granted the truth of an element of free will, of moral causation, of survival and responsibility and the non-inevitability of salvation had value in it.

Although there is no Personal God with the characteristics of omniscience, omnipotence and infinite goodness, there is the concept of a Mahā Brahmā (Mighty God) who is morally perfect and has very great knowledge and power but is not omniscient and omnipotent. Certain forms of theism, it is said, are put forward by teachers who are born on earth after dying from the world of such a being. Born here, they lead a homeless life of renunciation and meditation, see the heaven that they came from and teach a religion of fellowship with Brahmā (God). They believe that such a Brahmā is omnipotent (*abhibhū anabhibhūto*), omniscient (*aññadatthudaso*), the Mighty Lord (*vasavatti issaro*), Maker (*kattā*), Creator (*nimmātā*), the Most Perfect (*seṭṭho*), the Designer (*sañjitā*) and the Almighty Father of beings that are and are to be (*vasī pitā bhūta-bhavyānaṃ*) whose creatures we are.

The Buddha does not deny the existence of such a being; he is morally perfect but not omniscient and omnipotent. He is the chief of the hierarchy of Brahmās who rule over galactic systems and clusters of galactic systems. He is the regent of the cosmos who requests the Buddha to preach the pure and perfect Dhamma to the world, which will otherwise be destroyed. But he too is subject to the judgement of karma. According to the Buddha as reported in the *Brahmanimantanika Sutta* and elsewhere, Buddhahood is a state far exceeding the knowledge and power of any Brahmā. As the *Tevijja Sutta* points out, fellowship with Brahmā is not to be attained by petitionary prayers but by cultivating the divine life: "That those Brahmins versed in the Vedas and yet bearing anger and malice in their hearts, sinful and uncontrolled, should after death with the dissolution of the body attain fellowship with God who is free from anger and malice, pure in heart and has self-mastery—such a state of things can in no wise be" (DN 13.34–35/D I 248).

It is said that the cultivation of compassion in its purest form is called the divine life in this world (*Brahmaṃ etaṃ vihāraṃ idham-āhu*). It is also said that, when one lives the moral and spiritual life with faith in the Buddha, then one dwells with God (*Brahmunā saddhiṃ saṃvasati*). The Buddha came to establish "the rule of righteousness" or "the kingdom of righteousness" (*Dhamma-cakkaṃ pavattetuṃ*) in this world, which is elsewhere called "the kingdom of God" (*Brahma-cakkaṃ*). The Buddha and his disciples who have attained Nibbāna are said "to abide with self-become-God" (*Brahma-bhūtena viharati*). One who has attained Nibbāna, it is said, "may justifiably employ theological terminology" (*dhammena so Brahma-vādaṃ vadeyya*). The old theological terms are given a new meaning and significance in what is comparable to the modern death-of-God theology, which is currently gaining ground in the West with seekers after truth who can no longer with honesty and sincerity accept the old theology and the old dogmas.

Superfluous

Yet it is unnecessary and to some extent misleading to put Buddhism into a theological cast. Whatever we may mean by God and whether we say God exists or God does not exist, it is a fact that there is physical and mental illness. The right approach is to understand the nature of these illnesses, their causes, their cure and to apply the right remedies. Buddhism provides not palliatives but the right remedies for the gradual and complete eradication of all anxiety, insecurity and the mental illnesses we suffer from until we attain the completely healthy Nibbānic mind. If Nibbāna is God in the sense of being the Transcendent Reality, then those who are using these remedies cannot still comprehend it, while those who attain it do not need to.

9

Nibbāna

Nibbāna (Pali) or Nirvāṇa (Sanskrit) is considered to be the reality (*sacca*) or the ultimate reality (*parama-sacca*) in Buddhism. It is also a state of perfection (*parisuddhi*) or the highest good (*parama-kusala*), which, at least, a few can attain in this life itself. It is the ***summum bonum***, which not only all human beings but all beings in the universe should seek to attain. For unless and until they attain it, they are subject to the unsatisfactoriness and insecurity of conditioned existence, however pleasant it may be for a short or even a long period of time.

As with some of the other Buddhist concepts, the term *Nibbāna* has sometimes been misunderstood by scholars. It is also by no means clear that all Buddhists understand the meaning and significance of the term in the way in which it was understood in the early Buddhist texts. Some have considered Nibbāna to be a state of annihilation. Others deem it to be identical with Divinity and identify Nibbāna with the Brahman of the Upaniṣads. Yet others who regarded Buddha as an agnostic thought that he had no clear conception about the nature of Nibbāna or was, in fact, unconcerned about it, since what was important was to find a solution to the problem of human anxiety and suffering rather than be concerned with the nature of ultimate reality.

A knowledgeable Western psychologist, who recently made a careful and enlightening study of the psychology of Nibbāna in the light of the statements of the Pali Canon, arrived at the tentative conclusion that, "The Nibbāna of the Nikāyas is then a transformed state of personality and consciousness. In none of the innumerable cases where the attainment of Nibbāna is referred to as the destruction of the 'obsessions' is it ever suggested that this transformation is not enough: the new state is 'the end of suffering'" (Rune Johansson, *The Psychology of Nirvana,* London, 1969, p. 111).

Finally, there are those who would assert that Nibbāna is a transcendent state of reality, which the human mind, limited in its conceptions, cannot intellectually comprehend.

What then is the correct answer, if such an answer is possible? It is only a careful study of all the authentic texts, which can suggest an answer to this question.

The term *Nibbāna* is claimed in the Buddhist texts to be pre-Buddhist in origin, although the term as such is not to be found in the extant pre-Buddhist literature. The *Brahmajāla Sutta* (DN 1) refers to several schools of thought, which put forward different theories about Nibbāna that could be attained in this life (*diṭṭhadhamma-nibbāna-vāda*). The thinkers who posited these theories resembled in some respects the modern existentialist philosophers, who are concerned about the solutions to the problems of human anxiety and suffering and have found various theories concerning the nature of authentic living, which gives inner satisfaction to people and makes it possible for them to escape their boredom and anxiety. In other respects, these thinkers resemble the mystics of the different traditions, such as the Christian or Islamic (e.g. the Sufis), who claim to have found ultimate happiness in some contemplative mystic experience.

What concerns us here is the meaning of the term *Nibbāna*. The first school of thought held that the soul experiences the highest Nibbāna in this life (*parama-diṭṭhadhamma-nibbāna*) when it is fully engrossed and immersed in the enjoyment of the pleasures of the five senses. Some of the other schools, however, held that sense pleasures were not lasting and were a source of unhappiness and that the soul truly experiences the highest Nibbāna in a contemplative state in which one is detached from sense pleasures and aloof from morally evil states of mind. In these contexts we find that the term Nibbāna is used to denote a state of positive happiness conceived as the most desirable in the light of their respective philosophies.

On the other hand, when we examine the pure etymology of the term, we find that the word is formed of the components, the prefix *nis-* and the root *vā*, meaning "to blow." The word would, therefore, mean "blowing out" or "extinction." On the occasion on which the Buddha finally passed away into Nibbāna, Anuruddha described the Parinibbāna of the Buddha as, "The final liberation of mind was like the extinction of a lamp" (*pajjotass'eva nibbānaṃ vimokkho cetaso āhu ti*) (DN 16.6.10/D II 157).

In the word *Nibbāna*, therefore, we have a term which means both "extinction" as well as "the highest positive experience of happiness." Both of these connotations are important for understanding the significance of the term as it is employed in the Buddhist texts.

Annihilation?

The meaning of "extinction" easily lent itself to the annihilationist interpretation of Nibbāna. The individual, according to Buddhism, is in fact a process or a "stream of becoming" (*bhava-sota*) continuing from life to life, which in the human state was conditioned by heredity, environment and the psychological past of the individual. This process of conditioning was due to causal factors such as the operation of desires fed by beliefs. When the desires and beliefs ceased to operate, so it was argued, with the extinction of greed, hatred and ignorance, the individual was extinguished and ceased to exist for good. If the Buddha did not openly state this (so they say), it was because individuals being self-centred have a longing for life and personal immortality and would be frightened to hear of the truth.

There are some Buddhist scholars who virtually give the same explanation. They only object to the use of the word "annihilation" to describe "the ceasing of 'the individual' for good." They argue that annihilation is possible only if there is a being (*satta*) to be annihilated. But there is no such being. If there is no such being to be annihilated, there is no annihilation, for nothing or no one is annihilated. So what is wrong according to them is the use of the word "annihilation" to describe this state of affairs. They would not deny that the saṃsāric individual ceases to be for ever. This seems to be a merely verbal difference because, for all practical purposes, the individual is completely extinguished and if we are wrong (according to them) in saying so, it is because the individual did not exist in the first instance.

Such an interpretation leaves a lot of material unexplained in the early Buddhist texts. The Buddha certainly denied the persistence of an unchanging substratum or entity in the process of the individual but did not deny the phenomenal reality of the individual. The Buddha approves the use of the following language to describe the nature of individual existence on one occasion: "I did exist in the past, not that I did not, I will exist in the future, not that I will not and I do exist in the present, not that I do not" (*atthāhaṃ etarahi nāhaṃ natthīti*) (DN 9.49/D I 200). We must not forget that the Buddha held the view that "nothing exists" (*sabbaṃ natthi*) because everything passes away as one extreme point of view. The Buddhist criticism of the materialist's position was that the materialist posited without reason "the destruction of an existent individual" (*sato sattassa ucchedaṃ*).

When the Buddha himself was charged with being an annihilationist with regard to his teaching about Nibbāna, he counters it by saying that this was a gross misrepresentation of his teaching on the part of some of the other religious teachers (MN 22.37/M I 140). In the same context, the Buddha gives his reasons for saying so. When a person's (*bhikkhuṃ,* i.e. monk's) mind becomes finally emancipated (*vimutta-cittaṃ*), even the most powerful and intelligent Gods (*sa-brahmaka*) of the cosmos are unable to trace where the consciousness of such a Transcendent One (*Tathāgata*) is located (*anvesaṃ nādhigacchanti idaṃ nissitaṃ tathāgatassa viññāṇaṃ ti,* ibid.). It is stated that this is so even while he is living. For, says the Buddha, such a Transcendent One cannot be probed (*ananuvejjo*) even in this life.

When one's mind is emancipated, it does not become a dormant nonentity. If so the Buddha and the Arahats should have been apathetic individuals unconcerned about anything after attaining liberation. Instead, when the mind is purged of greed, hatred and ignorance it is transformed and shines with its natural lustre. It can then act spontaneously out of selflessness (*cāga*), compassion (*karuṇā*) and understanding (*paññā*).

The Transcendent One or the Tathāgata (a word used both of the Buddha and the Arahats) cannot be measured by the conditioned constituents of his personality (*khandha*) such as the body, the feelings, the ideas, the conative activities and the acts of cognition. Freed from reckoning in terms of these constituents of his personality, he is said to be "deep, immeasurable and unfathomable like the great ocean" (*gambhīro appameyyo duppariyogāho seyyathā pi mahāsamuddo*), (MN 72.20/M I 487). Qualities like compassion (*karuṇā*) and the other divine modes of behaviour (*Brahma-vihara*), we may note, are called "the infinitudes" (*appamaññāyo*).

Such an emancipated person, the depths of whose mind cannot be plumbed, it is said, cannot be considered to continue to exist after death (*uppajjati hoti parammaraṇā*) as an individual (whose existence is invariably self-centred and conditioned), nor to cease to exist or be annihilated at death (*na uppajjati na hoti parammaraṇā*). Neither description was apt for these reasons as well as for others.

The question as to whether the liberated person continues to exist for ever in time as a distinct individual or is annihilated at death is clearly posed in the *Suttanipāta*, where the Buddha is asked the question: "The person who has attained the goal—does he not exist or does he exist eternally without defect; explain this to me well, O Lord, as you understand it?" (Sn 1075). If annihilation was a fact or the person ceased to exist altogether, the answer would have been quite clear; it would have been, "He does not exist," but this is expressly denied. The reason given is that, "The person who has attained the goal is *beyond measure*" (*na pamāṇaṃ atthi*). Elsewhere, it is said that he does not come within time, being beyond time (*kappaṃ neti akappiyo*) or that he does not come within reckoning (*na upeti saṅkhaṃ*). In other words, we do not have the concepts or words to describe adequately the state of the emancipated person, who has attained the transcendent reality, whether it is when he lives with the body and the other constituents of personality or after death.

We may describe this situation in yet another way. Our minds function in this conditioned manner because they have become self-centred and corrupted by adventitious defilements (*upakkilesā*) and involvements (*upādāna*) in the course of our saṃsāric history. The mind, it is said, is naturally resplendent, though it has been corrupted by adventitious defilements (*pabhassaraṃ idaṃ cittaṃ taṃ ca āgantukehi upakkilesehi upakkiliṭṭhaṃ*). It is often compared in this respect to gold ore, which has the defilements of iron, copper, tin, lead and silver, but when it is purified it becomes pliant (*mudu*), flexible (*kammanīya*), resplendent (*pabhassara*) and not brittle (*na pabhaṅgu*).

So when the mind is cleansed of its defilements by meditative exercises and divested of its chief defilements, such as the obsessional attachment to sense-pleasures (*kāma-chanda*), aggressiveness (*vyāpāda*), apathy (*thīna-middha*), restlessness (*uddhacca-kukkucca*) and scepticism about moral and spiritual values and their rationale (*vicikicchā*), then it acquires a high degree of freedom, happiness, stability, serenity and awareness. Such a nature is in fact called "temporary Nibbāna" (*tadaṅganibbāna*). When the mind *is* further purified, it acquires certain extrasensory faculties such as telepathy, clairvoyance, etc., which are intrinsic to its nature. With the help of these faculties, it is possible to have an understanding of reality, which results in the mind being freed from the obsessions or inflowing impulses (*āsava*). Such a mind attains liberation. In the verses of the elders (*Thera-* and *Therigātha*) we find the testimonies of several monks and nuns who by these methods have gained emancipation.

Such a person is said to abide with his mind having transcended its bounds (*vimariyādikatena cetasa*). It is divested of personal strivings (*visaṅkhāra-gataṃ cittaṃ*), being wholly dominated with the greatest freedom and spontaneity by selflessness, compassion and understanding.

However, despite his liberation, since he is still limited by his conditioned psycho-physical individuality, it is called "the Nibbānic state with limitations still remaining" (*sa-upādisesa-nibbāna-dhātu*). Although his roots of greed, hatred and ignorance have been destroyed, he is still subject to pleasant and unpleasant experiences associated with his senses but not originating from his mind (It 2:27/p. 38).

God or Brahman?

The question as to what happens to his psycho-physical personality (*nāmarūpa*) at his final death is sometimes posed: "Where does the psycho-physical individuality cease to be without remainder?" The answer is given as follows: "Consciousness, without distinguishing mark, infinite and shining everywhere—here the material elements do not penetrate ... but here it is that the conditioned consciousness ceases to be" (DN 11.85/D I 223). Even the Commentary identifies the "infinite consciousness" with Nibbāna, saying that "it is a term for Nibbāna" (*nibbānassa taṃ nāmaṃ*; D-a II 393), while the second occurrence of the term "consciousness" is described as "the last stages of consciousness or conditioned consciousness" (*tattha viññāṇaṃ ti carimaka-viññāṇam-pi abhisaṅkhāraviññāṇam pi*; D-a II 393–94).

The *Brahmanimantanika Sutta* further corroborates the above interpretation. Here there is a dialogue between Buddha and Brahmā, and it is shown that the reality that the Buddha attains to is the ultimate and is beyond the ken even of Brahmā. The Buddha says: "Do not think that this is an empty or void state. There is this consciousness, without distinguishing mark, infinite and shining everywhere; it is untouched by the material elements and not subject to any power." The Buddha, it is said, can become invisible in it without being seen by any of the most powerful beings in the cosmos. In other words, it is the ultimate reality. We may recall the statement of the *Brahmajāla Sutta* that after the death of the body of the Transcendent One, gods and men would not see him. In other words, the Transcendent One does not cease to exist, though his existence is of a different order altogether. It is for this reason that the Mahayana texts represent this cosmic Buddha as an everlasting Father (see *Saddharmapuṇḍarīka Sūtra*).

However, all these phrases, "exists," "ceases to exist," etc. are misleading since they have a spatio-temporal connotation. Nibbāna is not spatially located (*na katthaci na kuhiñci*), nor located in time so that "one cannot say of Nibbāna that it is past, present or future." It is also not causally conditioned (*na paṭicca-samuppanna*). It is therefore not capable of conceptual formulation (*asaṅkhiyo*) or literal description.

So the explanations given to us who have not attained it are compared to the attempt to explain the nature of light or colour to a man born blind. To tell him that light or colour is not a sound, nor a taste, nor smell, nor touch, is literally true, but since he is only acquainted with sounds, tastes, smells and touches he may think that colours are nothing or cannot exist. The problem with Nibbāna is analogous. What we have to do with the blind man is to evolve a method of restoring his sight. When this is done, no explanation is necessary, but before that strictly no explanation was possible. So to explain Nibbāna by some form of rational demonstration is impossible—it falls beyond the pale of logic (*atakkāvacara*). So all one can do is to show the person who is anxious to attain Nibbāna the methods of doing so and then he is likely, if he carefully follows those methods, to have glimpses of it (e.g. *tadaṅga-nibbāna*) and perhaps eventually to attain it. At this stage no explanations would be necessary. This is precisely what the Buddha sets out to do and why he is averse to making detailed pronouncements about Nibbāna. As a result of this, the questions pertaining to the existence of the Transcendent One after death are treated as unanswered questions (*avyākata*).

However, certain brief indications are not lacking as we have seen from what we have stated above. In the *Udāna* we get some passages of this type. One of them reads as follows: "There is that sphere (*āyatanaṃ*) wherein is neither earth nor water nor fire nor air; wherein are none of the stages reached by *arūpa-jhāna* (impersonal mystical consciousness), where there is neither this world nor a world beyond nor both together, nor sun or moon; this, I say, is free from coming or going, from duration, arising or passing away; it has no foundation, no beginning and no object—this is, indeed, the end of unsatisfactoriness" (Ud 8.1/p. 80).

Again, it is said: "There is, O monks, the Unborn, the Unoriginated, the Unmade, the Uncompounded and if it were not for this Unborn, Unoriginated ... there would have been no salvation from the born, the originated, the made and the compounded" (Ud 8.3/p. 80–1).

These passages are sometimes interpreted as not having a positive connotation but as merely implying the possibility of attaining Nibbāna conceived as a state of nothingness, but such an interpretation would be incorrect in the light of what we have said.

Yet if we do so, it may be asked whether the Nibbāna of the Buddhist texts is in any way different from the conception of Brahman or God in the Upaniṣadic or theistic traditions. Here again, some scholars have claimed that there is no difference between the ultimate reality, or the Brahman of the Upaniṣads, and the Nibbāna of Buddhism. Some of the epithets used of Brahman such as *śānta* (peaceful) (Pali: *santa*), *śiva* (beneficial) (Pali: *siva*) are the same. While Brahman is said to have the characteristics of *sat* (existent), *cit* (intelligent) and *ānanda* (blissful), Nibbāna was called *sacca* (true or real), *ananta-viññāṇa* (infinite consciousness) and *parama sukha* (final bliss).

One who has attained Brahman is known in the Upaniṣads as *Brahma-prāpta* (*Kaṭha,* 6.18), while the Buddha is called *Brahma-patta* (MN 56.29/M I 386) in the Buddhist texts. The word *Brahma-patti* is also used of attaining Nibbāna (*majjhesitā brāhmaṇa Brahma-patti,* SN 7:9/S I 169). More frequently, those who have attained Nibbāna are called *Brahmabhūtena attanā viharati*, i.e. "abides with self become Brahman." Again, while the term *Nibbāna* is not found in the pre-Buddhist Upaniṣads, the *Bhagavadgītā* describes the ultimate reality as *Brahmanirvānaṃ.*

There is no doubt that Nibbāna is a transcendent reality beyond space, time and causation but despite the similarity between the two notions, an identification would be erroneous and misleading. Some of the final stages of jhānic attainment in Buddhism were achieved by Upaniṣadic seers and identified with Brahman. Buddhism points out their inadequacy and the necessity of going beyond. Besides, in some of the Upaniṣads we find a theistic interpretation of the ultimate experience and reality. For example, in the *Śvetāsvatara Upaniṣad* (6.10 = *Kaṭha*, 5.15 = *Muṇḍaka*, 2.2.10) we find the following description:

> *The sun shines not there, nor the moon and stars,*
> *These lightings shine not, much less this (earthly) fire!*
> *After Him, as He shines, doth everything shine,*
> *This whole world is illuminated with His light.*

In the *Udāna* we find a similar passage, which reads as follows:

> *Where earth, water, fire and air do not penetrate;*
> *There the stars do not glitter, nor the sun shed its light;*
> *The moon too shines not but there is no darkness there.*

Here there is no theistic interpretation of the experience and we earlier explained why such an interpretation would be erroneous. Besides, many of the metaphysical ideas about soul (*ātman*) which are rejected in Buddhism are to be found in the Upaniṣads, so that it would be quite misleading to identify the two.

The agnostic interpretation has also to be rejected. It was not that there was something that the Buddha did not know but that what he "knew" in the transcendent sense could not be conveyed in words because of the limitations of our concepts and of language. Nibbāna is, therefore, the Transcendent Reality, whose real nature we cannot grasp with our normal minds because of our self-imposed limitations. It is a state of freedom (*vimutti*), power (*vasī*), perfection (*parisuddhi*), knowledge (*aññā*) and perfect happiness of a transcendent sort. It is also said to be a state of perfect mental health, which we should try to attain for our personal happiness as well as for harmonious living.

10

The Buddhist View of Survival

It is necessary to have a clear and authentic formulation of the Buddhist view of survival as found in the early texts since there seem to be some misconceptions about this. We may briefly state some of these misconceptions.

Misconceptions

According to one view, the Buddha lived in a society in which the doctrine of rebirth was universally (or widely) taken for granted from time immemorial. The Buddha himself saw no reason to question this belief, which he accepted uncritically and dogmatically.

Another such misconception may be stated as follows: the Buddha's doctrine of *anattā* or no-soul was a denial of the existence of an animistic soul which survived the death of the body and transmigrated. Since nothing survived the death of the body, Buddhism is a form of materialism. The Buddha utilised the doctrines of rebirth and kamma prevailing in his society (so they say) to impart ethical teachings but did not himself believe in these doctrines.

There is yet another misconception. According to this view, the Buddha was not interested or held no specific views about the question of human survival or life after death. He roundly decried speculation about the past or the future (i.e. about prior or future lives) as unprofitable or mistaken. He was only concerned with man's present state of anxiety, suffering and dissatisfaction, and the solution for it.

These misconceptions can be cleared only by making a careful study of the authentic texts of Buddhism. When we do so we find that the Buddha did assert: (1) the continuity without identity of individuality due to the operation of causal factors; (2) the doctrine of *anattā*, which denied the existence of a physical, mental, psycho-physical or independent entity within or related to the psycho-physical aspects of personality; and (3) that mere metaphysical speculation about prior or future lives which did not result in the verification of facts about them was useless.

Historical Background

In order to understand the Buddhist view of survival it is desirable to have some knowledge of the views presented by pre-Buddhist thinkers, since the Buddhist conceptions were often presented in contrast to them.

It is a remarkable fact that in no other age in the history of thought was a solution to the problem of survival sought with such intensity as in this period and nowhere else can we find such a variety of views put forward.

Logically there are four possible points of view that we can adopt with regard to the question of survival. We may say (1) that we survive death in the form of discarnate spirits, i.e. a single after-life theory; (2) that we are annihilated with death, i.e. a materialist theory; (3) that we are unable to discover a satisfactory answer to this question or there is no satisfactory answer, i.e. a sceptical or positivist theory; and (4) that we come back to subsequent earth-lives or lives on other similar planets, i.e. a rebirth theory.

The Buddhist texts record several variants of each of these four types of theories. Let us take the variants of single after-life or one-life-after-death theories.

Single After-Life Theories

There are thirty-two of them listed in the *Brahmajāla Sutta.* According to what the philosophers or religious teachers who put these theories forward assert, they are broadly classified into theories which posit that the soul after death is (A) conscious (*saññī*), (B) unconscious (*asaññī*) and (C) superconscious (*nevasaññīnāsaññī*).

There are sixteen variants of (A) and eight of each of (B) and (C). The sixteen variants of (A) are due to

I. Variations regarding the *material form* of the soul:

- i. has a subtle material form
- ii. has no such form
- iii. has for some time a subtle material form and then has no such form
- iv. has no such form but has the power of manifesting one

II. Variations regarding the *duration* of the soul:

- i. comes to an end
- ii. is eternal

iii. changes its state after some time and becomes eternal
iv. does not exist in time

III. Variations regarding the *nature and extent* of consciousness:
i. is conscious of unity
ii. is conscious of diversity
iii. is of limited consciousness
iv. is of unlimited consciousness

IV. Variations regarding the hedonic tone of the experience:
i. is extremely happy
ii. is extremely unhappy
iii. is partly happy and partly unhappy
iv. does not experience happiness or unhappiness, i.e. has a neutral hedonic tone

Only variations I (i)–(iv) and II (i)–(iv) are considered applicable to those who hold that the soul was (B) unconscious or (C) superconscious after death.

The above classification appears to be a purely logical one, but the fact that many of these theories can be traced to pre-Buddhist literature proves that it is not just that.

Thus Prajāpati held, on the basis of rational and metaphysical speculation, that the soul was "conscious and having its own form after death" (*Chāndogya Upaniṣad* 8.12)—i.e. (A) I (i). Uddālaka held that the soul was "unconscious and without form" after death—i.e. (B) I (ii). The *Taittirīya Upaniṣad* holds that the soul has a subtle material form for some time after death and then ceases to have such a form—i.e. (A) I (iii). Yājñavalkya has tried to show that the soul is "neither conscious nor unconscious after death and has no form"—i.e. (C) I (ii). The *Brāhmaṇas* often speak of a "second death" after personal survival—i.e. (A) II (i).

The one-life-after-death theories held by people in the West who subscribe to different forms of theism or spiritualism are also classifiable as permutations and combinations of the above alternatives. Thus, the views held by those who subscribe to the belief that the soul survives as a discarnate spirit for all eternity, or those who say that the soul goes to heaven or hell for eternity after death, or those who maintain that the soul sleeps with the body till a day of judgement when its state is changed, or those who believe that the soul goes to purgatory till a day of judgement—all these views are classifiable under the above scheme.

In sharp opposition to those who held dualist theories of body and soul and claimed that there was only a single life after death were the materialists who denied a life after death altogether. Seven schools of such materialists are referred to in the *Brahmajāla Sutta* and some of them are independently referred to in the non-Buddhist literature.

The most extreme of them held that there is neither mind nor soul apart from the body, which was entirely a hereditary product of one's parents (*mātāpettikasambhavo*), and the material elements. What we call "mind" is the patterns of movements in our bodies. The modern version of this is called "central state materialism" (see J. J. C. Smart, *Philosophy and Scientific Realism,* 1963), which tries to do away with phenomenal factors such as "experience," "consciousness," etc. According to this theory, when we say that a person is happy, it refers not to a mental but to a physical state which has among its consequences that it causes a person to behave in a characteristically happy way.

Another school held that the mind is an emergent product which has a material basis and its condition is determined by the food we eat. They argued that, just as when we mix up certain chemicals in certain proportions there emerges the intoxicating power of liquor, even so the material particles of the body and the food we eat go to form the mind, which is an emergent by-product. There were also schools of mystic materialists who, by the use of drugs, claimed the possibility of achieving expansions of consciousness (called *micchā-jhāna* in the texts).

All these schools of materialists were characterised by the fact that they did not hold that mind and body were two different entities but were one and the same entity, either denying the reality of mental phenomena altogether or asserting that they were epiphenomena or accompaniments of the state of the body (for modern versions, see "The Identity Hypothesis—A Critique," in J. R. Smythies, *Brain and Mind,* London, 1965).

The dialectical opposition between the dualistic soul theorists, who asserted the reality of survival, and the monistic materialists, who denied survival, had already resulted prior to Buddhism in the rise of several sceptical schools of thought. The *Kaṭha Upaniṣad* states: "This doubt is there with regard to a man deceased—'he exists' say some; 'he exists not' say others" (1.20).

The four schools of sceptics (*amarāvikkhepikā*) in the *Brahmajāla*

Sutta adopted scepticism on the basis of various intellectual or pragmatic grounds. Some maintained that, in holding the view either that "there is survival" or that "there is no survival," there results an involvement or entanglement (*upādāna*) in a theory, and this promotes mental unrest. Others argued that in holding or denying the theory of survival one is led by one's prejudices for (*chanda, rāga*) or against (*dosa, paṭigha*) and that, therefore, truth demands that we do not come to any definite conclusions. Yet others avoided making definite pronouncements from fear of being engaged in debate. Others again like Sañjaya argued that statements about an after-life, about moral responsibility, or transcendent existence were not verifiable and therefore it was not possible to discover their truth or falsity.

Among those who held a dualist hypothesis and asserted "the eternity view" (*sassatadiṭṭhi*) were not only the single after-life theorists but those who held several variants of rebirth theories as well. It is important to bear in mind the fact that Buddhism was opposed to all these theories, including those on rebirth that had been propounded. The Buddha did not posit the existence of an unverifiable, unchanging entity to account for his theory of re-becoming and rebirth. Nor did he hold that the process of re-becoming was strictly determined by past kamma, by natural causes, or by the will of God. Causal factors were operative, no doubt, but they were not deterministic. Besides, some rebirth theories held that beings could be reborn even as "rice and barley, herbs and beans, sesame plants and trees" (*Chāndogya Upaniṣad* 5.10.6). The Buddha did not subscribe to such a point of view. In fact, it is doubtful whether he held that there was rebirth at the lowest levels of life. The Buddha later recounts as a mistaken view some of the beliefs of Jainism, which he put to the test prior to his enlightenment. In one place he says: "I used to walk up and down conscientiously extending my compassion even to a drop of water, praying that the dangerous bacteria in it may not come to harm" (*yāva udabindumhi pi dayā paccupaṭṭhitā hoti: mā'haṃ khuddake pāṇe visamagate saṅghātaṃ āpādessanti*), (MN 12.47/M I 78).

Buddhist Solution

It is in the historical context, outlined above, that the Buddha appeared on the scene and sought a solution to the riddle of life. It is, therefore, not correct to say (as many scholars have done) that the Buddha took for granted the belief in rebirth current in society at the time. As is evident from the Buddhist and the non-Buddhist literature, there was at the time a variety of views on the question of survival covering almost every possibility that one can think of.

Besides, the belief was not of very great antiquity. It is absent in the Vedas; it is merely hinted at in the *Brāhmaṇas* and the early Upaniṣads present a variety of views, some of which clearly reject rebirth. By the time of the Buddha, the materialists had made such an impact on society that he classifies the prevalent theories of his time as those of the eternalists and the materialists. In addition, scepticism was so rampant that the elite (*viññū-purisa*) did not subscribe to any specific belief. They were no doubt interested in the problem and people like Pāyāsi even performed experiments to test the validity of the belief in survival. One of these was that of weighing the body immediately before and after death. Finally, it is hardly consistent with the spirit of the *Kālāma Sutta,* where the Buddha asks people to adopt a critical attitude towards traditional beliefs.

The Buddhist theory of survival has its origin in the enlightenment of the Buddha and not in any traditional Indian belief. It is said that it was on the night of his enlightenment that he acquired the capacity to know his prior lives. It was when his mind was composed, clear, cleansed and without blemish, free from adventitious defilements, pliant and flexible, steadfast and unperturbed that he acquired this capacity to recall hundreds and thousands of prior lives and the prehistory of the universe, going back through the immensely long periods of the expansions and contractions of the oscillating universe. This is, in fact, called the first important item of knowledge, which broke through the veil of ignorance (*ayaṃ paṭhamā vijjā*).

As we have seen, the second important item of knowledge (*dutiyā vijjā*) was obtained by the exercise of the faculty of clairvoyance (*dibba-cakkhu*), with which the Buddha was able to see, among other things, the survival of beings in various states of existence, the operations of kamma, galactic systems, clusters of galactic systems and the vast cosmos.

The Five States of Existence

In the *Mahāsīhanāda Sutta,* there is a reference to the five states of existence. They are as follows: (1) the lower worlds (*duggati, vinipāta, niraya*); (2) the animal kingdom (*tiracchāna-yoni*); (3) the spirit-sphere (*petti–visaya*); (4) human beings (*manussa*); and (5) devas or higher, spirits.

While the "lower worlds" (*vinipāta*) are also called *niraya* (hells), we must not forget that "hells" (*pātāla*) in the popular sense are denied. It is said that the common man believes that there is a hell or nether world on the bottom of the ocean, but Buddha says that this belief is false and states that hell is a term for painful sensations. Yet elsewhere there is a reference to worlds which the Buddha claims to see in which everything one senses is unpleasant and the thoughts that come to one's mind are disagreeable and foul. In contrast, it is said, there are worlds in which everything one senses or experiences is pleasant. About the existence of devas, the Buddha says, when asked the question as to whether they exist, that he knows on good grounds that they do. When further questioned as to why he used the qualification "on good grounds," he says that it is because it is commonly taken for granted that devas or higher spirits exist (MN 100.42/M II 221f).

The five states of existence are graded according to the amount or degree of pain or pleasure experienced in them. According to this description, the human world is one in which one experiences "more pleasant than unpleasant experiences" (*sukhabahulā vedanā vediyamānaṃ*) (MN 12.40/M I 75). In the spirit-sphere it is more unpleasant than pleasant. In the animal it is unpleasant, since animals are supposed to live in a state of constant fear with strong unsatisfied instinctive desires such as hunger and thirst. In the lower worlds it is said to be very unpleasant. In the deva-worlds, on the other hand, it is extremely pleasant (*ekanta-sukha vedanā vediyamānaṃ*).

The person who is pictured as faring on in these states of existence is conceived as one who is oppressed by the heat, exhausted, afraid and thirsty. The lower worlds are compared to a pit of coals into which one falls; animal existence is a pit full of excrement; existence in the spirit-sphere is like coming under a tree in a desert without much shade; human life is compared to coming under a large and shady tree, while the deva-world is compared to a well-furnished and beautiful palace. In contrast, Nibbāna is said to be analogous to the above person, who is oppressed with heat, exhausted, afraid and thirsty, reaching a lake where the waters are cool and clear, bathing in it, quenching his thirst and sitting or lying down in an adjoining glade, experiencing extreme happiness (*ekanta-sukhā vedanā vediyamānaṃ*).

From the descriptions given in the early texts, the usual tendency is for a person to survive as a departed spirit or a discarnate spirit in the spirit-sphere and come back to an earth-life, since the normal character of human beings is a mixture of good and evil and the stage of evolution of one's consciousness is attuned to existence in these worlds. But it is possible to regress to animal or subhuman forms of existence by neglecting the development of one's personality or character and becoming a slave to one's passions. It is also exceptionally possible to attain to existence in the deva-worlds. In the *Saṅkhāruppatti Sutta* (MN 120), it is said that a person who is possessed of faith (*saddhā*), virtue (*sīla*), learning (*suta*), selflessness (*cāga*) and wisdom (*paññā*) can aspire to and attain to better states of existence among human beings or devas.

Intelligibility

The word used to describe the progression from existence to existence is "re-becoming" (*punabbhava*). Rebirth is only a special case of re-becoming when a person comes back to an earth-life. Rebirth in this sense takes place until a person attains a spiritual state of Non-Returner (*anāgāmi*) or Arahat. If there is any doubt about the interpretation of *punabbhava* as rebirth in these contexts, it may be dispelled by examining similar expressions such as "he does not come back to lie in the womb" (*na punar-eti gabbhaseyyaṃ*) (Sn 99), used of an Arahant.

The question has been raised by some philosophers as to whether a conception of survival after death either in the form of rebirth or as a discarnate spirit is at all intelligible. If we preserve someone's heart or kidney in a living condition after his death, we would not say in respect of such an organ that so-and-so is now alive. It is therefore necessary for there to be some sense in which the reborn person or discarnate spirit should be able to claim identity with the dead person (when he was alive), even though all that can be established is continuity and not identity even in this life. To say that both have the same soul will not help because the existence of such a soul as an unchanging agent or recipient of actions is unverifiable.

The solution to this problem lies in the criteria that we employ to claim personal identity. In a single human life we normally use two criteria. One is the spatio-temporal continuity of the body. On the basis of this we can claim that so-and-so is a person who as a child went to such-and-such a school, although there may be nothing in common between the two bodies as far as shape and content are concerned. The other criterion is memory; on the basis of which someone may claim that he was such-and-such twenty years ago. When one life is concerned the two criteria normally support each other.

In the case of the reborn person or discarnate spirit, it is the memory criterion alone which can establish the identity. In this case, when the body criterion is employed, we have to say that "he is not the same person," but when the memory criterion is employed, we would have to say "he is not another person." So according to Buddhism he is neither the same nor another (*na ca so na ca añño*) when we give a strictly accurate description, although in common parlance we may say that he is the same person.

The logical possibility of such personal identity without a soul is granted by Prof. A. J. Ayer, a logical analyst, who says, "I think that it would be open to us to admit the logical possibility of reincarnation merely by laying down the rule that if a person who is physically identified as living at a later time does have the ostensible memories and character of a person who is physically identified as living at an earlier time, they are to be counted as one person and not two" (see *The Concept of a Person*, London, 1963, p. 127).

As for the concept of a discarnate spirit, Prof. H. H. Price, following the ideas of some Hindu and Buddhist texts (as he admits) has given an intelligible account of how a "discarnate spirit" may be conceived of, consistent with findings of modern psychology and psychical research (see *Survival and the Idea of "Another World*," in J. R. Smythies, *Brain and Mind*, London, 1965, pp. 1–33).

Although the majority of modern psychologists attempt to explain the functioning of the brain on mechanistic models, they find it difficult to explain away the fact and role of consciousness. Despite the claim of some philosophers (e.g. G. Ryle, *The Concept of Mind*, 1949) the ghost from the human machine has not been exorcised. Prof. Sir John Eccles has made the following statement about the structure and functions of the brain: "the structure of the brain suggests that it is the sort of machine that a 'ghost' might operate" where the word 'ghost' is used 'to designate any kind of agent that defies detection by such apparatus as is used to detect physical agents" (*The Neurophysiological Basis of Mind*, London, 1953, pp. 278ff). We can do without the concept of a permanent soul, but it is doubtful whether consciousness can be explained away, where it functions as a causal factor in initiating plans, making decisions, etc.

The Buddha did not subscribe to the dualist hypothesis that, "the mind and body are different" (*aññaṃ jīvaṃ aññaṃ sarīraṃ*) nor to the identity hypothesis that "the mind and body are the same" (*taṃ jīvaṃ, taṃ sarīraṃ*) but found that there was partial truth in both. Consciousness is partly formed by the impact of the environment on the living body but in turn it determines bodily behaviour.

In rebirth and re-becoming there is continuity of the stream of consciousness (*viññāṇa-sota*) without identity (*anaññaṃ*), making the recall of prior lives potentially possible. It is, however, not a self-identical permanent substance, which is quite independent of the body with regard to its growth and development.

II

The Buddhist Doctrine of Kamma

I refer to this doctrine specifically as the Buddhist doctrine of kamma in order to distinguish it from the other non-Buddhist doctrines of kamma, which were taught by non-Buddhist thinkers prior to, during and even after the time of the Buddha. In this respect, it is important to note the significant differences between the Buddhist doctrine of karma and the doctrines of karma taught in Jainism, by certain Ājīvika thinkers as well as by the Brahmins.

Misconceptions

This is particularly necessary since the Buddhist doctrine of kamma is often confused with and assumed to be the same as the brahmanical one. People tend to speak of or criticise the doctrine of kamma as though there was only one such doctrine common to different religions such as Hinduism, Jainism and Ājīvikism, despite the fact that they profess different teachings about the nature, operations and attitude to the alleged phenomenon of karma.

Another misconception which is partly connected with the above misunderstanding is that the Buddhist doctrine of karma constitutes or implies a fatalist attitude to life and nature, a view put forward by some (not all) Western scholars and even subscribed to by some South Asian intellectuals both non-Buddhist and even Buddhist.

Yet another source of misunderstanding is the attempt on the part of certain scholars and other individuals to rationalise (quite unnecessarily) the doctrine of kamma by interpreting it to mean the social or biological inheritance of man or both, ignoring altogether and distorting the authentic teachings of the texts of the Buddhist Canon.

Meaning

In the pre-Buddhist literature the word kamma was used mainly in the sense of either religious rituals or the social functions and duties of man. In the latter sense the *Īṣa Upaniṣad* says: "Let a man aspire to live a hundred years, performing his social duties" (*kurvanneveḥa karmaṇi jijīviṣecchataṃ samāḥ*). This sense has survived in the Buddhist texts, where the word *kamma* is used in the plural to denote the different professions or occupations of men. Thus, Buddhism recommends people to take up "morally blameless occupations" (*anavajjāni kammāni*).

As a technical term, the word kamma is used in the early Buddhist texts to denote volitional actions. These actions may be morally good (*kusala*), morally evil (*akusala*), or morally neutral (*avyākata*). They may be actions which find expression in bodily behaviour (*kāya-kamma*), verbal behaviour (*vacī-kamma*) and psychological behaviour (*mano*).

The morally good and evil actions are said to be liable to give rise to consequences, individual as well as social, pleasant and unpleasant on the whole, as the case may be. The individual consequences may be manifested in this life, the next life or the lives to come unless their potentialities are extinguished or they do not find an opportunity for fruition.

Conscious volition (*cetanā*) is a necessary condition of such a morally good, evil or neutral act, but does not constitute the whole of it except when it happens to be purely mental. Thus, we would not be guilty of the crime of murder merely because we had the intention of murdering somebody. As the *Atthasālinī* (p. 98) points out: "There are five constituent factors in an act of killing: (1) the existence of a living being; (2) the awareness of the existence of such a living being; (3) the intention of killing; (4) the effort or the means employed to kill; and (5) the consequent death of the living being."

The intention is necessary but not sufficient to constitute an act of killing. As the Vinaya rules point out, where the intention is absent but one's actions are instrumental in causing the death of a person, one may be guilty of an act of negligence but not of murder.

So the word *kamma* is used to denote volitional acts which find expression in thought, speech or physical deeds, which are good, evil or a mixture of both and are liable to give rise to consequences, which partly determine the goodness or badness of these acts.

Basis for Doctrine

It is often assumed that the basis for the doctrine of kamma in Buddhism is a rational argument implicit in the *Cūḷakammavibhaṅga Sutta*. It is true that in this Sutta the Buddha seems to suggest purely rational grounds for believing in the doctrine of kamma, but it would be mistaken to believe that the doctrine is accepted as true or as representing the nature of things as they are on these grounds.

In this Sutta, a brahmin youth meets the Buddha and asks him for an explanation as to why among human beings some are short-lived while others are long-lived, some are sickly while others are healthy, some are ugly to look at while others are handsome, some have little power or influence while others are influential, some are poor while others are rich, some are of a lower social status while others are of a higher social status.

The question is posed in the form: "What is the reason and the cause for the inequality (*hīnappaṇītatā*) among human beings despite their being human?" The Buddha's reply was as follows: "Beings inherit their kamma and it is kamma which divides beings in terms of their inequalities."

We may argue that this embodies the following rational ethical argument, consisting of an empirical and ethical premise, viz. people are of unequal status, those of unequal status ought to be such only by virtue of their own actions—therefore, since this is not due to their actions in this life, it should be due to their actions in a prior life. This means that both kamma and pre-existence are the case.

It is also true that this kind of rational ethical argument has appealed to many thinkers. Maurice Maeterlinck (1862–1949), poet, dramatist and essayist, says: "Let us return to reincarnation ... for there was never a more beautiful, a juster, a purer, a more moral fruitful and consoling, nor, to a certain point, a more probable creed than theirs. It alone, with its doctrine of successive expiations and purifications, accounts for all the physical and intellectual inequalities, all the social iniquities, all the hideous injustices of fate" (see *Reincarnation, An East-West Anthology,* ed. Joseph Head and S. L. Cranston, New York, 1961, p. 200). Prof. Allan G. Widgery also speaks appreciatively of such an argument when he says: "For it affirms that men are not born equal ... and this affirmation appears to be more in accordance with the facts.... Men are regarded as different at birth: the differences being due to the manner in which in past lives they have built up their nature through the action of the law of karma" (ibid., p. 117).

But it would be mistaken to consider the passage in the above Sutta as presupposing a rational ethical argument with a concealed ethical premise. It is true as Ānanda has said of the Buddha that, "so far as anything can be attained by reasoning (*takka*), you have ascertained it" (*yāvatakaṃ takkāya pattabbaṃ anuppattaṃ tayā*) (SN 2:20/S I 56). But the doctrine of karma is not put forward in Buddhism as a product of mere speculative reasoning (*takka*), which is not adequate for the discovery of the facts of nature as the Buddha has elsewhere pointed out. The Buddha's statements even in this Sutta are based on clairvoyant observation and reasoning and not on mere rational speculation.

It is also mistaken to assume on the ground of the recognition of the fact of the known inequalities among mankind that Buddhism accepted the *status quo* of a static conception of society or denied the doctrine of what is known as "the equality of mankind."

For, as we shall see when we come to the social and political philosophy of Buddhism, Buddhism upholds the biological, social and spiritual equality of mankind and envisages a time in the future when with the economic, moral and spiritual regeneration of man there would come into being a social order in which people would be healthy and long-lived and the inequalities in power, wealth and social status would be greatly diminished.

In this context, we must not forget that one of the central teachings of Buddhism revolves round the conception of the destruction or elimination of the evil effects of kamma (*kammakkhaya*) by effecting a change in the basis of human motivation from that of greed (*lobha*), hate (*dosa*) and ignorance (*moha*) to selflessness (*cāga*), compassion (*karuṇā*) and understanding (*paññā*). Even the better social order of the future can be set up only by people who believe in moral and spiritual values and have to some extent cultivated the qualities of selfless service, kindness and wisdom.

Verifiability

As we have said above, the statements about the operations of kamma are made by the Buddha on the basis of inferences based on clairvoyant observation. The awareness of the nature of the operations of karma is said to be the second item of knowledge (*dutiya vijjā*) obtained by the Buddha on the night of his enlightenment.

It is said: "When his mind is thus composed, clear and cleansed, without blemish, free from adventitious defilements, pliant and flexible, steadfast and unperturbed, he turns and directs his mind towards an understanding of the death and rebirth (*upapāta*) of beings. Then with his pure, paranormal clairvoyant vision he sees beings—the high and the low, the beautiful and the ugly, the happy and the wretched—dying and being reborn according to their character (*kamma*)."

The threefold knowledge (*tisso vijjā*) acquired by the Buddha, which is crucial for the attainment of enlightenment, consists of the knowledge of pre-existence, of the operations of kamma and of the capacity to eliminate the inflowing impulses (*āsavakkhaya*). It is the same knowledge had by the Arahants attaining emancipation of mind (*ceto-vimutti*) and in the *Thera-* and *Therī-gāthā*, the verses of the elder monks and nuns, we constantly meet with the refrain: "I have attained the three-fold knowledge, I have done the bidding of the Buddha" (*tisso vijjā anuppattā kataṃ Buddhassa sāsanaṃ*).

The operations of kamma are, therefore, personally verified by the Buddha and his disciples. In the *Mahāsīhanāda Sutta,* the Buddha refers to the way he tested the theory of kamma as though he was testing a scientific hypothesis. It is said: "There are these five destinies, Sāriputta. What five? The lower worlds, the animal kingdom, the spirit-sphere (*pettivisaya*), human existence and the higher worlds. I know these lower worlds, the path which leads to them or the kind of conduct which takes you to that state of existence at death.... Herein, Sāriputta, I comprehend the mind of a certain individual with my mind as follows: 'This individual is set on behaving in such a manner and follows such a mode of conduct that he is likely to be born in one of the lower worlds at death on the destruction of the, body.' I then observe him at a later time by means of clear, clairvoyant, paranormal perception—the same individual born in one of the lower worlds at death experiencing great pain. Just as if there were a pit of coals and a man were to come along, tired and exhausted, taking a path leading straight to it and a man possessed of sight were to observe him and say to himself: 'This man is, surely, taking a path which will land him in a pit of coals,' and later see him fallen in that pit experiencing great pain; even so ... the animal world ... experiencing much unhappiness ... Just as if there were a cesspit and a man, tired and exhausted were to come along ...; even so ... the spirit-sphere ... experiencing more unpleasant than pleasant sensations. … Just as if there were a tree in a rugged place, with sparse foliage affording scanty shade and a man were to come along, tired and exhausted; even so … the human world … experiencing more pleasant than unpleasant sensations. … Just as if there were a tree with dense foliage in a pleasant spot and a man were to come along, tired and exhausted …; even so: … in a higher world … experiencing extremely pleasant sensations. … Just as if there were a palace with all the comforts and luxuries and a man were to come along, tired and exhausted…."

In the *Mahākammavibhaṅga Sutta,* the Buddha points out that certain yogins who have acquired the capacity for clairvoyant observation, nevertheless came to false conclusions and denied the fact of kamma since they made invalid inferences from the observed data. This is what he says:

"Herein a certain yogin as a result of his efforts and application, attains such a state of concentration that he sees with his clear, clairvoyant paranormal vision a man who has misconducted himself born at death on the dissolution of his body in a happier and better world. He concludes as follows: 'There are no evil actions (kamma) and no consequences of misconduct, for I have observed a man…. Everyone, whether he misconducts himself in this life or not, is born at death in a happier and better world.' I do not agree [says the Buddha] with the claim of this yogin that there are no evil actions and no future consequences of misconduct. I am prepared to grant that this yogin has observed a man who has misconducted himself in this life, born at death in a happier and better world, but I do not agree with his conclusion that, therefore, *all* people, whether they misconduct themselves in this life or not, are born at death in a happier and better world. The knowledge of the Transcendent One (*Tathāgata*) with regard to operations of kamma are different…. If a person who has misconducted himself in this life is born at death in a happier and better world, then he has either some time in his past done *good* deeds, which have resulted in these experiences, or at the time of his death has changed his ways and adopted the right view of life" (MN 136.14/M III 212.f).

The mistake that these yogins made, according to the Buddha, was to form generalisations on the basis of one or a few observations without observing a generality of cases and seeing that the apparent exceptions were explicable on other terms. The operations of kamma, it is said, are so complex that they are not fully comprehensible (*acinteyya*) (AN 4:77/A II 80) except to the vision and understanding of a Buddha. Even with regard to the universe (*loka-visaya*), we noted that the Buddha could observe clusters of galaxies and the vast cosmos, while Anuruddha the specialist in clairvoyance, could observe only a single galaxy.

Relation to Causal Laws

The operation of these laws of kamma was only a special instance of the working of causal laws in nature in which there were physical laws (*utu-niyāma*), biological laws (*bīja-niyāma*), psychological laws (*citta-niyāma*), karmic laws (*kamma-niyāma*) pertaining to moral acts and their consequences and laws pertaining to spiritual phenomena (*dhamma-niyāma*). But the pattern of events in nature, according to Buddhism, is neither deterministic nor indeterministic. So causal laws are only probable and statistical and not deterministic.

Karmic laws, therefore, state tendencies rather than inevitable consequences. Several of these correlations are stated in the *Cūḷakammavibhaṅga Sutta* (MN 135). The general principle is that morally good acts tend to be followed in the long run by pleasant consequences and morally evil acts by unpleasant consequences to the individual. Since it is of the nature of good acts to promote the material and spiritual well-being of mankind, it follows from this general principle that one cannot gain one's own happiness at the expense of others.

Among the specific correlations are the following. Those who harm and hurt living beings tend to be sickly, while those who are compassionate towards them tend to be healthy. Those who are angry and irritable, scowl at and abuse people tend to be ugly, while the others who are not so tend to be beautiful. Those who are envious and jealous of the honour and respect bestowed on others tend to lose respect, while the others tend to command it.

Medieval Analysis

In the *Abhidhammatthasaṅgaha,* a compendium of the medieval period, we find kamma classified firstly according to function (*kicca*), as what gives birth (*janaka*), what tends to support a tendency (*upatthambhaka*), what tends to obstruct a tendency (*upapīḷaka*) and what destroys (*upaghātaka*). Secondly, according to the manner in which they come into function (*pāka-dāna-pariyāya*), they are classified as weighty (*garuka*), proximate (*āsanna*), habitual (*āciṇṇa*) and residual (*kaṭattā*). Thirdly, according to the time of taking effect (*pāka-kāla*), there are four sorts that are experienceable in this life (*diṭṭhadhamma-vedanīya*), in the next life (*upapajja-vedanīya*), some time in the future (*aparāpara-vedanīya*), or never (*ahosi*). Fourthly, according to the place in which the effects occur, there is evil kamma finding fruition in the worlds of sense-gratification; similarly it is with good karma; and there is also good kamma which becomes effective in the subtle material worlds (*rūpa-loka*) and the immaterial, ideational worlds (*arūpa-loka*) (see *Abhidhammatthasaṅgaha* V.50ff).

Distinction

It is necessary to distinguish the Buddhist theory of kamma from the other non-Buddhist theories. Firstly, it has to be distinguished from the Jain theory, according to which man could not develop morally and spiritually without undergoing all the consequences of his previous evil kamma. The Jains hoped to achieve this by indulging in ascetic practises, which they believed helped to wear away the evil effects of past kamma. The value of a moral act likewise depended on its physical expression rather than the intention, which is not so in Buddhism.

The Buddhist theory has also to be distinguished from an Ājīvika theory, which asserted that all present actions and experiences are strictly determined by previous kamma. Kamma according to Buddhism, while being non-deterministic, was only one among many factors which conditioned the nature of the individual's experience of pleasure and pain. Among them was the physiological state of the body, which was partly a product of heredity or the biological laws (*bija-niyāma*) recognised in Buddhism. The other factors were changes in the physical environment (*utu-pariṇāma*), in social vicissitudes (*visama-parihāra*), the intentional activity of the individual (*opakkamika*) and lastly karma. Kamma, it would appear, could operate separately in a psychosomatic manner or in co-operation with the other factors.

Since a number of factors operated in conditioning man's experience, it was wrong to say that pleasure and pain were due entirely to one's own actions (*sayaṃ-kataṃ sukhadukkhaṃ*), nor were they due to the action of an external agent like God (*paraṃ-kataṃ*), nor to a combination of both (*sayaṃkataṃ ca paraṃkataṃ ca*), nor were they accidental (*adhicca-samuppanna*). Pleasure and pain were causally conditioned (*paṭicca-samuppanna*) and man by his knowledge of himself and nature could understand, control and master them.

Fatalism, Heredity and Kamma

Since karmic correlations were not deterministic, kamma was only one of many factors conditioning the nature of experience, while past karma was extinguishable and modifiable in the context of one's present actions. The Buddhist teaching of kamma was not fatalistic and was opposed to all forms of determinism: natural determinism (*sabhāva-vāda*), theistic determinism (*issara-karaṇa-vāda*) and kammic determinism (*pubba-kamma-vāda*) or any combination of them. According to one Brahmanical text, nature compels man to act as he does, while nature itself is under the control or will of God.

As we have seen, Buddhism states that man is conditioned by his heredity (*bīja-niyāma*), by his physical, social and ideological (*saḷāyatana-paccayā phasso*, etc.) environment, by his psychological past (*citta-niyāma*) including his kammic heritage (*kamma-niyāma*), but he is not determined by any or all of them. He has an element of free will (*attakāra*), or personal endeavour (*purisa-kāra*) by exercising which he can change his own nature as well as his environment (by understanding it) for the good of himself as well as others. In this sense man is master of his fate (*attā hi attano nātho*).

The laws of heredity, likewise, are not to be confused with those of kamma. Buddhism accepts both. As a result there may be situations in which the causal lines of kamma and heredity coincide. A person may have a certain trait because he inherits it from one of his parents and also because he has a particular kammic reason or affinity for it.

Sometimes in the case of mental traits, the origin may be karmic rather than hereditary. As C. D. Broad stated in his examination of the philosophy of McTaggart, who urged a belief in rebirth and karma on philosophical grounds in his books *The Nature of Existence* and *Some Dogmas of Religion*, McTaggart points out that the assumption of selective affinity between certain kinds of mind and certain kinds of organism would explain likenesses in mental characteristics between parents and children which are often ascribed to the direct influence of heredity. Owing to heredity a man's organism will resemble those of his direct ancestors more closely than those of other people. Now, similar organisms will be adapted to similar minds, and so zygotes which will develop into similar organisms are likely to attract similar minds and unite with them at conception. Broad added: "I think it must be admitted that this theory is ingenious and plausible" (*Examination of McTaggart's Philosophy*, Vol. II Part II, Cambridge, 1938, pp. 614–15). Besides, it can be seen how rebirth and kamma can explain the (sometimes marked) temperamental differences in identical twins, who when they happen to be Siamese twins have an identical and a common environment.

Central Teaching

It must, however, not be forgotten that the central teaching of Buddhism is not that of continuing to perform good kamma for the sake of rewards in continued saṃsāric existence (which cannot be enjoyed without the subsequent suffering from the evil which finds fruition), but the elimination of the effects of kamma (*kammakkhaya*).

The immediate ideal of the Buddhist should therefore be that of attaining the first stage of spiritual development (*sotāpanna*) by the elimination of attachment to notions of ego and ego-centred views (*sakkāya-diṭṭhi*); by the elimination of doubts regarding the Buddhist account of the nature and destiny of man in the universe (*vicikicchā*) through examination and inquiry into and partial verification of the truth of the Dhamma and the realisation that religion is part and parcel of one's daily living and experience and not of obsessional attachment to virtues and observances (*sīlabbata-parāmāsa*). Such a person is "not liable to fall below the status of human existence" (*avinipātadhammo*) and is destined to achieve the goal of enlightenment (*niyato sambodhi-parāyano*) before long. This is the path leading to the destruction of kammic effects (*kammakkhaya*) in which the good life is cultivated with the growth of selflessness, love and understanding for its own intrinsic worth and not for egoistic rewards.

12

The Case for the Buddhist Theory of Karma and Survival

If we use the word "rebirth" to denote the view that immediately or some time after death we return to an earth-life, then such rebirth is only a special case of re-becoming.

According to this Buddhist doctrine of re-becoming, there could be continuity of individuality in various planes of existence. We may survive as a discarnate spirit (Pali *gandhabba* = Skr. *gandharva*) in the spirit-sphere (*petti–visaya*), as a denizen of the sub-human world or as an angelic spirit in the celestial planes of existence. Such survival, as the *Katha-vatthu* explains, is either in the gross material world (*kāma-loka*), the subtle material world (*rūpa-loka*) or the immaterial world (*arūpa-loka*). There is no intermediate existence (*antarābhava*) apart from existence in one of these three planes of becoming.

As we have seen, since human existence is a mixture of good and evil, the usual pattern, as the texts make out, is to survive as a discarnate spirit and come back to a human existence. The practise of Buddhism by the cultivation of faith (*saddhā*), virtue (*sīla*), learning (*suta*), selflessness (*cāga*) and wisdom (*paññā*) makes it possible for a person to determine his future birth on the human or celestial planes. A person who has become a non-returner (*anāgāmin*) need not come back to human existence and an Arahant will not be born again in the spatio-temporally and causally conditioned cosmos.

Novel Theory

Besides, the Buddhist theory of survival is a novel theory which is not to be found in the pre-Buddhist literature. It was a doctrine of survival without the concept of a self-identical substance or soul. The physical form, perceptions, feeling, will or intellect were not the soul, nor did the soul own them, nor was a soul to be found within them, nor again were they to be located in a cosmic soul. There was no self apart from a complex of psycho-physical processes and man was defined as a bundle of dispositions (*suddha-saṅkhāra-puñja*). Though there was no self-identical (*anaññaṃ*) substance, there was a continuity (*santati, santāna*) of individuality, sometimes referred to as a stream of consciousness (*viññāṇa-sota*) or a stream of becoming (*bhava-sota*). Associated with a person's present body were the dispositions with potentialities for re-becoming (*ponobhaviko bhava-saṅkhāra*).

These planes of existence and the operations of karma were observed by the Buddha on the night of his enlightenment. His knowledge consisting of "the recall of prior lives" (*pubbenivāsānussati-ñāṇa*) is described as follows:

"When his mind is thus composed, clear and cleansed, without blemish, free from adventitious defilements, pliant and flexible, steadfast and unperturbed, he turns and directs his mind to the recollection of his former lives, viz. one life, two lives ... ten lives ... a hundred lives ... through evolving aeons, recalling in what place he was born, his name and title, his social status, his environment, experiences and term of life and dying there, in what place he was next born and so on up to his present existence, he remembers the varied states of his former lives in all their aspects and details. Just as a man who has travelled from his village to another and from that to yet another, when to his former village by the same route, remembers how he came from that village, where he stayed and rested, what he said and what he did; even so, when the mind is composed...." (DN 2.93/D I 81).

Since the Buddhist theory of survival *is* a composite theory, the case in support should include at least the arguments for survival as discarnate spirits as well as for rebirth.

Before we examine such arguments and the evidence, we have to meet the objection that the known facts of science concerning brain-mind phenomena suggest the impossibility of survival.

Two Views

There are two classical views regarding the relationship between the mind and the body. One is the identity hypothesis, which either denies the reality of mental experience or holds that such experiences are inseparable from aspects of neural or brain phenomena. The other is dualism, which holds that mental and neural phenomena interact.

The extreme form of the identity hypothesis, called central state materialism, tries to do away with such causal factors as "experience" or "consciousness" and explain psychological behaviour as being solely the functioning of the central nervous system. This is a purely mechanistic theory.

A less extreme view, which is still monistic, is the psychosomatic theory, according to which psychological experience and brain phenomena are merely the two aspects of one reality. According to this theory, the brain-mind combination does not function in a purely mechanical manner but, since brain and mind are two aspects of the same process, they both cease to function with the death of the person.

A modern form of the dualist theory would be the instrumental or the transmission theory, according to which the brain would function as the instrument of the mind, being itself affected by it.

Buddhism, which discards the monistic and the dualistic hypotheses, would hold that there is some truth in each without subscribing to either. For Buddhism the human being in normal consciousness is a psycho-physical unit, in which the physical and psychical phenomena are in a state of mutual dependence (*aññamañña-paccaya*). Yet at the same time aspects of will can control, govern and produce mental activity. Also, when the body is brought within control and is in a state of perfect composure with its activities stilled (*kāyasaṅkhārā niruddhā*), it can exercise its extrasensory powers of perception.

Buddhism, therefore, while rejecting the identity hypothesis that "the mind and the body are the same" (*taṃ jīvaṃ tam sarīraṃ*) and the dualist hypothesis that "the mind and the body are different" (*aññaṃ jīvaṃ aññaṃ sarīraṃ*) finds partial truth in each and thus puts forward a middle view.

Neurology

The ideal scientist in the field of neurology is not expected to subscribe to any particular point of view. As the neurologist Dr Wilder Penfield, said in 1957: "Any scientist who looks up from his work to declare, for example, that the truth is to be found in monism or dualism, or that there is a middle ground, ceases to be a scientist." (quoted from Prof. Hornell Hart, *The Enigma of Survival*, London, 1959, pp. 218–19).

This does not, however, mean that the findings of scientists have no bearing on these theories. The advances made over the last fifty years are due to new electro-physiological techniques which have made it possible to stimulate single nerve fibres and record responses from single nerve cells, the measurement of the electrical activity of the brain (EEGs); brain surgery and the study of the chemical basis of neural phenomena. They have shown that it is possible to alter somewhat the state of the personality or consciousness by physical or chemical means.

Consciousness, incidentally, cannot be argued or analysed away to the satisfaction of the extreme monists, for it is a brute fact that certain physiological processes such as aspects of brain phenomena are accompanied by consciousness or self-consciousness, though it could have been otherwise.

Memory

At the same time, this research has also shown that there is no one-to-one correspondence between phenomena and mental experience, as the psychosomatic theory would like to maintain. Thus, memory is not uniquely located in particular points of the brain. Dr H. O. Hebb stated in 1953 that "it is very difficult to conceive of memory as a function of a localised region" ("The Problem of Consciousness and Introspection," in Adrian, Bremer & Jasper, [Eds.] *Brain Mechanisms and Consciousness: A Symposium*, Springfield, 1954).

Dr Penfield records that, when a specific point in the brain of a woman patient was touched, she heard a mother calling her little boy. But eleven minutes later, when the same point was touched with the electrode, the patient no longer heard the mother calling her little boy but instead heard the voices of people calling from building to building. In another case, the patient heard the same song vividly when each of four different points in the brain were stimulated. Lord Brain, F.R.S., the eminent neurologist states: "Evidently in the brain, memory is not a unitary function nor is there any single part of the nervous system in which all memories are stored" (in "Some Aspects of the Brain-Mind Relationship," in *Brain and Mind,* London, 1965, p. 69).

The lack of specific localisation is not confined to memory but is to be found in other functions as well. In 1912, Yerkes found that habits registered in one part of the nervous system of an earthworm might shift later on to another part, and a similar versatility was to be found in human brains relative to the effects of brain damage in children by Klebanoff, Singer and Wilensky in 1954. A senior lecturer in zoology working mainly on the brains of rats reports as follows:

"Three of the preceding sections are headed respectively 'cortex,' 'limbic system' and 'reticular system,' but this anatomical arrangement does not correspond to the facts of function: the study of any of these systems soon becomes meaningless without reference to the others. During every few milliseconds, in the waking brain, information passes to and fro in a network of communication of which only the larger details are yet certainly known.... In such a flux we cannot, with our present knowledge, properly speak of localisation of function, but only of the specific effects of injury or stimulation.... A small injury can influence behaviour which certainly depends also on the functioning of the other parts; by contrast, some substantial injuries leave behaviour largely unaltered; and when behaviour is disturbed by lesions, there may be subsequent recovery due, evidently, to some compensatory process elsewhere. These facts at present defy explanation. All they do is to make accounts of neural function in terms of reflex arcs as absurd as interpretations of learning in terms of conditioned reflexes" (S. A. Barnett, A *Study in Behaviour*, London, 1963, p. 238).

Dr Grey Walter confessed a lack of knowledge about the nature of memory. He said: "No sketch of the contemporary world of brain research would be complete without a hue of mystery because this is what catches the mind's eye. For me there are two great obscurities in our picture: memory and sleep" (*Frontiers of Knowledge*, New York, 1966, p. 99). Recently (April 1968), Dr Penfield referred to the limitations of present scientific research. He says: "The more we learn about the mechanisms within the brain, the clearer it becomes that science has not thrown any real light on the nature of the mind.... The only way the neuro-physiologist works is to study the action of the brain on one side and the changing stream of mental activity on the other. You can see the parallelism of the activity but you cannot understand the interrelationship" (news report from *Times Weekender*, Toronto, 12 April 1968).

Instrumental Theory

The brain functions or is made to function as a whole and there is no one-to-one psychosomatic correspondence between brain phenomena and the concomitant experiences. So despite the recent advances in biochemistry and microbiology, mental phenomena cannot be considered to be just one aspect of a single process in the brain.

Prof. Sir John Eccles, who has been described by Sir Cyril Burt as "the most eminent of living neurologists who has specialised in the study of the brain," has observed that "the structure of the brain suggests that it is the sort of machine that a 'ghost' might operate where the word 'ghost' is used to designate any kind of agent that defies detection by such apparatus as is used to detect physical agents" (*The Neurophysiological Basis of Mind*, London, 1953, pp. 278ff).

This suggests that an instrumental theory of the brain cannot be excluded in the light of modern findings. We must not forget in this context that many physiological changes are initiated by the operation of aspects of will and that many diseases not only have a psychological origin (with or without a discoverable organic condition) but are curable by purely psychological means. We may note that physical pain with an organic basis can be relieved or removed by chemical means (i.e. drugs) or by the suggestions of hypnosis.

When in addition to all this, we have to take into account the realities of ESP (extrasensory perception), the identity hypothesis becomes almost untenable.

John Beloff has written: "This (i.e. parapsychological evidence), it seems to me, is the empirical reef on which the identity hypothesis is doomed to founder even if it can survive all other hazards. Most of its supporters do indeed recognise the danger but, like Feigl, pin their faith to the ability of science to explain the ESP phenomena eventually along more or less conventional lines (obscure brain functions, unsuspected sources of energy, etc.). Such faith though plausible enough twenty or thirty years ago is now increasingly unrealistic. The choice that confronts us today, I submit, is a very drastic one: either we must blankly refuse to credit the evidence or we must be prepared to accept a radical revision to the whole contemporary scientific world-picture on which materialism has taken its stand" (in *Brain and Mind*, pp. 50–1).

That the parapsychological phenomena constituting ESP have come to stay and are presently accepted as valid by leading scientists, psychologists and philosophers is evident from a recent publication of a book called *Science and ESP* by J. R. Smities (London, 1967).

The brain may be compared to a computer and electronic machines can be constructed to perform certain operations of abstract thinking (such as logical and mathematical calculations) with a greater speed, precision and accuracy than the human mind is capable. But however much such computers may stimulate human behaviour, they cannot have psychological experiences, express personal behaviour as opposed to mere imitation and have the degree of creativity and spontaneity that a human mind is capable of exhibiting.

Summing up recent scientific findings on the body-mind problem, Prof. Hornell Hart states: "To look at the body-mind problem without bias, it is essential that we recognise two pivotal facts: (1) that damage to brain structure may block or distort what the 'I' thinker wants to transmit; and (2) that the chemical condition of the brain has marked effects on the moods and attitudes of the 'I' thinker himself.... Whatever it is that thinks 'I' in any one of us is not a constant, unchanging reality. Nor is it something which progresses smoothly and consistently along a regular trend" (*The Enigma of Survival*, London, 1959, p. 219).

Buddhist View

All this seems to support the Buddhist theory of the mind, which holds that "conscious mental and cognitive phenomena function in dependence on their physical basis" (*yaṃ rūpaṃ nissāya manodhātu ca manoviññāṇadhātu ca vattati, Paṭṭhāna*), that certain aspects of will can direct, govern and produce mental activity as well as verbal and bodily behaviour and that, when the body and the brain are stilled with the attainment of the fourth jhāna (and sometimes even otherwise), the mind can exercise its powers of extrasensory perception which are potentially present.

So none of the modern findings with regard to the mind and its relation to the brain, or the assertions of modern brain physiologists, in any way preclude the empirical possibility of survival after death. This does not mean that survival after death is a fact but that it is an open possibility to be proved or disproved or made probable or improbable in the light of relevant evidence.

Other Objections

There are other objections that are raised specifically against the concept of rebirth. They fall into three categories: (1) that rebirth is a self-contradictory concept; (2) that it cannot account for the increase in the human population, which is a fact; and (3) that biogenesis or reproduction by fission at the lowest levels of life is inexplicable on the basis of the rebirth theory.

The first objection is that the concept of rebirth involves the identity of two or more persons one of whom lives now. It is held that the identification of two or more persons regarding them as one and the same person is either meaningless or self-contradictory. This is based on the belief that the identity of the person consists in the identity of the body, which is certainly the case in the law courts. But as the philosopher John Locke pointed out with specific reference to the case of rebirth, we also apply a mental criterion in our identification of persons.

If someone suffers from an attack of total amnesia, which involves a complete black-out of his past memories, resulting in a complete change of life, we would be inclined to say he is now a new person, that he is not the same person as before. For example, Dr Jekyll and Mr Hyde, who have the same body, are regarded as two different persons. This means that, as regards the identity of persons, we normally employ two criteria, that of the continuity of the body and that of the continuity of memory and mental dispositions. In the rebirth case all that is claimed is that in a significant sense there is a continuity (*santati*) of the mind of the individual from one earth-life to another.

This makes it meaningful to say that two persons, historically removed from each other in time, are one and the same individual because they have a continuous mental history. One modern positivist philosopher, Prof. A. J. Ayer of Oxford, granting the meaningfulness and the logical possibility of rebirth, says: "I think that it would be open to us to admit the logical possibility of reincarnation merely by laying down the rule that, if a person who is physically identified as living at a later time does have the ostensible memories and character of a person who is physically identified as living at an earlier time, they are to be counted as one person and not two" (*The Concept of a Person*, London, 1963, p. 127). The logical objection is, therefore, untenable.

The second objection is that it cannot account for the increase in human population. This objection would be valid if the theory requires that any human birth at present presupposes the death of a prior human being on this earth. Such a theory would also make it impossible for human beings to evolve out of anthropoid apes since the first human beings to evolve would not have had human ancestors (unless their saṃsāric ancestors were from other planes of existence). But according to the early Buddhist view of the cosmos, there are hundreds and thousands of galaxies spread out in space, containing "thousands of suns, moons, earths and other inhabited spheres." It is also the case according to the Buddhist theory of rebirth that the prior life of a human being may be animal. It is, therefore, possible according to this theory to account for the increasing number of present human births in terms of the deaths of human beings, animals or non-human beings in this as well as on other planets in the universe.

As regards the third objection from biogenesis, it can hardly affect the Buddhist theory. Although according to some Brahmanical theories, rebirth is possible even at the level of plants, it appears to be the case according to Buddhism that rebirth takes place at a higher level of evolution, when a "re-becoming mind" has been formed with the persistence of memory. After his enlightenment, the Buddha refers to some of his Jain practises as an aspirant to Buddhahood in the following words: "I used to walk up and down conscientiously extending my compassion even to a drop of water, praying that the dangerous bacteria in it (*khuddake pāṇe visamagate*) may not come to harm" (MN 12.47/M I 78). The context seems to suggest that this was a waste of time. Further objections arise in relation to the mind-body.

Body-mind Problem

The case against the possibility of survival in the light of what we know about the mind is fully stated in a book by Dr C. Lamont called *The Illusion of Immortality* (New York, 1950). A sound criticism of its contents is to be found in Chapter 13 of a book by Dr C. J. Ducasse called *A Critical Examination of the Belief in a Life after Death* (Springfield, 1961).

The Buddhist theory of the relationship between body and mind can account for the basic facts stated in Lamont's book as well as the criticisms of Ducasse. Lamont's case is based on the following facts:

1. that "the power and versatility of living things increase concomitantly with the development and complexity of their bodies in general and their nervous systems in particular."
2. that "the genes or other factors from the germ cells of the parents determine the individual's inherent physical characteristics and inherent mental capacities."
3. that "during the course of life the mind and the personality grow and change, always in conjunction with environmental influences, as the body grows and changes."
4. that "specific alteration's in the physical structure and condition of the body, especially in the brain and cerebral cortex, bring about specific alterations in the mental and emotional life of a man."
5. that "conversely, specific alterations in his mental and emotional life result in specific alterations in his bodily condition" (see Ducasse, op. cit., p. 114).

Ducasse shows that (5) contradicts Lamont's contentions against dualism. He further cites the case of psychosomatic disease to show that primarily mental states cause physical changes in the body. Psychosomatic medicine, for example, today recognises the fact that mental states such as anxiety, tension and worry sometimes cause painful stomach ulcers.

Now what is the Buddhist theory? Buddhism clearly holds that conscious mental and cognitive experiences function in dependence on a physical basis. A statement in the *Paṭṭhāna* reads as follows: "That physical basis in dependence on which the category of mental experience (*mano-dhātu*) and the category of cognitive experience (*mano-viññāṇa-dhātu*) function, this physical basis is to the category of mental experience and the category of cognitive experience and to phenomena associated with them, a condition by way of dependence" (*nissaya-paccaya*).

Because of this dependence it is not surprising that (1) is true and (4) occurs, namely the alterations in the physical basis resulting in alterations in consciousness.

Yet the dependence is not one-sided. As the Buddhist texts elsewhere state, "the mind follows in the wake of the body" (*kāyanvayaṃ cittaṃ*) and "the body follows in the wake of the mind" (*cittanvayo kayo*). The relation between the psyche (*viññāṇa*) and its hereditary psycho-physical basis (*nāmarūpa*) is one of mutual dependence (*aññamañña paccaya*). The will and other psychological factors can initiate some of the mental and physical changes that take place, as suggested in (5).

Again, since, according to Buddhism, the psycho-physical basis of our bodies is partly due to what is derived from mother and father and biological laws (*bija-niyāma*) operate, it is not surprising that (2) is partly true, namely that genetic factors condition our physical and some of our mental characteristics.

When the Buddha told Sāti that it was wrong to hold that consciousness fares on from life to life without change of identity (*anaññaṃ*), he illustrated this by showing that consciousness was causally conditioned. It is conditioned by the state of our body, which is partly a product of hereditary factors. It is also conditioned by the external environment. On account of the eye and visual phenomena, there arises in us visual consciousness. Similarly in respect of the other senses, there arise forms of consciousness associated with their respective sense-objects.

Likewise, it is said that on account of the impact on the conscious mind (*mano*) of ideas (*dhamma*), there arise various forms of conceptual consciousness. When these ideas do not come to us through language from our social and external ideological environment, they impinge on the conscious mind from our own unconscious. As a result of this our consciousness changes and grows and this in turn affects our subsequent behaviour. This is how the Buddha explains to Sāti that the psyche (*viññāṇa*) is not an unchanging entity but is in a state of dynamic growth and becoming in close association with the conditioning of the body.

In the case of visual stimuli, etc., they physically affect the senses in giving rise to their respective impressions (*paṭigha-samphassa*) but in the case of ideas that arise in the mind in remembering, imagining, thinking, etc., the contact with the conscious mind is said to be only nominal (*adhivacana-samphassa*).

It is these impressions and ideas and their by-products that accumulate in our memory and form part of our mind. So what is stated in (3), namely that "the mind and personality grow and change, always in conjunction with environmental influences, as the body grows and changes" is partly true. As we have seen above, it is stated in the Buddhist texts themselves.

So while Buddhism holds that the person is a psycho-physical unit (*nāmarūpa*), it does not subscribe to the identity hypothesis that the mind and the body are one and the same entity, or to the dualistic hypothesis that the mind and the body are entirely different.

Besides, Buddhism holds that, if awareness (*sati*) can be retained while the impressions and ideas that impinge on the conscious mind are inhibited, the activity of the body is gradually stilled and the emotions of sensuous love (*kāmacchanda*) and hate (*vyāpāda*) subside, then the mind being intrinsically resplendent (*pabhassara*) gradually acquires certain extrasensory powers of perception (*abhiññā*).

What we outlined earlier was the relationship of the conscious mind (*manodhātu, manoviññāṇadhātu*) to its physical basis, but we must not forget that according to the Buddhist theory the "stream of consciousness" has two components without a sharp division between them (*ubhayato abbocchinnaṃ*), the conscious mind and the unconscious, in which accumulate the emotionally charged experiences that we have had going back through childhood and birth into previous lives. Besides, with the expansion and development of consciousness (*vibhūta-saññī*), it attains a paranormal state.

How much of our memories in the unconscious are associated with the brain? Do they include the memories of prior lives as well? What is the nature of the association between the potentially paranormal mind and the brain? Does the paranormal mind function at its best when the activity of the brain and the body is quiescent (*kāyasaṅkhārā niruddhā*) and under its control? The total psyche (*viññāṇa*) of a person comprising the conscious mind, the memories and dispositions in the unconscious and the potentially paranormal mind is said to be "associated with and linked to the body" (*ettha sitaṃ ettha paṭibaddhaṃ*). But it is not clear how close or how loose the association of its several aspects are.

The Buddhist texts speak of two forms of telepathy, direct and indirect. Indirect telepathy, it is said, is had "by attuning oneself with the thought-vibrations of a person as he thinks" (*vitakkayato vitakka-vipphāra-saddaṃ sutvā*). Direct telepathy does not require this mediating process. Is the activity of the brain required for indirect telepathy while it is unnecessary for direct telepathy?

Previously we tried to show that the modern findings in regard to the mind and its relation to the brain do not preclude the possibility of survival after death. While reiterating this point we tried to give here a more detailed account of the Buddhist solution to the body-mind problem.

The arguments of the critics from the nature of the mind and its relation to the brain, if valid, would hold against any theory of survival after death, including the Buddhist. The other objections which we dealt with above could only be levelled against a rebirth theory. They were, that rebirth was a self-contradictory concept in that it claimed that many persons were one and the same person, that it could not account for the increase in the human population and that biogenesis or a-sexual reproduction at the lowest levels of life was inexplicable on the basis of a rebirth theory.

Another Objection

If any of the above arguments were valid, they would have shown that a rebirth theory was not merely improbable but impossible. But we saw that the arguments were based on false premises and did not affect the Buddhist theory of rebirth. Where there was continuity of mind in the form of actual or potential memory and mental dispositions, then, in popular parlance, we can speak of the many lives of one person. The increase of population would not present a difficulty where pre-existence could be in the form of animal lives or those of non-human beings in this as well as other planets in the universe. Biogenesis ceases to be a problem if rebirth takes place only at a higher level of biological evolution.

One of the commonest objections against a theory of rebirth, which implies pre-existence, is that we do not remember our past lives. The objection may take three different forms. Firstly, that we do not have any memory of prior lives and that, therefore, there is no evidence of our having lived in the past prior to our present birth. Secondly, that memory is indispensable to the identity of a person. Thirdly, that unless we have memory, rebirth is to no purpose, since no moral or other lesson is learnt in the process.

We may first dispose of the third form of this argument. We are concerned only with the question as to whether re-becoming or rebirth is a fact and not whether it is a good thing to be reborn. We cannot argue from what ought to be or what is best to what actually is the case. It is generally admitted that such an argument has no basis in fact, since, if it is true, the world would be very much different from what it is. Besides, there is a variety of rebirth theories and the question as to which one is true cannot be made on the basis of the ethical consideration as to which one is the best to believe in. For, quite apart from differences of opinion as to what is best (whether, for example, it would be better to remember or not to remember), there is no justification, as we have shown, in arguing that what is best is in fact the case.

The second form of the objection is that memory is indispensable to the identity of a person. If by this is meant that, unless a person has authentic memories of a past life, we cannot be at all certain that he is the same as one who lived before, there is some substance to this objection. But it would not be necessary to prove that this was so in the case of all people.

If a sufficient number and variety of people can be shown to have such authentic memories, then, although we may not be able to identify the prior lives of other human beings, it would be a reasonable presumption that they too had prior lives and are potentially capable of remembering this at some time or another.

To come back to the first form of the objection, that we have no memory of having lived before, then, if rebirth is a fact, it is certainly not true of all human beings that they do not recollect their prior lives. For there are at least a few who do while many others could be assisted to recall their previous lives.

It is possible, of course, to argue that the lack of memory regarding prior lives is no proof that we have not lived before, any more than lack of memory regarding the first year of our lives on the part of all or most human beings is no proof that we did not live in the first year of our life. It is true that mere absence of memory of a certain event or phase of life is no proof that such an event did not take place or that we did not live through such a phase of life.

Yet this is an argument from silence. In the case of our present life, we have another criterion to go on, namely the criterion of bodily continuity, and other people can testify to the fact that we existed in the first year of our lives and lived through certain experiences. But in the case of rebirth we have no evidence at all if we do not have actual or potential memories. Memory is, therefore, very relevant to the problem of rebirth.

However, it is necessary to point out that the word *memory* is used in two senses: in a secondary sense, "having memory" is a matter of retaining a skill or capacity that we acquired. If someone learnt how to swim when he was a child and can now swim very well without having to re-learn it and without even being able to recall that he learnt to swim as a child, we still say that he remembered how to swim, though he has forgotten that he had learnt it as a child.

If rebirth be the case, is it not likely that some of the capacities or skills we have or acquire without much difficulty in this life may be due to our having learnt them in a prior life, especially where they cannot be fully accounted for in terms of heredity or learning in this life?

The explanation not only of capacities and skills but of differences of temperament or weaknesses, which also fall into this category, would have to be the same. Now identical twins (as opposed to fraternal twins) are said to have the same heredity, and when they happen to grow up as Siamese twins conjoined to each other, they have more or less a common environment. Now if individual differences and variations are due entirely to the factors of heredity and environment alone, there should be identity of temperament and character on the part of these twins. At least there should not be marked differences in their dispositions and temperaments. But the facts are otherwise.

Thus H. H. Newman, who made a specialist study of twinning, says with regard to the original Siamese twins, Chang and Eng: "The author of a study made when the twins were in London was impressed with the lack of any strong resemblance between Chang and Eng. Much emphasis was placed on their different dispositions and temperaments. Chang was inclined to drunkenness, while Eng was a teetotaller" (*Multiple Human Births,* New York, 1940, pp. 64–5).

With regard to these identical twins, in general, his observations are as follows:

"In describing several pairs of these strange twins, writers have commented upon their lack of close similarity. Such twins have been regarded as the only kind of twins that are beyond question derived from a single egg and therefore surely identical in their hereditary make-up. One would expect such twins, since they have not only a common heredity but a common environment (for they must be in the same environment all the time), to be even more strikingly similar than pairs of separate twins that are not so intimately associated. The fact is, however, that Siamese twins are almost without exception more different in various ways than any but a few pairs of separate one-egg twins. One of the most difficult problems faced by the twinning specialist is that of accounting for this unexpected dissimilarity of the components of Siamese twin pairs" (ibid., pp. 67–8).

Could this difference not be due to a third factor other than heredity and environment, namely the psychological past of the two individuals? If so, is it not likely that even in other individuals as well there could be capacities, skills, temperaments, weaknesses, etc., which are due to memories (in the secondary sense defined above) of prior lives rather than to the factors of heredity and environment. Geniuses or child prodigies, whose extraordinary accomplishments cannot be accounted for in terms of heredity or environment would only be special cases of such a carry-over of skills from one life to another.

Apart from the use of the word "memories" in the above secondary sense, we use the word in its primary sense to denote the "recall of authentic experiences of one's past." In this sense there are quite a few who have claimed to have remembered experiences of their alleged prior lives. Some of them are spontaneous cases of recall while others are due to the intervention of hypnotists who have carried out age-regression experiments. How authentic are these memories and what reason have we to believe that they are potentially present in many if not all human beings? These are questions that we shall seek to answer.

Unsatisfactory Arguments

We need in due course to examine the evidence for recall of experiences from prior lives. Yet, before we proceed to do so, it is necessary to dispose of some unsatisfactory arguments that are sometimes adduced in support of the doctrine of rebirth. They may take many forms.

There is a tendency to urge that some belief is true because almost everybody holds it. Yet the universality of a belief does not entail its truth. Nor at the same time does it entail its falsity. It is sometimes maintained that many primitive peoples of the ancient world believed in survival or in the doctrine of rebirth. But this does not imply that the belief is either true or false. Its truth or falsity has to be established independently.

The relevance of the universality of the belief as evidence of its truth becomes more interesting when it is realised that people in a state of deep hypnosis give an account of experiences in alleged prior lives lived on earth, whatever their conscious beliefs may be. There is evidence that materialists and theists holding a variety of views on the subject of survival after death, without subscribing to the doctrine of rebirth or pre-existence, give alleged accounts of prior lives, recounting details of their experiences.

Does this imply the truth of the belief? Not necessarily, for it is possible that all their beliefs could be illusory, though the universality of such an illusion has to be accounted for. But the experiences they recount certainly constitute evidence for the truth or falsity of the belief in rebirth. We shall carefully examine this evidence later on.

Another form in which an argument for survival is presented, is that a human need or want implies the existence of what is needed or wanted. We need or want food. Therefore, it is suggested, there must be food. Many people feel the need for immortality or at least survival after death. Therefore, it is suggested, there must be such immortality or survival. However, this is an argument that cuts both ways. For others may argue that we believe in rebirth or survival because we need to believe or desire to entertain such a belief. But what we like to believe is not necessarily true, and, therefore, this is no evidence of the truth of the belief.

Freud in his work called *The Future of an Illusion* tries to show that people entertain certain religious beliefs, like the belief in the existence of God, for instance, because there is a deep-seated craving in us for security amidst the insecurity of life and the uncertainty of the beyond. According to him people believe in God dogmatically because of such a deep-seated craving. It is an object of wish fulfilment and, in this specialised sense, an illusion.

This does not, however, necessarily mean that the belief is false. As Freud himself pointed out, a girl may believe in the existence of a Prince Charming who may one day come and propose to her because she likes to believe this, but this does not necessarily mean that such a person does not exist. So the desire to believe in rebirth or survival does not necessarily show that the belief is false just as much as the desire to disbelieve in rebirth does not imply that the contrary belief is false.

The Buddhist view on this matter is both relevant and interesting. Our desires influence or condition our beliefs, to which we tenaciously cling (*taṇhā-paccayā diṭṭhūpādānaṃ*) but this does not necessarily mean that these beliefs are always false, for when they happen to be right beliefs (*sammā diṭṭhi*), they are in fact true.

So although desires affect our beliefs, this fact has no relevance to the truth or falsity of the beliefs. We have, however, because of our emotional involvement with these beliefs, to weigh the evidence for or against their truth or falsity without prejudice. As Buddhists we have to examine the truth even of the belief in rebirth objectively, without being prejudiced for (*chanda*) or against (*dosa*) or being affected by fear (*bhaya*), even if it be the fear of the beyond, or being guided by our erroneous beliefs (*moha*). So the desire to believe does not affect the truth or falsity of the belief, but we have to guard against the prejudice resulting from these desires in our quest for truth.

Authority and Revelation

Another set of arguments for survival is based on authority. It may be stated that many poets and mystics as well as rational thinkers, brought up in a tradition which condemned the belief, nevertheless professed it.

The classic case is that of Giordano Bruno, who is said to have stated in his profession of faith before the Inquisition: "I have held and hold souls to be immortal.... Speaking as a Catholic, they do not pass from body to body, but go to Paradise, Purgatory or Hell. But I have reasoned deeply, and, speaking as a philosopher, since the soul is not found without body and yet is not body, it may be in one body or in another, and pass from body to body. This, if it be not [proved] true, seems, at least, likely...." (See *Reincarnation: An East-West Anthology*, New York, 1961. According to this book, over two hundred and fifty well-known poets, philosophers and writers of the Western world have either held or professed some sort of belief in rebirth.)

All that this seems to suggest is that the belief is worth examining and it does not in any way imply the truth of the belief.

The argument from revelation is also unacceptable to science and Buddhism. It is true that certain texts in the Vedic tradition, particularly the middle and late Upaniṣads, profess a belief in rebirth, but there is a variety of views on the subject of survival in the Vedic tradition itself. In one of the early Upaniṣads, rebirth is denied. It is said: "There are these three worlds, the world of men, the world of departed spirits and the world of the gods. The world of men is obtained through a son only, not by any other means" (*Bṛhadāraṇyaka Upaniṣad*, 1.5.15).

While there are these contradictions within revelational traditions, the different theistic revelations also contradict each other on the problem of survival. So the doctrine of rebirth cannot be established by an argument from authority or revelation, since authority and revelation are not acceptable means of knowledge.

Metaphysical and Ethical Arguments

The metaphysical arguments are no better. Apart from the fact that they make use of unverifiable concepts like "soul," the arguments are of doubtful value and are generally discredited today. One of the traditional arguments for survival has been that the soul is a substance, substances are indestructible, therefore the soul is indestructible, i.e. immortal. But apart from the difficulty of the concept of a soul, the notion of an indestructible substance is discredited today.

With regard to rebirth, we have already met with a sample of such a metaphysical argument in that of Giordano Bruno. Such arguments, based on pure reasoning, intended to prove the truth of rebirth, are to be met with, for example, in the work of John McTaggart (*Some Dogmas of Religion,* London, 1906, Ch. IV). But they have little appeal today since it is recognised that matters of fact cannot be proved by pure reasoning (*takka*), as the Buddha himself pointed out (*mā takka-hetu*).

The ethical argument has a greater appeal but this is so only for those who accept its presuppositions. We have already stated this in the chapter on the Buddhist doctrine of kamma. There we pointed out that according to the Buddha kamma was one of the predominant factors responsible for human inequalities.

This has often been represented as embodying the following rational, ethical argument consisting of an empirical and ethical premise, viz. people are of unequal status; those of unequal status ought to be such by virtue of their own actions—therefore, since this is not due to their actions in this life, it should be due to their actions in prior lives. This means that both pre-existence and kamma are the case.

This is an argument that has appealed to many thinkers down through the ages, but most modern thinkers would not accept the second ethical premise, namely that "those of unequal status ought to be such by virtue of their own actions." This is because most people believe today that the universe of nature is amoral, and there is no ethical reason why anything should or should not be so. On the other hand many hold that ethical statements are neither true nor false. It is nevertheless a fact that many people brought up in a belief in the inherent justice of nature ask questions of the form, "Why should so-and-so be born healthy while I am in a state of ill-health from birth etc?".

It is only the modern scholars who have made an argument of this since the Buddha merely stated as an observed fact that the predominant cause of these inequalities was karma. The fact is, in principle, unverifiable, but the argument appeals to one's moral sense, and is of value only if such a moral sense is universally present and shared by all mankind.

Age-regression

The above arguments are, therefore, for one reason or another, unsatisfactory and have little force in proving the truth of rebirth or survival. The truth or falsity of rebirth, therefore, rests on the relevant empirical evidence. We may classify the main evidence into two sorts: (1) experimental and (2) spontaneous. The other evidence may be considered separately.

The experimental evidence is based on age-regression. In this experiment the subject is hypnotized and gradually taken back in time to the past. In the course of this the subject recalls and re-lives past experiences. Much of these experiences cannot be evoked by normal memory. These experiments have proved to the satisfaction of modern psychologists and psychiatrists that authentic memories of this life, which cannot be called to mind in normal consciousness, can be recalled by these means. Experiments have convinced psychologists and psychiatrists today that the authentic buried memories of one's childhood experiences, which cannot be called to mind in normal consciousness, can be unearthed by hypnosis.

It may be asked whether the subject is not just responding to the suggestion of the hypnotist and is merely play-acting or shamming. That this is not so has been proved experimentally.

H. J. Eysenck reports: "In one case it was found that when a twenty-year-old girl was regressed to various ages she changed the chalk to her left hand at the six-year level; she had started writing with the left hand, but had been forced to change over at the age of six" (*Sense and Nonsense in Psychology*, London, 1961, p. 48).

In another case, a thirty-year-old was hypnotised and regressed to a level of about one year of age on a chair arranged in such a way that with the release of a latch it would fall back into a horizontal position. When the latch was released the behaviour elicited was not that of an adult but of a child. An adult, it is said, would quite involuntarily extend both arms and legs in an effort to maintain balance. Since the subject made no movement of the limbs but screamed in fright and fell backward with the chair, urinating in the process, Eysenck comments: "It is unlikely that such behaviour is simply due to play-acting" (ibid., p. 49). Intelligence and achievement tests have been used to assess the nature of the behaviour of regressed subjects and it has been found that people tend to behave on tests of this type in a manner roughly appropriate to the given age. Eysenck's observations with regard to the possibility of faking such behaviour are as follows: "Such reactions, of course, could easily be faked, but it has been shown that when, for instance, the eye movements of subjects are photographed, a considerable lack of ocular co-ordination and stability is found when regression to a relatively young age occurs. Such physiological phenomena are characteristic of young children and are difficult, if not impossible, to produce voluntarily" (ibid.).

In the course of these age-regressions even the physiological condition of the body undergoes changes appropriate to the past time at which the subject is having the experiences concerned, even when the present state of the body or the physical environment cannot be responsible for this. To quote Eysenck again: "Even more impressive is another case of a subject who had had a colloid cyst removed from the floor of the third ventricle. Prior to this removal, the subject had been suffering from blindness in the left half of the right eye. After the operation, vision had become normal, but when the subject was regressed to a time shortly before the operation the visual defect again reappeared during the regression" (ibid.). The expected physiological reaction is not only appropriate to the age but reflects the physiological condition of the body at the time.

Drs Brennan and Gill report a case where a patient some months after being exposed to a particular situation was regressed back to that time hypnotically. It is stated that "the subject spontaneously began to perspire and complain of the heat: This was rather surprising in view of the fact that this particular phase of the study took place in winter. The experimenters then recalled that on the day to which the patient was now regressed, Kansas had experienced one of its hottest summer days" (*A Scientific Report on "The Search for Bridey Murphy,"* ed. M. V. Kline, New York, 1956, p. 185).

In the light of the experimental evidence Eysenck concludes: "Experiments such as those described in some detail above leave little doubt that there is a substantial amount of truth in the hypothesis that age regression does, in fact, take place, and that memories can be recovered which most people would think had been completely lost" (op. cit., p. 51). This is the consensus of opinion among orthodox psychologists today.

This is in fact the consensus of opinion among orthodox psychologists today on the basis of the experimental findings. Dr L. M. Wolberg observes: "The consensus at the present time is that 'regression actually does produce early behaviour in a way that obviates all possibility of simulation; this is the opinion of such authorities as Erickson, Estabrooks, Lindner, and Spiegel, Shor and Fishman. My own studies have convinced me of this fact, although the regression is never stationary, constantly being altered by the intrusion of mental functioning at other levels'" (*Medical Hypnosis*, Vol. I, New York, 1948).

So genuine memories not accessible to normal recall are generally evoked or the experiences relived at the suggestion of the hypnotist in age-regression. So at least as far as this life is concerned, to say that memories recalled under age-regression are hallucinatory or delusive is not correct.

Prior Lives

The majority of orthodox psychologists and psychiatrists, however, are reluctant to concede that accounts given of and the experiences lived through alleged prior lives are genuine. In such cases they tend to dismiss these accounts and experiences of prior lives as fantasy or a product of dramatization and role-playing based on material derived from the experiences of this life. They are prepared to grant that the subject's behaviour "will give the appearance of reincarnation" (F. L. Marcuse, *Hypnosis: Fact and Fiction*, London, 1961, p. 184) but deny that the reincarnationist interpretation is valid.

So the position is that many psychologists and psychiatrists are prepared to concede the fact that under age-regression a hypnotised subject will give detailed descriptions of an alleged prior life but would not agree with the validity of a reincarnationist interpretation of the data.

The main reason for this seems to be the logical and methodological difficulties involved in accepting an explanation in terms of the hypothesis of rebirth rather than a careful attempt on the part of these psychologists and psychiatrists to understand or explain the data itself.

Previously we have tried to show that neither the logical nor methodological difficulties are valid. We pointed out that the concept of rebirth does not lead to contradictions. Even a positivist philosopher such as Prof. A. J. Ayer has stated that the concept of rebirth is meaningful. Besides, as we have argued, there is a growing realisation that the phenomenon of consciousness cannot be explained away purely in terms of physico-chemical phenomena, while the validity of extrasensory perception precludes that psychological explanations be contained (where the data require this) within the narrow and limiting framework of mechanistic materialist assumptions. The data therefore require to be examined with an open mind.

There have been, however, a few psychiatrists who have accepted the reincarnationist explanation as valid. Dr Alexander Cannon refers to "one thousand three hundred and eighty-two reincarnation sittings to date" in his book *The Power Within* (London, 1950, p.183). His own reactions to these and the final conclusion he came to are summed up in the words: "For years the theory of reincarnation was a nightmare to me and I did my best to disprove it and even argued with my trance subjects to the effect that they were talking nonsense, and yet as the years went by one subject after another told me the same story in spite of different and varied conscious beliefs in effect until now, well over a thousand cases have been so investigated, and I have to admit that there is such a thing as reincarnation" (ibid., p. 170).

The Evidence

All important is the nature of the evidence and its authenticity and the legitimate conclusions that we can come to in explaining this evidence with the help of the various hypotheses that may be adduced to explain it. When hypotheses cannot be accepted or rejected outright, they may be held with varying degrees of probability according to relevant criteria.

One of the earliest recorded experiments of psychologists was that of Theodoure Flournoy, Professor of Psychology at the University of Geneva, who experimented with one of his subjects at the end of the nineteenth century and recorded the data and findings in a book published in 1899 (*Des Indes a la Planete Mars,* Geneva, 1899).

One of the prior lives of his Swiss subject was as an Arab chief's daughter who married a Hindu prince about four centuries before. The subject spoke and wrote in the languages (Arabic and Prakrit), which she knew in the regressed state but not in her normal life, and gave details of experiences in this life, re-enacting and reliving some of the scenes. The facsimiles of the writing are reproduced in pages 289 and 313 of the book.

Before we examine this case, we may turn our attention to a more popular work published in 1942. This would enable us to see the issues involved in the interpretation of the data more clearly. Since Buddhists are or ought to be interested only in objective facts or in "things as they are" (*yathābhūtaṃ*), it is important that we approach the subject with a critical mind without an initial bias for or against the theory of rebirth.

"Researches in Reincarnation and Beyond"

The work is by Rev. A. R. Martin, an ordained teacher of the Coptic Church, and is entitled *Researches in Reincarnation and Beyond* (1st ed., Pennsylvania, 1942). It is dedicated to "all seekers for truth or not it be in accordance with their former teachings or preconceived ideas" (p. 11). The book records the alleged experiences of people hypnotised by him or trained to recall their prior lives.

His comments with regard to the evidence and the records are as follows: "The questions and their answers thereto were carefully recorded, usually in shorthand, exactly as given. Great care was taken to ask no leading questions, thereby eliminating the possibility of implanting ideas in the mind of the reviewer, thus making certain to bring out only that which was recorded in the reviewer's subconscious mind. These correlations of important persons and events often occurring hundreds of years ago, were carefully checked in reference books, histories, encyclopaedias, etc., and were found correct as given by the reviewers. This information was known to come solely from the knowledge already in the reviewer's subconscious mind, for it was known that such knowledge was not contained in his intellectual mind of this present life" (ibid., pp. 7–8).

He claims that these explorations into the subconscious minds of various people, "worked out through powers of mind, absolutely without the use of any kind of drug," was attempted after a group of about twelve persons of various ages had for years examined various conflicting teachings of speculative philosophy on the subject of an after-life and were dissatisfied with them.

The author lists a number of beliefs about the nature of an after-life held by people in the West. The first was that "death ends all ..." (ibid., p. 4); the second that "the consciousness—soul—dies and is buried with the body and remains there until a time called the resurrection when all persons who have ever lived from the beginning of creation to the time of the resurrection will come forth, from the land or the sea or wherever they may be, to be judged and sent either to an eternal heaven or an eternal hell of fire and brimstone from which there is no escape" (ibid., p. 4); the third was the view "that there is an intermediate place of punishment or remorse from which the dead can be released through prayer and liberated into an eternal heaven ..." (ibid., pp. 4–5). Several other such views are listed. The author says that he "has lived all of his present life (to this time) in the United States" (ibid., p. 3), and was himself "raised to manhood under the instruction of the second belief" (ibid., p. 6), and that none of those who thus met regularly to investigate these matters "even leaned toward reincarnation" (ibid., p. 6).

If this is so, then, considering particularly the fact that "no leading questions" were asked, it is all the more remarkable that they were able to recall prior lives lived on earth. It is a curious fact, which calls for an explanation by itself, that those who in their normal conscious experience are materialists or theists, who do not believe in pre-existence or rebirth, give alleged accounts of prior lives under deep hypnosis. Where the subject is asked to concoct an account of an alleged prior life, this may be attributed to the suggestion of the hypnotist but where such prior lives are described without any express instructions on the part of the hypnotist to do so, this fact in itself calls for an explanation.

In the article "Can Reincarnation Be Proved by Hypnotism?" (in the magazine *Two Worlds,* May 1964, pp. 247–49) H. C. Miranda states:

"Sometimes the subject during what is called 'wakeful state' is not a reincarnationist, or even has never heard about such an idea, or else belongs to a creed that denies it emphatically.

"One very intelligent man, a Protestant, asked the hypnotist in a deep, booming, slow voice, 'Why do you ask such a question?' The question was repeated, 'Were you or were you not born for the first time?'

"He still hesitated as if to conquer a strong inner opposition, and then began to describe his life a couple of centuries ago in a monastery somewhere in Spain.

"When he awoke, slowly and by reversing the age-regression process, the tape was played back to him. He was amazed because he did not know about reincarnation and never thought it possible.

"A bright, beautiful, mature woman talked freely about reincarnation and other related subjects. When she listened to the playback she said, 'I must be crazy to say such things.' She is a diehard Roman Catholic."

Origin of Phobias

Granted that the experiences related in the above-mentioned book are authentic and factual, many of our problems in this life can be understood in terms of their causal origins in a prior life.

This is very much like the manner in which the submerged traumatic experiences of this life (as explained in Freudian psychology) are the causal factors which account for various symptoms.

Dr Eysenck records the case of a Mrs Smith who suffered from recurrent asthmatic attacks; her work necessitated her going into various hospitals but in doing so she experienced a very strong fear reaction. The sight of a pair of hairy arms or knives also produced such a reaction. Under hypnotic age-regression, she was able to recall and relive the incidents which were responsible for this condition. It was the shock caused by an operation for mastoiditis performed on her at the age of sixteen months, which she had forgotten. Dr Eysenck describes the situation as follows:

"During a self-induced trance one day, she was regressed to an early age, when she experienced a previously completely forgotten incident with unusual clarity. She seemed to be lying on a table under brilliant lights. A man was standing beside her holding a small knife. A vague, threatening object was descending from above her head, and settled down over her face. She was terror-stricken and tried to rise, but two hairy arms grabbed her and roughly forced her back. She continued to struggle, but was violently shaken and slapped repeatedly by someone. Finally, the object came down over her face and smothered her. On inquiry, it was found that at the age of sixteen months a mastoidectomy had been performed on her and that she had been very sick afterwards with complications caused by severe shock" (Eysenck, op. cit., pp. 51–2). The origin of this phobia was traced to a childhood incident in this life. But it is interesting to compare in this connection one of the experiences recorded in the above-mentioned book which locates the origin of a phobia in an incident of an alleged prior life. It is described as follows:

"A middle aged woman … when riding in a car driven twenty miles an hour or more, the motion produced such a fear within her that she would become very nervous and ready to jump out of the car. As a result she could ride only in cars driven around fifteen miles an hour. This fear of speed made it almost impossible for her to travel by train, bus, etc. Upon entering a past life review, she found herself to be a young girl travelling on a train with her parents, brothers and sisters. As, the train passed over a trestle bridge it was wrecked, killing all the members of the family but herself, along with many others who were on the train. Her injuries were so severe that she was badly crippled and rendered an invalid for the remainder of that life. The speed had been such a dominant factor in this accident and its impression was so deep that the subconscious fixation out-manifested in this life as intense fear whenever any degree of motion was felt by her" (ibid., p. 44).

We may recount some of the observations of a like nature made by Dr Cannon on the basis of his case studies. He says: "The majority of people do not benefit from psycho-analysis because the trauma lies not in this life but in a past life. Let me give you three examples: Mr A. is a business-gentleman of undoubted capabilities, but all his life he has suffered from a phobia or fear of going down in lifts. He is a common-sensed individual and has studied psychology and psycho-pathology quite seriously and intelligently, and yet he has gained no benefit from it and is at a loss to know why he has this fear of travelling in lifts. Hypnotic experiments reveal that some centuries ago he was a Chinese general who fell from a great height and was accidentally killed. This had resulted in the phobia or fear of descending lifts in this life" (op. cit., p. 171).

Karma?

If the experiences recounted in the Rev. Martin's book, *Researches in Reincarnation and Beyond,* are authentic and factual, they also appear to throw some light on the operations of karma.

In one case, five previous lives of a person are recorded. In the fifth life previous to the present, the person's first recollection was that of "awakening as a white baby in a log cabin" (op. cit., p. 90). The cabin was attacked by Indians, one of whom took her along and brought her up as a Indian maiden. Eventually, she was taken away by a British trader with whom she lived in a small hut until he decided to leave her and cross the mountains in search of gold. He offered to take her back to the Indian tribe, but conscious of her white parentage and coming motherhood she refused. Instead, faced with the prospect of being alone in the hut, it is said that she committed suicide by shooting herself on "the right side of her face."

In the very next birth, she is stated to have been born as a crippled child named Sammy, whose entire right side was paralysed. The subsequent birth is supposed to have been as a U.S. soldier of the South during the Revolution, when he was accosted by a British subject who stabbed him in the right side of the abdomen causing his death.

In the following birth, she was born as a girl named Nancy, whose mother worked for a wealthy family. A son of this family, it is said, fell in love with this girl and wanted to marry her, but his parents objected and had her married to a farmhand. She subsequently journeyed West in a covered wagon and settled in Illinois, where two children were born. Nancy died at the age of thirty as a result of abdominal disorders. Her next life was as a person who became well-known as an opera singer called "Miss Nellie," a daughter of a wealthy family near Baltimore, Maryland. She was happily married but before long her husband was shot dead and it is said that she "died of a broken heart." The author describes and comments on part of her present life as follows: "When she was fifteen years old, the first of these negative conditions resulted in a paralysis of the right side of the face and neck. At this age she knew nothing of reincarnation or of the influence of past lives upon the present. The overcoming of the paralysis, slight traces of which are still apparent, was accomplished in a period of six to seven years through rest and quiet" (ibid., p. 94).

If the facts are right, are we to attribute her birth as a child paralysed on the right side in her fourth previous life and her paralysis of the right side of the face and neck in this life as well as, perhaps, her deaths from abdominal injuries or disorders as karmic consequences of her suicide while being with child in her fifth previous life?

Taken literally, if the experiences recounted here are authentic and true records of prior lives, they exemplify the truths of both rebirth and kamma. But what justification have we for accepting these experiences at their face value?

Normal Hypotheses

A person with a sceptical frame of mind may very well indulge in doubt and claim that one of several hypotheses other than rebirth could adequately account for the alleged facts. Some may even doubt whether the book I refer to exists and whether all this is not a concoction of mine! This would be the extreme hypothesis of fraud. The reply to this is that the book is to be found in some libraries, for instance, the library of the University of Ceylon. A less extreme position that one could take would be to doubt whether the author of the book was not merely trying to bring out a sensationalist publication from which he might financially benefit and that he made it all up. One way of verifying this would be to contact the author and through him the people concerned as the author himself wants those interested to do (see ibid., p. 17). But this is unnecessary since this kind of evidence can be made available with the help of a suitable hypnotist and hypnotisable subjects.

Once it is established that the book contains an account of authentic experiences accurately recorded, we may still doubt the assumption that they are genuine memories of past lives. We may try to explain them as being due to the role-playing of the subject who has proceeded to give dramatised accounts of alleged prior lives on the basis of material drawn from this life. We would then resort to the hypothesis of fantasy or self-deception, unless the author *can* prove to us, as he says he could, that "it was known that such knowledge was not contained in his intellectual mind of this present life" (ibid., p. 8). This hypothesis would be difficult to exclude in the present circumstances unless it *can* be shown that specific items of knowledge later verified from encyclopaedias, etc., were not known to the subject (as the author claims to be the case). However, the fact that some of these alleged experiences solved some of the present psychological problems of some of these subjects is a factor to be taken into consideration in judging the genuineness of these experiences, though this test is by no means conclusive.

Another "normal" explanation would be to assume that such experiences can be derived genetically from one's ancestors. Apart from the fact that there is no independent evidence of such hereditary derivation of specific "memory experiences" (leaving out capacities and aptitudes), the hypothesis requires an ancestral link between the two personalities. This is very unlikely, at least in those cases in which the prior life is located in such countries as Iran or Egypt.

Paranormal Hypotheses

If the normal hypotheses fail to account for the facts, we have to resort to paranormal hypotheses to explain the evidence. Granted that the memories correspond with historical facts and knowledge of them is not derived from any experiences in this life, it is possible to suggest that they are the product of a telepathic clairvoyant or retrocognitive faculty operating along with dramatisation and role-playing. On such a hypothesis, these persons did not actually live in the past but acquired information about past events by paranormal or extrasensory means and dramatised such a past life. Such a hypothesis appears to be more extravagant than a simple one of rebirth. For, apart from not explaining all the data (e.g. the claim to identity, the serial nature of the recall in age-regression, etc.), there is little evidence of such wide and penetrative powers of telepathic, clairvoyant or retrocognitive perception except, perhaps, in a few extraordinary individuals.

For similar reasons, the hypothesis of spirit-possession appears to be less plausible in accounting for the data. For, in spirit-possession, the alleged spirit communicating through the medium claims to be a different person from the personality associated with the body. In the case where a claim to rebirth is made, this is not so.

If a paranormal explanation is to be preferred, rebirth, therefore, appears to be more plausible than the others, the data being what they are. But the data presented in Rev. Martin's book do not clearly rule out the possibility of explanation in terms of fantasy or self-deception, as defined above, unless it can be shown and not merely stated that specific items of knowledge regarding the past were not available to the subject in the course of his present life (for which in this book we have merely to take the author's word). This can be shown to be so in some of the better documented case studies, which we shall take up now.

As we said earlier, the evidence for rebirth (which is only a special case of re-becoming) falls into three categories: (1) the experimental evidence; (2) the spontaneous evidence; and (3) the other evidence.

The Experimental Evidence

We have already given samples of the experimental evidence. However, one may criticise these experiments as not being conducted under strictly controlled conditions, although the author mentions several precautions he had taken to eliminate subjective bias.

Let us now take examples where the experimental controls appear to have been more satisfactory. In the case investigated by Prof. Theodoure Flournoy, the account given reads as follows:

"It appeared that Helene Smith had twice lived upon the earth before her present incarnation. Once, five hundred years ago as an Arab chief's daughter (Simandini by name), she became the favourite wife of a Hindu prince. This prince, Sivrouka, reigned over the kingdom of Kanara and constructed in 1401 the fortress of Tchandragiri. This romance was developed with a wealth of detail and the astonishing features of it were, firstly, that research in old and little-known books on Indian history confirmed some of the details, such as the names of places and persons described; secondly, that Simandini uttered (in the trance automatisms) many Hindu words and phrases, sometimes appropriately used, sometimes mingled with other words which the experts failed to identify, and wrote also similar phrases in Arabic script. Further, the entranced medium would act the role of Simandini putting other members of the circle into the vacant places of the drama" (see William McDougall, *An Outline of Abnormal Psychology*, London 1952, p. 511).

In the professor's own words: "All this various mimicry and this exotic speech have so strongly the marks of originality, of ease, of naturalness, that one asks with stupefaction whence comes to this daughter of Lake Leman, without artistic training and without special knowledge of the Orient, a perfection of art which the best of actresses might attain only at the cost of prolonged studies or by residence on the banks of the Ganges" (ibid., pp. 511–12).

The professor confesses that he has not been able to resolve the mystery especially the Hindu language and the historical statements about the kingdom of Kanara which were verified in an old and rare book to which the subject had had no access. Yet he concludes that the "Hindu drama was a subconsciously elaborated fantasy, incorporating very skilfully fragments of knowledge picked up in haphazard fashion" (ibid., p. 512).

His explanation is the standard one resorted to by most orthodox psychologists when confronted with evidence of this sort, namely that here we get only dramatisation and role-playing based on elements of information picked up in this life. Prof. Flournoy is, however, constrained to "admit that some knowledge was displayed, the acquisition of which by normal means would seem to have been well nigh impossible" (ibid., p. 515).

Yet this does not seem to explain the ease, the spontaneity and the accuracy with which she sang Hindi (Prakrit) songs and wrote in a Prakrit script. Nor does it explain the factual information she gave, the claim she made that she was in fact the wife of a Hindu prince in her previous life and the serial account of the life and the incidents she gave.

Let us take another case, that of Mrs Anne Baker, reported by Dr Jonathan Rodney (*Explorations of a Hypnotist,* London, 1955). Mrs Baker, a Lancashire housewife, who has never studied French or been to France and whose education was very ordinary, spoke perfect French under hypnosis, referred to the death of Marie Antoinette as if it had just happened, gave her name as Marielle Pacasse and spoke of a street named Rue de St Pierre near Notre-Dame Cathedral.

Subsequent investigations revealed that the name Marielle is rare now but was much in vogue about 1794 and although there was no such street at present, there was in fact a street of that name in the vicinity 170 years back (see pp. 165–66). Here again a normal explanation would not do. Apart from the knowledge of French, one would have to say that the knowledge about the streets of Paris two centuries back was either acquired clairvoyantly or telepathically from the dead.

An explanation in terms of spirit-possession is also possible though highly improbable. One could say that the discarnate spirit of the dead Marielle Pacasse now inhabits the body of Mrs Baker. Normally, in the case of spirit-possession, the discarnate spirit claims to be a separate personality and possession is not continuous, whereas in this case, whenever Mrs Baker was hypnotised, she claimed to be Marielle Pacasse in her previous life. So to account for all the facts, rebirth is the simpler paranormal hypothesis.

Another case which cannot pass unnoticed is the famous Bridey Murphy case. When Mrs Virginia Tighe was hypnotised on six occasions, between November 1952 and August 1953, she recalled a life as Bridey Murphy in Ireland. It created a wide interest in rebirth. It will be interesting to see Prof. C. J. Ducasse's assessment of the case when it first came into the limelight and later after careful reflection, in the light of the verified facts.

In an opinion published in *Tomorrow* (Vol. 4, No. 4, pp. 31–3) in 1956, soon after the case became known, Prof. Ducasse suggests three hypotheses to account for it:

"That the former is a reincarnation of the latter is one hypothesis that would account for the veridicality of those details. A second hypothesis that would also account for their veridicality is that of illusion of memory; that is, the hypothesis that Mrs Tighe, in childhood or later, heard or read of the life of an Irish Bridey Murphy and then forgot this and that, under hypnosis, the ideas so acquired were recalled by Mrs Tighe; but not the manner in which she had acquired them, and hence, that they were indistinguishable by her from memories of events of a life of her own. A third hypothesis which would also explain the veridicality of the verified details is that while in deep hypnosis Mrs Tighe exercises powers of paranormal retrocognition latent at other times and vastly more far-reaching than those whose reality has been experimentally proved by Rhine, Soal and others."

Going on the assumption that Mrs Tighe's knowledge of Ireland was erroneous (as was thought at the time), Ducasse favoured the *second* hypothesis.

Later, when further investigations vindicated the truth of Mrs Tighe's statements and the attempts at debunking the rebirth theory were seen to be mainly inspired by religious prejudice and based on false assertions, Prof. Ducasse changed his views and favoured the first hypothesis (i.e. rebirth) without ruling out the possibility of the third. He does so in his book, *A Critical Examination of the Belief in a Life after Death* (Springfield, Illinois, 1961).

Here he refers to the items mentioned by Bridey which could not be easily explained away. One of the most significant was that in her previous life she bought foodstuffs from Farrs and John Carrigan. Extensive research on the part of Mr John Bebbington, Belfast Chief Librarian, disclosed the fact that these two grocers were found listed in a Belfast city directory for 1865–6. Besides, they were the only individuals of those names engaged in the foodstuffs business there at the time.

Bridey also referred to a rope company and a tobacco house, which were in operation in Belfast at the time, and this too was found to be correct. Another remarkable fact was that Bridey's statements, which according to experts on Ireland were irreconcilable with known facts, were shown after further investigation not to be so. Ten such facts are listed. To take one example, one was to the effect that her husband taught law at the Queen's University in Belfast sometime after 1847. *Life Magazine,* on the basis of so-called expert opinion, attacked this on the ground that there was no law school there at the time, no Queen's College until 1849, and no Queen's University until 1908. However, further investigation showed that this was incorrect. There was documentary evidence to show that on 19 December 1845, Queen Victoria ordained that "there shall and may be erected ... one College for students in Arts, Law, Physic ... which shall be called Queen's College, Belfast" (op. cit., p. 286). The Queen's University in Ireland was founded by her on 15 August 1850 (ibid.).

Such accuracy may be due to either extraordinary clairvoyant powers on the part of the subject or to the simple fact that these were genuine memories of her past life. Since she did not display any such clairvoyant powers in other respects during hypnosis, the latter appears to be the more plausible explanation.

Spontaneous Evidence

The spontaneous evidence consists of accounts given by individuals, mostly children, of their alleged prior lives, which when subsequently checked prove to be historical and accurate and could not have been derived from any normal source in this life.

There are several such cases from all over the world and reports of them are to be found in newspapers and magazines. But in coming to valid conclusions on their basis one has to rely on the trustworthy verified accounts of scientists. The evidence should be first recorded without bias and one should then see what theory best accounts for the data.

In this respect, one of the best studies so far is that of Dr Ian Stevenson. He makes a detailed study and evaluation of twenty cases in one of his books, *Twenty Cases Suggestive of Reincarnation* (New York, 1966).

Let us briefly review the case of Imad Elawar, as studied and reported in this book. Imad was born on 21 December 1958 at Kornayel and talked of a previous life when he was between a year and a half and two years old. He mentioned a considerable number of names of people and some events in this prior life as well as about certain items of property he claimed to have owned. He said he lived in the village of Khriby and had the name Bouhamzy. He had a woman (mistress) called Jamille, who was beautiful, and a brother called Amin, who lived at Tripoli, etc.

The father, however, discredited the story and scolded Imad for talking about an imaginary past life. Once, it is said, he even recognised a resident (Salim el Aschkar) of Khriby in the presence of his paternal grandmother. The parents attached more importance to Imad's statements after this. But no systematic attempt to verify the authenticity of Imad's statements were made until Dr Ian Stevenson undertook to investigate the case.

Khriby was situated about twenty-five miles away from Imad's home. The road from Kornayel was an extremely winding mountain road. The items were carefully recorded prior to the investigations at Khriby. It was ultimately revealed that, of the fifty-seven items mentioned, fifty-one were correct. In Dr Stevenson's own words: "Of the fifty-seven items in the first tabulation, Imad made ten of the statements in the car on the way to Khriby before we reached that village. But of these ten, three were incorrect. Of the remaining forty-seven items, Imad was wrong on only three items. It seems quite possible that under the excitement of the journey, and perhaps sensing some expectation of hearing more statements on our part, he mixed up images of the previous life and memories of his present life. In any case, his 'score' for this group of statements definitely fell below that for the forty-seven made before we left Khriby" (ibid., pp. 257–71).

Some of the items were very specific, as when he said that they were building a new garden at the time of his death and that there were cherry and apple trees in it, that he had a small yellow automobile, a bus, etc.

Besides the verification of these items of information, there were significant recognitions of persons and places, sixteen of which are listed. For example, we may note the recognition of the place where Ibrahim Bouhamzy (the previous personality) kept his dog and his gun. He also recognised the sister of Ibrahim, namely Huda, and the portrait of Ibrahim's brother Fuad. He was also able, it is said, to recall his last words before death, which his sister, Mrs Huda Bouhamzy, remembered and which were, "Huda, call Fuad."

When we consider the above as well as the similarity in the character traits between the previous and the present personalities, chance coincidence has to be virtually ruled out. Since neither fraud, self-deception nor racial memory could account for the evidence, a paranormal explanation is called for. And of all the different paranormal explanations, such as telepathy-cum-clairvoyance plus personation, spirit possession, etc., rebirth appears to be the most plausible. This was, in fact, Dr Stevenson's own general conclusion after studying several cases of this type.

In the spontaneous case there is no hypnotist to put any suggestion into the mind of the child. We may say, however, that the child's beliefs about a prior life are a product of his fantasy. But such an explanation ceases to be feasible in the above instances, when the so-called "fantasies" turn out to be historically true and they were not derived from any source in this life.

Other Evidence

We have already referred to other evidence for rebirth when we tried to suggest that temperamental differences in identical twins, which cannot be due to heredity and environment, may be accounted for in terms of the impact of the psychological past of the person, which goes back into prior lives. We have also seen how some phobias prevalent in this life have not only been traced to traumatic experience in prior lives but have been cured by reliving the experience and discovering the origin of it.

Although it is possible to give other explanations of the so-called *déjà vu* experiences, the experience of feeling "I have been here before," some of them, at least, seem to point to or call for an explanation in terms of pre-existence. There is a recorded case of an American couple who found that some parts of Bombay were extremely familiar to them, despite the fact that they were visiting the place for the first time. To test their knowledge, it is said they went to a certain spot where they expected to see a house and a banyan tree in the garden. They, however, did not find them but were told by a policeman in the vicinity that he recalled having heard from his father that they had been there and that the house belonged to a family named Bhan. Curiously, this couple had called their son Bhan, because they liked the name. (W. C. White, "Cruise Memory", in *Beyond the Five Senses,* ed. E. J. Garrett, J. B. Lipincott, New York, 1957; cited by Dr Stevenson.) Such stories are, however, anecdotal and one cannot attach much importance to them. They are of value only when one is certain of their authenticity.

Dr Raynor C. Johnson suggests that certain recurrent dreams may be memories of experiences had in prior lives (see *A Religious Outlook for Modern Man,* London, 1963, pp. 184ff). A brief excerpt from an account of one such dream reads as follows:

"The dream was of being a prisoner in a place that I knew to be the Tower of London. I had not seen it in real life, but I had no doubt where I was. It was very cold weather (in waking life, a hot summer). I was aware that I had been condemned to death.... This, I used to dream over and over again, and after being in the dream a vigourous man, to wake up and be a little girl felt rather strange. At last the dream changed, and I was standing on a scaffold which must have been newly erected as it smelt of sawdust. Everything was decorous and decent. The executioner knelt and apologised for what he was about to do. I took the axe from his hand and felt it, and handed it back, bidding him do his duty.... When I woke up I made a drawing of the axe, which was of a peculiar shape. Some time after this I asked to be taken to the Tower of London and I explained to a friendly gunsmith that I wanted to write history but could not understand the battles perfectly until I understood the weapons. 'You are right, Missy,' he said, and demonstrated to me the various uses of pike, lance, crossbow, etc. I then asked had he an axe that beheaded people? He said, 'Yes, this certainly beheaded the Jacobite Lords, but it is supposed to be very much older.' Somehow, I was not surprised that it proved to be the exact shape of the axe in my dream...." (op. cit., pp.184–85).

Here again we can suggest that this is not the only explanation possible but when one has read about several such dreams one begins to wonder whether they are not hang-overs from one's past-life experiences.

We have further evidence for rebirth from clairvoyants. The best attested case in the twentieth century is that of Mr Edgar Cayce. A general account of his life and doings is to be found in a book by Dr Gina Cerminara, *Many Mansions* (New York, 1950, p. 304).

There is good evidence that Cayce had remarkable clairvoyant powers with which he successfully diagnosed illnesses even without actually seeing the patient. But what is more remarkable is that he went on to give accounts of the prior lives of some of these individuals (some of which were historically verified). He also gave the alleged karmic causes of their present illnesses.

We have already seen how suicide had certain karmic effects in subsequent lives. Cayce in his readings[2] records the different kinds of karmic effects following in the wake of the different kinds of actions done in the past. In one case, it is said, a person was born blind in this life because in his third life previous to this, circa 1000 BCE, he was born in Persia as "a member of a barbaric tribe whose custom was to blind its enemies with red-hot irons, and it had been his office to do the blinding" (ibid., pp. 50–51).

---

2. The readings are still preserved and are available for study at the Association for Research and Enlightenment, Virginia Beach, U.S.A.

13

The Conditioned Genesis of the Individual

The term *paṭicca-samuppāda* denotes, in general, the Buddhist theory of causality. Here we are concerned with the special sense of this term, which came to denote the conditioned genesis of the individual. In this special sense, the term is used to denote the factors which condition and result in the process called "the individual" in the course of his *saṃsāric* existence.

There are four related senses in which the term is used. Firstly, it is used to denote what are known as the two principles of causal determination. Stated in an abstract and logical form, it reads as follows: "This being so, that is so" (*imasmiṃ sati idaṃ hoti*) and "This not being so, that is not so" (*imasmiṃ asati idaṃ na hoti*), i.e. whenever A, then B, and whenever not A, then not B. This may be called the "abstract formula of causal determination."

Secondly, it is used to denote the two principles of causal determination stated in a dynamic form as having application to the world of concrete reality: "This arising, that arises" (*imass'uppādā idaṃ uppajjati*) and "This not arising, that does not arise." This may be called the "concrete formula of causal determination."

Thirdly, it is used to denote the causal laws which operate in nature, whether they are physical laws (*utu-niyāma*), biological laws (*bīja-niyāma*), psychological laws (*citta-niyāma*), etc.

Finally, the word is used in a special sense to denote the causal laws which operate in bringing about the continued genesis of the individual. Here we are concerned primarily with this last sense of the term.

However, we must not forget that we cannot understand the full significance of this special use of the term to denote the conditioned genesis of the individual without calling to mind its general meaning.

We may recall here that Buddhism steers clear of the two extremes of strict determinism as well as of total indeterminism. At the time of the rise of Buddhism, there were thinkers who held the view that changes took place in nature without any pattern at all. According to them, all changes were haphazard, fortuitous, accidental and were due entirely to chance. These were the indeterminists.

On the other hand, there were thinkers who were utterly opposed to this point of view. They not only held that there was a definite pattern in the nature of the changes that took place, but argued that this pattern was rigidly determined. Among these rigid determinists were theists who argued that, since the world was created by an omniscient and omnipotent God, all events (including the actions of human beings) are due to the will of God. Besides theistic determinism, there was the natural determinism of the naturalists (*sabhāva-vāda*), according to whom everything that happened in nature was strictly determined by natural forces. In addition, there was karmic determinism, according to which everything that happened to a person was due entirely to his past kamma (*pubba-kamma-vāda*).

The Buddhist theory of causality was opposed to both these extreme points of view: to indeterminism, which denied any pattern altogether, as well as to the theistic and naturalistic forms of strict determinism, according to which there was a rigid pattern over which man had no control.

Buddhism is, therefore, opposed to the view that there is only the play of chance in the manifestation of phenomena, as also to the views that everything is due to the will of God or to the operations of rigid deterministic laws of nature. These ideas are important when we come to study the doctrine of the conditioned genesis of the individual. What happens to the individual and the changes wrought in him are not arbitrary and due to chance, nor are they due to the will of God nor, again, to the operation of rigid physical, bio-chemical and economic laws of nature over which he has no control at all. In keeping with the Buddhist theory of causality, man is conditioned by various factors, hereditary, psychological and environmental, but he is not determined by them.

Buddhism also avoided explanations in terms of agents, whether human or extra-human. Thus to say that pleasure and pain were caused by the agency of one's own soul or by an external agency such as God, or by one's own soul or self as well as by God, are all erroneous. On the other hand, to say that pleasure and pain were uncaused is equally erroneous. So all the following four alternatives are discarded as unsatisfactory, viz:

1. Pleasure and pain were caused by one's own self (*sayaṃ-kataṃ sukha-dukkhaṃ*)
2. Pleasure and pain were caused by an external agency (*paraṃ-kataṃ sukha-dukkhaṃ*)
3. Pleasure and pain were caused both by the self as well as by an external agency (*sayaṃ-kataṃ ca paraṃ-kataṃ ca sukha-dukkhaṃ*)
4. Pleasure and pain were not due to the self or an external agency but were fortuitous (*adhicca-samuppanna*), i.e. uncaused.

According to the Buddhist theory, pleasure and pain were causally conditioned (*paṭicca-samuppanna*). They may be causally conditioned by the physical environment, by the physiological condition of the body, by the social environment, by one's own present actions or by karma (or by any combination of them). So explanations are given in terms of causally conditioned factors without recourse to metaphysical concepts such as a soul or some sort of agency.

This idea is brought out in the *Śalistamba Sūtra*. Here it is said that, although "the element of heat" (*tejo-dhātuḥ*) is a causal factor in making a seed grow, it does not do this out of its own will. "It does not occur to the element of heat. 'I shall bring this seed to maturity,'" (*Ārya Śalistamba Sūtra*). Although the *Śalistamba Sūtra* is a Mahayana Sūtra, the same idea is to be found in the *Aṅguttara Nikāya* with regard to psychological causation. Here it is said that "a person who lacks remorse need not make an act of will (to the effect) 'let joy arise in me.' For, it is of the nature of things that joy arises to one who lacks remorse" (AN 10:2/A V 2). So, even in psychological causation, a conscious act of will was not always considered necessary in bringing about a subsequent psychological state.

In one place the Buddha points out that to say that "the experience and the one who experiences are one and the same" (*sā vedanā so vediyatīti*) (SN 12:18/S II 23), and therefore that the experience of pleasure and pain are one's own creation, is one extreme point of view. To say that "the experience and the one who experiences are different" (*aññā vedanā añño vediyatīti*), and therefore that the experience of pleasure and pain are due to an external agency is the other extreme point of view. The Buddha, it is said in this context, avoids these extreme points of view, which do not correctly represent the facts, and teaches the doctrine in the middle by means of conditioned genesis.

So the doctrine of conditioned genesis attempts to explain phenomena, as in science, in terms of causal correlations without recourse to explanations in terms of first causes or metaphysical substances such as a soul or agent.

In some of the pre-Buddhist Upaniṣads, which taught the doctrine of rebirth and kamma (though not exactly in the Buddhist sense), an attempt is made to explain rebirth and karma by having recourse to the doctrine of the soul, which was the common factor (as the unchanging agent) in the different lives of the individual. It was the agent of all actions as well as the recipient of reactions. So it was the same unchanging agent, which caused the actions and experienced their reactions.

These eternalists who posited the persistence of an unchanging agent or *ātman* were opposed by the materialists who denied the continuity of individuality altogether by saying that one who undergoes experiences in this life was different altogether from any previous person. The Buddha avoids these two extremes by means of the doctrine of conditioned genesis. The *Saṃyutta Nikāya* states: "In the belief that a person who acts is the same as the person who experiences ... he posits eternalism. In the belief that the person who acts is different from a person who experiences ... he posits materialism. Avoiding both these extremes, the Transcendent One preaches the doctrine in the middle: Ignorance conditions volitional acts" (SN 12:17/S II 20f).

So we see that the doctrine of conditioned genesis tries to explain phenomena in terms of causal correlations without assuming the existence of metaphysical entities like a soul.

It is, at the same time, an explanation of the origin and cessation of suffering or the unsatisfactory nature of conditioned existence. After stating the whole series of interrelated phenomena such as "ignorance conditions volitional acts, etc.," it is concluded: "In this manner there arises this mass of suffering ... and in this manner there ceases this mass of suffering" (SN 12:17/S II 20f).

We find in other religions and philosophies that many explanations of the present condition of the individual are in terms of metaphysical first causes or final causes. The theists try to explain the condition of the individual by asserting that the individual is a creation of God considered as a first cause. The materialists try to account for the individual in terms of purely material factors considered as a first cause in the evolution of the world. The dualists assume primordial first causes, such as Matter (*prakṛti*) and Spirit (*puruṣa*) in Sāṅkhya philosophy,

Yet, in the doctrine of conditioned genesis, ignorance (*avijjā*) is not a first cause in this sense. In this way, too, the doctrine is an attempt to explain phenomena "in the middle" without recourse to first causes or final causes. Explanations in terms of a first cause posit a cause such as God or Matter in the beginning of time, and explanations in terms of final causes try to explain things in terms of ultimate ends such as a goal or purpose which things serve. But in the doctrine of conditioned genesis, there are no first or final causes.

Ignorance is not a first cause, although it is selected as a convenient starting point to explain a series of interconnected phenomena.

Ignorance is to be found here and now in the present. It constitutes the sum-total of our erroneous beliefs, as well as true beliefs not amounting to knowledge, about the nature and destiny of man in the universe. We cannot know the first beginnings of such ignorance on the part of beings in an oscillating universe which expands and contracts without beginning or end. But we can know that our present ignorance is causally conditioned and that, by acquiring full knowledge and realization of our nature and destiny, we can put an end to our ignorance even in the present. As stated in the texts: "The first beginning of ignorance is not known (such that we may say) that before this there was no ignorance and at this point ignorance arose ... but that ignorance is causally conditioned (*idappaccayā avijjā*) can be known" (AN 10:51/A V 113).

Ignorance is, therefore, not conceived as a first cause except in the purely relative sense that we may start with ignorance, which is itself (as we shall see) conditioned by other factors. It is said that anyone who understands the causal process in the genesis and development of the individual would not seek for explanations in terms of first causes or final causes. After enumerating the doctrine of conditioned genesis, the Buddha asks the monks on one occasion the following rhetorical question: "Would you, O monks, knowing and seeing thus, probe [literally, run behind] the prior end of things ... or pursue [literally, run after] the final end of things?"

Buddhism starts with the present and explains specific phenomena in terms of general laws. This is also what the scientists try to do in their investigations into the nature of phenomena in their respective branches of study. In doing so, it does not try to give explanations in terms of first causes or other such unverifiable metaphysical entities. This is the distinctive contribution of Buddhism in its investigation of phenomena concerned with man's nature and destiny.

This is why the doctrine of causal genesis is considered to be the central teaching of Buddhism. It contains the truth about the nature of the individual and his destiny as discovered by the Buddha in the final stage of his enlightenment. In a stanza which was widely known, it is said that "the Transcendent One speaks of the causes of conditioned events which arise from causes." In one place the Buddha says: "He who sees the doctrine of conditioned genesis, sees the Dhamma, and he who sees the Dhamma sees conditioned genesis" (MN 28.28/M I 191).

It unfolds the predicament of man as he is found in the present, conditioned (but not determined) by his past experiences going back into prior lives, by heredity and the physiological condition of the body, the impact of the environment, physical and ideological, and the different kinds of desires which rage within him.

The explanation of specific events in the history of specific individuals is in terms of general causal laws or correlations. As we shall see when we examine this in detail, the statement, "ignorance conditions volitional activities" (*avijjā-paccayā saṅkhārā*), shows how our erroneous beliefs as well as our true beliefs (not amounting to knowledge) about the nature and destiny of the individual along with other factors condition our good and evil volitional actions of body, speech and mind. It is a statement whose truth can be at least partially verified by us when the different kinds of relations which hold between our beliefs and good and evil volitional acts are clarified.

Such relations between beliefs and volitional acts hold whether we observe or discover them, and whether we approve or disapprove of them. Such correlations are objective, for causation has the characteristics of objectivity (*tathatā*), empirical necessity (*avitathatā*), invariability (*anaññathatā*) and conditionality (*idappaccayatā*) (SN 12:20/S II 26). Hot things tend to get cold and cold things hot in a closed system, whether scientists observe or discover this and approve or disapprove of it. Those who observe such phenomena tend to deduce from them general causal laws.

In a similar fashion the Buddha states: "Whether Transcendent Ones arise or not, this order exists, namely the fixed nature of phenomena, the regular pattern of phenomena or conditionality. This the Transcendent One discovers and comprehends; having discovered and comprehended it, he points it out, teaches it, lays it down, establishes, reveals, analyses, clarifies it and says, 'look!'" (SN 12:20/S II 25).

This unique and central teaching of Buddhism was described by the Buddha as a doctrine which was "not only profound (*gambhīro*) but appears profound" (DN 15.1/D II 55). It is the failure to penetrate and realise this doctrine that has prevented beings enmeshed in *saṃsāric* existence from transcending the limitations of conditioned existence, which necessarily involves birth in lower realms of beings.

It is not surprising, therefore, that the majority of scholars who approached the study of this doctrine with the preconceptions of other religions and metaphysical systems failed altogether to understand it.

The mistake that many of them (e.g. Jacobi, Pischel, Schayer) made was to think of ignorance as the first cause in an evolutionary series accounting for the beginning and the development of cosmic phenomena emerging from the chaos of ignorance. Others thought of ignorance as the childhood condition of man and the series as representing stages in the growth of man, beginning with birth and culminating with his death. Yet others (Kern) considered ignorance as the state of sleep and the rest as what happens when we gradually awaken from sleep.

A sympathetic scholar of Buddhism, Dr Paul Dahlke, who had some remarkable insights into aspects of Buddhist philosophy, thought that "the whole chain of the conditions of origination represents one single karmic moment of personal experience." This, no doubt, leads to contradictions, as the Ven. Nyanatiloka pointed out (see *Guide through the Abhidhamma Piṭaka*, Colombo, 1957, p. 158). For if we say this, we find, for instance, that birth (*jāti*) as well as decay and death (*jarāmaraṇa*) must take place at one and the same moment. Dahlke seems to have been aware of these contradictions and the difficulties involved in his interpretation, for he speaks of "the apparent lack of logic, nay, the apparent contradictions" within the series. A local Buddhist scholar quotes this statement and adds: "To this statement of Dahlke the writer is ever so grateful," since he himself could not comprehend the traditional explanation.

The reason for his failure to comprehend the traditional explanation is interesting, since it is a common source of error. He says: "Unless I can comprehend the *paṭicca-samuppāda* as applicable in all its links to that reality which only is accessible to me—my present living—and, thereby, prove to myself its validity, I am afraid it is something that I will have to take upon faith."

The traditional explanation breaks up the twelve links into three lives, the first two being in the past, the next eight the present and the last two in the future. Yet, to imply that the past and the future are not accessible to me in the present is not correct since the present life, from the point of view of the past, is the future, and from the point of view of the future life, is the past. So we do not have to take the first two links or the last two on faith since they can be experienced in this life itself. We can be aware of our ignorance here and now, although ignorance was also present in our past life. What has to be taken on faith is the linkage between the past and the present as well as the past and the future.

Such faith is Buddhist since it is a "rational faith" (*ākāravatī saddhā*) which can be replaced with knowledge or realisation when one can develop the capacity to see one's past lives. If all that is taught in Buddhism must be accessible to our present experience, then there would be no necessity to develop higher knowledge (*abhiññā*) or extrasensory forms of experience.

All this does not mean that there are no scholars who have given a correct explanation of the doctrine of conditioned genesis. The one given by the Ven. Nyanatiloka is the best and the most authentic that I have seen so far.

This doctrine of causal conditioning should not seem so strange in a world dominated by science, which tries to explain specific phenomena as being causally conditioned in the light of general laws without recourse to metaphysical substances or agents or primordial first causes. However, as we have pointed out, we must not lose sight of the fact that causal conditioning as taught in Buddhism is not deterministic. So, despite the fact that we are conditioned by our psychological past, by heredity (*bija-niyāma*) and by the environmental present, both physical and ideological, we have an element of initiative or freedom (*ārabbha-dhātu*) by the exercise of which we can change the course of the future.

Yet, at the same time, we must not forget that no other doctrine has been so misunderstood and misinterpreted by scholars, some of whom were sympathetic towards Buddhism. If we take the first sentence of the formula describing the nature of the conditioning of the individual, viz. "ignorance conditions volitional activities" (*avijjā-paccayā saṅkhārā*), we find that most scholars took "ignorance" as a primordial first cause, despite the fact that this is explicitly denied in the Buddhist texts. For them, ignorance was the original state of unconscious existence in the beginning prior to evolution. With the process of evolution, there was blind groping on the part of all things or beings, but still no conscious awareness or purpose in their actions. So *"avijjā-paccayā saṅkhārā"* was interpreted to mean that a state of original ignorance was followed by that of blind groping in the history of evolution.

Another such explanation is that by ignorance is meant a state of deep sleep, while activities refer to our activity which follows our awakening from sleep. Still another explanation, which is favoured by some Sri Lankan scholars, is that ignorance, activities, as well as all the factors referred to in the formula, such as birth and death, co-exist in every single moment of our existence.[3]

However interesting all these explanations may be, they are all contradicted by, and are not consonant with, what is found in the early Buddhist texts and the interpretations of Buddhist tradition. It would, therefore, be wiser on our part to examine the explanations actually given in the Buddhist texts.

The Textual Explanation

What does *"avijjā-paccayā saṅkhārā"* actually mean? To understand this sentence it is necessary that one should, at least, understand what the words mean.

What is meant by *avijjā*? Or as the question is posed in the texts themselves, "*katamā ca avijjā*?" The answer given is that "by

---

3. Prof. Jayatilleke refers to the *Vibhaṅga's abhidhammabhājanīya* method of explaining *paṭicca-samuppāda* as taking place within a single mind moment; see *Vibhaṅga* commentary p. 199ff/§ 932–1009 (BPS ed.).

ignorance is meant lack of knowledge with regard to the unsatisfactoriness of things (*dukkhe aññāṇaṃ*), lack of knowledge with regard to the cause of the unsatisfactoriness of things, lack of knowledge with regard to the cessation of this sense of unsatisfactoriness and lack of knowledge with regard to the path leading to this cessation" (SN 12:2/S II 4).

The word *saṅkhārā*, on the other hand, means volitional acts. Although scholars have given all sorts of arbitrary translations of this term, its meaning has been clearly defined in the *Vibhaṅga* (p. 135). Here it is said that *saṅkhārā* constitute: (1) meritorious volitional actions (*puññābhisaṅkhārā*); (2) demeritorious volitional actions (*apuññābhisaṅkhārā*); and (3) imperturbable volitional actions (*āneñjābhisaṅkhārā*). These are subdivided into those which find expression through the body (*kāya-saṅkhārā*), speech (*vacī-saṅkhārā*) and the mind (*mano-saṅkhārā*).

Let us leave aside the imperturbable volitional actions, which are defined as "good volitional acts which occur in the states of impersonal mystical consciousness or *arūpa-jhāna*" (*kusalā cetanā arūpāvacarā*).

We then have meritorious volitional actions of body, speech and mind as well as demeritorious volitional actions of body, speech and mind. The meritorious volitional acts are defined in the *Vibhaṅga* as acts of good intention (*kusalā cetanā*) pertaining to the sensuous material world and the subtle material world, consisting of acts of charity (*dāna*), restraint (*sīla*) and mental culture (*bhāvanā*). The demeritorious volitional acts are defined as acts of evil intention (*akusalā cetanā*) pertaining to the sensuous material world (*kāmāvacarā*).

If we help someone in distress, do a charitable deed, say what we believe to be true, especially when this is helpful to others and not so helpful for ourselves, act with benevolence, even towards our enemies, then we are doing morally good actions or meritorious volitional acts. If, on the other hand, we cause harm to others out of malice, appropriate other people's property by fraudulent means, indulge in slander and hate people who may criticise us, then we are doing morally evil acts or demeritorious volitional actions.

Now, what the above statement says is that our lack of knowledge concerning the Four Noble Truths conditions our good and evil volitional acts. Lack of knowledge concerning the Four

Noble Truths is lack of knowledge concerning the nature and possible destiny of man in the universe. We lack knowledge concerning the nature and possible destiny of man in the universe when we entertain erroneous beliefs about man and his destiny in the universe and also when we have true beliefs about man and his destiny in the universe merely on the grounds of faith, whether rational or blind. The erroneous beliefs cannot be reckoned as knowledge because they are erroneous, and the true beliefs because they are mere beliefs not amounting to knowledge.

It is a fact that our beliefs condition our volitional acts. Many people, especially in the modern world, in the firm belief that this is the only life, do not believe that we are in any way responsible or accountable for our actions. Opportunism, expediency, the continued indulgence in the pleasures of sense and sex in the quest for pleasure as well as the multiplication and gratification of desires for the same end constitute their pattern of life. It is true that this kind of living, far from giving happiness, results in boredom, anxiety, conflict and tension. Yet, for them, the beliefs of all religions are superstitions of a by-gone age. Moral values do not exist. Their beliefs about the nature of man and the amoral ethic which accompanies these beliefs make them commit what is reckoned to be evil with impunity.

On the other hand, there are those who believe that good actions have their reward in an after-life and do good in the hope of attaining a better life in the next existence or in a heaven. So both good and evil actions are conditioned by our beliefs, which may be true or false.

Causal Correlation

According to Buddhism, those who act in the belief that there is no after-life or that there is an after-life are guided by ignorance. Those who deny an after-life are ignorant of the fact that there is one. On the other hand, those who merely believe in an after-life do not have knowledge of the fact. Both lack knowledge about the nature and destiny of man and are impelled by ignorance. Though impelled by ignorance, their actions are not strictly determined by ignorance since man has within himself the capacity to get rid of his ignorance.

So we see a causal correlation between ignorance and volitional activities, such that "whenever there is ignorance there is a tendency for volitional acts to come into being as a result of ignorance" (*avijjāya kho sati saṅkhārā honti, avijjā-paccayā saṅkhārā*) (SN 12:4/S II 7), and that "whenever there is no ignorance there are no volitional activities and with the cessation of ignorance there is a cessation of volitional activities" (ibid.). The Arahant or the perfect person does not experience the tensions of choice and decision which are involved in volitional actions; his actions are purely spontaneous (*kiriya-matta*) and are good by nature without involving a tendency to fruition in subsequent lives.

It may appear paradoxical to some as to how good actions may be caused by ignorance. There is no doubt that the early texts quite explicitly state that good as well as evil volitional actions can be performed under the influence of ignorance. It is said: "When a person under the influence of ignorance performs a meritorious volitional act, his consciousness tends to become meritorious; if he performs a demeritorious act, his consciousness tends to become demeritorious" (*avijjā gato yam purisa-puggalo puññaṃ ce saṅkhāraṃ abhisaṅkharoti puññūpagaṃ hoti viññāṇaṃ*) (SN 12:51/S II 82).

The question is posed rhetorically by Buddhaghosa in his *Visuddhimagga* (*Vism* XVII.109/p. 543), viz. "How can ignorance which has a decidedly undesirable effect and is blameworthy be the cause for meritorious action ...? How can sugarcane grow from a [bitter] neem-seed?" Buddhaghosa's answer is that there need not be a similarity between cause and effect, and therefore "this ignorance though it may have a decidedly undesirable result and is blameworthy in its intrinsic nature should be considered as a cause; so far as possible, of all meritorious actions...." Earlier, Buddhaghosa illustrates how this happens in the case of ignorance: "Craving for becoming is the specific condition of action which leads to a happy fate. Wherefore? Because the average man, overcome by the craving for becoming, strives to do the various kinds of deeds leading to a happy fate such as abstinence from taking life...." (*Vism* XVII.39/p. 525).

In a pictorial representation of the "wheel of becoming" (*bhava-cakra*) in an Ajanta painting (seventh-century), ignorance is depicted as a blind man with a stick. This is a very apt portrayal of the role of ignorance. Some stanzas from the ancient teachers (*porāṇā*) of the Buddhist tradition throw light on this illustration. They are quoted by Buddhaghosa in the *Visuddhimagga* and along with his preamble; the passage reads as follows:

"Blinded by ignorance, he is like a blind man who wanders about the earth, encountering now right and now wrong paths, now heights and now hollows, now even and now uneven ground, and so he performs acts now of merit, now of demerit and now imperturbable. Hence it is said:

As one born blind who gropes along
Without assistance from a guide,
Chooses a road that may be right
At one time, at another wrong,
So while the ignorant man pursues
The round of births without a guide,
Now to do merit he may choose
And now demerit in such plight.
But when the Dhamma he comes to know
And penetrates the Truths beside,
Then Ignorance is put to flight
At last, and in peace would he abide."

(*Vism* XVII.118–99/p. 544).

We may note that the blind man with the stick sometimes goes on wrong paths and sometimes on the right path, though he may not know that it is the right path. Volitional activities are here depicted as a potter with wheel and pots. This, again, is an apt illustration. These activities of ours are motivated partly by physiological and partly by psychological causes, of which we are not fully aware. All we do in turning them into volitional activities is to give them a push or restrain their momentum as the potter does with his wheel.

Elaborations

The different types of volitional activities, both good and evil, that we indulge in are well illustrated in a passage of the *Saṃyutta Nikāya.* According to the text, as a result of ignorance (*avijjā-paccayā*) we perform volitional acts of the body (*kāya-saṅkhārā*), of speech (*vacī*) or of the mind (*mano*), either of our own accord (*samaṃ*) or at the instigation of others (*pare*), with full awareness of what we are doing (*sampajāna*) or without full awareness of what we are doing (*asampajāna*) (SN 12:25.3/S II 40).

While the earliest texts of the Pali Canon define ignorance as "ignorance of the Four Noble Truths," as stated above, we find further elaborations in the *Abhidhamma Piṭaka* and the Chinese *Āgamas*. In the *Dhammasaṅgaṇī*, for instance, ignorance is defined not merely as ignorance of the Four Noble Truths but as ignorance regarding the past (*pubbante aññāṇa*), ignorance regarding the future (*aparante aññāṇa*), ignorance regarding the past and the future, ignorance regarding the conditioned nature (*idappaccayatā*) of causally conditioned events (*paṭicca-samuppannesu dhammesu*) (Dhs p. 1061). In the Chinese *Saṃyukta Āgama*, corresponding to the *Vibhaṅga Sutta* of the *Saṃyutta Nikāya* (SN 12:2/S II 2–4) of the Pali Canon, there is additionally mentioned ignorance of the interior, the exterior, both interior and exterior, action, consequence, both action and consequence, the Buddha, the Dhamma, the Saṅgha, etc. The Sanskrit version of this Sūtra was found in two brick inscriptions at Nālandā (see *Epigraphica Indica*, XXI, pp.179–99).

These further elaborations are only extensions of the original concept. A person who lacks knowledge regarding the Four Noble Truths may entertain a wide variety of false beliefs, or some if not all true beliefs about the nature and destiny of man in the universe. He may entertain or cling to any one of a variety of materialistic, sceptical or eternalist beliefs about the nature and destiny of man. He may believe in a variety of causes for man's predicament. He may or may not believe in an ultimate goal of existence. Even if he does believe in a goal, he may not be treading the Eightfold Path. He may believe that some goal is assured him by the grace of God or the necessity of evolution. He may not believe in causal conditioning, but instead hold to the view that the process of events in nature is entirely haphazard or one strictly determined by purely material causes. All these beliefs would have some impact on his values and volitional activities. This is what the statement, "Ignorance conditions volitional activities" (*avijjā-paccayā saṅkhārā*) implies.

Since only one view would be true, and an immense variety of views would be false, and we do not have knowledge of this one true view if it is a mere set of beliefs accepted on faith, we can imagine the extent of man's ignorance about his own condition, nature and destiny in the universe.

Errors

There are certain errors one must guard against in the interpretation of the causal formulae, of which "ignorance conditions volitional activities" is the first. It is not implied, as the texts quite clearly point out, that ignorance alone conditions our volitional acts. In Buddhist causal theory any causal situation is complex. What we pick out as a cause is only a predominant factor which operates along with other factors in bringing about an effect. Ignorance is a predominant factor because it is one of the impelling or motivating causes (*hetu*) of actions. The term *"hetu"* is used in the *Abhidhamma* in this specialised sense of motivating cause. The word is formed from the *hu-* "to impel" with the suffix *-tu* and means "impeller." Among the factors that motivate man's actions—good, evil, mixed and neutral—are, on the one hand, greed, hatred and ignorance, and, on the other, their opposites, namely selflessness, compassion and understanding. So, alongside ignorance, motivating man's actions are the desires.

The desires and beliefs together condition man's actions. When we desire a cool drink and quench our thirst by taking one, we are impelled by both desires and beliefs. There is, on the one hand, the desire to drink or the thirst which makes us restless and seek a drink. On the other hand, there are the beliefs (which may be true or false) that a drink may be had from the refrigerator, etc. So it is these two factors, namely desires and beliefs, which result in the activity which constitutes the quest for a drink.

Likewise, just as much as "ignorance conditions volitional actions," it is said that "volitional actions too reinforce our ignorance" (*saṅkhāra-paccayā pi avijjā*; *Vibhaṅga*, p. 141). Supposing we do an evil act under the influence of our desires and false beliefs. The evil act in turn reinforces our false belief and makes it harder to dislodge. We try to justify our evil act, and the belief impelling it (*hetu-paccaya*), associated with it (*sampayutta-paccaya*) and supporting it (*nissaya-paccaya*) becomes a rationalisation we cling to in the face of the evil act that we have done. If, for example, we scold someone in anger, we tend to hold and cling to the belief which led to the scolding, due to the tendency on our part to justify the scolding. So there is the relationship of mutual dependence (*aññamañña-paccaya*) as well between ignorance and volitional actions. So the causal correlation between ignorance and volitional actions involves several relationships (*paccaya*) between the two.

So the first statement of the causal formula means that "ignorance conditions volitional actions" as explained above. A careful study of and reflection on our volitional actions will reveal the desires and beliefs (erroneous or otherwise) lurking behind them, and the truth of the above statement can thereby be verified.

Partial Conditioned Experience

According to the Buddha, all this variety of opinion on this subject is due to the partial, relative and conditioned character of the thought of the thinkers who put forward these points of view. This is, in fact, what is said in the *Brahmajāla Sutta*, where the Buddha has classified the main views that thinkers put forward with regard to the nature and destiny of man in the universe.

The Buddha says that the religious teachers and philosophers, who were eternalists (*sassata-vādā*), semi-eternalists (*ekacca-sassatikā*), such as the theists (*issara-nimmāna-vādā*), who asserted that God was eternal while his creation was not; cosmologists (*antānantikā*) who asserted various theories about the extent of the universe; sceptics (*amarā-vikkhepikā*); indeterminists (*adhicca-samuppannikā*); primordialists (*pubbanta-kappikā*), who speculated about pre-existence and first-causes; eschatologists (*uddham-āghātanikā*), who speculated about survival and final causes; materialists (*ucchedavādā*), who believed in the annihilation of the personality at death; "and various existentialist moral philosophers (*diṭṭhadhamma-nibbāna-vādā*), who posited their various philosophies did so on the basis of conditioned and limited personal experience" (*chahi phassāyatanehi phussa phussa paṭisaṃvedenti*) (DN 1.3.70/D I 45).

As a result, the Buddha argues, their experiences have aroused their desires (*vedanā-paccayā taṇhā*), and these, in turn, have resulted in entanglements (*taṇhā-paccayā upādānam*) which result in further becoming (*bhava*) and rebirth (*jāti*). It is only, says the Buddha, when a person can understand the origin and limits of conditioned personal experience (*phassāyatana*), its values, its defects and how one transcends it that he can comprehend something higher than this (*ayaṃ imehi sabbeh'eva uttaritaraṃ pajānāti*) (DN 1.3.71/D I 45).

It is, therefore, not sufficient to have a merely intellectual appreciation of the Four Noble Truths or the central truths of Buddhism. Even such a person who entertains "the right view of life" (*sammā-diṭṭhi*) still has only a mere "view" (*diṭṭhi*). He may have true beliefs about the nature and destiny of man in the universe, but they are still mere beliefs not amounting to knowledge. So, while starting with right beliefs (*samma-diṭṭhi*) as the guide of life, one should try to attain right understanding (*samma-ñāṇa*).

Unless and until right understanding is attained, all people, whether they are Buddhists or non-Buddhists, entertain either erroneous beliefs or true beliefs (not amounting to knowledge) about the nature and destiny of man in the universe. As a result, they have diverse opinions about the reality of moral actions and the nature of good and evil. So their volitional actions, whether they believe in the value or moral efficacy of such actions or not, are conditioned by the various opinions they hold, which may be characterised as ignorance.

It is possible that they may not consciously or clearly hold such opinions; this would be the case if they do know what they believe about these matters, or are not very articulate in their beliefs; but even in such a case they are guided by ignorance in their volitional actions.

So this is the seemingly simple though truly profound truth expressed in the sentence "ignorance conditions volitional acts" (*avijjā-paccayā saṅkhārā*). As we have shown earlier, these volitional acts may be done of our own accord (*samaṃ*) or at the instigation of others (*pare*), with full awareness of what we are doing (*sampajāna*) or without full awareness of what we are doing (*asampajāna*) (SN 12:25.3/S II 40).

At the same time, we must not forget what we have already stated, namely that ignorance is only one of the main factors correlated with and conditioning our volitional activities. It is by no means the only factor, since another important factor conditioning our volitional actions are the different kinds of desires in us. In fact, it is the beliefs and desires together which largely motivate our behaviour and thereby condition our volitional activities.

Volitional Acts and Consciousness

The next statement of the formula of causal conditioning reads: "volitional acts condition consciousness" (*saṅkhāra-paccayā viññāṇaṃ*). The later explanation of this statement is to be found in the Commentaries, and the *Visuddhimagga* is somewhat sophisticated, but one of the earliest explanations, which has been neglected, is simple and straightforward. It says: "If a person under the influence of ignorance performs meritorious actions, his consciousness acquires a meritorious bent (*puññūpagaṃ hoti viññāṇaṃ*); if he performs demeritorious actions, his consciousness acquires a demeritorious bent; and if he performs imperturbable actions, his consciousness acquires an imperturbable bent" (SN 12:51/S II 82). If we take this explanation as valid, what it means is that the tone or moral tone of our consciousness is affected by the nature of the volitional actions performed by us.

The first verse of the *Dhammapada* underlines the importance attached to the factor of "will": "Psychological states are led by will, governed by will and are a product of will" (*manopubbaṅgamā dhammā manoseṭṭhā manomayā*). It is such willed actions which change our psychological nature and eventually cause our happiness or unhappiness in so far as happiness is kammically caused.

The *Nidāna Saṃyutta*, which deals extensively with causal formulae, has three sections devoted to the subject of will or intention (*cetanā*). What is stated in the first passage reads as follows: "What one wills (*ceteti*), decides (*pakappeti*) and registers in one's unconscious (*anuseti*) becomes an object for the persistence of consciousness (*ārammaṇaṃ hoti viññāṇassa ṭhitiyā*). When such an object is present, consciousness finds a footing in it (*ārammaṇe sati patittha viññāṇassa hoti*), and when consciousness is established therein and comes to maturity, there results a renewed birth in the future" (*tasmiṃ patiṭṭhite viññāṇe virūḷhe āyatiṃ punabbhavābhinibbatti hoti*) (SN 12:38/S II 65). We have translated the word "*anuseti*" as "registers in the unconsciousness." The meaning of the word as given in the *Pali Text Society Dictionary*, s.v. *anuseti,* is as follows: "1. to dwell on, harp on (an idea); 2. (of an idea) to obsess, to fill the mind persistently, to lie dormant and be continually cropping up." The word is formed from the prefix *anu-*, meaning on or under, and the root √*sī*, meaning "to lie down." Here what is meant is that these psychological states lie beneath the state of the conscious mind but continue to affect it.

What the above passage states is that when we perform willed actions, involving choice and decision, the form and tone of our consciousness is thereby changed and this tends to determine the nature of our next life. So there is a causal connection between will (*cetanā*), consciousness (*viññāṇa*) and the next life (*āyatiṃ punabbhavābhinibbatti*).

In the *Saṅkhārupapatti Sutta* of the *Majjhima Nikāya*, which deals with the question of "birth according to one's will" (*saṅkhārupapatti*), it is said that a person who is possessed of faith (*saddhā*), virtue (*sīla*), learning (*suta*), selflessness (*cāga*) and understanding (*paññā*) can acquire almost any kind of birth at will in his next life either among humans or in higher worlds among the galactic systems of the universe. When such a person wishes for some form of future existence, it is said, he fixes his mind on such thoughts (*taṃ cittaṃ dahati*), concentrates on such thoughts and develops such thoughts so that those acts of will (*saṅkhārā*) and that life of his (*vihāra*) when developed and often dwelt upon (*bhāvitā bahulīkatā*) tends to bring about such an existence (*tatr'upapattiyā saṃvaṭṭanti*) (MN 120.1–11/M III 99–100). Here again, the sequence is that of acts of will causing a growth in one's personality as reflected in his faith, virtue, learning, selflessness and wisdom resulting in the light of his wishes in a renewed form of existence which is to his liking.

Of the three passages we referred to in the *Nidāna Saṃyutta*, the second reads as follows: "What one wills, decides and registers in one's unconsciousness becomes an object for the persistence of consciousness. Such an object being present, consciousness finds footing in it, and when consciousness is established therein and comes to maturity, there is eventually an entrance into a new personality" (*tasmiṃ patiṭṭhite viññāṇe virūḷhe nāmarūpassa avakkanti hoti*) (SN 12:39/S II 66).

The third passage proceeds as above and then states: "When consciousness is established therein and comes to maturity it acquires a certain bent or tone (*nati*). This determines its activity (*āgatigati*, literally coming and going) and this in turn its decease and rebirth" (*cutūpapāta*) (SN 12:40/S II 67).

The sequence in all these passages is the same. The acts of will (*cetanā, saṅkhārā*) condition the nature and tone of our consciousness (*viññāṇa, citta*) and this, in turn, conditions the next life and the new personality (*āyatiṃ punabbhavābhinibbatti, nāmarūpassa avakkanti, cutūpapāta*). So while ignorance conditions our volitional activities (*avijjā-paccayā saṅkhārā*), as explained above, these volitional activities are the predominant factor in conditioning the nature and tone of our consciousness.

As we know, according to the Buddhist theory, consciousness is not an unchanging entity or soul, as explained in dealing with the heresy of Sāti in the *Mahātaṇhāsaṅkhaya Sutta* (MN 38/M I 256–71). It is constantly changing under the impact of the external world and our own past experiences. But the nature of our consciousness is not strictly determined by these factors which condition it, since predominant among the factors which determine the nature and direction in which our consciousness develops and matures are our will (*cetanā*) or acts of will (*saṅkhārā*). It is our own will or these acts of will which can or do make a tremendous difference to our future development. They can transform the nature of the human individual for good or for evil. Environment, heredity and our own psychological heritage from the past are, no doubt, factors which condition the nature of our consciousness, but the fundamental factor which governs our future is our will as expressed in our acts of will, which transform our nature or state of our personality or consciousness (*viññāṇa*).

Properly utilised, it is the most effective instrument that we possess in changing our future from what, out of neglect, it may otherwise be. So while the first statement of the causal formula taught that our beliefs or ignorance regarding the nature and destiny of man condition our volitional acts so that we tend to act in all sorts of ways and justify them, the second statement of the causal formula asserts the equally profound truth that our acts of will or volitional activities condition the nature, form and tone of our consciousness (*saṅkhāra-paccayā viññāṇaṃ*).

The meaning of the third statement of the causal formula, namely that the nature of our consciousness conditions the nature of the new individuality in the next life (*viññāṇa-paccayā nāmarūpaṃ*), should also be somewhat clear from the passages we have cited above, but before we examine this third statement, it would be worthwhile to consider another traditional explanation, which has been given to the statement "volitional activities condition consciousness."

Another Interpretation

Another interpretation is found in the *Visuddhimagga* of Buddhaghosa and the Commentaries, although it quotes in support certain statements of the *Dhammasaṅgaṇī,* which is the first book of the *Abhidhamma Piṭaka.*

The explanation is as follows: *Saṅkhārā* or acts of will are here treated as previous kamma. By consciousness is to be understood the five forms of consciousness associated with the senses such as visual consciousness, auditory consciousness, etc., as well as the consciousness which is a product of mental activity (*mano-viññāṇa-dhātu*) such as memory, reflection, imagination, reasoning, etc. Now, it is argued that acts of will constituting our previous kamma condition the nature of our consciousness in a subsequent life.

It is in this manner that Buddhaghosa explains the statement. He says: "In the statement 'volitional activities condition consciousness,' consciousness is of six kinds beginning with visual consciousness" (*Vism* XVII.121–22/p. 545). He quotes in support certain passages from the *Dhammasaṅgaṇī.* These passages are not directly relevant to the explanation of the formula of causal conditioning. For instance, one of them quoted from the *Dhammasaṅgaṇī* when taken in its context reads as follows: "What psychological states are morally neutral? When as a result of (*vipākaṃ*) good karma done and accumulated in the realm of sensuous existence there arises visual consciousness accompanied by a neutral tone and associated with visual objects...." (*Vism* XVII.122/p. 545; quoting *Dhs* p. 431).

Here visual consciousness among other forms of consciousness is represented as a product of previous good kamma. There is no doubt that kamma conditions the forms of consciousness that we have in subsequent lives. If we intentionally blind other people, then there is a tendency to be born blind. So our lack of visual consciousness would be due to a demeritorious act of will done in a past life. So there is, no doubt, a kammic connection between forms of consciousness and acts of will done in previous lives. It is in this sense that the Ven. Nyanatiloka, following Buddhaghosa, explains the statement "volitional activities condition consciousness" thus: "Here by 'consciousness' (*viññāṇa*) are meant only those classes of consciousness which are the results (*vipāka*) of wholesome or unwholesome kamma formations done in former existence ..." (*Guide through the Abhidhamma Piṭaka,* Colombo, 1957, p. 165). While not denying these facts of conditioning, and the possibility of explaining this statement in the aforesaid manner as well, it is important not to lose sight of the explanation given in the earliest authentic texts of the *Sutta Piṭaka*, which stress the fact that our volitional acts proximately change the nature and bent of our consciousness in this life itself quite apart from their remote consequences in subsequent lives, which are also not to be denied. Besides, acts of will considered as karmic factors should condition not only the state of our consciousness in subsequent lives but other factors in our lives as well.

Considering the citations that we have given, it would appear that the interpretation we gave earlier would be the more natural explanation, though the latter explanation does not contradict it. It merely supplements it. Another reason why this explanation appears to be more authentic would become clear when we examine the explanations given in the *Sutta Piṭaka* of the next statement of the formula, namely that "consciousness conditions the (new) individuality" (*viññāṇa-paccayā nāmarūpaṃ*).

From what we have cited already, it is clear that our acts of will condition the character of our consciousness. It is the nature and tone of our consciousness which conditions the nature of our successive personality. What one wills (*ceteti*), decides and registers in one's subconscious (*anuseti*) becomes an object for the persistence of consciousness. When such an object is present, consciousness finds a footing in it and "when consciousness is established therein and comes to maturity, there results a renewed birth (*punabbhavābhinibbatti*) in the future" (SN 12:38/S II 65). In another passage (already quoted), it was said: "When consciousness is established therein and comes to maturity, there is eventually an entrance into a new personality" (*nāmarūpassa avakkanti hoti*) (SN 12:39/S II 66). Or again: "When consciousness is established therein and comes to maturity, it acquires a certain bent or tone (*nati*), this determines its activity and this in turn its decease and rebirth" (*cutūpapāta*) (SN 12:40/S II 67).

All these passages confirm the fact that it is the nature of our consciousness, which refers to a phase, and the state of the dynamic stream of consciousness (*viññāṇa-sota*), to condition the nature and form of the new personality we inherit in our successive life. This subsequent life may be in various planes of existence, but since most people survive as a discarnate spirit (*gandhabba,* Skr. *gandharva*) and are reborn in an earth-life, the new personality is here depicted as rebirth in a human condition.

As we have already pointed out, three factors are necessary for a human birth: the presence of the ovum, its fertilisation by the sperm of the father as well as the interaction and integration of the zygote (i.e. sperm and ovum together) with the dynamic stream of consciousness (*viññāṇa-sota*), which is also called the discarnate spirit (*gandhabbo ca paccupaṭṭhito hoti*). So the new personality after integration (*avakkanti*) is a product of the two parents and the dynamic stream of consciousness, which in the later texts is called "the re-linking consciousness" (*paṭisandhi-viññāṇa*).

Modern biological science would not admit the existence of such a dynamic stream of consciousness charging and interacting with the zygote. It therefore assumes that the child conceived in the mother's womb is a purely hereditary product of the parental stock. At conception, a normal human being receives twenty-three chromosomes from the father's sperm and twenty-three from the mother's ovum. Each chromosome is composed of many individual determiners of heredity called genes. Modern biologists and psychologists consider the human person as being a product entirely of heredity and environment. It is, therefore, one of their basic assumptions that what cannot be due to heredity must necessarily be due to the environment.

It is now more or less established that physical characteristics at birth are due almost entirely to heredity, but it is assumed that the personality characteristics, such as temperament, are due to the interaction of the environment. In a study of identical twins (who have the same heredity because they are a product of the bifurcation of a zygote composed of one sperm and one ovum, a fact which is itself unexplained), it is said that "the authors came to the conclusion that the physical characteristics are least modified by the environment, intellectual characteristics somewhat more and personality characteristics most of all" (quoted from Ernest R. Hilgard, *Introduction to Psychology,* New York, 1962, p. 436). Buddhism, while granting that the laws of heredity (*bija-niyāma*) condition, on the whole, the physical and physiological characteristics of the person, holds that the temperamental and such personality characteristics, including aptitudes and skills, are on the whole conditioned by the psychological past of the individual. This is a theory that should be carefully examined by biologists and psychologists in the light of all the known facts since there is some significant evidence from science even at present in favour of the Buddhist theory. We have already cited some of this evidence.

We are presently trying to explain the statement that "consciousness conditions the (new) psycho-physical individuality" (*viññāṇa-paccayā nāmarūpaṃ*). According to the texts, there is mutual interaction and integration of the two in the formation of the new personality. It is said: "Just as much as two bundles of reeds are to stand erect supporting each other, even so conditioned by the (hereditary) psycho-physical factors is the consciousness, and conditioned by the consciousness are the psycho-physical factors" (SN 12:67/S II 114).

In the *Mahānidāna Sutta* of the *Dīgha Nikāya*, there occurs the following dialogue between the Buddha and Ānanda, which throws light on the relationship of the two:

> It has been stated that "conditioned by consciousness is the psycho-physical individuality" (*nāma-rūpa*). This assertion, Ānanda, is to be understood in the following manner: If consciousness did not come into the mother's womb, would the psycho-physical individuality spring up in the mother's womb?
>
> It would not, O Lord.
>
> If consciousness, Ānanda, comes into the mother's womb and departs, would the psycho-physical individuality be born into this world?
>
> It would not, O Lord.
>
> Therefore, this is the cause, the source, the origin and the condition [for the birth of the] psycho-physical individuality, namely the consciousness.
>
> Now, it is also stated that "conditioned by the psycho-physical individuality is the consciousness." This assertion is to be understood in the following manner: If, Ānanda, consciousness did not find a foothold in a psycho-physical individuality, would the arising again of birth, decay, death and suffering be manifested?
>
> It would not, O Lord.
>
> Therefore, Ānanda, this is a cause, a source, an origin and a condition [for the manifestation of] consciousness, namely the psycho-physical individuality.
>
> To this extent can one speak of one being born, decaying, dying, passing away and being reborn ... to this extent can one speak of a cycle of births in this world, namely owing to the mutual interaction of the psychophysical individuality with the consciousness (*nāmarūpaṃ saha viññāṇena*) (DN 15.19–24/D II 62–64).

The next statement of the causal formula asserts that "conditioned by the nature of our personality is our external world" (*nāmarūpa-paccayā saḷāyatanaṃ*). What we translate as the "external world" here is the term *saḷāyatana*, which is used to refer to both the five sense organs (such as the eyes, ears, nose, tongue and body-sensitivity), and the mechanism of the mind (*manāyatana*) as well as their objects, viz. visible forms, sounds, smells, tastes, tangibles as well as ideas, concepts, opinions and theories. This external world of ours is very much conditioned by our psycho-physical personality. For example, if we were born blind for psychological or physical reasons, then the world of colours and shapes would not exist for us. Likewise the world that we perceive through our sight is very much conditioned by our psychological natures. While what we actually see depends partly on the texture of the visual organs and the state of our brain, we may be conditioned to notice and pay greater attention to certain aspects of our visual environment owing to our past psychological conditioning and habits.

Likewise the ideas and concepts that we have depend partly on the condition of the basis of our mind (*manāyatana*), the ideas, opinions and theories we are exposed to in our social and ideological environment as well as the receptivity of our own mind as a result of which we may show a special interest in some sorts of ideas as against others.

A statement in the *Paṭṭhāna* also throws light on the nature of mental phenomena and their relation to the body and the external world. It is said: "The field of visual forms, sounds, smells, tastes and tangibles are, to perceptual activity and phenomena connected with it, a condition by way of prenascence (*purejāta-paccaya*). The physical base (*rūpa*), in dependence on which there arises perceptual activity (*mano-dhātu*) as well as conceptual activity (*manoviññāṇa-dhātu*), is a condition by way of prenascence for perceptual activity and phenomena connected with it; but for conceptual activity and phenomena connected with it, it is sometimes (*kiñcikāle*) a condition by way of prenascence (*purejāta-paccaya*) and sometimes not a condition by way of prenascence" (*Paccaya Niddesa*, 10).

What this means is that physical objects, sounds, smells, etc., exist prior to and independent of their being perceived and become a condition for perceptual activity and associated mental phenomena (such as feelings) to manifest themselves. Likewise, the physical basis of the mind exists prior to and becomes a condition for the arising of perceptual activity and associated phenomena (such as feelings). But the physical basis of the mind is not always prior to the conceptual activity of the mind (*mano-viññāṇa-dhātu*) such as memory, reasoning, imagination, etc., since their residues are present in the dynamic unconscious, which is prior to the formation of the physical basis of the mind, although their subsequent arousal and recall are dependent on the physical basis (*rūpa*) of the mind. It seems to follow from this that all conscious mental activity has a physical (i.e. physiological) basis, while all that is present in the dynamic unconscious of the stream of consciousness need not be located in this physical basis, although this consciousness is associated and connected with one's body (*ettha sitaṃ ettha paribaddhaṃ*).

The meaning of the next statement, which is to the effect that conditioned by the external world are the impressions (*saḷāyatana-paccayā phasso*), is fairly clear. The external objects impinge on our sense in the form of stimuli and when the mind is attentive to them produce sense-impressions. As the texts say, "On account of the organ of sight and visual objects there arise eye-consciousness and the meeting of the three constitutes a visual impression" (*cakkhuṃ ca paṭicca rūpaṃ ca paṭicca uppajjati cakkhu-viññāṇaṃ tiṇṇaṃ saṅgati phasso*) (SN 12:43/S II 72). The sense-impressions caused by the five senses are called "actual contacts" (*paṭigha-samphassa*), while the impressions caused by the manifestation of ideas or concepts in the mind are called "nominal contacts" (*adhivacana-samphassa*). On the basis of our conceptual activity and also as a result of our social and ideological environment, numerous ideas, concepts, opinions and theories pass through our minds. So we see that on account of the external world and the activity of our minds there arise various impressions.

These impressions give rise to or condition our feelings or sensations (*phassa-paccayā vedanā*), which may be pleasant, unpleasant or neutral. The feelings condition our desires (*vedanā-paccayā taṇhā*), the impressions (sensuous or mental) associated with pleasant feelings condition or arouse the desires for sensuous or sexual gratification (*kāma-taṇhā*) and the desires for egoistic pursuits (*bhava-taṇhā*) such as the desire for possessions, for power, for fame, for personal immortality, etc. On the other hand, the unpleasant feelings condition or arouse our desire for elimination or destruction (*vibhava-taṇhā*).

Then, these desires condition our entanglements (*taṇhā-paccayā upādānaṃ*). These entanglements may be with objects, places or persons (*kāmupādāna*), philosophical, religious or political ideas or theories (*diṭṭhupādāna*), habits, customs, rites or rituals (*sīlabbatūpādāna*) as well as our beliefs in soul or substance (*attavādupādāna*). For example, if our ego instincts (*bhava-taṇhā*) are strong, we hold on to or cling to some belief in a soul because this gratifies our desires for security and personal immortality in an insecure and uncertain world where we fear that death may be the end of everything. Likewise we cling to objects or persons when they afford us pleasure and gratify our various desires. So we cling to all the things, persons, habits and ideas which afford us pleasure by providing satisfaction for our desires and form sentiments of attachment around them in the vain hope that they would continue to be sources of pleasure since man acts on the principle of seeking pleasure and avoiding pain (*sukhakāmā hi manussā dukkhapaṭikkūlā*).

On the other hand, we are repelled by the things that cause displeasure. They become the objects of aggression or repulsion (*paṭigha*) and we direct our hatred (*dosa*) against them since they arouse our desire for elimination or destruction (*vibhava-taṇhā*). We form sentiments of hate around these things, persons, habits or theories, and so they too become our entanglements. The satisfaction of this desire for elimination and destruction also affords us sadistic pleasures.

Our entanglements may be of a higher order if we treat as secure states of personality, or as a soul, the higher stages of jhānic experience. So it is these kinds of things, persons, habits, theories or states of experience around which we formed entanglements which condition our future becoming (*upādāna-paccayā bhavo*) in different planes of existence. This becoming conditions our birth (*bhava-paccayā jāti*) and birth in these conditions results in decay and death (*jāti-paccayā jarāmaraṇaṃ*).

This is the "wheel of becoming" (*bhava-cakra*) that we are caught up in, but the emergence from this condition is also pictured as a process of conditioning. "Suffering is instrumental in arousing faith in moral and spiritual values, such faith results in gladness and composure of mind, giving rise to insight regarding reality and eventual salvation" (*dukkhūpanisā saddhā*) (SN 12:23/S II 31). However, in the last resort, it is the understanding of the nature of our conditioning that liberates us and makes it possible for us to attain the Unconditioned (*asaṅkhata*).

As we can see, the doctrine of conditioned genesis shows how we are conditioned by the environment, by our heredity (*bija-niyāma*) owing to the fact that our personality is made up of the fusion of the dynamic consciousness coming down from a previous life with what is derived from our parental stock, our psychological past going back to prior lives and the desires and beliefs which motivate our behaviour. Yet, although we are conditioned, we are not determined by these factors since we have an element of initiative (*ārabbha-dhātu*) or freedom from constraint which makes it possible for us within limits to control and direct our future course of *saṃsāric* evolution and make the future different from what it may otherwise be.

14

The Buddhist Ethical Ideal of the Ultimate Good

Moral philosophers use the term "good" in two important senses. There is the sense in which we speak of what is "good as an end" or what is "intrinsically good." There is also the sense in which we speak of what is "good as a means" or what is "instrumentally good." The two senses are interrelated. For what is instrumentally good, or good as a means, is necessary to bring about what is intrinsically good, or good as an end.

When the *Dhammapada* says that "health is the greatest gain" (*ārogyā paramā lābhā*), it is, in a sense, treating the state of health as being what is good as an end. For whatever our gains may be, most people are prepared to lose them, or use them in order to recover their health, if they fall ill. Besides, it is only if we are healthy that we can adapt the means to gain material or even spiritual riches. If health is a desirable end to achieve or is good as an end, then what is instrumental in achieving this state of health is good as a means. Since medicines, even when they are bitter, are often useful as a means to the cure of illnesses, they are deemed to be good as a means, or instrumentally good.

Although some people would regard a state of physical health in the above sense as being good as an end, others may say that good health is only a relative end since the ultimate end or goal that we should seek is happiness, and good health is only a necessary condition for happiness. So while no one would say that bitter medicine is good as an end, many people would regard a state of health as being good as an end only in a relative sense, as contributing to one's wellbeing and happiness. One's wellbeing and happiness would, therefore, be for them an ultimate end in a sense in which even physical health is not. Besides, in the world in which we live, we can enjoy a state of physical health only in a relative sense since we may fall ill from time to time and even healthy men eventually die.

In this chapter we shall be concerned only with what is ultimately good from the Buddhist point of view. Buddhism presents a clear conception of what is ultimately good and what is instrumentally good in order to achieve this. What is instrumentally good to achieve this end is regarded as good as a means. It consists mainly of right actions and the other factors that help in bringing about what is ultimately good.

These right actions may often be called good actions as opposed to evil actions. But we shall avoid the words "good actions" and consistently use the words "right actions" (as opposed to "wrong actions") in speaking about what is primarily necessary in order to achieve what is good as an end.

In the Buddhist texts, the terms that are most often used to denote right actions are *kusala* and *puñña*. *Kusala* means "skilful" and denotes the fact that the performance of right actions requires both theoretical understanding as well as practise. The person who has attained the ideal or the highest good is referred to as a person of "accomplished skill or the highest skill" (*sampannakusalaṃ parama-kusalaṃ*). *Akusala*, its opposite, means the "unskilful." *Puñña* as used of right action means what is "meritorious" as opposed to *pāpa*, which means "demeritorious." It is not a term that is employed to denote the highest good. In fact, the person who has attained the highest good is said to have "cast aside both meritorious and demeritorious actions" (*puñña-pāpa-pahīna*).

As we shall see in examining the nature of right actions, this does not imply that meritorious actions (as opposed to demeritorious ones) are not necessary for the attainment of the highest good, nor that those who have attained are amoral. The path to salvation or the path leading to the highest good in Buddhism is a gradual path, and although we may start with our egoistic or self-centred desires as a motive for self-advancement, they have progressively to be cast aside until eventually the goodness of the actions alone remains without the personal motivation for doing good.

If we acquaint ourselves with the nature of the ethical ideal or the conception of what is intrinsically good or good as an end, we would be in a better position to understand the Buddhist conception of right and wrong.

Moral philosophers have conceived of the ethical ideal in various ways. Some have thought of the ideal as pleasure and others as happiness. Yet others considered the notion of duty or obligation as central to ethics, while others again think of the goal as perfection.

What is the Buddhist conception of the ideal? Buddhism conceives of the ethical ideal as one of happiness, perfection, realisation and freedom. These ethical goals in fact coincide and the highest good is at the same time one of ultimate happiness, moral perfection, final realisation and perfect freedom. This is the goal to be attained in the cosmic or personal dimension of existence.

This is a goal for one and all to attain, each in their own interest as well as that of others. Besides, there is a social ideal which is also desirable to bring into existence. This is broadly conceived of as "the wellbeing or happiness of the multitude of mankind" (*bahujana-hitāya bahujana-sukhāya*). Here "wellbeing and happiness" are conceived of both materially as well as spiritually. The ideal society in which this wellbeing and happiness will prevail in an optimum form is conceived of as both socialistic, being founded on the principle of equality, and democratic, as affording the best opportunities for the exercise of human freedom. Such a society is also just, as it is based on principles of righteousness.

We shall explore the nature of these conceptions in greater detail when examining the social philosophy of Buddhism. We shall also examine in a later chapter the relationship that exists between the social ideal and the personal ideal. Although from an individualistic point of view "the path to the acquisition of wealth is one, while the path to Nibbāna is another" (*aññā hi lābhūpanisā aññā nibbānagāmini*), even the social ideal can be attained, it is said, only by people who are motivated to act in accordance with the ten virtues (*dasa-kusala-kamma*) in a society built on firm economic, political and moral foundations.

What is the role of pleasure and the performance of one's duties in relation to the Buddhist ethical ideal? Let us first take the role of pleasure. Buddhism recognises the importance of the hedonistic principle that man is predominantly motivated to act out of "his desire for happiness and his repulsion for unhappiness" (*sukha-kāmā hi manussā dukkha-paṭikkūlā*). In fact, the central truths of Buddhism, "the four truths concerning unhappiness" (*dukkha-sacca*), are formulated in the manner set forth so as to appeal to man's intrinsic desire for happiness and the desire to escape from or transcend his unhappiness.

Pleasure is classified in the Buddhist texts according to its different grades, and it is stated that "the most refined and most sublime form of pleasure" (*uttaritaraṃ paṇītataraṃ*) is the bliss of Nibbāna. This "experience of the bliss of freedom" (*vimutti-sukha-paṭisaṃvedi*) is so different from the conditioned pleasure and happiness of worldly existence that there is a reluctance on the part of the texts to use the word *vedanā* (feeling) in relation to it, since *vedanā* as represented in the formula of conditionality is always conditioned.

The attitude to pleasure in the Buddhist texts is a realistic one. It does not deny the fact or value of pleasure. The limited good (*assāda*) as well as the evil consequences (*ādīnava*) of even the gross forms of pleasure are recognised. The Buddha did not advocate a form of asceticism whereby we should shun all pleasures by closing our eyes and ears (and becoming like the blind and the deaf) to objects that arouse sensuous pleasure. Instead the Buddha wanted those who were addicted to such pleasures to realise their limitations.

One form of pleasure that we experience is by the gratification of our desires. We get satisfaction from time to time by gratifying our desire for sensuous pleasures and sex (*kāma-taṇhā*). We get such temporary satisfaction, again by gratifying our egoistic instincts (*bhava-taṇhā*) such as the desire for self-preservation (*jīvitu-kāma*), for security, for possessions, for fame, for personal immortality, etc. We also get satisfaction by gratifying our desire for destruction (*vibhava-taṇhā*) or aggression (*paṭigha*) or the elimination of what we dislike. The enjoyment of these pleasures is often accompanied by rationalisations or erroneous beliefs, such as, for instance, that we have been created for such a life of enjoyment of this sort or that we should eat, drink and be merry today for tomorrow we die.

What is important is not to shun pleasure or torment the body, but to realise for oneself the limitations of pleasures and the diminishing returns they afford, so that eventually we can transcend them by a life of temperance and restraint and enjoy the immaterial or spiritual forms of pleasure (*nirāmisa-sukha*), which accompany selfless and compassionate activity based on understanding. One must give up the gross forms of pleasure for the more refined and superior kinds of happiness. As the *Dhammapada* states, "If by renouncing a little pleasure we can find a great deal of happiness, then the prudent man should relinquish such trifling pleasures on discovering an abundant happiness" (*mattā sukha-pariccāgā passe ce vipulaṃ sukhaṃ, caje mattā sukhaṃ dhīro samphassaṃ vipulaṃ sukhaṃ*) (Dhp 290).

This is only an extension of the hedonistic principle that man has a tendency to seek pleasure and to recoil from pain and, therefore, that he ought to do what is both rational and possible by giving up the gross forms of pleasure for the more sublime forms until he eventually attains the supreme bliss of Nibbāna.

These more sublime forms of pleasure are correlated with forms of activity which are spiritually elevating and socially desirable. It is not always necessary that one should literally renounce the worldly life in order to cultivate them. Both laymen and monks can attain the first stage of spiritual progress (*sotāpanna*) as well as some of the later stages as well. A person who can perform the duties associated with his livelihood, provided it is a right mode of living (*sammā ājīva*), with a sense of selfless service to his fellow men out of concern, compassion and understanding can act without a narrowly selfish motivation and derive happiness from his work. The Buddha compared the spiritual gains to be had from the lay life and the life of the monk to agriculture and trade. Agriculture gives slow but steady returns, while trade gives quicker returns, though it is more risky. According to the Buddha, nothing could be worse than the outward renunciation of the lay life in order to live a life of corruption and hypocrisy as a recluse. Such a person, apart from the disservice he would be doing to the community, would be digging his own grave.

However, the ignorance that clouds the judgement of man is such that a man who enjoys the grosser forms of pleasure cannot experience anything "more refined or more sublime," since he is addicted to the grosser forms. So what often happens is that he experiences less and less of both pleasure and happiness because of his reluctance to go against the current (*paṭisotagāmī*) until eventually he becomes a slave to his passions, losing both his freedom and happiness as well as every other quality which can bring him closer to the ethical ideal.

While Buddhist ethics recognises, and appeals to, the hedonistic tendencies of man, it does not fall into the error of hedonism by asserting that pleasure alone, abstracted from everything else, is what is worth achieving. The hedonistic ideal of supreme happiness, for example, is also identical with the therapeutic goal of perfect mental health.

So the path to happiness is also the path to mental stability, serenity, awareness, integration and purity of mind. The Buddha classified diseases as bodily (*kāyika*) and mental (*cetasika*) and it is said that, while we have bodily diseases from time to time, mental illness is almost continual until arahatship is attained so that only the saint or a person with a Nibbānic mind can be said to have a perfectly healthy mind.

While the Four Noble Truths, as we have pointed out, on the one hand, indicate the path from unhappiness to perfect happiness, they have also the form of a medical diagnosis. From this point of view, the truths give an account of (1) the nature of the illness, its history and prognosis; (2) the causes of the illness; (3) the nature of the state of health that we ought to achieve; and (4) the remedial measures to be taken in order to achieve this. This diseased state of the mind is due to the unsatisfied desires and the conflicts caused by the desires that rage within our minds both at the conscious and unconscious levels. Thus, the desire for sense pleasures and selfish pursuits is found as a subliminal or latent tendency as well (*rāgānusaya*; cp. *kāmarāga, bhavarāga*). So is our hatred or aggression (*paṭighānusaya*). Mental serenity, stability and sanity can be achieved neither by free indulgence in our desires (*kāmasukhallikānuyoga*) nor by ascetic repression and self-torment (*attakilamathanuyoga*). When we become more aware of the way these desires operate in us by the exercise or practise of awareness (*satipaṭṭhāna*), we gradually attain a level of consciousness in which there is a greater degree of serenity and stability. The culmination of this development, when the mind is purged of all its defilements, is the perfect state of mental health which coincides with the experience of the highest bliss.

Buddhism points to the sources of unhappiness, or the causes of suffering, not to make us unhappy or brood over our lot, but in order that we may emerge from our condition with stronger, happier and healthier minds. Such people could say in the words of the *Dhammapada*:

> "So happily we live, free from anger among those who are angry,
> So happily we live in good health amongst the ailing,"
> So happily we live relaxed among those who are tense."
>
> *Susukhaṃ vata jīvāma verinesu averino,*
> *Susukhaṃ vata jīvāma āturesu anāturā,*
> *Susukhaṃ vata jīvāma ussukesu anussukā.* (Dhp 197–199)

The person who has attained the ideal is said to have fulfilled all his obligations (*kata-karaṇīya*) since the greatest obligation of everyone, whatever else he may do, is the attainment of the goal of Nibbāna. But, till he does this, man has all his social duties to perform towards the various classes of people in society. The duties and obligations of parents and children, employers and employees, husbands and wives, religious men and their followers etc. are given in the *Sigālovāda Sutta*, while duties and rights of a king or state and its citizens are recorded in the *Aggañña* and *Cakkavattisīhanāda Suttas.* Even such duties and obligations are to be performed in a spirit of selfless service, love and understanding, so that we are treading the path to Nibbāna in the exercise of these obligations.

So while the ultimate end is one of perfect happiness and mental health, it is not one in which one is obliged to perform one's duties for duty's sake. Likewise, when the Arahant serves society, as the several enlightened monks and nuns mentioned in the Thera- and Therīgāthā did, they did so out of a spontaneous spirit of selflessness, compassion and understanding.

It is, therefore, a mistaken notion to hold, as some scholars have held, that the Arahant is amoral and could even do evil with impunity. It is true that an Arahant casts aside both meritorious and demeritorious actions (*puñña-pāpa-pahīna*). By this is meant only that he does not do any acts whether they are good or evil with the expectation of reward nor do these acts have any efficacy for bringing about karmic consequences in the future. They are mere acts (*kiriya-matta*) of goodness, which flow spontaneously from a transcendent mind, which shines with its natural lustre with the elimination of craving, hatred and delusion and is wholly filled with selflessness (*cāga*), loving-kindness (*mettā*) and wisdom (*paññā*).

The following passage illustrates the process and nature of this attainment:

> In whatever monk who was covetous, covetousness is got rid of …, wrath, grudging, hypocrisy, spite, jealousy, stinginess, treachery, craftiness, … who was of evil desires, evil desires is got rid of, who was of wrong view, wrong view is got rid of…. He beholds himself purified of all these unskilled states and sees himself freed (*vimuttaṃ attānaṃ samanupassati*)…. When he beholds himself freed, delight is born; rapture is born from

> delight; when he is in rapture, the body is tranquil; when the body is tranquil, he experiences joy; being joyful the mind is concentrated. He dwells suffusing one direction with a mind of loving-kindness (*mettāsahagatena cetasā*), likewise the second, third and fourth; just so, above, below, across; he dwells having suffused the whole world everywhere, in every way with a mind of friendliness that is far-reaching, widespread, immeasurable, without enmity, without malevolence. He abides with a mind full of pity (*karuṇā*) ..., sympathetic joy (*mudita*) ..., equanimity (*upekkhā*) ..., without enmity, without malevolence. It is as if there were a lovely lotus pond with clear water, sweet water, cool water, limpid, with beautiful banks; and a man were to come along from the east, west, north or south, overcome and overpowered by the heat, exhausted, parched and thirsty. On coming to that lotus pond, he might quench his thirst with water and quench his feverish heat. Even so ... one who has come into this Dhamma and discipline taught by the Buddha, having thus developed loving-kindness, pity, sympathetic joy and equanimity attains inward calm (MN 40.7–13/M I 283–84).

We find it expressly stated of the saint that he is a "person of accomplished skill (*sampanna-kusala*), of the highest skill (*parama-kusala*), who has attained the highest attainment, an invincible recluse," who is endowed with "right aspirations (*sammā-saṅkappa*) such as compassion (*avihiṃsā-vitakka*), which do not require to be further disciplined (*asekha*)." The Arahant's state is, therefore, one of moral perfection, though it is not one of "conditioned morality, but natural or spontaneous morality"; he is said to be "naturally virtuous and not virtuous through conditioning" (*sīlavā hoti no ca sīlamayo*).

This state of bliss or ultimate happiness, perfect mental health and moral perfection is also described as a state of supreme freedom (*vimutta*) and realisation (*sambodhi, paññā*). The mind is master of itself (*vasī*) and one has supreme control over it. The inflowing impulses (*āsavā*) do not disturb it.

The criticism has been made that the quest for Nibbāna is a form of escapism. But this criticism is without basis since the person who attains Nibbāna does so with full understanding of the nature of the world as well as of himself. If he ceases to be henceforth attracted by the pleasures of the world, it is because he can assess their worth and their limitations. The real escapists are the people who cannot, in fact, face reality as a whole and try to drown their fears, anxieties and sorrows by indulging in their passions. They are easily upset by their circumstances and find consolation in some form of neurosis. But the person who has a Nibbānic mind, or is anywhere near it, is "unruffled by the ups and downs of the world, is happy, unstained and secure" (*phuṭṭhassa lokadhammehi cittaṃ yassa na kampati asokaṃ virajaṃ khemaṃ*).

In such a state one has no fear or anxiety (*abhaya*) at all. The highest good or the ethical ideal for each person is, therefore, conceived of as a state of bliss, mental health, perfection, freedom and realisation. It is a state that is stable (*dhuva*) and ineffable (*amosadhamma*) as well.

15

The Basis of Buddhist Ethics

Ethics has to do with human conduct and is concerned with questions regarding what is good and evil, what is right and wrong, what is justice and what are our duties, obligations and rights.

Modern ethical philosophers belonging to the analytic school of philosophy consider it their task merely to analyse and clarify the nature of ethical concepts or theories. For them, ethics constitutes a purely theoretical study of moral phenomena. They do not consider it their province to lay down codes of conduct, which they deem to be the function of a moral teacher, a religious leader or a prophet.

However, there are some philosophers, even in the modern world, as, for example, some of the existentialists, who consider it the duty of the philosopher to recommend ways of life or modes of conduct which they consider desirable for the purpose of achieving some end which they regard as valuable. Kierkegaard, for instance, considers that there are three stages of life, namely the aesthetical or sensualist, the ethical and the religious. He indirectly recommends in his philosophy that we pass from one stage to another. The aesthetical or sensualist way of life, according to him, leads to boredom, melancholy and despair, so it needs to be transfigured in the ethical stage, and so on.

In the philosophy of the Buddha, we have an analytical study of ethical concepts and theories as well as positive recommendations to lead a way of life regarded as "the only way" (*ekāyana magga; eso'va maggo natth' añño dassanassa visuddhiyā*), (Dhp 274) for the attainment of the *summum bonum* or the highest good, which is one of supreme bliss, moral perfection as well as of ultimate knowledge or realisation. This way of life is considered both possible and desirable because man and the universe are just what they are. It is, therefore, justified in the light of a realistic account of the nature of the universe and of man's place in it.

While this way of life in its personal or cosmic dimension, as it were, helps us to attain the highest good, if not in this very life, at least in some subsequent life, it also has a social dimension insofar as it helps the achievement of the wellbeing and happiness of the multitude or of mankind as a whole (*bahujana-hita, bahujana-sukha*). The wellbeing and happiness of mankind is another end considered to be of supreme, though relative, value in the Buddhist texts and this wellbeing and happiness are conceived of as both material and spiritual welfare.

Buddhist ethics, therefore, has a close connection with a social philosophy as well. This social philosophy is also fully developed. We have, in the Buddhist texts an account of the nature and origin of society and the causes of social change. There is also an account of the nature and functions of government, the form of the ideal social order and how it is likely to be brought about.

In dealing with the ethics and social philosophy of Buddhism, we are trying to give an answer to the question, "What should we do?" In our previous essays, we tried to give answers to the questions, "How do we know?" and "What do we know?" The question, "What should we do?" has a personal as well as a social dimension. In a Buddhist frame of reference, the question, "What should we do?" concerns, on the one hand, what the goal of life should be or is and what we have to do for self-improvement, self-realisation and the attainment of the highest good. On the other hand, the question has a social dimension and concerns what we have to do for the good of society or for the welfare and happiness of mankind. The questions, "What should we do for our own good?" and "What should we do for the good of others or society?" are mutually related and what the relationship is, according to Buddhism, we shall examine later on.

At the same time, we must bear in mind that the questions, "What should we do?" "What do we know?" and "How do we know?" are also interrelated. The majority of the essays in this series concerned the question, "What do we know?" The answer to this question constituted the Buddhist account of reality or the nature of man and the universe. It is a legitimate question to raise as to how we do know that reality was so and so. The answer to this was given in the earlier essays concerning the means of knowledge and the nature of truth.

Now, when we ask the question, "What should we do?" the answers we give presuppose a certain account of reality. Let us illustrate this. In one stanza in the *Dhammapada*, the sum and substance of Buddhist ethics is summed up as follows: "Not to do any evil, to cultivate the good and to purify one's mind—this is the teaching of the Buddhas" (Dhp 183). Now, someone may raise the question as to how we can be without doing what is called "evil" and cultivate what is called the "good" unless human beings have the freedom to do so.

If all our present actions, choices and decisions were strictly determined by our psycho-physical constitution,—which is partly hereditary, by our environmental influences, by our psychological past, or by all together—how is it possible for us to refrain from evil or to do good? The very possibility of our refraining from evil and doing good, therefore, depends on the fact that our choices and decisions are not strictly and wholly determined by such factors and in this sense are "free." So ethical statements become significant only if there is human freedom in this sense. But the question as to whether there is human freedom in this sense is a question pertaining to the nature of reality. Is man so constituted that he has the capacity for "free" action in the above sense without his actions being strictly determined by external and internal causes?

If not, these ethical statements cease to be significant. It does not make sense to ask a human being to refrain from evil, if, considering his nature, he is incapable of doing so. If, however, man is "free" in the above sense, it would be significant to ask him to exercise his choice in a certain way, which is what we do when we ask him to refrain from evil and to do good. But whether he is "free" or not in the above sense is not a question concerning ethics but a factual question concerning human nature. The answer belongs to the theory of reality and not ethics. This is an instance as to how ethics is related to the theory of reality. Or, in other words, how the answer to the question, "What should we do?" is related to the answer to the question, "What do we know about man and the universe?"

This question as to whether freedom in the above sense or free will is a fact is not the only one. There could be further questions. Even though one could, to some degree, refrain from evil and cultivate the good, despite all the influences external and internal that one is subject to, one may still ask what use it is for oneself to refrain from evil and do good.

One may maintain that if sporadic acts of evil or good do not change one's nature for the better or make one's lot happier and if death is the end of life, what purpose does it serve to refrain from evil, to do good and to cleanse the mind? Here, again, one of the answers would be that if this activity does not change our nature for the better or make our condition happier and death, in fact, is the end of life, there would not be much purpose in refraining from evil, doing good and cleansing the mind, even if we had the freedom or capacity to do so. So all this would be to some purpose only if such activity changed one's nature for the better and made one's condition happier in the long run, and if death was not, in fact, the end of individuality.

But the question as to whether this was so is a factual question: "Does refraining from evil and doing morally good acts tend to change one's nature for the better and make one's condition happier in the long run in a world in which physical death is not the end of individuality?" It is only if the answer to this question too is in the affirmative that it would seem worthwhile or desirable in a moral sense (as opposed to a merely social sense) of refraining from evil, doing what is good and purifying the mind.

Although it would appear to be worthwhile to do this if the answer is in the affirmative and there is human survival after death, and the refraining from evil, the cultivation of the good and the purification of the mind result in a happier state for the individual, it may still be asked whether there is an end to such a process. Is there a highest good or must the process of refraining from evil and cultivating the good go on forever with progression and regression? Here again, the question as to whether there is an end, which is one of supreme bliss, perfection and realisation of an unconditioned state of ultimate reality, is a purely factual question. It is only if there is such a state that an end to conditioned existence would be possible.

So an ethical statement, which recommends the attainment of a highest good, and lays down a way of life for such attainment, would be significant only if there is such a state which can be considered the highest good for each and all to attain, and if the way of life does, in fact, lead to it. The question as to whether there is such a highest good, and whether the way of life recommended leads to it, is, however, a factual question, which has to be established independently of the ethical recommendations.

It would, therefore, be the case that the ethics of Buddhism would be significant only if certain facts are true, viz.: (1) there is freedom or free will in the sense enunciated; (2) there is human survival or the continuity of individuality; (3) this continuity is such that the avoidance of evil and the cultivation of the good along with the purification of mind tends to make our nature better and our condition happier, while the opposite course of action has the reverse effect; and (4) there is a state, when the mind is pure and cleansed of all defilements—a state of bliss, perfection, realisation and ultimate freedom.

In examining the Buddhist account of reality, we have already shown the truth of (2), (3) and (4). We have shown that there is pre-existence and survival after death, constituting a "continued becoming" (*punabbhava*). We have shown that kamma (in the Buddhist sense) is operative and that morally good, evil and mixed acts make a difference to one's nature and are followed by pleasant, unpleasant and mixed consequences, as the case may be. We have shown that there is "that realm" (*atthi ... tad āyatanaṃ*) (Ud 8.1/p. 80) of Nibbāna beyond space-time and causation, which is the ultimate good that all should attain and without which it would not be possible to transcend conditioned existence.

It remains for us to examine more fully than we have done whether or not the Buddha asserts the reality of freedom or free will in the sense explained. By free will in a Buddhist context, it is not meant that there is a will, choice or decision which is unaffected by causal factors that affect it, but that our volitional acts or will, choice or decision, while being conditioned by such factors, are not wholly shaped or strictly determined by them, since there is in man "an element of initiative" (*ārabbha-dhātu*) or "personal action" (*purisakāra*) or "individual action" (*attakāra*), which can, within limits, resist the factors that affect it. If not for this factor of human personality, moral responsibility would be a farce and the forces that impel us to act would be responsible for our actions.

This is, in fact, what the Buddha says. On the one hand, he distinguishes the Buddhist theory of the "causal genesis" (*paṭicca-samuppāda*) of events from all forms of strict determinism, whether theistic or natural. According to the theistic version of strict determinism, every outcome in the universe is foreknown and predetermined by an omniscient and omnipotent Personal God. In such a situation all our experiences would be "due to the creation by God" (*issara-nimmāna-hetu*). If so, argues the Buddha, God is ultimately responsible for the good and evil that human beings do.

Such theistic determinists lived during the time of the Buddha. We must not forget that they are also found today. Dr Hastings Rashdall was such a theistic determinist. He says in one place in his book: "And after all a doctrine of free will which involves a denial of God's omniscience cannot claim any superiority over such a theistic determinism as I have defended on the score of avoiding a limitation of the divine omnipotence" (*The Theory of Good and Evil*, Vol. II, pp. 343–44 London, 1907). He is led to believe in determinism because of his total distrust of indeterminism at the time when scientists believed in deterministic causation, prior to the discoveries of quantum physics. Dr Rashdall, however, gives this scientific doctrine of his times an idealistic twist and says: "When the theory of determinism is held in connection with a philosophy which finds the ultimate ground and source of all being in a rational will, it is impossible to escape the inference that the will of God ultimately causes everything in the Universe which has a beginning—including therefore souls and their acts, good and bad alike" (ibid., p. 339).

Having taken up this position, he finds the consequences not too palatable and difficult to explain away, for he says: "Yet from the metaphysical or theological point of view we must admit also that the soul is made or caused by God: and one cannot help asking oneself the question why God should make bad souls, and so cause bad acts to be done" (ibid., p. 340).

He also admits the central difficulty of his position, which he tries to explain away unsatisfactorily, viz.: "We have seen then that the only point at which a difficulty is created either for Morality or for Religion by the acceptance of determinism lies in its tendency to make God in a sense the author of evil" (ibid., p. 345). So we see that the logic of theistic determinism is no different from the Buddha's time to the present.

The Buddha also rejects different forms of natural determinism. One such theory was that experiences of the good or evil we do is due to our (hereditary) physiological constitution (*abhijāti-hetu*). Another theory upheld psychic determinism (cp. Freud) and held that all our present acts and experiences are entirely due to our past actions (*pubbekata-hetu*). In addition, there were at the time of the Buddha natural determinists (*sabhāva-vādin*), who held that all events were strictly determined by natural forces. Pūraṇa Kassapa was a determinist (*niyati–vādin*) who held such a theory. As a result of his natural determinism, he was like the 19th century rationalists of Europe, an amoralist who denied that there was good or evil as such, since man was not responsible for his so-called "good" or "evil" acts.

It is important to remember that the Buddhist theory of causation was opposed to all such deterministic theories, both theistic and natural, as also to the theory of total indeterminism (*adhicca-samuppanna*) or Tychism, which denied causal correlations in nature altogether. As such, the Buddhist theory of causation seems to accept an element of indeterminacy in nature, which, in the case of human actions, manifests itself as the free will of the individual, which is conditioned but not totally determined by the factors that affect it.

While the Buddha distinguished his causal theory from determinism, he also faced the question of free will and asserted its reality in no uncertain terms. On one occasion, it is said, a certain brahmin (*aññataro brāhmaṇo*) approached the Buddha and told him that he was of the opinion that there was no free will on the part of himself (*attakāra*) or others (*para-kāra*). The Buddha admonished him and asked him how he could say such a thing when he himself of his own accord (*sayaṃ*) could walk up to the Buddha and walk away from him.

On this occasion, the Buddha says that there is such a thing as "an element of initiative" (*ārabbha-dhātu*) and as a result one can observe beings acting with initiative and this, says the Buddha, is what is called "the free will of people" (*sattānaṃ attakāro*). He also goes on to say that there is "an element of origination" (*nikkama-dhātu*), an "element of endeavour" (*parakkama-dhātu*), an "element of strength" (*thāma-dhātu*), an "element of perseverance" (*ṭhiti-dhātu*) and an "element of volitional effort" (*upakkama-dhātu*), which make beings of their own accord act in various ways and that this showed that there was such a thing as free will (AN 6:38/A III 337f).

We notice on the other hand that Makkhali Gosāla, the theist who held that the world was created by a divine fiat and continued to unfold itself like a ball of thread flung on the ground, held that beings were "devoid of free will" (*natthi attakāro*), "devoid of personal will" (*natthi purisakāro*), "devoid of power, effort, personal strength or personal endeavour" (*natthi balaṃ, viriyaṃ, purisathāma, purisaparakkamo*) (DN 2.19–20/D I 53). Those who denied the possibility and power of moral acts or, in other words, free will and its consequences were known at this time as *akiriya-vādins*. Thus, again, Makkhali Gosāla, the theist, is said to have held the doctrine that "there is no karma, there is no free action and no potentiality of action" (*natthi kammaṃ, natthi kiriyaṃ, natthi viriyaṃ*) (AN 3:135/A I 286). It is well-known, however, that the Buddha was accepted even by his brahmin opponents as a *kiriya-vādin*, a teacher of the efficacy of action.

All this goes to prove that the Buddha faced the problem of free will at the time and reiterated the view that asserted the reality of human freedom or free will without denying at the same time that this free will was conditioned but not wholly shaped or determined by factors which affected it. There are certain things beyond our powers but there are at the same time certain powers which one can exercise within limits. For example, I cannot, even if I tried my utmost, speak a thousand words a minute, but I can certainly vary my speed of utterance within limits merely to show that I have the power to do this. It is this power that we all have within limits for refraining from evil and doing good. The more we exercise this power, the more freedom and spontaneity we acquire.

Many scholars have failed to see that Buddhism upheld a theory of non-deterministic causal conditioning along with the doctrine of free will. As a result, Buddhism has been represented by some Western scholars as a form of fatalism because of their misunderstanding of the doctrine of kamma as well as the doctrine of causation.

This misunderstanding, however, is not limited to Western scholars. A local Sinhala Buddhist scholar, a layman, has represented the Buddhist teaching on this matter as follows in a paper read before a philosophers, conference: "What does Buddhism have to say regarding free will? The question does not seem ever to have been asked of the Buddha, but, if he had been asked, he would probably have answered that the question does not arise or that it is inaccurately put. There can be no such thing as a free will outside the causal sequence which constitutes the world process" (G. P. Malalasekera, "The Status of the Individual in Theravāda Buddhist Philosophy," in *The Status of the Individual in East and West*, ed. C. A. Moore, Honolulu, 1968, p. 73). Another local Buddhist scholar, a monk, says the following: "The question of free will has occupied an important place in Western thought and philosophy. But according to Conditioned Genesis, this question does not and cannot arise in Buddhist philosophy.... Not only is the so-called free will not free, but even the very idea of free will is not free from conditions." (Walpola Rāhula, *What the Buddha Taught*, London, 1959, pp. 54–5).

These three doctrines, namely upholding the reality of free will (*kiriya-vāda*) as opposed to the denial of free will (*akiriya-vāda*) in the sense specified, upholding the reality of survival after death (*atthi paro loko*) as opposed to the denial of survival (*natthi paro loko*) and upholding the reality of moral causation (*hetu-vāda*) as opposed to the denial of moral causation (*ahetu-vāda*), form the basis of Buddhist ethics. They are upheld because they are considered to be verifiably true.

It is these doctrines that make individual moral responsibility meaningful. Without them there is no sense in which we can be said to be morally responsible for our actions although we may be socially responsible. In the *Apaṇṇaka Sutta* (MN 60), where the Buddha addresses rational sceptics, he states that even if one is sceptical about free will, survival and moral causation, it would be pragmatic and rational to act on the basis that they are true rather than their opposites, for in such a case, whatever happens, we do not stand to lose. If we act on the basis that free will, survival and moral causation are true, then if they turn out to be true, we would be happy in the next life and if not true, praised by the wise in this life, whereas if we do not act on this basis, then, if they are true, we would be unhappy in the next life, and if they are not true, we would be condemned by the wise in this life for acting without a sense of moral responsibility.

While the ethics of good and evil (in a moral sense as opposed to what is merely socially good and evil) require the above three postulates, which, according to the Buddhist account of reality, are facts, the ethics of salvation from conditioned existence require the postulate of an Unconditioned Reality, which, according to Buddhism, is also a fact.

Man and the universe being what they are, the ethical and spiritual life (which in a sense is part of it) is both possible and the most desirable in our interests as well as of others.

16

The Buddhist Conception of Evil

We have shown that Buddhism considered the attainment of Nibbāna to be intrinsically good. It was the highest state of wellbeing, characterised by bliss, perfection, realisation and freedom. It was a condition in which our finitude comes to an end for "there was no criterion with which to measure the person who has attained the goal" (*atthaṃgatassa na pamāṇaṃ atthi*) (Sn 1076). It was the most desirable state to attain, and the highest aesthetic experience, although it was to be realised only by shedding our self-centred desires.

In contrast, what falls short of Nibbānic reality is, to that extent, afflicted with the evils of unhappiness or suffering, imperfection, ignorance and the bondage of finite self-centred existence. The degree to which those in conditioned forms of existence are affected by these evils varies with their level of existence and the extent of their moral and spiritual development.

So all sentient beings are subject to evil in its various forms until they attain Nibbāna. The evil they are subject to may be external and physical (natural or man-made), such as floods, accidents, nuclear weapons, etc., or they may be experienced in one's body in the form of illness. They may be psychological, such as the experience of pain or mental anguish. The evil may be moral such as the presence of undesirable traits in us, such as jealousy, hypocrisy, ingratitude, etc. Or the evil that affects and afflicts us may be social and political such as the experience of poverty, injustice, inequality or the lack of freedom.

Hell

Yet, whatever evils we may be subject to in our finite self-centred conditioned existence, there is no form of existence in the universe which is intrinsically evil, according to the Buddhist texts. Nothing could be more intrinsically evil than the sufferings of an everlasting hell, from which there is no escape for eternity, but there is no such place, according to the Buddhist conception of the universe.

In fact, the Buddhist conception of hell was both enlightened and rational. The Buddha denounced some of the superstitious popular beliefs about hell, held by the people at the time. For instance, he says in one place: "When the average ignorant person makes an assertion to the effect that there is a hell (*pātāla*) under the ocean, he is making a statement which is false and without basis. The word 'hell' is a term for painful bodily sensations" (SN 36:4/S IV 206).

This does not mean that we create our heavens and hells only in this life and that there is, in fact, no afterlife, for elsewhere the Buddha speaks of the worlds that he could observe with his clairvoyant vision, in which everything one senses and experiences (including the thoughts that occur to one) are foul, repulsive and ugly (SN 35:135/S IV 126), while other worlds are quite the opposite.

These are the "hells" of the Buddhist texts, apart from the experience of hell in this life itself. We learn from history about the existence of cannibalistic tribes in the past, not to speak of life in the concentration camps set up not so long ago in the centres of twentieth-century civilisation. As such, we need not necessarily look to other planets for the presence of sub-human forms of existence, which are "foul, repulsive and ugly." Yet none of these states is permanent, even though they exist.

Problem of Evil

The Buddha squarely faces the existence of evil in the universe. He sees things "as they are" (*yathābhūtaṃ*) and wants his disciples, too, to look at things in this way through the eyes of a realist. There is no escape into a world of make-believe, no undue pessimism nor facile optimism. The Buddha says: "There are religious teachers, who, because of their state of confusion, do not recognise the difference between night and day, but I would treat night as night and day as day" (MN 4:21/M I 21). Buddhism, therefore, frankly accepts the existence of both good and evil in the world of conditioned existence.

Evil becomes a problem only for a theist, who maintains that the world was created by a perfect being, omniscient, omnipotent, and infinitely good. In such a situation, it would be possible to account for evil by denying the omniscience, omnipotence or goodness of God, but then one would be denying that the world was the creation of a perfect being. So the problem is: *Si Deus bonus, unde malum*? If God is good, whence cometh evil?

In order to account for evil with these presuppositions, some have denied outright the fact of evil. Others have stated that evil is a privation or illusion, or has only a relative existence, while still others have maintained that evil is necessary as a component in the best of all possible worlds, which God necessarily creates. This last solution has, on the whole, been favoured by modern theists, but even this does not satisfactorily account for the suffering of animals, little children and innocent people within the framework of orthodox theistic beliefs.

What is the Buddhist solution to this problem? The problem does not exist in the above form for the Buddhist since he does not start with the theistic presumption that the world was created by a perfect being. Instead, he accepts the fact of evil and argues on its basis that the world with all its imperfections could not be the creation of a perfect being.

The argument is briefly stated as follows: "If God (Brahmā) is lord of the whole world and creator of the multitude of beings, then (1) why has he ordained misfortune in the world without making the whole world happy; or (2) for what purpose has he made a world with injustice, deceit, falsehood and conceit; or (3) the lord of beings is evil in that he has ordained injustice where there could have been justice" (J-a VI 208).

The Buddhist is under no compunction to deny or explain away the fact of evil. If we deny the existence of evil, there would be no reason or even the possibility of getting rid of it. If we justify it, it would still be unnecessary to try and eliminate it. But evil is real for the Buddhist and must be removed as far as possible at all its levels of existence for the good and happiness of mankind, by examining its causal origins.

This does not mean that Buddhism holds that all existence is evil. The Buddha is often represented by Western scholars as having said this or assumed such a stand.

The *Encyclopaedia of Religion and Ethics* says that, "existence ... seemed to the Buddha to be evil" (see article on Good and Evil, Ch. 16). Yet nowhere has the Buddha said that even finite conditioned existence is wholly evil. What he has often said is that such existence has its good side or pleasantness (*assāda*) as well as its evil consequences (*ādinavā*), and considering the possibility of transcending such finite conditioned existence, it was desirable to do so.

Primacy of the Good

Buddhism does not hold that evil predominates in nature. It is possible to take up different positions regarding the presence or primacy of good or evil.

We can say that (1) good predominates over evil, although both exist; or that (2) good alone exists but not evil; or that (3) evil predominates over good, although both exist; or that (4) evil alone exists but not good; or that (5) both good and evil exist with equal strength and vigour (dualism), and there is a perpetual battle in the universe between the forces of good and evil; or that (6) neither good nor evil exist in any strict sense (e.g. relativism, amoralism, illusionism [*māyāvāda*]).

Buddhism seems to favour the first point of view. It accepts the reality of both good and evil and seems to uphold the view that good predominates over evil.

The presence of some forms of evil such as suffering, it is said, has a tendency to awaken us from our lethargic state of existence and induce belief in moral and spiritual values (*dukkhupanisā saddhā*); (SN 12:23/S II 31).

We are attached to the world because of the joys and satisfactions it affords us by way of the gratification of our desires. But because of the disappointments, frustrations, anguish and suffering that we also experience in the process, we seek to understand and transcend our finite conditioned existence.

So some forms of evil such as suffering have a tendency to make us seek the good. But, in general, the problem of evil for the Buddhist is to recognise evil as such, to look for its verifiable causes and, by removing the causes, to eliminate evil as far as possible at all its levels of existence.

To look for the metaphysical causes of evil is deemed to be intellectually stultifying and morally fruitless. If we are struck with an arrow, our immediate task should be to remove it rather than investigate the credentials of the person who shot it. We may be in a better position to do so after we have been healed. The Dhamma, as the Buddha pointed out, is comparable to a raft which has to be thrown aside after we have attained Nibbāna with its help and have acquired a more comprehensive picture of the totality of things. In the meantime, the presence of evil is a challenge to us and our task should be to get rid of it: "One should conquer evil with good" (*asādhuṃ sādhunā jine*).

The baseless charge has been brought against Buddhism, namely that it is pessimistic, but it is a curious fact that it has given a less pessimistic account of both man and nature than some forms of theism. We have already pointed out that there is no conception of an "eternal hell" in nature according to Buddhist teachings. Even in respect of man, he has never been regarded as predominantly evil.

Man is fundamentally good by nature and the evil in him is an extraneous outcome of his saṃsāric conditioning. The mind of man is compared in the Buddhist texts to gold ore, which is said to have the defilements of iron, copper, tin, lead and silver but when these impurities are removed, then the gold shines, with its natural lustre. So does the mind when the evil is got rid of.

The Buddha states that, "the mind is naturally resplendent, though it is corrupted by adventitious defilements" (*pabhassaraṃ idaṃ cittaṃ taṃ ca kho āgantukehi upakkilesehi upakkiliṭṭhaṃ*). Man, therefore, despite the fact that he has committed sin (*pāpa*) and is capable of sinning is not addressed as a sinner but as a meritorious being (e.g. Sinhala, *pinvatā*) because of his potentiality for good.

Even the evil that he commits is not due to his basic depravity or wickedness but to his ignorance. This ignorance can be got rid of and man himself is capable of doing so. Buddhism does not agree with the theist who holds that man in his present condition is so degenerate by nature that he is incapable of saving himself without the grace of an external power. The future of man is in his own hands; he is master of his fate. In denying an eternal hell, in not regarding man as a sinner who is incapable of attaining salvation by his own efforts, Buddhism gives a less pessimistic account of man and nature than is to be found in some forms of theism.

Although in this respect, it upholds the primacy of the good, Buddhism is not an easy-going optimism which ignores the evil in man and nature. A realistic view of nature is partly pessimistic in that one has to take cognizance of the darker side of things as well. Many people, out of fear, do not wish to contemplate the fact that we are all liable to suffer from decay, disease and death. The Buddha, on the contrary, holds (like Socrates and Plato) that the contemplation of death (*maraṇānussati*) is of therapeutic value in making for mental stability and peace. To this extent, Buddhism recommends a partly pessimistic outlook (e.g. by contemplating the ugliness of the body, *asubhānupassiṃ viharantaṃ*) (Dhp 8) insofar as it is realistic and is a factor necessary to promote and establish one's personal happiness on firm foundations.

Māra

Buddhist realism, therefore, takes stock of all that is evil in man and nature, so that we may understand evil for what it is and overcome it at all its levels of existence insofar as this can be done.

Death (*mṛtyuḥ*) had been personified prior to Buddhism and the *Śathapatha Brāhmaṇa* refers to the legendary figure of "Death, the Evil One" (*mṛtyuḥ pāpmā*). This conception reappears in the Buddhist scriptures as "Māra Pāpimā," i. e. "Death, the Evil One," who signifies all the evil associated with or causally related to the phenomenon of death. Since all conditioned existence is subject to death, Māra is said to hold sway over the entire universe.

The term *māra* is formed of the root *mṛ*, to kill (cf. Latin, *mors*), and means "killer or death." In the scholastic tradition, the term is said to have four meanings. It may signify physical death (*maccu-māra*); it may denote the constituents of one's personality, which are subject to change and, therefore, to "death" in this wider sense (*khandha-māra*); it may mean moral evil or the defilements, which are the cause of repeated birth and death (*kilesa-māra*); or it may refer to the Evil One as a person (*devaputta-māra*), who tempts and obstructs people who seek emancipation from conditioned existence by means of a life of moral and spiritual development.

In this last sense, Māra symbolises all the opposition and obstruction that spiritual seekers have to contend with, whether this be internal (psychological) or external (physical, social). It is difficult to say that there is no such opposition towards those who seek to do good, when we know that outstanding teachers in history who tried to preach or establish a new universal ethic had to face not only opposition but even death at the hands of their own people, which provoked the Shavian remark that "It is dangerous to be too good."

The question is often asked as to whether Buddhism recognises the existence of such an Evil One as a person (such as Satan or the Devil). The forces (*sena*) of Māra as depicted in the Buddhist texts constitute merely the symbolic representation of evil in various forms. For example, the *Mahā Niddesa* speaks of the forces of Māra as consisting of lust (*kāma*), aversion (*arati*), hunger and thirst (*khuppipāsā*), desire (*taṇhā*), sloth and torpor (*thīna-middha*), fear (*bhīru*), doubt regarding moral and spiritual truths and values (*vicikicchā*), hypocrisy (*makkha*), hardness of heart (*thambha*), the gain, praise, respect and fame obtained by false pretences (*lābho siloko sakkāro micchāladdho ca yo yaso*) as well as "boasting about oneself while despising others" (*yo c'attānaṃ samukkaṃse pare ca avajānāti*; (Nidd I 96).

There are, however, situations in the Canon where Māra appears in person and criticises some of the teachings of the Buddha or propounds doctrines which are opposed to them. Does this not prove the personal existence of Māra? Even prior to Buddhism we find that the *Kaṭha Upaniṣad* employed the figure of Death or *Mṛtyuḥ* to impart an Ātman-doctrine. The entire teaching of the *Kaṭha Upaniṣad* is said to have been "declared by Death" (*mṛtyu-proktāṃ*;) (Kaṭha, 6.18), who does not appear in a derogatory role, probably because the functions of death, control and creation are in the hands of the Supreme Being. It would, therefore, not be surprising if the legendary figure of Māra is utilised as a literary device by the compilers of the Canon to indicate the Buddha's comments and criticisms of doctrines, belief in which was likely to prolong one's conditioned existence. On the other hand, we cannot rule out the possibility of higher intelligences in the cosmos who believe profoundly in and like to propagate some of the views attributed to Māra.

However, it is quite evident that the figure of Māra is often introduced in the Canon for purely didactic purposes and no personal manifestation of evil is meant. In the *Nivāpa Sutta* (MN 25.2–11/M I 151–59) it is said that a sower sows crops for the deer to come and eat. The first herd eats indulgently and fall an easy prey to the sower. The second herd, observing this, avoids the crops and repair to the forest close by but, weakened by hunger, is forced to come and eat the crops and do so with avidity and thereby falls a prey to the sower. The third herd, observing what happened to the first two, partakes of the crops without being infatuated and repair to a lair close by, which, however, is easily discovered by the sower, who is able to catch them. The fourth herd, observing the mistakes committed by the first three, repairs to a lair to which the sower has no access and thereby escape.

Here, the sower is said to be Māra, the Evil One, and the crops constitute indulgence in the pleasures of the senses. The four herds constitute four types of religious sects. The first finds nothing wrong in free indulgence in the pleasures of sense and becomes easy victims of Māra. The second resorts to asceticism but eventually returns to indulgence, the need for it being heightened by their repressions. The third exercises restraint in the enjoyment of sense-pleasures but their dogmatic beliefs about man and the world keep them within the realm and dominance of Māra. It is only the fourth who follow a Buddhist way of life who are successful in going beyond the clutches of Māra. There is nothing to suggest that Māra, in actual fact, operates as a personal entity here. The parable of the crops merely shows that ultimate salvation cannot be found within the realm of conditioned existence.

Destruction of Evil

The passage quoted from the *Niddesa* above, where various evils were figuratively referred to as "the forces of Māra," ends by saying that "It is only by conquering the forces of Māra that one attains happiness" (*jetvā ca labhate sukhaṃ*). The Buddha and the Arahants, it is said, have conquered Māra and, therefore, can recognise him and do not fall a victim to his wiles. The *Dhammapada* recommends that we "should fight Māra with the weapon of wisdom" (*yodhetha māram paññāvudhena*) (Dhp 40).

So the Buddhist attitude to evil is not to deny its presence or try to reconcile its existence with the creation of the world by a good God, but to observe its presence and, by studying its nature and causes, to eliminate it.

As far as one's personal evolution is concerned, one must develop the awareness and "the will to prevent the arising of evil states of mind not arisen, the will to eliminate evil states of mind which have arisen, the will to make arise good states of mind which have not arisen and the will to preserve, develop, refine and perfect good states of mind which have arisen" (SN 51:13/S V 268).

It is the same with social and political forms of evil. According to the Buddhist social contract theory of government, the people are ultimately responsible for the good government of the country. If the country is not properly governed, it is up to the people to ensure such a government in order to promote the material and spiritual welfare of the people by the promotion of the good and the elimination of evil in the body politic.

Buddhist Chants

We have so far dealt with realistic forms of evil. But some of our fears (which are themselves evil) are based on irrational foundations, such as the fear of the unknown. At the time of the Buddha, such fears were allayed by magical and ritualistic means with the help of the chants and incantations of the *Atharva Veda* or the resort to demonological practises. Where the people were not mentally equipped to give up these beliefs and practises, what the Buddha did was to substitute Buddhist chants (*paritta*, safeguard) of a more meaningful character, which developed into the institution of *pirit*.

Instead of chanting in an unintelligible language, the Buddha used the language of the people. In doing so, he used it as a vehicle of instruction as well. For example, the *Maṅgala Sutta* (chanted as *pirit*) is an attempt to answer the question, "What are the auspicious things?" The word *maṅgala* could also be translated as "superstitious observance" and in one place the Buddha, referring to the lay people at the time, says that they were superstitious" (*gihī maṅgalikā*) (Vin II 140). Now the list of "auspicious things or observances" given in the *Maṅgala Sutta*, far from being superstitions, were factors or practises which contributed to the social and personal advancement of people. To take but one stanza, the Buddha says: "A good education (*bāhusaccaṃ*), acquiring a technical skill (*sippaṃ*), a well-cultivated sense of discipline (*vinayo ca susikkhito*) and cultured speech (*subhāsitā ca yā vācā*)—these are the auspicious things" (Sn 261). The practises recommended are of relevance to any civilised society.

So while the people derived a psychological satisfaction and a sense of security by listening to this chant, they also received an education in the Dhamma. Those who listened with rapt attention, appreciated what was said and tried to live in accordance with the teachings would also have the protection of the Dhamma, for it is said that "The Dhamma protects him who lives in accordance with the Dhamma" (*Dhammo have rakkhati Dhammacāriṃ*) (Th 303).

17

The Criteria of Right and Wrong

We normally use the words "right" or "wrong" to denote classes of acts and sometimes the specific acts of human beings. Thus, what we mean when we say that "murder is wrong" is that the class of acts, which are classified as murder, are wrong. But sometimes we may say that his action in the specific situation in which he was placed was right. We do not use these words to denote the acts of animals, though, perhaps, the acts of some animals in rare situations may seem to us to be right or wrong, as the case may be.

Even with regard to human beings, we do not consider all their acts as being right or wrong. When a person eats bread instead of buns for his morning meal, when what he eats makes no difference to him or others, we do not consider this act of his right or wrong. We deem it to be morally neutral along with many of his actions, including reflex actions. Likewise, some of his actions may be partially right and partially wrong and therefore of a mixed character. So a man's actions may be classified as being morally right (*kusala*), morally wrong (*akusala*), morally neutral (*avyākata*) and morally mixed (i.e. both right and wrong, *vokiṇṇa*) in character.

It makes sense to speak of some acts as being right and others as being wrong or mixed in character, only if human beings were free to act within limits in a causally conditioned world. If a man's actions were mere responses to stimuli or merely reflected the hereditary structure or constitution of his body or were strictly determined by his psychological past, then it would not make sense to say that his actions were right or wrong, since they are constrained and not free. So if his actions are deemed to be right or wrong, it is because although his decisions and acts are causally conditioned by circumstances, they are not strictly determined and man has the freedom (*attakāra*) to act within certain limits in the universe in which he lives.

Besides, as we have shown in our previous essay, man and the universe are such that the moral and spiritual life is not only possible but is the most desirable. This is because in addition to the fact of freedom within a context of causal conditioning, there is ethicopsychological causation as well as survival after death. Our decisions, which result in right or wrong acts, make a difference to our nature and future. They have their own personal reactions in this life as well as in lives to come. These three facts, as often emphasised by the Buddha (e. g. *Apaṇṇaka Sutta,* MN 60), namely freedom (*kiriyavāda*), survival (*atthi paro loko*) and moral causation (*hetuvāda*), make moral responsibility a reality and self-development a practical possibility as well as a dire necessity. What we do by way of our mental, verbal and bodily acts makes a difference to our nature and regulates our future development.

This is what is often emphasised in the *Dhammapada*: "By oneself alone is evil done, by oneself alone is evil avoided and by oneself alone is one saved (lit. purified). Salvation and damnation depend on oneself (*paccattaṃ*), no one can save another" (Dhp 165). We are what we are not because of evolutionary necessity, God's grace or accidental happiness but because of what we can make of ourselves by the exercise of our own freedom and effort. So the teaching of the Buddha can help us only if we decide to follow it: "You yourselves must make the effort," says the Buddha; "the Transcendent Ones are only teachers; those who follow the path and meditate are delivered from the bonds of Māra" (Dhp 276).

This moral and spiritual development, as we have shown in one of our previous essays, is not an unending process, for its goal is Nibbāna, the ultimate good or the ethical ideal according to Buddhism, a goal which may be achieved by some in this life itself.

In this essay, we propose to examine the nature and the characteristics of these acts, which are designated "right" or "wrong." What makes right acts right and wrong acts wrong? What is the measure or what are the criteria which enable us to recognise and distinguish right acts from wrong?

We may state at the outset that moral philosophers have expressed a variety of opinions on this subject. Few thinkers are, in fact, in agreement about the nature of right or wrong acts or their analysis.

The objectivists have held that acts are right or wrong, irrespective of the person by whom or the time and place at which they are performed. Among the objectivist theories are metaphysical theories such as those of the theists. They have held either that right actions are right because this is God's will or that God has willed them because they are right or that God's will and what is right coincide. However, the conflicting accounts of God's will in the different theistic scriptures and the fact that some of the alleged divine commands do not appear to be right, apart from the objections from relativism, make this a difficult theory to accept. Other objectivists have put forward naturalistic theories. Some are sociological and hold that right actions are actions which are conducive to the survival of mankind. Still others, such as the utilitarians, assert that right actions are productive of a maximum amount of pleasure for human beings.

Among the objectivists many are intuitionists, who claim that the rightness or wrongness of actions can be directly apprehended by one's intuition like mathematical truths or can be perceived like perceiving the difference between the colours of objects, although the utilitarians or the proponents of evolutionary ethics are empirical in their approach.

In direct opposition to them are the subjectivists or emotivists, who believe that the rightness or wrongness of actions depend on the thoughts and feelings of human beings. Right actions are actions which all or most people like or approve of, whereas wrong actions are disliked or disapproved of.

The relativists take a different stand and put forward the view that the notions of right and wrong have differed in different periods of history and in different societies, though they have a relative objectivity within their frames of reference. The sceptics, on the other hand, claim that we cannot know anything regarding the nature of right and wrong, while logical positivists have dismissed ethical concepts as pseudo-concepts.

A positivist who says that they reject the subjectivist view states his point of view as follows: "The propositions which describe the phenomena of moral experience, and their causes, must be assigned to the science of psychology, or sociology. The exhortations to moral virtue are not propositions at all, but ejaculations or commands which are designed to provoke the reader to action of a certain sort" (A. J. Ayer, *Language, Truth and Logic*, London, 1958, pp. 103–04).

Modern analytic philosophers are evolving a more satisfactory analysis of ethical propositions, although this is by no means perfect as yet.

What is the position of Buddhism regarding ethical propositions and the notions of right and wrong? Is the Buddhist account objective, subjective, relativist, sceptical, positivist or something totally different? Only a careful study of the analysis of right and wrong in the scriptures can reveal the Buddhist point of view, which appears to be different from all of the above theories, although it may be compared with some of them in certain respects.

We have already stated that it is a necessary condition of right actions (or wrong actions) that they should be performed within a context of relative freedom, despite the causal conditioning. According to Buddhist conceptions, another necessary condition, which differentiates right actions from wrong ones, is the motive and intentions with which they are done. Suppose a person gets hold of a knife and cuts open another's body. Is this a right action or a wrong action? Some modern Western philosophers, who try to determine the rightness or wrongness of an action by virtue of the observable characteristics of the action itself or its consequences without reference to motive or intention, would find it difficult to answer this question. It is the motive and intention which make a tremendous difference to the nature of the act.

If the intention of the person was to injure or kill the other man and he was motivated by personal animosity, we would regard it as a wrong act (*akusala*). If, however, the intention was to prolong the other person's life by performing a surgical operation and he was motivated by a desire to be of service to a fellow man, then we would regard it as a right action (*kusala*). It is primarily the motive and intention (*cetanā*) which determines whether the act was right or wrong.

According to the Buddha, it is the motive and intention which ought to be a primary consideration in determining the rightness or wrongness of an action. But this is only a necessary condition and not a sufficient condition. Mere good intentions are not enough. The act must be performed as well before we can say whether a right action has been done. Besides, for the action to be a skilful (*kusala*) action, the act itself must be appropriate. Consider the case where a layman, who with the best of intentions gives his friend in an emergency a dose of medicine, which turns out to be poisonous because he gave the wrong dosage. Here he acted with the best of intentions and motives but did not do a totally skilful (*kusala*) act.

So in considering the skilfulness or rightness of an action one has to take into account not only the motive and intention but the nature of the act, the manner in which it was carried out, its consequences, the people it affected, etc. It is good to give but "one should give with discrimination" (*viceyya dānaṃ dātabbaṃ*), so that the most needy are benefited with the things that they most need. The motive and intention are, therefore, only a necessary condition in evaluating the rightness or wrongness of an action but there are other factors as well to be taken into account.

Predominant among these other factors is the tendency on the part of these right actions to bring about the ultimate good of the individual as well as of society. So one of the main criteria of a right action concerns the question as to whether it constitutes the right means towards the realisation of the ultimate good. The ultimate good for each individual is the attainment of Nibbāna, a state of highest happiness, moral perfection, supreme realisation, utter freedom and perfect mental health. The ideal for one is, in fact, the ideal for all.

The question may be raised as to whether the quest for such a goal is not narrowly egoistic. The answer is that it is not so, unless the goal is misconceived. The quest for Nibbāna necessarily implies the practice of other-regarding virtues, such as selflessness (*cāga*) and benevolence (*mettā*). So although the personal quest for Nibbāna may appear to be egoistic, it is a form of enlightened egoism, apart from the fact that the goal itself is permeated with selflessness. On the other hand, mere altruism may not be in the best interest of others. As the Buddha points out: "It is not possible for one who is stuck in the mud to help out another; it is only possible for one who is not stuck in the mud to help out another who is stuck in the mud. It is not possible for a man who has not saved himself to save another; it is only a man who has saved himself who can help save another" (MN 8.16/M I 45). Such unenlightened altruism would be illustrated in the activity of a foolish person with good intentions, who wishes to help his friend without being able to do anything of value. So enlightened altruism necessarily involves self-regarding activity.

The *Dhammapada* therefore firmly says, "One should first establish oneself in what is proper; then only should one instruct others. Such a wise man is not liable to be reproached. As he instructs others, so should he act himself" (Dhp 158–59). What Buddhism recommends, therefore, is the ideal neither of ethical egoism nor of ethical altruism. It may be called the ideal of ethical universalism. As the Buddha says on one occasion: "There are these four persons in the world. What four? He who is bent neither on his own welfare nor on the welfare of others. He who is bent on the welfare of others but not his own. He who is bent on his own welfare but not of others, and he who is bent on the welfare of oneself as well as of others. He who is bent on the welfare of oneself as well as of others is of these four persons the chief and best, topmost, highest and supreme" (AN 4:95/A II 95).

This is why right actions tend to benefit not only oneself, but others as well. When we state the truth, for example, on certain occasions it may not be of immediate benefit to us, though it would benefit the community. It is an action, therefore, which tends to bring about "the good and happiness of the multitude" (*bahujanahitāya bahujanasukhāya*) and indirectly benefits us. No doubt, we directly experience the reward of good conscience even if we derive no immediate material benefit by such an action. So in this sense, speaking the truth serves in the long run one's own welfare as well as that of others.

Viewing the individual and the social goods separately, a right action is, therefore, one which tends to bring about one's own ultimate good as well as contributes to the weal and welfare of society. The ten right actions (*dasa kusala kammā*), which have these characteristics, are stated as follows: (1) "He refrains from killing and abides full of mercy to all beings; (2) he refrains from stealing and is honest and pure of heart; (3) he refrains from sexual misconduct and does not transgress the social mores (*cāritta*) with regard to sex; (4) he refrains from lying and is devoted to truth. On being summoned as a witness before an assembly or a court of law, he claims to know what he knows, he does not claim to know what he does not know, he claims to have seen what he saw and does not claim to have seen what he did not see; he does not utter a conscious lie for the sake of himself, for the sake of others or for some gain; (5) he refrains from slander and holds himself aloof from calumny. What he hears here, he repeats not there in order to cause factions among people. He is a peacemaker, who brings together those who are divided, delights in social harmony and makes statements which promote harmony; (6) he refrains from harsh speech and uses language that is civil and pleasant to hear; (7) he refrains from idle gossip and speaks at the right time in accordance with facts what is meaningful, righteous and in accordance with the law; (8) he refrains from covetousness, does not covet another's property and is generous at heart; (9) he refrains from ill-will and is benevolent; (10) he refrains from holding false views and holds the right philosophy of life, believing in the reality of this world and the next, in moral recompense, moral obligations and values and in religious teachers who have led good lives and have proclaimed by their superior insight the nature of this world and the next" (MN 114.5–9/M III 47–52).

Right actions are, therefore, those which are instrumental in bringing about the ultimate good of one and all. Since happiness is one of the basic characteristics of this ultimate good, right actions are those that tend to promote the happiness of oneself as well as of others. But this happiness is not to be considered in isolation from moral perfection, realisation or knowledge regarding the nature of things, emancipation of mind, perfect mental health, etc.

Another account of right actions from the standpoint of the individual ultimate good as the goal is the Noble Eightfold Path, consisting of right beliefs (*sammā diṭṭhi*), etc. Here again, as the *Mahācattārīsaka Sutta* (MN 117/M III 71ff). points out, right effort (*sammā vāyāma*) is involved in trying to give up false beliefs. In dispelling these wrong beliefs and consciously adopting right beliefs as a basis for action, one is led by right awareness (*sammā sati*). These in turn, namely right beliefs, right effort, and right awareness, help in the cultivation of the other factors of the path. Thus, right beliefs help the cultivation of right aspirations, which in turn promote right speech and right action. Right action makes for a right mode of livelihood. This helps right effort, which in turn furthers right awareness or right mindfulness, which results in right meditation until eventually they culminate in right understanding (*sammā ñāṇa*) and right emancipation (*sammā vimutti*). So we see that right actions are right (*sammā*) in being the efficient means for the realisation of the good.

Wrong actions, on the other hand, constitute those that prevent or obstruct the realisation of the goal on the part of oneself and others (*attavyābādhāya saṃvaṭṭati paravyābādhāya saṃvaṭṭati*).

Although we said that right motives were a necessary condition of right action, we may note that they are included in the Eightfold Path as right aspirations (*sammā saṅkappā*), so that all right actions could be defined as what are instrumental in bringing about the ultimate good.

Since right actions constitute a middle path (*majjhima paṭipadā*) between two extremes, these extremes constitute wrong means for the attainment of the goal. The actions constituting them are, therefore, wrong actions. One wrong means constituting a set of wrong actions consists of causing pain to oneself (*attantapa*) or others (*parantapa*) or both. As the Buddha has shown in the *Kandaraka Sutta* (MN 51/M I 339ff) ascetics who mortify the flesh, hunters, fowlers and robbers who cause pain and suffering to others, kings who practise penance and burden their subjects with the performance of wasteful and cruel sacrifices, all fall into the category of people who do these wrong actions by causing pain to oneself, others or both.

In the other extreme are those who recommend free indulgence in one's desires, saying, for example, that "there is nothing wrong in indulgence in sensual pleasures" (*natthi kāmesu doso*) (MN 45.3/M I 305). Such persons, the Buddha says, enjoy limited pleasures in the present but because of their failure to see that indulgence gives diminishing returns by way of pleasure and results in our becoming slaves to our passions undergo suffering later. The Buddha says in the *Mahādhammasamādāna Sutta* (MN 45.6/M I 308) that those whose desires are strong are likely to achieve happiness in due course by restraining and curbing their desires in the present even at the cost of a little unhappiness. This exercise of restraint by the cultivation of one's emotions and meditative self-analysis is different from the mortification of the flesh. On the other hand, those whose desires are not strong, it is said, can easily achieve stable states of happiness by transforming themselves.

Right actions are right because they are based on a realistic understanding of man and nature, an awareness of the goal of human endeavour and of the correct means to realise it. Their rightness is to be judged by the nature of their motivation as well as the nature of their consequences. These consequences may be psychological or social and experiencable in this life or in future lives.

In my essays on "survival and kamma," I gave instances of the verifiable and verified personal consequences of such actions in future lives. In stating the kammic consequences of some of these wrong actions, the Buddha says that they tend to bring one's status down to sub-human levels of existence in subsequent lives but that if we are born among human beings, then one is likely to experience certain consequences of these wrong actions For instance, a habitual liar is likely to become the object of false accusations (AN 8:40/A IV 247). One who gossips is not likely to be accepted at his word. One who drinks heavily is likely to be born insane. Elsewhere, it is said that these consequences are to be expected in this life itself. The heavy drinker is said to end his days as an alcoholic and an insane person (Sn 398). The *Dhammapada* says: "Speak not harshly to anyone for those thus addressed will in turn retort" (Dhp 133).

If right action is a means to the attainment of an end which is the ultimate good, the question arises as to whether the means must not themselves be good. Buddhism does not seem to hold that ends are means or means are ends or that the means to be adopted to attain a good end must themselves be wholly good. There is a definite goal to be achieved, which is called "the end of unhappiness" (*dukkhass'anta*) or the "supreme state of happiness" (*parama-sukha*).

It may be argued that a good end can only be attained by means wholly good. But the fact is that we are not wholly good (if we were there would be no necessity to attain the end) and not being wholly good and not having a clear conception of the goal we cannot perform actions which are "perfectly right" (*parama-kusala*). Our right actions are, therefore, only approximations to what is perfectly right. It is only gradually that we refine them and doing so acquire clearer conceptions of the goal.

The desire for fame or happiness in this life or the desire to be born in a better state in the next life could provide the initial incentive for betterment. Even if we are developed enough to have our eyes on the goal we must have "the desire to attain the Ineffable" (*chanda-jāto anakkhāte*) (Dhp 218). "Desire is to be given up depending on desire" (*taṇhaṃ nissaya taṇhaṃ pahātabbaṃ*), namely the desire to end our self-centred desires. "Conceit is to be given up depending on the conceited wish (*mānaṃ nissaya mānaṃ pahātabbaṃ*) that I would attain the goal." A minimum of imperfection is, therefore, involved in our initial and sustained efforts to reach the goal. As the Buddha points out in the *Abhayarājakumāra Sutta* (MN 58), if a child has got something stuck in his throat, it may be necessary to cause a minimum of pain in order to get it out. Truth is not always pleasant and it is sometimes necessary to state unpleasant truths or remind ourselves of them in order to arouse others or to emerge from our own state of smug satisfaction.

The question may be raised as to how we may know that right actions are right and wrong actions wrong. One answer is that the Buddha and the Arahants have personally verified the nature of these actions and their consequences and that, in principle, we ourselves are in a position to do so.

Another answer that is often suggested is that our conscience tells us what is right and wrong. Theists hold that conscience is the voice of God, while psychologists and sociologists claim that conscience and guilt feelings are a result of conditioning from our childhood through our parents and the society in which we are brought up. The Buddhist view of conscience is something between the two. The Buddha says in one place that when we state a falsehood knowingly, then "our conscience knows whether what we say is true or false" (*attā te purisa jānāti saccaṃ vā yadi vā musā*) (AN 3:40/A I 149).

The mind, according to Buddhism, has a prior origin to our present human life. It has undergone a lot of *saṃsāric* conditioning and so its guilt feelings and its sense of uneasiness in certain situations are due to this conditioning, which extends beyond this life into the past. Its judgment, therefore, as to the rightness or wrongness of our actions, is not to be ignored, though it cannot always be trusted. Besides, the mind cleansed of its adventitious defilements possesses certain extrasensory intuitive powers, so that "when one's self is tamed it becomes a light to man" (*attā sudanto purisassa joti*).

There is another sense in which the "criterion of oneself" (*attūpamā*) may be employed in determining what is right and wrong. This is done extensively in the *Anumāna Sutta* (MN 15). For example, if a person boasts about himself and declaims others, such a person would be disagreeable and repulsive to me. So if I behaved in this manner, I would likewise be disagreeable and repulsive to others. Such actions, which cause unpleasantness, would be generally disapproved of and be deemed wrong actions.

Sometimes we find the criteria for deciding what are wrong actions stated as follows: (1) my conscience reproaches me if I do it (*attā pi maṃ upavadeyya*); (2) the wise would disapprove of it after examination (*anuvicca viññū garaheyyuṃ*); (3) one would tend to be born in states of downfall as a result of doing it (*parammaraṇā duggati pāṭikaṅkhā*).

Therefore, while motives and consequences are the predominant factors, the dictates of our conscience and the approval and disapproval of the wise may also be taken into account. So in deciding what is right and wrong, we are ruled by our conscience (*attādhipateyya*), by what the world says (*lokādhipateyya*) and by what the Dhamma states (*dhammādhipateyya*).

In the light of these findings, we shall explore the nature of Buddhist ethical theory as a whole in our next essay.

18

The Ethical Theory of Buddhism

Analytic philosophy is the current fashion in the English-speaking world. When this school of philosophy uses the term "ethical theory," it means nothing more than an analysis of moral language as it is found today among English-speaking peoples. Says one scholar: "Fully adequate ethical theory would analyse and systematise the whole variety of linguistic performances and commitments that are embodied in the use of moral language" (G. C. Kerner, *The Revolution in Ethical Theory*, London, 1966, p. 250).

Such an ethical theory obviously would not satisfy people who wish to know whether the nature of man, society and the universe makes a moral life possible for human beings, whether there are ends worth attaining and, if so, the proper means to attain them.

We see an attempt to meet this demand on the part of some existentialist philosophers who speak of "authentic living" as an end worth achieving and sometimes of the means of achieving it.

Marxists outwardly reject ethics. Apart from it being an adjunct of "bourgeois philosophy," the workings of dialectical materialism and economic determinism would make a moral life impossible or meaningless. The socialist state is a product of history and not of voluntary human action.

However, Marxists do make constant allusions and appeals to ethical values in their writings. The classless state is often considered an end worth attaining and as a means to it a proletarian revolution. So the proletarian revolution is also considered a relatively good end worth achieving and what is helpful for this purpose is deemed to be right or instrumentally good. The following paragraph from the Program of the Communist Party of Russia, adopted at the eighth party congress (March 1919), indicates the relevance of certain ethical traits (printed here in italics) in bringing about a certain desirable goal, thought of as a relatively good end: "To bring about the victory of the world-wide proletarian revolution it is essential that there should be absolute and *mutual trust*, the most intimate *brotherly alliance*, and the highest possible cohesion of the revolutionary activities of the working class in the more advanced lands" (N. Bukharin and E. Preobrazhensky, *The ABC of Communism*, Michigan, 1966, p. 377).

Mao Zedong's interpretations of Marxism and Leninism are also often deeply coloured by ethical values, which derive from the altruistic ethics of Mahāyāna Buddhism. Consider, for example, the following passage from the *Little Red Book:* "At no time and in no circumstances should a Communist place his personal interests first; he should subordinate them to the interests of the nation and of the masses. Hence, selfishness, slacking, corruptions, seeking the limelight, and so on, are most contemptible, while selflessness, working with all one's energy, whole-hearted devotion to public duty, and quiet hard work will command respect" (*Quotations from Chairman Mao Zedong*, New York, 1967, pp. 153–54).

Here we may note that "selfishness, slacking, corruption, seeking the limelight" are condemned as vices and some basically Buddhist virtues such as "selflessness, working with all one's energy," etc., are commended as virtues to be cultivated.

Even the theists cannot strictly speak of ethics. The history of a theistic universe (being a creation of God) is foreknown in all its ramifications, since God is held to be omniscient. At the same time, God is also entirely responsible for it, being omnipotent. Besides, if a man happens to be good, it is often claimed to be due to the grace of God. So, considering man's predicament in a theistic world, the performance of ethical actions on his part is strictly an impossibility since everything is due to God's will and real human freedom is incompatible with a theistic determinism.

However, theists, too, inconsistently with their theory, proclaim an ethic. They recommend virtues to be cultivated and condemn vices, which are to be eliminated under threat of divine punishment.

According to Buddhism, the events of history, including human actions, are not due to economic determinism or God's will. Economic factors, no doubt, affect and condition human behaviour; and according to the Buddhist philosophy of society, the economic factor constitutes one of the predominant factors (along with the ideological factor) in bringing about social change. But it is not the only factor. Nor does it strictly determine human behaviour. Hereditary, environmental and psychological factors condition man's actions according to the Buddhist account of conditioned genesis (*paṭicca-samuppāda*), but still, man has within himself an element of initiative (*ārabbha-dhātu*) or free will (*attakāra*), by the exercise of which he can make decisions, which make the future (including his own) different from what it would otherwise be.

This factor of freedom, along with human survival after death, and the correlation between moral acts and consequences (the good acts tending to bring about pleasant consequences and the evil acts unpleasant consequences) make individual moral responsibility a reality.

In fact, without survival and this correspondence between acts and consequences (which is known as *kamma* in a Buddhist context), a religious ethic promoting moral and spiritual development would be impossible. Prof. C. D. Broad states this explicitly in one of his essays on science and religion. He says:

> I will begin by remarking that, in my opinion, it is almost a *sine qua non* of any religious view of the world that some men at least should survive bodily death. I take it that one minimal demand of religion is that what we count to be the highest spiritual values shall not be merely ephemeral by-products of complicated material conditions which are fulfilled only occasionally in odd holes and corners of the universe, and are unstable and transitory when fulfilled. Another minimal demand is that there shall be at least rough justice, e.g. that evil deeds shall, in the long run, bring evil consequences on the doer of them, and not wholly or mainly on others. I do not see how either of these demands could be even approximately met if no man survives the death of his body.... Therefore, if science does make human survival impossible or very improbable, it does, in my opinion, deliver a fatal blow to all religion (*Religion, Philosophy and Psychical Research*, London, 1953, pp. 234–35).

It was also Sigmund Freud's view that ethics would be disregarded if virtue was not rewarded. Since Freud disbelieved in survival he thought that if ethics was to serve any purpose at all, virtue should be rewarded in this life itself. He says in his work, *Civilisation and Its Discontents*: "The variety of ethics that links itself with religion brings in at this point its promises of a better future life. I should imagine that as long as virtue is not rewarded in this life ethics will preach in vain" (London, 1957, p. 140).

As we tried to show in our essay "The Basis of Buddhist Ethics," the factors of freedom, survival, kamma and the ultimate good of Nibbāna make the moral and spiritual life both possible and the most desirable in the world in which we live.

When we, therefore, speak of the ethical theory of Buddhism, we cannot confine ourselves to an analysis of psychological and linguistic problems in ethics. Such analyses are, no doubt, relevant. Early Buddhism itself was known as the "philosophy of analysis" (*vibhajja-vāda*). It has forestalled some of the techniques of modern linguistic analysis and it would be possible to give the Buddhist analysis of the propositions of ethics. But we must not lose sight of the fact that Buddhism gives a positive account of the ends, both social and psychological, worth attaining and of the means of attaining them. We have already considered and given an account of the personal goal of the ultimate good. We shall examine the social goal of the ideal society and the conditions under which it is likely to be realised in our scrutiny of the social and political philosophy of Buddhism in our subsequent essays.

So an account of the ethical theory of Buddhism should indicate the ends to be achieved and the means of achieving them on the basis of the Buddhist theory of the nature and destiny of man in the universe. We have already done this in our previous essays of this series. It must also describe the general nature of this ethical theory. Is it egoistic or altruistic? Is it relativistic or absolutistic? Is it objective or subjective? Is it deotological or teleological? Is it naturalistic or non-naturalistic?

Before we do this, we may mention that the modern tradition of analysis in philosophy started as a reaction against metaphysics and ethical theories, which were closely associated with such metaphysical theories. One such example would be the ethics of self-realisation taught by Prof. F. H. Bradley of Oxford on the basis of his monistic metaphysics.

The Buddhist ethical theory is also based on its theory of reality but this theory of reality is not metaphysical in that it was, in principle, verifiable. It also does not commit the error of Kant, who tried to reconstruct his metaphysics on the basis of practical reason when pure reason failed him. The Buddhist theory, for instance, does not say with Kant that "ought" implies "can," i.e. that human freedom somehow must be a fact because moral propositions are for all practical purposes true and significant. What Buddhism says is that since human freedom is a fact, along with such other facts as survival, kamma and Nibbāna, moral propositions are significant. The ethical theory of Buddhism presupposes its theory of reality. But this theory of reality is independently established in the light of verifiable evidence. So obscure metaphysical presuppositions do not come into the picture, as in the case of the classical ethical theories based on metaphysical theories or assumptions.

We have already examined the question as to whether the Buddhist ethic was egoistic or altruistic. As we pointed out, it was a form of enlightened egoism or enlightened altruism, which could be best characterised as an ethical universalism. Of the four possible types—those who worked for their own good, for the good of others, neither or both—the Buddha held that the person who worked for the good of oneself as well as that of others was the best.

The Mahāyāna text *Sikṣāsamuccaya* also states that we should do good without distinction as to oneself or others: "When fear and pain are abhorrent to me as well as to others, what distinguishes my own self that I protect it and not others" (*yadā mama paresāṃ ca bhayaṃ dukkhaṃ ca na priyam, tadātmanaḥ ko viseso yattaṃ raksāmi netaraṃ*) (Ch. I). However, the texts often state that one should first try to better oneself before working for the general good. The *Dhammapada* states: "One should not, on the whole, hinder one's own welfare at the cost of serving others; perceiving one's own welfare, one should devote oneself to the sake of the general good" (Dhp 166). The reasons for this are that one cannot help others morally and spiritually very much unless one knows the art by one's own experience. Besides, one is likely to be an object of reproach if one does not practise what one preaches. At the same time, moral betterment or promoting one's own welfare is not possible without cultivating other-regarding virtues such as selflessness and compassion. So the egoist must develop altruistic virtues for his own good, while the altruist must cultivate his own good before he can effectively help others.

Is the Buddhist ethical theory relativistic or absolutistic? The answer to this question is given in the *Aggañña Sutta*, where it is pointed out that society undergoes change from time to time and as a result, "what is reckoned immoral at one time (*adhamma-sammataṃ*) may be reckoned to be moral at another time" (DN 27.16/D III 89).

The Buddha also recognised the fact that conventions differed in different countries or under different social systems. This was why he permitted that the minor rules of the Order may be changed to suit the different social and historical contexts.

So moral conventions may differ from time to time or from country to country. As long as the general principles of morality were not violated, these variations in mores do not seriously alter the basic values observed. To this extent, relativism is recognised and not considered as undermining the objectivity of values. But on the other hand, there could be "unrighteous epochs" or "unrighteous social orders" which in varying degrees violate the principles of morality due to ignorance of the true nature and significance of moral values. In this respect, we can speak of better or worse social orders as well as the best. Life in those social orders, which violate the principles of morality, would involve a greater degree of unhappiness according to the degree to which such principles have been violated. So while denying absolutism and recognising relativism, the objectivity of moral values is not denied.

If the objectivity of moral principles and values is recognised, the question may be raised as to the sense in which we may speak of their objectivity. Let us take an example. Buddhism holds, for instance, that drunkenness is an evil since it promotes one's own unhappiness as well as the unhappiness of others in due course. It also has its kammic consequence of making people insane or moronic in their subsequent lives. So a society in which drunkenness prevails is defective in this respect. The unpleasant psychological, social and kammic consequences of drunkenness would be there, irrespective of what the drunkard or his society may think of drunkenness or the habit of drinking. It may be that drunkenness is highly esteemed or approved of in such a society. But such opinions and attitudes would not in the least detract from the fact that drunkenness is objectively an evil. Its unpleasant consequences would be there whatever the people in that society or even the world at large may think or feel about drunkenness. It is in this sense that the consequences—psychologically, socially and kammically—would be there in the case of moral and immoral actions. The values embodied in the moral judgements are objective irrespective of the mental attitudes of people, including the agent.

This is not to deny the subjective element of morality, namely our own attitudes about ethical actions, including the reactions of our conscience. These attitudes and reactions may vary, though on the whole right actions which tend to bring about pleasant consequences to the agent as well as to others in due course are commended or approved of, while wrong actions which tend to bring about unpleasant consequences psychologically and socially are condemned or disapproved of. But there could be situations in which, as in the example about drunkenness cited above, when our commendation or approbation is misguided or mistaken. So while these subjective attitudes regarding morals are prevalent in society and, on the whole, give correct verdicts about the nature of moral values, they cannot always be trusted since the objective consequences determine the objectivity of the moral (or immoral) acts themselves.

We may next ask whether the ethical theory of Buddhism is deontological or teleological? A deontological theory of ethics is one in which the concepts of duty or obligation are of primary importance, while a teleological theory stresses the importance of motives and consequences.

The Buddhist theory appears to be teleological rather then deontological. It determines the nature of right and wrong actions in terms of motives and consequences rather than on the basis of their being done out of a sense of duty, regardless of consequences.

This does not, however, mean that it ignores duties and consequences. The Buddhist ethical theory considers it the fundamental duty of man to strive to attain the ultimate good and a person who has attained it is deemed to have discharged all his obligations (*katakaraṇīyā*).

In the meantime, man in society has various duties to perform towards the various classes of people with whom he is involved. The state, likewise, has certain duties to discharge towards its subjects, who are ultimately responsible for it. But all these duties become duties by virtue of the fact that they are right actions, which promote the "welfare and happiness of the multitude" (*bahujanahitāya bahujanasukhāya*). Yet they, too, should be performed not out of a cold sense of duty but as far as possible out of a desire for selfless service, love, compassion and understanding. This is not to deny that actions done with goodwill and with no expectation of reward are deemed to be better than those performed with the hope of egoistic rewards in this life or the life to come. Ultimately, the perfect person acts out of a spontaneous sense of selflessness, love and understanding and not out of any sense of duty or expectation of earthly reward or divine glory.

So the ethical theory of Buddhism is one of ethical universalism, which recognises the relativity of and the subjective reactions regarding moral values without denying their objectivity to be measured in terms of the motives with which the acts are done as well as their psychological, social and kammic consequences. It is teleological rather then deontological in character.

Lastly, we may briefly examine the Buddhist analysis of ethical propositions. Ethical propositions are of various sorts. Let us take a few standard examples. Take the statements, "Nibbāna is the ultimate good," "Puṇṇa is a good monk" and "It is right to refrain from slander, which causes divisions, and to make statements which promote harmony." According to the Buddhist analysis, such propositions would have two components, a factual component and an emotive-prescriptive component. The factual component would be of primary importance since the validity of ethical propositions would depend on the truth or falsity of the statements comprising this component. The emotive-prescriptive component would only have a secondary significance.

When we say that "Nibbāna is the ultimate good," the factual component consists of a statement of the characteristics (such as supreme happiness, moral perfection, ultimate realisation, utter freedom, etc.), whose co-presence justifies the use of the epithet "the ultimate good" for Nibbāna. It is, in fact, by virtue of the presence of these characteristics that we designate Nibbāna as the ultimate good. It is a factual question as to whether characteristics are present or not. We cannot observe or verify the presence of "the ultimate good" apart from these characteristics.

The Buddhist, therefore, cannot agree with the Moorean analysis that "good" is a unique unanalysable, non-natural quality. Hence the Buddhist ethical theory is not non-naturalistic. It is the same with the analysis of "good" in "Puṇṇa is a good monk." It is the presence of certain observable and verifiable traits and qualities in Puṇṇa which entitles us to describe him as "good" and not the presence of a unique natural quality which we can intuit.

However, stating the factual component does not exhaust the meaning of the word "good." There is an emotive-prescriptive component as well in the analysis of good. When I say that "Nibbāna is the ultimate good" or that "Puṇṇa is a good monk," I do not merely refer to the characteristics. I also show my appreciation and approval of them and try to evoke a similar attitude in others. It is this which makes the meaning of "good" not purely descriptive but emotive and prescriptive as well.

If we take the other statement, we would have to make a similar analysis in terms of factual as well as emotive-prescriptive components. Accordingly, the factual component of the other proposition is that "the class of actions which consist of refraining from slander, which causes divisions, and of making statements which promote harmony" (performed, no doubt, with a good motive) result in pleasant psychological, social and kammic consequences. Whether this is so or not is a factual question. The emotive-prescriptive component consists of the fact that in calling such a pattern of behaviour a right action, I am, in addition to making certain factual claims, approving such an action and recommending the approval of such an action on the part of others. But the significance of this emotive-prescriptive component is dependent on the truth of the factual component.

It follows from the above that the Buddhist ethical theory gives a naturalistic analysis of ethical propositions while asserting that such an analysis does not fully exhaust the meaning of ethical propositions, since they contain emotive-prescriptive components as well.

19

Some Aspects of the *Bhagavad Gīta* and Buddhist Ethics

Comparing the ethical teachings of the *Bhagavad-Gīta* (hereafter *Gīta*) with Buddhism, Radhakrishnan in his *Indian Philosophy* (pp. 526–27) makes the following observations: "Both protest against the absolute authority of the *Vedas* and attempt to relax the rigours of caste by basing it on a less untenable foundation. Both are manifestations of the same spiritual upheaval which shook the ritualistic religion, though the *Gīta* was the more conservative, and therefore a less thorough-going protest. ... In the descriptions of the ideal man the *Gīta* and Buddhism agree. As a philosophy and religion the *Gīta* is more complete than Buddhism, which emphasises overmuch the negative side. The *Gīta* adopts the ethical principles of Buddhism while it, by implication, condemns the negative metaphysics of Buddhism as the root of all unbelief and error."

The impression that this passage leaves in the mind of the reader is that the *Gīta*, though less critical of the Vedic tradition than Buddhism, nevertheless adopts, on the whole, the ethical principles of Buddhism and gives them a less extremist interpretation on the background of a more satisfying positive metaphysics. Now, whatever the difference of opinions that scholars have about the origin of the *Gīta*, they seem generally to agree that the work in its present form is eclectic in character and contains in it many strands of Hindu thought somewhat loosely knit together. As such it is not surprising that the *jñānamārga* (way of intuitive knowledge) of the *Upaniṣads* should be well represented. Now, it is from these passages that Radhakrishnan quotes (i.e. II.55–72; IV.16–25; V.18–28; XII.13–16) in support of his statement that "in the descriptions of the ideal man the *Gīta* and Buddhism agree." But this agreement in the content of these passages which idealise the *muni* or the "contemplative seer" (II.56; V.28; XII.19) is understandable, for there is much in common between the way of salvation in Buddhism and the *jñānamārga* of the *Upaniṣads*, and to this extent, the ideal man and the ideal life pictured in each is very much similar.

It may also be granted that the *Gīta* references to this life have a more Buddhist tone than the *Upaniṣads* in that phrases and concepts more typically Buddhist than Hindu such as *rāga-dveṣa* (II.64), *maitri* (XII.13), *kāruṇya* (XII.13) and *Nirvāṇa* (II.72) occur among them, betraying possible Buddhist influence on the *Gīta.*

But surely the Buddhist ideal is at variance with the *jñānamārga* of the *Upaniṣads*, if we go by the main trend of its thought and its special emphases, which show a persistent and distinct preference for the Personal conception of God as against the Impersonal, for devotion (*bhakti*) as against abstract meditation on the impersonal Absolute, and for the path of disinterested action based on moral imperatives (*karmayoga* and *svadharma*) as against the way of contemplative knowledge (*jñānamārga*). It is true that in this respect the *Gīta* contradicts itself or at least provides only a very loose synthesis of doctrines apparently mutually inconsistent. For instance, although it is essential and generally maintained that the worship of the Personal Lord is better than meditation on the Impersonal Being (XII.I.2), which is unmanifested (*avyaktaṃ*), yet it is expressly mentioned earlier that "men of no understanding think of Me, the Unmanifest (*avyaktaṃ*) as having manifestation (*vyaktiṃ āpannaṃ*) not knowing my higher nature" (VII.24).

These two conceptions of God show up the inconsistency of the *Gīta* teaching. On the one hand we are told that the highest intuition of God reveals his Being as Impersonal, and without this intuition salvation is not possible. On the other hand it is said that worship of God as Personal (which necessarily entails an erroneous conception of the divine being according to the former view) is the easier, the more proper and the natural path to salvation, thus implying that entertaining an erroneous conception is not only no bar to salvation but is in fact the better path to it.

The same inconsistency is manifest where the life of the *muni* or sage, who on attaining perfection is in no need of work that needs to be done (III.17), is represented, on the one hand, to be the ideal while the life of disinterested action is more often held up as the superior (V.2; VI.2), though both guarantee salvation (V.5).

Yet notwithstanding this divergence of doctrines in the *Gīta* we should not overlook the fact that the ideal man as portrayed in the main teaching of the *Gīta* is far removed from the *Upaniṣadic* ideal of the contemplative seer even though an *Upaniṣad* like the *Īśā* is almost an epitome of the religious philosophy of the *Gīta* while the contemplative seer finds a place, though not an important place, in the total background of *Gīta* teaching. The Gīta ideal is the man of action, who performs his social duties purely out of a sense of obligation and devotion to God.

In the circumstances it would be unfair both by the *Gīta* as well as by Buddhism to say that "in the descriptions of the ideal man the Gīta and Buddhism agree" merely on the ground of the similarity between the Buddhist sage and the contemplative seer of the *Upaniṣads* for whom the *Gīta* finds a not too important place in the scheme of things. If therefore we study the *Gīta* ideal in relation to the Buddhist, it is at the level of social ethics that we have to make the comparison, no doubt on the general background of the metaphysics of each.

Now, it would seem from the statements of Radhakrishnan (e.g. the passage quoted above) that even at the level of social ethics there is a similarity rather than a disparity in the ethical attitudes and outlook of the *Gīta* and Buddhism. I propose to show that this is by no means the case and that in this respect the ethics of the *Gīta* is to be contrasted rather than compared with the ethics of Buddhism. For this purpose I would like to show that there is a significant radical disparity between the attitude of the *Gīta* and that of Buddhism at least on the problem of war and the belief in caste.

But before we go into the details of these problems it is necessary to point out that the fundamental difference between the metaphysical background of the ethical doctrines of the *Gīta* and of Buddhism is not that the metaphysics of the *Gīta* is positive and that of Buddhism is negative, as Radhakrishnan has tried to point out, but that the *Gīta* metaphysics throughout maintains a deterministic view of the universe and of all events in it, while Buddhism on the contrary vehemently upholds free will though granting the causal relatedness of events. This seems to be the essential difference between the metaphysical standpoints of the *Gīta* and Buddhism touching ethics.

It would seem that one of the fundamental prerequisites of ethical action is that man should be free to choose between alternative courses of action open to him and should be solely responsible for the decisions he makes. If this is not granted moral injunctions would appear to lose their point. No one would deny that the *Gīta* contains moral advice, but this advice, it should be noted, is given in a context in which it seems on the whole to be taken for granted that the actions of men are strictly determined by nature (*prakṛti*), which is controlled by the fiat of God. Nothing is more striking than the advice that Arjuna, who has been seeking an answer to the moral question as to whether he should fight or not, gets in the last chapter, where he is told that he has no choice in the matter, for "If indulging in self-conceit you think, I will not fight,' vain is this your resolve. Nature will compel you (*prakṛtis tvāṃ niyokṣyati,* XVIII.59)" notwithstanding the statement that "he may ponder over it fully and do as he chooses" (XVIII.63).

This deterministic role or compelling power of *prakṛti* or Nature over which the individual has no control is one of the basic themes of the *Gīta* and reference is often made to it. Thus in making a case for the necessity for action (*karma*) one of the arguments employed is that for individuals action is inevitable "for no one can remain even for a moment without doing work; everyone is made to act (*karma kāryate*) helplessly (*avaśāḥ*) by the impulses born of Nature" (*prakṛtijaiḥ*) (XVIII.5). It would appear that individuals cannot help but act and that their actions are the mere working out of impulses generated by Nature (*prakṛti*) over which they have no control whatsoever—a fact which is clearly indicated by the term "*avaśāḥ,*" which implies that the individual "has no power of mind" to offset the force of the impulses which dominate his actions. Later in the same chapter it is argued that this dominant power of nature under whose yoke man can but only humbly submit afflicts even the man of knowledge for "even the man of knowledge (*jñānavān*) acts in accordance with his own nature (*prakṛti*). Beings follow their Nature (*prakṛtiṃ yānti bhūtāni*). What can repression accomplish?" (III.33). Saṃkara here interprets *prakṛti* to mean "the sum total of the good and evil mental dispositions due to past actions manifest in this life" (*Prakṛti nāma pūrvakṛtadharmādisaṃskāro vartamānajanmādāva-bhivyaktaḥ*). Radhakrishnan however explains that this verse seems to suggest the omnipotence of nature over the soul and requires us to act according to our nature, the law of our being, and adds that "it does not follow that we should indulge in every impulse. It is a call to find out our true being and give expression to it" (*The Bhagavadgīta*, London, 1948, p. 146). Yet if we take this verse for what it states in the context of the traditional comment of Saṃkara it is clear that *prakṛti* here does not mean "our true being" as opposed to our false nature, but our being as composed of all the modes which have potencies for both good and evil; and what the verse implies is not that we should not indulge in every impulse but that we cannot help but give vent to our impulses which we are unable to suppress, in that we are under the domination of *prakṛti*.

The relation of this *prakṛti* with the Supreme Being appears to be differently conceived in different contexts. On the one hand the omnipotence of the Supreme Being requires that he should be the ultimate cause and ground for the operations of *prakṛti*. On the other hand since the Supreme Being is transcendent though immanent in every individual it was necessary that his being should be conceived apart from the operations of *prakṛti*. We thus find it stated in one place that the Supreme Being sends forth the multitude of beings fixing the *prakṛti* of each: "I send forth again and again this multitude of beings who are helpless (*avaśaṃ*) under the power of *prakṛti* (*prakṛter vaśāt*) having fixed the *prakṛti* of each (*prakṛtiṃ svām avaṣṭabhya*).[4] But in another context, *svabhāva* or inherent nature, which is the same as *prakṛti* in connotation (see below), is said to operate independently of the Supreme Being: "The Lord does not create for the world agency or acts; nor does he connect acts with their consequences. It is inherent nature which works these out" (V.14).

Here the word *svabhāva* is used in a context in which *prakṛti* would have fitted equally well. *Svabhāva* or "intrinsic nature" is here regarded as the ultimate agent or cause of all action as well as what brings about the natural consequences of these, very much in the manner in which *prakṛti* was considered to perform this role in similar contexts (Cp. XVIII.59; III.33). But the use of the word, *svabhāva* is much more significant in this context, where *svabhāva* is said to function independently of the Lord, since the word seems in its origin to have reference to a theory which gave a purely mechanistic or deterministic account of the universe without theistic assumptions.

---

4. IX.8. Rādhakrishnan translates *prakṛtiṃ svām avaṣṭabhya* as "taking hold of nature which is my own." Even this translation would grant the ultimate power over *prakṛti* to God, but to take *svām* as "each one's own" is more consistent with the Sanskrit idiom.

The earliest reference we have is possibly the *Śvetāsvatara Upaniṣad* (I.2), where *svabhāva* along with time (*kāla*), fate (*niyati*), etc. are mentioned as possible alternatives to the theistic explanation of the universe. Again, Jñānavimala, commenting on the *Praśnavyākaraṇa Sūtra* (7), says that "some believe that the universe was produced by *svabhāva* and that everything comes about by *svabhāva* alone." Then in the *Tarkarahasya-dīpikā*, a commentary on the *Ṣaḍdarśana-samuccaya*, we find Guṇaratna quoting from the upholders of the theory of *svabhāva* a stanza which says, "What makes the sharpness of thorns and the varied nature of beasts and birds? All this comes about by *svabhāva*. There is nothing which acts at will. What is the use of effort?" (ed. L. Suali, Calcutta, 1905, p.13). This shows that the term "*svabhāva*" had reference to a theory which maintained that the universe was strictly determined and that all the processes in it were fully explicable in terms of such determinism and as a result denied free will and the value of human effort to alter the course of events.

We cannot be certain whether the author of the *Gīta* was trying to synthesise *svabhāva-vāda* as well into its general metaphysic. It is also difficult to determine the exact relationship between the workings of *prakṛti* or *svabhāva* and the Supreme Being of the *Gīta*, since on a monistic or monotheistic interpretation the *prakṛti* or *svabhāva* would be ultimately dependent on Deity, while on a dualistic Sāṅkhya analysis they would be independent (*prakṛtiṃ puruṣaṃ caiva/ viddhyanādyubhāvapi*) (XIII.19). And the *Gīta* does not seem to support wholeheartedly one interpretation, although the emphasis on a Personal God as the highest reality lends support to the monotheistic rather than the dualistic analysis. But so much seems to be clear, that whatever interpretation we adopt and whatever the import of moral injunctions in the *Gīta*, the *Gīta* metaphysic is thoroughly deterministic and as such is opposed to the doctrine of free will and to the possible value of human effort since human beings are helpless (*avaśāḥ*) in the predicaments in which they are placed.

It is, therefore, to be expected that in the last chapter, after a long-winded argument, Arjuna should be told that nature (*prakṛti*), over which he has no control, "will compel him" to fight. It is also not surprising that one of the arguments employed to urge Arjuna to fight should be that "his enemies are already slain by God before the event" (*mayi'vai' nihatāḥ pūrvam-eva)* (XI.33) or that "he should kill them and not desist since they are already doomed by him" (*mayā hātans tvaṃ jahi mā vyatiṣṭhāḥ*) (XI.34) and that he is not ultimately responsible morally for their death since "he is to be only an occasion (or an instrument) for God's action" (*nimittamātram bhava*) (XI.33). The metaphysical import and ethical significance of this argument has been well expressed in the words of Radhakrishnan himself, where he says that "the writer seems to uphold the doctrine of divine predestination and indicate the utter helplessness and insignificance of the individual and the futility of his will and effort. The decision is made already and Arjuna can do nothing to change it. He is a powerless tool in God's hands. ... Arjuna should feel, Nothing exists save your will. You alone are the doer and I am only the instrument," (*The Bhagavadgīta,* p. 280, 1).

Very much on the same lines is another argument as to why Arjuna should fight, namely that since salvation is predestined and assured for all beings including Arjuna there is no cause for worry and he should carry out his allotted task whatever this may be. "Beings originate in the unmanifest (*avyakta*), in the middle they are manifest and they would be immersed in the unmanifest in the end. So why worry?" (II.28). Attainment of the state of *avyakta* or the unmanifest, which is the highest state of the Absolute (VII.24), is equivalent to salvation, so that what is implied in this verse is that all beings would finally attain salvation in spite of the many vicissitudes they would have to go through in the course of their evolution and this is predetermined or predestined by the fiat of God.

If we compare this deterministic or fatalistic ethic and metaphysics with that of Buddhism, we find that the latter is totally opposed to it. Not only do the Buddhist texts repeatedly uphold the doctrine of free will and the value of human effort in offsetting the burden of the past and altering the course of the future, but they strongly condemn all types of metaphysical theories which give a deterministic or fatalistic account of the universe.

One such metaphysical theory, which is often singled out for criticism in the Buddhist texts, is that of Makkhali Gosāla and this theory is condemned because of its unmitigated fatalism. Now, in this respect, it would appear that there is much in common between the metaphysics of the *Gīta* and the philosophy of Makkhali. Makkhali denies the value of personal effort or human endeavour (*natthi attakāre* ... *natthi purisākāre* ... *natthi* ... *purisaparakkamo*) (D I 53); so does the *Gīta* when it says that "mental suppression (of the impulses) can accomplish nothing" (III.33). There is even verbal agreement in the description of the state of man and the processes of nature. "All beings" (*sabbe sattā, sabbe bhūtā*), according to Makkhali, "are devoid of the power of will" (*avasā*), an epithet frequently used in the *Gīta* to denote the same (e.g. *sarvaḥ* ..., *avaśaḥ*, everyone is devoid of the power of will; [III.5], *bhūtagrāmam* ... *avaśaḥ prakṛter vaśāt,* the multitude of beings helpless without the power of will on account of the power of *prakṛti*"). Man is thus impotent in the *Gīta* since he is subject to the power of *prakṛti* or *svabhāva*; in the philosophy of Makkhali all beings are impotent and helpless in that they are "subject to Destiny (*niyati*), Fate (*saṅgati*) and Nature (*bhāva-pariṇatā*) (D I 53). As A. L. Basham says, "*Bhāva* seems in this context to be synonymous with *svabhāva,* i.e. inherent character or nature. It suggests, below the fundamental category of *niyati*, sets of conditions and characteristics in each entity which, acting as factors subordinate to the great principle, control growth, development and rebirth" (*History and Doctrines of the Ājīvikas,* London, 1950, p. 226). There is yet another significant feature in respect of which the two philosophies seem to agree. Salvation as taught by Makkhali is predestined for each individual, "for, just as a ball of thread when thrown would unwind itself to the end, the wise and fools alike will attain salvation after journeying through *saṃsāric* states." (D I 54). This view has been called *saṃsāra-suddhi* (DN 2.21/ DI 54; cf. MN 12.57/M I 81) or salvation through transmigration and has been more explicitly referred to in a stanza in the *Jātakas* where the dependence of salvation on destiny is clearly brought out. "There is no open door to salvation, Bījaka. Await thy destiny (*niyati*). Joy or sorrow is obtained by destiny. All beings are purified through transmigration (*saṃsāra-suddhi*); so do not make haste (to attain) what is to come" (J-a VI 229).

It would be seen that these sentiments are very similar to what is found in a stanza of the *Gīta* (II.28), where it is said that "the beings who originate in the unmanifest reality and live in a manifest state in the middle will eventually attain the unmanifest reality. So why worry?" The context of this stanza of the *Gīta* reveals the import of the argument, namely that Arjuna should not desist from fighting since his ultimate salvation as well as that of all beings including his enemies is assured. In fairness to the *Gīta,* however, it must be mentioned that this doctrine of the inevitability of salvation appears to go against the grain of the moral advice of the *Gīta* (XVIII.64–6), although it is implicit in its deterministic metaphysics.

How strongly these doctrines, which denied free will and the value of human effort and proclaimed the inevitability of salvation, have been condemned in Buddhism may be seen by the references which Buddha makes to Makkhali and his theories in the Pali texts. In one place the Buddha says that he knows of no other person (than Makkhali) born to the detriment and disadvantage of so many people, comparing him to a fisherman casting his net at the mouth of a river for the destruction of many fish (AN 1:18/A I 33). In another passage his doctrines are said to be the worst of all the doctrines of the recluses (AN 3:135/A I 286).

There is also the pointed reference to and a criticism of aspects of these doctrines when taken up separately. Very often the denial of free will (*akiriyavāda*) is denounced. It is said that "the view that there is no free will when as a matter of fact there is free will, is a false view" (MN 60/M I 405). The value of personal effort (*attakāra*), no doubt in making the future course of events different from what they would otherwise be, is often stressed and it is maintained that there is such a thing as initiative (*ārabbha-dhātu*), enterprise (*nikkama-dhātu*), endeavour (*parakkama-dhātu*), courage (*thāma-dhātu*), perseverance (*thiti-dhātu*) and human instrumentality (*upakkama-dhātu*; AN 6:38/A III 337 ff) against the determinists who denied such a factor in human undertakings. The doctrine that salvation would be attained in due course by faring on in *saṃsāra* or the empirical states of existence is also severely criticised; it is said that "the goal of existence (i.e. salvation) where there is neither birth nor decay cannot be realised by merely faring on (*gamanena*) (AN 4:45/A II 48).

The main difference between the determinism of Makkhali and that of the *Gīta* is of course the fact that the latter is theistic. Though the *Gīta* would grant that all activity is directed by the operations of *prakṛti* over which we have no control, it would, as we have shown above, submit that *prakṛti* would find its ultimate sanction in the Divine Being, though there were passages betraying the dualistic Sāṅkhya analysis that the Divine Essence was quite separate from the workings of *prakṛti*. Saṃkara's comment that *prakṛti* was the sum total of good and evil mental dispositions of actions committed in the past (*pūrvakṛta*) is more in accord with the latter view and is an attempt to explain the present and the future in terms of the past activity of the individual. On the other view, which appears to be the dominant one, the *prakṛti* of each individual is fixed at creation in accordance with the prescience and providence of the divine will. Now, it is worth noting that Buddhism distinguishes between these two types of determinism, though condemning both of them unequivocally. One is the theory that our present actions are fully determined by the actions of the past (*pubbe-kata-hetu*) (AN 3:61/A I 173–5) and that we are in no sense free to act. The other is that an our actions are fixed in their entirety by the fiat of God (*issaranimmāṇavāda*) (ibid.); as Radhakrishnan (op. cit. p., 229) would say, "There is nothing however small or insignificant that has not been ordained or permitted by God even to the fall of a sparrow." Now, it is significant that both these theories are condemned in the Pali canonical texts (ibid) and with it the framework of *Gīta* metaphysics which appears to synthesise both these theories.

In spite of the deterministic background of the *Gīta* ethic, there is no doubt that there is much in common between the moral injunctions of the *Gīta* and of Buddhism and this is not surprising considering the eclecticism of the *Gīta*. But it is equally important to stress the differences especially when these differences are fundamental to the philosophy of each and reveal mutually opposed ethical attitudes to the problems of life. I propose to illustrate these differences by taking up the divergent attitudes that Buddhism and the *Gīta* adopt in respect to the problem of war and caste.

I would hold that the attitude to war in the *Gīta* is totally opposed to that of Buddhism. Yet, before we could illustrate the differences in the attitudes of each, it would be necessary to clarify the *Gīta* attitude to the problem of war. I would hold that the *Gīta* maintains that it is the moral duty of the soldier to fight in the event of any war in which the state is engaged. Radhakrishnan's interpretation of the *Gīta* appears to be fundamentally different in that he seems to believe that the *Gīta* speaks of war only in a metaphorical sense as referring to the moral struggle in man and nature and not to military action. Thus, commenting on the opening verse of the *Gīta*, Radhakrishnan (op. cit., p. 79) takes *dharma-kṣetre* to refer to the world instead of taking it as an epithet of *kuru-kṣetre*, the classical home of Vedic dharma. He says, "The world is *dharma-kṣetre*—the battle ground for a moral struggle." Then again, commenting on the phrase *māmānusmara yudhya ca* ("remember me and fight") (VIII.7), he says (op. cit., p. 229): "It is not a fight on the material plane that is intended here for it cannot be done at all times. It is the fight with the powers of darkness that we have to carry on perpetually." This metaphorical interpretation is often reinforced by frequent attempts to give the figurative meaning of otherwise literal statements. Thus *Gīta* I.14, which states that "Kṛṣṇa and Arjuna blew their celestial conches when stationed in their great chariot yoked to white horses" is to be taken metaphorically, for, says Radhakrishnan (p. 85), "throughout the Hindu and Buddhist literature the chariot stands for the psycho-physical vehicle. The steeds are the senses, the reins their controls, but the charioteer, the guide, is the spirit of real self, *ātman.* Kṛṣṇa, the charioteer, is the spirit in us."

However ingenious Radhakrishnan's attempt may be to give a metaphorical account of the *Gīta* injunctions to fight, it does not appear to be successful, for the greater majority of the passages containing references to war, far from admitting of metaphorical interpretation, have sense only when taken literally. On the other hand, the few passages which may possibly be interpreted metaphorically are so interpreted only at the cost of obscuring their meaning, especially when we consider their contexts. Thus the fact that Kṛṣṇa and Arjuna are stationed in their chariot is mentioned in a general description of the battlefield and the events taking place in it. If we interpret "chariot" here to mean the psycho-physical vehicle and Kṛṣṇa as representing the spirit in us, as Radhakrishnan does, it would be difficult to explain in similar terms the other paraphernalia of war mentioned, as well as the significance of the numerous other personalities besides Kṛṣṇa who are mentioned by name. And again the only passage which Radhakrishnan adduces as not admitting of a literal explanation (VIII.7) would be given a more natural interpretation if "*sarveṣu kāleṣu*" is taken as qualifying the nearest verb "*anusmara*" rather than "*yudhya*" and the stanza translated, "therefore remember me at all times but fight."

On the other hand an analysis of the positive injunctions to fight would show that it was at least incumbent on a soldier (*kṣatriya*) to fight in the event of a war in which the state is engaged, for fighting in such a war is always part of his dharma or social duty as being one of the demands made by the state on the soldier. It is said that "having regard to his own duty the kṣatriya should not falter, for there exists no greater good for a kṣatriya than a war enjoined by duty" (II.31). It is true that there are injunctions to the effect that the fight should be undertaken with selfless motives in a spirit of self-denial "free from desire and egoism" (III. 30; VIII. 7) and that fighting regardless of consequences "treating alike pleasure and pain, gain and loss, victory and defeat" brings with it no sin (II.38). Even if we grant that it is psychologically possible to engage in war "free from desire and egoism," the effect of these passages is more or less nullified by the numerous appeals made to selfish reasons as grounds for fighting. Thus moral grounds appear to be set aside when it is said that the refusal to fight amounts to "unmanliness" (II.3). Failure to answer the call to fight is "ignoble and un-Aryan and causes disgrace on earth" (II.2). Warriors who desist from fighting "incur ill-fame, and ill-fame is worse than death" (II.34–5). Could anything be sadder, it is asked, than hearing the taunts of his enemies (II.36), e.g. "If you are victorious you enjoy the earth (XI.33) and if slain you go to heaven" (XI.37). Fighting in a war enjoined as duty by the state is an open door to heaven (II.32). The general impression these passages seem to leave in the mind of the reader is that the *Gīta* is recommending the soldier to fight at any cost in a war in which the state is engaged. If he fights with selfless motives (and the psychological possibility of this many people would be inclined to doubt), he incurs no sin, whereas if he fights with selfish motives he would still stand to profit either by the gain and honour on earth or by the glory in heaven.

This teaching, that the soldier should fight at any cost in such a war, is reinforced by the metaphysical arguments in support of war. It is implied that Arjuna should not feel for the death of his enemies among who were his teachers and kinsmen, since "wise men do not grieve for the dead or the living" (II.11). Now, it is true that, according to the best teaching of the *Upaniṣads* and Buddhism, those who have transcended and overcome the world do not entertain thoughts of grief. But to argue that the soldier should likewise "not grieve for the dead" is to commit the fallacy that, since the wise do not grieve for the dead, those who do not grieve for the dead are wise. Then there are those arguments which seem to imply that the soldier is in fact not morally responsible for the act of killing either because he is not a moral agent as he is devoid of free will and is not morally responsible for his actions (as discussed above) or that since God is finally and solely responsible for the death of Arjuna's enemies in that "his enemies are doomed." Arjuna is only an instrument in God's hands (I.33–4). Finally, it is argued on metaphysical grounds that physical killing is not in reality killing, for the souls of people are eternal (II.12) and indestructible (II.17–25) and "one is not slain when the body is slain" (II.20).

The contrast between the *Gīta* attitude to war and the Buddhist is brought out in the advice Buddha gave when he was placed in a similar situation to that of Kṛṣṇa on the eve of a battle between his own people, the Sākyas, and their blood brothers, the Koliyas. The immediate cause for going to battle was that the Sākya and Koliya tribes were both making claims and demands on the waters of the river Rohiṇī, which flowed between their territories. The soldiers or *kṣatriyas* on each side were assembled (as the Kurūs and Pāṇḍavas had assembled) when the Buddha intervenes and asks them what the war was about. The answer was that it was over water and the Buddha asks them what the water was worth, to which it was replied that it was worth little. It turns out that both sides in their folly were prepared to sacrifice the invaluable lives of their soldiers for the sake of water, which was of little worth. And the futility of their war becomes apparent when the Buddha advises them in the words, "Why on account of some water of little worth would you destroy the invaluable lives of these soldiers?" (J-a V 412–4). The merits and demerits of the war as a whole are judged here by its possible consequences, and the suggestion seems to be that the causes for which wars are fought and lost are trivial in comparison with the human sacrifices involved. While the *Gīta* held that victory brings in its train honour and the gain of a kingdom (XI.33) while annihilation secures the reward of heaven (X.32), the Buddha (commenting on the war between kings Ajātasattu and Pasenadi) is supposed to have said that "victory arouses enmity and the defeated live in sorrow" (SN 3:14/S I 83). Wars result only in further wars, according to Buddhism, for "the victor obtains for himself a vanquisher" (SN 3:15/S I 85). War, as such, is condemned as an evil since it involves the destruction of invaluable human lives and such evils, we are told, should not be committed even though it be deemed that it is part of one's duties to one's king (*rañño rājakaraṇīyaṃ kātuṃ*) (MN 97.14/M II 188–191). It is therefore not surprising that the life of the soldier was looked down upon in Buddhism and even "trading in the weapons of war" (*sattha-vaṇijjā*) was considered a wrong mode of livelihood (AN 5:177/A III 208).

This seems to be the antithesis of the *Gīta* attitude to war and the fact may be further illustrated if we go into the details. It seems to have been an epic tradition that "the warrior who falls in the battleground while fighting attains heaven" (*Mahābhārata, Udyogaparva* 32.65). As such it finds expression in the *Bhagavad-Gīta*, where it is said that "if slain you shall go to heaven" (II.37) and "happy are the *kṣatriyas* for whom such a war comes of its own accord as an open door to heaven" (II.32). Now, this tradition finds mention in the Buddhist texts where a warrior chief (*yodhājīvo gāmaṇi*) tells the Buddha that he has heard from his ancestral teachers in the martial arts that the spirited soldier who fights with zeal and slays his opponents in battle is rewarded by being born in the company of gods in heaven. The warrior chief wants to know whether this is so and Buddha's reply is that on the contrary he is born in hell for his actions (SN 42:3/S IV 308 f).

It is therefore not surprising that it is Arjuna's attitude, which is condemned in the *Gīta*, that would appear to be similar to the Buddhist. Although *ahiṃsā* or non-violence is mentioned in the *Gīta* (X 5; XIII 7; XVI 2; XVII 14) as one among a list of virtues, nowhere is the concept woven into the central themes of *Gīta* philosophy and it is difficult to see how a soldier, whose duty is to fight and kill as many of the enemies as possible, can exercise *ahiṃsā* in these acts. The injunction to fight is therefore a negation of the ideal of *ahiṃsā* and the only representative, if at all, of the philosophy of *ahiṃsā* in the *Gīta* seems to be Arjuna. Arjuna's indecision and anxiety are not due to any lack of courage on his part but arises out of a moral conflict. On the one hand the love of his enemies for whom he feels compassion (I 28; II 2), a typically Buddhist virtue, makes him desist from the fight but on the other hand he is not sure whether it is not his duty to fight. The *Gīta* resolves the conflict by dismissing the former and making a case for the latter alternative. As such it would not be fair for Arjuna to call his a "mood of sentimental self-pity" (*The Bhagavadgīta,* p. 98), for, in a Buddhist context, Arjuna would have resolved the conflict by being a "conscientious objector" or non-resister who considered it his moral duty not to fight, without blindly obeying the dictates of his king or state and believing them to be part of his moral duties.

Left to his own devices Arjuna seems to favour the Buddhist solution, for he weighs the consequences of the war as a whole and finds them disastrous (I.38–43). He is by no means impelled by cowardice or selfish motives, for "he does not long for victory, kingdom or pleasures or even his own life" (I.32). Radhakrishnan (op. cit., p. 91) accuses Arjuna of "talking in terms of enlightened selfishness" but Arjuna, on the contrary, is prepared to offer non-resistance and sacrifice his life for the sake of what he considers at heart to be right without desiring the gains and glories of earth or heaven. "These I would not consent to kill though killed myself even for the kingdom of the three worlds; how much less for the sake of the earth? (I.35). "Far better would it be for me if the sons of Dhṛtarāṣṭra, with weapons in hand, should slay me in the battle while I remain unresisting and unarmed" (I.46). To do justice to Arjuna, one must say that except for his indecision and failure to apprehend clearly that it was no moral duty of his to fight and kill fellow human beings, his general attitude is Buddhist to the core. The *Bhagavad-Gīta,* in condemning this right along, therefore, takes up a position which is the antithesis of the Buddhist attitude to war.

Radhakrishnan (op. cit., pp. 570–71) sums up the Buddhist and *Gīta* teachings on caste by saying that "both attempt to relax the rigours of caste by basing it on a less untenable foundation." He is of course much less explicit when he elaborates on this point, for he says that "the *Gīta* recognises the caste divisions ... the *Gīta* broadly distinguishes four fundamental types of individuals answering to the four stages of the upward ascent. Basing caste on qualities the *Gīta* requires each individual to do duties imposed by his caste. ... The confusion of birth and qualities has led to an undermining of the spiritual foundation of caste." Here again I would hold that the *Gīta* attitude on caste is the very opposite of that of Buddhism and that while the *Gīta,* in keeping with the Vedic tradition, gives religious sanction to caste and attempts to provide an intellectual justification for it, Buddhism denies the validity of such a religious sanction and holds that there is no basis whatsoever for holding to caste distinctions. This would be clear if the specific arguments or assumptions on which caste is upheld in the *Gīta* were placed side by side with the relevant arguments against caste, as found in Buddhism. It may however be granted that the *Gīta* agrees with Buddhism in holding that people of all castes may obtain the highest spiritual attainments, but the important difference lies in the fact that while the *Gīta* upholds caste distinctions on religious and genetic grounds, Buddhism denies the reality and validity of these distinctions on these very grounds.

One of the arguments of Arjuna was that among the undesirable consequences of war was the possible danger of the "intermixture of castes" (*varṇa-saṃkara*). Since the prohibition of intermarriage as between castes was one of the principles of caste theory, it shows that according to the author of the *Gīta* the "intermixture of castes" was a disastrous consequence. In Buddhism, on the other hand, intermixture of castes, considered both as an historical fact and as a possibility, was adduced as an argument against the reality and validity of caste distinctions. It is said that even those who claim caste purity have had mixed ancestors, the implication being that the hereditary distinctions of caste are unreal (DN 3.1.15/D I 92–97). If this is an argument to show the historicity of caste mixture, the biological possibility of the mixture of castes, it may be mentioned, is also brought forward as an argument against the reality of caste distinctions (MN 93.12–15/M II 153–54). Arguing for the unity of mankind as against the distinctions of caste, the Buddha says that there are differences of species and genera among plants and animals, "although such distinctions are not found among humans" (*evaṃ n'atthi manussesu liṅgaṃ jātimayaṃ puthu*) (Sn 118).

Now, the crucial passage in the *Gīta*, which, according to Radhakrishnan, undermines the traditional Hindu basis of caste, is the one which says (to follow Radhakrishnan's translation): "The fourfold order was created by Me according to the divisions of quality and work" (*cāturvarṇyaṃ mayā sṛṣṭaṃ guṇa-karma-vibhāgaśaḥ*). Commenting on it, Radhakrishnan (op. cit. p. 160) says, "the emphasis is on *guṇa* (aptitude) and *karma* (function) and not *jāti* (birth). The *varṇa* or the order to which we belong is independent of sex, birth or breeding. A class determined by temperament and vocation is not a caste determined by birth and heredity." If this interpretation is intended for the two lines of the stanza quoted above, its absurdity would be apparent if its full implications are worked out. For, if it is correct, what is meant by these two lines is that there are four and only four types of individuals, each with a special aptitude for performing a special type of social duty which is obligatory on his part. Now, the references to the four types (as is evident from the word *cāturvarṇyam*) is obviously a reference to the four castes, viz. the *brahmins*, *kṣatriyas*, *vaiśyas* and *sūdras*. But, if as Radhakrishnan says "the *varṇa* or order to which we belong is independent of birth," then what is meant is that there may be brahmins who have the aptitude of *śūdras* and *śūdras* who have the aptitude of brahmins, so that it becomes the duty of these people who have been born in the wrong castes to do the work for which they have a special aptitude. This would cut the ground beneath the concept of *svadharma* in the *Gīta*.

Now, if the individual types were created in accordance with their *guṇas* or aptitudes and *karmas* or social functions, it is difficult to see why the number of types should be four and not less or more, for, if the types represented the *guṇas* there would have been three types corresponding to the *guṇas* of *sattva, rajas* and *tamas,* while if they represented the *karmas* or social duties surely many more.

But these two lines could be interpreted without absurdity in the general background of *Gīta* thought if they are construed as an attempt to give a religious sanction as well as a justification for the hereditary basis of caste. On such an interpretation it would appear that the fourfold caste structure of society (based on heredity) is fundamental, absolute and divinely ordained as being the creation of God himself, and is not a product of human conventions. The purpose of such a creation would be to ensure the stability and maximum efficiency of society since each caste had a special aptitude for performing the social duties they were expected to perform and it was the specific duty (*svadharma*) of the members of each caste to perform the duties for which they were so created.

This appears to be the more natural interpretation, but if so, it means that the *Gīta* not only holds that caste is a creation of God but attaches special sanctity to the four castes qua *four*. Now, both claims have been contested in Buddhism. The brahmin claim was that the brahmins were created from the mouth of God (*mukhato jātā ... brahmanimmitā*) (MN 93.5/M II 148), a theory which goes back to the *Puruṣa Sukta* of the R̥gveda (X.90), which says that the brahmin was the mouth of God (*brāhmaṇo'sya mukham āsīt*) and that all castes were created out of the Divine Person. This claim to a special association with Divinity was criticised by Buddhism on the grounds that the brahmins like the people of all the other castes were evidently born of human parents (*ditto*). But it is equally important to note that Buddhism held that there was nothing absolute even about the quarternity of castes. The Buddha argues that "among the Yonas and Kāmbojas and others living in the bordering territories there were only two castes (*dveva vaṇṇā*), namely the lords and serfs" (ibid). In fact it is asserted that caste names have only an occupational significance (Sn 119) and that birth is no index to caste (SN 7:7/S I 166) thus denying the hereditary basis of caste altogether, while the theory of caste as promulgated by the Vedic brahmins is referred to as a false and immoral view (*pāpakaṃ diṭṭhigataṃ*) (MN 93.18/M II 154–55). It would thus appear that while the *Gīta* tries to uphold, justify as well as give a religious sanction to the caste theory, Buddhism in countering these very arguments is presenting the opposite view so that it would be neither fair by the *Gīta* nor by Buddhism to say with Radhakrishnan that "both attempt to relax the rigours of caste by basing it on less untenable foundations."

20

Toynbee's Criticism of Buddhism

Prof. Toynbee in his work *An Historian's Approach to Religion* (Oxford, 1956) makes certain criticisms of Buddhism on the basis of what he believes to be the account given of the life and teaching of the Buddha in the Hīnayāna[5] scriptures. It is proposed in this article to examine these criticisms in light of the relevant material in the Pali Canon, which the Hīnayāna School holds in high regard as its main source of knowledge and inspiration with regard to the Buddha and his doctrine.

Toynbee's criticisms may be listed briefly as follows. He asserts that (a) there is a basic inconsistency between the life and teaching of the Buddha and that (b) it would seem that his life has at least more value than his teaching since (i) the account given of human nature in his teaching is wanting, (ii) the goal it sets forth would appear to be intrinsically unattainable and that (iii) even if it were attainable, it would not seem desirable.

Inconsistency between the Buddha's Life and Teaching

Let us examine the grounds on which these criticisms are made and see whether they are justified in light of the account given of the life and teaching of the Buddha in the Pali Canon.

Toynbee says that "the Buddha was an illogical evangelist" (p. 77) and speaks of his "sublime inconsistency" (p. 64) or "sublimely illogical practice" (p. 73). Now, what is the nature of his inconsistency? There seem to be three respects in which a religious teacher may be held to be inconsistent. His life may be inconsistent in the sense that his response or pattern of behaviour in some situations may be radically different from that of other situations which are essentially like them. His teaching may be inconsistent in

---

5. *Hīnayāna* is not a very happy term to denote the Theravāda School of the Southeast Asian countries, partly because it is a term of contempt, but mainly because it tends to presuppose the Mahāyāna metaphysics. I am using it, as no doubt Toynbee does, merely to denote by it the Southern School of Buddhism.

that there are at least two propositions in it, one of which or what it entails contradicts the other or what the other entails. Lastly, while his life may be perfectly consistent and his teaching a coherent whole when taken independently of each other, his life may not be compatible with his teaching and vice versa. When Toynbee speaks of the inconsistency of the Buddha, he seems to have this last sense in mind.

Strictly speaking there is nothing "illogical" in this kind of inconsistency since such a state of affairs is quite conceivable and perhaps not uncommon, since it is not everyone who for better or for worse practises what he preaches. Consider, for instance, the case of a person who says quite sincerely that it is bad to smoke but continues to smoke or says that it is good to have a regular medical check-up but does not himself do so. In both cases we find a person asserting that a certain proposition *p* is true and behaving as if he does not believe *p* or finds it difficult to live up to the demands that *p* makes on him. In such situations, however valid the grounds for asserting the truth of *p* may be, his behaviour seems to undermine or impugn it, since not only do his actions not seem to follow on the track of his beliefs but appear to go contrary to them. I suppose this is part of what Toynbee intends to convey by calling this relationship between teaching and practice "illogical." But perhaps he means more. Consider the case of the person who says that he has given up smoking but continues to smoke. Such a state of affairs is also quite conceivable and therefore cannot strictly be called "illogical," but his behaviour shows that his statement is false. In the previous case the statement "It is bad to smoke" could still be true even if he smoked, but the statement "I have given up smoking" cannot possibly be true in the light of his behaviour since his behaviour is directly relevant to the truth or falsity of his statement.

Consider Toynbee's own statement of the case he makes: "The Hīnayāna scriptures purport to be recording the Buddha's practise as well as his preaching; and if their record is true, we are bound to conclude from it that the Buddha was not preaching what he was practising. In preaching, if he did preach this, that man's paramount aim ought to be self-extinction, he was recommending to others a course of action which he had rejected for himself when the Tempter, after his attainment of Enlightenment, had suggested to him that he should make his exit into Nibbāna without delay. In choosing, instead, deliberately to postpone his own release from suffering in order to work for the release of his fellow sentient beings, the Buddha was declaring, in a positive act, that for himself, he believed that 'to suffer in the cause of love was a better course than to release himself from suffering through Self-extinction' (p. 292). In other words, if Buddha taught the proposition that "man's paramount aim ought to be self-extinction," (*p*), then in not extinguishing himself when he gained this knowledge he was acting as if he did not believe in *p* as far as he was concerned. Toynbee puts this argument in a slightly different form elsewhere. He says that if the attainment of Nibbāna involves the suppression of both good and bad desires, then after attainment there should be no motive or desire on his part to preach. If he does preach out of loving-kindness or compassion, this would be incompatible with his teaching about Nibbāna since there would be at least some desires (loving-kindness, compassion) which have not been suppressed and continue to influence his behaviour. Either his claim about the nature of Nibbāna as a state in which all desires (good and bad) are suppressed is false or his behaviour is not compatible with his teaching. So "if this impartial suppression of all desires, good and bad alike, was thus a logical consequence of the Hīnayāna Buddhist doctrine, the Buddha himself was guilty of a sublime inconsistency" (p. 64). In short, if the Buddha's teaching about the nature of Nibbāna and the means of achieving, it is true then his practise is not only quite incompatible with it but seems to show that this teaching was false.

It is worth pointing out that, although Toynbee sees an incompatibility between the teaching and practise of the Buddha, one of the points often stressed in the Pali Canon is that the Buddha "preached what he practised and practised what he preached" (*yathāvādī tathākārī yathākārī tathāvādī*) (It 122). Let us start at a point where Toynbee and the Pali Canon seem to agree, namely that what the Buddha suffered during the forty-five years of his ministry was inspired by his love for mankind. As Toynbee puts it, "Even if he did recommend in his teaching a self-centred pursuit of self-extinction, he was tacitly countermanding his words by his acts of self-devoting love" (p. 292). The Pali Canon makes frequent reference to the love and compassion of the Buddha. One of his lay disciples, Jīvaka, says on one occasion, "I have heard it said that

God is loving (*Brahmā mettāvihārī*), but I have seen with my own eyes how full of love the Blessed One is (*Bhagavā mettāvihārī*) (M I 369)." Where the Buddha converts the murderer Aṅgulimāla at the risk of his life, his kindness is referred to (*Buddho ca kāruṇiko;* M II 100), and it is often mentioned that the Buddha preaches not through desire for gain or glory but out of compassion and benevolence (*anukampako Bhagavā hitesī anukampaṃ upādāya dhammaṃ desesi*) (M II 238).

If the Buddha practised love, did he also not preach it? The injunctions to practise love and compassion towards our fellow beings are much more numerous in the Pali Canon than the references to his own example. The Buddha tells his followers, "Just as a mother loves her only child even more than her life, extend a boundless love towards all creatures" (Sn 149). The importance that he attaches to the cultivation of love for our fellow beings above all else is seen from the following statement that he makes: "None of the good works employed to acquire religious merit, O monks, is worth a fraction of the value of loving-kindness (*mettā)* It 19–21)." Then there is the well-known saying to his disciples: "Even if ruffians were to seize you and cut you limb from limb with a double-handed saw, you would not have carried out my bidding if you felt the slightest anger towards them" (M I 129, 186).

It would appear therefore that not only did the Buddha practise love but he preached it, and viewed in this manner, there does not seem to be any inconsistency between what he practised and what he taught. But Toynbee is now likely to raise the question as to how his teaching about self-sacrificing love would be compatible with the proposition: "If he did preach this, that man's paramount aim ought to be self-extinction" (p. 292). If love and pity along with selfish desires were to be extinguished in Nibbāna, how can they continue to influence a person after his attainment of Nibbāna? If the latter is true, the teaching about Nibbāna would be false.

In spite of Toynbee's use of the epithet "self-extinction" to denote the ideal set-up in Buddhism, it seems to be fairly clear from his references to the concept of Nibbāna (p. 62 f) that he quite rightly does not subscribe to the annihilationist view of Nibbāna, which has been discarded by scholars on the ground that it does not take account of the positive description of Nibbāna in the Pali Canon as also Buddha's own categorical denial that Nibbāna was annihilation. But Toynbee does not seem to take account of all the implications of this view. Just as much as it is man's duty to attain "self-extinction" it is equally a duty of his to attain ultimate reality, for "self-extinction" and "ultimate reality" are paradoxically synonymous. The Buddha's view seems to have been that the categories of logic do not apply to Nibbāna (*atakkāvacara*). As such Nibbāna cannot strictly be described by positive or negative epithets. Positive epithets suggest empirical reality and negative ones annihilation, both of which are misleading. Nibbāna is a transcendent reality beyond space (*na katthaci kuhiñci*), beyond time since "the distinctions of past, present and future do not apply to it," and beyond causation (*na paṭiccasamuppannaṃ*). The passage from our finite self-centred existence to Nibbāna is pictured as one from bondage to freedom (*vimutti*) and power (*vasī*), from imperfection to perfection (*parisuddhi, paramakusala*), from unhappiness to perfect happiness (*parama-sukha*), from ignorance to knowledge (*vijjā, aññā*), from finite consciousness to transcendent infinite consciousness (*ananta-viññāṇa*), from the impermanent to the permanent (*nicca*), from the unstable to the stable (*dhuva*), from fear and anxiety to perfect security (*abhaya*), from the evanescent to the ineffable (*amosadhamma*), from a state of mental illness to a state of perfect mental health,[6] from darkness to light (*āloka*), etc.

In Mahāyāna we are familiar with the conception of the Buddha as embodying infinite wisdom (*mahāprajñā*) and infinite compassion (*mahākaruṇā*) but this conception seems to have its roots in the Pali Canon, where Nibbāna is depicted not only as a state of perfect knowledge (*vijjā, aññā, jñāna*) but as a state in which the "boundless states" (*appamaññā*) of love (*mettā*), pity (*karuṇā*), sympathetic joy (*muditā*) and equanimity (*upekkhā*) find their fulfilment (M I 297). Nibbāna is frequently defined as a state in which craving (*lobha*), hatred (*dosa*) and delusion (*moha*) are completely extinguished, but with the elimination of hatred, for instance, perfect love (*mettā*) takes its place. One who has attained Nibbāna is therefore endowed with the finest qualities of compassion, utterly refined and removed from

6. A II 143. Here diseases are classified as bodily (*kāyika-roga*) or mental (*cetasika-roga*) and it is said that while we have bodily diseases from time to time, mental illness is almost continual until Arahantship is attained so that only the saint can be said to have a perfectly healthy mind.

the slightest tinge of selfishness. With the total elimination of the finite self-centred qualities of craving, hate and delusion, the transcendent mind, shining with its natural lustre (*pabhassaraṃ cittaṃ*), is wholly filled with perfect renunciation and charity (*alobha, arāga, cāga*), loving-kindness (*mettā*) and perfect wisdom (*amoha, paññā*). So with the eradication of the selfish desires love and pity find their perfect expression.

In other words, far from it being inconsistent for one who has attained Nibbāna to minister and preach unto others out of love and compassion, it would be quite natural for him to do so. He does this not out of earthly considerations of gain or glory or out of a sense of duty, for, as one who has attained the highest, he is described as one who is "free from debt" (*anaṇa*) and as one who has "discharged one's obligations" (*katakaraṇīya*) but because it would be just what such a person would quite naturally do by virtue of his attainment.

The role of love and compassion before and after the attainment of the ideal is not infrequently referred to in the texts. A person, for instance, who attains final salvation after the cultivation of these qualities of love, compassion and meditation is described as "one who is cleansed with an internal bathing" (*ayaṃ vuccati bhikkhave bhikkhu sināto antarena sinānena*) (M I 39)" and it is urged that this bathing is to be done not in the river but "in the waters of love and compassion for one's fellow beings" (*idheva sinähi brāhmaṇa sabbabhūtesu karohi khemataṃ*) (M I 39). Consider again the following passage:

> In whatever monk who was covetous, covetousness is got rid of, who was malevolent, malevolence of mind is got rid of, ... wrath ... grudging ... hypocrisy ... spite ... jealousy ... stinginess ... treachery ... craftiness ..., who was of evil desires, evil desire is got rid of, who was of wrong view, wrong view is got rid of. He beholds himself purified of all these evil unskilled states, he beholds himself freed (*vimuttaṃ attānaṃ samanupassati*). When he beholds himself freed, delight is born; rapture is born from delight; when he is in rapture, the body is tranquil; when the body is tranquil, he experiences joy; being joyful the mind is concentrated. He dwells, suffusing one direction with a mind of loving-kindness (*mettāsahagatena cetasā*), likewise the seconds, likewise the third, likewise the fourth; just so above, below,

across; he dwells having suffused the whole world everywhere, in every way with a mind of friendliness that is far-reaching, wide-spread, immeasurable, without enmity, without malevolence. He abides ... with a mind of pity (*karuṇā*), ... with a mind of sympathetic joy (*muditā*) ..., with a mind of equanimity (*upekkhā*) ... without enmity, without malevolence. It is as if there were a lovely lotus-pond with clear water, sweet water, cool water, limpid, with beautiful banks; and a man were to come along from the east, west, north or south, overcome and overpowered by the heat, exhausted, parched and thirsty and on coming to that lotus-pond might quench his thirst with water and quench his feverish heat. Even so ... one who has come into this Dhamma and discipline taught by the Buddha, having thus developed loving-kindness, pity, sympathetic joy and equanimity attains inward calm" (M I 283).

That love and pity cease or ought to cease with the attainment of Nibbāna is a basic misconception due to misunderstanding the nature of this ideal. It is quite expressly stated that the saint who has attained perfection (*sampannakusalaṃ paramakusalaṃ uttamapattipattaṃ samaṇaṃ ayojjhaṃ*) (M II 29) is endowed among other things with "right thoughts (*sammā-saṅkappā*) which do not require to be further disciplined" and these right thoughts include *ahiṃsā* (*avihiṃsa-saṅkappā*), which is a positive concept in Jainism and Buddhism.

That a person on attaining perfection, whether he be the Buddha or one of his disciples, ought to pass away immediately into Nibbāna without being a light unto the world by his example and teaching is an idea which is quite alien even to Hīnayāna ways of thinking. The Buddha exhorted his disciples who were Arahants to go and preach unto the world for the good and happiness of mankind (Vin I 21). Perhaps Toynbee was misled by the significance to be attached to the first "temptation" of the Buddha. According to the explanation in the Pali scriptures themselves, the Buddha's compassion is in no way compromised by his attainment of Nibbāna. He hesitates for a moment, wondering as to whether he should preach, not because of any lessening or lack of love on his part for his fellow beings nor because he thought that Nibbāna "was a prize to be clutched" (p. 293) but because he wonders whether the world, immersed in and getting satisfaction from its petty self-centred desires, hates and its cherished erroneous beliefs, would hearken unto a teaching which involves a total abnegation of all this. His thoughts on this occasion as recorded in the scriptures are as follows: "Should I teach what I have found with difficulty? This Dhamma is not readily comprehensible to those given to craving and hate. It goes against the current, is subtle, profound, and difficult of comprehension and as such those who are slaves to their desires and are enveloped in darkness would fail to see its truths" (M I 168). It is only after he looks into the hearts and minds of men and sees that there are among them those who would understand that he decides to preach.

Love and compassion as ideals exemplified in the lives of Buddha and his disciples, far from being incompatible with the teaching of the Buddha, have a central place in Buddhism both as a means to the attainment of Nibbāna and in a refined and transcendent form comprising the goal itself. Nibbāna was only the extinction of the fires of greed, hate and delusion in the infinite waters of transcendent and unconditioned love and wisdom. When the Buddha or one of his disciples attained this transcendent state, he came back to make use of his psycho-physical personality to serve others until it passed away. The theory that it would be an act of selfishness to seek to share one's spiritual gains with another is unequivocally condemned by the Buddha in a sermon on the ethics of teaching. The brahmin Lohicca holds the view, "If a religious person acquired some spiritual state, then he should tell no one else about it. For what can one man do for another? To tell others would be like the man who, having broken through an old bond, should entangle himself in a new one. Like that is this desire to preach to others; it is a form of selfishness. For what can man do for another?" (D I 224 ff). The Buddha dismisses this as a false and evil view (*pāpakaṃ diṭṭhigataṃ*) and among the reasons given for doing so is that such a person would be one who is lacking in love and sympathy for the welfare of others.

Lack of Value of the Buddha's Teaching

If the Buddha's life has value, as Toynbee grants, it would be difficult to see how his teaching, of which his life was an expression, lacks value. Here again Toynbee seems to entertain this view owing to a misunderstanding of Buddhist teaching. Let us consider his criticisms in detail. Toynbee says that the Hīnayāna account of human nature is defective: "If a twentieth-century inquirer, brought up in the Christian tradition, found oneself called upon to answer these questions as best as he could, no doubt he would be likely to declare in favour of Christianity and the Mahāyāna as against the Hīnayāna. On the question of fact, he would find the Hīnayāna's diagnosis superficial in its failure to distinguish between self-devoting and self-centred desires. He would find that a superficial diagnosis had led to a wrong valuation and a wrong prescription" (p. 291). Earlier in his work Toynbee seems to concede the distinction between good and bad desires, but both are to be suppressed for the attainment of Nibbāna: "If the Buddha was right as surely he was, in holding that absolute detachment can be achieved only through the extinction of all desire whatsoever, then the Hīnayāna must require not only the suppression of desires that are ordinarily regarded as being selfish, such as those of personal pleasure, prosperity, and power for oneself, but also the suppression of desires that are ordinarily regarded as being altruistic, such as love and pity for one's fellow sentient beings" (p. 64).

Although the analysis, classification and valuation of desires in Buddhism would not be the same as what Toynbee adopts, it would be quite incorrect to say that Buddhism fails to distinguish between self-devoting and self-centred desires. According to Buddhism, the springs of action are six-fold, comprising the three immoral bases of action (*akusala-mūla*), namely craving (*lobha, rāga*), hate (*dosa*) erroneous beliefs (*moha*) and the three moral bases of action (*kusala-mūla*) consisting of their opposites, selflessness (*alobha, cāga*), love (*adosa, mettā*) and wisdom (*amoha, paññā*). One of the terms generally translated as desire (*taṇhā*) literally means "thirst" (Skr. *tṛṣṇā*) and there are said to be three thirsts: the thirst for sensuous pleasures (*kāma-taṇhā*), the thirst for selfish pursuits (*bhava-taṇhā*) and the thirst for destruction (*vibhava-taṇhā*). Of these the thirst for sensuous gratification (*kāma-taṇhā, kāma-rāga*) and the thirst for selfish pursuits (*bhava-taṇhā*) such as the desire for self-preservation, self-continuity (personal immortality), self-assertion (power), self-display, self-respect, etc. arise from the basis (lit. root, *mūla*) of craving (*rāga*, i.e. *kāma-rāga, bhava-rāga*). The thirst for destruction (*vibhava-taṇhā*) springs from (the root of) hate. These are the three forms of thirsts or desires, which continually seek and find temporary satisfaction (*tatratatrābhinandinī*), though ever remaining unsatisfied, and provide the fuel for the process called the individual. The distinction made between these unwholesome desires (*taṇhā*) based on craving and hate, and righteous aspirations (*sammā-saṅkappā*) based on selflessness and love is so marked that the term "thirst" is not used to denote the latter. What springs from selflessness and love are not "thirsts," unlike the products of craving and hate. Love (*mettā*) is as such not termed a desire since a desire in the above sense of a "thirst" (*taṇhā*) is basically self-centred and its role would be to build the house that is the individual from birth to birth. Selflessness (*alobha, cāga*) and love (*mettā*), as the opposites of craving and hate when they occur in their purest form, do not have these characteristics and are hence not considered desires in the sense of "thirsts." In fact, by not doing so, Buddhism recognises the wide gulf that exists between the two. Desires are narrow and selfish (*pamāṇakataṃ*), while selflessness and love are boundless (*appamāṇā*) (M I 297). And what the Buddha recommends is the complete elimination and eradication of the former until the mind is entirely suffused by the latter in their most refined state. The distinction and opposition between the two as motives of action are often mentioned. For instance, it is said that "one's speech may be opportune or inopportune, true or false, gentle or harsh, useful or futile and inspired by love (*metta-citta*) or influenced by hate (*dosantarā*) (M I 26)." The narrow desires are in fact to be eliminated by the development of the latter, their opposites. It is said that "by cultivating love (*mettaṃ bhāvayato*), ill-will (*byāpāda*) subsides" (M I 424).

The criticism is sometimes made that although the cultivation of selflessness and love may be recommended as a means to an end, namely in order to expel craving and hatred, they too have to be given up in order to attain the state of perfect detachment, which is Nibbāna. There are passages in the Canon which *prima facie* appear to favour such a theory. It is said, for instance, that the mind's emancipation through love (*mettācetovimutti*) is conditioned (*abhisaṅkhata*) and as such, impermanent and liable to cease, and realising this, he attains the supreme secure state of Nibbāna (M I 351). To cite another instance, it is recommended that one should work for the cessation of evil habits (*akusalānaṃ sīlānaṃ nirodhāya paṭipanno*) as also for the cessation of good habits (*kusalānaṃ sīlānaṃ nirodhāya paṭipanno*) or for the cessation of good aspirations (*kusalānaṃ saṅkappānaṃ nirodhāya paṭipanno*) (M II 26)." It is perhaps passages of this sort which, if not carefully examined in their respective contexts, are likely to lead one to the conclusion that the Buddha recommends the suppression of both good and evil and that both are almost valued alike.

But if these very same passages are carefully studied in their contexts and on the general background of canonical thought, they would acquire quite a different meaning and significance. Let us take the passage that we have just referred to. Here the question is asked: "How should one conduct oneself in order to eliminate evil habits?" (M II 26). The answer given is that we should exercise our will (*chandaṃ janeti*) or master-desire as Toynbee would have it (see below) and, by a process of self-analysis and effort on our part, strive (a) to eliminate evil states that have arisen, (b) to be on our guard against the arising of evil states not arisen, (c) to make arise good states not arisen and (d) to preserve (*ṭhitiyā*), to not allow to fall into desuetude (*asammosāya*), to further develop (*bhiyyobhāvāya*), to bring to maturity (*vepullāya*), to cultivate (*bhāvanāya*) and perfect (*pāripūriyā*) good states that have arisen. Evil, in other words, is to be eradicated and prevented from influencing us and part of the means for doing so is to cultivate the good. Now, in this same passage when we come to the question, "How is one to conduct oneself in order to eliminate good habits?" the answer given is precisely the same as the above, comprising (a), (b), (c) and (d). Indeed it would look paradoxical as to how one can eliminate good habits (*kusalānaṃ sīlānaṃ nirodhāya paṭipanno*) were not the crucial distinction drawn in this passage between "conditioned virtue" (*sīlamayo*) and perfected "natural virtue" (*silavā*). It is said that the perfect saint who has attained final salvation (*cetovimuttiṃ paññāvimuttiṃ yathābhūtaṃ pajānāti*) is "naturally virtuous and not virtuous through conditioning" (*sīlavā hoti no ca sīlamayo*).

With regard to the elimination of the good aspirations, we find the same paradoxical statement that this is to be done by eliminating evil states of mind and cultivating the good states of mind to perfection and here again the saint "who has attained the highest perfection (*sampanna-kusalo*), the highest good (*parama-kusalo*) and the highest attainment (*uttama-pattipatto*)" is said to be, among other things, "endowed with righteous aspirations which do not need further refinement or disciplining (*asekhena sammā-saṅkappena samannāgato*)." This conception of the Arahant is surely far removed from that of a person who has attained a state of cold quietist indifference prior to extinction.

The distinction made in the Pali Canon is that of the conditioned (*saṅkhata*) goodness of those whose self-centred desires (i.e. the threefold thirsts) are not completely eradicated and the pure goodness of the perfect ones or the Arahants in whom these thirsts or desires have been completely extinguished. The conditioned goodness requires further disciplining (Pali *sekha*; Skt. *śaikṣya* from the root *śikṣ*, to discipline, train) while the perfect goodness (*parama-kusala*) of the saint does not require such disciplining or further refinement (*asekha*). The latter is naturally virtuous (*sīlavā*) while the virtue of those who have not as yet attained perfection is artificial and conditioned (*sīlamayo*). This is no denial of the importance of selflessness and love, the cultivation of which is necessary though not sufficient for the extinction of the self-centred desires but a recognition of the extent to which these same self-centred desires may condition and dominate much of our so-called acts of selflessness and love, so that it is only on attaining the detachment (*virāga*) of Nibbāna that our love and pity could be entirely disinterested. What passes for love and pity is influenced consciously or unconsciously by our desire for gain or glory in earth or heaven and other such self-centred considerations such as fear of man or God. Disinterested love and pity can arise only when the mind at all its levels is totally purged of all such self-centred desires and considerations.

Unattainability of the Buddhist Goal

Now, this goal, says Toynbee, "looks intrinsically unattainable." "Absolute detachment looks as if it might be intrinsically unattainable, because it is hard to see how the intensely arduous spiritual effort to detach oneself from all other desires can be achieved without attaching oneself to the single master-desire of extinguishing every desire save this. Is the extinction of the desire to desire nothing but the extinction of desire a psychological possibility?" (p. 64). To say that absolute detachment is intrinsically unattainable would of course imply that the claims made by the Buddha and some of his disciples to have attained such a state are in fact mistaken or false, but it is not primarily by an examination of these claims that Toynbee makes this assertion. Instead, he (i) asserts that the giving up of desires entails the presence of a single master-desire intent on eliminating all desires save this and (ii) questions the psychological possibility of extinguishing this master-desire.

That the giving up of desires is to be accomplished by attaching oneself to a master-desire is precisely what Buddhism states: "Desires are to be given up depending on desire" (*taṇhaṃ nissāya taṇhaṃ pahātabbaṃ*) (A II 146). This master-desire is more usually designated by the term "will" (*chanda*, sometimes translated as "desire," see *Kindred Sayings* V 239; also p. 243 fn.) and is defined as "the will to prevent the arising of evil states of mind not arisen, the will to keep out evil states of mind which have arisen, the will to make arise good states of mind which have not arisen and the will to preserve, develop, refine and perfect good states of mind which have arisen" (S V 268). In short, it is the will or desire to do away with the unwholesome desires ("thirsts," *taṇhā*) and to refine the wholesome states of mind to perfection by completely eliminating the impact of the former on the latter until these good states of mind (selflessness, love, wisdom) cease to be in the least affected by erroneous beliefs. This is the role of the master-desire, which in a wider sense comprises the acts of will (*chanda*), the physical and mental energy (*viriya*), the thoughts (*citta*) and the mental investigations and analyses (*vīmaṃsā*) directed towards the above end. So, on this count, the Buddhism of the Pali Canon would have no quarrel with Toynbee's assertion that a master-desire would be necessary to give up every desire save this.

The disagreement would be with the next step of Toynbee, namely his statement that it would be psychologically impossible to extinguish this master-desire. If by "the desire to desire nothing but the extinction of desire" Toynbee means "the master-desire," the objection would be: "Is the extinction of the master-desire a psychological possibility?" But why is this psychologically impossible? Apart from the mere suggestion, Toynbee does not seem to make it at all clear as to why this is so. He does not provide any empirical grounds or logical reasons for holding that this would be psychologically impossible. Would he say that from what we know of the psychology of man it would by no means be likely for one to have a desire to do away with desires or to extinguish a desire to do away with desires? Now, Buddhism would grant that in desiring to do away with desires one would be going against the natural current (*paṭisotagāmi*) of the mind, which continually seeks the gratification of its self-centred desires without ever finding satisfaction. But Buddhism would not grant that this is psychologically impossible and would point at least to the example of the Buddha and some of his disciples. It would be psychologically difficult particularly for those whose self-centred desires are strong but by no means psychologically impossible even for them.

On the other hand, is Toynbee's objection to the possibility of desiring the extinction of the master-desire primarily a logical one? Is he saying that, just as much as we need have a master-desire to extinguish desire, it would seem necessary to have a super-master-desire to extinguish the master-desire and that this would lead to an infinite regress? And is he also suggesting that the master-desire like the first-order desires cannot achieve permanent satisfaction? If the objection is in this form, it has already been raised and met in the Pali Canon itself. A Brahmin asks Ānanda how desire can be fully extinguished since the extinction of desire by desire would be an unending process.

> "What is it, Master Ānanda, for which the holy life is lived under Gotama, the recluse?"
>
> "For the sake of abandoning desire (*chanda*), Brahmin, the holy life is lived under the Exalted One."
>
> "But is there any way, is there any practise, Master Ānanda, for the abandoning of desire?"
>
> "There is a way, Brahmin, there is a practise for abandoning desire."
>
> "Pray, Master Ānanda, what is that way and that practise?"
>
> "Herein, Brahmin, a monk cultivates the basis of psychic power of which the features are desire (*chanda*) ... energy (*viriya*) ... thought (*citta*) ... investigation (*vīmaṃsā*) together with the co-factors of concentration and struggle. This, Brahmin, is the way, this is the practise for the abandoning of desire."
>
> "If that be so, Master Ānanda, it were a task without end not one with an end. That he should get rid of desire by means of desire is an impossible thing."

"Then, Brahmin, I will just question you on this matter. Do answer as you think fit."

"Now, what do you think, Brahmin? Was there not previously a desire in you (urging you) thus: 'I will go to the park?' When you got to the park was not that particular desire abated?"

"Yes, indeed it was, Master."

"Was there not previous energy (*viriya*) in you (urging you) thus: 'I will go to the park' ... thought (*citta*) in you ... deliberations (*vīmaṃsā*) in you ... When you got there did not energy ... thought ... deliberations subside?"

"Yes indeed, Master."

"Very well, then, Brahmin. That monk who is an Arahant ... who is released by perfect insight,—that desire which he had previously to attain Arahatship, now that Arahantship is won, that desire is abated ..." (*Kindred Sayings* V 243–5 = S V 271ff).

The argument is that logically the master-desire is not on the same footing as the first-order desires, for, unlike these self-centred desires which continually seek gratification without being permanently satisfied, the master-desire would achieve final satisfaction and be extinguished with the eradication of the self-centred desires.

Non-desirability of the Buddhist Goal

The next criticism is posed in the form of the question as to whether the pursuit of absolute detachment, if feasible, is also good: "They sought to detach themselves from every form of mundane society and beyond that from the lust of mundane life itself; and the very sincerity and resoluteness with which these Hīnayāna Buddhist philosophers pursued their spiritual quest raise two questions: Is absolute detachment an attainable objective? And supposing it to be attainable, is the pursuit of it a good activity?" (pp. 63–4). Perhaps this criticism, which was based on the misconception that loving-kindness and compassion were extinguished in Nibbāna along with the self-centred desires, is already met insofar as we have pointed out that these good states of mind, far from being effaced in Nibbāna are refined and perfected so that they are no longer dependent on the egoistic base of the self-centred desires.

Yet the objection may be raised in another form. It may be asked how love and compassion can be cultivated in the abstract by cutting oneself away from the life of society for the sake of one's own salvation. Is this not a radically egoistic pursuit in itself? Is not the ethic of Hīnayāna Buddhism rooted in the idea of achieving one's own salvation with no concern for others and even one may say at the expense of others who have to provide with their toil and sweat the basic necessities of life without which even their selfish ascetic existence would not even be possible?

This picture does not do justice to the Buddhist conception of the religious life. The Buddha does not say that the contemplative life (*vita contemplativa*), lived apart from the active life of society, was essential even to seek the goal of Nibbāna in this life itself, although there is no doubt that the contemplative life was recommended in view of the better opportunities that it provides the individual. The life of the Buddhist contemplative, i.e. the monk, is not the same as that of the ascetic who retires from the world. He dwells aloof from society but nevertheless in society, giving moral guidance and spiritual instruction to laymen. This work of his for society is considered as valuable as the production of mundane goods and services on the part of the other members of the society. Although he seeks to achieve the final goal by his own individual effort, yet the means of achieving it as well as the goal itself is stamped with selflessness. If he achieves his goal he continues to be of the greatest service to others because of his spiritual knowledge and attainments with no expectation whatsoever of earthly or heavenly reward.

Can such a life be called egoistic? Although the term "egoist" strictly refers to an individual who seeks his own welfare, we normally use the term to denote one who seeks primarily his personal material welfare even at the expense of others. But would a person who seeks primarily his own spiritual welfare at the expense of his material welfare or even his life, and seeks it partly by his selfless service in the present and in order to be of the greatest service to others in the future, rightly be called an egoist? Insofar as he seeks primarily his own spiritual welfare until he reaches the goal, he may be called an enlightened egoist. But insofar as he does this by cultivating a selfless love for his fellow beings, culminating in a state of perfect selfless love, which enables him to live the rest of his life solely in the service of others, it would at the same time be the life of an enlightened altruist. Buddhism holds to the principle that one cannot save another without first saving oneself. The Buddha tells Cunda, "It is not possible for one who is stuck in the mud to help another out but it is possible for one who is not stuck in the mud to help another who is stuck in the mud. It is not possible that a man who has not saved himself can save another but it is possible for a man who has saved himself to save another" (M I 46).

Toynbee says that "the Mahāyāna Buddhist's verdict on the Hīnayāna philosopher can be summed up in an inversion of the Scribes' and Pharisees' jibe at Christ on the Cross: "He saved himself; others he cannot save" (p. 65). The Hīnayāna philosopher's reply would be: "He saved himself so that others he can save." The Buddha first trained his disciples to be Arahants and then sent them into the world to work and preach for the good and happiness of mankind. It would seem odd to call these Arahants (who like Puṇṇa went among unknown peoples ready to meet the worst persecution and even death with hearts of love) egoists. The ethical ideal recommended in the Pali Canon, as representative of the Hīnayāna viewpoint, is that of enlightened egoism-cum-altruism, the one being dependent on the other. The Buddha says, "Monks, there are these four persons in the world. What four? He who is neither bent on his own welfare nor on the welfare of others; he who is bent on the welfare of others but not his own; he who is bent on his own welfare but not of others; and he who is bent on the welfare both of himself as well as of others. He who is bent on the welfare of oneself as well as of others is of these four persons the chief and best, topmost, highest and supreme" (A II 95). According to this valuation, the best of all people is he who works for his own good as well as for the good of others, there being no conflict between the two ends when the good happens to be moral and spiritual.

21

The Buddhist Attitude to Other Religions

The Buddhist attitude to other religions has from its very inception been one of critical tolerance. But what is significant is that it was able to combine a missionary zeal with this tolerant outlook. Not a drop of blood has been shed throughout the ages in the propagation and dissemination of Buddhism in the many lands to which it spread; religious wars either between the schools of Buddhism or against other religions have been unheard of. Very rare instances of the persecution of heretical opinions are not lacking, but they have been exceptional and atypical. Buddhism has also shown a remarkable degree of adaptability in the course of its historical expansion.

A student of Buddhism, a professor of philosophy, who made a special study of this aspect of Buddhism, has observed: "I refer to its remarkable elasticity and adaptability. Wherever Buddhism has gone it has manifested this characteristic, and manifested it in a superlative and unique degree. I do not think there is another religion that possesses so much of it. Buddhism has been emphatically a missionary religion. Its transplanting to new lands has been accomplished never through conquest or through migration but solely by the spread of ideas. Yet almost everywhere it has gone, it has so completely adapted itself to the new people and the new land as to become practically a national religion. This has been partly due to the tolerance and liberality of its thought, to which I have already referred, a tolerance which it has exhibited both within and without. With the most extremely rare exceptions, Buddhism has held no heresy trials and has carried on no persecutions. With a daring catholicity that approaches foolhardiness it has recognized every form of rival as a possessor of some degree of truth" (J. B. Pratt, *The Pilgrimage of Buddhism,* London, 1928, p. 719).

Speaking of the relevance for modern times of Buddhism and the cultural milieu in which it arose, namely Hinduism, Prof. Arnold J. Toynbee says: "Co-existence is mankind's only alternative to mass-suicide in the Atomic Age; and mankind means to save itself from committing mass-suicide if it can find a way. One open way is the Indian way; and it might therefore seem probable that, in the

Atomic Age, the spirit of Indian religion and philosophy will receive a welcome in the Western half of the world" (A. J. Toynbee, *America and the World Revolution,* London, 1962, p. 49). In one of his earlier works, Toynbee speaks of the religions of Southern and Eastern Asia as "Buddhaic religions" in contrast to the Judaic religions of Judaism, Christianity and Islam. He says: "There are three Buddhaic religions; the Hīnayāna Buddhism of Ceylon and South-East Asia; the Mahāyāna Buddhism of East Asia, Tibet and Mongolia; and the post-Buddhaic Hinduism of India" (A. J. Toynbee, *An Historian's Approach to Religion,* London, 1956, p. 272).

Perhaps what Toynbee had in mind in calling post-Buddhistic Hinduism a "Buddhaic religion" is the fact that Hinduism was deeply influenced by Buddhism, so much so that Hindus have claimed to have absorbed Buddhism rather than to have discarded it. Vaishṇavite Hindus have deified the Buddha and consider him the last (ninth) Avatar (Incarnation) of Vishnu. Saṃkara, one of the greatest philosophers of Hindu Vedānta, was so profoundly affected by Buddhist thought that he has been called a "concealed Buddhist" (*pracchanna-bauddha*), and the influence of Buddhism on recent Indian leaders like Mahātma Gandhi and Jawaharlal Nehru has been no less profound. Besides, millions of the so-called depressed classes, following their late leader Ambedkar, have consciously embraced Buddhism, attracted by its doctrine of social and spiritual equality. It is therefore worthwhile to examine the nature as well as the basis of the tolerant attitude of Buddhism towards other religions, despite its missionary zeal.

If we go into the historical origins of Buddhism, we note that Buddhism arose at a time when there was an interminable number of mutually conflicting theories about the nature and destiny of man in the universe. Some of them first arose as a result of the free speculations among the brahmins of the Āraṇyaka period, just prior to about 800 BCE, when knowledge came to be highly valued. Later, speculation on these and other matters spread in non-Brahmanical circles as well. It was from about this time that "dialectics" (*vākovākya*) became a separate branch of study among the Brahmins and the habit of debating religious and metaphysical topics in public became a recognised institution.

These theories are recorded or referred to in the Upaniṣadic and Jain texts. The Buddha summarizes the main views of his predecessors and contemporaries in the *Brahmajāla Sutta*, one of the oldest and most authentic of suttas in the Pali Canon. It is one of the few suttas to which the Buddha has given a title at the end and the only one for which several such titles are given. The Buddha says: "You may remember this exposition as the 'net of aims,' the 'net of doctrines,' the 'supreme net,' the 'net of religio-philosophic theories,' and 'the glorious victory in the war (of ideologies)'" (D I 46). The sutta and the doctrines contained in it are referred to elsewhere in the early portion of the Canon, the Nikāyas themselves (e.g. S II 227f; Sn 538), and a brief account of the circumstances in which it was preached is given in the proceedings of the First Council, reported in the *Vinaya Piṭaka*. The *Brahmajāla Sutta* is found in the Chinese *Āgamas* as well and may be presumed to belong to the common core of early doctrine.

I think that one of the reasons why Buddhism adopted a non-dogmatic attitude was that at its very inception it had to face a plurality of contending religio-philosophic theories about the nature and destiny of man. As a result, scepticism was rampant and the Buddha could not assume the truth of any particular religious philosophy in addressing the intellectual elite (*viññū-purisa*) of his age. A claim to authority would not have been seriously considered or accepted.

A Jain commentator, Sīlāṅka of the ninth century, speaks in the following vein of the reasons for the growth of the sceptical schools of thought during the time of Mahāvīra, who was the senior contemporary of the Buddha: "The sceptics say that those who claim knowledge cannot be making factual claims since their statements are mutually contradictory, for even with regard to the category of the soul, some assert that the soul is omnipresent and others that it is not omnipresent, some say it is of the size of a digit, others that it is of the size of a kernel of a grain of millet, some say it both has form and is formless, some that it resides in the heart and others that it is located in the forehead, etc. In respect of every category there is no uniformity in their assertions; there is no one with an outstanding intellect whose statements may be regarded as authoritative; even if such a person existed, he cannot be discovered by one with a limited vision according to the maxim that 'one who is not omniscient does not know everything,' for it is said 'how can one desiring to know that a certain person is omniscient at a certain time do so if he is devoid of that person's intellect, his knowledge and his consciousness" (see K. N. Jayatilleke, *Early Buddhist Theory of Knowledge,* London, 1963).

The very presence of such a variety of religio-philosophic theories at that time is a tribute to the tolerance of Hinduism in this period. The Vedic tradition at this time stressed the importance of knowledge (*jñāna*) whatever the form it may take, whether it be empirical, rational or intuitive, as the key to power or salvation. This was, no doubt, opposed by those who stressed the claims of social action and ritual (*karma-mārga*) as the way to salvation, but so long as the *jñāna-vādins* gave a nominal allegiance to the Vedic tradition they were not suppressed.

The *Āraṇyakas* for the first time proclaimed that what was important was not the actual performance of the various Vedic sacrifices but the understanding of their meaning and symbolism, which came to be interpreted to mean the understanding of the meaning of life. Eventually, in the *Upaniṣads* it is shown that there is no greater "sacrifice" (*yajna*) than that of understanding the meaning of life and living accordingly. The *Chāndogya Upaniṣad* says: "Now, what people call sacrifice (*yajña*) is really the religious life (*brahmacarya*), for only through the religious life does one who is a knower find that world" (8.5.1).

We may recall that when the Brahmin Kūṭadanta comes to the Buddha and wants to be instructed by him as to how to perform a really valuable sacrifice (Pali *yañña*, Skr. *yajña*), the Buddha explains that it would be a waste of valuable resources and a needless destruction of animals to perform a ritualistic sacrifice; he points out that the true "sacrifice" consists in leading the Buddhist way of life and adds: "There is no sacrifice that man can celebrate, O brahmin, higher and sweeter than this" (D I 147).

The thinkers of the *Āraṇyakas* and the *Upaniṣads* were not propounding one theory but a multiplicity of mutually contradictory theories about the nature and destiny of man in the universe. According to the independent attestation of the Buddhist scriptures, the Brahmins during this period were cultivating a "skill in metaphysics and logic," a branch of study which was known as *lokāyata,* a word which at this time meant "theories pertaining to the cosmos" but which later came to mean "materialist theories." Among these cosmological theories, which were being put forward by these Brahmins, according to the Buddhist texts, were the following:

(1) that everything exists (*sabbaṃ atthi*);
(2) that nothing exists (*sabbaṃ natthi*);
(3) that the world is a unity (*sabbaṃ ekattaṃ*); and
(4) that the world is a plurality (*sabbaṃ puthuttaṃ*) (S II 77).

The fact that they were putting forward and debating mutually contradictory views based on reasoning did not seem to have bothered orthodoxy at the time. Of the above theories, the first and the third are generally in keeping with Vedic assumptions, whereas the second and the fourth are characterized as materialist theories in the Buddhist commentarial tradition and would appear to contradict these assumptions. But it was agreed that evolving such diverse theories and living in accordance with them constituted worship of Brahman and complete intellectual freedom was thus allowed.

The above evidence is from Buddhist sources but it is confirmed from what we find in the Vedic tradition. The *Bhagavadgītā* speaks of "some who worship with offerings of knowledge, with (theories) of unity as well as of plurality" (*jñāna-yajñena cā'pyanye ... upāsate ekatvena pṛthaktvena*) (IX.15). As far as the Vedic scriptural tradition went, an idealistic monistic theory was apparently considered to be on the same footing as a materialist pluralistic theory.

We referred to the theory that "nothing exists" as a materialist theory. In the Buddhist canonical texts too one of the several materialist schools is said to hold that "neither this world existed nor the world beyond" (*natthi ayani loko, natthi paro loko*) (D I 55). It should appear strange that a materialist school of thought should deny the reality of this world, though it is understandable that it should deny the reality of the world beyond. The publication in 1940 of a work by Jayarāsi Bhaṭṭa called the *Tattvopaplavasiṃha* (eds. S. Sanghavi and E. C. Parikh, *Gaekwad Oriental Series* No.87, Baroda, 1940). has now settled our doubts. It is the only extant text of a materialist school hitherto discovered. It argues that even sense-perception (which was accepted by most materialist schools as the only valid means of knowledge) cannot be trusted, but that out of purely pragmatic considerations we must act on the assumption that there are only material things and values, though in actual fact even the reality of this world cannot be proved. This remarkable breadth of outlook on the part of the pre-Buddhist Vedic traditionalists, who permitted the widest degree of speculation within its fold, did not, however, last very long. Such absolute and untrammeled freedom of thought and expression was considered to be somewhat dangerous for orthodoxy; soon curbs and restrictions were believed to be necessary. Soon after the impact of Buddhism the *Maitrī Upaniṣad* states: "There are those who love to distract the believers in the Veda by the jugglery of false arguments, comparisons and paralogisms: with these one should not associate ... The world, bewildered by a doctrine that denies the self (*nairātmya-vāda*), by false comparisons and proofs, does not discern the difference between the wisdom of the Vedas and the rest of knowledge ... They say that there should be attention to a (new) Dharma, which is destructive of the teaching of the Vedas and the other scriptures ... Therefore what is set forth in the Vedas, that is the truth. On what is said in the Vedas, on that wise men live their life. Therefore a Brahmin should not study what is not of the Veda" (*Maitrī Up.* 7.8.10).

The *Lokāyata* speculations, likewise, led to the propagation of materialist theories of man and the universe in Brahmin circles and these were considered to undermine the Vedic tradition. The *Manusmṛti* therefore lays down the rule: "The Brahmin who despises the roots of the Vedic tradition because of his dependence on the science of reasoning should be expelled by the good Brahmins as a nihilist, who scorns the Vedas" (*Manusmṛti* II.11). After this, *Lokāyata* as a branch of study was taboo to Brahmin orthodoxy and the word survived to denote the materialist theories, which were once nurtured within the orthodox fold itself.

The free atmosphere for speculation and controversy generated by the pre-Buddhist Vedic tradition, however, had caused a hundred flowers to bloom both within as well as without the Brahmin intellectual circles. The variety of religio-philosophic views, which included several sceptical theories, as well as the unbounded freedom of thought and expression permitted at the time, no doubt left their mark on Buddhism.

This does not mean that the dawn of the Buddhist era was not without its dogmatists. In the welter of mutually contending theories, there were bound to be those who tried to peddle their own wares with dogmatic insistence. The *Suttanipāta* refers to "all those people who tenaciously cling to their respective religio-philosophical theories and argue, 'Here alone is the truth!" (*ye kec'ime diṭṭhi paribbhassānā, 'idam eva saccan' ti vivādayanti*) (Sn 896). There is also a reference to people who claimed to dispense salvation: "Here alone is salvation'—thus do they proclaim; they do not grant salvation in the religions of others" (*Idh'eva suddhi' iti vādiyanti, nāññesu dhammesu visuddhim āhu*)" (Sn 824).

The question of survival is central to religion, for unless there is some concept of survival after death the concept of salvation would be meaningless and we might as well dispense with religion. It would therefore be pertinent to illustrate the variety of views held on topics pertaining to religion by reference to the several solutions put forward at this time regarding this question. It will show the difference of the Buddhist point of view, with which some of these discarded theories are even today identified. Logically there are four possible points of view that we can adopt with regard to this question. We may say: (a) that we survive death in the form of discarnate spirits, i.e. a single after-life theory; (b) that we come back to subsequent earth-lives or lives on other similar planets, i.e. a rebirth theory; (c) that we are annihilated with death, i.e. a materialist theory; and (d) that we are unable to discover a satisfactory answer to this question or there is no satisfactory answer, i.e. a sceptical, agnostic or positivist theory.

The Buddhist texts record several variants of each of the above types. The *Brahmajāla Sutta* classifies the single after-life theories as follows:

It says that there are religious teachers, who assert that the soul after death is (a) conscious (*saññī*), (b) unconscious (*asaññī*) or (c) superconscious, lit. neither conscious nor unconscious (*nevasaññīnāsaññī*). There are sixteen variants of the conscious-theory and eight each of the other two. The following are the sixteen:

I. Variations regarding the form of the soul:

(i) has a subtle material form;
(ii) has no such form;
(iii) has a subtle material form for some time and then has no such form;
(iv) intrinsically has no such form but has the power of manifesting such a form.

II. Variations regarding the duration of the soul:

- (i) comes to an end, e.g. the theory of "second death" in the Brāhmaṇas;
- (ii) is of eternal duration;
- (iii) changes its state after some time and becomes eternal;
- (iv) does not exist in time.

III. Variations regarding the nature and extent of consciousness:

- (i) consciousness of unity;
- (ii) consciousness of diversity;
- (iii) of limited consciousness;
- (iv) of unlimited consciousness.

IV. Variations regarding the hedonic tone of experiences:

- (i) extremely happy;
- (ii) extremely unhappy;
- (iii) both happy and unhappy;
- (iv) not experiencing happiness or unhappiness.

Only variations I (i)–(iv) and II (i)–(iv) are considered applicable to those who held that the soul was (b) unconscious or (c) superconscious after death.

It would not be difficult to find instances of the above theories of survival put forward by religious teachers and philosophical thinkers of East and West. On first glance the above list looks artificial, but the fact that many of these theories can be traced to the pre-Buddhist literature proves that it is not. Thus Prajāpati held, on the basis of rational and metaphysical speculation, that the soul was "conscious and having its own form after death" (*Chāndogya Up.*, 8.12), i.e. (a)(I)(i).

Uddālaka held that the soul was "unconscious and without form" after death, i.e. (b)(I)(ii). The *Taittirīya Upaniṣad* asserts that the soul has a subtle material form for some time and then ceases to have such a material form (*Taittirīya Up.* 3.10.5), i.e. (a)(I)(iii). Yājñavalkya tries to show that the soul is "neither conscious nor unconscious after death" and has no form, i.e. (c)(I)(ii). Just as much as there are several single after-life theories, there are several rebirth theories in the pre-Buddhist traditions of the Upaniṣads, the Ājīvikas and Jains. They range from those who assert that the soul is reborn even as "herbs and trees" (*Chāndogya Up.* 5.10.6) to those who hold that the soul betters its status at each successive stage of rebirth, taking on "another newer and more beautiful form" (*Bṛhadāraṇyaka Up.*, 4.4.4).

On the other hand the several schools of materialists denied survival altogether. Seven such schools are referred to in the *Brahmajāla Sutta*. One of them, the most extreme, held that there is no mind or soul apart from the body, which is entirely a hereditary product of one's parents. What we call "mind" is the patterns of movement in our bodies. Another school held that the mind is an emergent product, which has a material basis, and its condition is determined by the food we eat. They argued that just as much as when we mix up certain chemicals in certain proportions there emerges the intoxicating power of liquor, even so the material particles of the body and the food we eat go to form the mind, which is an emergent by-product. This would be similar to a Marxist materialist conception of the mind. This emergent mind, however, was deemed to disintegrate on the dissolution of the body at death. There were also schools of mystic materialists, who believed in the possibilities of the expansion of consciousness but argued that since such forms of consciousness are dependent on the condition of the body, there is no survival after death.

The dialectical opposition between the soul-theorists, who asserted survival, and the various schools of materialists, who denied it, led to scepticism with regard to the question of survival and other such matters as well. The *Kaṭha Upaniṣad* says: "This doubt there is with regard to a man deceased—'he exists' say some; 'he exists not' say others" (*Kaṭha Up.* I.20). The sceptics adopted scepticism on the basis of various intellectual or pragmatic grounds or both. Some held that our experiences are subjective since they are based on our own individual perspective and that no objectivity in knowledge was possible since we cannot have any insight into the minds of others. Others held that on these matters one is led by one's prejudices for (*chanda, rāga*) or against (*dosa, paṭigha*) and that we are therefore unjustified in coming to definite conclusions. Yet others were of the opinion that in dogmatically accepting a theory of survival or denying it, we get involved with the theory and that such "involvement" is a source of mental unrest. Others found that we could argue rationally for or against survival and that therefore we are none the wiser. Sañjaya appears to have been of the view that the question of survival and similar questions are beyond verification and it is immaterial as to what we believe.

It would divert us from our task to give a detailed account of the Buddhist theory of survival and the grounds on which it is based. Suffice it to say, as it would appear to be evident from the above, that the Buddhist theory of survival was taught by the Buddha after examining all the alternative possible theories with regard to the question of survival. According to the information of the earliest texts, he did so after he was convinced of it on the basis of his capacity to recall his past lives and also to read by means of his clairvoyance the past lives of others. He trained several of his disciples to acquire these faculties and realise the truth of his discoveries for themselves.

It is a belief of many people today that religious dogmas cannot be empirically verified but have to be accepted on the basis of faith. It is therefore necessary to add that rebirth, which forms part of the Buddhist theory of re-becoming (*punabbhava*), is no longer in the realm of superstition and religious dogma. It is one thing which distinguishes Buddhism from other religions with the possible exception of certain forms of Hinduism. Rebirth has become philosophically respectable even to a modern logical analyst, who has expressly come out in favour of a concept of rebirth without a soul, which is exactly the Buddhist form of the doctrine. This professor of philosophy, A. J. Ayer, states his position as follows in one of his recent works: "I think that it would be open to us to admit the logical possibility of reincarnation merely by laying down the rule that if a person who is physically identified as living at a later time does have the extensible memories and character of a person who is physically identified as living at an earlier time, they are to be counted as one person and not two" (A. J. Ayer, *The Concept of a Person*, London, 1963, p. 127).

There are three sorts of empirical evidence for rebirth: the evidence from age-regression experiments conducted with subjects who allegedly recall minute historical details of experiences in prior lives without having obtained such information in this life, the evidence from authentic instances of the spontaneous cases of recall mostly on the part of children even from countries in which they are not predisposed to believe in rebirth, and finally evidential clairvoyance.

A psychologist refers to some of the case records of a psychiatrist, Dr Blanche Baker, in one of which the subject was regressed "through a total of forty-seven lives (twenty-three as a man and twenty-four as a woman)" and says, "literally hundreds of details of these lives have been verified in historical reference books. 'Coincidence' is the stock explanation offered by sceptics for these occurrences, but the explanation is at best inadequate in view of the frequency with which they occur" (Gina Cerminara, *The World Within,* New York, 1957, p. 28f). Dr Ian Stevenson selected forty-four cases in which there have been "apparent recollections of specific people, places and events in the life of a definitely identified other person, who died prior to the birth of the subject." He states his conclusion as follows after trying to account for the data in terms of several alternative normal and paranormal hypotheses: "I will say, therefore, that I think reincarnation the most plausible hypothesis for understanding cases of this series" (*The Evidence for Survival from Claimed Memories of Former Incarnations,* Essex, 1964, p. 84). The best attested case of evidential clairvoyance is that of Edgar Cayce, who gave detailed and accurate medical diagnoses of the illnesses of patients, some of whom he had not even seen. Later, when questions were put to him about the nature and destiny of man in the universe, he claimed to see and read the prior lives of himself as well as of others (Thomas Sugrue, *There Is a River*, New York, 1943, and G. Cerminara, *Many Mansions*, New York, 1960).

Rebirth is not a well-established scientific hypothesis universally accepted by psychologists as yet, but it is significant that it should be considered by at least some psychologists as "the most plausible hypothesis" to account for the empirical data.[7] I have digressed from my main theme in order to show that the Buddhist theory of rebirth can today be subjected to experimental investigation, and it would therefore be incorrect to say that it is a doctrine which has to be either accepted or rejected on mere faith.

To get back to my subject, I took this question of survival after death merely to illustrate the diversity of views regarding it prevalent at the time of the Buddha. Had I taken any other problem pertinent to

---

7. For a careful analysis of the evidence, see C. J. Ducasse, *A Critical Examination of the Belief in a Life after Death,* Springfield, Illinois, 1961, pp. 207–307.

religion, such as the problem of free will vs. determinism, moral responsibility vs. amoralism, theism vs. atheism, it would have been possible to illustrate a similar diversity of views prevalent at the time. At no other time in human history, unless it be in the present, was such a variety of views on matters pertaining to religion present together in the same epoch. No wonder that the Buddha referred to them as a "thicket of views, a wilderness of views, a tangle of views" (*diṭṭhi-gahanaṃ, diṭṭhi-kantāraṃ, diṭṭhi–visūkaṃ*) (M I 8). The opening verse of the *Visuddhimagga*, quoted from the Pali Canon, gives a beautiful and apt description of the plight of thinking men in that age:

> *The inner tangle and the outer tangle—*
> *This generation is entangled in a tangle.*
> *And so I ask of Gotama this question:*
> *Who succeeds in disentangling this tangle?*
>
> (*Path of Purification* I.1)

To have adopted a dogmatic attitude and to have accepted one or more of these views uncritically from one of the prevailing Vedic or non-Vedic traditions would have been self-defeating. So with those who were bewildered by the variety of religio-philosophical theories offered them during this age, the Buddha advocated a critical outlook, recommending that they test the validity of any particular religion or philosophy that appeals to them in the light of their personal experience. The sceptics had already taught that a man may be led by his prejudices for (*chanda*) or against (*dosa*) accepting or rejecting a theory. The Buddha showed them how one should examine things dispassionately without being led by attachment (*chanda*), hatred (*dosa*), ignorance (*moha*) or fear (*bhaya*) (D II 133). The following oft-quoted passage, which is not always accurately translated, contains the essence of the attitude recommended by the Buddha in choosing between conflicting ideologies as a basis for living:

> There are certain religious teachers who come to Kesaputta. They speak very highly of their own theories, but oppose, condemn and ridicule the theories of others. At the same time there are yet other religious teachers who come to Kesaputta and in turn speak highly of their own theories, opposing, condemning and ridiculing the theories of these others. We are now in a state

> of doubt and perplexity as to who out of these venerable recluses spoke the truth and who spoke falsehood."
>
> O Kālāmas, you have a right to doubt or feel uncertain, for you have raised a doubt in a situation in which you ought to suspend your judgement. Come now, Kālāmas, do not accept anything on the grounds of revelation, tradition or report or because it is a product of mere reasoning or because it is true from a standpoint or because of a superficial assessment of the facts or because it conforms with one's preconceived notions or because it is authoritative or because of the prestige of your teacher. When you, Kālāmas, realise for yourselves that these doctrines are evil and unjustified, that they are condemned by the wise, and that when they are accepted and lived by they conduce to ill and sorrow, then you should reject them..." (A I 189).

This critical attitude should be focused on Buddhism itself:

> "If anyone were to speak ill of me, my doctrine or my Order, do not bear any ill-will towards him, be upset or perturbed at heart; for if you were to do so, it would only cause you harm. If, on the other hand, anyone were to speak well of me, my doctrine and my Order, do not be overjoyed, thrilled or elated at heart; for if you were to do so, it would only be an obstacle in the way of forming a realistic judgment as to whether the qualities praised in us are real and actually found in us" (D I 3).

The later tradition often underlines this attitude. The following verse attributed to the Buddha is to be found in a Sanskrit Buddhist text called the *Tattvasaṃgraha* and a Tibetan work called the *Jñānasamuccayasāra*:

> Just as the experts test gold by burning it, cutting it, and applying it on a touchstone, my statements should be accepted only after critical examination and not out of respect for me.

This does not, however, mean that faith is no requirement at all in Buddhism. Far from it. One cannot test a theory unless one accepts it at least tentatively as one's basis of life. The Buddhist accepts the "right philosophy of life" (*sammā-diṭṭhi*) as the basis of his living because he finds it reasonable and in fact more reasonable than any other way of life. Such faith which eventually culminates in knowledge is called a "rational faith" (*ākāravatī saddhā*) as opposed to a blind or "baseless faith" (*amūlikā saddhā*).

Going along with this critical outlook is the causal conception of nature, which is conceived of as a causal system in which there operate physical laws (*utu-niyāma*), biological laws (*bīja-niyāma*), psychological laws (*citta-niyāma*) as well as moral and spiritual laws (*kamma-dhamma-niyāma*). These laws are said to operate whether a Buddha comes into existence or not, and all that the Buddha does is to discover them and reveal to us those which are of relevance to the moral and spiritual life, which is both possible and desirable in the universe in which we live. It is said:

> Whether Tathāgatas arise or not, this order exists, namely, the fixed nature of phenomena, the regular pattern of phenomena or conditionality. This the Tathāgata discovers and comprehends; having discovered and comprehended it, he points it out, teaches it, lays it down, establishes, reveals, analyses, clarifies it and says, "Look!" (S II 25).

This dispassionate and impartial but critical outlook (the causal conception of the universe and the conception of the Buddha as a being who discovers the operation of certain moral and spiritual laws and reveals them to us) may be said to be the first plank on which Buddhist tolerance rests. A scientist does not ask a fellow-scientist to accept a theory on faith, though his fellow-scientist must have enough faith in the theory on his preliminary examination of it before he thinks of testing it out. In the same way, the Buddha shows us the way but we have to do the hard work of treading it before we can get anywhere—*tumhe hi kiccaṃ ātappaṃ akkhātāro tathāgata.* The Dhamma is well-proclaimed (*svākkhāto*), *it* produces results without delay in this very life (*sandiṭṭhiko akāliko*), it invites anyone to verify it for himself (*ehipassiko*), it leads to the desired goal (*opanayiko*), and it is to be realised by the wise, each person for himself (*paccattaṃ veditabbaṃ viññūhi*). It looks as if the Buddha was addressing a modern mind of the twentieth century, for the outlook that the Buddha recommends is what we today call the scientific outlook, except for the fact that it does not make a dogma of materialism.

The concept of the Buddha as one who discovers the truth rather than as one who has a monopoly of the truth is clearly a source of tolerance. It leaves open the possibility for others to discover aspects of the truth or even the whole truth for themselves. The Buddhist acceptance of Pacceka-Buddhas, who discover the truth for themselves, is a clear admission of this fact. Referring to certain sages (*munayo*), who had comprehended the nature of their desires and had eliminated them, crossing over the waves of saṃsāric existence, the Buddha says: "I do not declare that all these religious men are sunk in repeated birth and decay" (*nāhaṃ bhikkhave sabbe samaṇa brahmaṇāse jātijarāya nivutā ti brūmi*) (Sn 1082). Yet, as it is pointed out, the Dhamma is to be preached to all beings, though all beings may not profit by it, just as much as all sick people are to be treated, although some may get well or succumb to their illnesses despite the medicines given (A I 120f). This is because there are beings who would profit only from the Dhamma.

This assertion of the possibility of salvation or spiritual growth outside Buddhism does not mean that Buddhism values all religions alike and considers them equally true. It would be desirable to determine the Buddhist use of the word for religion before examining this question. In early Buddhism, a religious doctrine was denoted by the word *dhamma. Diṭṭhi* was a "religio-philosophical theory" and for it the word *darsana* was later used in Indian thought. But for "religion," which includes both beliefs as well as practises, the word used was *dhamma-vinaya,* which literally means "doctrine and discipline." But the term which was common to the Vedic tradition as well was *brahmacarya,* which literally means the "religious life." It was used in a very wide sense, because of the intellectual tolerance of the Vedic tradition at this time, to denote any "ideal life." It could be interpreted to mean any way of life that was considered to be the ideal as a result of one accepting a certain view of life concerning the nature and destiny of man in the universe. In this sense, the way of life of a materialist is also an ideal life from his point of view.

Indian thought has been accused of failing to divorce religion from philosophy. The accusation is unjustified. For what happened in the history of Indian thought is that the theoretical aspect of each religion was considered its philosophy, whereas its practical aspect was the religion. Every philosophy including materialism thus had both a view of life as well as a way of life, and consistency was demanded not only in each sphere (i.e. within each "view of life" and within each "way of life"), but also between both. A materialist philosopher who did not live in accordance with material values was thus considered inconsistent. The Buddha claimed that there was consistency between his theory and practise (*yathāvādī tathākārī*). Western classical metaphysics on the other hand latterly came to be divorced from living. It was for this reason that existentialism had to come in to fill the void. In Indian thought, however, every philosophical system had its theory as well as its practise and a philosophy was not entertained in isolation from its practical bearing on life. Today we call those non-theistic philosophies (which have a practical bearing on life and often claim the sole allegiance of an individual) religion-surrogates since they take the place of traditional religions and act as substitutes for religion. Humanism, certain forms of existentialism not related to traditional religions and certain materialist philosophies like Marxism, which have a practical bearing on life, may be considered such religion-surrogates. Buddhism considers some of those religion-surrogates on the same footing as practical religions (*brahmacariya-vāsa*) in stating its attitude to various types of religion. In the *Sandaka Sutta* Ānanda, reporting the ideas of the Buddha, says that there are four pseudo-religions (*abrahmacariya-vāsā*) or false religions in the world and four religions which are unsatisfactory (lit. *anassāsikaṃ,* unconsoling) but not necessarily false.

The pseudo-religions are: first, materialism, which asserts the reality of the material world alone and denies survival; second, a religious philosophy which recommends an amoral ethic; third, one which denies free will and moral causation and asserts that beings are either miraculously saved or doomed; and fourth, deterministic evolutionism, which asserts the inevitability of eventual salvation for all (M I 515–18).

The four unsatisfactory but not necessarily false religions are presumably those which in some sense recognise the necessity for a concept of survival, moral values, freedom and responsibility and the non-inevitability of salvation. The first is one in which omniscience is claimed for its founder in all his conscious and unconscious periods of existence. The second is a religion based on revelation or tradition; the third a religion founded on logical and metaphysical speculation; and the fourth is one which is merely pragmatic and is based on sceptical or agnostic foundations.

We note here that the relativist valuation of religion in early Buddhism does not presuppose or imply the truth of all religions or religion-surrogates. Some types of religion are clearly condemned as false and undesirable, while others are satisfactory to the extent to which they contain the essential core of beliefs and values central to religion, whatever their epistemic foundations may be. Those based on claims to omniscience on the part of the founder, revelation or tradition, metaphysical speculation or pragmatic scepticism, are unsatisfactory insofar as they are based on uncertain foundations.

Revelations and revelational traditions contradict each other and it is said that they may contain propositions which may be true or false. In the case of religions based on metaphysical arguments and speculations, "the reasoning may be valid or invalid and the conclusions true or false" (*sutakkitaṃ pi hoti duttakkitaṃ pi hoti tathā pi hoti aññatha pi hoti*) (M I 520). Buddhism is, therefore, by implication a religion which asserts survival, moral values, freedom and responsibility, and the non-inevitability of salvation. It is also verifiably true.

I do not propose here to examine any of the specific doctrines of another religion and compare or contrast them with Buddhism, but it will be observed that the definition of the Buddhist "right view of life" (*sammā-diṭṭhi*) comprehends the basic beliefs and values of the higher religions. The definition reads as follows: "There is value in alms, sacrifices and oblations; there is survival and recompense for good and evil deeds; there are moral obligations, and there are religious teachers who have led a good life and who have proclaimed with their superior insight and personal understanding the nature of this world and the world beyond" (M III 72). This "right view of life" (*sammā-diṭṭhi*) is said to be of two sorts: (a) one of which is mixed up with the inflowing impulses (*sāsavā*), and (b) the other not so mixed up. These impulses are the desire for sensuous gratification (*kāmāsavā*), the desire for self-centred pursuits and for continued existence in whatsoever form (*bhavāsavā*), and illusions (*avijjāsavā*). Thus a right view of life mixed up with a desire for personal immortality in heaven or a belief in sensuous heavens would be a *sāsava-sammā-diṭṭhi*.

The above summary of the right philosophy of life, it may be observed, is comprehensive enough to contain, recognise and respect the basic truths of all higher religions. All these religions believe in a Transcendent, characterised as Nibbāna, which is beyond time, space and causation in Buddhism, as an impersonal monistic principle such as Brahman or Tao in some religions, and as a personal God in others. They all assert survival, moral recompense and responsibility. They all preach a "good life," which has much in common and whose culmination is communion or union with or the attainment of this Transcendent. The early Buddhist conception of the nature and destiny of man in the universe is, therefore, not in basic conflict with the beliefs and values of the founders of the great religions so long as they assert some sort of survival, moral values, freedom and responsibility and the non-inevitability of salvation. But at the same time it is not possible to say that in all their phases of development, and in all their several strands of belief in varying social contexts, they have stood for this central core of beliefs and values. This applies to Buddhism as well, particularly when we consider some of the developments in Tantric Buddhism.

One of the last questions put to the Buddha was by the wandering ascetic Subhadda. He wanted to know whether the leading philosophies and religions proclaimed in his day by the six outstanding teachers, who each had a large following were all true, all false or whether some were true and some false. The Buddha did not give a specific answer to this question since he generally avoided making specific criticisms of particular religions unless he was invited or challenged to do so. He says, however, that any religion is true to the extent to which it would incorporate the Noble Eightfold Path: "In whatever religion the Noble Eightfold Path is not found, that religion would not have the first saint, the second, the third, and the fourth; in whatever religion the Noble Eightfold Path is found, that religion would have the first, second, third and fourth saints. Void are these other religions of true saints. If these monks were to live righteously, the world would never be devoid of saints" (D II 151). The first saint, the stream-enterer or *sotāpanna*, is the person who has given up preconceptions about a soul to be identified with or located within aspects or the whole of his psycho-physical personality, is convinced that no permanent and secure existence is possible within the cosmos of becoming (i.e. has given up *sakkāya-diṭṭhi* or personality belief), has by study and understanding cleared his doubts about the Buddha, Dhamma and the saintly Sangha (i.e. has got rid of *vicikicchā*), has given up obsessional attachments to religious virtues and observances (i.e. has discarded *sīlabbata-parāmāsa*), and leads a pure moral life. As such he is not likely to fall below the level of human existence in any of his future births (*avinipāta-dhammo*) and is assured of final realization. The third saint[8] is the person who, in addition to the above, tends to act out of selfless charity (*cāga*), compassion (*karuṇā*) and understanding (*vijjā*) rather than out of greed (*lobha*), hatred (*dosa*) and ignorance (*moha*). Ignorance comprises all the erroneous beliefs and illusions we entertain about the nature and destiny of man in the universe. Hatred is the source of our aggressive (*vibhava-taṇhā*) tendencies and greed includes the desire for sensuous gratification (*kāma-taṇhā*) as well as the desire for self-centred pursuits (*bhava-taṇhā*), such as the desire for power, fame, etc. The fourth saint, the arahant, is the person who attains final realization in this life itself.[9]

Leaving out Nigaṇṭha Nātaputta, the founder of Jainism, the other five outstanding teachers in the day of the Buddha represent standard types of philosophies or religions. In Sañjaya, we have the sceptic or agnostic or positivist who argued that questions pertaining to survival, moral responsibility and values, spiritual beings and transcendent existence were beyond verification. Ajita Kesakambalī was a materialist who denied any value in religious activities, denied survival, moral recompense and moral obligations, and denied that there were any religious teachers who had led a good life and who have proclaimed with their superior insight and understanding the nature of this world and the world beyond. His view was that the fools and the wise alike were annihilated at death. Makkhali Gosāla has been called a theist (*issara-kāraṇa-vādi*); as a theist who believed in God he seemed to have argued that salvation is eventually predestined for all. Everything is preplanned and takes place in accordance with the fiat of God; it is like the unraveling of a ball of thread thrown on the ground. Fools and wise alike evolve in various forms of existence, high and low, in the course of which

---

8. The non-returner to the world of sensuality (*anāgāmi*). He has fully eliminated the fetters of sensuous desire and ill-will, which are still present, though weakened, in the second saint (once-returner), who is not mentioned in this text (editor).

9. The arahant has fully eliminated all the remaining five fetters: desire for fine-material and immaterial existence, conceit, restlessness and ignorance (editor).

they gather experience under the impact of diverse forces, living in accordance with the sixty-two philosophies of life in different lives. Man himself has no will of his own since everything is predetermined by the divine will, which guarantees final salvation for all.

The theism of Makkhali is severely criticized since it gives a false sense of security to people and encourages complacency by denying free will, the value of human effort and ensuring eventual salvation. The Buddha says that he knows of no other person than Makkhali born to the detriment and disadvantage of so many people, comparing him to a fisherman casting his net at the mouth of a river for the destruction of many fish (AN 1:18/A I 33).

There are two arguments against belief in such a personal God (*īsvara*) mentioned in the Buddhist scriptures. The first is that the truth of theism entails a lack of man's final responsibility for his actions: "If God designs the life of the entire world—the glory and the misery, the good and the evil acts—man is but an instrument of his will and God is responsible" (J-a V 238). The other is that some evils are inexplicable if we grant the truth of such a theism: "If God is the lord of the whole world and creator of the multitude of beings, then why has he ordained misfortune in the world without making the whole world happy? For what purpose has he made a world that has injustice, deceit, falsehood and conceit? The lord of the world is unrighteous in ordaining injustice where there could have been justice" (J-a VI 208).

The fact that such a theistic philosophy is severely criticized does not mean that all forms of theism are condemned. A theistic religion and philosophy which; (1) stresses the importance of human freedom, responsibility and effort; (2) encourages the cultivation of moral and spiritual values and the attainment of moral perfection; and (3) offers the hope of fellowship with God (Brahmā), who is represented as a perfect moral being (wise and powerful but not omniscient or omnipotent) is to be commended on pragmatic grounds. Addressing some personal theists among the Brahmins, the Buddha describes the path to fellowship (*sahavyatā*, lit. companionship) with God (Brahmā) and speaks of the necessity of cultivating selflessness, compassion, freedom from malice, purity of mind and self-mastery for this purpose:

> Then you say, too, Vāseṭṭha, that the Brahmins bear anger and malice in their hearts and are impure in heart and uncontrolled, whilst God is free from anger and malice, pure in heart and has self-mastery. Now can there be concord and harmony between the Brahmins and God?"
>
> "Certainly not, Gotama!"
>
> "Very good, Vāseṭṭha. That those Brahmins versed in the Vedas and yet bearing anger and malice in their hearts, sinful and uncontrolled, should after death, when the body is dissolved, attain fellowship with God, who is free from anger and malice, pure in heart and has self-mastery—such a state of things can in no way be" (Tevijja Sutta, D I 247–8).

Whatever the basis of the theistic myth they believed in, so long as these Brahmins could be persuaded to cultivate these virtues grounded in their faith in God, it was a step in the right direction. Thus on pragmatic grounds the belief in a personal God is not discouraged insofar as it is not a hindrance but an incentive for moral and spiritual development. At the same time we must not forget that, even according to the Buddhist conception of the cosmos, such a heaven had a place in the scheme of things, though the God who ruled in it, worshipped as the Almighty, was only very wise, powerful and morally perfect, though not omniscient and omnipotent.

It will be worthwhile drawing attention to this conception of the cosmos in order to clarify this statement. The early Buddhist description of the cosmos, as far as the observable universe goes, is claimed to be based on extrasensory clairvoyant perception. It is remarkably close to the modern conception of the universe:

> As far as these suns and moons revolve shedding their light in space, so far extends the thousand-fold universe. In it there are thousands of suns (*sahassānaṃ suriyānaṃ*), thousands of moons, thousands of inhabited worlds of varying sorts … thousands of heavenly worlds of varying grades. This is the thousand-fold minor world system (*cūlaṇikā loka-dhātu*). Thousands of times the size of the thousand-fold minor world system is the twice-a-thousand middling world system (*majjhimika loka-dhātu*). Thousands of times the size of the middling world system is the thrice-a-thousand great cosmos (*mahā loka-dhātu*) (A I 227–28).

This conception of the universe as consisting of hundreds of thousands of clusters of galactic systems containing thousands of suns, moons and inhabited worlds is not to be found in the Hindu or Jain scriptures and was much in advance of the age in which it appears. In later Theravāda it gets embedded in and confused with mythical notions about the universe. In the Mahāyāna, the conception is magnified and there are references to the "unlimited and infinite number of galactic systems (*loka-dhātu*) in the ten quarters" (*Sukhāvatī-vyūha,* I), but the original conception of a "sphere of million millions of galactic systems" (*Vajracchedikā,* XXX) survives. Brahmā occupies a place in the highest of heavens, and although he is morally perfect, he is still within the cosmic scheme of things and his knowledge does not extend as far as that of a Buddha.

In the *Brahmajāla Sutta*, the Buddha points out that the origins of some forms of theistic religion and philosophy are to be traced to the religious teachings of beings from this heaven, who are born on earth and lead a homeless life preaching a doctrine which leads to fellowship with Brahmā. It is said that in the ages past Sunetta (Fair-Eyed) and five other such teachers taught the path to heaven and fellowship with God (A III 371). Such teachings are commended since they help man in bettering his condition.

On the other hand, when the Buddha addressed materialists, sceptics, determinists or indeterminists, who denied survival, freedom and responsibility, he does not presuppose the truth of these latter concepts but uses a "wager argument" reminiscent of Pascal. This shows that on pragmatic grounds it is better to base one's life on the assumptions of survival, freedom and responsibility; for, otherwise, whatever happens, we stand to lose whereas on the other alternative we stand to gain (*Apaṇṇaka Sutta,* MN 60).

It would be possible for scholars and students of Buddhism to take these texts in isolation and, ignoring the rest of the material in the Canon, argue that either the Buddha was a theist or an agnostic, a sceptic or a materialist, as the case may be. There seem to be even "Buddhists" who, on the basis of the erroneous belief that the doctrine of *anattā* (no-soul) precludes any possibility of a belief in survival, argue that the Buddha could not have entertained any belief in survival. This would make Buddhism a form of materialism, perhaps a dialectical materialism with the emphasis on the doctrine of impermanence (*anicca*) or a scepticism, doctrines from which Buddhism has been clearly distinguished in all its phases of expansion. It has even been said that rebirth is not taught in the First Sermon, which no one dared tamper with, whereas even this sermon quite clearly refers to "the desires which tend to bring about rebirth or re-becoming" (*taṇhā ponobbhavikā*). So does the last sermon to Subhadda emphasize the Noble Eightfold Path, whose first member is "the right view of life," which underlines the reality of this world as well as the world beyond (*atthi ayaṃ loko, atthi paro loko*).

Likewise, on the question of theism, we find that a scholar like Mrs. Rhys Davids latterly believed that Buddhism was no different in principle from a theistic religion, making the Buddha a personal theist. Radhakrishnan saw in the Buddha an impersonal theist or implicit monist. For Keith, the Buddha was an agnostic and for Stcherbatsky an atheist. In actual fact none of these labels is adequate to describe Buddhism, which transcends them all. It is important to distinguish Buddhism from all of them, for the Buddhist attitude to other religions would depend on the view we take of Buddhism itself.

It is important to distinguish Buddhism on the one hand from personal theism and on the other hand from atheistic materialism, although Buddhism has common ground with both. The Buddha was quite emphatic about this. He referred to the former as *bhava-diṭṭhi,* "the personal immortality view," and the latter as *vibhava-diṭṭhi,* "the annihilation view." Distinguishing Buddhism from both these views, which he says are found in the world and are mutually opposed to each other, the Buddha states: "These religious teachers who do not see how these two views arise and cease to be, their good points and their defects and how one transcends them in accordance with the truth are under the grip of greed, hate and ignorance … and will not attain final redemption from suffering" (M I 65).

We have already talked about the common ground that Buddhism has with some forms of theism in urging the validity of moral and spiritual values and of a transcendent reality. It will be worthwhile summarizing the common ground that Buddhism has with some forms of materialism. The Buddha refused to preach to a hungry man. What Buddhism requires of man in society is the pursuit of one's material as well as spiritual well-being (such a quest being practicable), where one's wealth is righteously earned and spent for one's good and that of others, without squandering or hoarding it. The man who is valued is the person who "possesses the capacity to acquire wealth that he could not acquire before and also to increase it and at the same time possesses that insight which makes it possible for him to distinguish good and evil" (*Puggalapaññatti*, III). Buddhism upholds the reality of this world as well as the next, and the Buddha speaks of the happiness of the average man as deriving from economic security (*atthi sukha*), the enjoyment of one's wealth (*bhoga-sukha*), freedom from debt (*anaṇa-sukha*) and a blameless moral and spiritual life (*anavajja-sukha*). All forms of asceticism that mortify the flesh are condemned even for monks since a strong and healthy body is necessary for both material and spiritual endeavours.

The Buddha was the first to proclaim the equality of man in the fullest sense of the term. There are differences of species, points out the Buddha, among plants and animals, but despite differences in the colour of the skin, the shape of the nose or the form of the hair, mankind is biologically one species (*Vāseṭṭha Sutta, Suttanipāta*). There was absolute spiritual equality as well for man, for anyone could aspire to become a Brahmā or a Buddha; there are no chosen castes, chosen churches or chosen individuals.

The Buddha gives a dynamic conception of society and holds that the economic factor is one of the main determinants of social change. Social disintegration and the division of the world into the haves and the have-nots, resulting in tensions, the loss of moral values in human society and destructive wars, originate from the misdistribution of goods: "As a result of goods not accruing to those bereft of goods, poverty becomes rampant; poverty becoming rampant, stealing becomes rampant ..." (D III 65). Tracing the cause of this poverty, which leads to such dire consequences, it is said that the mistake that the kings made was to consider that their task was merely to preserve law and order without developing the economy; the king "provided for the righteous protection and security of his subjects but neglected the economy" (*dhammikaṃ rakkhāvaraṇaguttiṃ saṃvidahi, no ca kho adhanānaṃ dhanaṃ anuppadāsi*). (D III 65). The ideal state was one in which there was both freedom as well as economic security. This freedom embraces the recognition of human rights, the freedom to propagate any political or religious doctrine, as well as freedom for "birds and beasts" (*migapakkhīsu*) to live without being wantonly attacked by humans.

In advising a king, the Buddha says that the best way to ensure peace and prosperity in one's kingdom is not by wasting the country's resources in performing religious sacrifices but by ensuring full employment and thereby developing the economy (see D I 135). The Emperor Asoka, who was imbued with these ideals, has been credited with being the first king in history to conceive of a welfare state. Imbued with these same ideals Sinhalese kings set up tremendous irrigation works for the welfare of man. It was King Parākramabāhu who said: "Truly in such a country not even a little water that comes from the rain must flow into the ocean without being made useful to man … for a life of enjoyment of what one possesses, without having cared for the welfare of the people, in no wise befits one like myself" (see Wilhelm Geiger, *The Cūḷavaṃsa,* Colombo, 1953, p. 277).

I think these few observations will suffice to show how strongly Buddhism stresses the importance of the material realities of life and how practical the advice has been. Both freedom as well as economic security are necessary ingredients for man's material and spiritual advancement. And freedom includes the freedom to criticise each others' political or religious philosophies without rancour or hatred in our hearts.

I said earlier that the dispassionate and impartial quest for truth, the causal conception of the universe and the conception of the Buddha as a discoverer and proclaimer of truth were some of the planks of Buddhist tolerance. Another has been compassion. We cannot force the truth on others. All we can do is to help them to discover it, and the greatest help we can give others especially in imparting spiritual truth is to try not to speak out of greed, hatred and ignorance but out of unselfishness, compassion and wisdom.

> Truth is immortal speech—this is the eternal law.
> *Saccaṃ ve amatā-vācā—esa dhammo sanantano.*
> Hatred does not cease by hatred—hatred ceases by love.
> This is the eternal law.
> *Na hi verena verāni—sammantīdha kudācanaṃ*
> *Averena ca sammanti—esa dhammo sanantano.*

22

Buddhism and Peace

What Buddhism has to say on the theme of peace and the concepts of truth, freedom, justice and love is, I believe, particularly appropriate to our times. This view, I also believe, would be shared by most of you in respect of your own religions.[10] This raises a number of problems. Are we all saying the same thing? Or are we saying a number of things which complement and supplement one another, each of us contributing some aspect of truth regarding these concepts, values and ideals? Or can it be that only one of us (or none of us) is right and the rest are wrong? Or is it the case that our talk about these things is devoid of meaning and has only an emotive significance for us and some of our hearers? We cannot hope to solve all these problems, but I believe that discussions of this sort can go a long way to help us see one another's points of view and clarify our own views about them.

It is evident that there is a common content in the higher religions. All these religions profess a belief in a Transcendent Reality, in survival, in moral responsibility and moral values, and in a good life, despite the differences when we go into details. The Christians and Muslims seek communion with God, the Hindus seek union with Brahman, and the Buddhists seek to attain Nibbāna. It is equally evident that on matters on which they disagree they cannot all be true—unless it can be shown that the disagreements are purely verbal. Christianity believes in one unique Incarnation; Hinduism in several. To Islam the very idea is blasphemy. To the Buddhist it depends on what you mean. Now, what I have to say on the concepts of peace, truth, freedom, justice and love in Buddhism belongs partly to the common content and partly to the disparate element which distinguishes Buddhism from other religions. It would be necessary for me to point out both, if I am to give a clear picture of the account given of these concepts in Buddhism.

---

10. Talk given on 8 April 1961 at the seminar on religion and peace at Oxford University, organised by the International Fellowship of Reconciliation.

Peace is a central concept in the religion of the Buddha, who came to be known as the "*santi-rājā*" or the "Prince of Peace." For on the one hand the aim of the good life, as understood in Buddhism, is described as the attainment of a state of "peace" or "*santi*," which is a characteristic of Nibbāna or the Transcendent Reality. On the other hand, the practice of the good life is said to consist in "*sama-cariyā*" or "harmonious (lit. peaceful) living" with one's fellow beings. It was this doctrine, which gave "inward peace" (*ajjhatta-santi*) (Sn 837). and resulted in "harmonious living" (or "righteous living"—*dhammacariyā*—as it is sometimes called), which the Buddha for the first time in the known history of mankind sought to spread over the entire earth when he set up as he claimed "the kingdom of righteousness" (*dhamma-cakkaṃ,* lit., rule of righteousness) or "the kingdom of God" (*brahma-cakkaṃ*).[11]

The Buddha, who in the earliest texts is said to have been "born for the good and happiness of mankind" (*manussaloke hita-sukhatāya jāto*) (Sn 683), first trained sixty-one of his disciples to attain the highest spiritual goal in this life itself and then sent them out, requesting that no two of them were to go in the same direction. They were "to preach this good doctrine, lovely in the beginning, lovely in the middle and lovely in its consummation." It is necessary to stress the importance of this training, which was intended to bring about the moral (*sīla*), intuitive (*samādhi*) and intellectual-spiritual (*paññā*) development of the person. For it was only those who had attained the "inward peace" who were considered fit to preach, since according to Buddhism "it is not possible for a man who has not saved himself to (help) save another" (M I 46). Those who went out on such missions were to train themselves in such a way that, "if brigands were to get hold of them and cut them limb by limb with a double-edged saw," they should not consider themselves to have done the bidding of the Buddha if they showed the slightest anger towards them (M I 129).

The practise of *mettā* or loving-kindness was thus an essential part of the training. The worth placed on love in Buddhism may be gathered from the following remark of the Buddha: "None of the good works employed to acquire religious merit is worth a fraction

---

11. *Brahmā* means here "the highest" or the "most sublime" without theological connotations.

of the value of loving-kindness" (It 19–21). The word *mettā* is the abstract noun from the word *mitra,* which means "friend." It is, however, not defined just as "friendliness" but as analogous to a mother's love for her only child. "Just as a mother loves her only child even more than her life, so extend a boundless love towards all creatures." The practise of the "highest life" or the "God-life" (*brahma-vihāra*) is said to consist in the cultivation of feelings of loving-kindness towards all beings, sympathy towards those in distress who need our help (*karuṇā*), the ability to rejoice with those who are justly happy (the opposite emotion to that of jealousy, envy, etc.) (*muditā*) and impartiality towards all (*upekkhā*). The person who has successfully developed these qualities is said to be "one who is cleansed with an internal bathing" after bathing "in the waters of love and compassion for one's fellow beings" (M I 39).

When the Buddha's disciple Ānanda suggested to him that half of the religion of the Buddha consisted in the practise of friendliness, the Buddha's rejoinder was that it was not half but the whole of the religion. It was this emphasis on compassion which made it possible for Buddhism to spread its message over the greater part of Asia without resorting to military force or political power. It is the proud boast of Buddhism that not a drop of blood has been shed in propagating its message and no wars have been fought for the cause of Buddhism or the Buddha. It was able to convert people to its view by its reasonableness and the inspiring example of those who preached it.

Differences of opinion there were with regard to the interpretation of the texts among the Buddhists themselves, and this was inevitable in a religion which gave full freedom of thought and expression to man. But these differences did not result in fanaticism and an attempt on the part of one party to persecute the other. History records the fact that those who subscribed to the ideals of Mahāyāna or Theravāda Buddhism were able to study side by side in the same monastery. In world conferences of Buddhists, Mahāyānists and Theravādins come together despite the known differences in their views. Another aspect of this practise of compassion on the part of the Buddhists is the fact that they were the first in history to open hospitals in India, Sri Lanka and China for the medical treatment not only of human beings but of animals as well, thus translating into action the saying of the Buddha that "He who serves the sick serves me" (*Vinaya Pitaka*, Mahāvagga VIII. 26).

The effect that this doctrine of compassion had on the Buddhist emperor Asoka may be seen when he says: "All men are my children, and, as I desire for my children that they obtain every kind of welfare and happiness both in this world and the next world, so do I desire for all men." Here was a king, unique in history, who on his conversion to Buddhism gave up military conquest as an instrument of policy not after defeat but after victory. Asoka had conquered an area almost the size of Europe, but he did not extend his conquest to the southernmost part of India or try to annex Sri Lanka, although he could have easily done so.

The Rock Edict XIII contains a personal confession of his remorse at the sight of the suffering and carnage which his military campaigns involved. When he embraced Buddhism, he indulged in spiritual conquest, saying that "the reverberation of war drums" was now replaced by the "reverberation of the drum of the dharma." It appears as if Asoka was trying to emulate the example of the righteous "universal monarch" (*cakkavatti-rāja*) as depicted in the Buddhist texts. The Buddha had said that "it was possible to rule a country in accordance with dharma without resorting to harsh punitive measures or engaging in military conquests" (S I 116).[12]

The "universal monarch," who is called a "king of righteousness" (*dharma-rāja*), governs his country as a model state in which there is both economic prosperity as well as the practise of righteousness. The idea and fame of this Just Society spreads over the earth until the entire world follows its example and comes under a single rule "without the necessity for arms or the sword" (*adaṇḍena asatthena*). In any case Asoka seems to have been impressed by the sentiments about war expressed in the Buddhist texts. The Dhammapada says:

> *Victory breeds hatred,*
> *for the conquered sleep in sorrow;*
> *casting aside victory and defeat,*
> *the peaceful one dwells at ease"* (Dhp 207).

---

12. According to Buddhist tradition, there are periods in the world cycles when human beings are at the peak of moral and intellectual development, and at such times a world ruler (*cakkavatti*) is able to govern in righteousness, without the use of force.

> *The conqueror gets someone who conquers him"* (S I 85).
> *Hatred does not cease by hatred—*
> *hatred ceases by love—*
> *this is the eternal law"* (Dhp 5).

The Mahāyāna work, the *Suvarṇabhāsottama Sūtra*, contains a plea for peace and concord among "the 84,000 kings of India."

The Buddha not only preached against war but actually intervened on one occasion to prevent a war—the first practical lesson in non-violence (*ahiṃsā*) in the field of politics. Two tribes, the Sakyas and the Koliyas, who lived on either side of a river, were making warlike preparations to destroy each other because they could not agree on dividing the waters for their use. It is on this occasion that the Buddha intervened and brought about a settlement after asking the warmongers what they considered to be of greater worth—water or human lives? It is these acts of compassion of the Buddha, who gave up a kingdom to show humanity the way to enlightenment, which made one of his contemporaries say of him, "I have heard it said that God is compassionate but I have seen with my own eyes how full of compassion the Blessed One is." It is not surprising therefore that in the Mahāyāna, the Buddha should be conceived of as the incarnation of the "highest compassion" (*mahā kāruṇika*).

The idea of compassion has its origins in pre-Buddhist thought. It is first met with in the *Chāndogya Upaniṣad*, where it is said that one should practise non-violence (*ahiṃsā*) towards all creatures with the sole exception of holy places (*Chāndogya Up.* 8.15)—in other words, animal sacrifices to God were permitted. The concept of *ahiṃsā* also finds a central place in Jainism, where the Jain ascetic goes to extremes in practising this virtue. But it was Buddhism which made *ahiṃsa* basically a virtue to be practised in human relations and introduced the new word *mettā* (loving-kindness) to denote this concept. But the object of one's *mettā* is not only human beings but all beings both higher and lower than the human, and it came to mean the completely selfless but boundless compassion of a Buddha.

The concept of "beings higher than the human" is unintelligible except in the background of the Buddhist cosmology. According to the Buddhist conception of the cosmos, there are an innumerable number of world-systems. This is a conception that partially coincides with the modern physicist's view of the cosmos, with its hundreds of galactic systems or island universes, whether we accept the interpretations of Bondi and Hoyle or Ryle.

The compassion of the Buddhist is to be extended not only to the humans and animals on our earth but to the beings in all these worlds. All beings within the cosmos, however low their state of evolution may be, are said to have the capacity to evolve up to the very highest state and, however high their stature may be, are said to be subject to death so long as they remain within the cosmos—both these facts teach us the same lesson, namely that it is each one's duty to help his fellow beings and that no one has any right or valid grounds to despise another.

At the human level the need for mutual help is much greater. Buddhism taught the doctrine of the equality of mankind at a time when human inequality was taken for granted. We find here for the first time the biological argument that mankind was one species. The Buddha says, "Know the grasses and trees ... the marks that constitute species are for them and their species are manifold. Know the worms and the moths and the different sorts of ants, the marks that constitute species are for them. ... As in these species the marks that constitute species are manifold, so among men the marks that constitute species are not found. ... Not as regards their hair, head, ears. ... Difference there is in beings endowed with bodies, but amongst men this is not the case—the difference amongst men is nominal (only)" (*Suttanipāta*, tr. Fausböll, SBE, X, pp. 111–13).

The Hindu conception of society was static and was dominated by the idea of caste. This was given a divine sanction by being considered a creation of God: "God created the fourfold castes with their specific aptitudes and functions" (*Bhagavad Gīta*, IV.13). Against this was the dynamic evolutionary conception of society as pictured in early Buddhism. The Buddha countered the arguments that the hierarchical fourfold division of society was fundamental by pointing out that in certain societies (e.g. among the Yona-Kambojas, i.e. certain Persian states), there were only two classes, the lords and the serfs and that even this was not rigid for "sometimes the lords became serfs and the serfs lords" (M II 157).

While the theists at that time urged that men were created unequal by God, the Buddhists turned the arguments of the theists against them. Aśvaghoṣa, a brahmin convert to Buddhism, writes in his *Vajrasūci* (circa 1st century BCE), a polemic against caste, that the fatherhood of God should imply the brotherhood of man. He says, "Wonderful! You affirm that all men proceeded from One, i.e. God (Brahmā); how then can there be a fourfold insuperable diversity among them? If I have four sons by one wife, the four sons having one father and mother must be all essentially alike." We also find moral and spiritual arguments for equality to show that all people, irrespective of caste, race or rank, were capable of moral development and the highest spiritual attainments. The Buddhist idea of fellowship or *mettā* is thus founded on the conception of the oneness of the human species, the equality of man and the spiritual unity of mankind.

The Buddhist undertaking to refrain from killing is not a negative precept and has its positive side when fully stated, viz. "One refrains from killing creatures, laying aside the stick and the sword, and abides conscientious, full of kindness, love and compassion towards all creatures and beings" (D I 4). A Buddhist layman has to follow a righteous mode of living (*sammā ājīva*) and this meant that certain professions were not open to him. According to the texts five trades are forbidden: he should not engage in the sale of arms (*sattha-vijjā*), the sale of human beings or animals (*satta-vijjā*), the sale of flesh (*maṃsa-vijjā*), the sale of intoxicating drinks (*majja-vijjā*) and the sale of dangerous and poisonous drugs (*visa-vijjā*) (A III 208). The order of monks were exhorted to practise the following, which are said to promote unity—to be compassionate in their behaviour, their speech and their thoughts towards one another and to have all things in common (M I 322).

I said that the ideal in Buddhism was to attain a permanent state of mind described as the "inward peace" not in the remote future but in this life itself. This is not a passive apathetic state of quietism, as some Western critics of Buddhism have thought. For the passage from our finite self-centred existence to Nibbāna is pictured as one from bondage to freedom (*vimutti*) and power (*vasī*), from imperfection to perfection (*parisuddhi, parama-kusala*), from unhappiness to perfect happiness (*parama-sukha*), from ignorance to knowledge (*vijjā, aññā, ñāṇa*), from finite consciousness to infinite transcendent consciousness (*ananta-viññāṇa*), from the impermanent to the permanent (*nicca*), from the unstable to the stable (*dhuva*), from fear and anxiety to perfect security (*abhaya*), from the evanescent to the ineffable (*amosadhamma*), from a state of mental illness to a state of perfect mental health, etc. It is a peace that passes understanding, for it is the result of what is paradoxically described both as the extinction of one's self-centred desires and the attainment of an ultimate reality. Let me explain. According to Buddhism, the springs of action are sixfold, comprising the three immoral bases of action (*akusala-mūla*) and the three moral bases of action (*kusala-mūla*), viz. (1) immoral bases: (a) *rāga* (craving): *kāma-rāga* or *kāma-taṇhā*, the desire for sense gratification; *bhava-rāga* or *bhava-taṇhā*, the desire for selfish pursuits; (b) *dosa* (hatred): *vibhava-taṇhā*, the desire for destruction; (c) *moha* (delusion): erroneous beliefs; and (2) moral bases: (a) *arāga* (non-craving) or *cāga* (charity); (b) *adosa* (non-hatred) or *mettā* (love); (c) *amoha* (non-delusion) or *vijjā* (knowledge).

Toynbee has said that the Buddha failed "to distinguish between self-devoting and self-centred desires" (*An Historian's Approach to Religion*, London, 1956, p. 29). But the distinction between the two is so marked in Buddhism that the former (the moral bases) are not even called "desires." "Desires" or "thirsts" are threefold—(1) the desire for sense-gratification (*kāma-taṇhā*), (2) the desire for selfish pursuits (e.g. self-preservation, self-continuity, self-assertion, self-display, etc. (*bhava-taṇhā*), and (3) the desire for destruction (*vibhava-taṇhā*). These desires continually seek and find temporary satisfaction (*tatra-tatrābhinandinī*), though ever remaining unsatisfied, and provide the fuel for the process called "the individual." They are said to be narrow and limited (*pamāṇa-kataṃ*) (M I 297), while their opposites—charity and love—are boundless (*appamāṇa*; M I 297). Now, the Buddha urges only the total extinction of these self-centred desires (i.e. 1 a & b) and the complete elimination of ignorance or delusion (i.e. 1–c). This is done by gradually cultivating and developing the opposite traits of charity, love and knowledge until the mind at all its levels is finally purged of all such self-centred desires and considerations.

The mind is said to be "divided into two compartments" (*ubhayato abbhocchinnaṃ*) (D III 105): the conscious and the unconscious. As long as it is affected by the threefold desires, there is an influx of defiling impulses (*āsava*) into the conscious mind, and it is in a state of tension and unrest. Now diseases are classified as twofold, bodily disease (*kāyiko rogo*) and mental disease (*cetasiko rogo*). It is said that we suffer from bodily disease from time to time, but that mental illness is continual until the final state of sainthood is attained. This is the concept of the healthy mind as understood in Buddhism—a state in which the self-centred desires are utterly extinguished and the mind enjoys an "inward peace," which is said to be one of indescribable happiness.

Toynbee has said that this goal "looks intrinsically unattainable" (Toynbee, op. cit., p. 64) since desires cannot be given up without cultivating the desire to give them up. This criticism has already been forestalled and met in the Pali Canon itself. The self-centred desires are to be eliminated by depending on desire (*taṇhaṃ nissāyataṇhaṃ pahātabbaṃ*) (A II 146)—namely the desire for Nibbāna. But this latter master-desire, it is pointed out, is not on the same footing as the first-order desires, for unlike the self-centred desires, which continually seek gratification from time to time without being permanently satisfied, the master-desire would achieve final satisfaction and be extinguished with the eradication of the self-centred desires and the attainment of Nibbāna, which coincides with it. This is the "inward peace" spoken of in the Buddhist texts. It is a word full of meaning but it has meaning only to those who have experienced it, partially or fully. To others it is devoid of meaning in the same way in which the formulae of a physicist would be devoid of meaning to one who does not understand this subject.

This brings us to the problem of meaning and truth in Buddhism. The two are related, for, before we can say that a statement is true or false, we are obliged to ask whether it is meaningful or significant. It is to the credit of the Buddha that he was one of the first thinkers of the East or West to discuss the problem of the meaning of statements, particularly of the statements of religion. We cannot go into this in detail, and we may state briefly that, according to the Buddha, a statement is meaningful if it is in principle verifiable in the light of experience, sensory or extra-sensory. A statement should also have a basis in a person's experience before he can meaningfully assert it, so that the same statement may be meaningful in one context and meaningless in another. Meaningful statements may be true or false. Truth is said to have the characteristic of "correspondence with fact" (*yathābhūtaṃ*). If I believe that there is a next world, and it is the case that there is a next world, then my belief is true and otherwise false (MN 60/M I 402–03). Truth must also be consistent; it is said that "truth is one and there is no second truth" (Sn 884). But consistency is not enough, for it is possible to have several internally consistent systems of thought, mutually contradicting one another. For this reason any religion based on pure (a priori) reasoning (*takka*) is said to be unsatisfactory, for, even if the reasoning is sound (*sutakkitaṃ pi hoti*) (M I 520) and internally consistent, the theory may be false if it does not correspond with fact.

While Buddhist tolerance is partly derived from its emphasis on compassion, it also has its roots in its attitude to truth and its general conception of man. If men did wrong, it was because they were ignorant rather than sinful, and it is, therefore, our duty to enlighten the ignorant and reform them rather than punish them for their wrongdoing. Ignorance again cannot be replaced with knowledge by imposing one's beliefs on others, even if they were true. People have to grow up and discover the truth themselves, and the most that others can do (even the Buddha) is to help them to do this. Far from being detrimental, the scientific outlook was considered to be essential for the moral and spiritual development of man; and our critical faculties should be exercised to the fullest extent in the discovery of religious truth. The Buddha tells a questioner, on more than one occasion:

> You have raised a doubt in a situation in which you ought to suspend your judgement. Do not accept anything because it is rumoured so, because it is the traditional belief, because the majority holds it, because it is found in the scriptures, because it is a product of metaphysical argument and speculation, because of a superficial investigation of facts, because it conforms with one's inclinations, because it is authoritative or because of the prestige-value of your teacher" (A I 191).

Even his own teaching was no exception, and the Buddha did not demand a blind faith in or allegiance to it. "One must not," he says, "accept my Dhamma (teaching) from reverence but first try it as gold is tried by fire."

The sincerity and frankness on which a truly religious life should be grounded demanded healthy criticism and continual self-examination, and the importance of such an outlook is nowhere so well emphasised as in the following exhortation: "If anyone," says the Buddha, "were to speak ill of me, my doctrine or my order, do not bear any ill-will towards him, be upset or perturbed at heart, for, if you were to be so, it would only cause you harm. If, on the other hand, anyone were to speak well of me, my doctrine and my order, do not be overjoyed, thrilled or elated at heart, for, if so, it would only be an obstacle in your way of forming a correct judgement as to whether the qualities praised in us are real and actually found in us" (D I 3). There is a distinction drawn in the Buddhist texts between a "rational faith" (*ākāravati-saddhā*) in what is verifiable and worth trying out and a "baseless faith" (*amūlika-saddhā*) in unverifiable dogmas—the former is commended and the latter condemned.

Buddhism parts company with other religions in holding that moral and religious truths (with one exception) are not different in principle from scientific truths. Paradoxical as it may seem, it was the Buddha—i.e. a religious teacher—who was the first in the history of thought to state formally the two principles of causal determination, namely that A and B are causally related: if whenever A happens B happens and B does not happen unless A has happened. The theory of causation is central to the understanding of Buddhism. The Buddha tells us "the causes of things that arise from causes" and adds that "he who understands causation understands the Dhamma and vice versa." Causation, however, is not strictly deterministic since the mind (with its acts of will) can often divert and direct the operation of causal processes and the mind is said to have the capacity to act with degrees of freedom according to its state of development. The Buddhist concept of causation, therefore, stands midway between indeterminism (*adhicca-samuppāda*, Skt. *yadṛccha*) on the one hand and strict determinism (*niyati*) on the other.

There were three forms of determinism prevalent at the time to which Buddhism was opposed—one was natural determinism (*svabhāva-vāda*), which held that everything that happens is due to the innate constitution of things; another was karmic determinism (*pubbekata-hetu*, Skt. *purātana-karma-kṛtaṃ*), which held that everything that happens to an individual was due to his past karma; lastly, there was theistic determinism (*issara-nimmāna-vāda*), which held that all that happens was due to the fiat or will of a Personal God who has created the universe and sustains it.

In the universe there operate physical laws (*utu-niyāma*), biological laws (*bīja-niyāma*), psychological laws (*citta-niyāma*) and moral and spiritual laws (*dhamma-niyāma*). While the natural scientists tell us about the first three, the Buddha discovers and reveals the latter. It is said that, whether the Buddhas appear or not, these laws operate and we are subject to them. All that the Buddha does is to discover (or re-discover) them. What is thus discovered is said to be verifiable by each and every one of us, by following the path that leads to their discovery. It is a contingent fact that the moral and spiritual life (i.e. the religious life) is both possible and desirable in the universe in which we live. If the universe were different from what in fact it is (e.g. if indeterminism or strict determinism were the case, if the soul were identical with the body or were different from it, if there were no transcendent reality), then the religious life might not have been possible and would not have been desirable.

One of the spiritual truths stated in Buddhism is the law of kamma. As understood in Buddhism it merely states that there is an observable correlation between morally good acts and pleasant consequences to the individual and morally evil acts and unpleasant consequences. It does not state that all our present experiences are due to our past kamma. This is in fact emphatically denied, where it is shown that many of our experiences are due to our own actions in this life or to causal factors (such as the weather, our state of physical health), which have nothing to do with our kamma. The law of kamma as stated is a causal correlation, which guarantees the fact of individual moral responsibility. It is said to be a correlation that is observable and verifiable by developing one's faculty of retro-cognition, i.e. the ability to recall one's past lives. This faculty and others are said to be within the reach of all of us to develop by the practise of meditation. What evidence is there to believe in rebirth? Since rebirth or "reincarnation" is said to be a meaningful concept and a logical possibility (see A. J., Ayer, *The Problem of Knowledge*, London, 1957, pp. 193 f.), the problem is whether it is the case or not.

Briefly, the evidence today is of two sorts: (1) there are cases of spontaneous recall of previous lives, especially on the part of young children, which have been verified and claimed to be found true; (2) there is also experimental evidence. People under deep hypnosis are able to recall not only the lost memories of this life but of previous lives as well. Several interpretations are possible of these experimental data, but I believe that the simplest and best hypothesis to account for the data I have seen so far is that of rebirth. It is hoped that with more and better experimentation on this verifiable theory of survival, we shall be able to know the truth about it before long.

While the *Upanishadic* thinkers interpreted the mystic experiences that they had as being due to the grace of God (*dhātuḥ prasādāt, Kaṭha Upaniṣad* 2.20), Buddhism explains these experiences as due to the natural development of the mind. For Buddhism they result from the operation of causal processes relating to religious experience. They are, however, not considered subjective and are held to be of great value, though Buddhism does not subscribe to the metaphysical and theological interpretations given to them in the Upaniṣhads and the rest of mystical literature in the East and West. One of the prerequisites for developing these experiences, which give meaning to the religious life, is the absolute moral integrity of the individual.

I have tried to illustrate what I mean by saying that for Buddhism spiritual truths were on a par with scientific truths. There is, however, one "experience," if it may be called an experience, which is beyond the empirical, phenomenal and causal. This is the experience of Nibbāna, which is called "the Truth" (*sacca*). This illumination is said to be comparable to that of a man born blind obtaining sight after a physician has treated him. It is described as a flaring up of a great light (*ālokā udapādi*) and is said to coincide with the extinction of the fires of greed, hatred and delusion, and the attainment of the peace that causes understanding. It is not a conditioned causal experience, since Nibbāna is said to be the Unconditioned (*asaṅkhata*), the Uncaused (*akataṃ, na paṭicca-samuppannaṃ*) and the Timeless (*nibbānaṃ na vattabbaṃ atītan ti pi anāgataṃ ti pi paccuppannan ti pi*), not located in space (*na katthaci, kuhiñci*). To say that one exists (*hoti, upapajjati*) in Nibbāna or ceases to exist (*na hoti, na upapajjati*) are both said to be wrong.

The question was put to the Buddha in his own lifetime: "The person who has attained the goal—does he cease to exist, or does he exist eternally without defect; explain this to me, O Lord, as you understand it." The Buddha explains: "A person who has attained the goal is beyond measure; he does not have that with which one can describe him" (*Yena naṃ vajju taṃ tassa natthi*) (Sn 1076).

Elsewhere, the Buddha explains that the question is meaningless. It is the concepts with which we are familiar that make us ask it. We can only conceive in two alternatives—the annihilation of the individual at some point of time or his eternal duration in time. The Buddha illustrates what he means with an example. If someone, who has seen a fire in front of him go out, were to ask in which direction the fire has gone—northern, southern, eastern or western—it is a question which cannot be answered, since the question itself is meaningless. Wittgenstein takes the same example to illustrate the same point: "Thus it can come about that we are not able to rid ourselves of the implications of our symbolism which seems to admit of a question like 'Where does the flame of a candle go when it is blown out? Where does the light go?...' We have been obsessed with our symbolism. We may say that we are led into puzzlement by an analogy, which irresistibly drags us on" (*The Blue and Brown Books*, Oxford, 1958, p. 108).

The Buddha classified questions into four types: (1) questions which can be answered categorically; (2) questions which can be answered only after analysis; (3) questions which must be answered with a counter-question; and (4) questions which have to be put aside as meaningless. The question whether the saint exists in Nibbāna or not is said to be meaningless, although there is a psychological urge and a linguistic reason for asking it. Another set of questions which the Buddha set aside as meaningless were the questions, "Is the soul identical with the body?" and "Is the soul different from the body?" Having discarded as an empiricist and a "verificationist" the concept of the soul or substance as meaningless, these questions too are meaningless since they contain a meaningless concept. The traditional explanation says that these questions are like asking whether "the child of this barren woman is fair or dark." It was not agnosticism which made the Buddha discard these questions but a realisation of their very nature. It is not that there was something that he did not know but that he knew only too well what he was talking about. Where language failed, the Buddha literally followed the dictum: "Whereof one cannot speak, thereof one must be silent," but his silence was more eloquent than words. To those who had attained Nibbāna, no explanation was necessary; to those who had not, no explanation was possible.

The Buddha was very meticulous in the use of language. He often reformulated questions or removed ambiguities in words before answering them in order to remove misleading implications. He claimed that he was not a dogmatist (*ekaṃsa-vādo*) but an analyst (*vibhajja-vādo*). The truth of Nibbāna or the ultimate reality is thus strictly inexpressible, but all else that belongs to the realm of moral and spiritual truth can be stated and stated precisely.

The final state of "inward peace" is also a state of perfect freedom (*sammā-vimutti*), for the mind then ceases to be conditioned by the load of its past and the desires raging within it. It becomes master of itself. In the state of normal everyday consciousness we are finite conditioned beings. According to what the texts say, we are conditioned by what we inherit from mother and father, by the store of unconscious memories going back to our childhood and our previous lives, by the desires and impulses which agitate within it and by the stimuli which come from the "six doors of perception," i.e. the data of the five senses, our environment and the ideas that we imbibe and respond to. But despite the fact that the ordinary man is thus largely conditioned by his inner nature and environment, he has a certain degree of freedom to act within limits.

During the time of the Buddha there were violent disputes about this problem between two schools of thought. There were *akiriya-vādins* who denied free will because they were determinists in some sense or another, and in the opposite camp were the *kiriya-vādins* who upheld free will. The Buddha held that man was possessed of a degree of free will, while not denying that he was largely conditioned. What is meant by attaining salvation in Buddhism is the attainment of full freedom from our relative state of bondage. This is possible because of the very fact that we possess a degree of free will, and the processes of sublimation and de-conditioning are causal processes, which can be understood and directed by the mind. It also means that man's salvation lies in his own hands and that he cannot and should not depend on an external saviour. As the Dhammapada says:

By ourselves is evil done
By ourselves we pain endure
By ourselves we cease from wrong
By ourselves we become pure.

> *No one saves us but ourselves*
> *No one can and no one may*
> *We ourselves must tread the path*
> *Buddhas only show the way* (Dhp 165).

The Buddha says that there are four false religions and four unsatisfactory religions in this world (*Sandaka Sutta*, MN 76) . One of the four false religions is that which denies causation and asserts that "beings are miraculously doomed or saved" (*natthi hetu natthi paccayo sattānaṃ saṅkilesāya ... visuddhiyā*) (M I 516). Buddhists pray that "all beings may be happy" (*sabbe sattā sukhitā hontu*); but they do not pray for salvation either to the Buddha or to anyone else. When our salvation depends on what we ourselves do with our free will, prayer is superfluous and is nothing more than a pious wish or hope. The Buddha compares a person who prays to God for salvation to one who wishes to cross a river and get to the other bank, but hopes to achieve this by incessantly calling on the other bank to come to him (D I 244f).

Religious truths, with the exception of the truth about Nibbāna, are thus "statable." They are all verifiable and have meaning only to those who verify them. There is individual moral responsibility and, therefore, justice in the universe. We have freedom in a limited sense, which makes it possible for us to attain freedom in the absolute sense. Seeking our own salvation may appear to be a selfish pursuit, but it is a paradoxical fact not only that we can attain this only by living in a completely selfless manner but that the goal itself is one in which our self-centred individuality is lost in a state "beyond measure." Selfless charity (*cāga*), compassionate love (*mettā*) and enlightened behaviour (*vijjācaraṇa*) *is* what we have to develop in attaining this goal.

The Buddhist monk does not cut himself away completely from society. His isolation is intended to provide him with the leisure to develop his mind and spiritual vision. He is thus in a position to speak from direct experience about the nature of spiritual truths and give guidance and advice to his fellow beings. He is one who is expected to specialize in his field of inquiry as much as the physicist specialises in his. The development of the mind is a full-time job, and the findings of these explorations are of no less interest and value to society than the findings of the natural scientist working in his laboratory. Both have something to offer to society; and monasticism, if understood rightly, has a big part as yet to play in the moral and spiritual regeneration of mankind.

There is no easy solution to the problem of how we can have peace on earth and goodwill among mankind. The West believes that their military potential is keeping the communist monster at bay, while the communists in turn are convinced that their military might prevents the capitalist demon from swallowing them. Each side is certain that war is the lesser evil to being dominated by their opponents. The great powers are working for peace by forging the weapons of war and talking about peace for propagandist purposes. But the real alternative to peace today is the destruction of mankind. What is really happening is that, while half the world is spending colossal amounts of money on armaments, the other half is dying of starvation, malnutrition and disease in an age when all this can be prevented if the resources are available and goodwill is present. People and governments tend to do what is expedient rather than what is morally good. Can we say that, in such a world, people have much faith in moral and spiritual values? There is hope in the possibility that the very fear of the dire consequences of the next war may prevent it. It would be too much to hope for a great power to have the moral courage and the spiritual strength to disarm unilaterally without fear of the consequences, but for those who love humanity more than themselves or nations, there seems to me to be no other alternative but to work unreservedly for pacifism.

23

The Significance of Vesākha

Vesākha is traditionally associated with the birth, enlightenment and Parinibbāna of the Buddha, who renounced a life of luxury to solve the riddle of the universe and bring happiness to man as well as to other beings. As in the case of other religious teachers of antiquity, his birth is enshrouded in myth and legend, the later accounts found in the *Lalitavistara,* for instance, containing descriptions of more miraculous happenings than in the earliest accounts in the Pali Canon. As Buddhists, who have to believe only in things as they are, and therefore in verifiable historical truths, we are not obliged to believe in all these myths and legends. The truths of Buddhism stand or fall to the extent to which the Dhamma contains statements which can be verified as true, and the veracity of Buddhism, therefore, does not depend on the historical accuracy of legendary beliefs about the birth or death of the Buddha. Besides, the Buddha encouraged self-criticism as well as a critical examination of his own life on the part of his disciples. Even with regard to matters of doctrine or discipline, textual criticism was encouraged. For instance, a monk who claimed to have heard something from the Buddha himself was asked to examine its authenticity in the light of the Sutta and Vinaya (a collection of texts regarding doctrinal and disciplinary matters made during the time of the Buddha himself), since his personal recollections and interpretations may not have been altogether trustworthy.

Historical Facts

This does not mean that we need to dismiss all the statements associated with the birth, life and demise of the Buddha as mythical or legendary. Some of us may feel that if we were closer in time to the Buddha we would have had a better opportunity of apprehending the historical facts about him. But in a way we are better placed today, for we can study the historical development and expansion of Buddhism and also compare the life of the Buddha and contrast it with that of other great religious teachers and philosophers of mankind. Some of the legends may have a kernel of historical truth. Human imagination seems to have worked in a very similar way with regard to some of the heroes of history. At least a hundred years after the death of the Buddha we find in the *Mahāvastu* the statement that "the Buddha's body was immaculately conceived" (*na ca maithuna-sambhūtaṃ sugatasya samucchritaṃ*) or in other words that the Buddha had a virgin birth, but if we trace the origin of this idea to the texts of the Pali Canon, we find it stated that the mother of the Buddha had no thoughts of sex after the Buddha-child was conceived, which may quite possibly be historically true.

Some of the claims are certainly historically significant. Everyone would admit today that the Buddha was the first religious teacher in history with a universal message for all mankind and that he was the founder of the concept of a world religion. Asita's prophecy that the Buddha was "born for the good and happiness of the human world" (*manussaloke hita-sukhatāya jāto*) may be seen today in all probability to be true, although, at the time that it found its way into the text, it was a mere prophecy. It was also a historical fact that the birth of the Buddha was marked by a spiritual awakening of the whole human race. In Greece, Pythagoras conceives of philosophy as a way of life and establishes a brotherhood. The prophet Isaiah in Israel dreams of the brotherhood of man and an era of universal peace. In Persia, Zoroaster, who conceives of the world as a battleground between the forces of good and evil, is convinced of the eventual victory of good over evil. In China, we find Confucius preaching a new ethic of human relationships and Lao Tse speaks of the necessity of living in conformity with eternal principles and values. In India itself from about 800 BCE, there was a persistent quest for truth, light and immortality:

> *From the unreal lead me to the real!*
> *From darkness lead me to light!*
> *From death lead me to immortality!*
>
> (Bṛhad Āraṇyaka Upaniṣad, I, 3. 28)

It is in answer to this quest that the Buddha declares: "Open for them are the doors to immortality" (*aparutā amatassa dvārā*). So when the prophet Isaiah contemporaneously says that a people who walked in darkness have seen a great light and speaks of a child who shall be called the Wonderful, the Counsellor, the Mighty God, the Everlasting Father and the Prince of Peace, someone has only to point out that the Buddha claimed or it was claimed of the Buddha that he was the Wonderful Person (*acchariya-puggala*), the Counsellor of gods and men (*satthā-devamanussānaṃ*), the God among gods (*brahmātibrahmā*), the Everlasting Father (*adhipitā*) and the Prince of Peace (*santirāja*). Similarly, the Buddhists of China have seen in a text attributed to Confucius a prophetic utterance alluding to the Buddha, which reads: "Among the people of the West there is a Sage. He does not speak and is yet spontaneously believed, he does not (consciously) convert people and yet (his doctrine) is spontaneously realised. How vast he is!" Are these texts interpolations or do they support the historical veracity of the Buddhist legend that the world at this time was eagerly awaiting the birth of an Enlightened One.

Last Days

Let us now turn to the last days of the Buddha on earth, as reported in the *Mahāparinibbāna Sutta* (DN 16). Here again we find fact with an occasional admixture of legend. Here again, it is difficult at times to distinguish the hard core of fact from legend. The Buddha, it is said, was transfigured just prior to his death. His robes, it is said, were aglow when touching the body. Is this fact or fiction? We do not know. But there are a number of significant statements about the Dhamma whose historicity is self-authenticated. It is said that the Buddha did not want to pass away until he had brought into existence a set of monks who were learned in the Dhamma, had realised its fruits and were competent to deal with any criticisms levelled against it.

When the sal flowers from the twin sal trees under which he lay wafted over his body, it seemed as though nature were paying him homage. Today we Buddhists worship the Buddha by offering flowers before his image. But the Buddha says that one does not really pay homage to the Transcendent One (*Tathāgata*) by such offerings. It is the disciple, whether man or woman, who follows in the footsteps of the Dhamma and lives in accordance with it who truly reveres and pays the highest homage to the Transcendent One. When Ānanda is worried as to how the funeral rites should be performed, the Buddha asks him not to worry about these rituals but to strive hard to attain the good goal (*sadattha ghaṭatha*), for Ānanda had not as yet become an Arahant.

Most instructive is the Buddha's last sermon, which was to Subhadda, the wandering ascetic (DN 16.5.23ff.). The question he asked was very interesting: Did all the six outstanding teachers who were contemporaries of the Buddha understand the truth? Or is it the case that only some understood or none? In the order in which they are mentioned, there was Purāṇa Kassapa, who was an amoralist because he thought that everything was strictly determined by natural causes; Makkhali Gosāla, who was a theist who believed that everything happened in accordance with God's will; Ajita Kesakambalī, the materialist, who denied survival, moral values and the good life; Pakudha Kaccāyana, the categorialist, who tried to explain the world in terms of discrete categories; Sañjaya Bellaṭṭhiputta, the agnostic sceptic or positivist, who held that moral and religious propositions were unverifiable; and Nigaṇṭha Nātaputta, who was a relativist and an eclectic. The significance of the question comes to this: Are amoralism, theism, materialism, categorialism, agnosticism and eclecticism all true? Or is none true? Or are one or some of these theories true?

The True Religion

Elsewhere, in the *Sandaka Sutta* (MN 76), there is a clear-cut answer to this question. There, Ānanda says that in the opinion of the Buddha, there are four false religions in the world and four religions which are unsatisfactory though not necessarily totally false, while Buddhism is distinguished from all of them. The word for religion here is used in a wide sense, as in modern usage, to denote theistic and non-theistic religions as well as pseudo-religions or religion-surrogates, i.e. substitutes for religions such as, say, Marxism, existentialism, humanism, etc.

The four false religions or philosophies inculcating a way of life are, first, materialism, which denies survival; second, amoralism, which denies good and evil; third, any religion which asserts that man is miraculously saved or doomed; and last, theistic evolutionism, which holds that everything is preordained and everyone is destined to attain eventual salvation.

The four unsatisfactory religions in some sense uphold survival, moral values, moral recompense as well as a relative freedom of the will. They are, first, any religion that claims that its teacher was omniscient all the time and knows the entirety of the future as well;

second, any religion based on revelation, since revelations contradicted each other and were unreliable; third, any religion based on mere reasoning and speculation, since the reasoning may be unsound and the conclusions false; and fourth a pragmatic religion based on purely sceptical foundations, which is, therefore, uncertain. On the other hand, Buddhism is to be distinguished from all of them by virtue of the fact that it is realistic and verifiable. Its truths have been verified by the Buddha and his disciples and are open to verification (*ehipassika*) by anyone who wishes to do so.

The answer to Subhadda's question, however, is different. There is no examination of the relative claims of materialism, theism, scepticism, etc. Instead the Buddha says, leave aside the question as to whether these several religions and philosophies are all true or false or that some are true. In whatever religion the Noble Eightfold Path is not found, in that religion one would not get the first, second, third or fourth stages of sainthood and in whatever religion the Noble Eightfold Path is found, in that religion one would get the first, second, third and fourth stages. Finally, there is a very significant remark: "If these monks lead the right kind of life, the world would never be devoid of Arahants" (*ime ca bhikkhū sammā vihareyyuṃ asuñño loko arahantehi assa*) (D II 151).

The Buddhist view is that any religion is true only to the extent to which it contains aspects of the Noble Eightfold Path. Let us take one of the factors of the path—the necessity for cultivating right instead of wrong aspirations. Right aspirations consist in the cultivation of thoughts free from lust and sensuous craving and the cultivation of creative and compassionate thoughts. Wrong aspirations consist of the cultivation of lustful thoughts and sensuous craving as well as of destructive and malevolent thoughts. Now if any religion asserts that one may indulge in lustful, destructive and malevolent thoughts and yet be saved if one professes faith in the creed, then such a religion, according to the Buddha, is not to be trusted. It is the same with each of the other factors of the path. The net result is that there is no salvation outside the Noble Eightfold Path. It is the one and only way for the salvation of beings and the overcoming of suffering.

First Saint (Sotāpanna)

What kind of person is the "first saint" spoken of here? It is none other than the person who attains the stream of spiritual development (*sotāpanna*), as a result of which his eventual salvation is assured and he does not fall into an existence below that of a human being. Such a person, it is said, sheds three fetters on attaining his spiritual insight. They are; (1) the fetter of believing in a substantial ego somehow related to aspects or the whole of one's psycho-physical personality (*sakkāya-diṭṭhi*); (2) the fetter of doubting the veracity and validity of the Dhamma (*vicikicchā*), and (3) the fetter of clinging to the external forms of religion (*sīlabbata-parāmāsa*). The belief in an ego satisfies a deep-seated craving in us—the craving of our egoistic impulses (*bhava-taṇhā*). Misleading implications of language tend to make us believe that there is an "I" and a "me" (which is unchanging) when in fact there is only a constantly changing psycho-physical process. We certainly exercise a certain degree of control over ourselves, which makes us believe that there is an "I" who controls, but such control is only an aspect of the conative functions of our conditioned psycho-physical process. A dispassionate analysis would ultimately expose the hollowness of this belief. Shedding our belief in such an ego does not, however, mean that we get rid of conceit (*māna*) altogether, for the "conceited" view "I shall try to attain the goal," it is said, is necessary to spur us on up to a point. He gets rid of this "conceit" (*māna*) only in a later stage of his spiritual evolution. Doubt has to be got rid of in Buddhism not by blind belief but by critical inquiry and by living the Dhamma. Such inquiry and the personal experience of verifying aspects of the Dhamma give us the inner conviction that we are treading on the right path. Overcoming such doubt through conviction does not, again, mean that we have totally got rid of ignorance (*avijjā*), which we can do only at a later stage in our spiritual evolution. Religion, likewise, becomes for such a person not a matter of conforming to external ritual and forms of worship, not a form of obsessional neurosis (to use Freudian terminology), but a matter of day-to-day living of the Dhamma. It is such a person who is said to have entered the stream of spiritual development, a state which is within the capacity of any of us to attain.

When we ponder over these admonitions of the Buddha in his last days on earth, we see how far the modern Theravada tradition in Sri Lanka has strayed from the true path of the Dhamma. Are we not preserving the Dhamma in its pristine purity only in the books when we try to rationalise our belief in caste, for instance, with the help of opinions which go contrary to the teachings of the Buddha? Are we not rationalising our disinclination to live the Dhamma by fostering false beliefs that Arahantship is not possible today, when this is contrary to the assertions of the Buddha himself?

Enlightenment

If we turn from the birth and the last days of the Buddha to his enlightenment, it strikes us that it was not a revelation from above but an illumination from within. Part of the realisation was of the nature of causal laws operative in nature and in us.

When we come to the first sermon, we are again confronted with the Noble Eightfold Path as the right path leading to emancipation, happiness and realisation. It is the straight and narrow road between indulgence of our desires and ascetic deprivation. The most obvious way to happiness appears to be in the gratification of desires but unfortunately there is a law of diminishing returns which operates here. Gratification gives temporary satisfaction but continued gratification gives less and less of it. Besides, we become slaves of our passions and lose our freedom and self-control while our minds become unclear and confused. Ascetic deprivation, on the other hand, results in repression and self-inflicted suffering. It substitutes one kind of suffering for another. The way out or the way to transcend suffering is by a watchful self-control exercised by a person guided by the Noble Eightfold Path.

Another significant fact about the first sermon is the claim of the Buddha that it was to set up the kingdom or rule of righteousness (*dhammacakkaṃ pavattetuṃ*), which shall in the fullness of time be established on earth and neither Brahmā (God), nor Māra (Satan), nor anyone else in the world could prevent this. In spite of many reverses, truth and justice shall win in the end. As one of the Upaniṣads puts it: "Truth alone shall conquer and never untruth" (*satyam eva jayate nānṛtam*).

It is not possible to measure the enlightenment of the Buddha. As he said in the Siṃsapā forest, taking a few leaves into his hand and saying that what he knew but did not teach us was like the leaves in the forest, while what he taught amounted to the leaves in his hand. What he taught was only what pertained to man's emancipation, happiness and understanding.

Since the Buddha's ministry was spread over forty-five years, this teaching in itself is vast, as is evident from the Buddhist scriptures. If we take its essence, we can see the immense worth of the Buddha's teaching and hence the true significance of Vesākha, which mankind has yet to comprehend. In these teachings we have a theory of knowledge, a theory of reality giving an account of the nature and destiny of man in the universe, an ethical system, a social and political philosophy and a philosophy of law.

Let us take the most significant teachings in each of these fields.

Theory of Knowledge

Take the theory of knowledge. Nature is conceived as a causal system in which there are to be found non-deterministic causal correlations. The events of nature are not haphazard, nor are they due to the will of an omnipotent God nor again to rigid deterministic causal laws. The Buddhist theory of conditioned genesis (*paṭicca-samuppāda*) steers clear of the extremes of indeterminism (*adhicca-samuppāda*) on the one hand and of strict determinism (*niyati*), whether theistic or natural, on the other. Understanding, therefore, is the key to salvation and not blind belief in unverifiable dogmas. And for understanding we need an impartial outlook. We must not be influenced by our prejudices for or against (*chanda, dosa*), by fear (*bhaya*), whether it be fear of nature or of the supernatural, nor by our erroneous beliefs (*moha*). To gain personal knowledge, we must not rely on authority—whether it is revelation, tradition, hearsay, conformity with scripture, the views of experts or our revered teachers. We must not rely on pure reasoning alone, nor look at things from just one standpoint nor trust a superficial examination of things nor base our theories on preconceived opinions. Personal verification and realisation are the way to truth.

Here was man's charter of freedom, which makes Buddhism the most tolerant of religions and philosophies. It recommended an outlook which we today call the scientific outlook. So there have been no inquisitions, heresy trials or witch hunts in Buddhism as in some theistic traditions and positively there has been the recognition of human dignity and freedom. The Buddha, again, was the earliest thinker in history to recognise the fact that language tends to distort in certain respects the nature of reality and to stress the importance of not being misled by linguistic forms and conventions. In this respect, he foreshadowed the modern linguistic or analytic philosophers. He was the first to distinguish meaningless questions and assertions from meaningful ones. As in science, he recognised perception and inference as the twin sources of knowledge, but there was one difference. For perception, according to Buddhism, included extrasensory forms as well, such as telepathy and clairvoyance. Science cannot ignore such phenomena and today there are Soviet as well as Western scientists who have admitted the validity of extrasensory perception in the light of experimental evidence.

Theory of Reality

If we turn to the theory of reality, the Buddha's achievements were equally outstanding. Buddhism recognises the reality of the material world and its impact on experience. Conscious mental phenomena have a physical basis in one's body. Life (*jīvitindriya*) is a by-product (*upādā-rūpa*) of matter. The economic environment conditions human relationships and effects morality. Like modern psychologists, the Buddha discards the concept of a substantial soul and analyses the human personality into aspects of experience such as impressions and ideas (*saññā*), feelings or hedonic tone (*vedanā*), conative activities (*saṅkhāra*) as well as cognitive or quasi-cognitive activities (*viññāṇa*). There is a dynamic conception of the mind and the stream of consciousness (*viññāṇa-sota*) is said to have two components, the conscious and the unconscious. The first explicit mention of unconscious mental processes and the unconscious (*anusaya*) motivation of human behaviour is in the Buddhist texts. The Buddhist theory of motivation may be compared with that of Freud, although it is more adequate than the latter.

Man is motivated to act out of greed, which consists of the desire to gratify our senses, and sex (*kāma-taṇhā*, comparable with the libido of Freud) as well as the desire to gratify our egoistic impulses (*bhava-taṇhā*, comparable with the *ego-instincts* and *super-ego* of Freud). He is also motivated to act out of hatred, which consists of the desire to destroy or eliminate what we dislike (*vibhava-taṇhā*, comparable with the *thanatos* or *death-instinct* of Freud) and also out of erroneous beliefs.

Both men and nature are in a state of perpetual flux. As such, personal existence is insecure and there is no permanent soul or substance that we can cling to despite our strong desire to entertain such beliefs.

Owing to the causal factors that are operative, man is in a state of becoming and there is a continuity of individuality (*bhava*). Morally good and evil acts are correlated with pleasant and unpleasant consequences, as the case may be. Man is conditioned by his psychological past, going back into prior lives, by heredity and by the impact of his environment. But since he is not a creature of God's will or a victim of economic determinism, he can change his own nature as well as his environment.

There is no evidence that the world was created in time by an omniscient, omnipotent and infinitely good and compassionate God. In fact, the evidence clearly tells against the existence of such a God and the Buddhist texts mention two arguments in this connection. Although evil is logically compatible with the existence of a good God, there are certain evils (such as the suffering of animals and of little children, for instance), which are inexplicable on the assumption of the existence of a merciful God, who is also omniscient and omnipotent. Besides, the universe created by such a God would be a rigged universe in which human beings were mere puppets devoid of responsibility.

According to the Buddhist theory of the cosmos, it has no origin in time. This Buddhist conception of the cosmos, which is a product of clairvoyance, can only be compared with the modern theories of the universe. The smallest unit in it is said to be the minor world-system (*cūḷanīka-loka-dhātu*), which contains thousands of suns, moons, inhabited and uninhabited planets. Today we call this a galaxy. The next unit is the middling world-system (*majjhimikā-loka-dhātu*), which consists of thousands of such galaxies, as we find in Virgo, for instance. The vast cosmos (*mahā-loka-dhātu*) consists of thousands upon thousands of such clusters of galaxies. This cosmos is said to undergo periods of expansion (*vivaṭṭamāna-kappa*) and contraction (*saṃvaṭṭamāna-kappa*). So the universe is in a state of oscillation, continually expanding and contracting without knowable beginning or end in time (*anamatagga*).

Recent findings based on observations made from radiotelescopes have shown that the "big-bang" theory (fancied by theists) and the oscillating theory are preferable to the steady-state theory. But of the "big-bang" and oscillating theories, the latter is to be preferred on scientific and philosophical grounds. It does not involve the concept of the creation of the dense atom out of nothing and it does not have to face the problem of an infinitude of time prior to creation.

While the Buddhist conception of the cosmos foreshadows the modern astronomer's conception of it, it goes beyond the latter in speaking of a subtle-material world (*rūpa-loka*) and a non-material world (*arūpa-loka*) which are not accessible to science.

Similarly, Buddhist atheism is not the same as materialistic atheism in that Buddhism speaks of the objectivity of moral and spiritual values and of a transcendent reality beyond space, time and causation. Neither the Buddha nor those who attain Nibbāna cease to exist, according to Buddhist conceptions. When the Buddha was asked whether the person who has attained Nibbāna does not exist or exists eternally without defect, his answer was: "The person who has attained the goal is without measure; he does not have that, whereby one may speak about him."

Ethics

If we turn to Buddhist ethics and examine its system, we find that according to Buddhist notions, the propositions of ethics are significant. There can be no ethics without a concept of moral responsibility. But there cannot be moral responsibility unless: (1) some of our actions are free (though conditioned) and not constrained; (2) morally good and evil actions are followed by pleasant and unpleasant consequences, as the case may be; and (3) there is human survival after death to make this possible with justice. Now, the question as to whether these conditions are fulfilled or not is a purely factual one. If there was no free will and human actions were strictly determined, there would be no sense in our talking about moral responsibility for our actions. According to Buddhist conceptions, nature is such that all these conditions are fulfiled and, therefore, moral responsibility is a fact. Buddhism considers human perfection or the attainment of arahantship as a good in itself and likewise the material and spiritual welfare of mankind. Whatever are good as a means in bringing about these good ends are instrumentally good and these are called right actions, defined as those which promote one's own welfare as well as that of others. Right actions consist in refraining from evil, doing what is good and cleansing the mind. The goal of perfection is also therapeutic in that only a perfect person, it is said, has a perfectly healthy mind. Hence the necessity for cleansing the mind, which consists in changing the basis of our motivation from greed, hatred and ignorance to selfless service, compassion and understanding. The Buddha emphatically pointed out that what he showed was a way, a way to achieve this change in motivation by a process of self-analysis, meditation and self-development. Men and women are classified into different psychological types and different forms of meditation are prescribed for them to achieve this end. The aim of Buddhist ethics therefore is the attainment of personal happiness and social harmony.

The Buddhist theory of reality and its ethics are summed up in the Four Noble Truths.

Society, Polity and Law

The social and political philosophy of Buddhism is equally relevant and enlightening. Again, the Buddha was the first thinker in history to preach the doctrine of equality. Man was one species and the division into social classes and castes was not a permanent or inevitable division of society, although it was given a divine sanction at the time. Historical and economic factors brought about, as the Buddha relates in the *Aggañña Sutta,* the division of people into occupational classes which later became castes. All men are capable of moral and spiritual development and should be afforded the opportunity for this. The doctrine of equality does not imply that all men are physically and psychologically alike, for they are obviously not, but that there is a sufficient degree of homogeneity amongst men in terms of their capacities and potentialities as to warrant their being treated equally and with human dignity (*samānattatā*). It is a corollary of the doctrine of equality that there should be equality before the law, in educational opportunities and in the enjoyment of other human rights such as the right to employment, etc.

Society, according to the Buddhist, like every other process in nature is liable to change from time to time. The factors that determine this change are economic and ideological, for men are led to action by their desires and beliefs. It is the duty of the state to uphold justice and promote the material and spiritual welfare of its subjects. There is a social contract theory of society and government. Ultimate power, whether it be legislative, executive or judiciary, is vested with the people but delegated to the king or body of people elected to govern. If the contract of upholding law and order and promoting the good of the people is seriously violated, the people have a right to revolt and overthrow such a tyrannical government (see *Padamānavakusala Jātaka*).

Sovereignty is subject to the necessity to conform to the rule of righteousness. The rule of power has to be dependent on the rule of righteousness (*dharmacakraṃ hi nisrāya balacakraṃ pravartate*). Punishment has to be reformatory and only secondarily deterrent and never retributive. In international relations the necessity for subjecting sovereignty to the rule of righteousness requires that no nation be a power unto itself, while in its dealings with other nations it always has the good and happiness of mankind at heart. The ideal just society is both democratic and socialistic and ensures human rights as well as economic equity and the well-being of the people. It is likely to come into existence after a catastrophic world war, when the remnant that would be saved will set up a new order based on a change of heart and a change of system.

Such in brief is the message of the glorious religion and philosophy of the Buddha, whose value and full significance the world has yet to realise. Such is the message of Vesākha.

24

Buddhism and the Race Question

K. N. Jayatilleke and G. P. Malalasekera

Man's Place in the Universe

The texts of both the Theravāda (i.e., the southern) as well as the Mahāyāna (i.e. the northern) schools of Buddhism often speak of man in the context of a larger concourse of sentient beings who are considered as populating a vast universe. Although speculations about the origin and extent of the universe are discouraged, the vastness of space and the immensity of time are never lost sight of. It is said that, even if one moves with the swiftness of an arrow in any direction and travels for a whole lifetime, one can never hope to reach the limits of space (A IV 428). In this vastness of cosmic space are located an innumerable number of worlds. As far as these suns and moons revolve, shedding their light in space, so far extends the thousandfold world-system. In it are a thousand suns, a thousand moons, thousands of earths and thousands of heavenly worlds. This is said to be the thousandfold minor world-system. A thousand times such a thousandfold minor world-system is the twice-a-thousand middling world-system. A thousand times such a twice-a-thousand middling world-system is the twice-a-thousand major world-system (A I 227f; A IV 59f). These galactic systems (if we may use a modern term which seems to approximate very closely to this conception of the world-systems) are however never static or lasting; they are in the process of being evolved (*saṃvaṭṭamāna*), or of being dissolved (*vivaṭṭamāna*). These processes take immensely long periods of time measured in aeons (*kappa*) (S II 181), until eventually cosmic catastrophes put an end to them (A IV 100–03). But time, we are told, is not the same everywhere, for fifty earth years are equivalent to one day and night in one of the heavenly worlds, while in another a day and night are equivalent to no less than 1,600 earth years (A IV 429).

Several attempts are made to classify this vast array of beings. One such classification speaks of human beings, as well as some of the higher and lower beings, as falling into the class of beings who are different and distinguishable from each other in mind and body. There are other classes where the beings are different in body, but one in mind. Yet others are alike in body but different in mind, while there are some who are alike both in body and in mind. A further set of four classes of beings mentioned are formless. All these are described as the several stations which the human consciousness can attain (*viññāṇaṭṭhiti*) (A IV 39–40), and find renewed existence after death. Another such classification puts beings into the several classes of the "no-footed, the two-footed the four-footed, the many-footed, those having or lacking material form, the conscious, the unconscious and the super-conscious" (A III 35). The human worlds are always represented as standing midway in the hierarchy of worlds. Life in these human worlds is a mixture of the pleasant and the unpleasant, the good and the evil, while the pleasant and good traits are intensified in the higher worlds and the unpleasant and evil in the lower.

If we contemplate the vastness of cosmic space and the seemingly endless number of worlds of which the human worlds form a very small part, the problems of race would appear in a different light and seem very trifling indeed. One is reminded of a comparison the Buddha made when he rebuked a section of his monks who felt superior to the rest in that they had more fame and gain than the others; he likened them to worms who, born in dung, bred in dung, and living on dung, feel superior to other worms who are not so privileged in this respect. Whatever the picture we may get from a cosmic perspective of humanity "crawling over the surface of the earth and trying to eke out an existence on it," humility is one of the lessons we have to learn from it. Kingship on earth is a beggarly existence in comparison with the joys of the heavenly worlds (A IV 254). The span of life of mortal men is insignificantly small in comparison with cosmic time and may be compared in its duration to a line drawn on the earth (A IV 138).

But although human life appears insignificant from a cosmic standpoint, yet it is constantly pointed out in the Buddhist texts as being of tremendous worth, as man has within him the capacity of gaining the highest knowledge, or of attaining a moral pre-eminence which can make him worthy of becoming a "ruler of a world-system." This is not possible for those in lower-than-human states of existence, whose actions are instinctive and too preoccupied with securing elementary needs; nor is it possible for those in the higher worlds who are too distracted by the joys of the present for serious contemplation to be possible. This is why a human birth is so valuable, although in the cosmic scheme of things it is all too rare. In the course of our *saṃsāric* evolution we have been born, as it is said, hundreds of times as animals (S II 188), and it is rare that we emerge into a human existence: "Birth as a human being is a rare event" (*dullabhaṃ manussattaṃ*). It is therefore the duty of humans to make the most of the precious human life that they have acquired. Man has within him the potentiality of discovering the deepest truths about the cosmos for himself. A person who has realised such potentialities is the Buddha, who is not only the best among humans but the highest among all sentient beings. When the Buddha was asked whether he was man or god, he answered that he was neither since he was the Buddha (A II 38). The intellectual, moral and spiritual heights that man can attain are so great that those who have attained them are as different from ordinary men as men are from animals. Yet such men are not mere freaks nor have they been specially favoured by any divine agency. They have attained such heights by dint of effort directed towards developing their intellectual, moral and spiritual nature extending over many lives. And what has been achieved by one or a few is within the capacity of all to achieve. As the Mahāyāna texts put it, it is not only men but all sentient beings down to the very lowest who are potential Buddhas, in that a Buddha nature (*Buddha-bhāva*) is present within them. If only for this reason, no one has a right to despise a fellow creature, since all are subject to the same laws of existence and have ultimately the same nature and the same potentialities, though they are in varying stages of growth or development and their rates of growth may differ from time to time.

At the human level the lessons that man can learn by realising his position in the universe are not only that he needs to be humble, but also that he need not despair, since he has the power to understand the world and overcome it and cease to be a mere mechanism within it. Both these lessons, the realisation of our common plight as well as the potentialities within each of us, teach us but one moral—namely that it is everyone's duty to help his fellow beings, and that no one has any right or valid grounds to despise another.

The Biological Unity of Mankind and the Case Against Racism

A special emphasis is placed in Buddhism on the worth and dignity of human existence in view of the opportunities and potentialities that man possesses for self-development. The unity of mankind is emphasised, and a distinction drawn between human beings and the animal and plant kingdoms.

It is argued on biological grounds that—unlike in the case of the plant and animal kingdoms, where differences of species are noticeable—mankind is one species. This view accords remarkably with the findings of modern biological science. Not only is it in disagreement with the scientific pretensions of the biologists of the eighteenth and early nineteenth centuries, who tried to classify men into different races which could be graded like species of animals into the higher and lower, but it cuts the ground beneath the very foundations of any racist doctrine which would divide human beings into more or less isolated groups and argue that their varying human characteristics are in their entirety genetically determined. The following passage occurs in a polemic against the pretensions of the Brahmanic caste theory and incidentally shows by implication how the Brahmins were claiming superiority for themselves on genetic grounds:

> *'We have a controversy regarding (the distinctions of) birth, O Gotama! Bhāradvāja says, one is a Brahmin by birth, and I say by deeds; know this, O you clearly-seeing!*
>
> *'We are both unable to convince each other, (therefore) we have come to ask you (who are) celebrated as perfectly enlightened."*
>
> *'I will explain to you—O Vāseṭṭha, so said Bhagavat, 'in due order the exact distinction of living beings according to species, for their species are manifold: Know ye the grass and the trees, although they do not exhibit (it), the marks that constitute species are for them, and (their) species are manifold.*
>
> *'Then know the worms, and the moths, and the different sorts of ants, the marks, that constitute species are for them, and (their) species are manifold.*
>
> *'Know you also the four-footed (animals), small and great, the marks that constitute species are for them, and (their) species are manifold.*

"Know you also the serpents, the long-backed snakes, the marks that constitute species are for them, and (their) species are manifold.

"Then know you also the fish which range in the water, the marks that constitute species are for them, and (their) species are manifold.

"Then know you also the birds that are borne along on wings and move through the air, the marks that constitute species are for them, and (their) species are manifold.

"As in these species the marks that constitute species are abundant, so in men the marks that constitute species are not abundant.

"Not as regards their hair, head, ears, eyes, mouth, nose, lips, or brows.

"Nor as regards their neck, shoulders, belly, back, hip, breast, female organ, sexual intercourse,

"Nor as regards their hands, feet, palms, nails, calves, thighs, colour or voice are there marks that constitute species as in other species.

"Difference there is in beings endowed with bodies, but amongst men this is not the case, the difference amongst men is nominal (only).

"For whoever amongst men lives by cow-keeping—know this, O Vāseṭṭha—he is a husbandman, not a Brahmin.

"And whoever amongst men lives by archery—know this, O Vāseṭṭha—he is a soldier, not a Brahmin.

"And I do not call one a Brahmin on account of his birth or of his origin from a (particular) mother. ..."

(*Vāseṭṭhasutta*, Sn, tr. Fausböll, SBE, X, pp. 111-13)

What is apparent from the above is that, according to the Buddha, there are no distinguishing characteristics of genus and species among men, unlike in the case of grasses, trees, worms, moths, fishes, beasts, birds, etc. As Chalmers says: "Herein, Gotama was in accord with the conclusion of modern biologists that 'the Anthropidae are represented by the single genus and species, Man'—a conclusion which was the more remarkable inasmuch as the accident of colour did not mislead Gotama, (JRAS, 1894, p. 346). The Buddha goes on to show that the apparent divisions between men are not due to basic biological factors but are "conventional classifications" (*samaññā*). The distinctions made in respect of the differences in skin colour (*vaṇṇa*), hair form (*kesa*), the shape of the head (*sīsa*) or the shape of the nose (*nāsa*), etc., are not absolute categories. One is almost reminded of the statement of the scientists that "the concept of race is unanimously regarded by anthropologists as a classificatory device ..." (*The Race Concept*, UNESCO, p. 38).

It would thus appear that Buddhism is in accord with the findings of the modern biologists who explored the doctrines of racism and would urge the biological unity of mankind in support of the concept of a common humanity. So when Buddhism asks us to treat all man, irrespective of race or caste, as our fathers, mothers, brothers and sisters or as one family, there seems to be a deeper truth in this statement than that of a mere ethical recommendation.

While the above passage brings out the Buddhist attitude to the problem of race, it is not possible to say that early Buddhism was confronted with a racial problem as such. The problem was no doubt there in Rgvedic society, where the race-conscious Aryan who spoke derisively of the dark-skinned and noiseless aborigines treated them as an inferior race. But by the time of the rise of Buddhism this race-consciousness had given place to a caste-consciousness and it was the Brahmin in particular and the "higher" castes in general, who were probably derived largely from Aryan stock, who claimed superiority by virtue of their light skin colour. It was claimed by the Brahmins to be one of the hereditary characteristics of a Brahmin that he was handsome (*abhirūpo*), fair (*dassanīyo*), endowed with an excellent complexion (*paramāya vaṇṇapokkharatāya samannāgato*), and of the fairest colour (*brahmavaṇṇī*) (D I 119) by virtue of which he claimed superiority over those of a dark complexion.

The terms "Aryan" (*ariya*) and "non-Aryan" (*anariya*), are frequently found in the Buddhist texts, but never in a racial sense. The racial sense of superiority associated with the word "Aryan" is completely eclipsed by the moral and spiritual sense of superiority, which the word in a Buddhist context connotes, devoid of any associations of race or birth. Thus Aṅgulimāla, a brutal brigand and a person of a "low" caste who struck terror in the territory of the king of Kosala by his wanton acts of cruelty, is described after being converted by the Buddha as "*ariyāya jātiyā jāto*," which means "reborn with a spiritual birth," though if the words are taken literally the phrase would mean "born in the Aryan race." The use of the word "Aryan" in the sense of "noble" and "spiritual" and "non-

Aryan" in the sense of "ignoble" and "immoral" is an eloquent testimony of how Buddhism ignored racial claims and distinctions. Thus "Aryan quest" (*ariya-pariyesana*) means "spiritual quest," which is defined as "the quest of one who being subject to birth, decay and death realises the evil consequences thereof and seeks the immortal and secure haven of Nibbāna" (M I 162f). The "Aryan haven" (*ariya-uccāsayana-mahāsayanaṃ*) means the "spiritual haven," which is "the state of being free from lust, hatred and delusion" (A I 182).

There is, however, a philosophical theory of racism held by some of the religious teachers in the Buddha's time which is mentioned and criticised in the Buddhist texts. It is associated with two teachers, both of whom denied free will to man. One was Purāṇa Kassapa, who denied man's capacity for moral action in virtue of the fact that he had no free will. The other was Makkhali Gosāla, who denied both free will and causation and argued that beings were miraculously saved (*ahetū appaccayā sattā visujjhanti*) or doomed. They argued that human beings belonged to one or another of six species (*abhijāti*) (A III 383) or specific types; in virtue of which they had certain genetic constitutions, physical traits and habits and psychological natures which they were incapable of altering by their own will or effort. The six types were designated by six colours. They were the black species (*kaṇhābhijāti*), the blue species, the red species, the yellow species, the white species and the pure white species. Whether these colours denoted differences in their physical complexions is not clear,[13] but that they were genetically different physical and psychological types is what is implied by the classification. To the black species belonged the butchers, fowlers, hunters, fishermen, robbers, and executioners and all those who adopt a cruel mode of living. They were, incidentally, among the lowest castes and their complexion was on the whole the darkest. The other five specific types differed in virtue of their degree of wickedness or saintliness, which was not in their power to alter. The pure white species were reckoned to be the perfect saints, though their saintliness was considered to be natural to them as

---

13. *Mahābhārata*, *Śantiparvan*, where it is said that "the colour of the Brahmin was white, that of the Ksatriyas red, that of the Vaisyas yellow and that of the Sudras black." The commentator, however, explains these colours as psychological characteristics in terms of Sāṃkhya philosophy.

much as their physical constitutions, and was in no way achieved by any effort of will on their part. In the opinion of these typologists, human beings who suffered pain in this life were so born to suffer as a result of their inheriting certain physical constitutions and psychological natures (M II 222).

Arguing from the reality of free will and the capacity that man has within himself of becoming either moral or immoral or even happy or unhappy by transforming himself or degenerating morally as the case may be, the Buddha denies that there are such fixed human types genetically determined. There are no men who are intrinsically good or evil by nature and must necessarily remain so, for the evil can turn into good and the good degenerate into evil. The six types of human beings that the Buddha would recognize do not have fixed natures genetically determined but are the six classes of beings, namely the evil who remain evil, the evil who become good, the evil who transcend good and evil (and enter Nibbāna), the good who become evil, the good who remain good and the good who transcend both good and evil (and enter Nibbāna)—all of them no doubt by the exercise of their free will. The emphasis is not on what a man is born with but what he does with himself since man, irrespective of his physical constitution and psychological nature at birth, can—given the opportunity and effort—change for better or worse. The racist tenor of the former theory is thus denounced in the Buddha's classification, where the merits of people are to be judged not in terms of what they are born with but what they do with themselves.

The Dignity and Equality of Mankind and the Case against Caste

Although it should be clear from the above that Buddhism upholds the biological unity of mankind and denies any genetic basis for discrimination between different "racial" groups, it may be noted that the statements about race quoted above were not made in an encounter with any racial problem as such, for the racial conflict between the Aryan and non-Aryan had been reduced in the time of the Buddha, mainly to a caste conflict between the Brahmins or the "higher" castes versus the "lower." It is in such a context that the problem is generalized and discussed in the background of the biological doctrines which caste theory appeared to espouse or take for granted.

In the previous section we referred to the possible racial origin of much of caste prejudice, and showed the strong similarity between the prejudice and discrimination in matters of caste as in race. The case against caste discrimination and prejudice as presented in Buddhism applies as much against caste as against racial prejudice and discrimination.

The course that Buddhism adopted in combatting caste prejudice and discrimination was to ignore it in practice and denounce its theory by means of rational persuasion. We shall take up the former aspect of the question in the next section and confine ourselves here to the scientific, ethical and religious arguments adduced against the theory of caste as advanced by the Brahmins. The scientific arguments may conveniently be classified as the biological and the sociological.

The Biological Arguments

The thesis that we do not find differences of species among human beings as we do among plants and animals and that mankind is one species forms the crux of the biological argument. Found in the earliest texts (as quoted above), this argument is expanded in subsequent polemics against caste written by Buddhists. Thus Aśvaghoṣa in his *Vajrasuci* (circa first century CE) says:

> "All that I have said about Brahmins you must know is equally applicable to Kshatriyas; and that the doctrine of the four castes is altogether false. All men are of one caste.
>
> "Wonderful! If you affirm that all men proceeded from one, i.e. Brahmā, how then can there be a fourfold insuperable diversity among them? If I have four sons by one wife, the four sons having one father and mother must be all essentially alike. Know too that distinctions of race among beings are broadly marked by differences of conformations and organization. Thus, the foot of the elephant is very different from that of the horse; that of the tiger unlike that of the deer and so of the rest, and by that single diagnosis we learn that those animals belong to very different races. But I never heard that the foot of a Kshatriya was different from that of a Brahmin or that of a Sudra. All men are formed alike, and are clearly of one race. Further, the generative organs, the colour, the figure, the ordure, the urine, the odour

and the utterance of the ox, the buffalo, the horse, the elephant, the ass, the monkey, the goat, the sheep, etc., furnish further diagnostics whereby to separate these various races of animals: but in all those respects the Brahmin resembles the Kshatriya, and is therefore of the same race or species with him. I have instanced among quadrupeds the diversities which separate diverse genera. I now proceed to give some more instances from among birds. Thus, the goose, the dove, the parrot, the peacock, etc., are known to be different by their diversities of figure, and colour, and plumage and beak; but the Brahmin, Kshatriya, Vaishya and Sudra are alike without and within. How then can we say they are essentially distinct? Again, among trees, the Vata and Bakula, and Palasha and Ashoka, the Tamala and Nāgakeshara, and Shirisha and Champaka and others, are clearly contradistinguished by their stems, and leaves, and flowers, and fruits and barks, and timber, and seeds, and juices and odours; but as Brahmins, and Kshatriyas and the rest are alike in flesh, and skin, and blood, and bones, and figure, and excrements, and mode of birth it is surely then clear that they are of one species or race. Again, tell me, is a Brahmin's sense of pleasure and pain different from that of a Kshatriya? Does not the one sustain life in the same way, and find death from the same causes as the other? Do they differ in intellectual faculties, in their actions or the objects of those actions, in the manner of their birth or in their subjection to fear and hope? Not a whit. It is therefore clear that they are essentially the same. In the Udumbara and Panasa trees the fruit is produced from the branches, the stem, the joints and the roots. Is one fruit therefore different from another, so that we may call 'that produced from the top of the stem the Brahmin fruit, and that from the roots the Sudra fruit'? Surely not. Nor can men be of four distinct races because they sprang from four different parts of one body" (From H. H. Wilson, *Indian Caste,* London, 1877, pp. 302–03).

The differences in skin colour (*vaṇṇa*), hair (*kesa*), shape of nose (*nāsa*) or head (*sīsa*) were indeed small in comparison with the differences among the various species of plants and animals. Caste names were merely conventional designations signifying occupational differences and, since men were free to change their occupations, these differences had no hereditary or genetic basis. As Aśvaghoṣa says: "The distinctions between Brahmins, Kshatriyas, Vaishyas and Sudras are founded merely on the observance of diverse rites and the practise of different professions" (ibid. pp. 303–04). One who engages in trade comes to be known as a merchant, one who indulges in military pursuits is known as a soldier, and one who administers the country, as a king. It was not by birth that one becomes merchant, soldier or king but by the actions that one performs or the job one does.

Caste theory tried early to lay down that there were specific hereditary occupations (karma) suitable for people born into the different castes, and since they had a special aptitude (*guṇa*) for these types of occupations it was the specific duty (*svadharma*) or obligation of those born in their respective castes to perform their respective tasks and no others. A son of Sudra (outcast) parents must always do a menial job for which he has been created with a special aptitude, and the son of Kshatriya parents an administrative job. Even the Bhagavadgītā says: "The fourfold order was created by Me (i.e. God) according to the divisions of quality and work" (*The Bhagavadgita*, Radhakrishnan ed., London, 1948, p. 160), meaning thereby that God created the four castes with certain aptitudes (*guṇa*) and functions (karma) and it was their duty to perform their respective functions and not swerve from this path of duty.

The analogy with racist theory is that the "superior" races are born to rule, with a special aptitude for this task, while the "inferior" races are born to serve their masters, who rule them. It was such a theory that Buddhism denounced, on the grounds that it had no basis in fact; since people are not born in their respective castes with such aptitudes genetically determined and are under no obligation to do the work assigned to their castes and no other. The job one does and that one is free to choose should give one's "caste" name (*kammanā khattiyo, vasala hoti*), but it is merely a conventional designation denoting one's occupation and is of no genetic significance; since one does not follow a vocation or have an aptitude for it merely because one was born of parents who followed the same (Sn 650).

Man is biologically one species. There are no separate castes (or races) radically different from each other and created from the beginning. The concept of pure castes (analogous to that of pure races) is dismissed on the grounds that most of us cannot in the least be sure whether caste purity, or intermarriage strictly within the caste alone, was observed by our parents and grandparents even up to seven generations (D I 92–99). Devala the Dark, who is quoted as one of the Brahmin seers opposed to the caste theory formulated by some of the Rigvedic Brahmins, questions the latter in the course of a discussion about caste as to whether they remember whether their parents and grandparents were of the same caste even up to seven generations, to which it is replied that they do not. It is then concluded that in such circumstances "we do not know who we are" (*na māyaṃ jānāma keci māyaṃ homa*) (M II 156) and therefore we have no right to maintain the reality or purity of castes. We also find the Buddha arguing with Brahmins who claimed caste purity, showing them that some of their ancestors did not marry within the caste (*Ambaṭṭha Sutta*, DN 3) and that the claim to purity was therefore a myth and not a fact.

It also follows from the biological unity of mankind that intermarriage between castes or races is both possible and not necessarily undesirable. This was again a point on which the caste theorists, like the racists, held strong views—severely condemning intermarriage between castes on the ground that this would have disastrous consequences. The Buddha on the other hand not only argued against claims to caste purity in view of the fact that intermarriage between castes was both a possibility and a historical fact, but even seems to have held that it was not necessarily undesirable. The products of such caste mixture would resemble both parents and in such situations we cannot say from observing the physical or genetic constitutions to which caste the child belongs.

The *Ambaṭṭha Sutta* (DN 3) exposes the myth of the purity of caste of which the Brahmins were so conscious. Ambaṭṭha was a Brahmin youth who was so conscious of his high Brahmin lineage that he did not observe the usual courtesies in talking to the Buddha, whom he despised on the ground that he was not a Brahmin. In the course of the conversation with him, which turns round caste, the Buddha points out that the so-called purity of his ancestry was a myth. "If one were to follow up your ancient name and lineage," says the Buddha, "on the father's and mother's side, it would appear that one of your ancestors was the offspring of one of the slave girls of the Sakyas" (D I 92). Later Buddhist polemics against caste continue such arguments. Aśvaghoṣa says: "Do you say that he who is sprung from Brahmin parents is a Brahmin? Still I object that, since you must mean pure and true Brahmins, in such case the breed of Brahmins must be at an end, since the fathers of the parent race of Brahmins are not, any of them, free from the suspicion of having wives who notoriously commit adultery with Sudras. Now, if the real father be a Sudra, the son cannot be a Brahmin, notwithstanding the Brahminhood of his mother" (H. H. Wilson, op. cit., p. 298).

Although the physical constitution of the child is held to be due to a combination of genetic factors derived from both parents, it is important to note that the prenatal growth of the child takes place, according to Buddhism, in conjunction with the psychic factor constituting the impressions of former births, so that in addition to the effects of biological heredity and environment there is the influence of the psychic factor on the development of the personality. This fact is also made use of by means of a reduction absurdum to argue against the reality of caste. It is said that the psychic factor or the spirit seeking rebirth (*gandhabbo*) cannot be considered as belonging to any particular caste (M II 137), so that the essence of one's personality is beyond caste distinctions.

The Sociological Arguments

Another way of combatting caste theory revolves round the investigation of the nature and origins of human society and of caste divisions.

The Hindu conception of society was static and was dominated by the idea of caste. The traditional fourfold order of priests, soldiers and administrators, merchants and agriculturists and menial workers was considered not only to be absolute, fundamental and necessary to society but was also given a divine sanction by being considered a creation of God (Brahmā). "God created the fourfold caste order with their specific aptitudes and functions", with the result that people born into the different castes have certain special biologically inherited aptitudes which eminently fit them to perform the caste functions which it is their duty to perform.

Against this was the dynamic evolutionary conception of society as pictured in early Buddhism. The fourfold order is here not considered absolute since, as the Buddha says, in certain societies there are only two classes (*dve'va vaṇṇā*)—the lords and the serfs or the masters and the slaves, and that not too rigid a division since "the masters sometimes become slaves and the slaves masters" (ibid). Nor is caste divine in origin. The belief that caste was a creation of God and that the Brahmins were the chosen legitimate children of God, "born of the mouth of Brahmā," a conception which is as old as the Rigveda, is denied in the Buddhist texts, where it is said that the birth of Brahmins, as is well known, is in no way different from that of other human beings (M II 149), and that the Brahmins are referred to ironically as "the kinsmen of God" (*brahma-bandhu*). In place of this conception of a divinely ordained fourfold order, Buddhism conceived of caste divisions as being occupational divisions which arose owing to historical circumstances and considered the perpetuation of caste prejudice and discrimination as being due largely to the sanctions given it by the early Brahmin priesthood.

This is well brought out in the story of Devala the Dark, a well-known priest himself, who was scorned because of his colour by the other priestly seers who are said, in the words of the Buddha, to have got together and formulated the following false and evil view (*pāpaka-diṭṭhigataṃ*), namely that the Brahmins were the highest caste while the others were low caste, the Brahmins were "whites" while the others were "blacks," the Brahmins alone were saved while the others were not, and the Brahmins alone were the only chosen legitimate children of God (M II 156). If this legend contains a germ of historical truth, then in the words of Ghurye: "Caste in India must be regarded as a Brahmanic child of the Indo-Aryan culture, cradled in the land of the Ganges and then transferred to the other parts of India by the Brahmin-prospectors (*Caste and Race in India*, London, 1932, p. 143)."

In place of a static conception of a fourfold order created by God, a Buddhist myth of genesis (found in the texts of both schools of Buddhism) gives an evolutionary account of society and shows how what later became caste divisions arose from a necessary division of functions in society at a certain stage of social evolution. To quote from Prof. Rhys Davids' brief summary of the myth: "Then successively fine moss, and sweet creepers, and delicate rice appeared, and each time the beings ate thereof with a similar result. Then differences of sex appeared; and households were formed; and the lazy stored up the rice, instead of gathering it each evening and morning; and the rights of property arose, and were infringed. And when lusts were felt and thefts committed the beings, now become men, met together, and chose men differing from the others in no way except in virtue (*dhamma*), to restrain the evildoers by blame or fines or banishment. These were the first Kshatriyas. And others chose to restrain the evil dispositions which led to the evil-doing. And these the first Brahmins, differing from the others in no way, except only in virtue (*dhamma*). Then certain others, to keep their households going, and maintain their wives, started occupations of various kinds. And these were the first Vessas. And some abandoned their homes and became the first recluses (*samaṇas*). But all were alike in origin, and the only distinction between them was in virtue" (*Dialogues of the Buddha*, I, p. 106). As Prof. Rhys Davids comments: "We may not accept the historical accuracy of this legend. Indeed a continual note of good-humoured irony runs through the whole story. ... But it reveals a sound and healthy insight and is much nearer to the actual facts than the Brahmin legend it was intended to replace" (ibid.).

The Buddhist texts constantly refer to the theory of caste which the Brahmin priesthood tried to impose on society—justifying on religious grounds and attempting to perpetuate caste prejudice and discrimination—as a mere propagandist cry (*ghoso*) (M I 89) on their part. Such propaganda was met by the Buddhists by appealing to the historical facts about the origins of caste, which gave no basis for the rigidity of caste structure or for prejudice and discrimination between castes, since caste names were in origin and even in the time of the Buddha designations denoting differences of occupation.

It has been argued with some justification that the social organization of eastern India was possibly different from the west, where Brahminism held sway (R. Flick, *The Social Organization in North-East India in Buddha's Time*, tr. by S. Maitre, Calcutta, 1920, p. 13 ff). But from the Brahmanical works it is evident that theory was different from practise even in regions where Brahmanism held sway, for we find that, although certain restricted duties and occupations were considered to be suitable for Brahmins, in actual fact the professions of Brahmins were multifarious and there were among them not only tradesmen and military advisers but even butchers and carriers of corpses, professions which were being confined to the Sudras in the laws drawn up by the Brahmin priests (*Laws of Manu*, SBE, Vol. 25, III.150–68).

Under these circumstances the Buddhists tried to uphold the cause of the social equality of man, illustrating their case against the Brahmanical attack by pointing to actual conditions prevailing in the society of the time. They pointed out that the ability to command the services and labour of others depended not on one's caste or high birth, which ipso facto made the Brahmins or the Kshatriyas the masters, but on the wealth that one had. A Sudra who could command enough wealth could easily have a Brahmin or Kshatriya servant to attend to him and be a menial in his household (M II 85). There was no intrinsic reason why a Sudra should be born to serve others, since in society it was economic power that counted and not caste superiority in requisitioning the services of others. It was shown that all were in fact, and should be, equal before the law. Even the Laws of Manu (III 150) speak of "Brahmins who are thieves and outcasts" and who on this account lose their right to be Brahmins. This shows that, even where Brahminism held sway, to some extent at least, it was their deeds and not birth that mattered. In the Buddhist texts, however, it is said that such robbers, irrespective of whether they were born of Brahmin or Sudra parents, were executed, burnt or exiled by the king quite regardless of their pedigree (M II 88).

Although Brahmins were denying the Sudras admission into their religious orders, and even the possibility of salvation or moral development, on the grounds that Sudras were born to serve and their nature was untruth itself, non-Brahmanic religious orders represented by the Samaṇas (the Garmanes of Megasthenes) admitted people of all castes (J-a III 381; IV 392), even the Sudras, and it is said that such people were honoured as "religieux" even by the kings (M II 89). In contrast to the Brahmins, who were trying to make a monopoly of religion, the Buddhists idealize a society in which all men irrespective of their social standing or birth were free to join religious orders and receive equal recognition as men of religion.

While the Brahmins argued that only people of the different castes were capable of or suitable for performing certain functions, which were considered to be obligatory on their part by virtue of their birth, the Buddhists tried to show that this was by no means so. It is said, for instance, not without some sarcasm, that people of all castes whether "high" or "low" are capable of kindling a fire and that a fire that men of the so-called "low" castes would kindle would be no less bright than the fires kindled by the so-called "higher" castes (M II 151 f.). The choice of "kindling a fire" as the example is probably an ironical reference to the Brahmins, who specialized in the kindling and tending of sacrificial fires.

The hollowness of the magical notions associated with the concept of caste pollution is exposed by the empiricist stand of Buddhism. The only sense of cleanliness or pollution, barring the spiritual sense (see below), was the physical sense and it is said with biting irony that people of all "castes," even the Sudras can soap themselves and bathe in the river and be equally clean (M II 151), so that Sudras are not at a disadvantage in their ability to be clean.

Thus, according to Buddhism, all men, irrespective of their caste or race, had equal rights and deserved equal opportunities for development as members of a single social order which embraced a common humanity. It was a man's social status as determined by the wealth that he possessed, and not his birth in a particular caste or racial group, which made it possible for him to command the services of others whatever their pedigree might be. All men likewise, irrespective of race or caste, should be equal before the law. The aptitudes of people do not depend on their birth in a particular caste or race. The moral worth of a person should receive social recognition regardless of the caste to which he belonged and all men should receive equal opportunity for moral and spiritual development since all men were capable of it.

It was in these terms that Buddhism proclaimed the equality of man as a member of human society. The constant refrain that we find in these discussions, which are intended to counter the Brahmin claims to superiority by virtue of their birth, is that considering the capabilities of men of all castes "people of all castes are on an equal footing" (*evaṃ sante ime cattāro vaṇṇā samāsama honti*), and that "there is no distinction whatsoever among them in these respects" (*nesaṃ ettha kiñci nānākaraṇaṃ samanupassāmi*) (M I 85–9).

Ethical and Religious Arguments

As mentioned above, Buddhism denied in the light of historical facts the special prerogatives that the Brahmins claimed in matters of religion. Their claim to be the chosen children of God by virtue of their birth and their exclusive claim to salvation were shown to be false, since people of castes, given the opportunity, were capable of attaining the spiritual heights required for salvation. In place of the Brahmin claim that "Brahmins alone were saved and not others," we find it stated in the words of the Brahmin opponents to Buddhism that the "recluse Gotama proclaims the possibility of salvation to all men of all four castes" (*Samaṇo Gotamo cātuvaṇṇiṃ suddhiṃ paññāpeti*) (M II 147). All men irrespective of caste were capable of spiritual development, and a man whether born in a "high" caste or "low" "can develop within him loving thoughts towards all beings" (M II 151). Such religious exercises were within the capacity of all and make for their spiritual progress. Similarly the claim to a divine origin for caste was condemned as mere propaganda on the part of the Brahmin priests and as having no basis in view of the gradual evolutionary origins of society.

All men are likewise equal before the moral law: Men are judged in the hereafter by the good and evil they do, and not by the stations of life in which they were placed by virtue of their birth. The reward and punishment are strictly in proportion to the good and evil done, and caste whether "high" or "low" does not matter in the least. A Sudra (outcast) who does good in this humble station enjoys later the pleasant fruits of his actions, while a Brahmin who does evil suffers. The magical concept of cleanliness and pollution associated with caste is given an ethical twist; what matters is not even external cleanliness but purity of heart or the absence of pollution within (Sn 43). Moral and spiritual development is not a prerogative of people who are specially favoured by their birth, but is open to all and is within the reach of all.

The Spiritual Unity of Mankind

Biologically man is one species. As members of a common human society all men deserve to have equal rights and opportunities, which include the opportunities for moral and spiritual development. But man is more than a biological specimen or a social being. Deep within his desires to satisfy his biological needs and social instincts is his quest for security, immortality and a lasting peace and happiness.

What brings men together is the realization of their common lot and their common humanity. All men of whatever race are subject to disease, decay and death. All men are likewise impelled by the desires within them—the desire for sense-gratification, the desire for life or personal immortality and the desire for domination over death. Man's quest for security and lasting happiness never ceases, but it is never satisfied by pandering to his desires, as a result of which he is continually in a state of unrest. But deep within this fathom-long body, says the Buddha, is the final goal we all seek and it is only by discovering this eternal peace and happiness within us that we realise the highest that we are capable of.

All people, whatever their caste or racial origins may be, are in need of and capable of this self-same salvation. The king of Kosala once questioned the Buddha on this subject:

"There are these four castes, sir—Kshatriyas, Brahmins, Vaisyas and Sudras. Let us suppose them to be imbued with the five forms of strenuous exertion to attain salvation. In this case would there be any distinction, sir, any difference between them (in regard to the quality of their salvation)?"

"Here, too, sir," replies the Buddha, "I do not admit any difference whatsoever in regard to the nature of their salvation. Just as if, sir, a man were to kindle a fire with dry herbs, and another man were to kindle a fire with dry sal-wood, and a third were to kindle a fire with dry mango-wood, and a fourth with dry fig-wood—what think you, sir, would these diverse fires kindled with diverse woods show any difference whatsoever in respect of their flame, hue or brightness?"

"No difference at all, sir."

"Even so, sir, is the inward illumination which is kindled by effort and nursed by strenuous exertion. I say that there is no difference whatsoever herein in regard to their salvation" (M II 129–30).

All men have the capacity to attain salvation, irrespective of the race or caste to which they belong, and it is this quest for eternal happiness which constitutes the religious quest of man.

It is the realization of this quest which should be the ultimate aim of man, for it is only on attaining it that his mental conflicts are at an end and he has found salvation, a state to be attained in this life itself and not necessarily in the hereafter. "Man," says the Buddha, "is subject to both bodily and mental disease. Bodily disease afflicts him only from time to time, but except for those who have attained salvation the others cannot claim to have perfect mental health even for a second" (A II 143). But such perfect control and poise of mind, which awakens in us a peace that passes understanding, can only be found by those who practise love and charity to all beings and engage in the development of their minds by following the process of self-analysis as recommended in Buddhism. And being obsessed by one's "superior" birth in respect of the race or caste to which one belongs is one of the first obstacles that has to be put away in the interests of our own mental health as well as of the world. The outcast as described in Buddhism is not one who is born in a particular caste but "one who hardens his heart by virtue of his birth in a particular race (*jāti-tthaddho*), or by virtue of his wealth (*dhana-tthaddho*) or caste (*gotta-tthaddho*), and despises his neighbour" (*saṃñātiṃ atimaññati*) (Sn 104).

So when we consider differences among human beings it is not the shape of their limbs, the colour of their skins, their parentage or social status that matters, but the question of how far each human being is from his goal, which is also the goal of all mankind, and which gives him real happiness and perfect mental health. Are we progressing towards this goal or away from it? It is solely in virtue of the degree of moral and spiritual attainment of people, irrespective of race or caste, that Buddhism classified human beings as superior or inferior—although this classification too is not rigid inasmuch as each person is constantly changing and has within himself the power to change for better or for worse. The superior ones are those who have attained the goal or are near it or are progressing towards it, while the inferior ones are those who are far from the goal or are going away from it. And, significantly enough, it is said that those who are "bound by racial prejudices" (*jāti-vāda-vinibaddha*) or "bound by caste prejudices" (*gotta-vāda-vinibaddha*) have strayed "far from the way of salvation" (*arakā anuttarāya vijja-caraṇa-sampadāya*). (D I 99).

It is also a characteristic of the superior ones that they do not assert or make personal claims of their moral and spiritual superiority over others (Sn 782, 918). This does not, however, mean that they are conscious of their superiority but merely do not show it, for it is said that those who have attained salvation cease to think of themselves in terms of "being superior" (*seyyo*), "being inferior" (*niceyyo*) or "being equal" (*sarikkho*). (Sn 918). The morally and spiritually inferior ones, on the other hand, shut their minds to the possibility of a spiritual awakening and cease to make any moral or spiritual progress as a result of their asserting or claiming superiority over their fellow beings on baseless grounds, and thus bringing unhappiness both on themselves and on others by causing baseless divisions among men. The degree of moral and spiritual progress is therefore the only criterion by which men should be classified as being superior or inferior—though such classifications are not absolute since men are changing and can change.

Thus we have no right to despise another. Even a hardened criminal like Aṅgulimāla, the outcast murderer, who was converted by the Buddha, may have deep within his nature strong potentialities for undergoing a relatively quick spiritual transformation. The truly superior being is never conscious of his superiority, nor does he claim it. Such people are the true Brahmins, regardless of their origins, and not those who are obsessed by their claims to a "pure" birth.

There are several such classifications of mankind on the basis of their varying moral and spiritual attainments in the Buddhist texts. We may refer to one which classifies individuals into seven grades:

"There are these seven persons to be compared with those immersed in water, viz., one who is once drowned is drowned, one who is drowned after emergence, etc....

"(1) How is a person who is once drowned just drowned? Here a certain person is possessed of absolutely black immoral qualities. Such a person being once drowned is drowned.

"(2) How is a person drowned after emergence? Here a certain person emerges with faith, with modesty, with conscientiousness, with energy, with insight, as regards good (moral) qualities, but his faith, his modesty, conscientiousness, energy or insight neither persists nor grows, but decreases. Such a person is drowned after emergence.

"(3) How does a person persist after emergence? Here a certain person emerges with faith, with modesty, with conscientiousness, with energy, with insight; as regards good qualities and his faith, his modesty, conscientiousness, energy, or insight neither decreases nor grows, but persists. Such a person persists after emergence.

"(4) How does a person look about and around after emergence? Here a certain person emerges with faith, with modesty, with conscientiousness, with energy, or with insight, as regards good qualities. By complete destruction of three fetters he becomes a stream-attainer, no more liable to fall into a woeful state, but sure to win enlightenment as his final end and aim. Such a person looks about and around after emergence.

"(5) How does a person swim on after emergence? Here a certain person emerges with faith, with modesty, with conscientiousness, with energy, or with insight, as regards good qualities. By complete destruction of three fetters and by the destruction of passion, hatred, and delusion he becomes a once-returner, who coming back but once to this world makes an end to suffering. Such a person swims on after emergence.

"(6) How does a person reach a fixed footing after emergence? Here a certain person emerges with faith, with modesty, with conscientiousness, with energy or with insight, as regards good qualities. By complete destruction of five fetters causing rebirth in the lower worlds, he becomes a being of apparitional rebirth attaining the final release in that state, and is not liable to return from that world. Such a person reaches a fixed footing after emergence.

"(7) What sort of person is he who as a true Brahmin after emergence crosses to the other shore and establishes himself in fruition? Here a certain person emerges with faith, with modesty, with conscientiousness, with energy or with insight, as regards good qualities. By destruction of sinful tendencies, he lives in possession of emancipation of will, of emancipation, of insight, free from those sinful tendencies and having come to know and realise them by his own efforts in this very existence. Such a person is a true Brahmin crossing after emergence and going to the other shore and establishing himself in fruition" (*Puggala Paññatti*, tr. *Human Types*, pp. 99–100).

The Practical Policy of Buddhism towards Racism and Caste

As we tried to show in the previous chapter, Buddhism from the first proclaimed the oneness of mankind and denied that birth in a particular race or caste was or should be an obstacle towards anyone developing his potentialities as a man or as a spiritual being. "Race" names and "caste" names were convenient misleading designations, but they were not absolute divisions. Caste names had only an occupational significance and from what appears in the texts the people at that time were still relatively free to choose or change their occupations. Caste prejudice and discrimination were still in the formative stage; their foundations were being laid by the Brahmin priesthood, who were formulating the required religious and legal sanctions for perpetuating the system. In the circumstances, we find the Buddha and his disciples completely ignoring the claims attached to birth with regard to dispensation of the Order of Monks—while fighting caste prejudice and discrimination, fanned by the Brahmin priesthood in the prevalent social order, by the methods of rational persuasion and example.

As Prof. Rhys Davids says, the Buddha "ignores completely and absolutely all advantages or disadvantages arising from birth, occupation or social status and sweeps away all barriers and disabilities arising from the arbitrary rules of mere ceremonial or social impurity" (*Dialogues of the Buddha*, I, p. 100). People of all castes were freely admitted to the Order and in doing so people had to change even their names and designations associated with their rank or birth. There were possibly a few who while being members of the Order of Monks were still conscious of their "high" birth or lineage and tried to claim special privileges on these grounds but such attempts were always checked and sternly denounced. It is said that a section of monks who were conscious of their "high" rank as civilians tried to monopolize lodgings, thereby leaving out the senior elders of the Order. The Buddha inquiring into the matter asked them, "Tell me, who deserves the best lodging, the best water, and the best rice, brethren?" Whereupon some answered, "He who was a noble-man before he became a brother," and others said, "He who was originally a Brahmin, or a man of means." The Buddha's reply was: "In the religion which I teach, the standard by which precedence in the matter of lodging and the like is to be settled, is not noble birth, or having been a Brahmin, or having been wealthy before entry into the Order ..." (*The Jātaka*, Vol. I, pp. 92–3).

Some of the most distinguished members of the Order were from the so-called "low" castes. Upāli, who was the chief authority on the rules of the Order after Buddha himself, had formerly been a barber, one of the despised occupations of the "lower" castes. Puṇṇā and Puṇṇikā, who joined the Order of Nuns, had been slave girls. The members of the Order, whether male or female, do not seem however to have been drawn exclusively from the "lower" castes. An analysis of the social position of the nuns mentioned in the *Psalms of the Sisters* shows that 81 percent of the whole number were "base-born." Prof. Rhys Davids says: "It is most likely that this is just about the proportion which persons in similar social rank bore to the rest of the population" (op. cit., p. 102). Perhaps it would be nearer the truth to say that if 81 percent of the contributed poems were composed by and express the religious joy that the members of the despised castes felt on joining the Order and realizing the fruits of the training that it gave, then the actual percentage of the women of "low" birth in the Order would have been very much larger, since the social class from which they were drawn was mostly illiterate. As Mrs. Rhys Davids says in the introduction to the sister work, the *Psalms of the Brethren*: "That a large proportion of these men of "letters" should belong to the class who were the custodians of religious lore and sacred hymns was inevitable. The really interesting feature is that the residuum, consisting of noblemen trained in war, governance, and sports, of merchants, craftsmen, and the like, occupied with business, commerce and constructive work, and of the illiterate poor, should be as numerous as it is. Or, indeed, that there should have been any of the last-named group at all as composers of verses deserving inclusion in the Canon. In fact, it would not be entirely unreasonable to conclude that if 4 percent of the canonical poets were drawn from the poor and despised of the earth, from whom no such products as verses could be expected, then the proportion of monks, in general, coming from that class may have been considerable" (*Psalms of the Brethren*, PTS, p. xxix).

How the Buddha called men and women from the lowliest walks of life and made them realise the richness of their spiritual heritage as human beings even though they were despised and reckoned as only fit for menial work by some of their fellow men—who ought to have known better—is best described in the words of those who received such gifts not as a matter of grace but as a fruit of their own efforts. Sunīta, for example, was a scavenger and the following is a brief account of his life and successful quest told in verse in his own words:

Humble the clan wherein I took my birth
And poor was I and scanty was my lot;
Mean task was mine, a scavenger of flowers,
One for whom no man cared, despised, abused,
My mind I humbled and I bent the head
In deference to a goodly tale of folk.

And then I saw the All-Enlightened come,
Begirt and followed by his Bhikkhu-train,
Great Champion entering Magadha's chief town.

I laid aside my baskets and my yoke,
And came where I might due obeisance make,
And of his loving kindness just for me,
The Chief of men halted upon his way.

Low at his feet I bent, then standing by,
I begged the Master's leave to join the Rule
And follow him, of every creature Chief.

Then he whose tender mercy watch the all
The world, the Master pitiful and kind,
Gave me my answer: "Come, Bhikkhu!" he said,
Thereby to me was ordination given.

Lo! I alone in forest depths abode,
With zeal unfaltering wrought the Master's word,
Even the counsels of the Conqueror.

While passed the first watch of the night there rose
Long memories of the bygone line of lives.
While passed the middle watch, the heavenly eye,
Purview celestial, was clarified.

While passed the last watch of the night, I burst
Asunder all the gloom of ignorance.

Then as night wore down at dawn
And rose the sun, came Indra and Brahmā,
Yielding me homage with their clasped hands:
Hail unto thee, thou nobly born of men!
Hail unto thee, thou highest among men!

Perished for thee are all the intoxicants;
And thou art worthy, noble air, of gifts.
The Master, seeing me by troop of gods

Begirt and followed, thereupon a smile
Revealing by his utterance made response;
"By discipline of holy life, restraint
And mastery of self: hereby a man
Is holy; this is holiness supreme!" (ibid., p. 273).

It was the same with the women. To quote a few extracts from the utterances of Puṇṇā, who was once a slave girl:

Drawer of water, I down to the stream,
Even in winter went in fear of blows,
Harassed by fear of blame from mistress.

Lo! To the Buddha I for refuge go,
And to the Norm and Order. I will learn
Of them to take upon my self and keep
The Precepts; so shall I indeed find good.

Once a son of Brahmins born was I
Today I stand Brahmin in every deed.
The nobler Threefold Wisdom[14] *have I won,*
Won the true Veda-lore, and graduate
Am I from better Sacrament returned,
Cleansed by the inward spiritual bath.
(*Psalms of the Sisters*, PTS, p. 117–19.)

The training for realizing their spiritual potentialities which they received as members of the Order was such that not only did race or caste consciousness have no place in it but such prejudices actually hindered the awakening of spiritual insight and the cultivation of the moral life. As we said before, "Those who are obsessed with the prejudices of race or caste are far from the moral life and the attainment of supreme spiritual insight." Such obsessions, which are the accumulated products of acquired erroneous beliefs, are among the intoxicants (*avijjāsavā*) of the mind and have to be got rid of by a process of self-analysis and conscious elimination. Intoxicants are to be eliminated by seeing and recognizing them as they affect our mind and not by being blind to them (M I 7). This requires watchfulness (*sati*) on our part, the acquiring of right views (*dassana*)

14. I.e. (i) the faculty of seeing one's past births, (ii) clairvoyance and (iii) the knowledge of one's inner mental processes.

to replace the erroneous ones, constant vigilance over our thoughts (*saṃvara*) and the cultivation of our mind (*bhāvanā*). The practise of *mettā* or loving-kindness towards all beings, and of *upekkhā* or equanimity or impartiality towards all, would be considered impossible on the part of those who have not freed their minds of the initial prejudices associated with race or caste.

How Buddhism set about to explode the theory of caste by adducing historical, scientific, ethical and religious arguments against it we have mentioned already. If we consider these arguments we see that they do not merely represent a trend of Kshatriya opposition to Brahmin claims to superiority, for it is constantly pointed out that men of all castes are on an equal footing (*samasama*) with regard to their capabilities; and the Kshatriya and Vaisya claims to superiority are as much denounced in this respect as those of the Brahmins. There is however one statement which in the opinion of the authors has sometimes been misinterpreted to mean that Buddhism championed the cause of the superiority of the Kshatriyas over the Brahmins and all else. It occurs in a discourse against caste which ends on the theme that what really matters is moral superiority and not the pretensions of "high" birth. "The Kshatriya is the best of those among his folk who put their trust in lineage. But he who is perfect in wisdom and righteousness, he is the best among gods and men" (D I 99). It would of course be possible to explain this text away by attributing it to the work of some of the editors of the Canon who were unconsciously influenced by notions of superiority based on birth, but this would be unnecessary if the statement is carefully studied in its context. It would then be seen that what the Buddha does in this discourse is to employ a dialectical method of argument whereby he takes up some of the criteria which the Brahmins (he is arguing with a Brahmin) accept as proof of caste superiority and showing that when they are actually applied to the context of society it would show the superiority of the Kshatriya and not the Brahmin—thus proving that the Brahmin claim to superiority in respect of these criteria was baseless. Lineage is of little or no account but if lineage (as defined here) is taken as the criterion, then it is the Kshatriya who should claim superiority and not the Brahmin. The fact that, as Hutton says, "the Brahmin in the Rigveda seems to have been second in social importance to the Rajanya" (J.H. Hutton, *Caste in India*, Cambridge, 1946, p.156) lends historical support to this deduction. In any case the point of this quotation is that he who is supreme above all is the one "who is perfect in wisdom and righteousness, a supremacy not based on the claims of birth."

The attempt at influencing public opinion by rational persuasion and example was not backed up merely by the exemplary organization of the Buddhist Order of monks and nuns, who did away with all distinctions or claims based on birth. The monks and nuns visited the homes of people of all castes, "high" or "low," for purposes of preaching and having their meals, sometimes at the cost of personal discomfort: the Buddha was sometimes railed at by Brahmins for visiting their homes to beg for meals, and his invariable answer as to what was his race or caste was "Ask me not for my birth" (*ma jātiṃ puccha*). (Sn 462). Sometimes he visited Brahmin villages without getting a morsel of food. The disciples did the same, and ignored caste distinctions and practises in their relations with their fellow human beings. The following incident is recorded of Ānanda, one of the immediate disciples of the Buddha, who rehearsed the dhamma at the first Council: "Now the elder Ānanda dressed early and taking his bowl and robe entered the great city Sāvatthī for alms. After his round and having finished his meal, he approached a certain well. At that time a Mātaṅga (outcast) girl named Prakṛtī was at the well drawing water. So the elder Ānanda said to the Mātaṅga girl, 'Give me water, sister, I wish to drink.' At this she replied, 'I am a Mātaṅga girl, reverend Ānanda.' 'I do not ask you, sister, about your family or caste but if you have any water left over, give it me, I wish to drink.' Then she gave Ānanda the water. ..." (*Divyāvadāna*, p. 611, ff, quoted in E. J. Thomas, *The Life of Buddha*, London, 1952, p. 242).

It is not only the monks and nuns who have to practise compassion but the lay disciples as well. The following are among the sentiments expressed in stanzas recited frequently by lay Buddhists even today:

"Whatever living beings there are, either feeble or strong, long or great, middle-sized, short, small or large. Either seen or which are not seen, and which live far (or) near, either born or seeking birth, may all creatures be happy-minded.

"Let no one deceive another, let him not despise (another) in any place, let him not out of anger or resentment wish harm to another.

"As a mother at the risk of her life watches over her own child, her only child, so also let everyone cultivate a boundless (friendly) mind towards all beings" (SBE, vol. X, p. 25).

The cultivation of such sentiments is incompatible with the harbouring of any racial prejudice or hatred. Lay disciples were admonished to give up conceit based on notions of "high" birth, or in other words racial or caste pride. In a sermon which distinguishes between the characteristics of the man who progresses and the man who degenerates, this is reckoned among one of the many causes for the downfall of man: "The man who, proud of his birth, wealth or family, despises his neighbour is degenerate" (Sn 104) and this conceit would be the cause of his downfall. It is also not surprising that among the trades forbidden to Buddhists is the slave trade or "trafficking in human beings" (*satta-vanijjā*) (A III 308), as this would not be in keeping with the right mode of livelihood (*samma-ājīva*), which every Buddhist must follow. The treatment of the servants in one's household too should be such that their human dignity is recognized. "They should not be overburdened with work, they should be well provided with their meals and wages, they should be looked after when they are ill, the food and delicacies should be shared with them and they should be given enough leave and leisure" (D III 191). Thus did Buddhism lighten the lot of a class of people who were considered to have been born or created to serve their masters and to be expelled at will (*kāmotthāpyaḥ*) or to be slain at will (*yathākāmavaddhyaḥ*), according to the texts of the Brahmins.

It was in keeping with these Buddhist ideals and principles that in the third century BCE the great Buddhist emperor Asoka modelled his policy towards the lower strata of society in his kingdom, the subject races, the forest tribes and the border peoples. Quoting the Buddhist saying that the "gift of the Dhamma excels all other gifts," we find his Rock Edict 12 calling attention before all else to the just treatment of servants and slaves: "There is no gift that can equal in merit the gift of Dhamma, ... from it follow the right treatment of slaves and servants, service to mother and father ..." (*Edicts of Asoka*, tr. G. Srinivasa Murti, Adyar, 1951, p. 33). And what he preached he seemed to have practised himself to judge by the record of his inscriptions.

Believing in the equality of man as an adherent of the Dhamma he seems to have treated his subjects, irrespective of race or social status, equally before the law, not withstanding what was prescribed in Hindu legal codes: "It is most desirable," he says in pillar edict IV "that there should be absolute equality for all in all legal proceedings and in the punishments awarded ..." (ibid., p. 95). He extends this equality of treatment even to the border tribes, in Edict II, making the following declaration: "All people are my children. Just as I desire on behalf of my own children that they should be fully provided with all kinds of comfort and enjoyment in this world as well as in the other world, similarly I desire the same on behalf of all people. Those who live on the borders of my dominions, and have not been conquered by me, may wonder what exactly is my disposition towards them. My disposition towards them is this: they should be told that the King desires thus: 'Let them not be afraid of me. Let them be made to feel confident that they need expect only happiness from me and not misery.' They should again be told thus: 'The King will forgive their faults that can be forgiven. May they be induced to practise Dhamma for my sake and thereby attain happiness in this world and in the next.' ... Your action should be shaped accordingly and the borderers should be comforted and consoled and inspired with confidence and with this idea: 'The King is like our father. He cares for our welfare as much as he cares for himself. We are to him, like his own children'" (ibid., pp. 62–3, 65). In the ninth Rock Edict (*Girnar*) Asoka recommends the practice of the law of piety and discourages vain ritual and ceremonies, which possibly included the practise of caste rites: "Men are practising various ceremonies during illness or at the marriage of a son or daughter, or at the birth of a son, or when setting out on a journey; on those and other occasions men are practising various ceremonies. And women are practising many and various vulgar and useless ceremonies. Now, ceremonies should certainly be practised. But ceremonies like these bear little fruit indeed: But the following practise bears much fruit, namely, the practise of morality. Herein the following (are comprised): proper courtesy to slaves and, servants, reverence to elders, gentleness to animals ..." (E. Hultzch, *Inscriptions of Asoka*, London, 1925, pp. 112–13). He proclaims "that those of the humblest origins, even among the border tribes, are capable of experiencing the highest spiritual joy," and in the Brahmagiri and Rupnath Edicts he enjoins his people to exert themselves in this direction: "Men in Jambudīpa, who were till now unmingled, have now been mingled with the gods. This is certainly the fruit of my exertion. Nor is it correct to hold that it can be achieved only by the great ones, for even the smallest person can achieve the ideal of heavenly bliss by force of exertion. It is for this purpose that this proclamation has been proclaimed thus: 'Let the humble and the great exert themselves to achieve this ideal. May my border people understand this. May this spirit of exertion endure everlastingly'" (ibid., pp. 70–1).

The care and concern with which he referred to the weaker aboriginal tribes dwelling in the hills and borderlands of his territory, was indeed enlightened beyond much modern practise. He regarded them not as savage beasts who deserved to be exterminated or as fierce peoples who should be kept in check by the fear and force of arms but as human children who were to be made to understand that they were under his care and protection. In Rock Edict XIII he says: "Devanampriya considers that even he who wrongs him is fit to be forgiven of wrongs that can be forgiven. And even the forest inhabitants included in the dominions of Devanampriya, who submit, he pacifies and converts (by kind methods), duly informing them of his power to punish them, in spite of his compassion. And what for? In order that they may feel ashamed of their past conduct, and not be killed. Because Devanampriya desires that all beings should be left unhurt, should have self-control, have equal (impartial) treatment and should lead happy lives" (ibid. p. 44f).

Buddhism was from the first a missionary religion which sought to bring the message of truth and love to all mankind: "Go forth," said the Buddha to his disciples, "I am delivered from all fetters, human and divine. You are also delivered from all fetters, human and divine. Go now and wander for the gain of the many, for the welfare of the many, out of compassion for the world, for the good, for the gain and for the welfare of gods and men. Let not two of you go the same way" (*Vinaya Texts*, I, p. 112f). And they were to go, as they did go, to all manners of peoples and tribes, regardless of the hazards of such journeys and the dangers of trying to understand and convert strange peoples. Yet the only weapons they were allowed to take and have with them were the weapons of truth and love. Their training in the practice of compassion should be such that, in the words of the Buddha: "They would not have done his bidding if they were to manifest the slightest irritation or anger even if wily robbers were to get hold of them on the way and cut them limb by limb with a double-edged saw" (M I 129). The Buddha's interrogation of Puṇṇa just before he set out on such a dangerous mission, which however achieved amazing success, was as follows:

"With this concise teaching from me, Puṇṇa, in what country will you take up your abode?"

"In Sunāparanta, sir:"

"They are a fierce and violent race, Puṇṇa in Sunāparanta. If they were to abuse you and revile you there, what would you think?"

"I should think, Lord, that the good folk of Sunāparanta were really nice people, very nice people indeed, in that they forbore to strike me."

"But if they strike you?"

"I should think, Lord, that the good folk of Sunāparanta were really nice people ... if they forbore to pelt me with clods."

"But if they pelt you with clods?"

"I should think, Lord ... forbore to cudgel me."

"But if they cudgel you?"

"I should think, Lord ... forbore to knife me."

"But if they knife you?"

"I should think, Lord ... forbore to take my life."

"But if they take your life?"

"If they did, Lord, I should think that there are disciples of the Lord who, in their tribulation and despair, are on the look-out for someone with a knife, and that I have found him without having to hunt about. This is what I should think, Lord; that would be my thought, Blessed One."

"Good indeed, Puṇṇa. With such a command of yourself, you will be able to live with the folk of Sunāparanta" (M III 268, tr. Lord Chalmers, *Further Dialogues of the Buddha*, Part II, p. 308).

How fast Buddhism succeeded by these methods of gentle persuasion and example in stemming the tide of caste in India is a problem about which we do not wish to be dogmatic, for, especially after the Asokan era, Brahmanism gradually came back into its own, and with it the sanctions for the hardening of the caste structure. But if the account of a great Chinese saint and traveller of the fifth century is to be trusted, on the whole a Buddhist atmosphere prevailed in India even then. He says: "The people are numerous and happy, they have not to register their households or attend to any magistrates or their rules; only those who have to cultivate the royal land have to pay (a portion of) the gain from it. If they want to go, they go; if they want to stay, they stay. The king governs without decapitation or [other] corporal punishments. Criminals are simply fined, lightly or heavily, according to the circumstances (of each case). ... The king's bodyguards and attendants all have salaries ..." (James Legge, *A Record of Buddhist Kingdoms*, Oxford, 1886, p. 42f). Mention is however made of the Caṇḍālas, who are fishermen and hunters, and live apart from the rest of the population, but this does not necessarily imply the extensive division of the whole population into numerous castes. Such accounts are meagre, however, and it is not possible to say how much caste prejudice and discrimination were present even though the caste structure was still fairly flexible.

But it is very likely that when the Gītā throws open the road to salvation to all castes this is due to the influence of Buddhism. Early Brahmanism denied religious instruction to the Sudras and thought them incapable of salvation, and in the Buddhist books the Brahmins are quoted as saying of the Buddha that "the recluse Gotama proclaims salvation to all castes." Ghurye, following Fick (op. cit.) (who only examined part of the material of the Jātakas and left out the major portion of the Canon), holds that "it is wrong to look upon the Buddha as a social reformer and Buddhism as a revolt against caste" (op. cit., p. 67), but he grants that "the actions of Buddha had a general, liberalizing effect" (ibid.) and as regards the possibility of salvation for all says that "the necessity of closing up the ranks against the onslaught of Buddhism and of assuring individual salvation for all led to the formation of two slightly differing philosophies of caste" (ibid., p. 60). It is therefore very likely that, to a great extent at least, the Buddhist movement was responsible in relaxing the rigours of caste in this direction.

Buddhism has spread in many lands and among many races during the 2,500 years of its history, though its light has mainly been confined to the East. The work it did during these years is perhaps partly responsible for knitting these races closely together in one Asian spirit, and in so far as non-aggressiveness and tolerance are to some extent characteristic of this spirit (however dangerous such generalizations may be) they transcend the boundaries of Buddhist lands and embrace the whole earth. This unity is certainly not the unity of orthodox beliefs, for Buddhism never sought to inculcate such orthodoxies and curb the free spirit of inquiry in man. The verdict of one pilgrim traveller in Buddhist lands, Hiuen-Tsiang was: "In agreement with the mysterious character of this doctrine the world has progressed in its higher destiny; but distant peoples coming to interpret the doctrine are not in agreement. The time of the Holy One is remote from us, and so the sense of his doctrine is differently expounded. But as the taste of the fruit of different trees of the same kind is the same, so the principles of the schools as they now exist are not different." (*The Life of Hiuen-Tsiang*, transl. by Samuel Beal, London, 1911, p. 31). This view is reiterated by another such pilgrim of the twentieth century, Pratt, who in his "The Pilgrimage of Buddhism" says: "Not so obvious, perhaps, are those persistent characteristics which help to make it in all its ramifications and all its history still one religion. I shall not, of course, maintain that all those who burn incense in Buddhist temples or employ Buddhist monks at funerals are Buddhists, any more than I should hold that every icon-worshipper is necessarily a Christian. What I mean, is that there are certain qualities of character and feeling, of point of view, conduct, and belief, which may properly be called Buddhist, and that these are not confined to any one school of Buddhism, whether Hinayana or Mahayana, but are to be found in all those who by common consent would be considered typically Buddhist in all the lands we have studied from southern Sri Lanka to northern Japan. These qualities, I hold, transcend not only nations but centuries, and unite the earnest follower of the most up-to-date Japanese sect with the earliest disciples of the Founder."

Pratt adds that "Taken together, they constitute what, in a rough and general way, may be called the Spirit of Buddhism" and goes on to describe that what is particularly characteristic of this spirit is the lack of aggressiveness and the love of life: "This lack of aggressiveness is one of the most marked of Buddhist traits. ... There is a kind of gentleness in the Buddhist nature which I think everyone must feel. But this is not the gentleness and non-aggressiveness of weakness. It is not fear that prompts it. ... The non-aggressiveness of the typical Buddhist is a kind of strength in reserve; it is the gentleness of the strong man who refuses to push his own way in a crowd, or of the reflective man who is convinced the game is not worth the candle. Partly as an outgrowth of this gentleness of spirit, partly in obedience to the never forgotten exhortations of the Founder, partly out of contagion from the example and influence of his mesmeric personality, Buddhism in all the lands to which it has gone has never ceased to preach and to practise universal pity and sympathy for all sentient life."

With the exception of Sri Lanka, where a caste structure prevails side by side very uneasily along with Buddhism, such divisions are wholly absent in Buddhist lands. In fact those who have lived and moved among the peoples in these lands have often been struck by the equality of man in countries steeped in Buddhism and unaffected by the Hindu caste structure. Fielding Hall, writing of the Burmese, says: "There was, and is, absolutely no aristocracy of any kind at all. The Burmese are a community of equals, in a sense that has probably never been known elsewhere" (*The Soul of a People,* London, 1903, p. 54).

In Sri Lanka the proximity of South India was perhaps largely influential in the emergence of a caste structure in society (see Ananda Coomaraswamy, *Medieval Sinhalese Art*, p. 21ff), which later became more rigid with the rule of South Indian kings who relied on Hindu legal codes. Yet it is interesting to observe that the classical Sinhalese treatise on caste, the *Janavaṃsa*, a Sinhalese poem of the fifteenth century, endeavours, as Ananda Coomaraswamy says, "to show that all men are really of one race though occupied in different ways," stress is being laid on the well known saying of the Buddha "not by birth does one become a Vasala [outcast], not by birth does one become a Brahmin ..." (ibid. , p. 22).

The resultant effect of these historical circumstances is a situation which is summed up by Bryce Ryan (*Caste in Modern Ceylon,* New Brunswick, 1953, p. 34) in the following words. "Informed Buddhists, of the laity and clergy alike, repudiate sacred foundations for the caste hierarchy. Nor will an ignorant villager, even under the most stringent questioning, admit religious or perceptual basis for the organization of society into castes. The intelligentsia today will relate caste purely to secular foundations, usually noting that such a system is contrary to the Buddha's teaching, and in this context deplore this departure from both the spirit and teachings of the religion. The less sophisticated may not deplore caste organization, but find it from the religious point of view irrelevant. Thus an intelligent villager responds, 'Caste is not of the Buddha, it is of the kings.' Unlike his educated fellow he is not confronted with the necessity of conventionalizing religious views and secular practises. At no intellectual level do Sinhalese believe that Buddhism supports caste, and in general Western observers have considered the caste system as existing in opposition to religious principles. In any case the mildness of caste in Sri Lanka in contrast to what obtains in India is only too apparent. Untouchability is absent, and there is full freedom of worship for people of all castes who sit together in the preaching halls to listen to sermons."

Conclusion

In the foregoing pages we have tried to show that Buddhism stands for the oneness of the human species, the equality of man, and the spiritual unity of mankind. The differences among the so-called races as far as their physical characteristics go are negligible. The differences in cultural attainment are due to historical circumstances and not to any innate aptitudes with which some of the "cultured" races, whether of the East or West, are favoured by nature or God. All men likewise, irrespective of their race, caste or class, have the capacity to reach the heights of moral and spiritual attainment.

Man's destiny is to develop as a spiritual being and therefore what really matters is the degree of his moral and spiritual development. This has no connexion with birth in any particular race or caste since the "meanest," "humblest" of mankind may have the potentialities for attaining the very highest in this respect in this life, so that we have no right to despise any person whatever his station in life may be. The harbouring of racial and caste prejudice is moreover detrimental to one's mental health and spiritual state and it is a characteristic of the spiritually enlightened that they shed them and act with love and impartiality towards all. Race and caste discrimination are also inimical to social progress since they bring about artificial and unreal divisions among human beings where none exist and hinder harmonious relations.

The close analogy between racial and caste prejudice and discrimination and the possible racial origin of much of the latter has been referred to; although in essence 'caste prejudice is an aspect of culture prejudice, while race prejudice—as distinguished from culture prejudice—is colour-and-physique prejudice" (O. C. Cox, *Caste, Class and Race,* New York, 1948, p. 350). In fact, even class prejudice within the same "racial" group can have strong affinities with racial prejudice so that the problems of race, caste and class cannot be divorced from each other. The history of mercantilism shows how far an economic motive can form the basis for the exploitation of one class of people by another, even of a homogeneous racial group. As Cox points out, "The mercantilist feared the prospects of the labourer's getting out of his place. It was felt that some class of people should be depended upon to do the common work, and that the status of this class as common workers should remain permanent. It was some tendency in the working class to be independent which called forth reactions akin to racial antagonism. Writing in 1770, William Temple says: 'Our manufacturing populace have adopted a notion that as Englishmen they enjoy a birth-right privilege of being more free and independent than any country in Europe. ... The less the manufacturing poor have of it, the better for themselves and for the estate. The labouring people should never think of themselves as independent of their superiors for, if a proper subordination is not kept up, riot and confusion will take the place of sobriety and good order.' That is, let us interpose, precisely the idea of 'the Negroe's place' in the United States" (ibid., p. 340). To keep them in their place they had to be denied the right to be educated, for, as Bernard Mandeville said in 1723 in his *Fable of the Bees*: "To make the society happy and people easy under the meanest circumstances, it is requisite that great numbers of them should be ignorant as well as poor." Only a rationalisation in the form of a race myth or a caste myth was needed in order to numb the consciences of the ruling classes and offer them an "explanation" of their lot to the labouring classes. And such a rationalization would have been an easy affair when the downtrodden class was "racially" different from the ruling class.

The Buddhist way of solving these problems is to seek for the causes and conditions which bring them about or accentuate them and then proceed to eradicate these causal factors. The Buddhist diagnosis would be that the causes are found in man as an individual as well as in society as an organization. According to Buddhism the springs of action of human individuals are greed, hatred, and delusion (or erroneous beliefs) as well as their opposites. The Buddhist view is that unless the former are entirely replaced by their opposites—charity, love and wisdom—man is in need of salvation and that in any case unless the former are toned down no just society can be founded. The greed for economic and political power can be so great as to blind people to the nature, feelings and needs of individuals other than themselves or of human groups other than those they (erroneously) identify themselves with. Hatred can also find an easy outlet towards human beings or groups considered as alien or hostile to oneself or one's group. And, as the Buddhist texts say, greed and hatred nurture erroneous beliefs or delusions ("rationalisations") such as the racial and caste myths which we evolve out of our imagination with no basis in fact. These myths or erroneous beliefs in turn encourage our racial hatred and lust for power at the expense of our fellow men. Add to this the ignorance of the fact that we are prejudiced, as well as the costs of prejudice, and the process goes on within our minds, warping our personalities, shutting the door to spiritual experience and causing division and disharmony in human society. A change of heart and a change of outlook and attitude at the level of the individual is the solution to this problem. But such a transformation cannot be achieved by waiting for the operation of evolutionary processes or the grace of a divine being but only by putting forth effort on our own part. The erroneous beliefs that we entertain about race or caste have to be replaced by awareness of the facts before greed can give place to true charity and hatred to love.

But if a change of heart and outlook is essential on the part of individuals who harbour such prejudices, it is equally important that a change in the organisation of human society should be made. Buddhism conceives of society as a changing process subject to causal laws and it can change for better or worse. It is a popular misconception of Buddhism in the Western mind that it is only concerned about salvation and in the higher spiritual life and not in social reformation at all. The numerous sermons to laymen on the subject of their social well-being and the discourses on the nature of a righteous government and of a just society, coupled with the example of Asoka, leave no doubt that this aspect has received serious attention in Buddhism.

While the importance of the ideological factor as a social determinant is recognized, the world is led by ideas or ideologies (*cittena loko niyati*); it is significant that social evils as well as the growth of hatred in society are ultimately traced to the presence of poverty in human society or the misdistribution of economic goods. It is said in a sutta (sermon) which deals with the subject in an allegorical form and a prophetic tone: "Thus, brethren, as a result of the misdistribution of goods, poverty grows rife; from poverty growing rife stealing increases, from the spread of stealing violence grows apace, from the growth of violence the destruction of life becomes common ... lying ... evil speaking ... adultery ... abusive and idle talk ... covetousness and ill-will ... false opinions ... incest, wanton greed and perverted lust ... till finally lack of filial and religious piety. ... Among such humans keen animosity will become the rule ..." (DN 26). The elimination of economic inequalities in human society will therefore be an essential precondition for the emergence of harmonious relations among human beings, so that what is required is both a change of heart as well as a change of system.

Such sweeping changes can however only be brought about by—as they are the responsibility of—those who at present wield economic and political power in the world. The individual can only make decisions for himself and employ in his own way the weapons of rational persuasion and example.

Except when truly Buddhist kings like Asoka were in power, when political and legal methods were possible, these were the weapons that the Sangha or the Order of Monks and Nuns as well as lay Buddhist individuals employed. The Sangha is the oldest historical institution which has had as its members people of diverse races, castes, classes and tribes who have shed their racial prejudices for the universalism of the Order. In reflecting the Buddhist conception of the equality of man, its structure is democratic. As Mookerji says, "The Pali texts furnish interesting information of the working of the Buddhist Sangha in strict and minute conformity with genuine democratic principles" (R. K. Mookerji, *Hindu Civilisation,* New york, 1936, p. 209). It is not controlled by a pope or hierarchy of ecclesiastics of any particular nation. When new countries were converted the sons of the soil took over very soon after, so that we do not find for instance a Chinese Church of Japan or a Ceylonese Church of Burma.

It is also noteworthy that there were no crusades in Buddhism, which never lent itself to imperial expansion and the subjugation of peoples. There has been no military or political campaign or conquest with the idea of spreading Buddhist culture and civilization.

The pacifism of Buddhism, as well as the absence of an "out-group" feeling directed towards non-Buddhists on embracing Buddhism, is perhaps largely responsible for this, as is also the fact that the Dhamma is not considered a unique revelation which alone contains the sole truth. The Buddhist definition of "the right philosophy of life" was comprehensive enough to contain, recognize and respect whatever truth other religions may have. According to the Buddhist conception of conversion, each person has to realise the truth for himself and rather than be hostile towards the ignorant one has to be compassionate and helpful towards them. The use of threats or force or the utilisation of economic and social incentives for conversion was evidently considered futile for such a purpose.

25

The Principles of International Law in Buddhist Doctrine

The Origins of Buddhism and the Relevance of Buddhist Epistemology for Law

It is proposed in this series of five lectures to give a brief account of the Buddhist attitude to law and the Buddhist conception of law, including international law.[15]

I may mention at the outset that one early scholar, who worked mainly on the Pali source material, has expressed the view that there is no Buddhist law. The view presented here on the basis of the evidence adduced gives, on the contrary, a different account altogether. In fairness to the point of view expressed by that scholar, I would like to quote him in his own words: "In the strict sense of the word, there is no Buddhist law; there is only an influence exercised by Buddhist ethics or changes that have taken place in customs. No Buddhist authority, whether local or central, whether lay or clerical, has ever created or promulgated any law. Such law as has been administered in countries ruled over by monarchs nominally Buddhist has been custom rather than law; and the custom has been in the main pre-Buddhist, fixed and established before the people became Buddhist. There have been changes in custom. But the changes have not been the result of any enactment from above. They have been brought about by changes of opinion among the people themselves. …"[16]

I would maintain on the contrary that the monastic code consisted of laws insofar as it consisted of enforceable rules of conduct, precisely stated and codified, there being a set procedure

---

15. I would like to record my gratitude to (i) Dr C. F. Amerasinghe, Senior Lecturer in Law, University of Ceylon, for permitting me to sit in at his lectures on international law, (ii) Dr Richard A. Gard, for providing me with a "Short Bibliography of Buddhist Jurisprudence and Legal Thought" and suggesting topics for consideration and (iii) Senator C. D. S. Siriwardena for the illuminating discussions I had with him.

This essay was first published in *Recueil des Cours*, Tome 12, pp. 300–426. The Hague Academy of International Law, The Hague, Netherlands, 1967.

16. I. Hastings, *Encyclopaedia of Religion and Ethics*, s.v. Law (Buddhist).

laid down in the constitution for trial and conviction in case of infringement. As a student of jurisprudence observes:

> "The Buddhist Sangha also gave rise to a body of laws, which were codified under the *Pātimokkha*. An objection might be raised as to whether the *Vinaya* or *Pātimokkha* can be called laws in the proper sense of the term. Can they not be conveniently called the valid rules of a private body as well? The answer to this question is not far to seek. We have already shown that though the Buddhist Sangha developed out of a common ascetic society, it had obtained a peculiar dignity only to be found in a republican state. No doubt, it being primarily a religious body its outlook on life as well as the aim of such associated life differed from that of a political state. … Still the laws of the *Vinaya* can claim all the dignity and prestige of jurisprudence as far as the Sangha and the relations of the Sangha to the state were concerned. The laws of the *Vinaya* had also the sanction of the state, wherein lies the validity of all laws. Kauṭilya tells us that the laws of a Sangha and Kula were binding on the king and he had to inflict punishment on those who broke them. … The Chinese traveller, I-tsing, informs us that once a person entered the Sangha, his name was no longer to be found in the register of the states; henceforward the Sangha was fully authorized to tackle all problems issuing through his misbehaviour or the difficulties he encountered. The authority of the Sangha as sanctioned by the state is also proved by an episode in the *Vinaya*. Once a Licchavi wife committed adultery. Her husband resolved to kill her. So she went to Sāvatthī and succeeded in getting *pabbajjā* (ordination). When the husband knew it, he went and lodged a complaint at the court of king Pasenadi. The king said that as the woman had become a nun no punishment could be inflicted on her. … The monks were thus allowed by a long succession of tradition to submit to their own law without outside interference" (Bhagvat, pp. iv–v).

Besides the monastic laws, secular legal texts were composed by Buddhist monks in Burma and these laws were adopted by the state. These were based on Hindu legal texts, whose content and character were altered in the light of Buddhist doctrines. Kings enacted codes of secular law and formulated constitutions on the basis of Buddhist ethical principles. The criminal and civil laws were to some extent transformed in conformity with Buddhist ethics during certain periods. The attitude to war and the conduct of war was affected by Buddhism. Besides, there is a developed philosophy of the state and law in Buddhist texts and a statement of the principles that should govern interstate relations.

It seems both necessary and desirable for several reasons that a clear outline be given of the relationship between Buddhism and law before the principles of international law in Buddhist doctrine are enunciated. Firstly, the relationship between a theistic religion and law follows more or less a standard pattern, where the essence of the law constitutes or is intimately related to the divine will, although man-made laws may often be considered to be in conflict with it. Buddhism, on the contrary, is not a religion or philosophy which can be rightly described as either theistic or atheistic.

Secondly, while the positivists would study the law for what it is, without introducing any extralegal considerations, Buddhist conceptions of law are closely related to its ethics and social philosophy. Although it is possible to study the law in isolation from the latter, law becomes meaningful only on the basis of the ethics. Buddhism, we shall see, regards the law as an instrument for achieving certain ends, which are held to be socially desirable. What these ends are, or should be, is a matter for ethics. A system of ethics, in turn, becomes significant only on the background of a certain theory of reality. An ethic, for example, which asserts that a person ought to become perfect would be meaningless if either man is an automaton or man's personality terminates with his death. A theory of reality, again, derives its validity from a theory of knowledge and both these, as we shall see, can have a bearing on the conception of law. Buddhism, while distinguishing these branches of study, does not fail to note their interrelations.

Thirdly, it may be stated that while this approach to the problem of international relations and international law may appear to be philosophical, we cannot today under rate the importance of philosophy for law. It was the political philosophy of Locke which inspired much of the content of the American constitution and every one of the varying systems of law, if examined, will be seen to have its own philosophical basis. Certain ideological disputes, though springing from a variety of causes, political, economic, social and psychological, are also partly philosophical insofar as the dispute revolves round or presupposes the question as to which ideology is true or is to be followed.

The ideological conflict, therefore, concerns law inso far as the different ideologies present differing conceptions of law.

Buddhism is a religion with a philosophy. It recommends a way of life, which follows from its view of life, which is justified on the basis of the philosophy of Buddhism. It has been said that "Ancient India ... had no word for 'religion'" (Ingalls, p. 34). But it is difficult to agree with this view. The term *brahmacariya* (Pali) was used in the Buddhist texts to denote a religion in general. It is taken from the Upaniṣadic *brahmacarya* (God-life), which meant the "religious life" in a restricted sense (*Chāndogya Upaniṣad*, 8.5.1; TPU p. 266). But Buddhism gave it a wider connotation to denote the religion or way of life of a theist, agnostic or even a materialist. When the word was used to denote the way of life of the materialist, it was used in the form "pseudo-religion" (*abrahmacariyāvāsa*) / (M I 515 ff). This word for "religion" was, therefore, used in the sense of "the ideal life" or any way of life which anyone may consider to be the ideal as a consequence of his holding a certain set of beliefs about the nature and destiny of man in the universe. We also find the word *Dhamma-vinaya* used extensively (PED, s.v. *vinaya*) to denote a religion and this term if literally translated means "doctrine-cum-discipline" or "philosophy-cum-law," since *Vinaya* was the word used in the general sense of "discipline" and in the special sense of "the law and constitution" of the Community (Sangha) of monks and nuns.

An examination of the Buddhist principles of law, including international law, in the light of its philosophy is, therefore, relevant to a jurisprudence which has to face the legal needs of the contemporary world in that, as Prof. F. S. C. Northrop has shown, "an adequate contemporary jurisprudence must ground itself on the basic concepts—that is, in the philosophy of the world's cultures." (Northrop, p. 15).

Buddhism originates with the teachings of Siddhartha Gotama, who gave up a princely life of luxury in order to seek a solution to the problem of suffering and the riddle of the universe. When he gained enlightenment after six years of experimentation with himself, the Buddha or "the Enlightened One" taught at the deer-park at Benares that the path to happiness, peace and supreme realisation lay in avoiding the two extremes of self-indulgence and self-mortification and the adoption of the right philosophy of life, right aspirations, right speech, right action, right mode of livelihood, right effort, right mindfulness and right meditation, which culminate in right realisation and right emancipation. He then trained sixty monks to attain emancipation of mind and addressed them as follows: "Go ye forth for the welfare and happiness of mankind, out of compassion for the world, for the weal, welfare and happiness of gods and men. Let not two of you go in the same direction" (Vin I 21).

The first sermon has been called by the Buddha himself "the setting into motion of the Supreme Wheel of the Law, which cannot be turned back by any religious teacher, angel, Satan (Māra), God (Brahmā) or anyone in the world." The term *Dhamma-cakka*, here translated as "the Wheel of the Law," can be more accurately rendered as "the rule of righteousness" since the *cakka* or the "wheel" is the emblem of authority of the sovereign. The phrase has also been translated as "(the founding of) the kingdom of righteousness" or even as "the kingdom of God" since the term *Brahma-cakka* has been used synonymously with it (M I 69). But it must be borne in mind that Brahma here means the "highest" or "most sublime" and has no theological connotations.

This conception of the "rule of righteousness" is, as we shall see, extremely important for the Buddhist attitude to and conception of law. Of similar importance is the conception of "the welfare and happiness of mankind, out of compassion for the world," for this is the first time in Indian history that the idea of a "general good" or a "common good," not only affecting the common man but also pertaining to the peoples of the world, is envisaged.

The Buddha also set up an order of monks and nuns on democratic foundations with a constitution and code of laws governing their conduct. We can see from the statements of the Buddha himself the need for and the purpose of such legislation. When one of his disciples wanted to know why the religion of some enlightened teachers lasted long while others did not, his reply was that those teachers whose religious dispensation lasted long had given a detailed exposition of their teachings and also "enacted a code of rules or precepts" (*paññattaṃ sikkhāpadaṃ*) and "enforced legislation binding on them" (*anuddiṭṭhaṃ pātimokkhaṃ*).[17] Whereupon this disciple requests the Buddha to enact these rules and enforce such legislation. The reply given on this occasion was that the time was not yet ripe for legislation since at the time even the least of the 500 brethren had gained the first stage of moral and spiritual evolution and that such legislation would be necessary only when the Community (Sangha) would be of long standing and had attained full development. For it is only when the Community has become very prosperous and acquired great learning (it is said) that those misdemeanours would arise, which it would be necessary to curb by enacting rules and enforcing legislation. At a very much later stage of the history of the Sangha (Community), the observation is made that the number of monks who have gained final emancipation is proportionately less, although the code of laws has expanded in size (S II 223; KS II pp. 151–52).

We notice here that legislation was considered unnecessary or superfluous, where conformity can be ensured without it but that legislation makes for the perpetuity of an institution and of the aims and aspirations for which it stands. At the same time there is the constant reminder that legislation alone is of no avail. Legislation itself contributes to a legalistic frame of mind. People tend to conform to the letter of the law, forgetting the spirit in which the laws were enacted. Others find ways and means (as happened in the Sangha during the time of Buddha himself, contributing to the growth of the law) of evading the law by conforming to the letter of the law and violating the spirit. The moral that is generally drawn is that law-abiding behaviour must result eventually from charity, love and understanding and not from a fear of the sanctions of the law.

When the Buddha eventually enacts legislation as and when situations arise, he gives ten reasons for doing so: "I am enacting rules of training (*sikkhāpada*, precepts) for the monks (i) for the well-being of the Community, (ii) for the convenience of the Community, (iii) in order to curb miscreants, (iv) for the ease of well-behaved monks, (v) in order to restrain misbehaviour in the present, (vi) in order to check future misbehaviour, (vii) in order that those who have no faith (in this religion) may acquire faith, (viii) in order that those who have faith may be further strengthened in

---

17. Vin III 9; BD p. 17. *Pātimokkha*, left untranslated here by Miss Horner, means "bond" and refers to the "binding legislation," lit. "that which shall be made binding"; see PED, s.v.

their faith, (ix) in order that the good Doctrine (Dhamma) may last long and (x) for the promotion of discipline." (Vin III 21)

We observe a utilitarian and pragmatic motive behind the legislation.[18] Besides, the rules are meant to serve the interests of the Community as a whole, while making things easy for those whose behaviour is good and serving as a deterrent to others. The legislation is also inspired by public opinion and seeks to promote public confidence in the institution, whose life is said to be prolonged by the legislation concerned. It is also said to serve the discipline, which is considered a good in itself.

Just before his demise the Buddha tells Ānanda that it was possible that they may think that after his death they would be without a teacher and adds: "You should not look at things in this light. The Dhamma (i.e., the Doctrine of Righteousness) that has been taught and the Vinaya (i.e., the constitution and the code of laws) that has been laid down by me should serve as the Teacher after I pass away." Further, it is added, "If the Sangha so desires, it may abolish the minor rules of the Community after my death" (D II 154).

Both these conceptions are of significance for the Buddhist ideas about secular law. The Buddha sets up the Sangha, the oldest international society in history, which is to function after his death in accordance with its Constitution (Vinaya), drawn up for the furtherance of the rule of righteousness and the teachings of the Buddha (i.e., the Dhamma). Now, while the Buddha is said to have been "born for the welfare and happiness of mankind" (*manussa-loke hita-sukhatāya jāto*)/(Sn 683), where the "welfare" is primarily the spiritual welfare and secondarily the material welfare, there is in Buddhism the conception of a world-ruler or world-statesman, who is likewise said to "be born for the welfare and happiness of mankind, for the weal, welfare and happiness of gods and men" (A I 76). It is stated that he sets up a just social order and a righteous government with worldwide ramifications, which is not inherited by a person but continues to function on the basis of a world-wide adherence to a political philosophy and constitution (Dhamma) on

---

18. Cp. "Besides, there are a number of laws in the Khandhakas relating to health, sanitation, medicine, etc. ... their aim is the 'attainment of some practical end' ..." Bhagvat, p. 34.

the part of the states, embodying the principles of such a just world order. This conception of an international order will be examined in a later paper.

The other statement of the Buddha to the effect that the minor rules may be abrogated after his death if the Sangha so desired enshrines the principle that the laws regarding matters of lesser importance have to be flexible and adapted to suit different historical and social contexts without being too rigid. It had interesting repercussions for the history of Buddhism. Since the question as to whether the Buddhism of the two great schools, Theravāda (Hīnayāna) and Mahāyāna, could be treated as one religion may legitimately be raised, it is worth briefly stating the reason for the division into these two schools in order to remove certain misconceptions.

The First Council held soon after the death of the Buddha discussed the question of abrogating the minor rules but it was discovered that there were serious differences of opinion as to what the minor rules were. As such, it was finally decided not to make any changes especially since the Sangha would lay itself open to public criticism on the score that rules were being abrogated no sooner the Buddha passed away (Vin II 154). But with the spread of Buddhism the need for such changes in the monastic laws was widely felt and when the Second Council was convened, a schism took place between the orthodox conservative Elders (Thera), who resisted any change and the liberals who outnumbered them. The latter, who were called the Mahāsaṅghikas (Great Community) owing to their numbers, held a separate convocation called the *Mahā-saṅgīti* (Great Convocation). Judging by what is said, they seem not only to have made changes in the legal code but also to have adapted the original teaching in order to bring Buddhism to the masses in a form intelligible to them. This was the *raison d'etre* for the emergence of Mahāyāna.

The origins of Mahāyāna are to be traced to this "Great Convocation," composed of a dissident group of both laymen and monks (Beal, II p. 164) held about a hundred years after the death of the Buddha. It is one of the early schools of the above Mahāsaṅghikas, called the Lokottaravādins (Transcendentalists), who were the first to adopt a docetic theory about the birth of the Buddha, holding that the "Buddha's body was immaculately conceived" (*na ca maithuna-sambhūtaṃ sugatasya samucchritaṃ*) (*Le Mahāvastu*, p. 170), although the Pali canonical scriptures had merely stated that the mother of the Buddha had no thoughts of sex after the Buddha-child was conceived.

The widespread belief among Western scholars that Mahāyāna Buddhism originated from about the beginning of the Christian era and bears a radically different character from the earlier religion is not borne out by the facts. Buddhism has recognized the necessity for distinguishing between literal or absolute truth (*paramārtha-satya*) and conventional or symbolic truth (*saṃvṛti-satya*). It has recognized the need for the literal truths to be so presented to hearers as to suit their capacity to receive it and the skill in doing so has been designed by a special term, *upāya-kauśalya*, i.e., the skilfulness as to the means adopted in teaching the doctrine.

The recognition of such a difference in the standpoint from which the Dhamma (i.e., the teaching of the Buddha) may be presented naturally had its repercussions in the diversity of presentations suited to people of different temperaments, interests, capabilities and cultural milieux but the basic principles taught and the fruits of such teachings are considered to be the same. A Chinese pilgrim of the seventh century, Hiuen Tsiang, observes: "The time of the Holy One is remote from us and so the sense of the doctrine is differently expounded but as the taste of the fruit of different trees of the same kind is the same, so the principles of the schools as they now exist are not different" (Beal, II p. 164). A knowledgeable twentieth-century Western observer records that "not so obvious, perhaps, are those persistent characteristics which help to make it, in all its ramifications and all its history, still one religion ..." (Pratt, p. 50).

The Theravāda Buddhists recognize the value of the predominantly altruistic path to salvation in Mahāyāna but observe that "he who is bent on the welfare of oneself as well as others is ... the chief and best, topmost, highest and supreme" (A II 95) and hold that there is but one way (*ekāyano maggo*)/(S V 168) to salvation, namely the eradication of greed, hatred and ignorance by the practise of restraint and meditation. The Mahāyānist, while recognizing the value of Hīnayāna (Theravāda), holds that the Buddha "by an able device holds forth three vehicles and afterwards leads all to Nibbāna by the one great vehicle" (*eka-yāna*)." (*Saddharma*

Puṇḍarīka, III, 38; Tr. p. 82)

All later developments of Buddhism, including Zen (which was a continuation of Jhāna Buddhism through Chinese Ch'an) and Jodo (Pure Land), starting out from the early Buddhist conception of the "Pure Lands" (*Suddhāvāsa*), the importance of faith in Buddha and the exceptional value attached to one's last thoughts prior to death in determining one's future birth (*Amitāyurdhyāna Sūtra*, 30; BMT, pp. 127–28)—are traceable to their origins in the Pali Nikāyas and Chinese Āgamas, whose contents contain the common core of the early teaching. The Mahāyānist writer who quoted Sir Charles Eliot on this subject was quite correct when she said: "These ideas (of Mahāyāna) are all to be found in the Nikāyas, sometimes as mere seeds, sometimes as well-grown plants. But between early Buddhism and the Mahāyāna there is a great difference in emphasis" (B. L. Suzuki, p. 17).

These differences in presentation have ultimately to be justified, explained and established on the basis of the propositions expressing the literal truths to be found in the original teaching of the Dhamma contained in the Pali Nikāyas and the Chinese Āgamas. The emphasis of the modern scholars of Japan has also been "on the original Buddhist texts and on the return to the purity of the religion, which had been obscured by later elaboration and by the development of sects" (Ware, p. 894).

While some of these later elaborations may not be totally legitimate or justified, they do not affect the common core of fundamental tenets and the apparent difference in the Mahāyānist conceptions is due to the failure to see them as full-blooded symbolic descriptions of literal truths stated more precisely in early Buddhism.

Thus the belief that a mere human teacher in Theravāda Buddhism becomes a Cosmic Person in Mahāyāna is incorrect. In the early Buddhist texts, the Buddha denies that he is a human being and claims that he is a Buddha, in the sense that he is a human being whose nature is transformed into that of an enlightened being (A II 38–9). It is said that the Buddha when freed from the conceptions of bodily form, sensations, impressions and ideas, conative activities and cognitive states, is "deep, immeasurable and unfathomable like the great ocean" (M I 487). Nibbāna is a transcendent reality beyond space, time and causation. Consistent with this conception, it is held that it is incorrect to say that "one exists" or "one does not exist" in nibbāna since such a state (indirectly referred to by the concept of Tathāgata) is not a kind of personal existence in time nor is it annihilation. When the question was asked of the Buddha: "The person who has attained the goal—does he not exist or does he exist eternally without defect?" the reply given is as follows: "The person who has attained the goal is without measure—he does not have that whereby one may speak of him" (Sn 1076). So it is wrong to say that the Buddha becomes extinct in nibbāna and it is this idea that is picturesquely conveyed in the Mahāyāna conception of the eternal cosmic Buddha.

In these lectures, we shall confine ourselves to conceptions common to both schools of Buddhism and in doing so, we may conveniently discuss the relevance of this material for the Buddhist philosophy of law under the heads of the theory of knowledge, the theory of reality, ethics, and the social and political philosophy.

Buddhism recommends the importance of a critical, impartial outlook in the quest for truth, which can be best illustrated by some passages in the texts:

> "There are certain religious and philosophical teachers who come to Kesaputta. They speak very highly of their own theories but oppose, condemn, and ridicule the theories of others. At the same time there are yet other religious and philosophical teachers who come here and in turn speak highly of their own theories, opposing, condemning and ridiculing the theories of these others. We are now in a state of doubt and perplexity as to who spoke the truth and who spoke falsehood."
>
> "O Kālāmas, you have a right to doubt or feel uncertain, for you have raised a doubt in a situation in which you ought to suspend your judgement. Come now, Kālāmas, do not accept anything on the grounds of revelation, tradition or report or because it is a product of mere reasoning or because it is true from a standpoint or because of a superficial assessment of facts or because it conforms with one's preconceived notions or because it is authoritative or because of the prestige of your teacher. When you, Kālāmas, realise for yourself that these doctrines are evil and unjustified, that they are condemned by the wise and that when they are accepted and lived by, they conduce to ill and sorrow, then you should reject them" (A I 189).

This critical attitude should be focussed on Buddhism itself and criticisms should be dispassionately assessed:

> "If anyone were to speak ill of me, the Dhamma or the Sangha, do not bear any ill-will towards him, be upset or perturbed at heart for if you were to be so, it will only cause you harm. If, on the other hand, anyone were to speak well of me, the Dhamma or the Sangha, do not be overjoyed, thrilled or elated at heart, for if so, it will only be an obstacle in the way of forming a realistic judgment as to whether the qualities praised in us are real and actually found in us" (D I 3).
>
> "Just as the experts test gold by burning it, cutting it and applying it on a touchstone, my statements should be accepted only after critical examination and not out of respect for me" (*Tattvasaṃgraha*, verse 3588).

The faith that one should have in adopting the Buddhist philosophy of life is therefore described as a "rational faith" (*ākāravatī saddhā*) as opposed to a blind or "baseless faith" (*amūlikā saddhā*) (M II 170).

The importance of this critical impartial outlook is further emphasised where it is shown that "the four ways of falling into injustice or untruth" (*cattāri agatigamanāni*) (A II 18) are prejudice, hatred, ignorance and fear. It was felt that in the administration of justice the judge should administer the law without fear, favour, folly or antagonism and as such the Mahāvastu gives the following advice to a king who is hearing a lawsuit: "When a dispute arises he should pay equal attention to both parties to it, and hear the arguments of each and decide according to what is right. He should not act out of favouritism, hatred, fear or folly. He should hear the arguments of each side and act according to what is right" (*The Mahāvastu* I, p. 228).

This advice has left its mark on Buddhist legal systems. For instance, the *Nīti-Nighaṇḍuva*, a Sinhalese work on law which contains a summary of the legal principles of Kandyan Buddhist law (civil), has a chapter on "the four avenues of injustice" (pp. 3–4). Each mode of committing an injustice is briefly illustrated and defined. For example, it is said that a judge fails to uphold justice through hatred if he deprives a rightful owner of his property or pronounces an innocent man guilty because he had a long-standing grudge against him or because he was irritated over something or another. Likewise, it is said that he will fall into injustice through ignorance if he deprives a rightful owner of his property or pronounces an innocent man guilty or fails to convict a guilty person on the basis of some ideas that may come into his head without applying legal principles (*yukti-ayukti*) to the facts of the case. The judge is admonished to come to a decision after carefully considering several factors and a quotation from the Buddhist texts is cited to show that a judge who succumbs to any one or more of these modes of injustice is likely to lose prestige in the country and suffer loss of status among his colleagues, while a judge who administers the law with impartial justice will have his reputation enhanced.

All schools of Buddhism accept perception and inference as the two sources of knowledge, although perception included not only sensory perception but extrasensory perception such as telepathy, clairvoyance and retrocognition (the capacity to recall the experiences of prior lives) as well (EBTK, Ch. IX). It is true that the inhibition of reflective and discursive thinking at a certain stage of the meditative development of the mind was considered necessary for the expansion of consciousness but this does not make Buddhism irrational.

On the other hand, Buddhism has criticised the species of rationalism which held that truth about reality can be had by *a priori* reasoning (EBTK, p. 271 ff). Such reasoning was criticised on the ground that "the reasoning may be valid or invalid" (*sutakkitam pi hoti, duttakkitam pi hoti*) and even if valid, the conclusions may be "true or false of reality" (*tathā pi hoti aññathā pi hoti*) (M I 520). This was because consistency was a necessary but not a sufficient criterion of truth and for a view to be true, it had to correspond to reality in addition to being consistent. Factual propositions were classified in Buddhism as true or false, useful or useless and pleasant or unpleasant (EBTK, p. 351 ff). It also distinguished between meaningful (*sappāṭihāriya*) and meaningless (*appāṭihāriya*) propositions holding that propositions verifiable in the light of reason and experience were meaningful but those not so verifiable were meaningless but the distinction was not the same as that of the logical positivist (EBTK, p. 326 ff).

The above observations have had little repercussions on legal thought in the East. But they seem to indicate that Buddhism would not view a positivistic conception of law with disfavour. Stating the law as it is in a verifiable and consistent form is in the interests of both clarity and justice. Justice demands consistency both in the statement of the law as well as in its application. But according to Buddhism consistency alone would not be a criterion of good law since the legal principles must conform with moral experience if the law is to promote justice rather than prevent or inhibit it. It means, of course, that with the evolution of moral experience legal systems must be changed. Such changes have to be effected on the basis of changing value-systems reflecting the growth of man's moral stature (regression and degeneration are also possible) and cannot stem from within the positivist system of law itself.

There is a parable in the Buddhist texts to illustrate the necessity for progressively exchanging better views for worse, even though we may have been accustomed to entertain certain views for a long time for personal or traditional reasons. It is said that two men went out in search of treasure. They came to a certain spot where they discovered a heap of hemp thrown away. They both agreed to bundle it up and carry it on their heads. As they proceed a little further they discover hempen thread thrown away. Here the progressive person discards the bundle of hemp and makes a fresh bundle of hempen thread while the conservative person says: "I've brought this load of hemp a long way, friend, and it's well tied up—that's enough for me; you choose for yourself." As they proceed they discover at each stage a heap of hempen cloth, a heap of flax, linen-thread, linen-cloth, cotton-down, cotton thread and calico, iron, copper, tin, lead, silver and finally gold. At each spot the progressive made a change for the better while the other insisted on retaining the hemp, which he had carried on his back for longer and longer distances. Eventually when they returned home it is said: "There the person who brought a load of hemp pleased neither his parents, nor his family, nor his friends, and won neither pleasure nor happiness. But the other with his load of gold both gave and won pleasure" (DB, II 369–70). The progressive is held up as the ideal of the Buddhist who should gradually discard ideas which are of lesser value for those which are better.

Apart from the transcendent, the world in space-time is said to be a causal system in which there operate physical laws (*utu-niyāma*), biological laws (*bīja-niyāma*), psychological laws (*citta-niyāma*) as well as moral (*kamma-niyāma*) and spiritual (*dhamma-niyāma*) laws. What the Buddha claims to do is to discover these causal correlations insofar as man's moral and spiritual life is concerned and to reveal them. It is said: "What is causation? On account of birth arises decay and death. Whether Tathāgatas arise or not, this order exists, namely the fixed nature of phenomena, the regular pattern of phenomena or conditionally. This the Tathāgata discovers and comprehends; having discovered and comprehended it, he points it out, teaches it, lays it down, establishes, reveals, analyses, clarifies it and says 'Look'!" (S II 25). These causal laws are said to be non-deterministic (*na niyati*) and since these are non-deterministic causal correlations, the pattern of events is at the same time not indeterministic (*adhicca-samuppanna,* EBTK, s.v. Index). The objectivity of causation is emphasized: "Causation has the characteristics of objectivity, empirical necessity, invariability and conditionality" (*tathatā avitathatā anaññathatā idappaccayatā ayaṃ vuccati... paṭiccasamuppādo*) (S II 26). Its closest parallel to modern Western theories of causation is the regularity theory; the activity and entailment theories are clearly discarded (EBTK, p. 449 ff). It is abundantly clear at the same time that causation is said to operate not merely in the moral karmic realm but in psychological, biological and physical processes as wel. (EBTK, p. 351). These ideas have been translated into Chinese and the Chinese Āgamas refer to the operation of causal laws in the organic and physical realms (Kalupahana, Ch. VI).

Misled by the scholar Berriedale Keith,[19] Joseph Needham has remarked in connection with his studies in causal theory and law in China that the concept of causal law was applied by the Buddhists exclusively to the moral sphere in the law of karma. It is interesting to note that Needham conceived of the possibility of the Stoic conception of the *koinos nomos* or "universal law" being influenced by the Buddhist conception of law but dismissed the idea in the mistaken belief that the Buddhist conception of law "was never applied to non-moral, non-human phenomena."[20] The above conception of the universe as a causal system, in which the operation of the moral law of karma is, as we shall see, a special case, is relevant to the notion that Buddhism has a conception of natural law in the juridical sense (see *Northwestern University Law*

---

19. Needham J. and Wang L., p. 572. For a criticism of Keith's view, see EBTK, pp. 450 ff.
20. Needham J. and Wang L., p. 535.

Review; cp. Northrop, pp. 161 ff, 168 ff). But since the concept of "natural law" is ambiguous and vague, we shall try to analyse and clarify it later.

Two of the outstanding developments in logic in the twentieth century have been first that logic was shown to be a discipline fundamentally like mathematics and that the valid formulae of a system of logic (which form the basis of sound reasoning) constituted a deductive system and secondly that there could be three-valued or n-valued systems of logic. Yet all Western legal systems have developed under the belief that there could be one and only one system of logic and that the laws of this system, which reveal the structure of reality, have been discovered by Aristotle. Although the positivist movement in law was influenced by scientific empiricism and historical materialism (see Rommen, Ch. VI) and Kelsen is concerned with developing law as a logical system derived from an extra-legal basic norm, the framework of logic presupposed by the legal positivists was a two-valued system of two alternatives.

If we take the logical speculations of Ancient Indian thinkers along with the modern developments, we may classify systems of logic into two sorts: (i) categorical and (ii) relativistic. A relativistic logic is a logic which makes the fundamental presupposition that a proposition may be true from one standpoint but false from another; thus a law may be just from the point of view of an earlier age and unjust from the point of view of a later age. Categorical logic would fall into two types: viz. *(a)* logic in which the number of values would be equivalent to the number of logical alternatives and *(b)* logic in which the number of values would not be equivalent to the number of alternatives.

Buddhist thinkers have operated with both these types of logic and it is the second type that is of relevance to us here. It is known as the "logic of four alternatives" (*catuṣkoṭi*) (see EBTK, Ch. VII) and assumes that the values "true" or "false" are applicable to four possible logically alternative forms of the proposition. We do not have the space to elaborate this at any length but merely to indicate its significance for law. On a two-valued logic of two alternatives, we can, for example, have the pair of propositions, which are mutually exclusive and together exhaustive of the possibilities: (i) the universe is finite; (ii) the universe is not finite.

But Buddhist logic proposes that with regard to this proposition the mutually exclusive and together exhaustive alternatives would be brought into better focus by a fourfold form of predication as follows:

(i) the universe is finite (in all dimensions);
(ii) the universe is infinite (in all dimensions);
(iii) the universe is (partly) finite and (partly) infinite, i.e., finite in some dimensions and infinite in others;
(iv) the universe is neither finite nor infinite, i.e., both "finite" and "infinite" cannot be predicated of the universe because the universe or space is unreal.

The above example is one actually given in the texts (D I 22–3), but in a legal context, we may say:

(i) this act is lawful;
(ii) this act is unlawful;
(iii) this act is (partly) lawful and (partly) unlawful;
(iv) this act is neither lawful nor unlawful.

It will be seen that proposition (iii) appears to be though not actually, of the form p.-p and (iv) of the form -p.- -p, both of which are necessarily false or contradictions on the basis of a two-valued logic of two alternatives. Yet there is little doubt that experience and language warrant their usage. They are considered empirically meaningful or contingent propositions in ordinary usage. Thus, Sir Ernest Barker says of Rousseau that "he may be said both to belong and not to belong to the school of Natural Law" (Barker, p. xxxix), while a professor of English law makes the statement: "... in a strict sense any action of the Secretary of State was neither lawful nor unlawful...." Both these propositions, taken by themselves, would be plain contradictions in Aristotelian logic but it is evident that their authors did not intend them to be so.

The third alternative of the form S-is-and-is-not-P as well as the conception that truth lies generally though not necessarily in the middle of two extreme points of view (see EBTK, p. 359 ff) is of special interest to Buddhism. For according to Buddhism to say that "everything exists" (*sabbaṃ atthi*) is one extreme view and to say that "nothing exists" (*sabbaṃ natthi*) is another, the truth being that everything is *becoming*. This notion has its repercussions in law in that in some types of disputes between two parties both sides are to blame and the unilateral conviction of one party as the "guilty" party to the exclusion of the other not only fails to do justice in giving a wrong (morally) verdict but may lead as a result of the verdict to estrangement between the parties concerned. There is a sense in which the accused in the dock may justifiably say that he is partly guilty and partly not to some charge made against him. It has been said that "in the *less rationalistic* systems of many Asian countries legal rules have a less rigid character and are open to much adjustment and compromise" (Syatauw, p. 23). But in actual fact this has nothing to do with rationalism except on the presupposition that an Aristotelian two-valued logic is the only valid logic. What would be irrational in the light of the modern developments in logic would be to sacrifice life and experience at the altar of a system of logic, which at best has to be used in the light of its limitations with care without resorting to Procrustean methods.

Prof. Northrop has referred to "the ethics of the 'middle path' of Buddhist culture with its preference for and present persisting practise of the mediational, rather than the codified litigational method of settling disputes" (Northrop, p. 190). He traces it to a nominalistic epistemology and tries to show that the difference in the approach to law of the Confucian and legalistic schools in China is also derived from a difference in epistemological outlook, the former stressing the uniqueness of particulars and the latter the need for categorizing in class-concepts. Buddhism, however, does not deny the utility of class-concepts and the need for categories. In fact, Buddhist philosophy makes abundant use of them (EBTK pp. 301 ff). The logic of two alternatives as well as the logic of four alternatives are used side by side according to the nature of the material studied (ibid., pp. 302–04). All that Buddhism would point to is that certain logics are more satisfactory than others for specified purposes in classifying certain aspects of experience with a minimum of distortion.

The relativistic logic in its extreme form was adopted in Jainism but it had its repercussions in Buddhism as well as in its doctrine of two truths, absolute and conventional or literal and metaphorical. As we shall see later, Buddhism considered the concept of a person as an unchanging entity to be mistaken but recognised the fact that we may speak of a person in a conventional sense. It is therefore no contradiction to say that from a literal standpoint there is no person but that from a conventional or legal point of view there is. In fact, the word "self" (*atta*) is sometimes used in a way in which it would make sense to refer to a state of normal consciousness of an individual as one "self" and to a state of mystical consciousness of the same individual qualitatively different from it as another "self." This relativism makes it possible for Buddhism to conceive of a person in his private capacity as a legal entity different from the same individual in his official or any other capacity so long as such a concept had conventional utility.

The Relevance of the Buddhist Theory of Reality for Law

In the previous section we tried to show the relevance of the epistemological and logical theories of Buddhism for law. In this we shall take up the question of the relevance for law of the Buddhist theory of reality.

Buddhism arose at a time when there was a welter of mutually conflicting philosophies and religions, each giving a different account of the nature and destiny of man's place in the universe. A brief reference to some of the main ideologies prevalent at the time is relevant to our study for more than one reason.

Firstly, these ideologies can be seen to be not different in essence from those prevalent today. Buddhism grew up in opposition to them and therefore can be seen in better focus in distinction from them. Secondly, one's attitude to law is at least partly determined by the ideology to which one subscribes. It follows from this that a change in one's attitude to law may partly be a consequence of an acceptance or rejection of some of these ideologies. Thirdly, the Buddhist philosophy of law and polity is developed partly out of a criticism of one of these ideologies. Lastly, we can see the predominant role that ideology is playing in the international scene, so much so that the problem of ensuring international peace has become partly a question of resolving or containing the conflict of ideologies, which is more political than religious today, though in the past (as far as the West was concerned) it was more religious than political. The question as to which philosophy of law we are to follow depends partly on which ideology we can subscribe to and unless the great powers are going to settle the ideological war on the political and military plane, the conflict has to be resolved at the level of reason and experience. If so, what Buddhism says on the subject is of great relevance.

It is said in the texts that there were six outstanding teachers who were contemporaries of the Buddha with a large following each. Since these teachers or their doctrines are mentioned in the non-Buddhist literature as well, we need not doubt the historicity of their existence. Makkhali Gosāla is said to be a theist (*issara-nimmāṇa-vādin*), who taught that everything happens in accordance with the divine will and beings, who do not have any real free will of their own, will gradually evolve through various states of existence and eventually attain salvation, the whole process being viewed as the unravelling of a ball of thread when flung on the ground. For all things are foreknown and preordained by the will of the omniscient and omnipotent deity. Ajita Kesakambalī was a materialist, who held that the personality of man ceases to be with the death of the body since only the material forces could be counted as real and there was no value in the so-called "good-life" prescribed by religious teachers. Sañjaya Bellaṭṭhiputta was a sceptic (*ajñāna-vādin, amarāvikkhepika*), who held that since propositions about right or wrong, propositions pertaining to an after-life or propositions pertaining to the transcendent were unverifiable, one should always suspend judgement on these matters. Among the others, Pūraṇa was an amoralist and a natural determinist (*svabhāva-vādin*), Pakudha was a categorialist like Empedocles or Aristotle, who tried to explain man and the world in terms of discrete categories, while Nigaṇṭha Nātaputta, the founder of Jainism, is described as an eclectic who adopted a relativistic logic holding that there was some truth in mutually contradictory points of view.

All these philosophies had their implications for man's living and Buddhism used the word for "religion" for any one of them. For Buddhism held that a man's actions are motivated partly by his desires and emotions and partly by the ideology to which he subscribes. It is said: "A man's ideology ... be it sound or unsound, is what induces him to actions corresponding with it. For people find expression through their words and actions of the various decisions made in line with their ideologies. And for this reason people should follow an ideology which is true and good (*saddṛṣṭiḥ*) and reject false and evil ideologies, which are a source of calamity" (*Jātakamālā*, I, p. 153, xxiii, 58–9).

In a classification of "religions" in the above sense of the term, it is said that there are four pseudo-religions (*abrahmacariyāvāsā*) in the world and four religions which are unsatisfactory (*anassāsikaṃ*, lit. unconsoling) but not necessarily totally false.

The pseudo-religions are first materialism, which asserts the reality of the material world alone and denies individual freedom and responsibility, survival, and the good life. Secondly, a philosophy which recommends an amoral ethic, holding that everything is strictly determined by nature (*svabhāva*). Thirdly, a religion which denies free will and moral causation and asserts that beings are miraculously saved or doomed. Fourthly, predestinarian deterministic evolutionism, which asserts the inevitability of eventual salvation for all.

The four unsatisfactory but not necessarily false religions are those which in some sense recognize the necessity for a concept of survival, moral values, freedom and responsibility and the non-inevitability of salvation. They are described as follows. The first is one in which omniscience at all times (*suttassa ca jāgarassa ca,* i.e., "whether awake or asleep") (M I 519) is claimed for its founder. The second is a religion based on revelation or tradition. The third is a religion founded on logical and metaphysical speculation and the fourth is one which is merely pragmatic and is based on sceptical or agnostic foundations.

We note that some types of "religion" are clearly condemned as false and undesirable, while others are satisfactory to the extent to which they contain the essential core of beliefs and values central to religion, whatever their epistemic foundations may be (*Sandaka Sutta*, M I 515–21). Revelations and revelational traditions contradict each other and may contain propositions which may be true or false. In the case of religious ideologies based on metaphysical arguments and speculations, it is said that "the reasoning may be valid or invalid and the conclusions true or false." Buddhism is here presented as a religion which asserts survival, moral values, freedom and responsibility, the non-inevitability of salvation and is verifiably true. We may observe that even the formula repeated by Buddhists down the ages in taking refuge in the Dhamma results in this life itself without delay, it is verifiable (*ehipassika*, lit. has the characteristic "come and see"), it leads to the intended goal, it should be realised by the wise, each person for himself' (*Svākkhāto bhagavatā dhammo sandiṭṭhiko akāliko ehipassiko opanayiko paccattaṃ veditabbo viññūhi*).

Despite the number of ideologies put forward at this time, sixty-two of which are mentioned in the *Brahmajāla Sutta* (D I 1–46), there is little doubt that the predominant teachings of the time were on the one hand like today, that of theism holding to the doctrine of the immortality of the soul (*bhava-diṭṭhi*) and materialism, which asserts that personality is annihilated with the death of the individual (*vibhava-diṭṭhi*). The Buddha recognizes the value of each of these doctrines but considers that the Dhamma, while embodying their merits and lacking their defects, transcends them both: "These religious and philosophical teachers who do not see how these two views (which are said to be opposed to each other) arise and cease to be, their good points and their defects and how one transcends them in accordance with the truth, are under the grip of greed, hate and ignorance ... and will not attain final redemption from suffering" (M I 65).

The necessity for singling out materialism as the ideology diametrically opposed to theism is due to the wide prevalence of this philosophy during that period. The intellectual elite seem to have had an open mind and not subscribed to any particular ideology at the time (EBTK, pp. 374–75). The *Brahmajāla Sutta* mentions no less than seven schools of materialists. One of them held that there is no mind or soul apart from the body, which is entirely a hereditary product of one's parents. What we call "mind" are the patterns of movement in our bodies. Another school maintained that the mind is an emergent by-product, which has a material basis and its condition is determined by the food we eat. They argued that just as much as when we mix up certain chemicals in certain proportions there emerges the intoxicating power (*mada-śakti*) of liquor, even so the material particles of the body and the food we eat go to form the mind, which is an emergent by-product and which disintegrates on the dissolution of the body at death. There were also schools of mystic materialists, who believed in the possibilities of the expansion of consciousness but argued that, since such forms of consciousness are dependent on the condition of the body, there is no survival after death and therefore no objectivity in moral values.

The materialists held that the material pleasures derived from the gratification of the senses were the highest good but these ancient Indian materialists (see Chattopadhaya, *Lokāyata*) were said to be divided on the question of the means to be adopted in maximizing the attainment of such pleasure. The individualistic school of materialists, who have been nicknamed "the rogues" (*dhūrta*), held that one should seek one's own material pleasure in this world even at the expense of or by the exploitation of others but there was another section called "the gentlemen" (*suśikṣita*), who held that in the quest for material pleasure it was in each person's material interest to help others to gain their goal of maximising their pleasure. It is evident that the former would have little use for the law, which they would try to circumvent or make use of, as the case may be, for gaining their own ends, while the latter would have conceded the utility of laws which safeguard the common interest since the interests of each person including themselves would be thereby safeguarded.

There is also evidence for the existence of schools of political materialism among the nobility, which, according to the Buddhist texts, taught *khatta-vijjā* (D I 9) or the "science of power" and this has been interpreted in the commentary as *niti-sattha*, which means both "political science" and "law." This term is independently mentioned in the *Chāndogya Upaniṣad* as *kṣatra-vidyā* and Śaṃkarācārya has interpreted this to mean "military science" (*dhanur-veda*). This "science of power" included both military and political science as well as the study of law, considered as an instrument for the retention and advancement of power. Here the principle of expediency based on one's material interests were to be the guiding principles behind military strategy, political power and law. This philosophy is referred to as follows in an early Buddhist text: "Fools thinking themselves learned say that there is the 'rule of might' (*khatta-vidhā*) in the world; one may sacrifice mother, father, elder brother, children and wives if one's material interests demand it" (*attho ca tādiso siyā*) J-a V 240).

The importance of military power for political realism and the necessity to adjust our values to meet the requirements of such power is a recurrent theme of political scientists even today. A well-known historian says that "military power, being an essential element in the life of the state, becomes not only an instrument, but an end in itself" (Carr, p. iii). Another writer says that "the honest realist who accepts the proposition that military power is a concomitant of the state system assumes the obligation to appraise military power according to the strictest canons of *both* political necessity *and* human values" and observes that the "large scale mobilisation of military power invariably means the sacrifice of economic, moral and cultural values" (Olson & Sondermann, pp. 190, 192).

Another passage of a later date in the Buddhist tradition, in which there is a pun on the word *kauṭilya,* meaning "crookedness," and, therefore, possibly a reference to Kauṭilya, minister and political adviser of Candragupta and the author of the well-known work *Arthaśāstra,* which dates from the 4th century BCE,[21] reads as follows: "Another on the pretext of instructing him on the duties of the king (or the state) wholeheartedly recommends the practises that are taught in the 'science of power' (*kṣatravidyā*) and which, following the crooked (*kauṭilya*) ways of political science, are soiled by cruelty and are contrary to righteousness (*Dharma-virodhiṣu*): 'You must make use of men in the way you utilise shady trees. You should try to extend your glory by showing them gratitude only as long as you need them; they should be appointed to their tasks only in the manner of beasts used for a sacrifice'" (*Jātakamālā,* xxiii, 21; cp. transl. p. 207).

The study of politics, law, international relations and military strategy were all disciplines within the "science of power" and the *Arthaśāstra* or the "science of material interests" of Kauṭilya has treated all these branches of study within it. The book refers to the contents of several treatises on *arthaśāstra* composed by ancient teachers and states its scope in its opening sentence as follows: "This single work on *arthaśāstra* is written summarising in it as much of the contents as possible of the *arthaśāstra-s* composed by ancient teachers for acquiring and administering the territory of the (entire) earth" (*pṛthivyā lābhe ca pālane ca*) (1.1). The ideal set before a sovereign ruler of a state was nothing short of world hegemony. The work deals with internal politics and administration in Books I, II, IV, VIII and XI; municipal law, civil and criminal, in Book III; international relations and international law in Books V, VI and VII; and military strategy, including espionage and the conduct of war, in Books IX, X, XII, XIII and XIV.

---

21. On the date of the *Arthaśāstra*, see Appendix I, Thapar, pp. 218–25.

From the references to ancient teachers (*pūrvācārya*) and to different schools of thought in Kauṭilya's *Arthaśāstra*, it is evident that there were different and conflicting views on the nature and significance of the "science of power." Kauṭilya mentions in Book I, Chapter II, that the schools of Manu, Bṛhaspati and Usanas differed from each other about the classification and the relative importance of the different branches of study, Kauṭilya himself suggesting a separate view of his own. While Aristotle regarded "the science of politics" as "that study which has most authority and control over the rest" since its end was "the good" (Thomson, p. 26), we find the school of Usanas asserting that "political science" (*daṇḍanīti*) was the only science since "all sciences originate from it and are connected with it" (*Kauṭilīyas Arthaśāstra,* p. 6). Yet we have very little information about these schools and it is clear that Buddhism criticises the main theses of the *Arthaśāstra* as later recorded in Kauṭilya's work, although in substance they were pre-Kauṭilyan.

It is evident in this work that all respect for moral values was subservient to the ends of power and expediency. The quest for power as an end in itself and the employment of any means whatsoever to gain these ends were against the principles of Buddhist ethics. At the same time the political philosophy of Buddhism develops partly out of a criticism of the Machiavellian political realism of the doctrines of the *Arthaśāstra.*

Buddhist texts accept much of the political wisdom of the *Arthaśāstra*, including the need for efficient administration and vigilance on the part of the king or state in regard to both internal and foreign policy. But they reverse the roles of power and moral values. While values were subservient to the ends of power in the *Arthaśāstra*, power is said to be ultimately subservient to the rule of righteousness in the Buddhist texts. This idea is forcefully expressed in the principle that "the wheel of power turns in dependence on the wheel of justice" (*bala-cakraṃ hi niśrāya dharma-cakraṃ pravartate*) (*The Mahāvastu*, p. 277). The state must be vigilant but human rights must not be interfered with. That power is subservient to the ends of justice does not mean that everything that is done by a state is necessarily just but that, the universe being what it is, injustice will in the long run be seen to be inexpedient. This point of view may be briefly illustrated by some passages in the texts.

The king's duty is to maximize the national economy without overstepping the bounds of righteousness and to work for the material and spiritual welfare of his subjects according to the Buddhist concept of the king's Dhamma. This should be his internal policy for reasons of expediency. In doing so, he ensures a strong and prosperous kingdom:

> This world rests on two foundations—the acquisition of wealth not yet acquired and the conservation of what is acquired.
>
> Therefore (the king is told) to acquire wealth and conserve what you have gained, make firm efforts within the bounds of righteousness. The realm of that king who rules unrighteously becomes weakened and rent on all sides,
>
> But the realm of the king who rules righteously is strong, prosperous, flourishing and populous."[22]

In foreign policy, he should give up all aggressive intentions and act with friendliness towards all nations with which he has dealings instead of following the policies recommended in the *Arthaśāstra* of making peace only when he is weak and of setting up one state against the other for the sake of furthering his imperialistic ambitions:

> A kingdom where insidious enemies are at work becomes split up into five realms. Do not trust them, and do not be led astray by them. The noble who is led astray and obeys the wills of others falls into the power of his enemies, and later has cause for regret.
>
> To win power for yourself, and out of regard for your kingdom, examine all matters yourself, even though you thus incur the displeasure of your foes.
>
> Speak, whether by day or by night, only after due deliberation; for men stand about to listen, and will use what they hear to confound you. O king, do not foster hostility towards neighbouring kings. Whoever hates will be repaid with hatred by his foes.
>
> Cultivate ties of friendship (*mitra-bandhaṃ ca kuryāsi*) with neighbouring kings, O mighty lord, for other peoples honour kings who are steadfast in friendship.

---

22. *Le Mahāvastu.*, pp. 277–78; cp. *The Mahāvastu,* I, pp. 230–31. The translation, "acquisition, without avarice, of wealth ...," is incorrect.

> Keep your counsel secret, and always conceal it, O king. For princes who reveal their counsel come to great harm" (*The Mahāvastu,* pp. 229, 231).

There is reason to think that the criticisms of the Buddhists among others modified to a great extent the recommendations made and the advice given in the *Arthaśāstra* on the grounds of political expediency, although the modifications do not seem to have gone far enough to meet all the Buddhist criticisms. The Hindu scholar Dr Shamasastry, who made an exhaustive study of the contents of the *Arthaśāstra*, has observed:

> Owing partly to the influence of the highly moral and philanthropic teachings of the Buddhists and partly to the precepts of the Dharmaśāstra and the Vedānta of the reviving or reformed Brahmanism, a number of practises and customs previously existent seem to have gradually disappeared between the birth of Buddha and the close of the third or fourth century of the Christian era. The political practises which disappeared during this period appear to be the institution of espionage with its evil consequences; the vices of the harem life resulting in the cold-blooded murder of kings, princes, ministers and other high officers; the evils of the passport system; the taking of a census of men, women, children and beasts;[23] the levy of a number of taxes, benevolences and special taxes to replenish empty treasuries; oppressive taxes on trade; the exaction of religious taxes and the robbing of temple money by imposing upon the credulity and superstition of the people; the confiscation of the property of the rich under the plea of embezzlement or of tiding over famine and other national calamities; the slaughter of beasts on a large scale for the supply of flesh to the people, including even the Brahmins; state-owned drinking saloons to supply liquor to men, women and children of all castes; torture of criminals to elicit confession; deceitful treaties and treacherous battles; the evils wrought by spies in creating distrust between man and man; and the use of destructive gases,

---

23. As envisaged in the *Arthaśāstra*, II, 35, the census denied the privacy of the individual.

medicines and poisons to murder people or to render them infirm either in war or in peace" (Shamasastry, p. xvii).

Buddhism has claimed to be an ideology to end all ideologies. It asks man to develop his cognitive faculties to the fullest and to see things as they are (*yathābhūta*) and regards ignorance (*avijjā*) or the failure to see reality as it is, the source of all conflicts, personal, inter-personal and international. Whatever the validity of this claim, the above would suffice to illustrate the importance of the relationship between ideologies and the law. The attitude to law differs with different ideologies. It also differs with conflicting interests. To speak of the "rule of law" in the abstract or to ask merely for what the law is, regardless of its sources and the interests it seeks to promote, does not make sense to the Buddhist. According to Buddhism, many of the ideologies we cling to are disguised rationalisations of greed and hatred, which seek to promote.

Therefore, some pertinent questions that the Buddhist would ask in regard to any set of laws would be:—By whom were they enacted? Whose interests were they intended to promote? On what ideology are they justified? This does not mean that Buddhism is opposed to the "rule of law." For, as we shall see, it emphasises the importance of ensuring that the rule of law, when necessary, should reflect the rule of righteousness and is grounded on an ideology, which is universally valid.

This belief in a rule of righteousness on the part of a non-theistic religious philosophy may be confusing to Western thinkers, who have associated the concept of righteousness with theism, with the exception of those who subscribe to a purely humanistic ethic. The view put forward by many Western scholars that in the history of Buddhism an original atheistic philosophy turned into a theistic religion with the birth of Mahāyāna is also a gross mistake. It would, therefore, be worth clarifying these confusions in order to illustrate the fact that Buddhism does not subscribe to a theistic origin of the law, while speaking of the necessity for the rule of righteousness.

The belief that Theravāda is atheistic while Mahāyāna is theistic is, however, not confined to Western scholars. For we find this view being propagated by Radhakrishnan as well, when he says: "While for Mahāyāna Buddhism the Supreme is of a transcendent character, it also believes in a personal God. The Buddha ceases to be a human teacher, a historical person. He is the essence of all being (*Dharma-kāya*). ... Salvation for Mahāyāna is not annihilation but eternal life" (*Lalita Vistara*, pp. v–vi).

We have already referred to the fact that the supreme state of Nirvāṇa is of a transcendent character both in Theravāda and Mahāyāna (see Chapter I). The Buddha is called the "essence or the embodiment of righteousness" not only in Mahāyāna but in Theravāda as well: "The description 'the embodiment of righteousness' is a term for the Tathāgata (Transcendent One)" (*Tathāgatassa h'etaṃ adhivacanaṃ—Dhamma-kāyo iti pi...*) (D III 84)—says the Buddha himself in the early Pali canonical scriptures. We have cited evidence to show that the conception of salvation as a state of annihilation or extinction is utterly mistaken, according to the early texts themselves (see Chapter I). In the *Brahmanimantanika Sutta*, the Buddha claims that, being one with the transcendent infinite consciousness beyond the reach of the material world and the empirical mind, he cannot be seen even by Brahmā, the regent of the cosmos (MN 49). Radhakrishnan's statement that salvation in Mahāyāna is "eternal life" is also mistaken if it is taken to mean a durational existence in time. The two *Sukhāvatī-vyūha*-sūtras, which are the chief authority of the Jodo and Shin-shiu sects (see *Buddhist Mahāyāna Texts*, pp. v–vi), make it quite clear that people born in the Pure Land are born there only "till they have reached Nibbāna" (ibid., Larger *Sukhāvatī-vyūha*, sec. 24) and "are bound to one birth only" (ibid., sec. 28), they are "never to return again and are bound by one birth only" (ibid., Smaller *Sukhāvatī-vyūha*, sec. 10; cp. sec. 17). Here we have nothing more than the early Buddhist conception of the Anāgāmin or the "Non-Returner," who may be born in the Pure Lands (*Suddhāvāsa*, D II 50) from which there is no return here, a state which the layman could attain (S V 177–78).

The Buddha attains the transcendent in his lifetime and becomes invisible to beings within the cosmos at death. But this does not make him a Personal God who creates the universe and is responsible for it, either in Theravāda or Mahāyāna. In fact, the concept of a Personal Creator God (Īśvara) is criticised both in the Theravāda as well as in the Mahāyāna texts. Early Buddhism had adduced two arguments against belief in a Personal Creator God. One is that the universe created in time by an omniscient and omnipotent deity will be a rigged universe in which everything will ultimately happen in accordance with the will of God, resulting in even human beings being puppets (J-a V 238). The other is that in such a world the existence of certain evils cannot be explained (J-a VI 208). In this sense, "the world is without refuge and without a God" (*attāṇo loko anabhissaro*) (M II 68). All these arguments and more are found in the Mahāyāna texts. Aśvaghoṣa, who seems to belong to a Mahāyāna school of thought stemming from the Mahāsaṅghikas (*The Buddhacarita,* II, p. xxxi ff), uses the former argument: "So others say that creation proceeds from Īśvara. What is the need in that case for action by men?" (ibid., ix, 63; p. 136). In the *Mahābodhi Jātaka* of the *Jātakamālā* several variants of the above two arguments are given but there is a further argument, which concerns the question of the creation of Dhamma: "Further, the sovereignty of the Lord must rest either on the lawful order of things (Dhamma) or on something else. If on the former, then the Lord cannot have existed before the Dhamma. If effected by some external cause, it should rather be called 'bondage'; for if a state of dependency should not bear that name, what state may not be called 'sovereignty'" (op. cit., p. 211).

The universe in Theravāda Buddhism is without known beginning because the earlier one goes back in time, there is a possibility of going back still further. This is so even with retrocognitive clairvoyance. Mahāyāna, however, goes a step further in saying that the universe "is without beginning or end" (*anavarāgra*). There is no sense, therefore, in saying that either Theravāda or Mahāyāna is a personal theism. Prof Slater has quite rightly quoted a Mahāyānist scholar who flatly says: "Buddha has never believed in a creator-Buddha or a creator-God" (quoted in Slater, p. 109). There can be, therefore, no conception of a divine law-giver in Buddhism and, in the absence of such a divinity, of a human law-giver who is divinely inspired. Buddhism would point to the babel of laws, all claiming to be of divine origin but conflicting with each other as further evidence of the folly of such a belief, however impressive a myth giving divine sanction to law may be in enforcing a rule of law.

It is necessary to add, however, that, although Buddhism was distinguished from both scepticism and agnosticism on the one hand and from personal theism on the other, it tried to accommodate both the sceptic as well as the theist. With the sceptic, the Buddha used a wager argument (M I 406–08) to the effect that, if one is uncertain about moral responsibility, values and an after-life, still it was better from a pragmatic point of view to live one's life on the assumption of the reality of responsibility, values and survival than that of the opposite view, since in that case we have nothing to lose whatever happens. The theist in the early Buddhist texts is represented as a person who believes in God in Heaven and seeks to attain "fellowship with God" (*Brahma-sahavyatā*) as the end of his religious life. It is said the theist believes that "God (Brahmā) in Heaven is the Mighty God (Mahā-brahmā), the Omnipotent (*abhibhū anabhibhūto*), the Omniscient (*aññadatthu-dāso*), the Controller (*vasavatti*), the Lord (*issaro*), Maker (*kattā*), Sustainer (*nimmātā*), the Perfect or the Most High (*seṭṭho*), the Creator (*sajitā*), the Almighty Father of beings that are and are to be (*vasī pitā bhūta-bhavyānaṃ*) (D I 18)." The Buddha argues that although Brahmā is nominally the highest being within the cosmos, he is lower in spiritual status to a Buddha or an Arahant in that he has not attained the transcendent. He is morally perfect but is not omniscient or omnipotent. He then shows that man can attain fellowship with such a being not by prayer or by calling on his name but by being "free from anger and malice, being pure in heart and gaining self-mastery" (D I 50). For only then would there be concord and harmony between the nature of man and his God so as to make it possible for man to have fellowship with God.

Thus, according to Buddhist conceptions, Brahmā in Heaven is a morally perfect being, wise and powerful but not omniscient or omnipotent. As regent of the cosmos it is he who requests the Buddha, according to the texts, to preach the Dhamma to the world but he is himself subject to the judgement of Dhamma or righteousness. He is not a creator or saviour, although, it is said, his devotees believe him to be so, and what is more, any person on earth can aspire to and attain this high office just as much as any person can aspire to and attain the status of a Buddha. It means that even in the cosmos as a whole, it is merit and desert that counts and all are equal before the cosmic justice of Dhamma. The universe is conceived on the democratic and not a monarchical or aristocratic model.

These conceptions have certain implications for the Buddhist conception of law. It means that ultimate sovereignty resides not in any ruler, human or divine, nor in any body governing the state nor in the state itself but in Dhamma, the eternal principles of righteousness. This is not to be interpreted to mean that Dhamma is some sort of mysterious entity but that it is only to the extent to which states conform with Dhamma in their internal and foreign policy that man can achieve his legitimate aspirations for peace, prosperity and happiness. Since man is free to choose and the power and right to govern is vested in the people according to the Buddhist social contract theory, it would be the responsibility of man to set up such states.

Since sovereignty does not reside in the king or body delegated to govern the state, Buddhism does not view with favour the belief that they are immune from the operations of the laws they enact. Another corollary of this theory is that it would not be consonant with the Austinian conception of the law as the command of a sovereign. Our allegiance to a law-making body is always qualified and the unjust legislation of such a body need not justify obedience.

We have so far stated primarily what Buddhism is not, with regard to its theory of reality. It will, therefore, be necessary to touch on the central teachings of Buddhism concerning the theory of reality and indicate their relevance for its attitude to and conception of law.

Scholars have sometimes stated that the Buddhist theory of reality is such that Buddhism is unconcerned with social problems, suggesting that its attitude to law cannot be anything but anarchist. For example, one scholar writes: "It is in fact surprising that such a body of doctrine as the Buddhist, with its profoundly other-worldly and even anti-social emphasis … can have become even as 'popular' as it is in the modern Western environment" (Coomaraswamy, p. 48). Another scholar poses the problem as follows: "One of the features of the study of Buddhism most frustrating to the Western mind is the effort necessary to discover a social philosophy within it. The question suggests itself: *Is* there any?" (King, p. 176). and proceeds to suggest the answer: "To tell the truth the Buddha had little either of concern for society as such or of firm conviction of its possible improvability" (ibid., p. 177). The impression created in the Western mind has been summed up in the statement: "Buddhism generally stands aloof from the affairs of the world" (*Life Magazine*—Issue on "Buddhism," 7 March 1955). If Buddhism is anti-social or unconcerned with the social order, it follows that it will show little interest in law since "legal arrangements are a variety of social organisation" (Vinogradoff, p. 12).

Dissentent opinions are not lacking but rare. We may quote the statement of an emeritus professor of Harvard who has summed up Buddhist sentiment on this subject in the following words: "Buddhism is concerned with the reformation of society as well as the salvation of the individual, and this means a regard for what might be done to establish world order" (Slater, R. L., "The Implications of Buddhist Ethics for International Relations," unpublished paper, p. 52). The theoretical basis of this view should be clear from this series of five lectures, where I have tried to indicate in outline the Buddhist views about the duties of the state, the rights of the people and of individuals, the principles on which the civil and criminal laws should be founded, the just social order, inter-state relations and world government.

Yet there is a sense in which the life of a Buddhist has to be led only partly in a social dimension and partly in what may be called a cosmic dimension. Buddhist ethical recommendations speak of happiness *in this world and the next* as the consequence of following in the footsteps of the Dhamma. The *Dhammapada* says: "He rejoices here, he rejoices hereafter; he who has done good rejoices in both worlds" (Dhp 18), The same is said in the inscriptions of Emperor Asoka: "This inscription of *Dhamma* has been engraved so that any sons or great grandsons that I may have should not think of gaining new conquests, and in whatever victories they may have gained should be satisfied with patience and light punishment. They should only consider conquest by *Dhamma* to be a true conquest, and delight in *Dhamma* should be their whole delight, for this is of value *in both this world and the next*" (Thapar, pp. 256–57).

Buddhist ethics is founded partly on the notion of social concern and partly on the notion of the perfectibility of the individual. An idea of what this "cosmic dimension" is can be appreciated only by giving a brief account of the Buddhist conception of reality and of the nature and destiny of man in the universe.

Early Buddhism upheld the reality of the material world and life (*jīvitendriya*) was considered to be a derivative (*upādārūpa*) of the basic material forces. The world of matter is said to be causally conditioned (*sappaccayaṃ saṅkhataṃ*) and existing externally to the mind and mental phenomena (*acetasikaṃ cittavippayuttaṃ*) (Dhs 135). The human individual is described as a "psycho-somatic unit" (*nāmarūpa*), whose "psyche" is analysable into four aspects of mental experience or phenomena such as hedonic tone (*vedanā*), impressions and ideas (*saññā*), conative dispositions (*saṅkhārā*) and cognitive as well as quasi-cognitive acts (*viññāṇa*). The total mind conceived of as a flux of mental phenomena is called "the stream of consciousness" (*viññāṇa-sota*). This stream of consciousness is said to be divided without discontinuity (*ubhayato abbhocchinnaṃ*) into two parts, the conscious and the unconscious, and along with the physical aspect of one's personality constitutes "the stream of becoming" (*bhava-sota*). Conscious mental phenomena have a physical basis (*rūpaṃ nissāya vattati*) with which they are in a state of mutual dependence (*aññamañña-paccaya*). The unconscious constitutes a section of the mind containing emotionally charged memories or conative dispositions going back into prior lives. Since the individual as a psychosomatic unit is in a perpetual state of flux under the conditioning of environmental, hereditary and psychic factors, it is senseless to talk of a person as an unchanging entity or soul. The strong belief in such an entity is traced in the Buddhist texts to linguistic confusions and the need to satisfy certain deep-seated cravings in us. This does not, however, affect the legal concept of a personality since these psychosomatic units do not get mixed up with each other and preserve a relative independence.

This relative independence of the individual is preserved, according to Buddhist conceptions, not only in this life but throughout our cosmic existence so that each "stream of consciousness" has a history which does not begin with one's physical birth in this life or end with death. In this continued becoming of the individual through many lives, it is said that there is an observable correlation between moral acts and consequences, such that morally good acts have pleasant consequences and morally evil acts unpleasant consequences on the whole. This is said to be verifiable by a person acquiring by means of meditation a capacity to recall one's prior lives,[24] and also by developing the faculty of clairvoyance, which makes it possible to verify this in the case of others.[25]

The detailed correlations are of a specific sort and have relevance for the Buddhist conception of natural law. Thus, it is said that a person who kills living creatures tends to be short-lived while a person who is compassionate towards others tends to be long-lived. A person who is angry and of an irritable disposition tends to be ugly in appearance while a person who is not so tends to be beautiful (M III 203). It is strictly incorrect to regard karmic consequences as rewards or punishments, for this would imply the existence of a dispenser of rewards and punishments, which would be an anthropomorphic concept which has no place in the operation of causal correlations. But if we speak of unpleasant consequences as "punishments" in a figurative sense, then it is important to emphasize the fact that such "punishments" are strictly individual and do not involve the friends and relatives of the sinner.

In a book written by Hsi Ch'ao called *The Essentials of Religion* (*Feng-fa Yao*) historical examples (from Chinese history) are adduced to show that the consequences of good and evil deeds do not pass on to sons and grandsons and that karmic recompense or retribution was purely individualistic. The author deduces from this the legal principle that collective punishment is unjustified. He says: "That the four punishments do not extend to (the culprit's relatives) has been a constant rule for a hundred generations. When a sage monarch rules the world there are already no excesses (in the

---

24. "When his mind is thus composed, clear and cleansed without blemish, free from adventitious defilements, pliant and flexible, steadfast and unperturbed, he turns and directs his mind to the recollection of his former lives, viz., one life, two lives ... ten lives ... a hundred lives through evolving eons, recalling in what place he was born, his name and title, his social status, his environment, experiences and term of life and dying there, in what place he was next born and so on up to his present existence, he remembers the various states of his former lives in all their aspects and details. Just as a man who has travelled from his village to another and from that to yet another, when he returns to his former village by the same route, remembers how he came from village to village, where he stayed and rested, what he said and what he did, even so, when the mind is composed ..." (D I 81).

25. "When his mind is thus composed ... he directs his mind to the knowledge of the death and rebirth of beings. By means of his clear paranormal perception he sees beings dying and being reborn, the high and the low, the rich and the poor, the beautiful and the ugly, each according to his character ..." (ibid., p. 82).

application of punishments). ... Not to take the circumstances into consideration but to cause punishments and rewards to be applied in a disorderly way so that good and evil are without distinction is to violate the true principles most seriously." Speaking of the Ch'in, "who instituted the punishment involving the whole family," the author says that "that would be a way of legislation not only intolerable to the sacred scriptures, but also certainly rejected by (the legalist philosophers) Shen (Pu-hai) Han (-fei tzu)" (Zürcher, p. 169).

Thus in the operation of karmic laws, there is no distinction between individuals. The *Assalāyana Sutta* points out that a priest, a nobleman, a merchant or a worker is subject to karmic recompense equally irrespective of their status (M II 149–50). The Mahāyāna *Dharma-Saṅgīti Sūtra* states: "The law (i.e., karma) is equal for all beings. The low or middle or high the law cares for nothing. The law has no preferences" (De Bary, pp. 182–83).

As we stated earlier (see section I), the universe, according to Buddhism, is a causal system in which there operate non-deterministic causal laws. The operations of karma are deemed to be of the same sort and occur in the realm of volitional acts and their consequences to the individual. These karmic laws are non-deterministic in the sense that the initial volitional acts are conditioned but not determined and are therefore "free" within limits, while the consequences of these acts may be inhibited, prevented or promoted by background conditions such as time, place, opportunity and the potentialities of later and present volitional acts. The view that all our present experiences of pleasure and pain are due to past karma is criticiased. It is held that such experiences may be the product of physiological causes, environmental, physical or social causes or the result of our willed actions in the present; karma is only one of the possible causes which may act independently or in co-operation with the other causes (A II 87). Karma as a natural law in Buddhism is not different in principle from a law in the natural sciences. In fact, it would be misleading to call it a "moral law" since it does not constitute a divine command, a categorical imperative or a norm.

Karma operates in the course of the re-becoming (*punabbhava*) of the individual in various states of existence in the cosmos, which is not confined to subsequent earth-lives. There is a gradation of these states of existence according to the general level of pleasure or pain experienced in them. It is said that "in the human worlds" (*manussesu*) "one has pleasant experiences on the whole" (*sukha-bahulā vedanā vediyamānaṃ*) (M I 75). Hell in the popular sense is rejected. It is said that superstitious people believe in the existence of a hell (*pātāla*) underneath the ocean but that there is no such place and that "hell" is a term for painful sensations (S IV 206). Elsewhere it is said that the Buddha with his clairvoyant vision can see worlds describable as "hells," in which everything one experiences is unpleasant and repulsive and yet other worlds describable as "heavens" in which everything one experiences is pleasant and charming (S IV 125–26). The value of human life, which is a rare thing in the cosmos, is often emphasised. It is said that it is a difficult thing for man who has gone down the scale of existence to a subhuman condition to emerge as a man again: "Because here prevails no practise of righteous or equitable living but just cannibalism, the stronger preying on the weaker creatures" (S V 456).

The cosmos in which these various states of existence are found is described as follows: "As far as these suns and moons revolve, shedding their light in space, so far extends the thousand-fold universe. In it there are thousands of suns (*sahassaṃ suriyānaṃ*), thousands of moons, thousands of inhabited worlds of varying sorts ... thousands of heavenly worlds of varying grades. This is the thousand-fold Minor-World-System (*cūlaṇikā lokadhātu*). Thousands of times the size of the thousand-fold Minor-World-System is the twice-a-thousand Middling-World-System (*majjhimikā lokadhātu*). Thousands of times the size of the Middling World System is the thrice-a-thousand Great Cosmos (*mahā-lokadhātu*)" (A I 227–28). In the Mahāyāna the conception is magnified and there are references to "the unlimited and infinite numbers of world-systems of the ten quarters" (Larger *Sukhāvatī-Vyūha*, I, BMT, p. 1) but the original conception survives except for the fact that "thousand" is replaced by "million" in the *Vajracchedikā* (XXX, ibid., p. 142), which speaks of "a sphere of million millions of world (-systems)." If we leave aside the notion of the "heavenly worlds" and translate these concepts into modern terms, a Minor-World-System would be a galactic system, a Middling-World-System a cluster of such galaxies and the Great Cosmos, the modern universe of astronomy, in which there are thousands of such clusters.

At first sight it may seem that the above theory of reality has little connection with law, studied as an autonomous discipline. But I have given the main outlines of it because karmic natural law is claimed to be meaningful and verifiable and the question may be legitimately raised as to whether it can withstand the criticisms of legal positivism. Besides, the Buddhist value-system is significant only on the basis of the above conception of reality and the Buddhist attitude to and conception of law is intimately connected with its value-system. And although, *prima facie,* it would appear that the connection between law and the cosmos is very remote, the decision on the part of many an individual as to whether he should be law-abiding or not may depend on what view he takes of the nature of the cosmos.

If modern criticisms about the reliability of the Buddhist literary records and the findings of modern science undermine this theory of reality, the Buddhist value-system would crumble, for one cannot cash in for long on a value-system whose ideological basis is shattered.

The most radical criticism against the view that Buddhism was founded by Gautama Buddha in the fifth and sixth century BCE is to be found in the *Soviet Encyclopaedia*, which says: "Buddhist religious literature (Tripitaka, Sutra, Jataka) attributes the founding of Buddhism to the Buddha, Shakya Muni, in the fifth and sixth centuries BCE. Reactionary bourgeois science reiterates this version. Analysis of Buddhist literature and archaeological data from 200–100 BCE indicates irrefutably that the myth about Buddha Shakya Muni was created by the Buddhist clergy relatively late, in order to propagandize Buddhism more successfully..."[26] This criticism has little historical basis.

As for the literary records, the Calcutta-Bairat Rock inscriptions of Emperor Asoka have cited seven passages from the canonical scriptures that have come down to us in the third century BCE. (Hultzsch, pp. 172–74). These passages as well as several sentences and phrases quoted in the inscriptions (Barua, pp. 29 ff) are to be found in the Pali Canon, whose *Nikāyas* (from which we have quoted in these lectures) have an almost identical content with the greater portion of the Chinese Āgamas, traceable to schools which separated a hundred years after the death of the Buddha. On literary,

26. *Bolshaya Sovetskaya Entsiklopediya,* VI, 2nd ed., 1951, s.v. "Buddism," pp. 228–30.

linguistic, ideological, sociological and historical evidence the contents of the early portions of the Pali *Nikāyas* go back to the fifth or sixth century BCE.[27]

The Buddha is referred to as "the recluse Gotama" in the early books of these Pali *Nikāyas*, although claims are made that he and some of his disciples have attained mystical states of experience and the transcendent as well as certain forms of extrasensory perception.

Except for these claims, Buddhism resembles modern scientific humanism. As for these claims, it is worthy of note that a leading modern analytic philosopher considers the concept of rebirth meaningful.[28] The evidence from age regression experiments in which subjects recall their alleged prior lives has been analysed by another leading philosopher who finds the material significant but not conclusive (Ducasse, pp. 207–99). An empirical study of spontaneous cases of recall suggestive of rebirth has led a professor of psychiatry to the conclusion that "rebirth" is the most plausible explanation that could be given of the evidence after a careful consideration of the various possible alternative normal and paranormal hypotheses.[29]

If further experimental study establishes the validity of "rebirth," the natural law of karmic recompense will be at least in principle verifiable.

---

27. DB II, pp. ix-xx; cp. M. Winternitz, *A History of Indian Literature,* tr. S. Ketkar and H. Kohn, University of Calcutta, 1933, p. 18; E. Lamotte grants a primitive core of remarkably uniform material common to the Pali *Nikāyas* and the Chinese *Āgamas*, see *Histoire du bouddhisme indien*, I, Louvain, 1958, p. 171. For a sceptical view, see J. Brough, *The Gāndhārī Dharmapada,* London, 1962, pp. 32 ff.
28. "I think that it would be open to us to admit the logical possibility of reincarnation merely by laying down the rule that if a person who is physically identified as living at a later time does have the ostensible memories and character of a person who is physically identified as living at an earlier time, they are to be counted as one person and not two"—A. J. Ayer, *The Concept of a Person,* London, 1963, p. 127.
29. I. Stevenson, *Twenty Cases Suggestive of Reincarnation,* New York, 1966, p. 362; cp. "I will say, therefore, that I think reincarnation the most plausible hypothesis for understanding cases of this series. This is not to say that I think they prove reincarnation either singly or together. Indeed, I am sure they do not. But for each of the alternative hypotheses I find objections or shortcomings which make them for me unsuitable explanations of all cases, although they may apply to some." I. Stevenson, *The Evidence for Survival from Claimed Memories of Former Incarnations,* 2nd Impression, London, 1961, p. 34.

The Relevance of Buddhist Ethics for Law

Except for the legal positivist and for those for whom the law is an instrument or an expedient to preserve or further the interests of one's nation or class, there is a close relationship between moral and legal notions. They would hold that one ought to obey the law either because it is the law (Hobbes) or because it is or it reflects to some extent at least the divine will (theocracies) or again because it is right to do so (natural law theorists).

The Buddhist texts distinguish between *law* and what is (morally) right, using the words *nīti, nyāya* or *vinaya* for the former and *dhamma* (Skr. *dharma)* for the latter. This distinction is to be found in the Sinhalese language as well, which uses the word "*nītiya*" to denote "law" and "*yuktiya*" to denote "justice." While the same distinction is to be found in English, which distinguishes *law* from *right,* in all European languages the terms for law and right coincide (Vinogradoff, p. 19). It is not possible to draw any significant conclusions from these linguistic facts. For example, we cannot say that those who did make or failed to make the distinction in language have had more just laws than the others. But a study of the political philosophy of Buddhism shows that according to Buddhism the relationship of the state with its subjects as well as with other states was to be founded on Dhamma or the principles of righteousness rather than that of short-term expediency, not because of Utopian reasons but because it was considered, *inter alia,* expedient in the long run to do so. Prof. Ghoshal is quite justified on the evidence when he says that "the most important contribution of the early Buddhist canonists to the store of our ancient political thought consists in their 'total' application of the principle of righteousness to the branches of the king's internal and foreign administration" (Ghoshal, p. 69).

It is, therefore, necessary to clarify and distinguish the Buddhist conception of Dhamma or righteousness from the Hindu conception of Dharma in order to be able to see the significance of the Buddhist contribution in better focus. It is all too frequently assumed that the two conceptions are the same or that Buddhism as a protestant movement merely cleared up certain confusions and corruptions that had crept into the Hindu notion of Dharma at the time. But a careful study of the term in all its uses, religious, ethical, social, legal and political, would show that the Buddhist concept was not only different but radically different. This does not, however, mean that Buddhism did not accept any notions at all from pre-Buddhist Hindu conceptions. Here as elsewhere Buddhism appears to have followed the general principle of taking what it considered to be sound and good and developing it, while leaving out what was unsound or evil.

For instance, if we take the legal sense, we find that Buddhism stressed the importance of equality before the law and the fact that the law should serve the best interests of society as a whole without granting special privileges or immunities to a favoured class (see "The Story of the Brahmin" in *The Jātakamālā*, pp. 109–14; cp. Ghoshal, p. 349). On the other hand the Hindu law-books sanction inequalities, laying heavier burdens on the poor (See Chapter 24) and granting immunities and privileges to the brahmins (Ghoshal, pp. 58–9). Yet at the same time, one of the basic notions of the law, namely that it should not serve the interests of the strong against the weak, can be traced to the Upaniṣads, where it is said: "He created still further a better form, Law (Dharma). This is the power (*kṣatra*) of the ruling class (*kṣatra*), viz., Law. Therefore, there is nothing higher than Law. So a weak man controls a strong man by law, just as if by a king. Verily that which is Law is truth. Therefore, they say of a man who is speaking the truth 'He speaks the Law' or of a man who speaks the Law 'He speaks the Truth.' Verily both these are the same thing". (*Bṛhadāraṇyaka Upaniṣad*, 1.4.14; TPU, p. 84). The idea that the law should safeguard the rights of the weak is developed in their own way in the Hindu and Buddhist literature. But in Buddhism the idea is radically transformed since the ruling class becomes the community of people who have equal rights and who delegate their power to the state, and the concept of Dhamma itself gets magnified because it is superior and anterior to a Personal God, who, therefore, cannot create it.

In this section, we shall examine the ethical sense of Dharma, which formed the basis of the Buddhist sense of Dhamma in all its different uses.

Ethics is concerned with the notions of right, duty, good and just, all of which are used in connection with the acts of persons, while the latter two are used in reference to persons themselves or with corporate concepts such as a social order, state or a government. We do use all these notions in reference to laws as when we say that it is right on our part or it is so-and-so's duty to obey the law or question whether the laws are good or bad, just or unjust.

The idea of a person, whether used in reference to the psychosomatic personality of the human individual or the "group personality" of a corporation, is a legal concept and is made use of in Buddhist monastic law. These laws mention offences against persons such as defamation and slander, murder and assault or sexual offences, offences against property such as theft or damage and offences against the corporate body of the Sangha (Community of Monks and Nuns) such as causing schisms, flouting legal authority, etc. (Bhagvat, pp. 20–21).

The Sangha is deemed a juristic person: "The Buddhist Sangha was undoubtedly a juristic person and was capable of holding property in the same way as a private person could ... the ordinary formalities of gift were observed by the donor when he wanted to dedicate any property to the Buddhist congregation, and the gift was accepted on behalf of the Sangha by its head or representative. The property did not become the private property of the ostensible donee, nor could it be said to belong jointly to all the monks who were members of the congregation at that particular time. It was the property of the congregation itself which could not but be deemed to be a separate entity for this purpose and which continued to exist even if all its members died out or were replaced by other people" (Mukherjee, p. 24). These observations of a Hindu jurist are consonant with the facts about the Sangha as we find them in the texts. That all property was vested in the universal Sangha and loaned to the individual for use is clear from several passages, of which we may cite the following: "Monks, the Sangha is the owner of the bowl and robes of a monk who has passed away. But truly those who tend the sick are of great service. I approve of your giving through the Sangha the three robes and the bowl to those who tended the sick and also of your distributing through the (resident) Sangha in their presence the light goods and the light requisites that are there; but whatever heavy goods and heavy requisites that are there, these belong to *the Sangha of the four quarters of the present and the future*—they are not to be disposed of and not to be divided up" (Vin I 305). But it would be misleading to speak of the congregation as a separate entity altogether from its actual and possible members. Such a conception of the Sangha or of the state is repugnant to Buddhist analytic thinking. For Buddhism, while granting that the corporate body of the "Sangha of the four quarters, present and future" could be deemed to have legal existence in a conventional sense, would not say that there can be a Sangha without actual or possible members.

While property is owned by or transferred to juristic persons, individual or corporate, some rights such as the right to life, to free speech, to personal freedom, etc., cluster around the notion of individual personality.

The question of the Buddhist concept of the "person" in a moral and legal sense is, therefore, fundamental to Buddhist conceptions of law and ethics. It needs to be clarified especially since Buddhism rejects the notion of a person as a metaphysical entity and holds that the notion of an "I" (*ahaṃ*) or "mine" (*mama*) is ultimately a source of error. At first sight it would appear that the doctrine of "no-soul" (*anattā*) is incompatible with the concept of personal responsibility. But it is shown that it is not so. The psycho-physical processes continue in a state of flux and maintain a relative individuality within cosmic existence. To distinguish one series of processes from another we use the term "person" in a conventional sense despite the lack of a persisting substratum. This fact, coupled with the relative "freedom" of volitional acts and the karmic causal correlations, is what makes moral responsibility a reality. If any one of the three factors, freedom, karmic correlations and the serial individuality is denied, moral responsibility would be a meaningless concept. This is the reason why when a monk entertained the thought that "since body, feelings, ideas, dispositions and consciousness is without self, what self can deeds not done by a self affect," the Buddha considered this an unwarranted corollary of his teaching (M III 19).

Not to speak of an abiding unchanging entity within us because no such entity is observable is not to deny an "evolving consciousness" (*saṃvattanika-viññāṇa*). To regard any one of the five constituents of personality with which we are acquainted as an abiding entity or soul or as being owned by a soul or as being located within a soul or to think of a soul as residing within any one or all of them is deemed to be mistaken. It is said to be equally mistaken to conceive of the individual apart from them. For conventional purposes, therefore, we may call the personality analysable into the constituents as a "person." In one Sutta, the five constituents are said to be "the burden" (*bhāra*), and the "bearer of the burden" (*bhāra-hāra*) is said to be "the person" (*puggala*) of such and such a name and such and such a family (S III 22), which according to the commentators of different schools such as Buddhaghosa, Vasubandhu, Candrakīrti and Yaśomitra is a designation for the "constituents" of the living individual.[30] The Buddha points out that the error of believing in a soul in one of the above senses is traceable partly to language (EBTK, p. 319), which categorises dynamic reality, and partly to our self-centred desires (e.g., the desire for security), which makes us seek solace in comforting metaphysical theories (EBTK, p. 430). There is, however, no objection to the use of person-words in conventional senses because of their conventional utility so long as one does not get confused by their misleading implications. The Buddha says that words denoting persons or entities are "expressions, terms of speech, terms in common use in the world, which the Buddha makes use of without being led astray by them" (D I 202).

But at the same time, it is stated that the laying down of the burden, which consists in eradicating the desires for sense-gratification, self-centred pursuits and the desire for destruction does not result in annihilation but in the attainment of the transcendent, a person who has thus attained the transcendent or Nibbāna being described as "beyond measure" and "deep, immeasurable and unfathomable." The relationship between this transcendent and the person consisting of the constituents cannot be spoken about since in speaking about it we are imposing our empirical concepts and categories onto it, as we do when we talk of a relationship between the two.

This concept of a person is by no means confined to the Theravāda tradition. While Theravāda uses empirical, analytic techniques to show that a person is a congeries of ever-changing

30. B. Keith, however, says, "... to say that the aggregates are the bearer is to contradict the text" but gives no reason for accepting his point of view since the text does not state that the person is different from the constituents but merely points to the living physical personality as "the person" (*Buddhist Philosophy in India and Ceylon*, Oxford, 1923, p. 82).

psychosomatic constituents, maintaining a certain individuality in one life or in a succession of lives without any underlying identity, the same idea is often conveyed in the form of a paradox in the Mahāyāna texts: "... the idea of a living being or a person is no-idea ... there are neither beings nor no-beings. And why? Because those who were preached as beings, beings indeed, they were preached as no-beings by the Buddha and therefore they are called beings" (*Vajracchedikā*, XXI, in BMT, p. 138). The intention of these paradoxical utterances is to draw our attention to the misleading implications of language, which seems to suggest a world of discrete entities, where in fact there are only interdependent dynamic processes and ultimately the transcendent.

There is, therefore, no problem as regards the concept of moral and legal responsibility in Buddhism since in a conventional sense the legal reality of a person can be asserted. In fact, according to Buddhist usage the different personalities that the same individual can have at different times may be designated different "selves" (*attā*). This idea can be extended to grant that there could be a legal relationship between a private individual and the same individual in some official capacity.[31]

As we stated earlier it was with Buddhism that there emerged for the first time in Indian history the conception of a universal good embracing the whole of mankind. This universal good was conceived of not only as spiritual welfare but as material welfare as well. The Buddha's doctrine of righteousness was intended to serve primarily the spiritual welfare and secondarily, in view of its social philosophy, the material welfare of humanity. But in the Buddhist texts there is also a frequent reference to the concept of a world-ruler, who sets up a just social order embracing the whole earth, working primarily for the material and secondarily for the spiritual welfare of humanity. In one place it is said: "There are those two persons who in being born in the world are so born for the good and happiness of mankind, for the weal, good and happiness of gods and men. Which two? The worthy and perfectly enlightened One who has attained the transcendent and the universal monarch" (A I 76).

---

31. Saloman v. Saloman & Co. Ltd. (1897), A.C. 22; 1895–99, *All England Law Reports*, REP., pp. 33 ff. (H.L.).

Goodness is therefore partly understood in terms of the utilitarian principle of what contributes to the weal and welfare of the multitude. Works of social utility and help extended to those in distress are thus reckoned to be good:

> Planters of groves and fruitful trees
> And they who build causeway and dam
> And wells construct and watering-sheds
> And (to the homeless) shelter give—
> Of such as these by day and night
> For ever doth the merit grow.
> In righteousness and virtue's might
> Such folk from earth to heaven go.
>
> (S I 33; tr. KS I p. 46)

While the welfare of others or the good of the multitude was one end to be aimed at, the other was self-perfection or the attainment of Nibbāna. To those for whom Nibbāna was too difficult a goal to strive for in this life itself and especially for the laymen, the ideal of self-betterment, which makes for happiness in this life and the next, was presented. For the mundane person the pursuit of material gain was deemed to be compatible with the good life, provided the wealth was gained by just means and the wealth so acquired was spent for one's good as well as the good of others without squandering or hoarding it. The man "who possesses the capacity to acquire wealth that he could not acquire before and also to increase it and at the same time possesses that insight which makes it possible for him to distinguish good and evil" (Pp III) is well spoken of.

The eightfold path to happiness and realisation requires that one adopts a "right mode of livelihood" (*sammā-ājīva*). The "wrong mode of livelihood" (*micchā-ājīva*) is described in one place as that of acquiring wealth "with the idea of adding gain to gain by resorting to trickery, fraud and hypocritical talk" (M III 75). It is suggested that a good Buddhist should not undertake "trade in armaments (*sattha-vaṇijjā*), the slave-trade (*satta-vaṇijjā*),[32] trading in meat, intoxicants and poisons" (A III 208).

---

32. This term, which literally means "trading in living beings," is explained in the Commentary as "*manussa-vikkaya*," i.e., buying and selling of human beings, s.v. PED.

Buddhism upholds the reality of this world and the next (*atthi ayaṃ loko atthi paro loko*) (M III 71) and the Buddha speaks of the happiness of the average man as depending on his economic security (*atthi-sukha*), the enjoyment of one's wealth (*bhoga-sukha*), freedom from debt (*anaṇa-sukha*) and the blameless moral and spiritual life (*anavajja-sukha*) (A II 69). Here the happiness of economic security is said to derive partly from the feeling that his wealth was earned by just means and by the sweat of his brow, while the happiness of enjoying one's wealth is said to be partly that of doing good to others with it. We see here that welfare is conceived in terms of both material and spiritual welfare, an idea which is of importance in connection with the Buddhist conception of human rights.

Although the spiritual goal of human endeavour, namely Nibbāna, was a state beyond space, time and causation (*na paṭicca-samuppanna*) and therefore strictly beyond description, analogical accounts are given of it and the passage from our finite self-centred existence to Nibbāna is pictured as one from bondage to freedom (*vimutti*) and power (*vasa*), from imperfection to perfection (*pārisuddhi, parama-kusala*), from unhappiness to perfect happiness (*paramasukha*) and bliss (*siva*), from ignorance to knowledge (*vijjā, aññā*), from finite consciousness to transcendent infinite consciousness (*ananta-viññāṇa*), from the impermanent to the permanent (*nicca*), from the unstable to the stable (*dhuva*), from fear to freedom from fear (*abhaya*), from death to immortality (*amata*), from the evanescent to the ineffable (*amosa-dhamma*), from a state of mental illness to a state of perfect mental health,[33] from darkness to light (*āloka*), etc. It is the final goal of ethical and spiritual endeavour and is called reality (*sacca*), the excellent (*paṇīta*), the wonderful (*acchariya*) and the marvellous (*abbhuta*). The attainment of Nibbāna has been compared in the texts to that of the wonder experienced by a man born blind gaining his sight, and although it is the extinction of the self-centred desires, aggressive tendencies and ignorance, which coincides with the attainment of Nibbāna, the

33. A II 143; here diseases are classified as bodily (*kāyika*) and mental (*cetasika*) and it is said that while we have bodily diseases from time to time mental illness is almost continual until Arahantship is attained, so that only the saint can be said to have a perfectly healthy mind.

translation of the term as "extinction" has given a wrong impression to the reader.[34]

Nibbāna being the goal for each is the goal for all. It is the Summum Bonum and is referred to as a state of utter Freedom, Happiness, Perfection, Knowledge, etc., and a state "beyond measure."

A wrong act or (literally) an unskilful act (*akusala*) is defined as what tends to hinder the self-development of oneself (*atta-vyābādhāya saṃvattati*) as well as of others (*para-vyābādhāya*) and a right or skilful act is its opposite. It is said: "A wise person does not think of hindering one's self-development or of others' or of both oneself and others' self-development but he would always think of the welfare of oneself, of others, of both oneself and others and in fact of the welfare of the whole world" (*sabba-loka-hitameva*) (A II 69). Thus any act which obstructs the quest for freedom, happiness, perfection, knowledge, security, peace, etc., is a wrong act and one which promotes or helps the quest for freedom, etc., is a right act.

We see that the Buddhist ethical theory is teleological insofar as its conceptions of right and wrong are goal-determined by the notions of the summum bonum and the good of mankind. At the same time Buddhist ethics has also been stated from a deontological standpoint, where men in society, including monks and nuns, are said to have certain duties to perform by virtue of the stations in life they occupy, although the fundamental obligation of all should be to seek finally to attain Nibbāna, for it is only then that one's obligations are over (*kata-karaṇīya*). Man's social duties are to be performed not merely out of a sense of duty but as far as possible out of a spirit of service (*cāga*), love (*mettā*) and understanding (*paññā*), the opposite of greed, hatred and ignorance.

The Buddhist ideology is pragmatic insofar as it is to serve as a basis for action, its view of life pointing to a way of life. A man is considered inconsistent not only if his professed ideology is internally inconsistent but if his actions are not compatible with the ideology he professes. For to be a Buddhist, it is not sufficient to subscribe to a view of life since it involves commitment to a way of life.

---

34. *Nirvāṇa* is from *nir* (out) and √ *vā*, to blow, but the word was also used by nibbāna or the hedonists at the time to denote presently experienced happiness.

The task of Buddhism is therefore to help man transform himself from what he is to what he ought to be. In this Buddhism recognises the role both of conflicting ideologies by which human beings are attracted as also the different natures and stages of development of different individuals, despite their fundamental equality. A materialist ideology may hold that the nature of man can be changed only by the transformation of his material, mainly economic environment constituting the modes of production, distribution and exchange and that the most that men can do is to quicken the inevitable historical process by an understanding of history. A theistic ideology may hold that the nature of man can be changed only by his deep faith and submission to the will of God, the author of his being. A sceptical ideology may hold that human nature cannot be changed and that the most that we can do is to do our best with it, taking human nature for what it is. These ideologies will have different conceptions of the nature and role of law though they may agree to a basic minimum of law for purposes of coexistence.

Buddhism was aware from the earliest times of ideological conflicts arising from "people tenaciously clinging to their respective ideologies, holding 'here alone is the truth'" (Sn 895). One of the basic problems of international law today in fact, is that of finding an agreed basis of faith in international law (which does not contravene principles of justice) as a means of resolving inter-state problems and disputes without resort to unilateral or factional solutions based on force or the threat of force in the face of both conflicting interests and ideologies. Buddhism holds that there is some truth in all these ideologies, more truth in some, but insists that the ideological conflict cannot be settled on the military and political planes without detriment to the interests of mankind. It can only be settled ultimately in the light of reason and experience. Buddhism does not hold to the inevitability of war in the future because there have been wars in the past. The whole message of Buddhism is that we have been born to die in the past but that we need not be born to die in the future. There is hope in the thought that some of the ideologies contending for supremacy today also do not think that war is inevitable or that ideological disputes can be settled by war. Lenin thought that peaceful coexistence would provide favourable opportunities for the development of the class struggle in the capitalist and dependent countries but he denounced war as a means of settling ideological disputes: "But ideological and political disputes between states must not be settled through war" (*World Marxist Review*, Vol. III, No. 12, Dec. 1960).

Physiological and bio-chemical studies alone cannot give us a comprehensive account of the nature and potentialities of man. We need a new philosophy of man based on his achievements in all cultural traditions which can form a subject of further exploration and experimental study. Laws are meant for men and the extent to which the tools of law can be utilized or dispensed with depends on what man really is and what he can make of himself. Legal systems have to be empirically examined and used in the light of their efficacy without stifling the creativity of man. As a student of Soviet jurisprudence observes: "Man is not uniformly the dependent and growing youth of Soviet law, nor is he uniformly the reasonable man of our (i.e., Western) legal tradition" (Berman, p. 384). Buddhism has a significant contribution to make towards such a philosophy of man.

Buddhism admits that there are individual variations in the nature of man, owing to differences in the impact of his environment, heredity and saṃsāric history or psychic past going back into prior lives. Nevertheless, there is a basic similarity in the nature of man which is susceptible of analysis.

Man's fundamental nature is said to be good and in this respect the mind of man is compared to a piece of gold ore, which is said to have the defilements of iron, copper, tin, lead and silver, but when it is purified it shines with its natural lustre (A II 16), as when he attains the transcendent mind. These defilements are classified as gross, medium and subtle (*sukhuma*). The gross defilements consist of misconduct with regard to body, speech and mind; the medium defilements are lustful and covetous thoughts, thoughts of destruction and ill-will and the subtle defilements consist of racial feelings (*jāti–vitakka*), national feelings (*janapada-vitakka*) and egotism or personal and national pride (*avaññatti*) (A I 254). We note here how our preoccupations with thoughts concerning our race or state are considered harmful to the concept of a common humanity.

Wars and disputes ultimately have their origins in the minds of men. And the Buddha points out that, although men suffer from bodily disease from time to time, they are continually subject to mental conflicts or mental disease until they attain perfection, which is conceived as a state of perfect mental health. The roots of this diseased state of mind are said to be the lack of a realistic understanding of the nature of man and his place in the universe (ignorance), the continual onrush of unsatisfied cravings (greed) and the aggressive tendencies (hatred) which demand and receive temporary satisfaction from time to time but are never allayed. The goal of Buddhism is therefore partly conceivable as the goal of the psychotherapist seeking to create a relative or complete sanity of mind as a prerequisite of personal happiness and social harmony. The Buddhist analysis of our springs of action is as follows:

1.Greed (*lobha*):
  (i) desire for sensuous gratification (*kāma-taṇhā*);
  (ii) desire for self-centred pursuits (*bhava-taṇhā*, e.g., desire for power, fame, wealth, personal immortality, etc.).

2. Hate (*dosa*).

3. Ignorance (*moha*, i.e., erroneous beliefs regarding man and his place in the universe, "illusions," "rationalisations").

4. Selfless service (*cāga*, lit. charity, selflessness).

5. Wisdom, understanding (*paññā*).

6. Friendliness (*mettā*).

The pleasure that we get from satisfying our desires for sensuous gratification, self-centred pursuits and aggression or by entertaining illusions or rationalisations which go hand in hand with or promote the above constitute much of the enjoyment of modern man. The Buddha says that it is in the nature of man "to seek pleasure or happiness or recoil from pain or a source of unhappiness" (*sukha-kāmā hi manussā dukkha-paṭikkūlā*) (M I 341). So the quest for happiness as such is not condemned. But it is pointed out that there is a law of diminishing returns which operates in the search for happiness by continual gratification of the desires, while it is held there is a greater happiness of a more serene and stable sort, which wells from selfless service, friendliness and a realistic view of life. The *Dhammapada,* therefore, says: "If by renouncing a little pleasure, one finds a greater happiness, then let the wise man renounce the little pleasure in finding a greater happiness" (Dhp 290). We go with the current in acting and reacting out of greed, hatred and ignorance but our endeavour should be to go against the current (*paṭisotagāmi*) and replace greed with selfless service, hatred with friendliness and ignorance with wisdom as our springs of action.

It is said that "desire should be eliminated by depending on desire" (*Taṇhaṃ nissāya taṇhaṃ pahātabbaṃ*) (A II 146). We have to cultivate a longing (*chanda*) to act out of selflessness and friendliness and make an effort to eliminate greed and hatred. Likewise, ignorance must be replaced with right beliefs or the commitment to the right philosophy of life. The cultivation of meditation and self-analysis, it is said, results in increased self-awareness and control of one's actions, which is believed to be the path leading to personal happiness, social harmony and international understanding. While laws may be useful for peaceful coexistence, international friendliness and understanding can grow only as a result of a deliberate effort on our part to get rid of the sources of hatred and misunderstanding both within and without us. It is claimed that those who can achieve this transformation here and now can honestly say in the words of the *Dhammapada:* "Happily we live without anger among those who are angry" (Dhp 197) and "happily we live in sound (mental) health among those who are ailing" (198).

It is, no doubt, recognised that only a highly intellectual type of individual could profit by such a method of self-analysis. But individuals are of different types. As opposed to the intellectual types (*buddhi-carita*), there is a mention of the passionate types (*rāga-carita*) and the aggressive types (*dosa-carita*), etc. Individuals are also in varying stages of moral and spiritual development. In a work called *Puggala Paññatti* (tr. *Human Types,* pp. 99–100), which forms part of the Canon, seven grades of individuals in varying stages of moral and spiritual evolution are referred to. Different types of meditative exercises are prescribed for the different psychological types and the doctrine is presented in different forms to those of little understanding in ways which appeal to them.

This philosophy of man had important repercussions in law for brief periods at least in Buddhist legal and social history. The belief in the inherent goodness of man led to the view that, if man was educated in right and wrong, he is likely to be law-abiding. The belief in the possibility of transforming human nature, the need to approach the criminal with mercy and understanding and the doctrine that officials are morally responsible for the acts they do even in their official capacities (*raññо rājakaraṇīyaṃ hetu*) (M II 186–88) resulted in the abolition of capital and sometimes even corporal punishment, based on the reformatory theory of punishment, only secondarily deterrent.

We may briefly illustrate the effect that some of these teachings had on Japanese legal history. In Japan, "it is with Prince Shōtoku that we come to know something of laws in the modern sense" (Nakamura, p. 22). Shōtoku Taishi is credited with having drafted the "Constitution of Japan" (von Mehren, p. 53). and this had a profound effect on subsequent legislation and the spirit of the people. Prof. Hajime Nakamura speaks of Shōtoku in the following terms: "Prince Shōtoku, the real founder of the centralized state of Japan proclaimed the Seventeen-Article Constitution in CE 604. This was the first legislation in Japan ... adopting the civilisations and thought of China and India sufficiently for their purposes, based chiefly upon the spirit of Buddhism. This is so to speak the *Magna Carta* of Japan. ... It has been confirmed by scholars that there is a close connection between the spirit of Shōtoku's constitution and the political regime established at the Taika Innovation, which brought about the unified state of Japan" (Nakamura, p. 23). The second article of Shōtoku reads as follows and we see him in its latter part stressing the inherent goodness of man: "Sincerely revere the Three Treasures, i.e., the Buddha, Dhamma and Sangha. These three constitute the final ideal of all living beings and are the ultimate foundation of all nations. What man in what age can fail to revere this truth. *Few men are really vicious.* If only we teach them what is good and right the great majority would be able to follow it. How shall their crookedness be made straight unless we take refuge in the Three Treasures."[35]

The restraint in Japanese criminal law is traced to the influence of Buddhism and the abolition of capital punishment during the ninth and tenth centuries is also due to it: "The restraint found in Japanese criminal law undoubtedly stems from the underlying character of traditional Japanese culture. In Europe criminal law

35. "Jushichijo Kempo," in *Mochizuki Bukko Dai-jiten*, ed. Mochizuki (S.), revised ed. 1954, Kyoto, Japan, Vol. III, 22576. I am indebted to Mr. S. Mori, Assistant Editor, *Encyclopaedia of Buddhism*, Peradeniya, Ceylon, for the translation.

originally developed to satisfy the desire for retribution. But in tracing the history of criminal law in Japan prior to the importation of Western institutions, one does not encounter retributive law, probably because the highly developed and non-retributive penal law of China was taken over at a very early period in Japanese legal development.... This original difference became even greater as the Western European tradition was influenced by the strict individualistic morality of Christianity, while Japanese culture derived its inspiration from permissive Buddhism and practical Confucianism" (von Mehren, pp. 290–91).

The essence of the Buddhist ethical teaching is summed up in the words of the *Dhammapada:* "To refrain from all evil, to cultivate the good and to cleanse the mind—this is the teaching of the Enlightened Ones" (183). A more elaborate version of what is meant by refraining from all evil and cultivating the good is summarised in the form of the Ten Virtues, which are extensively referred to in the Theravāda and Mahāyāna scriptures and has been the basis of legislation in some Buddhist countries. These Ten Virtues, the observance of which at least in the negative form in every country, are deemed to be an essential prerequisite of social stability, international understanding and peace, read as follows when stated in both the positive and negative forms, in which they are to be found in the texts:

1. He refrains from killing and abides full of mercy to all beings.
2. He refrains from stealing and is honest and pure of heart.
3. He refrains from sexual misconduct and does not transgress the social mores (*cāritta*) with regard to sex.
4. He refrains from lying and is devoted to truth. On being summoned as a witness before an assembly or a court of law, he claims to know what he knows, he does not claim to know what he does not know, he claims to have seen what he saw and does not claim to have seen what he did not see; he does not utter a conscious lie for the sake of himself or for the sake of others for some trifling gain.
5. He refrains from slander and holds himself aloof from calumny. What he hears here, he repeats not there in order to cause factions among people. He is a peacemaker, who

brings together those who are divided, delights in social harmony and makes statements which promote harmony.

6. He refrains from harsh speech and uses language that is civil and pleasant to hear.
7. He refrains from idle gossip and speaks at the right time in accordance with facts, what is meaningful, righteous and in accordance with law (*vinaya-vādi*).
8. He refrains from covetousness, does not covet another's property (and is generous at heart).
9. He refrains from ill-will (and is benevolent).
10. He refrains from holding false views and holds the right philosophy of life, believing in the reality of this world and the next, in moral recompense, moral obligations and values and in religious teachers who have led good lives and have proclaimed by their superior insight the nature of this world and the next" (M III 47–52; BMT, pp. 167, 197; Zürcher, p. 165).

Of the above precepts recommended to all humanity, it will be noted that the first three find expression through the body, the next four through speech and the rest in the mind. If we compare this set of Ten Virtues or skilful actions (*kusala*) with the Decalogue, we can see that the first corresponds with the sixth commandment, the second with the eighth, the third with the seventh, the fourth with the ninth, and the eighth with the tenth, while part of the tenth (the obligations to mother and father) corresponds to the fifth commandment. There is nothing corresponding to the fifth, sixth, seventh and ninth in the Decalogue.

We have already seen that Buddhism does not favour a command theory of the law (Chapter II). In contrast to the commands of the Decalogue, the desirability of basing one's conduct on the Ten Virtues or "skilful actions" is recommended on the grounds of self-interest and expediency and a person voluntarily decides to take upon himself these precepts. The appeal is to the egoist to follow the path of enlightened egoism in his own interests, but such enlightened egoism necessarily involves other-regarding activity. Likewise, the altruist who wants to save the world and work for its sake is quietly reminded that no one can help save another unless he has saved himself.[36]

So enlightened altruism necessarily involves self-regarding activity. The net result is an ethical universalism which regards the best person as one who works for his own welfare as well as of others. This involves for both the egoist and the altruist the rooting out of greed, hatred and ignorance so that he progressively acts out of a sense of selfless service, love and understanding.

These Ten Virtues formed the basis of legislation in some Buddhist countries. The first great ruler of Tibet, King Sron-btsan-sgam-po, who reduced spoken Tibetan to a system of alphabetic writing and with whom written Tibetan begins, is said to have "promulgated laws to harmonise with the Ten Virtues prescribed by Buddhism"[37] in the seventh century CE.

The Hindu tradition stressed the importance of sanctions for law based on the deterrent and retributive theories of punishment. It upheld the theory that law is force incarnate. The study of law was itself called the "science of punishment" (*daṇḍa-nīti*). The *Mahābhārata* says: "Force or the fear of punishment rules all beings, force alone protects them; when people are asleep it is force that keeps awake, the wise recognize the law to be force" (*daṇḍaṃ dharmaṃ vidurbudhāḥ*). (*Mahābhārata, Śāntiparvan*, 15.2). Ultimately all law and order depends on force or the fear of punishment. It is said that people do not commit crimes for four reasons, viz., the fear of punishment by the king, the fear of divine vengeance, the fear of the other world and the fear of society (ibid., 15.5).

In contrast, Buddhism holds that, although sanctions have a place in law, the law itself is based on consent resulting from understanding, friendliness and mutual interest. The role of sanctions is secondary. Buddhism speaks of virtuous behaviour arising out of respect for the dictates of our conscience (*attādhipateyya*), respect for public opinion (*lokādhipateyya*) and respect for righteousness or Dhamma (*dhammādhipateyyo*) (A I 147) in the Buddhist sense of the term. Conscience for Buddhism is a by-product of our accumulated and recurrent experiences in many lives and is generally deemed trustworthy but sometimes misleading (Vin

36. "It is not possible for one who is stuck in the mud to help out another ... it is possible for a man who has saved himself to (help) save another" (M I 46).

37. Bapat, pp. 73–4; cp. Yu Li, pp. 127–28; only some of the virtues are represented in the "Sixteen Articles of Law."

III 62–3). While Buddhism thus promotes a frame of mind in which there would be respect for just laws out of love and understanding, it is not unmindful of the fact that there is a class of people who refrain from crime mainly out of the fear of punishment in this life. The Buddha refers in one place to a class of people who "out of fear of punishment in this life do not plunder the goods of others" (A I 48). Although the goal of Buddhism is a state in which there is freedom from fear (*abhaya*), it recognises the importance of cultivating a sense of moral shame (*hiri*) and moral dread (*ottappa*) in the initial stages of one's moral development.

Although the Ten Virtues are considered necessary for social stability and peace, they have been further watered down in the form of the Five Virtues, known in Buddhist tradition as the *Pañca Sīla*. They include the first four of the Ten Virtues stated negatively along with the precept to refrain from drinking and gambling. Since they concern the overt behaviour of the individual, they would form the basis of legislation in countries with a Buddhist cultural tradition.

We have seen how Buddhist ethics is based partly on the notion of the perfectibility of man. The universe being what it is, it is said that the quest for perfection is both possible and desirable. Besides, in such a universe, it is expedient on the part of the individual to avoid evil, to do good and to cleanse the mind by gradually eliminating his self-centred desires and erroneous beliefs. While one axis of ethical action turns round the notion of perfectibility the other revolves round the utilitarian and humanist conception of the good of mankind. The two ends are not at variance with each other because the means adopted for attaining these ends are the same, namely the cultivation of selflessness (*cāga*), friendliness (*mettā*) and wisdom (*paññā*).

We have also seen one fundamental difference between Hindu Dharma and Buddhist Dhamma, in that according to Buddhism the state must be founded as far as possible on the principles of love and understanding rather than on that of the fear of punishment, although fear too plays a minor role. This implies, *inter alia,* that penal laws must be based on a primarily reformatory and only secondarily deterrent theory of punishment.

It is evident that if the laws of the state as well as international law must be based on the principles of Dhamma, Buddhism upholds a theory of natural law. But the Buddhist theory has to be distinguished from many of the Western conceptions of natural law in several respects. The Western conceptions for the most part have been vague and ambiguous. Slavery has been both supported and opposed on the ground that this accords with natural law and Aquinas, while considering slavery to be contrary to natural reason, yet considers it reasonable *secundum alicuam utilitatam consequentem.* (Micklem, p. 76).

Buddhism holds that human law must have a universally acceptable moral basis to be deemed binding. Every individual is morally responsible for his private or official actions. This responsibility is personal and one is not obliged to perform unrighteous or iniquitous acts either for the sake of the king or state (*rañño hetu*) or for the sake of one's parents or children (M II 18–88). The Buddha advises monks to obey the orders of the king or state (Vin III 138) in so far as they are not morally repugnant.[38] The Buddhist monks of China were charged with lawlessness for refusing to bow before the emperor but they were able to persuade the emperor that the encouragement of Buddhism was highly beneficial to the state because Buddhist laymen will be good law-abiding citizens since "their five prohibitive rules (i.e., *pañca sīla*) virtually assist the ruler in exerting his transforming influence."

It will be clear from what we have said so far that the moral basis of the law is not due to its being the will of a personal creator God. If we may briefly outline the senses in which Buddhism upholds a theory of natural law, we may formulate the Buddhist conceptions as follows.

Firstly, it may be said that Buddhism propounds a theory of natural law by virtue of the fact that karmic correlations are a special instance of causal correlations in nature, which is an ordered system. In these correlations as described in the Buddhist texts, morally good actions tend to be followed by pleasant consequences to the individual and to society, morally evil actions by unpleasant consequences and actions which partake of both good and evil (i.e., are of a "mixed" nature = *vokiṇṇa*) by a mixture of pleasant and

---

38. "He should not obey any injunction of a king contrary to the Dhamma" (Vinaya Commentary III, p. 138)—ed. I. Paññāloka, *Mahāvagga Vaṇṇanā*, Colombo, 1916, p. 222.

unpleasant consequences. Nature being so, it is in the interest of the individual in the long run to avoid evil and to do good.

As a result the individual is not to imitate nature by returning evil for evil and good for good but to so develop himself that he returns good for evil. The penal laws of the state as well should reflect this enlightened attitude and not copy the justice of nature by demanding an eye for an eye. The wrong doer should be punished primarily with a view to reform and secondarily for deterrent reasons. The wrong doer is morally and legally responsible for his acts but since, according to Buddhism, such wrong doing has been conditioned by psychological, social and economic causes and those who sit in judgement have to act out of compassion in their own interests as well as that of the wrong doer, penal laws must be so framed that punishment is directed at the reformation of the wrong-doer. Nature's method of causing suffering is said at times to result eventually in the moral and spiritual reformation of the individual[39] but man is not to copy the methods of nature. It is, therefore, misleading to regard the human secular law as a *jus naturale* participating in a divine law working in nature (Rommen, p. 38). The secular criminal law is to be grounded on love and understanding, while nature's methods in the operations of karma appear to be different. It is true that human justice may be faulty due to prejudice and error in the administration of justice as compared with karmic justice.

It is, therefore, incorrect to say with Dr Zürcher that "the concept of inexorable justice, the existence of the 'natural law' of karma 'is' the cosmic counterpart of worldly government" (Zürcher, p. 133). Karma being non-deterministic and modifiable is not inexorable, nor is worldly government to be a copy of karmic natural law. Besides, the "natural law" of karma, which operates with equality to all beings, is a causal law in Buddhism and should not, of course, as Prof. Nakamura has pointed out, be identified with the *jus naturale,* which is secular law in the juridical sense.[40]

---

39. "Suffering is instrumental in arousing faith in moral and spiritual values, such faith results in gladness and composure of mind giving rise to insight regarding reality and eventual salvation" (*dukkhūpanisā saddhā* ...) (S II 31). Here "suffering" is not necessarily used in the sense of physical or mental pain but in the general sense in which all conditioned existence is unsatisfactory and therefore suffering.

Secondly, Buddhism upholds a natural law theory in recognizing that man's conscience is generally aware of right and wrong even though conscience is admitted to be sometimes fallible: "Your conscience (*attā*) is aware whether it is truth or falsehood ... therefore be guided by one's conscience (*attādhipateyya*) as well as by public opinion (*lokādhipateyya*) and the Dhamma (*dhammadhipateyya,* A I 149–50)." Reason also forbids what is condemned by righteous law. In the *Anumāna* (Inference) *Sutta,* the principle is laid down that one should not do unto others what one does not wish others to do unto oneself by a series of inferences of the following form: "If a person boasts about himself and belittles others, such a person is disliked by me; therefore, if I were to boast about myself and belittle others, I would be disliked by others." (M I 97) Thus, a rational person who would not like to be disliked by others, would not boast about himself and belittle others. In this way a Kantian categorical imperative (Broad, pp. 127–28) would compel us to hold that it is wrong to boast about oneself and belittle others and so it would be with the actions we generally penalize according to the criminal law. But the main reason why such actions are considered to be wrong is that they are verifiably wrong, social repercussions and karmic correlations being in principle verifiable.

Thirdly, Buddhism upholds a natural law theory in the sense that it puts forward a social contract theory of the origin of the state and all that it implies. We shall examine the nature of this theory in our next chapter.

---

40. "Here one may find an analogue of this Buddhist idea of the law in Hugo Grotius' *jus naturale* or 'natural law.' His natural law is supposed to be impartial to any person or nation and unchangeable under any circumstances. Even God cannot alter this product of his reason. But it should be remembered that natural law regulates human existence. The law is valid without necessarily referring to God's authority so long as it is clear to reason as a universal principle necessary in governing the relations of human beings in this world. The Buddhist law of nature, on the other hand, is not the law regulating the relations of individual human beings but it is the law controlling the relations between the state of ignorance (which is inevitably attached to individual human existence and behaviour) and the way of deliverance from it. Though Grotius' natural law and the Buddhist law of nature are similar in form, they are quite different in essence"—Nakamura, p. 16.

The Buddhist Conception of Society, Law, and Human Rights

Although no answers are forthcoming as regards absolute origins, there is no doubt that we can talk about relative origins of the universe from the Buddhist point of view. As we stated earlier, the smallest unit in the universe was the minor-world-system (*cūlaṇikā-lokadhātu*), in which there were thousands of suns and thousands of inhabited worlds. If we replace "thousands" by "millions" (as some of the Mahāyāna texts do) a minor-world-system would be a galactic system. The next unit, the middling-world-system (*majjhimikā lokadhātu*) would be a cluster of galaxies and the vast universe (*mahālokadhātu*) would be a cluster of such clusters. This vast universe is said to undergo periodic changes with time, measured in immensely long periods called eons (*kappa*). In one long eon of the birth and death of a universe, there are two main stages described, that of the "opening out" (*vivaṭṭamāna*) and that of the "closing in" (*saṃvaṭṭamāna*) and destruction of the universe. But the destruction is only a prelude to a new birth, and in the course of each cycle of the expansion and contraction of this oscillating universe, the beings within the universe are said to evolve up to the status of radiant beings. From there those who fail to attain Nibbāna fall into lower states of existence with the new expansion of the universe. It is said that some of them come down attracted by the beauty, smell and taste of the earth and gradually acquire gross bodies, due to the gradual increase of their greed, conceit and lust coupled with the diminishing abundance of the earth. It is at this stage that they form a contract of society.

The context of this sermon (in the *Aggañña Sutta*, D III 80–98, tr. DB, pp. 77 ff) shows that the Buddha intended to expose the falsity of the claim to superiority on the part of the Brahmins by going back into the historical origins of human beings. For in origin all human beings were alike and what later became caste or class distinctions were originally due to a division of or a differentiation into specific occupations on the part of human beings who were all "like unto themselves and not unlike" (*anaññesaṃ sadisānaṃ neva no asadisānaṃ*) (D III 80–98, tr. DB p. 93).

Two other themes run through the whole account. One is the fact of the gradual change and the evolution of the earth. At a certain stage of evolution, the earth was without vegetation or animal life and was like "the scum that forms on the surface of boiled milky rice that is cooling" (ibid., p. 82). Very much later "outgrowths" (*bhūmi-pappaṭaka*) like "mushrooms" (*ahicchattaka*) spring up and later still creepers (*badālatā*) and by the time settled human society has come into existence, there is a reference to animals, for some take to hunting (*luddācāra*). The other is a moral relativism "for what is reckoned immoral at one time is reckoned moral at another time" (D III 89). These changes in the moral condition of man are due partly to changes in human nature such as the gradual growth of greed, etc., and partly to changes in the physical and economic environment such as loss of abundance in nature and the lack of *lebensraum*.

It is at this critical stage of settled life that there is a contract of society. The description in the text reads as follows: "Come now, let us divide off the rice fields and set boundaries thereto! And so they divided off the rice and set up boundaries round it. Now some being of greedy disposition, watching over his own plot, stole another plot and made use of it. They took him and holding him fast said: Truly, good being, thou has, wrought evil in that, watching thine own plot, thou hast stolen another plot and made use of it. See, good being, that thou do not such a thing again! Ay, sirs, he replied. And a second time he did so. And yet a third. And again they took him and admonished him. Some smote him with the hand, some with clods, some with sticks. With such a beginning did stealing appear, and censure and lying and punishment became known" (DB, p. 88).

The contract of society,[41] however, proved inadequate to the task of ensuring property rights and securing just, efficient and deterrent punishment, which became necessary. It is, therefore, followed by a contract of government, described as follows: "Now those beings gathered themselves together, and bewailed these things, saying: From our evil deeds, sirs, becoming manifest, inasmuch as stealing, censure, lying, punishment, have become known, what if we were to select a certain being who should be wrathful when indignation is right, who should censure that which should rightly be censured and should banish him who deserves to be banished? But we will give him in return a proportion of rice.

41. Cp. "The theory of a contract of government really postulates, as a prior condition, the theory of a contract of society" (Barker, pp. xii, xiii).

Then those beings went to the being among them who was the most handsome, most charming, most attractive and most capable and said to him: Come now, good being, be indignant at that whereat one should rightly be indignant, censure that which should rightly be censured, banish him who deserves to be banished. And we will contribute thee a proportion of rice. And he consented, and did so, and they gave him a proportion of their rice. Chosen by the whole people is what is meant by *Mahāsammata* (the Great Elect); so the Great Elect was the first standing phrase to arise. Lord of the fields is what is meant by *Khattiya*; so *Khattiya* (lit. the holder of power, the Sovereign) was the next expression to arise. He brings happiness to others by Dhamma—is what is meant by Ruler (*rāja*); so this was the third standing phrase to arise" (DB, p. 88).

This account of the origin of society and the state is found in all schools of Buddhism and was widely known.[42] In all these versions the main themes reappear with minor and sometimes local variations.

In the earliest Mahāyānist version, for instance, found in *The Mahāvastu* (pp. 285–301), the changes are only in the words and phrases and not in the substance when compared with the version in the Pali Canon. Thus, where the Pali version speaking of the changing conceptions of morality in different epochs, speaks of "what is reckoned immoral" (*adhamma-sammataṃ*) at one time, the Sanskrit version in *The Mahāvastu* speaks of "what is reckoned immoral, irreligious and unlawful" (*adharma-sammataṃ ayajñasammataṃ ca avinayasammataṃ ca*) (ibid., p. 342) at one time.

What is emphasised in this theory is a democratic conception of the state and the law. The king is said to be the "Great Elect" because he is elected "by the people as a whole" (*mahājana-sammato*), as the Pali version puts it, and "by the great body of the people" as the Sanskrit version says. The king, likewise, is after the election merely a *primus inter pares* being "like unto themselves and not unlike" because of the equality of man despite the fact that the person so elected has a handsome and commanding personality. The king is of the people, is to act in the interests of and for the

42. Ghoshal, pp. 62–5, 66–8, 258–60, 337–38; Saletore, 1963, pp. 322–25; Vallee Poussin, pp. 203–06; Prasad, pp. 202–20; Lingat, pp. 284–87; Han, pp. 13–16; *Nīti-Nighaṇḍuva,* pp. 4–8.

people and for this task has been elected by the people. Āryadeva in his *Catuḥ Sataka* says that the king should not feel any pride because he is "the servant of the community" (*gaṇa-dāsa*), for whose services the people give in taxes one-sixth of their produce (*Catuḥ Śataka,* IV, 77). It is said in *the Jātakas* that "just as an aged father ought to be cared for by an able-bodied son, so too ought all the people to be protected by the king" (*The Jātaka,* III, p. 305).

In contrast to the Buddhist theory, the Brahmanical legal literature of the time posits the theory of the divinity of kings. Manu says that the king "is a great deity (*mahatī devatā*) in human form" (*Mānavadharmaśāstra,* VII, 8). The masses on the whole were led to believe in the divinity of kings.[43] However, in the *Śāntiparvan* of the *Mahābhārata* there are two theories put forward, the one contradicting the other. One of these is a compromise with the social contract theory and Prof. Basham describing the two along with the Buddhist theory, which he mentions first, says: "Midway we meet the king as a divinely appointed figure, but appointed by the will of the people and at their request; and finally, at the other extreme, the king is entirely divine and is inspired from on high without reference to the wishes of his subjects, in order to keep the people pious."[44]

While Buddhism conceived of the king as human, certain texts concede the fact that people believe royalty to be divine in classifying gods (*deva*) into three sorts, of which the first is "gods by convention" (*sammuti-devā*), namely kings and princes. A Theravāda work of the medieval period says that the first elected king must be a bodhisattva on the grounds that it was a position of eminence and must have been held by such a being but it would be a mistake to associate this concept with divinity for anyone can become a bodhisattva and such a being has to act with selfless devotion for the good of others. The closest that the Buddhist texts come to associating the king with the gods, which is not the same as

---

43. "In India the divinity of kings, however small their domain, has always been accepted by the masses. The banner of authority inspires awe, fear or admiration" (Gonda, p. 1.). Gonda, however, has failed to present the Buddhist point of view with any degree of accuracy.

44. "In the Buddhist story the king is merely the servant of the people, and is entitled to levy taxes only in return for fulfilling his task of protection" (Basham, p. 16).

ascribing divinity, especially considering the role of gods in the Buddhist theory of reality, is in the *Suvarṇaprabhāsottama Sūtra.* Here it is said that a king is styled a deva-putra or a "son of a god" because the gods decide who is to be born as a king before he is conceived but we cannot infer from this that the king's authority was divine in origin (cp. Ghoshal, pp. 261–62) since the whole of this particular chapter stresses the king's responsibilities and the author says that "whether the king be a man, god, spirit, devil or outcast he must suppress evil" (XII, 14) in his kingdom.

Secondly, the theory draws attention to the fact that the king becomes a legislative, judicial and executive authority by virtue of the fact that he represents the people and his actions have their implicit consent, so long as he fulfils his contract. Part of his contract consists in his administration of justice and the maintenance of law and order. The person chosen in addition to being handsome and having a commanding personality is said to be endowed with intelligence (*buddhisampanna*) and capable of reproving and recompensing people (*paṭibalo niggahapaggahaṃ kātuṃ*).[45] The Tibetan version found in the *Dulva* (III) mentions that, under the contract of society, some people warn the transgressor of property rights up to a third time, then arrest him and bring him before the people. The people let him off with a warning after which the transgressor brings up a counter-charge of arrest, whereupon the people let him off with a warning. This is evidently intended to show on the one hand the unsatisfactory nature of individual punishment and on the other the fact that the power to legislate, administer and execute the law is vested in the people but delegated to the king, so that justice may be impartial, effective and fair.

Another fact that may be noted is that the punishments mentioned are humane and confined to reproving, warning and banishment, with no mention of corporal or capital punishment on the part of the king, despite the fact that mutilation, torture and capital punishment were rife at the time. This is due to the Buddhist ethics of punishment. Punishment has to be in the best interests of the community but based on love and understanding of the criminal. It follows from this that punishment has to be primarily

---

45. *Visuddhimagga,* p. 419. The idea of recompense is found in the *Mahāvastu,* op. cit., p. 348.

reformatory and secondarily deterrent but never retributive or vindictive, despite the fact that the karmic consequences may appear to be retributive.

The *Jātaka* states that "at all times in the tradition of the democratically elected kings (*mahāsammatarājakula*) there was no greater punishment than that of beating, warning and banishment (*tāḷana-garahaṇa-pabbājana*); there was, indeed, no cutting off of hands and feet and execution (*hattha-pāda-cchedana-ghātana*) and these things came into existence afterwards during the times of cruel kings" (J-a IV 192). In the *Ratnāvalī*, which is a "discourse to a king" (*rāja-parikathā*) (p. 307), Nāgārjuna, the well-known Mahāyāna philosopher states the Buddhist attitude to the criminal: "You must punish them out of compassion and from a desire to turn them into worthy persons as you do as regards worthy sons; and you must not be moved by hatred or by the desire for material gain."[46] As a consequence of compassion, mercy should be shown to those who are punished, imprisoned or beaten in accordance with the law (*nyāyato*), prisoners should be well looked after,[47] no one should be imprisoned for life (*Ratnāvalī*, v. 33) and there should be no mutilation or execution of criminals, though banishment is permitted (v. 37).

This social contract theory of the origin of society and the state was propounded by the Buddha in a context in which he was trying to show two Brahmins who had entered the Order the falsity of the Brahmanical claims to the superiority of the Brahmins (cp. Vallée Poussin, pp. 319–20), on the basis of which they were accorded privileges and immunities in law. The Buddhists insisted on "the application of the absolute and universal standard of Buddhist ethics to the question of class privileges" (Ghoshal p. 349) based on a conception of the equality of man.

This conception is of importance for the doctrine of human rights and the notion of the equality of sovereign states, which is derivative from the notion of the equality of man. We would,

46. "The *Ratnāvalī* of Nāgārjuna," p. 436, v. 36: cp. "With your compassion, O King, you must always bend to righteousness the mind ... even of those who have committed terrible sins" (v. 31).

47. Ibid., v. 35: "Up to the time of their discharge let them enjoy a pleasant imprisonment and the comfort of barbers, baths, drinks, food, medicines and garments."

therefore, briefly outline the nature of this Buddhist doctrine.

While Buddhism recognizes that all beings in the cosmos have something in common by virtue of the fact that they are all subject to insecurity and suffering and at the same time have potentialities of attaining the very highest, human existence, which is said to be a rare thing (*dullabhaṃ manussattaṃ*), is considered to be of the greatest value. There is a conception of a common humanity embracing the whole earth. The people of the four classes (Basham, p. 6) or castes and people of "diverse races" (*nānājaccā*) are said to be equal. The Buddha says: "The facts being what they are, the people of all four classes (or castes) are absolutely equal (*samasamā*) and I do not see any difference between them at all in these respects" (M II 86).

This sense of equality will become clear if we briefly indicate the arguments used in the texts. Firstly, there is a biological argument used to show that man was a single species. The Buddha says in the *Vāseṭṭha Sutta* that, although there are different species among plants and animals, man constitutes one species, despite the minor observable differences in the nature of the hair, colour of the skin, shape of the head, etc. (Sn 116–19). Contrasting the different plant and animal species with the human species, the Buddha says: "Thus there are no characteristics indicating differences of species (*liṅgaṃ jātimayaṃ*) among human beings (*manussesu*) in the way in which there are such characteristics indicative of differences of species among the (several) species (*jātisu*) (of plants and animals)" (Sn 607). Secondly the anthropological argument, which we have met with above in the *Aggañña Sutta* traced the historical origins of class or caste to divisions of labour and occupational distinctions which arose with settled society "among beings who were like unto themselves and not unlike." The theory was intended to counter the Brahmanical claim that the fourfold class or caste structure of society was absolute and created by God from the very beginning of time. It followed from the Brahmanical theory that each person had certain hereditary functions to perform by virtue of his birth, called "one's own duties" (*svadharma*), and man was not free to choose his occupation. The Buddhist condemnation of this idea is seen where it is said that the Order of Recluses[48] (*samaṇā*) was formed by people

48. The Buddha himself belonged to this Order and was known as "the Recluse Gotama" (*Samaṇo Gotamo*).

from all the four occupational classes "despising (the concept of) their own duty" (*sakaṃ dhammaṃ garahamāno*) (D III 96).

Thirdly the sociological argument was intended to show that the fourfold class or caste structure was not universal since among the bordering states (*janapada*) of the Yona-Kāmbojas (i.e., in some Persian states adjoining the North-Western border of India), there were "only two classes" (*dve'va vaṇṇā*), namely the lords and the serfs, and this too was not rigid since "the lords sometimes became the serfs and the serfs lords" (M II 149).

Fourthly, the legal argument was to the effect that, to whatever caste or class a person belonged, he was held liable and punished for an infringement of the criminal law with the same type and degree of punishment (M II 88). This seems to depict a time or social setting different from what is presupposed in the Hindu civil and criminal law, which lays down different scales of punishment and reward for people of the four classes,[49] the punishments for the "lower" classes being harsher (Mookerji, p. 138; cp. *Āpastamba Dharmasūtra,* ii, 16–17, 27). Fifthly, the moral argument was that all were equally liable to karmic consequences (M II 86). Sixthly, the ethical argument maintained that all were capable of good and evil (D III 250–51) and none was to be treated as a means to an end "like beasts in a sacrifice" (*Jātakamālā*, p. 207). Lastly, the religious or spiritual argument was that all were capable of attaining salvation or spiritual development despite individual differences in their capacities, which had little relationship to the classes or castes to which they were born (M II 147).

Buddhist monks and nuns ignored caste and racial discrimination both within the Sangha and in their relationships with the laity and openly preached and practised the doctrine of the equality of man (Malalasekera & Jayatilleke, pp. 55ff). Aśvaghoṣa in his *Vajrasūci,* which is a polemic against caste and racialism, utilizes among others the arguments of the theists against them when he says: "You affirm that all men proceeded from the One, i.e., Brahmā (God)—how then can there be a fourfold insuperable division among them? If I have four sons by one wife, the four sons having one father and mother must be all essentially alike" (ibid., pp. 40–1).

---

49. Cp. "This Sacred Law lays down different scales of punishment and reward and different standards of conduct for the four classes because they are different species of beings ..." (Basham, p. 7).

The fatherhood of God does not necessarily lead to the concept of the brotherhood and equality of man. It may also be used to support an attitude of paternalism or even sheer inequality when it is used to justify caste, apartheid or racial discrimination.

Buddhism, therefore, upholds the equality of man in the sense that man's essential nature is the same whatever the individual differences due to heredity, environment or karmic factors may be. His basic needs, material, psychological and spiritual, are also fundamentally the same, although men may differ in their interests and capacities due to their divergent historical evolution, and could contribute in their own way by developing their talents to enrich the life of mankind. He therefore needs to be treated equally and afforded equal opportunities for developing his potentialities and serving mankind. Even the cosmic perspective is for the Buddhist democratic, for any man of his own free will may aspire to and attain the status of a Brahmā or Buddha. So the Buddhist conception of the equality of man allows for no chosen caste or class, chosen race, chosen creed or chosen individual.

Women were also considered to have similar potentialities to that of men. When King Pasenadi complained to the Buddha that his queen had given birth to a daughter his comment was:

> A woman child, O Lord of man, may prove even a better offspring than a male" (KS, p. iii).

Both men and women were equally capable of attaining Nirvana:

> And be it woman, be it man for whom such chariot doth wait, by that same car into Nibbāna's presence shall they come" (S I 5).

As Miss Horner says: "There seemed to have been no real doubt in his mind as to the equality of the powers of man and women" (Horner, p. 104). Both men and women joined the Sangha and their achievements as well as those of laymen and laywomen are listed on a footing of equality (A I 23–26). The initial reluctance on the part of the Buddha to admit women to the Sangha cannot be interpreted as being due to any belief on his part of the inferiority of women. Buddhism had to contend with an environment in which the people as a whole were full of prejudices and superstitions. A clear example of the compromises that Buddhism had to make in order to thrive in such an environment can be seen from the fact that, although a rule was laid down that monks need not bless people or each other with the words "May you live long!" (*jīva*) when they sneeze in their presence because this was not going to prolong their life, the rule had to be modified to exclude the public from the application of this rule because of public criticism, on the ground that as the Buddha said "the lay people were superstitious" (*gihī maṅgalika*) (Vin II 140).

The organization of the Sangha or the Community of monks and nuns interests us because of the importance attached to the value of the individual within the Community, the role of law in furthering the aims and objectives and the life of the Community, the fact that it was modelled on that of a democratic political state and the concept of the international Sangha, which has an analogy for the Buddhist conception of the international society.

The Sangha was established primarily to give the individual a training in the higher morality, in the cultivation of the higher mind by a process of self-analysis and meditation and in the development of the higher understanding. It is suggested that the person who enters the Sangha with such aims and aspirations would not find it difficult to observe the 150 odd rules or precepts (A I 230; cp. BD II, p. xiii). At the same time, the Community was to hand down the scriptures to posterity and preach the message of Buddhism throughout the world. Their relative isolation from secular society was not an end in itself. The Sangha was dependent on the laity for their material needs and in turn had to perform the duty of educating the public and giving them moral, spiritual and psychological guidance (D III 191) with the therapeutic aim of creating people with healthy minds.

Although the Sangha has been designated "a system of government formed by the Bhikkhus (monks), for the Bhikkhus and of the Bhikkhus" (De G., p. xv) and therefore a "democracy," it will be more correct to say that it was a democratic institution set up by the Buddha for the good of its members as well as of mankind so that it may continue to function on a democratic basis after his death. The Buddha says that the Dhamma or the Buddhist theory of knowledge, reality and ethics as well as the Vinaya or the Constitution and code of laws were to function in the role of the Teacher after his death (D II 154). When a question is raised as to how, in the absence of a refuge, there could be unity in the Buddhist

Community since the Buddha had not appointed a head and a successor to function in his place after his death, a disciple replies that they are not without a refuge, for the Dhamma was their refuge.[50] Such an idea was a novel one and was unknown to the political or religious organizations contemporary or prior to Buddhism (Dutt p. 116).

At first admission to the Sangha as well as the higher ordination was given by the Buddha himself and no legislation, it is said, was enacted since the Sangha consisted entirely of monks who had attained one of the four stages of moral and spiritual development (Vin III 10). It was only later whenever the occasion arose that rules were laid down "regulating the outward conduct of the Sangha" (Vin I, p. xiii). These were in the form of "rules of training or precepts" (*sikkhāpada*) voluntarily accepted as binding on themselves by the monks. But with the growth of missionary activity, the monks brought persons from various quarters (*nānādisā*) and from "different states" (*nānājanapadā*) for admission and ordination but, since this was troublesome for all of them, the Buddha requested that they may be admitted and ordained by the monks themselves by the repetition of a formula of refuge in the Buddha, Dhamma and Sangha (Vin I 22). Later when the rules or monastic laws were codified and the set of legally binding rules (*Pātimokkha*) was formally recited every fortnight (Dhirasekera, see Ch. VIII) at a formal meeting of each Sangha, admission and ordination took a more formal character. After a brief period of probation an experienced and capable monk of a particular Sangha proposed at a formal meeting of the Sangha that such and such a person be ordained by such and such a preceptor. The matter was placed before the assembly in the form of a formal motion which was read thrice and with none dissenting was deemed to have been unanimously passed. The jurisdiction of each Sangha extended only as far as its geographical boundaries or "territorial limits" (*sīmā*), which were strictly defined and this was another innovation of the Buddha (Ariyasena, p. 21). The concept of the "Sangha" appears to have been taken over from its political use for a democratic republican state (Jayaswal, pp. 33–55) and the idea of the territorial

---

50. M III 9; cp. Pande p. 330: "Buddha's institution of an Order without a supreme head was a revolutionary novelty in this respect."

limits of a state was known at this time (see later). These Sanghas extended beyond the limits of the national states (*janapada*) and there was constant intercourse between them. The singular word Sangha was used to denote all of them collectively and was designated "the Sangha of the four quarters, of the present and the future" (*āgatānāgatassa cātuddisassa saṅghassa*) (Vin II 147). They all abided by the same Dhamma and the same Vinaya, except for the fact that those rules which were proposed and adopted by one Sangha and having only a local relevance were not binding on another Sangha unless that Sangha decided to adopt them (Bhagvat, pp. 87–8).

Legislative, judiciary and executive powers are vested in the Sangha and the decisions of the Sangha, if necessary, were enforced by the secular state (Dutt, p. 145), which did not in any way interfere with the authority or jurisdiction of the Sangha over its members (Bhagvat, p. v). Four formal sources of law (*cattāro mahāpadesa*) (D II 123–25) are mentioned, namely the claim that a rule was promulgated (i) by the Buddha, (ii) by a unitary Sangha, (iii) by a body of learned doctors of the law (*vinaya-dhara*) and (iv) by a single learned doctor of the law, but it is said that such claims should be confirmed and the laws adopted only if they are in conformity with the spirit of the existing Dhamma and Vinaya.

In the codified form the penal offences are listed according to the gravity of the type of offence. Within each type the specific offences are stated in a definite form. First, there is a case history leading to the promulgation of the law along with the penalty for its infringement. This is followed by a legal definition of the terms and phrases of the law as formulated. Then we find further casehistories in which the penalty for breaking the rule or some lighter penalty is incurred and finally a list of cases which entail no offence against the rule. In general, motive and intention are necessary but not sufficient conditions for the violation of the law but the degree of offence depends on the degree to which the physical act is carried out. There is no offence if there was no motive and intention involved but if the physical act has been committed there may be penalties for a lesser offence such as negligence. The punishments are humane and consist of confession, asking for forgiveness even from a layman, placing on probation, deprivation of rights, privileges or property, banishment to another Sangha (compulsory change of residence), public proclamation, social boycott (*brahmadaṇḍa*) and expulsion (Bhagvat, pp. 103–11).

We have already shown that the Sangha was a juristic person having a legal personality of its own. Property was owned by the Sangha and it was possible to commit offences against it. The importance of the Sangha could be gauged by the fact that the Buddha himself when he was given a robe wanted it to be given to the Sangha. Yet except for the expulsions of the persons who were deemed no longer to be in communion (*asaṃvāsa*) with the Sangha, the interests of the individual are not sacrificed for the interests of the Community.

Every individual is given a fair trial and the principles of natural or moral justice, as conceived in Buddhism, are scrupulously observed. Formal acts of the Sangha could be either disciplinary or non-disciplinary (Dutt, pp. 136–38; cp. Bhagvat, pp. 96 ff). These acts are deemed invalid if the constitutional procedure laid down is violated. One of the first requirements of a disciplinary act is that the trial should be held in the presence of the accused, who has to be confronted with four things: "Monks, a formal act of guidance or banishment or reconciliation or suspension should not be carried out against monks without confrontation" (Vin II 73). Confrontation (*sammukha-vinaya*) involved four things, viz., (i) confrontation with the full assembly authorized to conduct the trial, the consent of those entitled to send their consent having been obtained and no member of the assembly being challenged by any other, (ii) and (iii) confrontation with the letter and spirit (i.e., moral basis) of the law under which the accused is charged along with an account of the procedure for settlement as laid down by the Teacher (Buddha) and (iv) confrontation with the complainant (Vin II 93–94). Secondly, an attempt should be made to secure a confession by reminding the person of the circumstances in which the offence was committed, as far as the assembly was aware. This is followed by the formal charge, after which the trial proceeds, giving a full opportunity for the accused to present his case and point of view. The formal nature of the proceedings may be seen from the following description:

> "And thus, monks, should it be carried out. First, the monks who are followers of Paṇḍuka and Lohitaka should be reproved; having reproved them, they should be made to remember;

> having helped them remember, they should be charged with an offence; having charged them with an offence, the Sangha should be informed by an experienced, competent monk, saying: 'Honoured sirs, let the Sangha listen to me. … If it seems right to the Sangha, the Sangha may carry out a (formal) act of censure against the monks who are followers of Paṇḍuka and Lohitaka. This is the motion (*ñatti*). … A (formal) act of censure … is being carried out by the Sangha. It is pleasing to the Sangha … therefore it is silent. Thus do I understand it."
>
> "Monks, if it is possessed of three qualities a (formal) act of censure comes to be not legally valid and not disciplinarily valid and one that is hard to settle: (that is to say) if it is carried out without the confrontation, if it is carried out without interrogation, and if it is carried out without the acknowledgement (of the accused). … Further, if it is possessed of these three qualities a (formal) act of censure comes to be … hard to settle: (that is to say) if it is carried out without having reproved him, if it is carried out without having made him remember, if it is carried out without charging him with an offence" (Vin II 2–3. BD, V, pp. 2–4).

The logically possible attitudes that the accused may take up (which are not merely that of "guilty" or "not guilty") and the procedure to be followed in each case is precisely laid down (Dutt, pp. 136–38).

Another democratic feature of the trial is that it is carried out by members who were fully ordained (*upasampanna*) after their periods of probation and who had one vote each. Voting was always on a resolution formally moved once or thrice according to the importance of the matter under discussion. A special officer called the "arbitrator" (*salāka-gahāpaka*—lit. vote-taker), noted for his impartiality, knowledge of the law and voting procedure was unanimously elected by a formal resolution of the assembly to take charge of the voting. Every attempt was made to secure unanimity in the voting but if a division appeared inevitable, the motion was put to the house and decided by the majority vote (*yebhuyyasika*). Voting could be by secret ballot (*gūḷhaka*), open ballot (*vivaṭaka*) or by "the whispering method" (*sakaṇṇa-jappaka*). The arbitrator, who enjoyed the confidence of the whole assembly, had the privilege of deciding how the voting should be conducted and also had the right to advise members on matters legal and moral, if he feared a breach of justice. From the powers given to the arbitrator we can see that it was not merely the consent of the majority that mattered but the conformity of the decision with the spirit and the letter of the law, i.e., with Dhamma and Vinaya. If in the course of the proceedings the assembly felt that it was difficult to come to a decision, they could appoint a committee (*ubbāhikā*) to settle the matter but if the committee found it impossible to decide the matter delegated to it, they had to report back to the Sangha, who could then settle it by a vote of the majority (Dutt, pp. 129 ff).

Buddhism has been acquainted with a republican democratic form of government at its inception and with the monarchical form in its origin and development. Yet in its social contract theory it conceives of the state as democratic. While the Buddhist doctrine of impermanence applies to society and the state as well, there is little doubt that Buddhism considers democracy to be the best form of government, while any form of government would be good to the extent to which it follows the principles of the Buddhist political Dhamma. But the democracy that Buddhism favours is not merely a rule of the majority but the rule of the majority in conformity with the Dhamma or the principles of righteousness which the majority is acquainted with and tries to live by.

While the state was in origin not divine but democratic and the Sangha was set up on democratic foundations, the concept of the Sangha appears to have been derived from that of a democratic political state. The Buddha on one occasion (D II 72–77) speaks very appreciatively of the Vajjian state. He says that as long as the Vajjians meet frequently and regularly, assemble, disperse and conduct their business in unity, make no revolutionary changes in their statutes and administer justice in accordance with their ancient Vajjian constitution (*porāṇa vajjidhamma*), look after the aged, respect their women, revere their religious monuments and protect the rights of holy men to free access in their realm, their prosperity was to be expected and not their decline.

The reference to the "ancient Vajjian constitution" is interesting because of the comment made in the Commentary, which reads as follows: "As for the 'ancient Vajjian constitution' it is said that when a thief was brought before the ancient Vajjian rulers, they handed him over to the judicial officers (*vinicchaya-mahāmatta*). They investigated the facts and if they thought that he was not a thief they released him but if they suspected that he was a thief, they handed him over to the magistrates (*vohārika*) without making any statement themselves. They in turn investigated matters and if they thought he was not a thief they released him but if they suspected that he was a thief they made him over to the justices (*sutta-dhara*) ... they in turn to a panel of eight judges (*aṭṭha-kulika*) ... they in turn to the president, who investigated the case and if he thought that he was not a thief, released him but if he was convinced that he was a thief called for the book of precedents (*paveṇi-potthaka*). There it is written down that such and such was the punishment for such and such an offence. The president, thereupon, compared his offence with those and ordered the appropriate punishment. Thus the people who abided by the ancient Vajjian constitution had no grouse (against the state) because justice was done in accordance with the ancient tradition and they felt that if anyone was at fault it was themselves and not the officials (of the state). And as a result they performed their tasks with a sense of responsibility. In this way the state prospered" (D-a 519).

This reveals an ancient system of justice in which the accused was presumed innocent until his guilt was proved beyond doubt and the Vajjian Dhamma, which in this context means the "Constitution," guaranteed this.

As we have seen from the analogy of the Sangha, Buddhism would recognise the need to distinguish the corporate personality of the state in a conventional legal sense from the individual but at the same time it would not hold that the state existed apart from the individuals comprising it. A reductivist analysis in terms of the actions of individuals would, therefore, be possible when we speak of the actions of states. A Hegelian conception of the state would be unthinkable from the Buddhist point of view.

At the same time (as we have stated earlier) according to the Buddhist ethic a person acting in his official capacity would not be exempt from the moral responsibility of his acts, although the moral value of the act would have to be differently assessed owing to the difference in motivation. One is still responsible for the evil done "for the sake of the state in the course of the performance of one's duties" (*rañño rājakaraṇīyaṃ hetu*).

Apart from the concept of a state as a Sangha or a political organisation, the concept of a sovereign state is known to the early Buddhist texts. There is a reference to two kings who confront each other on a road in neutral territory beyond "the territorial limits" (*paccanta-sīmā*) (J-a II 3) of their respective states. They cannot pass each other for the road is too narrow and the question as to which of the two should have precedence is raised. In this context, a comparison is made of the two states in respect of (i) the extent of the territory of the state (*rajja-parimāṇa*), (ii) the military strength (*bala*), (iii) the economic resources (*dhana*), (iv) the prestige (*yasa*) and (v) the qualities of the king such as nobility of birth, age, etc. It is said that each king was "a sovereign ruler (*sāmi*) of a state with a perimeter (*parimāṇa*)[51] of three hundred leagues" (*tiyojanasatikassa rajjassa sāmino*). Here the state is conceived of as having people resident within certain territorial limits, having a sovereign ruler and a government with economic and military resources to defend its sovereignty.

Later in Kauṭilya's *Arthaśāstra* the constituents of sovereignty are said to be seven in number, viz., "the sovereign ruler (Skr. *svāmi* = Pali *sāmi*), the ministers (*amātya*), the realm or territory (*janapada*), the fortifications (*durga*), the treasury (*kośa*), the army and police (*daṇḍa*) and the allies (*mitra*)" (*Arthaśāstra*, VI, I). This concept of the constituents of sovereignty is accepted in the Buddhist texts as well (e.g. *Buddhacarita,* Part I, Ch. II, v. 45).

According to the Buddhist theory of social contract, sovereignty in the sense of the supreme legislative power is vested in the people as a whole. We saw that, according to the Tibetan version of the theory, when the person who stole was arrested and brought before the people and charged with theft, it was the people who tried him and warned him for breaking the contract of society. Subsequently, when the thief made a counter-charge of arrest it was the people who in turn warned those who arrested him presumably for arresting a fellow-being without having the authority to do so. It is

---

51. The extent of the territory was evidently measured by the length of the boundary. *Parimāṇa* (*pari* and √ *mā*, to measure = perimeter); cp. "At the basis of international law lies the notion that a state occupies a definite part of the surface of the earth, within which it normally exercises, subject to the limitations imposed by international law, jurisdiction over persons and things to the exclusion of the jurisdiction of other states" (Brierly, 1963, p. 162).

then that in the interests of fairer and more efficient justice, among others, that the people elect a king and delegate their legislative, judiciary and executive functions to him. The king now becomes the symbol (*paññāṇaṃ,* S I 41) of sovereignty, which is vested in the people as a whole and is ultimately derived from Dhamma. According to Buddhist conceptions, therefore, the constituents of sovereignty enumerate the factors necessary in a monarchical state representing the interests of the people to guarantee its integrity. The reference to "allies" is possibly an admission that a sovereign state needs recognition by others.

It is said that if the king or the state fails to fulfil the contract, which is presumed to exist, and instead of providing good government betrays the trust that the people have placed on the king or state, the people have a right to depose the king or overthrow the state. In such a situation, the Bodhisattva addresses the people as follows:

> Let town and country folk assembled all give ear
> Lo! Water is ablaze. From safety cometh fear.
> The plundered realm may well of king and priest complain
> Henceforth protect yourselves. Your refuge proves your bane.
>
> (*The Jātaka*, III, 305)

This is the only place in the texts in which the use of violence seems to be considered a necessary evil for the overthrow of a corrupt regime. Such violence or the incitation to violence is, however, incompatible with the life of a monk and would be unnecessary in a democratic state (which is upheld as the ideal in Buddhism) since such a state would provide mechanisms for securing justice by non-violent means. There is no doubt that on the analogy of the principles recommended for inter-state relations (see Section V), non-violent resistance would be considered to be superior to the use of violence to overthrow even a corrupt tyrannical government.

It is interesting to note, however, that the statement, *attaguttā viharatha*, i.e., "it is up to you to protect yourselves," is here used in a clearly political context. For the statement is made to the "general public" (*mahājana*), who are told that the king is defrauding the people when he ought to protect them and work for their welfare. The commentarial explanation reads as follows: "Although there should be security from the king, he has become a source of danger. 'It is up to you to protect yourselves' means that now you are without protection, so instead of permitting yourselves to be destroyed become your own protectors and guard the wealth and the corn that belongs to you" (J-a III 513–14).

It was the duty of the first king to maintain law and order for the welfare of the people as a whole. However, it was also said that the king "brings happiness to others by means of Dhamma." Part of what is meant here by Dhamma is the administration of justice which involved the punishment of those deserving punishment and the compensation of those deserving compensation. But the duty of the king is not limited to that of preserving law and order in the Buddhist texts. Positively encouraging and contributing to the economic and spiritual welfare of the subjects is also considered to be an important duty of the state.

While the Brahmins often advised kings to perform religious sacrifices to secure such welfare, the Buddha's advice was that such measures were a waste of time and resources. Prosperity and the elimination of crime were possible only by ensuring full employment and thereby developing the economy. This, for example, is the advice of the Buddha on one occasion:

> The king's country, sirs, is harassed and harried. There are dacoits abroad who pillage the villages and townships, and who make the roads unsafe. Were the king, so long as that is so, to levy a fresh tax, verily his majesty will be acting wrongly. But, perchance, his majesty might think: "I'll soon put a stop to these scoundrels' game by degradation and banishment, and fines and bonds and death!" But their licence cannot be satisfactorily put a stop to so. The remnant left unpunished would still go on harassing the realm. Now there is one method to adopt to put a thorough end to this disorder. Whosoever there be in the king's realm who devote themselves to keeping cattle and the farm, to them let his majesty the king give food and seed-corn. Whosoever there be in the king's realm who devote themselves to trade, to them let his majesty the king give capital. Whosoever there be in the king's realm who devote themselves to government service, to them let his majesty the king give wages and food. Then those men, following each his own business,

> will no longer harass the realm; the king's revenue will go up; the country will be quiet and at peace; and the populace, pleased with one another and happy, dancing their children in their arms, will dwell with open doors" (DB, pp. 175–176).

That planning the economic welfare was part of the functions of the king or state is clearly emphasised where it is shown that things went wrong because the king "provided for the righteous protection and security of his subjects but neglected the economy" (lit. "did not provide means for wealth to accrue to those devoid of wealth") (*Dhammikaṃ rakkhāvaraṇaguttiṃ saṃvidahi, no ca kho adhanānaṃ dhanaṃ anuppādāsi*) (D III 65).

The Mahāyāna texts develop this same philosophy of the state. Parodying the *Arthaśāstra* of Kauṭilya, it is said that the predominant aim of the king or state should be to maximize the economy and conserve the gains but do so within the bounds of righteousness: "The world rests on two foundations: the acquisition of wealth not acquired and the conservation of what is gained. Therefore to acquire wealth and conserve what you have gained make firm efforts within the bounds of righteousness" (*The Mahāvastu*, I, p. 230).

While the Machiavellian realism of the *Arthaśāstra,* which greatly influenced the Hindu philosophy of the state, was based on the theme that "might or what was expedient was right," the Buddhist political philosophy was founded on the principle that "the wheel of might turns in dependence on the wheel of righteousness" (*balacakraṃ hi niśrāya dharmacakraṃ pravartate*). The constant reminder is that the pursuit of the doctrine of narrow political expediency is inexpedient in the long run, both in one's internal policy as well as in one's inter-state relations.

The way of righteousness in politics required as far as the state's internal policy was concerned that the king and his officials act out of selflessness (*pariccāga*), rectitude (*ajjava*), mercy (*akkodha, avihiṃsā, maddava*) and political wisdom (*prajñābala*), whose importance is greatly stressed. One list of the ten qualities of rulers (*dasarājadhamma*) mentions the above characteristics, while another list of the same name mentions the several duties of rulers towards different classes of persons and beings, including citizens in the town and country, religious teachers as well as "birds and beasts" (*miga-pakkhīsu*). The four bases of service, which everyone especially officials were to cultivate, were charitable-mindedness (*dāna*), affability (*piyavacana*), work for the welfare of society (*atthacariyā*) and a sense of equal respect for all (*samānattatā*) (PED, s.v.).

While the state has duties to its citizens, the *Sigālovāda Sutta* outlines the duties that citizens have to each other, the performance of which the state has to encourage by education and other means in pursuing welfare-state policies. The reciprocal duties of parents and children, teachers and pupils, husbands and wives, friends and acquaintances, employers and employees, religious teachers and their followers are outlined. While their content would need to be modified in changed social circumstances, the basic values they embody still remain valid. Thus, employees are to be treated as follows: "By assigning them work according to their strength; by supplying them with food and wages; by tending them in sickness; by sharing with them unusual delicacies; by granting them leave at times" (DB III). Commenting on the question of leave, the Commentary says, "i.e., constant relaxation so that they need not work all day, and special leave with extra food and adornment for festivals, etc." A husband's duties to his wife are stated by the Buddha as follows: "In five ways should a wife ... be ministered to by her husband: by respect, by courtesy, by faithfulness, by handing over authority to her (*issariya-vossaggena*), by providing her with adornment" (DB III). While rights imply obligations, obligations need not necessarily confer rights but we can see from modern labour legislation that what was deemed to be an obligation for a Buddhist employer from the 6th century BCE is today a matter of a right of the employee.

While the notion of contract runs through the mutual relationships, the basic obligation of each person to attain Nibbāna requires the cultivation of selflessness, love and understanding and all these duties, including the duties of the state, should ultimately be performed in such a spirit of service (*cāga*), love (*mettā*) and understanding (*paññā*). Of these qualities, the importance of *mettā* is greatly stressed. This word appears to have been coined by the Buddhists to replace the negative term *ahiṃsā* (which also has a positive content).[52] It is an abstract noun meaning "friendliness" formed from the word "*mitra*" meaning "friend." It is man-centred

52. One of the best studies of the meaning of the term *ahiṃsā* is to be found in Tāhtinen, p. 192.

and positive in connotation. The nature of a kingdom founded on the "strength of friendliness" (*maitri-bala*) is illustrated in the *Maitrībala Jātaka* of the Mahayanist work, the *Jātakamālā* (Ch. VIII).

The political philosophy outlined above is pregnant with the conception of human rights, although the Buddhist approach is more humanistic than legalistic. Buddhism would not place much faith in mere legislation from above since according to Buddhist conceptions laws must not only be based on what is morally right but also have the consent and approval of the people. The ideal state is a democracy working for the material and spiritual welfare of the people, guaranteeing political, religious and personal freedoms as well as economic security with full employment.

While Western classical liberal thought held that the maintenance of law and order was the only legitimate function of the state, Friedmann analyses the functions of the modern state as that of (i) protector, (ii) dispenser of social services, (iii) industrial manager, (iv) economic controller and (v) arbitrator (Friedmann, pp. 387 ff). Buddhism has stressed the first, second and fourth of these functions, the other two being in fact corollaries of the first and the fourth. But in addition to them Buddhism considers it a duty of the state to promote righteousness. This it should do by education (without indoctrination), by basing its policies on the principles of righteousness or Dhamma and by affording opportunities for the moral and spiritual life, which will add new dimensions to human personality and help base human relations on the foundations of selfless service, love and understanding rather than that of the fear of the sanctions of the law. It was in pursuance of this political Dhamma that the Buddhist emperor Asoka adopted welfare-state policies. Max Weber has made the following observations about them: "For the first time in the Hindu culture area there appeared the idea of the 'welfare state,' of the 'general good' (the promotion of which Asoka regarded as the duty of the king). 'Welfare' was, however, partially understood to mean spiritual welfare (as the furtherance of salvation chances), and partially to mean charities, but also rational and economic action. The tremendous irrigation works of the Ceylonese kings, however ... were thoroughly fiscal in orientation, i.e., intended to augment the number of taxpayers and the capacity to pay taxes, not to implement welfare politics." Weber erred in failing to see that Asoka was merely trying to follow the political Dhamma of Buddhism as is evident from his inscriptions themselves. He is also mistaken in thinking that the Ceylonese kings were not imbued with the same ideals from the same source. A quotation from a speech attributed to one of these kings in the early written history of Ceylon gives us a glimpse of the ideas which inspired them: "Truly in such a country not even a little water that comes from the rain must flow into the ocean without being made useful to man. … For a life of enjoyment of what one possesses, without having cared for the welfare of the people, in no wise befits one like myself" (*The Cūḷavaṃsa*, p. 277).

Buddhism contends that it is only such a political philosophy or ideology which will provide a firm basis for a rule of law, which reflects the rule of righteousness or Dhamma, within the state. The sovereignty of the state derives from the will and consent of the people in whose interests it shall govern but sovereignty is subject to the rule of righteousness, for "the wheel of power has to turn in dependence on the wheel of righteousness" (*balacakraṃ hi niśrāya Dharmacakraṃ pravartate*).

Buddhism and International Law

As we tried to show in some of the previous chapters of this series, there emerged with Buddhism the concept of a common good, embracing the whole world and conceived as both material and spiritual welfare. Going along with this idea there was the concept of a common humanity transcending national and racial barriers. All men were equal (*samasamā*). Man belonged to one species. Owing to his oneness, of which he is ignorant, national pride (*avaññatti*), racial feelings (*jātivitakkā*) and national feelings (*janapada-vitakkā*) were ultimately mistaken notions. The social contract theory of the origin of society, the state and law made it obligatory for the state to serve the best interests of the people and of mankind. Sovereignty was vested in the people and was limited by the requirement to conform to the rule of righteousness or Dhamma. The conception of the welfare state was conceived for the first time.

There also came into being the concept of an "international Sangha of the present and the future" (*āgatānāgata cātuddisa saṅgha*). This organization modelled on a political Sangha and set up on democratic foundations survived the death of its founder, its monastic laws being designed to make it last for a long time. The relations between the Sanghas, which transcended the boundaries of states, were regulated by laws and all the Sanghas abided by a common philosophy known as the Dhamma and a common constitution and code of laws called the Vinaya. This Vinaya was considered binding on all the Sanghas for 100 years after the death of the Buddha, after which they split into two great schools, the conservative and the liberal.

One of the most important Buddhist concepts relevant to international law and international relations is that of the world-ruler or world-statesman (*rājā cakkavatti*), both because of the inherent value of the ideas centred around him and also because of the messianic expectations it has given rise to (Sarkisyanz, 1965, Chs. XIV, XV; cp. Sarkisyanz, 1955). He is depicted as a person like the Buddha who comes at a time, when the conditions are historically ripe, and just as much as the Buddha secures primarily the spiritual welfare of mankind, the world-ruler was to work primarily for the material welfare of mankind. And just as much as the Buddha sets up democratic Sanghas without appointing a supreme head to function on the basis of a common philosophy and constitution, the world-ruler is supposed to set up an ideal government in his kingdom, which is followed by a series of such governments having similar political philosophies and constitutions throughout the world, forming a network or basis of an international political order which is to ensure the peace and prosperity of mankind for a long time to come.

Unlike, however, the moral and spiritual teachings of the earliest scriptures, which are plain and matter of fact with little or no mythological accretions, the ideas about the world-ruler are partly enshrouded in myth but the mystical accretions can be easily dispensed with, leaving a conception of society and the state consistent with the naturalistic and causal conceptions we meet with elsewhere in Buddhism.

According to Buddhist conceptions, society like every other institution or process was a changing complex, changing in accordance with certain causal factors. The static conception of society, which prevailed at the time, was based on the idea that there was an eternal fourfold hereditary class or caste order in society divinely ordained. The Buddha opposed this by presenting a dynamic evolutionary conception of society. The Buddhist account of genesis, as we have seen, presents such an account of society and shows how what later became caste or class divisions arose from a division of functions in settled society at a certain stage of social evolution, which necessitated such occupational divisions, the recognition of property rights, the law and the guardians of law. It was the economic factor such as the growing demand for land and its produce, which made it necessary to institute private property and eventually to safeguard the rights to such property.

From the accounts given of the causes of social change we find an important place given to the economic and the ideological factors. "The world," it is said, "is ruled by ideas" (*cittena loko nīyate*). In a myth about the possible future of society, the causal factors affecting social change are well illustrated. Here it is stated that, with the maldistribution of goods, there is likely to be economic inequality, resulting in a division of the world into the rich and the poor or the haves and have-nots. Due to the failure to meet each others' demands, tension and organized violence springs up between the two factions and there is a gradual loss of values in human society. This reaches a climax in a catastrophic war in which the greater part of humanity is likely to be destroyed. The remnant who manage to survive learn a bitter lesson from history and proceed to build the Just Society on firm moral and economic foundations. The text reads as follows:

> "Thus from goods not accruing to those devoid of goods, poverty becomes rampant. From poverty being rampant, stealing becomes rampant ... violence ... killing ... lying ... slander ... sexual misconduct ... abusive and idle talk ... covetousness and ill-will ... false view of life ... wanton greed and perverted lust ... till finally filial and religious piety and lack of regard for authority. ... Among such humans the ten immoral courses of conduct will flourish excessively; there will be no word for "moral" among such humans—far less any moral agent. Among such humans it is to them who lack filial and religious piety and show no respect for authority that homage and praise will be given. The world will fall into promiscuity ... keen enmity will become the rule, keen ill-will, keen animosity, passionate thoughts even of killing ... in a father towards his child and a child towards his father. ... Among such humans there will arise a war of seven days, during which

> they will look on each other as wild beasts. Dangerous weapons will come into their hands and they, regarding each other as beasts, will deprive each other of life. ... But to those to whom it would have occurred, "Let us not slay each other"—they would betake themselves to dens of grass or dens in the jungle, or holes in trees, or river fastnesses, or mountain clefts, and subsist on roots and fruits of the jungle. And they will do so for those seven days. And at the end of those seven days, coming forth from dens and fastnesses and mountain clefts, they will embrace each other, and be of one accord comforting one another and saying: Hail, O mortal, that thou livest still! Then it will occur to those beings that it was only because they had gotten into evil ways that they had this heavy loss of kin. They will then decide, "Let us, therefore, now do good" ... So they will practise these virtues ... and they increase in length of life, in comeliness and prosperity. ... Among such humans there will be only three kinds of disease—unfulfilled wishes, natural hunger and decay. Among such humans, this India (v.l. this world) will be mighty and prosperous, populous and with plenty of food and having numerous villages, towns and cities" (D III 70–75).

All things and institutions in the cosmos are causally conditioned, according to Buddhism, and the above passage illustrates the impact of man's material economic environment on his life and on society. Man's economic inequalities cause tension and instability in human society and lead to a loss of values, belief in which is essential for a just social order. Man whose inner nature is essentially good eventually comes to regard his fellow beings as beasts, descending into a Hobbesian state of nature while being in society, in utter disregard of law. Economic inequalities on the one hand promote racial pride (*avaññatti*) and on the other create resentment, which offends the principle of "equal respect for all" (*samānattatā* or *isotimia*). The erroneous belief that the path to happiness lies in the continued gratification without restraint of the desire for sensuous pleasures (*kāma-taṇhā*), the desire for self-centred pursuits (*bhava-taṇhā*) and the aggressive impulses (*vibhava-taṇhā*) leads to blind indulgence unaware of the operation of the principle of diminishing returns, which operates in the mere gratificatory quest for happiness, resulting in mental instability, tension and boredom.

These desires in turn promote the rationalisations or the belief in ideologies, which are only partially true and are based only on partial conceptions of justice. For man is "conditioned by his desires to hold on to ideologies" (*taṇhā paccayā diṭṭhūpādānaṃ*) (see EBTK, p. 430). While his economic condition tends to make him accept or reject certain ideologies, these ideologies in turn tend to make him act in certain ways. For "a man's creed, be it true or false, is the motive which induces him to actions corresponding with it. For people show the tenets of their belief by their words and actions, since their purposes comply with the line of conduct, prescribed by their creed" (*Jātakamālā*, p. 215).

While man's actions are conditioned by economics and ideology, it is important not to forget the fact that man's actions are not determined by them. For according to the Buddha man's actions are not determined either in a natural (*sabhāvavāda*) or a theistic sense (*issara-kata*), so that what happens is not due to economic determinism or God's will. During the time of the Buddha it was generally believed that this age was the Kali Yuga or one of corruption and decline but the Buddha counters this fatalistic view by calling this "the fortunate age" (*bhaddakappa*) of opportunity in which an Enlightened One has been born (D II 2). In the earliest texts, "predictions" are given about the future in the form of logically probable optimistic and pessimistic possibilities and it is suggested that man should try to make the optimistic possibilities real. One's self is one's own master (*attā hi attano nātho*); man is the master of his fate.

Although in certain things optimistic possibilities have been realised, as for instance in the preservation of the texts for posterity, there is a grave danger that unless man can change his nature for better rather than worse and see the world anew, there is a likelihood of the pessimistic possibilities about the future of human society becoming realities, if the Buddhist account of reality is basically correct.

The passage quoted above is also intended to show that the world-ruler is born like the Buddha at a period in history when as a result of the lessons of history man has realised his supreme folly and longs for a just international social and political order. It is said that such a world-ruler "admonishes the world girdled by the oceans." In this same Mahāyāna Sūtra there is a chapter on the "science of government" (*rāja-śāstra*), which is said to "promote the welfare of all beings" (*sarvahitaṃkara*) and which emphasises the fact that it is part of the duty of the king "to make unrighteousness subside, as one who prevents evil and establishes beings on the righteous path" (*Suvarṇaprabhāsottama Sūtra*, p. 135). The work expresses the hope that it may circulate in India (the world?) for the good and happiness of beings so that all the kings of the world being delighted with it may rule their realms in such a way that "the world would be peaceful (*kṣema*), prosperous and beautiful and that all over the world all beings would become happy" (ibid. p. 100). What is meant is that, if the political philosophy of Buddhism is made the philosophy of each state, there would be international peace and prosperity.

There are two important facts about such a world-ruler and it is here that Buddhism makes an altogether new contribution in the history of Indian political thought. One is that such a ruler is able to extend his authority "over the whole earth girdled by the oceans without the rod or the sword through the victory of Dhamma" (*imaṃ paṭhaviṃ sāgarapariyantaṃ adaṇḍena asatthena dhammena abhivijiya*) (D III 59). The other is that such a world-ruler, as the Buddha says, sets up "a kingless authority" (*arājaka-cakka,* A I 109).[53] When the question is asked, "Who, then, is the king of the world-ruler" (*Ko pana ... rañño cakkavattissa rājā?*), the reply given is that "it is the Dhamma" (*Dhammo bhikkhū ti*). This conception of a non-ruler state based on a political philosophy and constitution, it is said, "came to be the object of derision of political writers of Hindu India. The ideal of this legislation was that Law was to be taken as the ruler and there should be no man-ruler. The basis of the state was considered to be mutual agreement or social contract between the citizens. This was extreme democracy, almost Tolstoian in ideal" (Jayaswal, quoted in Saletore, 1963, p. 139).

The idea is that the world-statesman sets up a state on the basis of the Dhamma, which in this context means "a political philosophy and constitution founded on the principles of righteousness." And just as much as the Buddha sets up an international Sangha, based on the Dhamma, its religious philosophy and the Vinaya, the constitution and code of laws, the world-statesman sets up an

53. I am taking the v.l., which alone makes sense of the question subsequently asked.

international order in which all states have a common political philosophy and constitution.

Although the idea of such a democratic state based on a constitution has been ridiculed by some Hindu writers unfamiliar with the nature and value of such democratic states, the idea hardly needs to be defended today, when India is a democratic state with a constitution modelled on a Lockean political philosophy borrowed from the West. The only comment that needs to be made is that the Buddhist conception is neither Tolstoian nor Utopian.

The essentials of the political Dhamma of the world-ruler needs to be briefly outlined here. It is said that he first sets up a model state in his own country. When this is done, the idea proves to be infective and his prestige spreads in the four quarters of the world, a fact which is symbolically expressed by the movement of the "wheel"—the symbol of his political Dhamma and sovereignty—in all four quarters of the world. What is meant is that other nations establish similar states with similar political philosophies and constitutions and acknowledge his leadership. This is the essence of the concept as it appears in the Buddhist texts of both schools of thought.

Such a ruler, it is said, honours, reveres, faithfully abides by and is led by the righteous political philosophy embodying the ethical principles of the Ten Virtues (*dasa-kusala-kammapatha-dhamma*) (D-a 849) and based on the need of the state to work for the good of the people with selflessness, love and understanding imparting impartial justice and promoting both material and spiritual welfare on the principle of the equality of man.

The essence of the duties and functions of such a state is summed up in the form of four requirements. First, the necessity to provide "righteous care, ward and protection to all citizens, including the people of all professional classes, religious teachers and the army" (D III 61). This care and protection are to be extended to "birds and beasts" (*miga-pakkhīsu*) as well.[12] Here "care" (*rakkha*) is explained as treating all subjects "with forgiveness, tolerance, friendliness and kindness" (*khantiyā avihiṃsāya mettācittatā anuddayatā*) (D-a 850) on the principle that the state which "cares for its subjects would safeguard its own interests" (*paraṃ rakkhanto attānaṃ rakkhati ti* ...) (ibid.); "ward" (*āvaraṇa*) is defined as the insurance of property such as housing, clothing, etc., and "protection" (*gutti*) as protection against loss and other calamities (*upaddava*). It comes to mean not only the safeguarding of persons, property and human rights but the institution of welfare services such as the care of the aged, the sick,[54] etc. It is interesting to note that freedom of movement and the freedom to propagate their faith should not be limited to Buddhist monks but that this should be extended to all "recluses and brahmins" (*samaṇa-brāhmaṇā*), a term used to denote all religious teachers and philosophers, some of whom were materialists and sceptics and included those propounding Machiavellian theories of the state. As for "birds and beasts," it is said that even "birds and beasts must be made to feel secure by granting them freedom from fear (*abhaya-dāna*)" (D-a 850).

Secondly, the state has to ensure that there is no crime: "let not a person in the state act unrighteously" (*mā ca te vijite adhamma-karo pavattittha*) (D III 61). This according to Buddhist conceptions has to be done both by removing the social causes of crime, mainly inequalities of wealth and unemployment, as well as the psychological by a training in values which has to be both theoretical and practical (psychological).

Thirdly, the state has to ensure that there is no unemployment or lack of wealth amongst any of its citizens: "The state should adopt means for the acquisition of wealth on the part of those devoid of wealth" (*ye ca vijite adhanā assu tesañ ca dhanam-anuppādajjeyyāsi*) (D III 61) so that there is an abundance of goods in the country and the people "can enjoy these goods as much as they like" (*yathābhuttaṃ ca bhuñjatha*) (D III 62).

Fourthly, all state policies must be based on righteous principles and therefore it behoves the state to act in consultation with enlightened religious teachers and philosophers in determining policy (D III 61).

All this is written in the language and idiom of India of the sixth century BCE and if it is translated into modern terms it means that the state must be an enlightened democratic welfare state guaranteeing freedom and economic security and promoting

54. It was this principle, for example, which inspired some kings of Buddhist countries to establish such institutions (cp. *Cūḷavaṃsa*, I, p. 128): "In Pulatthinagara he built of his great pity a large hall for the sick, and likewise in Padāvi, each provided with a maintenance village, also halls for cripples and the blind in different places."

righteousness. Since the state had to perform these functions and duties, it follows that the philosophy and constitution or the Dharma-Vinaya[55] of the state must embody these rights.

Before we examine the implications of this political philosophy for international law, it may be worthwhile briefly to indicate the impact it has had on the countries influenced by Buddhist culture. While the religious teachings of the Buddha seeped down to the masses modifying and eliminating existing cults and superstitions, the influence of the political philosophy, on the whole, remained peripheral and sporadic but decisively felt. There are several reasons for this. The Buddha himself did not think that religious teachers living on the alms of the faithful should devote their life to the study of a science like that of "the science of power" (*khatta-vijjā*) (D I 9). The Mahāyānist work, *Śikṣāsamuccaya,* says: "It has been stated by the Blessed One in the *Jñānavaipulya Sūtra* that only sciences which are useful should be studied and that sciences which are useless (for the religious life) should be avoided, viz.,... political science (and law) (*daṇḍa-nīti-śāstrāṇi*)" (*sikṣāsamuccaya of Śāntideva*).

The political philosophy in the Buddhist texts themselves was taught, no doubt, to kings and the laity and this in turn leads to changes in the policies of the kings as in the case of Emperor Asoka in India and several such Buddhist kings of South-East Asian countries in particular, not to speak of China and Japan. But no sustained study of existing non-Buddhist political ideologies appears to have been made in order to criticise them and show their specific defects and replace them with the Buddhist. Another reason was the widespread influence of Manu's *Dharmaśāstra* in South-East Asian Theravāda countries and of Confucianism in the Mahāyāna countries. Likewise, it was not the primary task of the Buddha or the monks to set up an ideal political order, which concerns the laity and kings and the world-ruler, if and when he comes. Quite apart from all this, the Buddhist political philosophy with its social contract theory had politically dangerous potentialities for kings, who would have preferred to believe that they had a divine right to rule. It was, therefore, left to the lay Buddhist movement in the modern world in Asia at a critical period in the history of Buddhism and human

---

55. In a political context, the king is told: "Betake yourself to the Dharma, its Vinaya makes its road a lovely one" (*Jātakamālā*, p. 154).

civilisation to espouse the cause of this political philosophy of righteousness (Ling, Benz 1966).

Although Buddhism failed to replace the Hindu theory of the state, there is reason to think, as we have already shown, that it modified the extremist recommendations of the *Arthaśāstra* of Kauṭilya. The impact of Buddhism on Asoka, who has been called "the greatest of kings" (Wells, p. 95) by a historian is too well known for any detailed comment. Inspired by the Buddhist ideals of social equality and mercy he remarks in one of his edicts that "it is most desirable that there should be absolute equality for all in all legal proceedings and in the punishment awarded and I have ordered from now the respite of three days to those on whom punishment has already been passed ..." (Murti & Aiyaṅgar, p. 95). Asoka's welfare-state policies and his political Dhamma can be directly traced to the Buddhist texts. A careful perusal of the ancient Sinhalese history as recorded in the *Mahāvaṃsa* and *Cūḷavaṃsā* also shows the extent to which this same political Dhamma has influenced them.

In Ceylon "the laws of Manu" (*Manu-nīti*) appear to have been followed in the late medieval period (Geiger, p. 132) but earlier there is some evidence of Buddhist principles of justice being observed. In the third century CE king Tissa, the lawgiver (*vohārika*), is said to have been the "first in this country to make a law to set aside (bodily) injury (as penalty)" (*Mahāvaṃsa*, p. 258). This seems to have been set aside at least four centuries later but there is again a mention of the abolition of capital punishment and life imprisonment in the thirteenth century under King Parākramabāhu II (Geiger, p. 145). Paraṇavitana conjectures on inscriptional evidence that there may be some substance in the observations of Solinus Polyhistor about ancient Ceylon in the first century CE when he says that "the sovereign was strictly elective and not hereditary. Moreover, though the monarch had ever so great a regard for justice, he was never permitted singly to dispense it but in all matters of life and death was assisted by a council of 40, and there was finally a court of appeal presided over by 70 judges."[56] But we have firm evidence only for saying that there is a reference to

56. Quoted from Pridam, *Ceylon and Its Dependencies*, I, p. 8 in Paranavitana, "Two Royal Titles of the Early Sinhalese," *J.R.A.S.*, 1936, p. 458.

a "President of a Court of Justice," judicial precedents written down in books and a code of laws compiled in the thirteenth century (Geiger, p. 146). However, the belief that the king was the servant of the people as stated in the theory of social contract seems to have weighed in the minds of the people when they rebelled against a king who violated the right of sanctuary claimed by Buddhist monasteries whereupon it is said that the king had to obtain the pardon of the monks in question (Geiger, p. 148).

In Thailand we again meet with the impact of the Buddhist philosophy of the state in the inscriptions of King Ram Khamhaeng of the thirteenth century.[57] In this inscription, which is said to be the first in which the Thai language is used and is conjecturally claimed to be "the first Thai constitution," there is a mention of welfare-state policies, impartial and easy justice in an atmosphere of freedom: "The ruler taxes not his people on travel. They drive oxen to trade; they ride horses to sell. Whoever wants to deal in elephants, deals ... When common folk of the realm, nobles or princes fall out, are at dispute, the king sifts the truth and decides in honesty. He sides not with the stealer, favours not the converter. He covets no man's rice, envies no man for his wealth. ... Over there, at the gateway a bell is hung. If any folk of the realm seek court with their king, having anguish in the stomach, grievance in the heart, there is no difficulty. Go ring the bell hung there. ... Whoever wants to play, plays. Whoever wants to laugh, laughs. Whoever wants to sing, sings. ... He nurtures the children of the land, folk of the realm, equally in accordance with the law."[58] There is also a mention of the humane treatment of prisoners of war in this inscription: "When foes, enemies are captured, he kills them not, nor beats them."[59] It is not clear whether the motivation was partly the social contract theory when the "free Tai kingdoms" in which there were no slaves were established in Siam.[60] Similarly, in Tibet as we pointed out

57. The original stele is presently preserved in the National Museum, Thailand.
58. "Father King Ram Khamhaeng's Stone Inscriptions" in *Bangkok World of Sunday*, 29 May 1966, pp. 4–5—A new translation by M. R. Seni Pramoj (former Prime Minister). See also, Wood, pp. 54–58.
59. Ibid., p. 4; cp. ibid., p. 60: "King T'ammarāja was a lover of peace ... he won less renown by his military prowess than by the humanity with which he treated his prisoners. ..."

earlier King Sron-btsan-sgam-po introduced writing and promulgated laws to harmonise with the Ten Virtues of Buddhism. In Cambodia, "the Khmer king Jayavarman II attempted at the close of the twelfth century CE to enforce ideas similar to those once expounded by Asoka" (Thapar, p. 216) without having even heard of the example of Asoka.

In Burma, we find that the monks adapted the *Dharmaśāstra* (textbook of law) of Manu, the divine lawgiver of India, changing the form of the law in accordance with the principles of Buddhist legislation. The obligation for the observance of law is traced to the social contract theory and Manu is represented as the legal adviser of Mahā-sammata (see Ch. IV), the Great Elect who was the first king chosen by the people. Manu is here "a counsellor well versed in the art of administering justice" (Lingat, 1949, p. 296). Hindu theology is discarded: "The Wagaru (Code) mentions neither Brahma, nor the Vedas, nor the sacrificial fire, nor any point denoting influence of the Brahmins and of civil and religious institutions peculiar to Brahmanical India" (Forchhammer, p. 58). The law is simplified and rationalised by being "reduced to a collection of elementary rules judiciously selected so as to be easily understood" (Lingat, 1949, p. 292). There is equality before the law. Marriage is not a sacrament but a contract which can be dissolved by mutual agreement or even by the will of either party and remarriage of women is allowed and unlike in Hindu law both husband and wife have coparcenary rights to the common property.[61] Corporal punishments are done away with, the criminal being considered to be in need of reformation, and losses are compensated in proportion to the loss: "The Buddhist lawgivers ... based their theory of punishment on the doctrine of karma, which, as will be remembered, takes the past and future existences of the individual into account. With this doctrine in mind they thought out a system of legislation to defend the social order without inflicting what must be, according to their theory, unjustified, useless, illogical penalties. Their system is described as a civil code punishing every crime or offence with fines, demanding compensation which is

60. Ibid., p. 49; see also pp. 67–8, 71–2.

61. Lingat, op. cit., p. 293. The author's statement that "it is impossible to see in this book anything else than a Mon code" on these grounds is to close one's eyes to the traditions of Buddhist law.

proportionate to the amount of damage occasioned by one person to another" (Bode, pp. 85–6). Under the circumstances it is not surprising if the Buddhist text *Mohavicchedanī* (by Rājabala-kyaw-din, 1832), without mentioning Manu, "presents the substance of the Manu *Dhammathats* as the law preached by the Buddha" (Eliot, 1957, p. 67). It may also be noted that the judge was morally (*karma*) to blame if his judgements were not impartial and in accordance with the letter and spirit of the law but also to some extent, the responsibility was his if, whatever the law, he inflicted capital punishment since this was incompatible with mercy towards the criminal. The relations between the Sangha and the state and the duty of the state to consult enlightened religious teachers in regard to right and wrong when carrying out the policies of the state is seen from the comment of the author in respect of the Burmese experience: "The Sangha has always shown a laudable reserve in interfering directly with politics, but in former times the king's private chaplain was a councillor of importance and occasionally matters involving both politics and religion were submitted to a chapter of the Order" (Eliot, 1957, p. 71).

In the early history of Buddhism in China, the idealized figure of Asoka made some impression on the Chinese cultured public since it was consonant with "the traditional Chinese ideal of the saintly ruler who by following the rules of the ancient sages brings peace and prosperity to his people, so that finally the whole world comes to submit to his authority" (Zürcher, p. 277). The Buddhist conception of punishment also influenced some kings for "in 65 CE the emperor Ming decreed that all those who had committed crimes warranting the death penalty were to be given an opportunity to redeem their punishment" (ibid., p. 27). But there is an instance where the Buddhist monks appear to have compromised and taught that "the rogues and irresponsibles whom the civilising influence does not reform, when they are guilty of a crime, they must be put to death" (ibid., pp. 121–22).

In Japan, as we have already seen, it was the Buddhist Prince Shōtoku who is credited with having drafted the "Constitution of Japan" in which he lays down certain principles of legal and social justice that have to be observed and speaks with reverence of the Buddha, Dhamma and Sangha as "the final ideal of all living beings and the ultimate foundation of all nations." The articles are of both

Confucian and Buddhist origin and stress the importance of harmony (1), impartial justice (5), punishment and reward to deter the wicked and encourage the good (6), a division of labour based on individual capacities (7), sincerity (9), tolerance of individual differences (10), recompense strictly in accordance with desert (11), selfless friendly co-operation (15), while the seventeenth and the last emphasises the importance of democratic discussion before decisions on important matters are arrived at: "No problem must be decided arbitrarily but it must be freely discussed with one another. As a trivial matter is unimportant it is not always necessary to confer with others. Only on the occasion of determining a great matter, there is anxiety about any unexpected failure owing to an arbitrary decision. Consequently if we hold a mutual discussion, our opinions can be reasonable without fail."[62]

Shōtoku's conviction that "the Three Treasures" would be the ultimate foundation of all nations finds an echo in the great religious teacher Nichiren, who in the thirteenth century foresaw a time when righteousness shall be the basis of the philosophy of all states: "When the Law of kings shall merge with the Law of Buddha, when ruler and people alike shall hold to the Three Great Mysteries ... Thus the moral law will be established in actual life" (Eliot, 1935, p. 430).

The impact of the political teachings of Buddhism was thus felt throughout Asia but the influence was sporadic and not sustained. According to the theory, sovereignty is vested with the people, who delegate the legislative, judiciary and executive functions to a person or body of persons who represent the government. In a monarchy the king is the symbol (*paññāṇa*) of sovereignty and in a democracy Parliament. But the sovereign is subject to the requirement of acting in conformity with Dhamma and therefore the power of the sovereign national state both as regards internal and foreign policy is not absolute. The sovereignty of the state is not absolute because of the necessity to conform to the principles of righteousness or Dhamma. A state is an entity only in a conventional legal sense, for in reality it is an artificial barrier separating man from man. Therefore "thinking in terms of one's own state" (*janapada-vitakka*)

---

62. "Jushichijō Kempō," in *Mochizuki Bukkō Dai-jiten,* ed. Mochizuki (S.), revised ed., Ill, Kyoto, Japan, 2257*b*-2258*c*.

in matters affecting humanity has been deemed in Buddhism to be a subtle defilement (*upakkilesa*) of the mind, as we have shown earlier. It is also an ethical principle of Buddhism that "a person who seeks to find happiness for himself by inflicting pain on others gets entangled in the meshes of hatred and does not escape from the consequences of hatred" (Dhp 291). What is true in this respect of one person is also true of a group of persons and, therefore, of a state. It follows from this that aggression against other states is not justified in one's own self-interest in the long run. For as Brierly points out "any state that attempted to pursue a policy of more coercion against others would unite the others against itself" (Brierly, 1958, p. 45). Since it is one's fellow human beings who are members of other states, it is not only an obligation to coexist without hostility but to co-operate with them as well for the good of mankind.

This is an idea that has been particularly stressed by Mahāyāna Buddhism in its ethical and religious literature. This has been aptly expressed by Archbishop Shodo Okano, the present leader of the Kodo Kyodan Buddhist movement in Japan, who says in the preface of one of his books that "in 1945 with the conclusion of the Second World War a democratic Japan was born, and this led to the appearance of Buddhist movements suited to the new age" (*An Introduction to Kodo Kyodan Buddhism,* Yokohama, 1967, p. i). In his own words:

> In order for one man to be saved it is necessary that the whole society be saved. This is the Mahayana ideal, and it was clearly expressed in a parable given by Saicho, the founder of Japanese Tendai Buddhism. He stated that 'the single mesh of a net cannot catch a bird." ... What Saicho's parable teaches is that we, as the individual meshes, must not follow personal inclinations alone, but that as part of the vast net of society we must work for the welfare of the whole. Unless we think and act in terms of a bigger world, personal happiness can never be ours.
>
> When we understand all the meshes of a net—you and I, father and mother, brother and sister, friends and neighbours—are equally important in the fabric of life, we come to respect all peoples and wish for their well-being in the same way as we wish for our own happiness.

In the contemporary world we realise that life would be impossible, if we should lead a completely isolated existence; a single grain of rice, a single piece of clothing, a single rooftop, are the products of countless men in both the past and present worlds. Thus, it is clear that the happiness of one man involves the happiness of the whole world, and the unhappiness of one man contributes to the unhappiness of the whole world. This is especially true of the modern world which has shrunk in size due to the progress in communication and transportation. A hydrogen bomb experiment in one corner of the world has dreadful implications for all mankind.

If we seek individual happiness, then we must consider the happiness of the rest of mankind. This means that the quest for personal fulfilment must be based upon Mahayana Buddhism, for this is the teaching par excellence which advocates that the salvation of the single man does not exist apart from total salvation. The final summary of Sakyamuni Buddha's fifty years of missionary life is contained in the Lotus Sūtra, which reveals the path of salvation for the individual and society" (Ibid., pp. 26–8).

The principles on which inter-state relations should be based by any particular state have, therefore, been stated briefly as follows in the *Mahāvastu*: "O king, do not foster hostility towards neighbouring kings. Whosoever hates will be repaid with hatred by his foes. Cultivate ties of friendship (*mitrabandhaṃ ca kuryāsi*) with neighbouring kings, O mighty lord, for other peoples honour kings who are steadfast in friendship" (p. 229). Thus, non-aggression and co-operation in international relations is recommended on the grounds of expediency, though at the same time it is an obligation following from the observance of Dhamma just as much as in internal policy the pursuit of Dhamma was both obligatory and expedient: "Sire, the realm of that king who rules unrighteously becomes weakened and rent on all sides. But, sire, the realm of the king who rules righteously is strong, prosperous, nourishing and populous" (p. 231).

The question as to how the state is to meet aggression is also dealt with. There is a mention of two policies, each of which has been pursued by kings who "rule their realm with righteousness" (*dhammena rajjaṃ kārento*). These principles are enunciated in a *Jātaka* story called "Advice to Kings" (*rājovāda*). The kings of two states meet on neutral territory on a road outside their territorial limits and the question of precedence is raised since it was necessary for one to give way. Since it is discovered that "the extent of the territory" (*rajjaparimāṇa*) of their states, their military strength, economic resources, prestige and the nobility of birth and age of the kings are the same; there is a discussion about their policies. At this stage the policy of one is summed up as follows: "He meets force with force, mildness with mildness; he wins over the good with good and conquers the evil with evil." The policy of the other is stated in the following words: "He conquers wrath with kindness, evil with good, greed with charity and falsehood with truth" (J-a II 3–4). This latter policy is acknowledged as the superior and the former voluntarily gives way.

The former is the policy of meeting aggression with military force in a war of self-defence without indulging in aggression oneself. It will be noted that Buddhism does not talk about a Utopian state and recommends a policy of disbanding the army. Despite the peace, security and prosperity of his kingdom, the king keeps his army satisfied and in a state of military preparedness and good humour. For "a prince who, having no reason to complain of his army, fails to honour it and disregards his military men who have shown their valour on the battlefield and are renowned for their skill in the science of arms, surely such a king will be deserted by victory in battle" (*Jātakamālā*, p. 217). The army is there purely to meet aggression but it is said that the chances are that such a friendly, just, powerful, prosperous and wisely run state is unlikely to be attacked: "On friendliness does his strength rest, not on his motley-bannered army, which he keeps only to comply with custom. He knows no anger, nor does he speak harsh words. He protects his land in the proper manner. Righteousness is the rule of his actions, not political wisdom, that base science" (ibid., p. 59).

Despite the fact that a wise king may counter aggression with military force, passive resistance is held up as the better ideal. The *Mahāsīlava Jātaka* (No. 52, J-a I 132) states that "when the king of Kosala appeared outside the city and sent a message to the king bidding him either yield up the kingdom or give battle" (which, incidentally shows that it was the custom at the time to make a formal declaration of war before fighting) (Viswanatha, pp. 128–30).

the reply was: "I fight not ... let him seize my kingdom." Finally after a series of events when the king is in a position to overpower his foe but does not, it is said that "the usurper's heart was moved within him" and the king regains his kingdom. The moral of the story is that passive resistance would be eventually triumphant if tried.

The Buddhist conception of Dhamma as well as the Buddhist attitude to war differs from that of the classical texts of Hinduism such as the *Dharmaśāstras*, the *Arthaśāstra* and even the *Śāntiparvan* of the *Mahābhārata*. In them we breathe a different atmosphere from what we find in the Buddhist texts. Following the martial tradition of the Aryan conquest of India reflected in the stories of the "imperial conquests" (*digvijaya*) of the Rgvedic war-god Indra, the *Arthaśāstra* holds out the ideal of imperial domination by conquest. There is a dynamic conception of the varying military strengths of any "circle of states" (*maṇḍala*) and the sixfold policy recommended is based on it. It is clear from the policy that peace is only a temporary expedient for a state that feels that it is not strong enough to defeat another state: "Whoever is inferior to another shall make peace with him; whoever is superior in power shall wage war; whoever thinks, 'No enemy can hurt me, nor am I strong enough to destroy my enemy,' shall observe neutrality; whoever is possessed of necessary means shall march against his enemy; whoever is devoid of necessary strength to defend himself shall seek the protection of another; whoever thinks that help is necessary to work out an end shall make peace with one and wage war with another. Such is the aspect of the six forms of policy" (*Kauṭilya's Arthaśāstra,* p. 293). This is not the doctrine of maintaining a balance of power to keep the peace. It follows from this *maṇḍala* theory that only a state which was reputed to be stronger than any other could escape attack and it is on this principle that the Buddhist recommendation referred to above was made. The Dharma (Hindu) of a king requir him to wage war for "conquering in battle" was one of the duties of a king[63] and engaging in a war of aggression is even counted a meritorious deed:

63. *The Mahābhārata*, VIII, *Śāntiparvan,* Part I, p. 210; cp. "A king whose power has been consolidated and who is confident of his own strength should assail a neighbour that is weaker than himself but never one who is stronger" (p. 214).

"Gifts, study and sacrifices bring prosperity to kings. Therefore, a king who desires to acquire religious merit should engage in battle" (*The Mahābhārata*, p. 135). And the Commentary explains: "For without battle he cannot extend his kingdom and acquire wealth to give away and meet the expenses of sacrifices" (ibid., p. 135, fn). The Gītā teaches that if a soldier "fights with selfless motive (and the psychological possibility of this many people would be inclined to doubt) he incurs no sin, whereas if he fights with selfish motives he would still stand to profit either by the gain and honour on earth or by the glory in heaven."[64]

The Buddha's attitude to war is an antithesis of the above. The Buddha intervened on one occasion in a war between the Śākyas and Koliyas, which was to be waged on the question of the right to the use of the waters of the river Rohini, which flowed between their territory. He settled the issue by peaceful means and in the course of it commented: "Why on account of some water of little worth would you destroy the invaluable lives of these soldiers" (J-a V 412–14; cp. Chapter 22 "*Buddhism and Peace*,"). Human lives are more precious than the spoils of war. Commenting on a war between two kings on another occasion he says: "Victory arouses enmity and the defeated live in sorrow" (S I 83). Wars result only in further wars: "The victor obtains for himself a vanquisher" (S I 85). While the Epic tradition held that "the warrior who falls in the battleground while fighting attains heaven" (*Mahābhārata*, *Udyogaparvan*, XXXII, 65). and while the Gītā taught that "if slain (in battle) you will go to heaven," the Buddha tells a warrior-chief in connection with this traditional belief that a person who exerted himself in battle with the thought of exterminating his foes is born in a hapless condition after death (S IV 308–09). A man is not absolved from moral responsibility for killing on the score that "he was carrying out the duties of the state" (*rañño rājakaraṇīyaṃ kātabbaṃ*) (M II 186). The Buddha condemned not only "the slave-trade" (*satta-vaṇijjā = manussa-vikkaya*) but also "the manufacture and sale of weapons of war" (*sattha-vaṇijjā*) as a mode of livelihood unsuitable for the Buddhist layman (A III 208).

---

64. See Ch. 19 "Some Aspects of the Bhagavad-Gīta and Buddhist Ethics," above; cp. Bhagavadgītā, II, 31, III, 30, VIII, 7, II, 38, II, 2, II, 3, II, 5, II, 34, XI, 33, II, 37.

In a later Commentary it is said that the Śākyas as the followers and relatives of the Buddha had the reputation of not killing their enemies (*asattughātaka*) and it is said that in a war they did not shoot to kill, although they were skilled archers, but only to put the enemy to flight (Dhp-a I, p. 358). Whatever the historicity of this claim may be it seems likely that the humanitarian ethics of Buddhism affected the conduct of war. In a Sinhalese work of the ninth century[65] there is a reference to a custom prevailing at the time of not putting to death in battle a person who "bites a straw."[66] This is explained as revealing an important principle followed in the conduct of war in ancient times, namely of not fighting with a person who is "biting a straw" in the battlefield as a sign of defeat. There is a similar reference in a book entitled "The War with the Portuguese" (*Paraṅgihaṭana*) in the seventeenth century[67] to the same custom. The *Mahāvaṃsa* records that King Duṭṭhagāmaṇī decided to fight with King Eḷāra himself (p. 175).

These are ancient customs recorded in the *Śāntiparvan* of the *Mahābhārata* and the above references indicate that they were followed in the course of battle. The relevant passages read as follows:

> It is laid down that a king should fight one that is a king. One that is not a king should never strike one that is a king ...
>
> An enemy should not be deceived by unfair means. Nor should he be wounded mortally. ... A soldier must not put on armour for fighting a soldier unclad in mail. One should fight one and abandon the opponent when the latter becomes disabled. If the enemy comes clad in mail, his opponents should also put on mail. ... If the enemy fights aided by deceit, he should be met with the aid of deceit. If, on the other hand, he fights fairly, he should be resisted with fair means. One should not on horseback proceed against a car-warrior. ... When an antagonist has fallen into distress, he should not be struck; nor should one that has been frightened, nor one that has been vanquished. Neither poisoned nor barbed arrows should be

65. *Dhampiyā-aṭuvā-gäṭapadaya,* see C. E. Godakumbura, *Sinhalese Literature,* Colombo 1955, p. 31.
66. Hettiaratchi D. E., *Vesaturu Dā Sannē,* Colombo 1950, p. 17.
67. C. E. Godakumbura, op. cit., pp. 232–34.

> used. These are the weapons of the wicked. One should fight righteously without yielding to wrath or desiring to slay. A weak or wounded man should not be slain, or one whose weapon has been broken; or one that has fallen into distress; or one whose bow-string has been cut; or one that has lost his vehicle. A wounded opponent should either be sent to his own home, or if brought to the victor's quarters, should have his wounds attended to by skilful surgeons. When in consequence of a war between righteous kings, a righteous warrior falls into distress (his wounds should be attended to and) when cured he should be set at liberty. This is an eternal duty. Manu himself, the son of God (Brahman) has said that battles should be fought fairly. … If a soldier whose duty it is to fight righteously wins a victory by unrighteous means, he becomes sinful. …
>
> Bhishma said—"A king should never desire to subjugate the earth by unrighteous means, even if such subjugation were to make him the sovereign of the whole earth …" (*The Mahābhārata*, pp. 217–20).

Viswanatha remarks that "there could not have been much fair fighting on either side" (p. 13) in Rgvedic times. If so, these customs would have come into vogue later and it seems likely that the Buddhist ethos helped to establish these customs, at least.

The effect that Buddhism had on the foreign policy of Emperor Asoka is clearly seen from his statements in the inscriptions. He gives up war as an instrument of policy at the height of his power because he felt remorse at the sufferings caused by war. In his own words:

> When he had been consecrated eight years the Beloved of the gods, the king Piyadassi, conquered Kāliṅga. A hundred and fifty thousand people were deported, a hundred thousand were killed and many times that number perished. Afterwards, now that Kāliṅga was annexed, the Beloved of the gods very earnestly practised *Dhamma,* desired *Dhamma,* and taught *Dhamma.* On conquering Kāliṅga the Beloved of the gods felt remorse, for, when an independent country is conquered, the slaughter, death, and deportation of the people are extremely grievous to the Beloved of the gods, and weighs heavily on his mind. What is even more deplorable to the Beloved of the gods

> is that those who dwell there, whether brahmans, śramaṇas, or those of other sects, or householders who show obedience to their superiors, obedience to mother and father, obedience to their teachers and behave well and devotedly towards their friends, acquaintances, colleagues, relatives, slaves and servants—all suffer violence, murder and separation from their loved ones. Even those who are fortunate to have escaped, and whose love is undiminished (by the brutalizing effect of war), suffer from the misfortunes of their friends, acquaintances, colleagues and relatives. This participation of all men in suffering weighs heavily on the mind of the Beloved of the gods. ... Today if a hundredth or thousandth part of those people who were killed or died or were deported when Kāliṅga was annexed were to suffer similarly, it would weigh heavily on the mind of the Beloved of the gods. The Beloved of the gods believes that one who does wrong should be forgiven as far as it is possible to forgive him. ... For the Beloved of the gods wishes that all beings should be unharmed, self-controlled, calm in mind, and gentle. The Beloved of the gods considers victory by Dhamma to be the foremost victory. And moreover the Beloved of the gods has gained this victory on all his frontiers to a distance of six hundred *yojanas* (i.e., about 1500 miles), where reigns the Greek king named Antiochus, and beyond the realm of that Antiochus in the lands of the four kings named Ptolemy, Antigonus, Magas, and Alexander; and in the south over the Coḷas and Pāṇḍyas as far as Ceylon ... everywhere the people follow the Beloved of the god's instructions in Dhamma ... What is obtained by this is victory everywhere, and everywhere victory is pleasant. ... This inscription of Dhamma has been engraved so that any sons or great grandsons that I may have should not think of gaining new conquests, and in whatever victories they may gain should be satisfied with patience and light punishment. They should only consider conquest by Dhamma to be a true conquest, and delight in *Dhamma* should be their whole delight, for this is of value in both this world and the next (Thapar, pp. 255–57).

It has been said that the concept of Dharma-vijaya is found in the *Arthaśāstra* (XII, I; cp. Dikshitar, pp. 128–30) but as Barua has shown the Brahmanical Dharma-vijaya was undoubtedly a conquest by the sword. Asoka rightly characterized it as a milder method of conquest where forbearance (*kṣānti*) and light punishment (*laghu-daṇḍatā*) were to be practised and preferred. The Buddhist Dhamma-vijaya was to be achieved, on the other hand, "without the employment of the sword or armed force" (*adaṇḍena asatthena*) .... (see Barua, 1955). Besides, it is clear from the above passage that the Dhamma referred to can only be the Buddhist Dhamma for historical reasons since it is to propagate this Dhamma that Asoka sent missionaries to the countries mentioned.

There have been no wars of aggression waged by Buddhists on religious grounds against others or amongst themselves. Monks were forbidden to have more than the minimum to do with armies,[68] and there has been no struggle for power between the Sangha and the state. Ho Shang-chih argued in 435 CE in order to prove the practical value of Buddhism that "it is well known that the numerous smaller and greater Buddhist countries in the West have always peacefully lived together without encroachment" (Zürcher, p. 264). The *Cūḷavaṃsa* says that "between the countries of Laṅkā (Ceylon) and Rāmañña (Burma) there had never been a dissension since they were inhabited by people who held the true faith" (*Cūḷavaṃsa*, II, pp. 64–5). But this occurs as a preamble to explain that the envoys sent on one occasion (twelfth century) were not treated with the customary courtesies and in fact were maltreated and that as a result the king had recourse to war. Here again the influence of the Buddhist political philosophy has only been sporadic and not sustained. We can cite in contrast to the above that "when Ayutia was the capital of Siam, the Siamese fought with the Burmese twenty-four times" (Thein, pp. 124–96). Prof. Mukherjee has conjectured on the basis of some statistics that "wars are far less frequent in the historical East than in the West" (Mukherjee, p. 25) but accurate comparisons are difficult. Yet there is little doubt that Buddhism succeeded to some extent in curbing the desire for conquest on the part of some kings at least, despite the widespread influence of the political theories of the *Arthaśāstra,* according to which all states are in a state of nature and war is the prerogative of

---

68. Horner, 1967, p. 3. On the basis of Buddhist tolerance, see Phra Khantipālo, 1964.

the strong and peace the obligation of the weak.

Asian states have had diplomatic relations with each other on a footing of equality from the earliest times. Some of these have been with the West. (Saletore, 1958). Dr Hultzsch concludes from one of the inscriptions of Asoka that he "maintained ambassadors not only in the frontier states ... but the foreign courts named in section Q, viz., those of the five Greek kings, the Coḷas, and Pāṇḍyas and the island of Ceylon. Similarly, Dionysius may have been the ambassador of Ptolemy II Philadelphus of Egypt at Asoka's court" (Hultzsch, pp. xxxv, xli). Pliny gives an account of Sinhalese envoys sent to Rome in the reign of Emperor Claudius (or Augustus?) and says that "the king particularly admired the Romans and their emperor as men possessed of an unheard-of love of justice" (Sastri, p. 50). Some of the missions seem to have been sent for cultural reasons. Ibn Shahriyar writes in his *Ajaib Al-hind* (*circa* 953 CE): "When the peoples of Ceylon... came to know of the Prophet of Islam's message, they selected an able person from among themselves and sent him to Arabia to get information at first hand" (Imam, S. A., "Ceylon-Arab Relations," in *The Ceylon Observer,* 30 May 1965).

Wang Gungwu has given a list of clearly dated missions to China sent between 400 to 960 CE by India and South-East Asian countries and of them eleven are from Ceylon and two from a South Indian state, the Pallava kingdom of Kāñci (Gungwu, pp. 120 ff).

The earliest historically recorded mission to China from Ceylon was in 395 CE to the court of Emperor Hsiao-wu, which Dr Zürcher has called "a remarkable happening known from various independent sources and of unquestionable historicity."[69] In 426 and 429 CE Sinhalese nuns arrived in Nankin and in 434 CE women were ordained as nuns in China for the first time. Treaties have been signed, alliances made and the principle of *pacta sunt servanda* followed. In the eleventh century, for example, there was "the creation of a Triple Alliance of Śrī Vijaya (in Malaya), Siṃhala (i.e., Ceylon)[70] and Pāṇḍya directed against the Coḷa from whose yoke they had been but recently liberated" (Paranavitana p. 50).

69. Zürcher, p. 152; cp. Paranavitana, p. 15: "According to some authorities, embassies from Ceylon are said to have been sent to China in CE 97, 120 and 121, but the accounts of these embassies cannot be taken definitely as referring to Ceylon."

70. "Ceylon" is derived from the Portuguese equivalent for "Siṃhala."

To sum up, according to the Buddhist theory of the state, sovereignty is subject to Dhamma, which in the Buddhist sense meant the obligation to promote the material and spiritual welfare of its subjects in internal policy. Therefore, it follows that the state has to guarantee human rights, extending security to birds and beasts as well. In foreign policy the state has an obligation not to commit aggression and to co-operate with other states for the common good of mankind. This policy of maximising material and spiritual welfare and acting in a spirit of friendly co-operation with other nations is held up not as a Utopian ideal but as one that is expedient and fruitful of beneficial results. By it one strengthens the power of one's state and the bonds of humanity. The Buddhist doctrine of equality, the democratic origin and basis of the state, with the ruler as "one elected by popular consent" (*mahā-sammata*) and as "the servant of the people" (*gaṇadāsa*), the doctrine of social contract, which gives the people the right to oust a government which is not working for the welfare of the people and demand certain rights, the conception of the common good viewed as promotion of both material and spiritual welfare and the idea of a common humanity together entail that these ideals would find their fulfilment in a network of worldwide democratic and socialistic states, each acting in accordance with a Dhamma or political philosophy and a constitution embodying these ideals.

Buddhism would uphold the doctrine of human rights as embodied in the universal declaration of human rights adopted by the General Assembly of the United Nations (1948), including all rights that flow from them. It would interpret the right to life (Article 3) and the right not to be subjected to inhuman punishment (Article 5) as entailing the abolition of the death penalty, based on a rational and humane approach to the problem of the criminal. It would, in fact, stress the importance of devising ways and means of extending this right to live without fear (*abhaya-dāna*) to birds and beasts as well. Thus, there was legislation for the protection of fauna in ancient Ceylon based on Buddhist principles and this bit of legislation continued up to the eighteenth century. While Buddhism would hold that everyone has the right to work and employment, this should not be so interpreted as to prevent a person from living a life of a monk or priest of any religion, whose life and work may be of a different character, though of value to the community.

At the same time since sovereignty is vested in the people, the state representing the people has a right to curb any abuse of any human rights on the part of individuals and to restrict the right to property (Article 17) in the public interest without infringing Dhamma. Another fact that has to be borne in mind is that for a Bill of Rights to ensure the actual observance of human rights in any society, it is imperative that the spirit behind the legislation as well as the legislation itself have the approval and support of the people. The rules enacted in the monastic code of laws of the Sangha were voluntarily accepted as "precepts" (*sikkhāpada*) by the members, who considered them binding. They were meaningful because they were based on a system of values universally acknowledged and the values were significant in the light of the Buddhist theory of reality and knowledge, which was verifiable and not dogmatic. When there was an alleged infringement of the law, the procedure for trial required that the accused be made to recall (*sāretabbaṃ*) the circumstances in which the alleged transgression occurred and be confronted with (*sammukhā-vinaya*) both the letter and spirit of the law before he was formally charged.

It is also imperative that the law should be accessible. In fact, this should be one of the most basic human rights (if the rule of law is to reflect the rule of righteousness), namely that a victim of discrimination should be in a position to seek redress and justice without being hampered by educational and pecuniary disabilities. Good Buddhist kings had a bell outside their palace gates which anyone with a strong sense of grievance against a judgement given in a lower court could ring. Legal remedy is reduced to a farce if the people cannot understand or afford it through no fault of their own.

Take a situation in which the laws are written down and administered in a language not understood by over 90 percent of the people, where the cost of litigation makes legal remedy available only to a small proportion of the remaining 10 percent, where the police do not take a sympathetic view of complaints lodged by common people who do not have sufficient political influence or pecuniary means at their command and where the laws have been imposed on them and are partly based on moral convictions they do not share. In a situation such as this,[71] an introduction of a Bill of Rights in the Constitution is only likely to help an articulate and privileged class to perpetuate its privileges.

While according to Buddhist concepts the state would have a corporate personality in a conventional legal sense (like each Sangha, whose "territorial limits" were defined), there would be no state apart from the individuals. Although, according to traditional positivist doctrine, states alone are subjects of international law, we should not forget that, in the final analysis, those laws affect only the lives and interests of individuals and are interpreted by individuals acting in their official capacities. The recognition of human rights by all nations would entail that individuals should also be recognised as possible subjects of international law.[72] This would not conflict with the Buddhist doctrine of state sovereignty in so far as the sovereignty of the state is subject to Dhamma, which embodies the necessity to uphold human rights. Besides, officials are morally responsible for their actions and the fact that they are "carrying out their official duties or the orders of the state" (*rañño rājakaraṇīyaṃ kātabbaṃ*) does not altogether absolve them from blame and they should, therefore, be liable to prosecution and conviction in international law for crimes against peace, war crimes and crimes against humanity.

The Buddhist doctrine of the equality of man and its concept of the state entail in one sense the equality of states since states are conventional legal entities. In another sense they entail the proportionate representation[73] of the state in certain bodies, since the state cannot have actual existence apart from the actual and possible individuals composing it. The sources of obligation in international law are both consent and conformity with Dhamma, whose ethical principles can be claimed to be of universal validity and could be precisely formulated if the problems are approached without prejudice, hatred, fear and ignorance of facts and values.

---

71. This is not a purely hypothetical situation since it partly reflects the state of affairs in my own country at present.

72. Cp. "It would, therefore, appear that to the extent to which the Charter incorporates obligations to respect the fundamental human rights and freedom, it amounts to recognition of individuals as subjects of international law" (H. Lauterpacht, *International Law and Human Rights*, p. 35; cp., G. Ezejiofor, *Protection of Human Rights under the Law*, London, 1964, pp. 26 ff).

73. Cp. Clark & Sohn, pp. xix ff. To treat the People's Republic of China, which has a population about twice as great as the U.S.A. and U.S.S.R. put together, on the same footing with each of the latter does not appear to be justified.

Consent alone is not enough even if all the states agree, although a legal positivist would consider this the only criterion.

Prior to the advent of the Western nations, the Eastern states had diplomatic relations with each other on a footing of equality and followed a civilised code of behaviour in their dealings. If established customs were violated there were reprisals. It has been shown that early relations between the South East Asian powers and the European nations was on a footing of equality and were governed by international law.[74]

Subsequently, the majority of these states lost their independence to European powers. Aggression was rationalised by Christian missionaries as a divine opportunity for civilizing and saving benighted heathens. As one learned Christian missionary put it: "Why have India, Burma and Ceylon ... been placed under the control of the British sceptre? ... We cannot doubt that ... nations have been placed under our authority that we ought to carry on with better effect the good work of the world's conversion from darkness to light and from the powers of Satan unto God" (Hardy, p. 6).

With the regaining of independence these countries have resumed their status of being sovereign national states. While they can look back to their past civilisations for inspiration they realise the need to get on their feet once again. Despite their domestic problems and the ideological wars in which they tend to get caught up, they have found it difficult to agree wholly with the international law of the Western nations as it stands nor reject the need for international law as a binding force for the good and happiness of all nations. The criticism that "they have begun to claim the right to select from among its rules only those which suit their interests or which arise out of agreements to which they have themselves been parties" (Brierly, 1963, p. 43) is somewhat misplaced (Syatauw, Ch. IV). If law is not wholly an instrument to further sectional interests, it is desirable that, despite the clash of interests in the ideological, political and economic plane, a workable common body of rules regulating the relations between states be formulated.

---

74. C. Alexandrowicz, "Treaty and Diplomatic Relations between European and South Asian Powers in the Seventeenth and Eighteenth Centuries," *Recueil des Cours*, II, 1960, p. 207; cp. R.Higgins, *Conflict of Interests*, London 1965, pp. 32, 33.

The nuclear deterrent cannot be expected to ensure a lasting peace. In the context of a bipolarization of power blocs, there can be only one of four possible outcomes. The first and second would be victory for one of the two in the event of war, the third would be a virtual defeat of both involving dire destruction for humanity and the fourth would be to co exist in a framework of international law until inequalities are removed, freedom is not denied and human rights are respected throughout the world and the states would co-operate with each other materially and culturally on a footing of equality for the good and happiness of mankind.

Considering probabilities the third is the pessimistic view and the last the optimistic view. The task of traditionally Buddhist states would be, while putting their own houses in order, to do all they could to make the fourth possibility a reality. The doctrine of *Pañca Sīla* (which is a traditionally Buddhist term) embodies the Buddhist concepts of inter-state relations in speaking of the equality of states and the necessity for peaceful coexistence, based on non-aggression, non-interference, mutual respect for each others' sovereignty as well as mutual benefit (Syatauw, pp. 212–219).

It was Nehru and U Nu who put forward the Buddhist point of view in urging the doctrine of *Pañca Sīla* at the Bandung conference. Whatever may have happened since, Nehru's words still remain true:

> We must avoid war and peace should be the decisive factor in the policy of every country. This is not a mere flowery statement, because we can actually bring about a real change in the world and cement the foundations of peace. India, on her part, will not take part in a future war unless she were attacked. If every country were to side with either of the two power blocs, war would thus be inevitable. But if every country maintained its integrity, it would be thus helping in allaying the possibility of war. The moral strength of Asia and Africa is indeed an important factor which should stand for peace. It has been said that the Pañca Sīla—the five principles upon which Gandhi's policy was based—should prevail. This, in fact, is not new as all great ideas are not new. Coexistence, however, has dominated the minds, because it is more in conformity with modern trends. There is no other way to avoid war.[75]

Non-commitment is not a cult practised for the sake of being in a bargaining position (H. A. Kissinger, "The New Cult of Neutralism," in Olson & Sondermann, pp. 353–60.) It is a positive role which many a state has to play in the present juncture if it has the welfare of humanity at heart.

As a late premier of Ceylon put it:

> I do not like the word "uncommitted." We know, of course, the meaning the word conveys. But we are very much "committed"—we are committed to the hilt—to peace in a positive form, to friendship amongst all nations and to the peace and prosperity and happiness of all mankind. We are committed quite so much as anyone else, perhaps even more so (Bandaranaike, p. 445).

---

75. *The First Asian-African Conference Held at Bandung, Indonesia* (18–24 April 1955), report published by League of Arab States, Imprimerie Misr S.A.E., 1955, pp. 103–04.

Bibliography to Pali Texts and Translations

Pali Canonical Texts

Unless marked otherwise, all references are to the editions and translations of the Pali Text Society, London. The texts forming its early portion called the *Sutta* have been translated under the following titles:

Dialogues of the Buddha, Vols. I–III.
Middle Length Sayings, Vols. I–III.
Kindred Sayings, Vols. I–V.
Gradual Sayings, Vols. I–V.

The section called the *Vinaya,* containing the constitution and the monastic laws of the Sangha (i.e., Community of monks and nuns), is listed below (see under "Translations").

Secondary works

Pali-English Dictionary, T. W. Rhys Davids and W. Stede (eds.), PTS, London, 1921–25.

Abbreviations

Pali Texts

Unless marked otherwise, page and volume numbers refer to the Pali Text Society editions, for example, D I 84 = Dīgha Nikāya, book I, page 84.

A	Aṅguttara Nikāya
A-a	*Aṅguttara-aṭṭhakathā*, i.e., *Manorathapurāṇī*
D	Dīgha Nikāya
D-a	*Dīgha-aṭṭhakathā*, i.e., *Sumaṅgalavilāsinī*
Dhp	Dhammapada
Dhs	Dhammasaṅgaṇī
It	Itivuttaka
J-a	*Jātaka-aṭṭhakatthā*
M	Majjhima Nikāya
Nidd I	Mahā-Niddesa
S	Saṃyutta Nikāya
Sn	Suttanipāta
Ud	Udāna
Vibh	Vibhaṅga
Vin	Vinaya Piṭaka

Translations, etc.

BD	*Book of Discipline*, tr. I. B. Horner.
BMT	*Buddhist Mahāyāna Texts,* tr. E. B. Cowell, etc.
DB	*Dialogues of the Buddha.*
EBTK	*Early Buddhist Theory of Knowledge,* K. N. Jayatilleke.
JRAS	*Journal of the Royal Asiatic Society.*
KS	*Kindred Sayings.*
PED	*Pali-English Dictionary,* ed. Rhys Davids and Stede.
PTS	Pali Text Society.
RV	Ṛg Veda
SBB	*Sacred Books of the Buddhists.*
SBE	*Sacred Books of the East.*
TPU:	*The Thirteen Principal Upanishads*, tr. R. E. Hume.

Bibliography to Chapter 25

Original Texts

Catuḥ Śataka by Āryadeva, ed. H. P. Sastry, Calcutta, 1914.

Chinese Āgama-s or the Chinese Canonical Texts—These have been published in: *Taisho Shinshu Daizokyo,* Vols. I and II, Photoprint, Taiwan, 1955.

Jātakamālā, I, ed. Kern H., Harvard Oriental Series, 1891.

Kauṭilīyam Arthaśāstram, ed. Sastri R. S., Mysore 1919, *Le Mahāvastu,* ed. E. Senart, Paris, 1882.

Nīti-Nighaṇḍuva (Sinhalese), ed. P. Tikiribandara, Colombo, 1879.

Sikṣāsamuccaya of Śāntideva, ed. C. Bendall, Reprint 1957, 'S-Gravenhage.

The Visuddhimagga of Buddhaghosa, ed. Rhys Davids C. A. F., London, 1921.

Translations (the relevant sections or pages are indicated)

Book of the Discipline, tr. I. B. Horner, Parts I–V, SBB, Vols. X, XI, XIII, XIV, XX.

The Buddhacarita, tr. E. H. Johnston, Part II, Calcutta 1930, pp. xxxi ff.

Buddhist Mahāyāna Texts, tr. E. B. Cowell, F. Max Müller, and J. Kakakusu, SBE, Vol. XLIX, 1894.

Cūḷavaṃsa, Parts I and II, tr. W. Geiger, Colombo, 1953.

Dhammapada, tr. Bhikkhu Khantipālo, Bangkok, 1966.

Dialogues of the Buddha. Part I–III, tr. T. W. and C. A. F. Rhys Davids, SBB, Vol. IV—Read Nos. 27, 31 and 26.

Human Types, tr. B. C. Law, PTS, London, 1924.

The Jātaka, Vols. I–VI, tr. under ed. E. B. Cowell, London—Read especially No. 151; also Nos. 51, 77, 258, 301, 303, 334, 353, 457, 462.

Jātakamālā by Ārya Sūra, tr. J. S. Speyer, SBB, Vol. I.

Kauṭilya's Arthaśāstra, tr. R. Shamasastry, 7th ed., Mysore, 1961.

Kindred Sayings, tr. C. A. F. Rhys Davids, PTS, London.

L'Abhidharma de Vasubandhu, L. de la Vallée Poussin, I–VI, Paris, 1921–1931, Ch. III

Lalita Vistara, ed. P. L. Vaidya, *Buddhist Sanskrit Texts I*, Durbhanga, 1958, pp. v–vi; Foreword by S. Radhakrishnan.

The Mahābhārata, tr. K. M. Ganguli, VIII, 1883–1896, Calcutta.

Mahāvaṃsa, The Great Chronicle of Ceylon, tr. W. Geiger, Information Dept., Colombo, 1950.
The Mahāvastu, Vol. I, tr. J. J. Jones, SBB, Vol. XVI, London 1949—Read pp. 225–35, 285–301.
"The *Ratnāvalī* of Nāgārjuna," G. Tucci , *J.R.A.S.,* 1934.
Saddharmapuṇḍarīka or the Lotus of the True Law, tr. H. Kern, SBE, Vol. XXI.
Suvarṇaprabhāsottama Sūtra, text and tr. J. Nobel, Leiden, 1944.
Tattvasaṃgraha, ed. E. Krishnamacharya, Gaekwad Oriental Series, Baroda, 1926.
The Thirteen Principal Upanishads, R. E. Hume, Oxford University Press, London, etc., reprint 1934.
Vinaya Texts, T. W. Rhys Davids and H. Oldenberg, SBE, Vol. XIII, Oxford, 1881.
Visuddhi Magga, the Path of Purity, Vol. II, tr. P. Maung Tin, PTS, London—read Ch. XIII.

Monographs and Articles

Ambedkar, B. R., *The Buddha and His Dhamma,* Bombay, 1957.
Ariyasena Thera, "The Early Buddhist Bhikkhu Organisation" (*Purātana Bauddha Bhikṣu Saṃvidhānaya*) in *Cultural Researches (Saṃskṛtika Vimarśana),* I, X, 1966.
Bandaranaike, S. W. R. D., *Speeches and Writings,* Colombo, 1963.
Bapat, P. V., ed., *2500 Years of Buddhism,* New Delhi, 1956.
Barker, E., *Social Contract,* Oxford University Press, 1947.
Barua, B. M., *Asoka and His Inscriptions,* 2nd. ed., Calcutta, 1955.
Basham, A. L., *Aspects of Ancient Indian Culture,* Bombay, 1966.
Beal, S., *Si-Yu-ki, Buddhist Records of the Western World,* repr. New Delhi, 1983.
Benz, E., *Buddhism or Communism, which holds the future of Asia?,* London, 1966.
Berman, H. J., *Justice in the U.S.S.R.,* rev. ed., Harvard, 1963.
Bhagvat, D. N., *Early Buddhist Jurisprudence,* Poona, 1939.
Bode, M. H., *The Pali Literature of Burma,* London, 1909, Ch. VI.
Brierly, J. L., *The Basis of Obligation in International Law,* Oxford, 1958, p. 45.
—. *The Law of Nations,* 6th ed., Oxford, 1963.
Broad, C. D., *Five Types of Ethical Theory,* London, 1944.
Carr, E. H., *The Twenty Years' Crisis, 1919–1939,* London, 1951.

Chan Toon, *Principles of Buddhist Law*, 2nd ed., Rangoon, 1902.

Clark, G. and Sohn, L. B., *World Peace through World Law*, Harvard, 1960.

Chattopadhaya, B., *Lokāyata, A Study on Ancient Indian Materialism*, New Delhi, 1959.

Coomaraswamy, A. K., *Hinduism and Buddhism*, New York, 1943.

De G., *Democracy in Early Buddhist Sangha*, Calcutta University, 1955, p. xv.

De Bary, W. T., *Sources of Indian Tradition*, New York, 1958.

Dhirasekera, J. D., *Buddhist Monastic Discipline*, Colombo, 1982 (repr.).

Dikshitar, V. R. R., *Mauryan Policy*, 1932.

Ducasse, C. J., *A Critical Examination of the Belief in a Life after Death*, Illinois, 1961.

Dutt, S., *Early Buddhist Monarchism*, New Delhi, 1st Indian ed., rev., 1960.

Eliot, C., *Japanese Buddhism*, London, 1935.

—. *Hinduism and Buddhism*, Vol. III., London, repn., 1957.

Forchhammer, E., *An Essay on the Sources and Development of Burmese Law from the Era of the First Introduction of the Indian Law to the Time of the British Occupation of Pegu*, Jardine Prize Essay, Rangoon, 1885.

Friedmann, W., *Law in a Changing Society*, London, 1964.

Furnivall, J. S., "Manu in Burma: Some Burmese Dhammathats," *Journal of the Burma Research Society*, Vol. 30 (1940), pp. 351–70.

Gard, R. A., *Buddhism*, New York, 1961.

Garratt, G. T., ed., *The Legacy of India*, Oxford, repr., 1938, Introduction by the Marquess of Zetland.

Geiger, W., *Culture of Ceylon in Medieval Times*, ed. Heinz Bechert, Wiesbaden, 1960, Part III, Ch. III.

Ghoshal, U. N., *A History of Indian Political Ideas*, Oxford University Press, 1959, Chs. IV, XIV and XIX.

Gonda, J., *Ancient Indian Kingship from the Religious Point of View*, Leiden, 1966.

Gungwu, Wang, "The Nanhai Trade," *JRAS*, Malayan Branch, XXXII, Part 2.

Han, B., "Burmese Cosmogony and Cosmology," *Journal of the Research Society*, Vol. XLVIII, Part I, June 1965.

Hardy, R. S., *The British Government and the Ideology of Ceylon*, London, 1841.

Higgins, R., *Conflict of Interests, International Law in a Divided World,* The Bodley Head, 1965.

Horner, I. B., *Women under Primitive Buddhism,* London, 1930.

—. *Early Buddhism and the Taking of Life,* BPS, Kandy, 1967.

Hultzsch, E., *Inscriptions of Asoka,* Corpus Inscriptionum Indicarum, Vol. I, Oxford, 1925.

Ingalls, D. H. H., "Authority and Law in Ancient India," *Journal of the American Oriental Society,* Baltimore, Supplement No. 17, July–September 1954.

Jayaswal, K. P., *Hindu Polity,* Bangalore, 1978.

Jayatilleke, K. N., *Early Buddhist Theory of Knowledge,* London, 1963.

—, *Buddhism and Peace,* BPS, Kandy, 1962.

—, "Some Aspects of Gītā and Buddhist Ethics," *University of Ceylon Review,* Vol. XIII, Nos. 2 & 3, April-July 1955, pp. 135–51.

Kalupahana, D. J., *Causality: The Central Philosophy of Buddhism,* Honolulu, 1975.

King, W. L., *In the Hope of Nibbāna, An Essay on Theravāda Buddhist Ethics,* Illinois, 1964.

Leidecker, K. F., *Buddhism and Democracy,* BPS, Kandy, 1963.

Lin Yi, *A Short History of China 1840–1919,* Foreign Languages Press, Peking, 1963.

Ling, T., *Buddha, Marx and God,* St. Martin's Press, New York, 1966.

Lingat, R., "Evolution of the Conception of Law in Burma and Siam," *The Journal of the Siam Society,* Bangkok, Vol. XXXVIII, Part I (1950), pp. 9–31.

—, "The Buddhist Manu or the Propagation of Hindu Law in the Hīnayānist Indochina," *Annals of the Bhandarkar Oriental Research Institute,* Poona, Vol. XXX (1950), Nos., 3–4, pp. 284–97.

—, "La conception du droit dans l'Indochine Hīnayāniste," *Bulletin de L'École Française d' Extrême-Orient,* Tome XLIV, 1947–1950 (1951), pp. 165–87.

—, "L'influence juridique de l'Inde au Champa et au Cambodge," *Journal Asiatique,* 1949, pp. 273–90.

Majumdar, R. C., *Corporate Life in Ancient India,* Calcutta, 1922.

Maḷalasekera, G. P., and Jayatilleke, K. N., *Buddhism and the Race Question,* English and French editions, UNESCO Race Series, Paris, 1958. Republished by the BPS, Kandy, 1974 (Wheel Publication 200–201).

McCrindle, J. W., *Ancient India as described by Megasthenes and Arrian,*

Calcutta, 1926.
McCrindle, J. W., *Invasion of India by Alexander the Great,* Westminster, 1893.
Micklem, N., *Law and the Laws,* London, 1952.
Moffat, A. L., *Mongkut King of Siam,* New York, 2nd ed., 1962.
Mookerji, R. K., *Hindu Civilisation,* 1936.
Mukherjee, B. K., *The Hindu Law of Religious and Charitable Trust,* Calcutta, 1952.
Mukherjee, R. *Democracies of the East,* London, 1923.
Murti, G. S., and Aiyaṅgar, A. N. K., *Edicts of Asoka,* Adyar, 1950.
Nakamura, H., "The Indian and Buddhist Concept of Law," Unpublished Paper read at Edward F. Gallahue Conference on World Religions, Princeton, 3 May—II, 1966.
Needham, J., *Science and Civilisation in China,* Vol. I, Cambridge, 1954, Ch. 18.
—and Wang, L., *Science and Civilisation in China,* Vol. II, Cambridge, 1956.
Northrop, F. S. C., *The Complexity of Legal and Ethical Experience,* Toronto, 1st ed., 1959.
Northwestern University Law Review, July-August 1953, Vol. 48, No. 3.
Okano, Archbishop S., *An Introduction to Kodo Kyodan Buddhism,* Yokohama, 1967.
Olson, W. C,. and Sondermann, F. A., *The Theory and Practice of International Relations,* New Jersey, 1966.
Pande, G. C., *Studies in the Origins of Buddhism,* Allahabad, 1957.
Paranavitana, S., *Ceylon and Malaysia,* Colombo, 1966.
Phra Khantipālo, *Tolerance,* Rider & Co., London, 1964.
Prasad, B., *Theory of Government in Ancient India,* Allahabad, 1968.
Pratt, J. B., *The Pilgrimage of Buddhism,* London, 1928.
Ray, N., *Theravada Buddhism in Burma,* Calcutta, 1946.
Rhys Davids, T. W., *Buddhist India,* 6th ed., India, 1955.
Rommen, H. A., *The Natural Law,* London, repr. 1959, Ch. VI.
Saletore, B. A., *Ancient Indian Political Thought and Institutions,* New York, 1963.
—, *India's Diplomatic Relations with the West,* Bombay, 1958.
Sarkisyanz, E., *Buddhist Backgrounds of the Burmese Revolution,* The Hague, 1965.
—, *Russland und der Messianismus des Orients. Sendungsbewusstein und Chiliasmus des Ostens,* Tübingen 1955.

Sastri, K. A., ed., *Foreign Notices of South India from Megasthenes to Huan,* University of Madras, 1939.
Shamasastry, R., *Kauṭilya's Arthaśāstra,* 7th ed., Mysore, 1961, Introductory Note.
Sharma, R. S., *Śūdras in Ancient India,* New Delhi, 1958.
Slater, R. L., *World Religions and World Community,* New York, 1963.
Sternbach, L., *Juridical Studies in Ancient Indian Law,* New Delhi, 1965.
Sarkisyanz, E., *Buddhist Background of the Burmese Revolution,* The Hague, 1965.
—. *Russland und der Messianismus des Orients,* Tübingen, 1955.
Suzuki, B. L., *Mahāyāna Buddhism,* with an Introduction by D. T. Suzuki, London, 1948.
Suzuki, D. T., *Zen Buddhism,* New York, 1956.
Syatauw, J. J. G., *Some Newly Established Asian States and the Development of International Law,* The Hague, 1961.
Tachibana, S., *The Ethics of Buddhism,* Oxford, 1926; 2nd ed. Colombo, 1953.
Tāhtinen, U., *Non-Violence as an Ethical Principle,* Turku, 1964.
Thapar, R., *Asoka and the Decline of the Mauryas,* Oxford, 1961.
Thein, U. A., "Our Wars with the Burmese," *Journal of the Burma Research Society,* Dec. 1955.
Thomson, J. A. K., *The Ethics of Aristotle,* London, repr. 1963.
Vallée Poussin, L. de la, *Bouddhisme, Études et Matériaux, Cosmologie: Le Monde des Êtres et le Monde-Réceptacle,* Bruxelles, 1919.
Vinogradoff, Sir P., *Common Sense in Law,* 3rd ed., Oxford, repr. 1961.
Viswanatha, S. V., *International Law in Ancient India,* London, New York, Toronto, 1925.
Von Mehren, A. T., *Law in Japan—The Legal Order in a Changing Society,* Harvard, 1963.
Ware, C. F., Panikkar, K. N., and Romein, J. M., *The Twentieth Century,* UNESCO, 1966.
Wells, H. G., *A Short History of the World,* London, 1946.
Wigmore, J. H., *A Panorama of the World Legal Systems,* Washington, 1928, pp. 224–42.
Wood, W. A. R., *A History of Siam,* Bangkok, 1924.
Yu Li, Shih-yü, "Tibetan Folk Law," *Journal of the Royal Asiatic Society,* London, 1950, Nos. 3 and 4, pp. 127–48.
Zürcher, E., *The Buddhist Conquest of China,* text and notes published separately, Leiden, 1959.

Kulatissa Nanda Jayatilleke

Born: 1st November 1920—Died: 23rd July 1970.

Education:

Royal College, Colombo 1930–38.

University College and University of Ceylon 1939–43. B.A. First Class Honours in Indo-Aryan 1943.

Christ College, Cambridge University, 1945–48. Moral Science Tripos, Parts I and II, Second Class Honours.

B.A. Honours in Western Philosophy, University of London, 1948. M.A.: 1951; Ph.D.: 1961.

Academic Positions, etc. (selected):

Professor of Philosophy & Head, Dept. of Philosophy, University of Ceylon, 1963–70

Editor, *University of Ceylon Review,* 1952–60

Fellow of the Royal Asiatic Society of Great Britain and Ireland, 1960

Visiting Professor of Philosophy, University of North Carolina, U.S.A., 1965

Advisory Editor, *Philosophy East & West,* University of Hawaii, U.S.A., 1967

Other Publications

Early Buddhist Theory of Knowledge, George Allen and Unwin Ltd., London, 1963, pp. 520.

Of Related Interest from the BPS

The Vision of Dhamma

Nyanaponika Thera

This volume brings between two covers the author's original writings from the BPS's Wheel and Bodhi Leaves series. These writings offer one of the most mature, comprehensive, and authoritative expressions of Buddhism by a contemporary Western monk, the co-founder of the BPS.

BP 414S 374 pp.

The Discourse on The All-Embracing Net of Views

The Brahmajāla Sutta and Its Commentaries

Translated by Bhikkhu Bodhi

The Brahmajāla, one of the Buddha's most important discourses, weaves a net of sixty-two cases capturing all the speculative views on the self and the world. The massive commentary and subcommentary allow for a close in-depth study of the work. The book contains a lengthy treatise on the Theravada conception of the Bodhisattva ideal. The long introduction is itself a modern philosophical commentary on the sutta.

BP 209S 370 pp.

The Great Discourse on Causation

The Mahanidāna Sutta and Its Commentaries

Translated by Bhikkhu Bodhi

The Mahanidāna Sutta is the Buddha's longest discourse on dependent arising, often taken to be the key to his entire teaching. The commentary treats this doctrine according to the Abhidhamma method, explained in an appendix. A penetrative introduction lays bare the sutta's structure and the philosophical significance of dependent arising.

BP 211S 160 pp.

THE BUDDHIST PUBLICATION SOCIETY

The BPS is an approved charity dedicated to making known the Teaching of the Buddha, which has a vital message for all people.

Founded in 1958, the BPS has published a wide variety of books and booklets covering a great range of topics. Its publications include accurate annotated translations of the Buddha's discourses, standard reference works, as well as original contemporary expositions of Buddhist thought and practice. These works present Buddhism as it truly is—a dynamic force which has influenced receptive minds for the past 2500 years and is still as relevant today as it was when it first arose.

For more information about the BPS and our publications, please visit our website, or write an e-mail or letter to:

The Administrative Secretary
Buddhist Publication Society
P.O. Box 61
54 Sangharaja Mawatha
Kandy • Sri Lanka

E-mail: bps@sltnet.lk
web site: http://www.bps.lk
Tel: 0094 81 223 7283 • Fax: 0094 81 222 3679

The Discourse on The All-Embracing Net of Views

The Brahmajāla Sutta and Its Commentaries
Translated by *Bhikkhu Bodhi*
The Brahmajāla, one of the Buddha's most important discourses, weaves a net of sixty-two cases capturing all the speculative views on the self and the world. The massive commentary and subcommentary allow for a close in-depth study of the work. The book contains a lengthy treatise on the Theravada conception of the Bodhisattva ideal. The long introduction is itself a modern philosophical commentary on the sutta.
BP 209S, 2007, 370 pp

A Similes of the Buddha

An Introduction
By *Hellmuth Hecker*
This book is an introductory guide to the rich, wonderful, and profound world of Buddhist similes. The Buddha used many similes as a skilful means to facilitate the understanding of teachings that otherwise could appear overly abstruse and dry to his listeners. Thus, contemplation of the similes and the explanations as given in this book will widen and deepen one's understanding of the Teaching of the Buddha.
BP 427S, 2009, 216 pp.

Collected Wheel Publications

Various Authors
Each volume contains fifteen retypeset numbers of the renowned Wheel Publication series, dealing with various aspects of the Buddha's Teaching such as Buddhist philosopy, psychology, ethics, history, etc., as well as translations from Buddhist scriptures. The authors are Nyanaponika Thera, Francis Story, Bhikkhu Bodhi, etc..

Our complete catalogue can be viewed or downloaded from our website at www.bps.lk